Er. D.C. Gupta

Heat & Thermodynamics

for JEE Main & Advanced

(Study Package for Physics)

Fully Solved

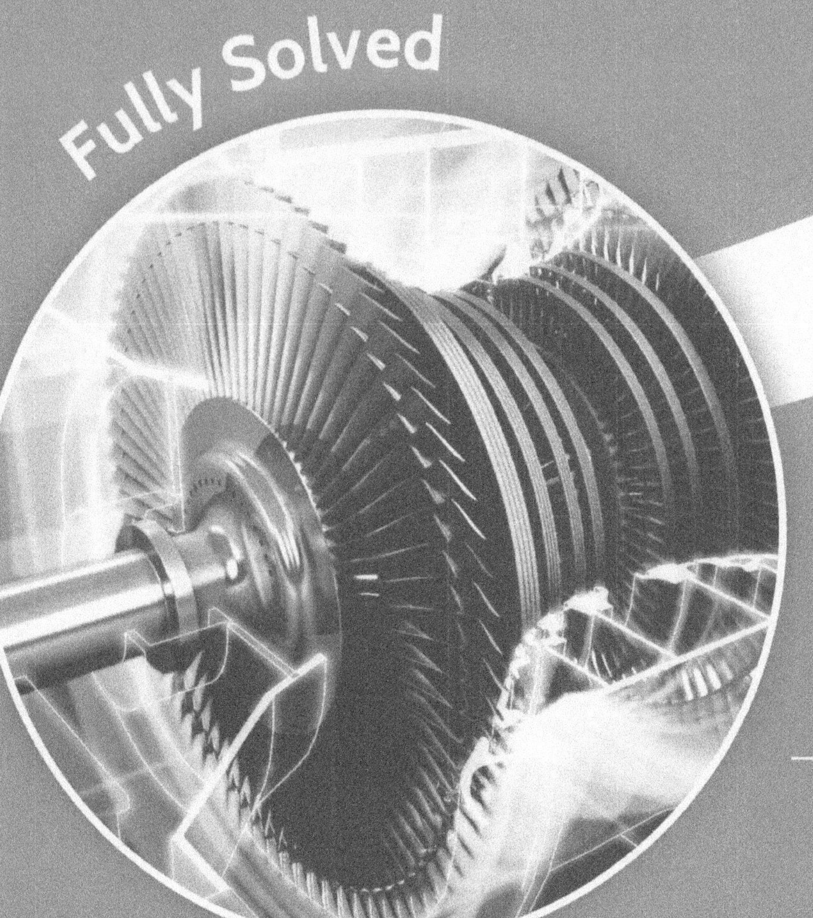

Includes Past
JEE & KVPY Questions

Useful for Class 11,
KVPY & Olympiads

- **Head Office :** B-32, Shivalik Main Road, Malviya Nagar, New Delhi-110017
- **Sales Office :** B-48, Shivalik Main Road, Malviya Nagar, New Delhi-110017
  Tel. : 011-26691021 / 26691713

Page Layout : Prakash Chandra Sahoo

Typeset by Disha DTP Team

Printed at: **Repro Knowledgecast Limited, Thane**

For further information about the books from DISHA,
Log on to **www.dishapublication.com** or email to **info@dishapublication.com**

STUDY PACKAGE IN PHYSICS FOR JEE MAIN & ADVANCED

Booklet No.	Title	Chapter Nos.	Page Nos.
1	Units, Measurements & Motion	Ch 0. Mathematics Used in Physics Ch 1. Units and Measurements Ch 2. Vectors Ch 3. Motion in a Straight Line Ch 4. Motion in a Plane	1-202
2	Laws of Motion and Circular Motion	Ch 5. Laws of Motion and Equilibrium Ch 6. Circular Motion	203-318
3	Work Energy, Power & Gravitation	Ch 7. Work, Energy and Power Ch 8. Collisions and Centre of Mass Ch 9. Gravitation	319-480
4	Rotational Motion	Ch 1. Rotational Mechanics	1-120
5	Properties of Matter & SHM	Ch 2. Properties of Matter Ch 3. Fluid Mechanics Ch 4. Simple Harmonic Motion	121-364
6	Heat & Thermodynamics	Ch 5. Thermometry, Expansion & Calorimetry Ch 6. Kinetic Theory of Gases Ch 7. Laws of Thermodynamics Ch 8. Heat Transfer	365-570
7	Waves	Ch 9. Wave – I Ch 10. Wave –II	571-698
8	Electrostatics	Ch 0. Mathematics Used in Physics Ch 1. Electrostatics Ch 2. Capacitance & Capacitors	1-216
9	Current Electricity	Ch 3. DC and DC circuits Ch 4. Thermal and Chemical effects of Current"	217-338
10	Magnetism, EMI & AC	Ch 5. Magnetic Force on Moving Charges & Conductor Ch 6. Magnetic Effects of Current Ch 7. Permanent Magnet & Magnetic Properties of Substance Ch 8. Electromagnetic Induction Ch 9. AC and EM Waves	339-618
11	Ray & Wave Optics	Ch 1. Reflection of Light Ch 2. Refraction and Dispersion Ch 3. Refraction at Spherical Surface, Lenses and Photometry Ch 4. Wave optics	1-244
12	Modern Physics	Ch 5. Electron, Photon, Atoms, Photoelectric Effect and X-rays Ch 6. Nuclear Physics Ch 7. Electronics & Communication	245-384

Contents

Study Package Booklet 6 - Heat & Thermodynamics

Thermometry, Expansion & Calorimetry (365- 414)

5.1 INTRODUCTION

Mechanics deals with the quantities like; acceleration, force, mechanical energy (external energy) and Newton's second law and conservation of energy. Thermodynamics deals with temperature, heat, internal energy, entropy and the first and second law of thermodynamics. The fundamental quantity in thermodynamics is temperature, so we start our study by developing the concept of temperature from its foundation.

5.2 TEMPERATURE

Temperature is a macroscopic quantity of thermodynamics which gives the sensation of hotness or coldness. Its SI unit is kelvin. The lowest temperature that has achieved in lab is 2×10^{-8} K, in the process, called nuclear spin. Scientist are trying to see how close they can come to absolute zero temperature. The highest laboratory temperature is 10^8 K.

Zeroth law of thermodynamics : Thermal equilibrium

A system is said to be in the state of thermodynamic equilibrium if the variable describing the thermodynamic state of a system do not change with time. A system in thermal equilibrium have no unbalanced force between the system and the surroundings and each part of the system and the surrounding are at the same temperature. According to zeroth law of thermodynamics, if two bodies A and B are in thermal equilibrium with third body C separately, then bodies A and B are also be in thermal equilibrium. The zeroth law, came in light in 1930 s, after the first and second laws of thermodynamics had been discovered. Temperature on being central concept should have the lowest number, hence the zero.

Measuring temperature

Any device which is used to measure the temperature is called thermometer. A thermometer makes use of some property like; length of mercury column, pressure of gas etc. whose variation with temperature is defined by a law. There is no property which varies by a law for all range of temperature. Therefore we need different properties and hence different thermometers.

Fixed points on a temperature scale

The old method was based on two fixed points of temperature which can be easily reproduced in laboratory. The temperature of melting ice at 1 atm (called ice point or freezing point) and the temperature of boiling water at 1 atm (called steam point or boiling point). On Celsius scale the freezing point is assumed as 0 °C and the boiling point as 100 °C.

Suppose a property 'X' which is defined by assuming a linear relation with t as

$$X_t \;=\; at + b \qquad\qquad \ldots (i)$$

If X_0 and X_{100} denote the values of property at 0°C and 100°C respectively, then from equation (i), we have

$$X_0 \;=\; a \times 0 + b \qquad\qquad \ldots (ii)$$

and

$$X_{100} \;=\; a \times 100 + b \cdot \qquad\qquad \ldots (iii)$$

After solving equations (ii) and (iii), we get

$$b \;=\; X_0$$

and

$$a \;=\; \left(\frac{X_{100} - X_0}{100} \right).$$

Substituting these values in equation (i), we get

$$t \;=\; \left(\frac{X_t - X_0}{X_{100} - X_0} \right) \times 100 \text{ degree.}$$

Here property X may be length of mercury column, resistance of metal etc.

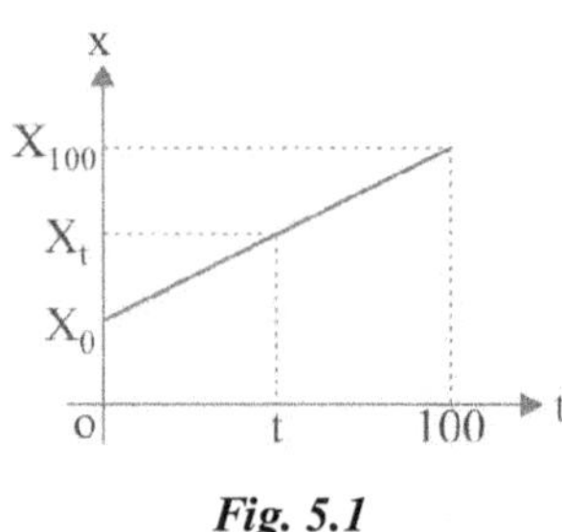

Fig. 5.1

1. **Mercury thermometer**

   Its working is based on the fact that mercury expand uniformly on heating. If ℓ_0, ℓ_{100} and ℓ_t be the lengths of mercury column at 0°C, 100°C and at unknown temperature t°C respectively, then the unknown temperature t can be calculated as

   $$t = \left(\frac{\ell_t - \ell_0}{\ell_{100} - \ell_0}\right) \times 100.$$

   The range of mercury thermometer is quite large because of low freezing point (–39°C) and high boiling point (357°C).

2. **Platinum resistance thermometer**

   The electric resistance of metal wire increases with temperature as, $R_t = R_0(1 + \alpha t)$, where α is the temperature coefficient of resistance. If R_0 and R_{100} denote the resistances of metal wire at 0°C and 100°C respectively, then we can define the temperature as

   $$t = \left[\frac{R_t - R_0}{R_{100} - R_0}\right] \times 100 \text{ degree}.$$

   Platinum resistance thermometer can be used in temperature range – 170°C to 200°C.

Temperature scales

1. **The Celsius scale**

   On this scale, the lower fixed point is taken as 0°C the upper fixed point as 100°C. The interval between these fixed points is divided into hundred equal divisions and each division is called 1 °C.

2. **The Fahrenheit scale**

   On this scale lower and upper fixed points are taken 32 °F and 212 °F respectively. The interval between these fixed points is equally divided into 180 division. The each division is equal to 1 °F.

3. **The Kelvin scale**

   On this scale the lower and upper fixed points are taken as 273.15 K and 373.15 K respectively. The interval between these fixed points is divided equally in 100 divisions. Thus each division represents 1 K.

   1 division of C = 1.8 division of F = 1 division of K

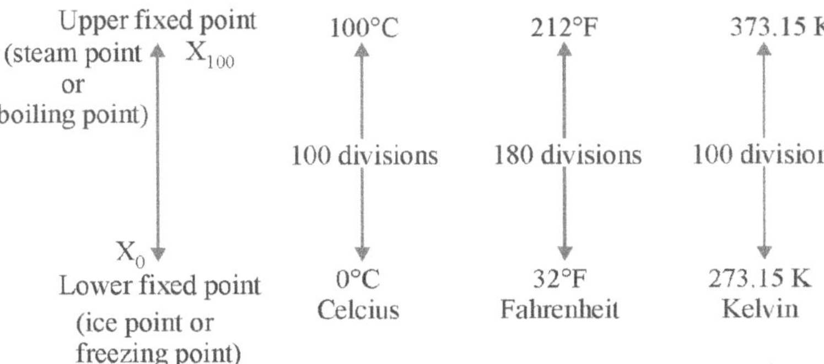

Fig. 5.2

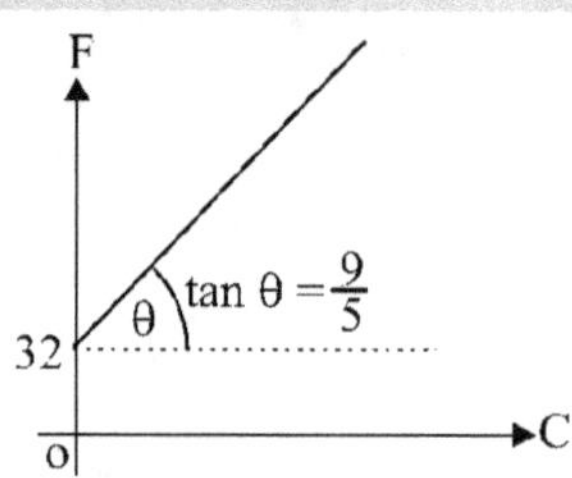

Fig. 5.3

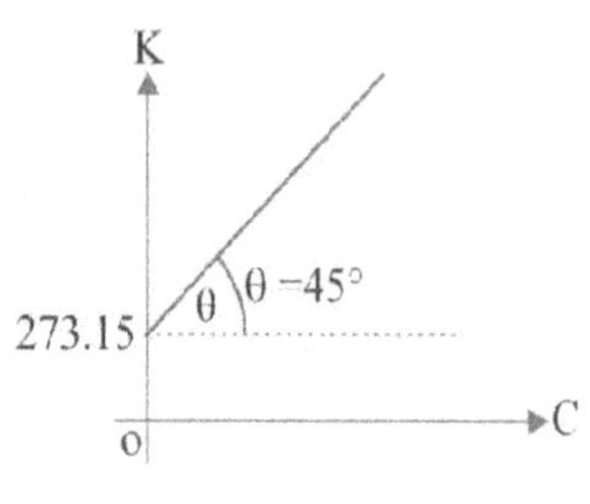

Fig. 5.4

Conversion of temperature from one scale to another

This can be done by using following relation

$$\frac{\text{Temerature on any scale - lower fixed point}}{\text{Upper fixed point - lower fixed point}} = \text{Constant for each scale}$$

Thus we

$$\frac{X - F.P.}{B.P. - F.P.} = \frac{C - 0}{100 - 0} = \frac{F - 32}{212 - 32} = \frac{K - 273.15}{373.15 - 273.15}$$

Here X is the temperature on any scale. F.P. and B.P. stand for freezing point and boiling point of water respectively.

From the above equation, we have

$$\frac{C}{5} = \frac{F - 32}{9} = \frac{K - 273.15}{5}$$

or

$$F = \frac{9}{5}C + 32$$

and

$$K = C + 273.15$$

Absolute zero and absolute scale of temperature

According to kinetic theory of gases $v_{rms} = \sqrt{\dfrac{3RT}{M}}$. The gas is supposed to have no molecular motion (Also zero volume and zero pressure) at $T = 0$. This temperature is called **absolute zero temperature**. Kelvin scale is called absolute temperature scale.

Triple point of water

The triple point of water is the state at which the three phases of water namely ice, water and vapour are co-exist in equilibrium. It is unique because it occurs at a specific temperature of 273.16 K and at a pressure of 4 mm of mercury. Thus for water.

$$T_r = 273.16\,\text{K or } 0.01°\text{C}$$
$$P_r = 4\,\text{mm of mercury}$$

Note:

In modern thermometry, the triple point of water is chosen to be one of the fixed points. The melting point of ice and boiling point of water both change with pressure but triple point is characterised by a unique temperature and pressure, so it is preferred over the conventional fixed points.

In the absolute scale, the triple point of water is assigned the value 273.16 K. The absolute zero is taken as the other fixed point on this scale.

Constant volume gas thermometer : Ideal gas temperature

If P and P_r are the pressures of constant volume of a gas at temperatures T and at the triple point T_r respectively, then by Charle's law, we have

$$\frac{T}{T_{tr}} = \frac{P}{P_{tr}}$$

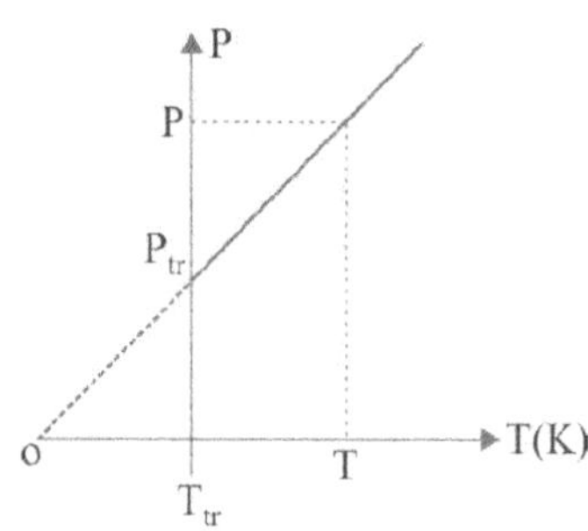

Fig. 5.5

or

$$T = T_{tr}\frac{P}{P_{tr}}$$

or

$$T = 273.16\left(\frac{P}{P_{tr}}\right)\text{K} . \qquad ...(1)$$

The temperature defined by the above equation depends slightly on the nature of the gas and its pressure. But at high temperature and low pressure, in the limit $P_{tr} \to 0$, all the different gas thermometers give the same value of temperature $373.15\ K$ for steam point. So we define a temperature scale by the equation

$$T = \lim_{P_{tr} \to 0} 273.16 \left(\frac{P}{P_{tr}} \right) K. \qquad ...(2)$$

The temperature scale defined by equation (2) is called ideal gas temperature.

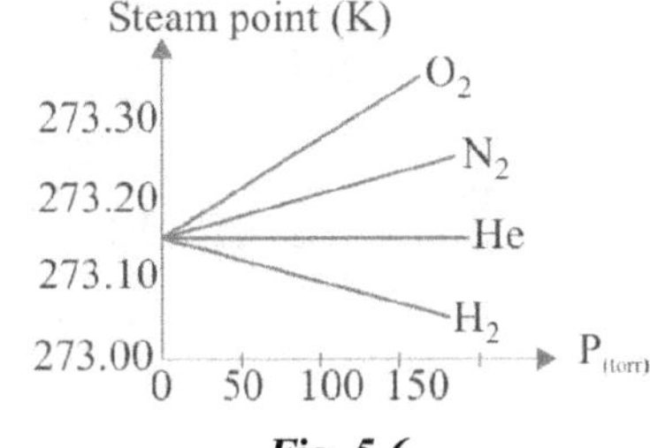

Fig. 5.6

Note:

One can also define a centigrade scale with gas thermometers. Suppose P_0 and P_{100} are the pressure of a constant volume of gas at melting ice and in a steam bath respectively, then temperature t corresponding to pressure P_t of the gas is defined by

$$t = \left[\frac{P_t - P_0}{P_{100} - P_0} \right] \times 100°C$$

Radiation pyrometer

It is based on Stefan's law, which states that the radiation emitted by a black body per unit area per second is proportional to the fourth power of the absolute temperature i.e., $E = \sigma T^4$, where σ is called Stefan's constant. By noting the radiation E we can calculate temperature T as

$$T = \left[\frac{E}{\sigma} \right]^{\frac{1}{4}} K.$$

The main advantage of the pyrometer is that it is capable of measuring the temperature, however high it may be and whatever the distance of the object from the pyrometer. It can accurately measure temperature greater than $1000\ K$.

Ex. 1 What is the value of the following in °F?
(i)   40 °C temperature,
(ii) 40 °C difference of temperature.
Sol.

(i)   We know that $F = \dfrac{9}{5}C + 32$

$$\therefore \qquad F = \frac{9}{5} \times 40 + 32$$
$$= 104\ °F$$

(ii) 1 °C difference is equal to
$$= 1.8\ °F$$
$\therefore$ 40 °C difference is equal to
$$= 1.8 \times 40$$
$$= 72\ °F$$

Ex. 2 A faulty thermometer reads freezing point and boiling point of water as 5 °C and 95 °C respectively. What is the correct value of temperature as it reads 60 °C on faulty thermometer?
Sol.

If X is the value of temperature on faulty thermometer, then

$$\frac{X - F.P.}{B.P. - F.P.} = \frac{C - 0}{100 - 0}$$

or $\dfrac{60 - 5}{95 - 5} = \dfrac{C}{100}$

After solving , we get
$$C = 61.11\ °C \qquad \qquad \textbf{\textit{Ans.}}$$

Ex. 3 The electrical resistance in ohm of a certain thermometer varies with temperature according to the approximate law:

$$R = R_0[1 + 5 \times 10^{-3}(T - T_0)]$$

The resistance is 101.6Ω at the triple point of water and 165.5Ω at the normal melting point of lead (600.5 K). What is the temperature when the resistance is 123.4Ω?
Sol.

At $T = 273\ K, R = 101.6\ \Omega$

$\therefore \quad 101.6 = R_0\,[1 + 5 \times 10^{-3}\,(273 - T_0)] \qquad ...(i)$

When $T = 600.5\ K, R = 165.5\ \Omega$

$\therefore \quad 165.5 = R_0[1 + 5 \times 10^{-3}\,(600.5 - T_0)] \quad ...(ii)$

After solving equations (i) and (ii), we get
$$T_0 = -49.3\ K$$

Substituting the value of T_0 in equation (i), we get
$$101.6 = R_0(1 + 5 \times 10^{-3}\,(273 + 49.3)]$$

or $R_0 = \dfrac{101.6}{(1 + 5 \times 10^{-3} \times 322.3)} = 38.9\ \Omega$

For $R = 123.4\ \Omega\ ;$
$$123.4 = 38.9\ [1 + 5 \times 10^{-3}\,(T + 49.3)]$$

After solving, we get
$$T = 384.8\ K \qquad \qquad \textbf{\textit{Ans.}}$$

Ex. 4 Two ideal gas thermometers A and B use oxygen and hydrogen respectively. The following observations are made:

Temperature	Pressure thermometer A	Pressure thermometer B
Triple point of water	1.250×10^5 Pa	0.200×10^5 Pa
Normal melting point of sulpher	1.797×10^5 Pa	0.287×10^5 Pa

(a) What is the absolute temperature of normal melting point of sulphur as read by thermometer A and B?

(b) What do you think is the reason for slightly different answers from A and B?

Sol.

(a) For thermometer A;

$T_{tr} = 273$ K , $P_{tr} = 1.250 \times 10^5$ Pa

and $T = ?, P = 1.797 \times 10^5$ Pa

We have

$$T = \frac{P}{P_{tr}} \times T_{tr}$$

$$= \frac{1.797 \times 10^5}{1.250 \times 10^5} \times 273 = 392.46 \text{ K}$$

For thermometer B;

$$T_{tr} = 273 \text{ K},$$
$$P_{tr} = 0.200 \times 10^5 \text{ Pa}$$
$$T = ?, \qquad P = 0.287 \times 10^5 \text{ Pa}$$

We have

$$T = \frac{P}{P_{tr}} \times T_{tr}$$

$$= \frac{0.287 \times 10^5 \times 273}{0.200 \times 10^5} = 391.75 \text{K}$$

(b) The slight difference in the temperatures as read by two thermometers are due to the fact that oxygen and hydrogen do not behave like an ideal gas.

5.3 THERMAL EXPANSION OF SOLIDS

Substances expand on heating. The atoms of a solid are held together in a three dimensional lattice by interatomic forces. The individual atoms vibrate about these lattice. When solid is heated, the amplitude of vibration of atoms increases, and so the average interatomic separation increases. This result in the thermal expansion of solid.

Coefficients of expansion of solid

1. **Coefficient of linear expansion:**

$$\alpha = \frac{\text{Increase in length}}{\text{Original length} \times \text{rise in temperature}}$$

or

$$\alpha = \frac{\Delta L}{L_0 \Delta T}$$

If L_0 and L_t are the lengths at $0°C$ and $t°C$ respectively, then $\Delta L = L_t - L_0$ and $\Delta T = t - 0 = t°C$

$$\therefore \qquad \alpha = \frac{L_t - L_0}{L_0 \, t}$$

or

$$L_t = L_0(1 + \alpha t)$$

Note:

1. In differential form α can be written as ; $\alpha = \frac{1}{L_0} \frac{dL}{dt}$

2. The above equation is applicable for small value of t ($t < 100\,°C$), till the expansion of the material can be taken uniform. For higher range of temperature, L_t is given by; $L_t = L_0(1 + \alpha_1 t + \alpha_2 t^2 + ...)$, where $\alpha_1 > \alpha_2 > ....$

2. **Coefficient of superficial expansion**

$$\beta = \frac{\text{Increase in area}}{\text{Original area} \times \text{rise in temperature}}$$

or

$$\beta = \frac{\Delta A}{A_0 \Delta T}$$

If A_0 and A_t are the areas at 0°C and t°C respectively, then $\Delta A = A_t - A_0$ and $\Delta T = t - 0 = t°C$

$$\therefore \qquad \beta = \frac{A_t - A_0}{A_0 \, t}$$

or

$$A_t = A_0(1 + \beta t)$$

3. Coefficient of cubical expansion

$$\gamma = \frac{\text{Increase in volume}}{\text{Original volume} \times \text{rise in temperature}}$$

or

$$\gamma = \frac{\Delta V}{V_0 \Delta T}$$

If V_0 and V_t are the volumes at 0°C and t°C respectively, then $\Delta V = V_t - V_0$ and $\Delta T = t - 0 = t°C$

$$\therefore \qquad \gamma = \frac{V_t - V_0}{V_0 \, t}$$

or

$$V_t = V_0(1 + \gamma t)$$

Note: Value of α, β and γ depends on material of the body.

Variation of γ with temperature

The value of γ is not constant at all range of temperature. The variation of cubical expansion of copper with temperature is shown in *Fig. 5.7*.

At high temperature (above 500 K) its value becomes almost constant.

Relationship between α, β and γ

(i) Consider a sheet of length a and width b, the area of the sheet

$$A = ab \qquad \qquad ...(i)$$

For small change in area (ΔA), we can write

$$\frac{\Delta A}{A} = \frac{\Delta a}{a} + \frac{\Delta b}{b} \qquad \qquad ...(ii)$$

Dividing both sides of the equation by ΔT, we have

$$\frac{\Delta A}{A \Delta T} = \frac{\Delta a}{a \Delta T} + \frac{\Delta b}{b \Delta T}$$

or

$$\beta = \alpha_1 + \alpha_2$$

where α_1 and α_2 are the coefficients of linear expansions along length and width respectively. For a material having expansion coefficient same in all directions, we have $\alpha_1 = \alpha_2 = \alpha$

$$\therefore \qquad \beta = 2\alpha$$

(ii) Take a cuboid of sides a, b and c respectively its volume ,

$$V = abc \qquad \qquad ...(i)$$

We can write,

$$\frac{\Delta V}{V} = \frac{\Delta a}{a} + \frac{\Delta b}{b} + \frac{\Delta c}{c} \qquad \qquad ...(ii)$$

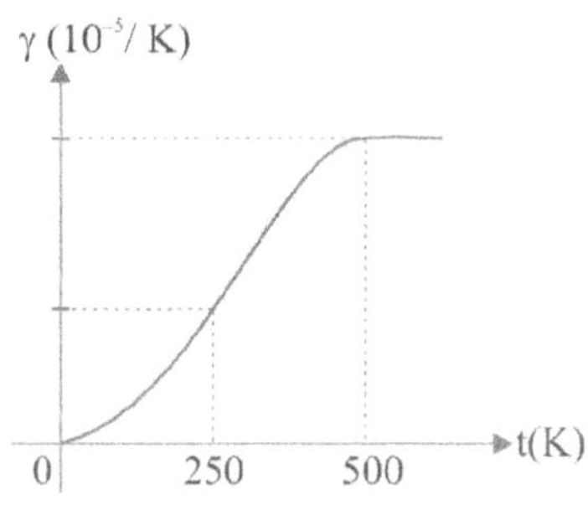

Fig. 5.7

Dividing both sides of the equation (ii) by ΔT, we have

$$\frac{\Delta V}{V\Delta T} \;=\; \frac{\Delta a}{a\Delta T} + \frac{\Delta b}{b\Delta T} + \frac{\Delta c}{c\Delta T}$$

or
$$\gamma \;=\; \alpha_1 + \alpha_2 + \alpha_3$$

For a material having expansion coefficient same in all directions, we have,
$$\alpha_1 = \alpha_2 = \alpha_3 = \alpha$$

$\therefore$
$$\gamma \;=\; 3\alpha$$

Note :

It is difficult to determine β and γ directly. For solids, the value of α is determined and value of β and γ are taken approximately equal to 2α and 3α respectively.

Variation of density with temperature

(i) Suppose ρ_0 is the density of the substance at 0°C. At any temperature, let it becomes ρ_t. As mass of the substance remains constant at any temperature, so we have

$$\rho_0 V_0 \;=\; \rho_t V_t$$

Here V_0 and V_t are the volumes of the substance at 0°C and t°C respectively.

Also
$$V_t \;=\; V_0(1+\gamma t)$$

$\therefore$
$$\rho_0 V_0 \;=\; \rho_t\{V_0(1+\gamma t)\}$$

or
$$\rho_t \;=\; \frac{\rho_0}{(1+\gamma t)}$$

We can write,

$$\rho_t \;=\; \rho_0(1+\gamma t)^{-1}$$

For small value of γ, we can approximate, it as;

$$\rho_t \;\simeq\; \rho_0(1-\gamma t)$$

(ii) If ρ_1 and ρ_2 are the densities at t_1 and t_2 respectively, then we can write

$$\rho_1 V_1 \;=\; \rho_2 V_2$$

or
$$\rho_1 V_0(1+\gamma t_1) \;=\; \rho_2 V_0(1+\gamma t_2)$$

or
$$\rho_1 \;=\; \rho_2 \frac{(1+\gamma t_2)}{(1+\gamma t_1)}$$

$$=\; \rho_2(1+\gamma t_2)(1-\gamma t_1)$$

$$=\; \rho_2[1+\gamma(t_2 - t_1)]$$

$$\{\text{neglecting } \gamma^2 \text{ on being small}\}$$

$\therefore$
$$\gamma \;=\; \frac{\rho_1 - \rho_2}{\rho_2(t_2 - t_1)}$$

5.4 EXPANSION OF LIQUIDS

When a liquid is heated, the containing vessel also expand and hence the observed increase in volume of the liquid is the apparent increase in volume. Thus:

Real expansion of liquid = Apparent expansion of liquid + expansion of vessel.

Coefficient of real expansion of liquid (γ_r)

If V_0 and V_t are the volumes of liquid at 0°C and t°C respectively, then

$$\gamma_r = \frac{\Delta V}{V_0 \Delta T}$$

Here,

$$\Delta V = V_t - V_0 \text{ and } \Delta T = t - 0 = t$$

$$\therefore \quad \gamma_r = \frac{V_t - V_0}{V_0 t}$$

or

$$V_t = V_0(1 + \gamma_r t)$$

If γ_a and γ_g are the apparent coefficients of expansion of liquid and volume coefficient of expansion of container respectively, then

or

$$\gamma_r = \gamma_a + \gamma_g$$

Determination of γ_a

Method - I : By Dilatometer

Let V_0 and V_t are the apparent volume noted (volume w.r.t container) at 0°C and t°C respectively, then

$$\gamma_a = \frac{V_t - V_0}{V_0 t}.$$

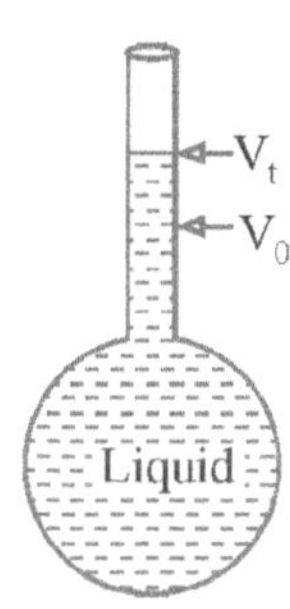

Fig. 5.8

Determination of the coefficient of real expansion of liquid by Dulong and Petit's method

The apparatus consists of a long glass tube. The tube contains the liquid whose coefficient of real expansion is to be determined. Let the temperature of the cold and the hot limbs are t_1 °C and t_2 °C respectively. Again let h_1 and h_2 be the height of liquid columns and ρ_1 and ρ_2 be the densities of the liquids at temperatures t_1 and t_2 respectively, then

$$\text{Pressure at } B = \text{Pressure at } C$$

$$\Rightarrow \quad P_a + h_1 \rho_1 g = P_a + h_2 \rho_2 g \qquad \ldots(1)$$

where P_a is the atmospheric pressure.

The equation (1) reduces to

$$h_1 \rho_1 = h_2 \rho_2 \qquad \ldots(2)$$

Here,

$$\rho_1 = \frac{\rho_0}{1 + \gamma_r t_1} \text{ and } \rho_2 = \frac{\rho_0}{1 + \gamma_r t_2}$$

$$\therefore \quad h_1\left[\frac{\rho_0}{1 + \gamma_r t_1}\right] = h_2\left[\frac{\rho_0}{1 + \gamma_r t_2}\right]$$

or

$$h_1(1 + \gamma_r t_2) = h_2(1 + \gamma_r t_1)$$

$$h_1 + h_1 \gamma_r t_2 = h_2 + h_2 \gamma_r t_1$$

$$\gamma_r(h_1 t_2 - h_2 t_1) = h_2 - h_1$$

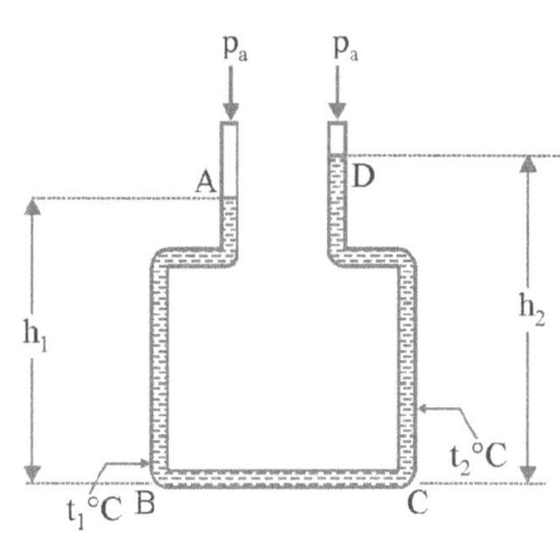

Fig. 5.10

$$\text{or} \qquad \gamma_r = \left(\frac{h_2 - h_1}{h_1 t_2 - h_2 t_1} \right)$$

If $t_1 = 0$, $h_1 = h_0$ and $t_2 = t$, $h_2 = h$, then $\gamma_r = \dfrac{h - h_0}{h_0 t}$

Determination of the coefficient of real expansion of liquid : Second method

With the experimental set-up and data given in the figure, we have to find the value of γ_r
In the *Fig. 5.11* t_1, t_2, t_3 and t_4 denotes the temperatures.

If ρ_0 is the density of mercury at $0°C$, then

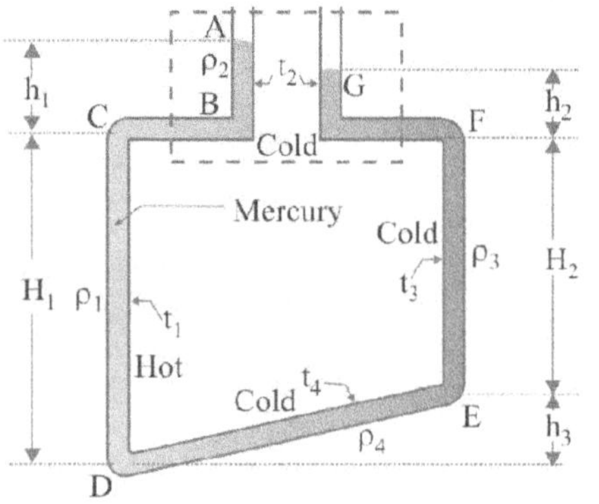

$$\rho_1 = \frac{\rho_0}{1 + \gamma_r t_1}; \qquad \rho_2 = \frac{\rho_0}{1 + \gamma_r t_2}; \qquad \rho_3 = \frac{\rho_0}{1 + \gamma_r t_3}; \qquad \rho_4 = \frac{\rho_0}{1 + \gamma_r t_4}$$

It is clear from the figure that, the pressures at D due to the columns of mercury in the hot and cold limbs must be equal .

$$\therefore \qquad h_1 \rho_2 g + H_1 \rho_1 g = h_2 \rho_2 g + H_2 \rho_3 g + h_3 \rho_4 g$$

$$\text{or} \qquad h_1 \rho_2 + H_1 \rho_1 = h_2 \rho_2 + H_2 \rho_3 + h_3 \rho_4 \qquad \text{... (1)}$$

Substituting values of ρ_1, ρ_2, ρ_3 and ρ_4 in equation (1), we have

$$h_1 \left(\frac{\rho_0}{1 + \gamma_r t_2} \right) + H_1 \left(\frac{\rho_0}{1 + \gamma_r t_1} \right) = h_2 \left(\frac{\rho_0}{1 + \gamma_r t_2} \right) + H_2 \left(\frac{\rho_0}{1 + \gamma_r t_3} \right) + h_3 \left(\frac{\rho_0}{1 + \gamma_r t_4} \right)$$

$$\text{or} \qquad \frac{h_1}{1 + \gamma_r t_2} + \frac{H_1}{1 + \gamma_r t_1} = \frac{h_2}{1 + \gamma_r t_2} + \frac{H_2}{1 + \gamma_r t_3} + \frac{h_3}{1 + \gamma_r t_4}$$

$$\text{or} \qquad \frac{h_1 - h_2}{1 + \gamma_r t_2} + \frac{H_1}{1 + \gamma_r t_1} = \frac{H_2}{1 + \gamma_r t_3} + \frac{h_3}{1 + \gamma_r t_4}$$

By putting the values of heights and temperatures, the value of γ_r can be calculated.

Anomalous expansion of water

Most of the substances expand on heating. But water contracts instead of expanding, when heated from $0°C$ to $4\ °C$, after which it expands in the usual manner. Thus water has its least volume and maximum density at $4\ °C$. It can be seen from the *Fig. 5.12*.

Correction for barometric reading

The scale of barometer is usually calibrated at $0°C$. If observation is taken at a different temperature, then there need correction for brass-scale. Suppose the height of mercury at $0°C$ is H_0 and true scale reading is H. If α is the coefficient of linear expansion of brass, then true height of brass scale at temperature t,

$$H_t = H(1 + \alpha t) \qquad \text{...(1)}$$

As atmospheric pressure is constant at all temperature, so we have

$$\text{Pressure at } 0°C = \text{Pressure at } t°C$$

$$\text{or} \qquad H_0 \rho_0 g = H_t \rho_t g \qquad \text{...(2)}$$

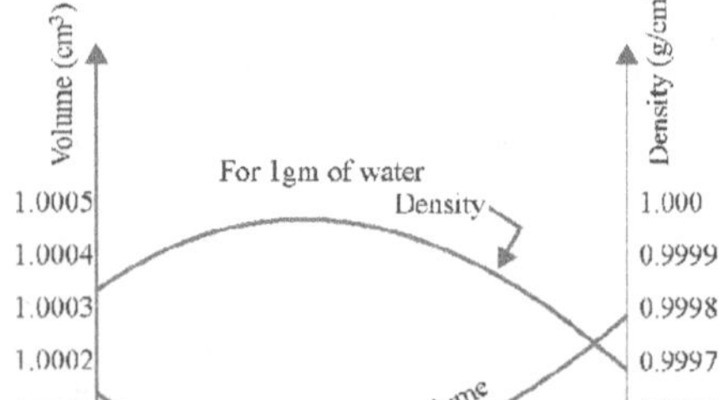

Fig. 5.11

Fig. 5.12

Here ρ_0 and ρ_t are the densities of mercury at 0°C and t°C respectively. Also we have

$\rho_t = \dfrac{\rho_0}{1+\gamma t}$, γ being volume coefficient of mercury. Thus from equations (1) and (2), we have

$$H_0\rho_0 g \ = \ H(1+\alpha t)\dfrac{\rho_0}{1+\gamma t}\, g$$

or $$H_0 \ = \ H(1+\alpha t)(1+\gamma t)^{-1}$$

$$H_0 \ = \ H(1+\alpha t)(1-\gamma t)$$

$$H_0 \ = \ H[1+\alpha t-\gamma t-\alpha\gamma t^2] \simeq H[1-(\gamma-\alpha)t]$$

Since α and γ both are small $(\sim 10^{-5}/°C)$, so their product becomes very small, and therefore can be neglected.

$\therefore$ $$H \ = \ \dfrac{H_0}{[1-(\gamma-\alpha)t]}$$

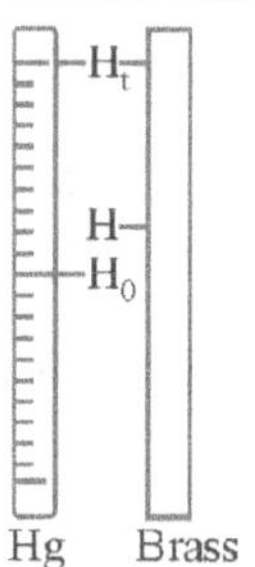

Fig. 5.13

Bimetallic strip

Bimetallic strip is made of two metal strips placed in contact (see *Fig. 5.14*). The strip works as an electric contact breaker in an electrical circuit.

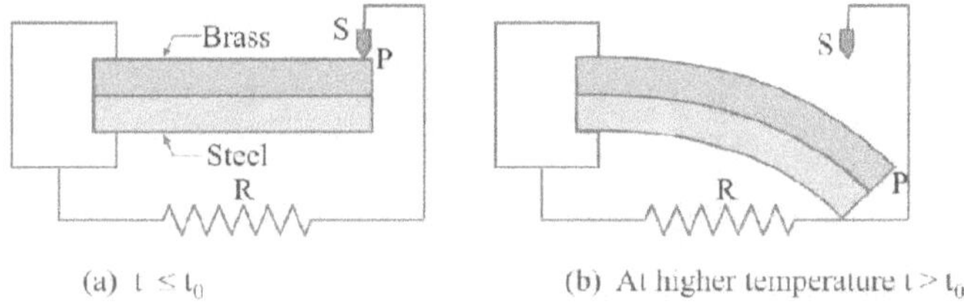

Fig. 5.14

When bimetallic strip is heated, it curves due to the difference in the coefficients of linear expansion of the two metals, and the circuit breaks (figure b).
The metal of higher coefficient of expansion bends more than the other of lesser coefficient of expansion. When temperature falls, the bimetallic strip contracts and the contact at P is restored.

Ex. 5 The coefficient of cubical expansion of mercury is 0.00018 /°C and that of brass 0.00006/°C. If a barometer having a brass-scale were to read 74.5 cm at 30 °C, find the true barometric height at 0°C. The scale is supposed to be correct at 15 °C.

Sol. Coefficient of linear expansion of brass,

$$\alpha \ = \ \dfrac{\gamma}{3}=\dfrac{0.00006}{3}$$

$$= \ 0.00002/°C$$

The brass scale is true at 15 °C, therefore at 30 °C its graduation will increase in length and so observed reading will be less than true reading by,

$$\Delta\ell \ = \ \ell\alpha\Delta t = 74.5\times 0.00002\times 15$$

$$= \ 0.02235 \text{ cm}$$

$\therefore$ True reading at 30 °C,

$$\ell_{30} \ = \ \ell_{observed}+\Delta\ell$$

$$= \ 74.5+0.02235$$

$$= \ 74.522 \text{ cm}$$

As pressure is constant at all temperature, so

Pressure at 0°C $\ = \ $ Pressure at 30 °C

or $$h_0\rho_0 g \ = h_{30}\rho_{30}g$$

$\therefore$ $$h_0 \ = \ \dfrac{h_{30}\rho_{30}}{\rho_0} = \dfrac{h_{30}}{\rho_0}\times\dfrac{\rho_0}{(1+\gamma_{Hg}t)}$$

$$= \ \dfrac{74.522}{1+0.00018\times 30} = 74.122 \text{ cm} \quad \textbf{\textit{Ans.}}$$

Fact to know :

Invar is an alloy of nickel and steel which has very small coefficient of expansion. That is why the pendulum clock provided with invar pendulum, whose length and therefore time period remains almost constant.

Ex. 6   The difference between length of a certain brass rod and that of a steel rod is claimed to be constant at all temperature is this possible?

Sol.

Yes, let ℓ_1 and ℓ_2 are the lengths of brass and steel rods at $0°C$ and α_1 and α_2 are their respective coefficients of expansion. If change in lengths of the rods are equal, then their difference remain constant at all temperature. i.e.,

$$\Delta\ell_1 = \Delta\ell_2$$

or

$$\ell_1\alpha_1 t = \ell_2\alpha_2 t$$

or

$$\ell_1\alpha_1 = \ell_2\alpha_2$$

5.5 EXPANSION OF GASES

When gases are heated, they may change in pressure and volume both. Hence there are two coefficients of expansion of a gases.

(i)   **Volume coefficient of a gas, γ_v :**

It can be defined as ;

$$\gamma_v = \frac{\text{Increase in volume (keeping pressure constant)}}{\text{Original volume} \times \text{rise in temperature}}$$

$$= \frac{\Delta V}{V_0 \Delta T}$$

If V_0 and V_t are the volumes of gas keeping pressure constant at $0°C$ and $t°C$ respectively, then

$$\Delta V = V_t - V_0, \ \Delta T = t - 0 = t$$

$\therefore$

$$\gamma_v = \frac{V_t - V_0}{V_0 t}$$

or

$$V_t = V_0(1 + \gamma_v t)$$

Value of γ_v for an ideal gas :

For an ideal gas, $\qquad PV = nRT \qquad \qquad$ ...(1)

At constant pressure

$$P\Delta V = nR\Delta T \qquad \qquad ...(2)$$

Dividing (2) by (1), we get

$$\frac{\Delta V}{V} = \frac{\Delta T}{T}$$

or

$$\frac{\Delta V}{V \Delta T} = \frac{1}{T}$$

As

$$\frac{\Delta V}{V \Delta T} = \gamma_v$$

$\therefore$

$$\gamma_v = \frac{1}{T} = \frac{1}{273}/°C$$

At

$$T = 273 + 0$$

$\therefore$

$$V = V_0$$

(ii)   **Pressure coefficient of gas, γ_p :**

It can be defined as ;

$$\gamma_p = \frac{\text{Increase in pressure (at constant volume)}}{\text{Initial pressure} \times \text{rise in temperature}}$$

$$= \frac{\Delta P}{P_0 \Delta T}$$

If P_0 and P_t are the pressures at 0°C and t°C respectively, then

$$\Delta P = P_t - P_0, \ \Delta T = t - 0 = t$$

$$\therefore \quad \gamma_p = \frac{P_t - P_0}{P_0 t}$$

or

$$P_t = P_0(1 + \gamma_p t)$$

Value of γ_p for an ideal gas :

$$\gamma_p = \frac{1}{273}/°C$$

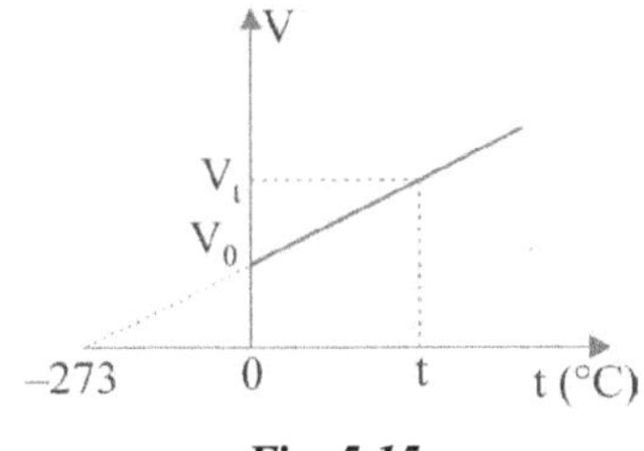

Fig. 5.15

If P_1 and P_2 are the pressures, of a given mass of gas at temperatures t_1 and t_2 respectively, then

$$P_1 = P_0(1 + \gamma_p t_1) \ \text{ and } P_2 = P_0(1 + \gamma_p t_2)$$

$$\therefore \quad \frac{P_2}{P_1} = \frac{1 + \gamma_p t_2}{1 + \gamma_p t_1}$$

After solving, we get

$$\gamma_p = \frac{P_2 - P_1}{P_1 t_2 - P_2 t_1}.$$

Unoccupied length of tube

Suppose x_0 be the length of mercury column at 0°C and x_t at t°C.
Let a_0 and a_t are areas of cross-section of tube at 0°C and t°C respectively, then

$$a_t = a_0(1 + \beta_g t) = a_0(1 + 2\alpha_g t)$$

where α_g is the linear coefficient of expansion of glass.

Length of glass tube unoccupied by mercury

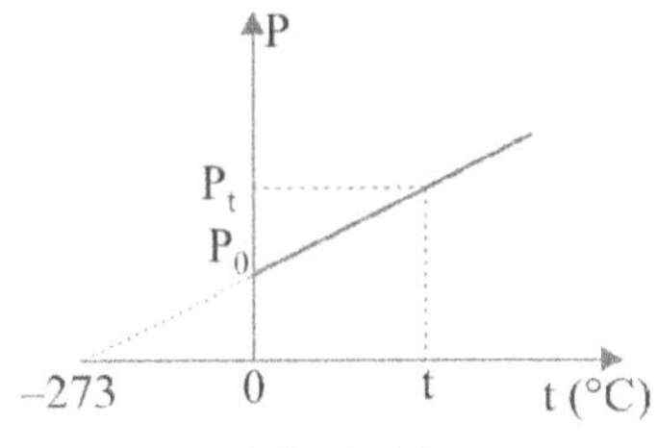

Fig. 5.16

$$\Delta \ell = AB = \ell_t - x_t$$

$$= \frac{(V_{\text{glass}})_t}{a_t} - \frac{(V_{Hg})_t}{a_t}$$

$$= \frac{(V_{\text{glass}})_0(1 + 3\alpha_g t) - (V_{Hg})_0(1 + \gamma_{Hg} t)}{a_0(1 + 2\alpha_g t)}$$

$$= \frac{a_0 \ell_0(1 + 3\alpha_g t) - a_0 x_0(1 + \gamma_{Hg} t)}{a_0(1 + 2\alpha_g t)}$$

$$= \frac{\ell_0(1 + 3\alpha_g t) - x_0(1 + \gamma_{Hg} t)}{(1 + 2\alpha_g t)}$$

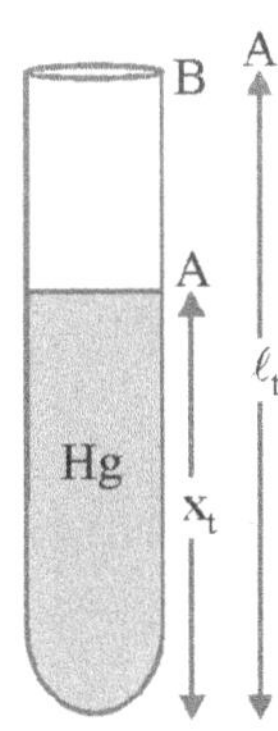

Fig. 5.19

$$= \ell_0(1 + 3\alpha_g t)(1 + 2\alpha_g t)^{-1} - x_0(1 + \gamma_{Hg} t)(1 + 2\alpha_g t)^{-1}$$

$$\simeq \ell_0(1 + 3\alpha_g t)(1 - 2\alpha_g t) - x_0(1 + \gamma_{Hg} t)(1 - 2\alpha_g t)$$

Neglecting product $(\gamma_{Hg}\alpha_g)$ and α_g^2, we have

$$\Delta \ell = \ell_0(1 + \alpha_g t) - x_0[1 + (\gamma_{Hg} - 2\alpha_g)t]$$

$\Delta \ell$ to be constant at all temperature, so

$$\frac{d(\Delta \ell)}{dt} = 0$$

$$\frac{d}{dt}[\ell_0(1 + \alpha_g t) - x_0\{1 + (\gamma_{Hg} - 2\alpha_g)t\}] = 0$$

$$\text{or} \quad \frac{d}{dt}[\ell_0(1+\alpha_g t) - x_0\{1+(\gamma_{Hg}-2\alpha_g)t\}] = 0$$

$$\ell_0\alpha_g - x_0(\gamma_{Hg}-2\alpha_g) = 0$$

$$\therefore \quad x_0 = \left(\frac{\ell_0\alpha_g}{\gamma_{Hg}-2\alpha_g}\right)$$

Change in time period of simple pendulum

If ℓ_0 be the length of the pendulum at 0°C, then its time period

$$T_0 = 2\pi\sqrt{\frac{\ell_0}{g}} \qquad \ldots(1)$$

At any temperature t, the time period of the pendulum is given by,

$$T = 2\pi\sqrt{\frac{\ell}{g}}$$

Here,
$$\ell = \ell_0(1+\alpha t)$$

$$\therefore \quad T = 2\pi\sqrt{\frac{\ell_0(1+\alpha t)}{g}}$$

$$= 2\pi\sqrt{\frac{\ell_0}{g}}(1+\alpha t)^{1/2}$$

$$= T_0(1+\alpha t)^{1/2} \qquad \ldots(2)$$

$$\simeq T_0\left(1+\frac{\alpha t}{2}\right)$$

$$\text{or} \quad \frac{T}{T_0}-1 = \frac{\alpha t}{2}$$

$$\frac{T-T_0}{T_0} = \frac{\alpha t}{2}$$

$$\text{or} \quad \frac{\Delta T}{T_0} = \frac{\alpha t}{2}$$

$$\therefore \quad \Delta T = \left(\frac{\alpha t}{2}\right)T_0$$

(i) If temperature increases, time period also increases and clock runs slow, so here is loss in time.

(ii) If temperature decreases, time period also decreases and clock runs fast, so there is gain in time.

Apparent weight of body at any temperature

Suppose a body of weight W in a submerged in liquid, its apparent weight at any temperature t is given by

$$W_t = W - F_t \qquad \ldots(1)$$

Here F_t is the buoyant force exerted by liquid

At 0°C, $$F_0 = V_0 \rho_0 g \qquad \ldots(2)$$

Here ρ_0 is the density of liquid and V_0 is the volume of the body at 0°C.

At t°C, $$F_t = V_t \rho_t g$$

Here V_t is the volume of body at t°C, which is;

$$V_t = V_0(1+\gamma_s t)$$

Here γ_s is the coefficient of cubical expansion of body, ρ_t is the density of liquid at t°C, which is given by;

$$\rho_t = \frac{\rho_0}{1+\gamma_\ell t}$$

Here γ_ℓ is the coefficient of cubical expansion of liquid.

$$\therefore \qquad F_t = V_0(1+\gamma_s t)\left(\frac{\rho_0}{1+\gamma_\ell t}\right)g$$

$$= V_0\rho_0 g(1+\gamma_s t)(1+\gamma_\ell t)^{-1}$$

$$\simeq F_0(1+\gamma_s t)(1-\gamma_\ell t)$$

$$= F_0(1+\gamma_s t-\gamma_\ell t-\gamma_s\gamma_\ell t^2)$$

Neglecting $\gamma_s\gamma_\ell t^2$ on being small.

$$\therefore \qquad F_t \simeq F_0[1-(\gamma_\ell-\gamma_s)t] \qquad \ldots(3)$$

Substituting this value in equation (1), we get

$$W_t = W - F_0(1-(\gamma_\ell-\gamma_s)t \qquad \ldots(4)$$

It is clear from equation (3) and (4) that with increase in temperature of the system buoyant force decreases and apparent weight increases. If $\gamma_s = \gamma_\ell$, $W_t = W - F_0$, at all temperatures.

Thermal expansion : An atomic view

Graph shows the potential energy U of two neighbouring atoms in a solid and their interatomic separation r_0.

At $T_0 = 0\ K$, the atoms remain at the equilibrium separation r_0 and their energy E_0 is minimum (only P.E). At the higher temperature, under the influence of thermal energy, atoms vibrate about their mean positions, the amplitude of vibrations increase with increase in temperature. Referring to *Fig. 5.20*, at temperature T_1, the amplitude of vibration is $a_1 b_1$ and at T_2 ($T_2 > T_1$), the amplitude is $a_2 b_2$ The corresponding mean spacing between the atoms are giving by r_1 and r_2 respectively. As the repulsive force is short range in nature as compared to the attractive force, the potential energy curve is steeper on the left side of r_0 than on the right side. The equilibrium position shift to the right of the curve i.e., $r_0 < r_1 < r_2$. In other words, the material exhibits thermal expansion.

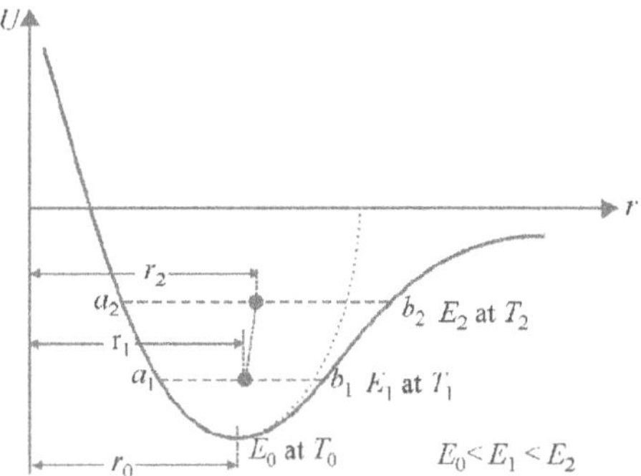

Fig. 5.20

Ex. 7 The *Fig. 5.17* shows a rectangular plate of size $(a \times b)$ from which two circular holes of radii R_1 and R_2 has been cut. The separation between the holes is x. If a', b', R_1', R_2' and x' are the respective values at higher temperature t, then find

$$\left(\frac{a'}{a}\right), \left(\frac{b'}{b}\right), \left(\frac{R_1'}{R}\right), \left(\frac{R_2'}{R_2}\right) \text{ and } \left(\frac{x'}{x}\right).$$

Sol.

If given data are at 0°C, then at any temperature t,

$$a' = a(1 + \alpha t)$$

$$b' = b(1 + \alpha t)$$

$$R_1' = R_1(1 + \alpha t)$$

$$R_2' = R_2(1 + \alpha t)$$

and

$$x' = x(1 + \alpha t)$$

$$\therefore \quad \frac{a'}{a} = \frac{b'}{b} = \frac{R_1'}{R_1} = \frac{R_2'}{R_2} = \frac{x'}{x} = 1 + \alpha t$$

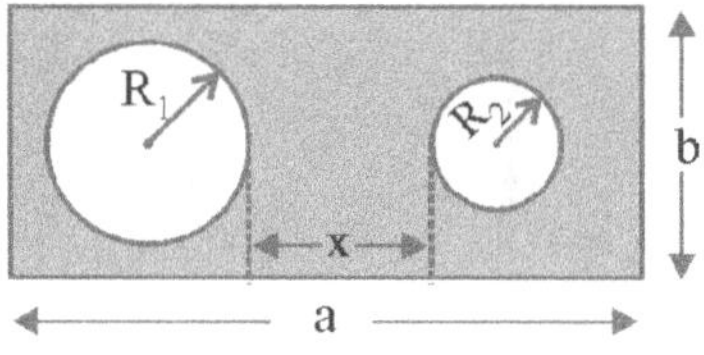

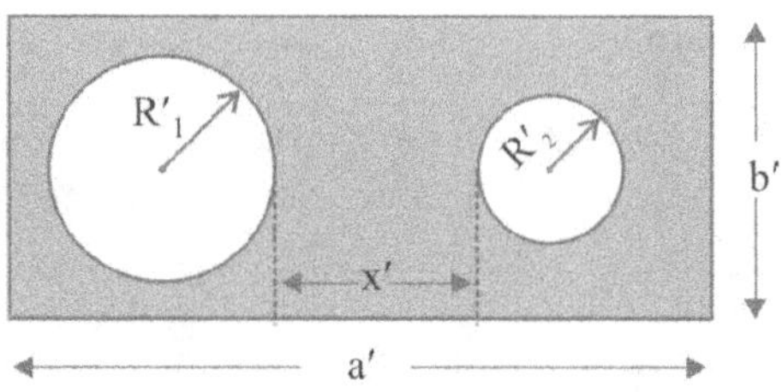

Fig. 5.17

Ex. 8 A bimetallic strip is formed out of two identical strips, one of copper and the other of brass. The coefficients of linear expansions of two metals are α_C and α_B. On heating, the temperature of the strip goes up by ΔT and the strip bends to form an arc of radius R. Find R.

Sol.

Let ℓ_0 be the length and t the thickness of each strip. On heating, length of brass rod

$$\ell_1 = \ell_0(1 + \alpha_B \Delta T)$$

By the geometry of the figure, we have

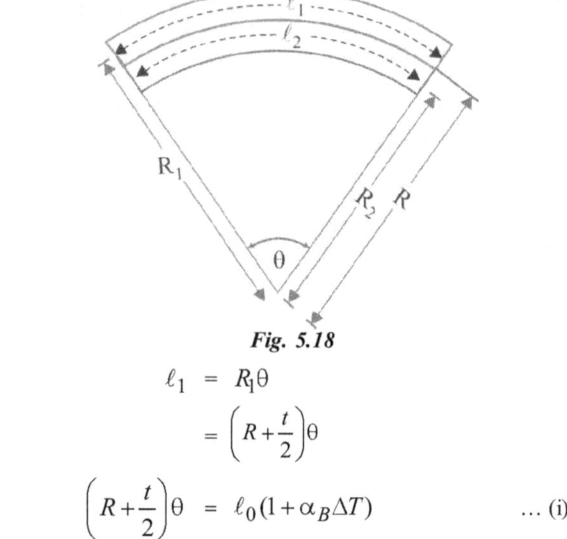

Fig. 5.18

$$\ell_1 = R_1\theta$$

$$= \left(R + \frac{t}{2}\right)\theta$$

$$\therefore \quad \left(R + \frac{t}{2}\right)\theta = \ell_0(1 + \alpha_B \Delta T) \qquad \ldots \text{(i)}$$

Similarly for copper strip, $\ell_2 = \ell_0(1 + \alpha_C t) = R_2\theta$

$$\text{or} \quad \left(R - \frac{t}{2}\right)\theta = \ell_0(1 + \alpha_C \Delta T) \qquad \ldots \text{(ii)}$$

Dividing equation (i) by (ii), we get

$$\Rightarrow \quad \frac{\left(R + \dfrac{t}{2}\right)}{\left(R - \dfrac{t}{2}\right)} = \frac{1 + \alpha_B \Delta T}{1 + \alpha_C \Delta T}$$

$$\Rightarrow \quad \left(R + \frac{t}{2}\right)(1 + \alpha_C \Delta T) = \left(R - \frac{t}{2}\right)(1 + \alpha_B \Delta T)$$

$$\Rightarrow \quad R + R\alpha_C \Delta T + \frac{t}{2} + \frac{t}{2}\alpha_C \Delta T = R + R\alpha_B \Delta T - \frac{t}{2} - \frac{t}{2}\alpha_B \Delta T$$

If ΔT is small, α is still small, so we can neglect their product. And, therefore, we have

$$R\alpha_B \Delta T - R\alpha_C \Delta T = t$$

$$\text{or} \quad R = \frac{t}{(\alpha_B - \alpha_C)\Delta T} \qquad \textit{Ans.}$$

Ex. 9 A long mercury glass tube with a uniform capillary bore has in it a thread of mercury which is 1 m long at 0°C. What will be its length at 100°C if the real coefficient of expansion of mercury is 0.000182 and coefficient of cubical expansion of glass equal to 0.000025/°C

Sol.

Suppose V_0 and V_t are the volumes of mercury thread at 0°C and t°C respectively, then

$$V_t = V_0(1 + \gamma_r t)$$

Let a_0 and a_t are the areas of cross-section of the tube at 0°C and t°C respectively, then

$$a_t = a_0(1+\beta t)$$

$$= a_0(1+2\alpha t) \qquad \{\beta = 2\alpha\}$$

The length of the thread at 0°C,

$$\ell_0 = \frac{V_0}{a_0}$$

The length of thread at t°C,

$$\ell_t = \frac{V_t}{a_t}$$

$$= \frac{V_0(1+\gamma_r t)}{a_0(1+2\alpha t)}$$

$$= \ell_0(1+\gamma_r t)(1-2\alpha t)$$

Substituting the given values, we get

$$\ell_t = 1(1+0.000182\times100)\left(1-2\times\frac{0.000025}{3}\times100\right)$$

$$= 1.0182 \times 0.9983$$

$$= 1.016\,\text{m} \qquad\qquad \textit{Ans.}$$

Ex. 10

A cube of coefficient of linear expansion α_s is floating in a bath containing a liquid of coefficient of volume expansion γ_ℓ. When the temperature is raised by ΔT, the depth upto which the cube is submerged in the liquid remain the same. Find the relation between α_s and γ_ℓ showing all the steps.

Sol.

Suppose initially ℓ be the length of the cube and y the depth of the cube submerged. Then by law of floatation.

Weight of cube = Weight of liquid displaced

$$\text{or} \qquad Mg = (\ell^2 y)\rho_\ell g \qquad\qquad \ldots\text{(i)}$$

With the increase in temperature, the weight remain constant. Thus at higher temperature

$$Mg = (\ell'^2 y)\rho'_\ell g \qquad\qquad \ldots\text{(ii)}$$

From equations (i) and (ii)

$$(\ell^2 y)\rho_\ell g = (\ell'^2 y)\rho'_\ell g$$

$$\text{or} \qquad \ell^2\rho_\ell = \ell'^2\rho'_\ell$$

$$\text{But} \qquad \ell' = \ell(1+\alpha_s\Delta T),\ \rho'_\ell = \frac{\rho_\ell}{(1+\gamma_\ell\Delta T)}$$

$$\therefore \qquad \ell^2\rho_\ell = [\ell(1+\alpha_s\Delta T)]^2\frac{\rho_\ell}{(1+\gamma_\ell\Delta T)}$$

$$\text{or} \qquad 1+\gamma_\ell\Delta T = (1+\alpha_s\Delta T)^2$$

As $\alpha_s\Delta T \ll 1$, so by binomial theorem we can write

$$1+\gamma_\ell\Delta T = 1+2\alpha_s\Delta T$$

$$\therefore \qquad \gamma_\ell = 2\alpha_s \qquad\qquad \textit{Ans.}$$

Ex. 11

A bar with a crack at its centre buckles as a result of temperature rise of 32 °C. If the fixed distance L_0 is 3.77 m and the coefficient of linear expansion of the bar is 25×10^{-6} /°C find the rise x of the centre.

Sol.

Consider one half of the bar, its initial length

$$\ell_0 = \frac{L_0}{2}$$

Its length after increase in temperature Δt,

$$\ell = \ell_0(1+\alpha\Delta T)$$

By Pythogoras theorem

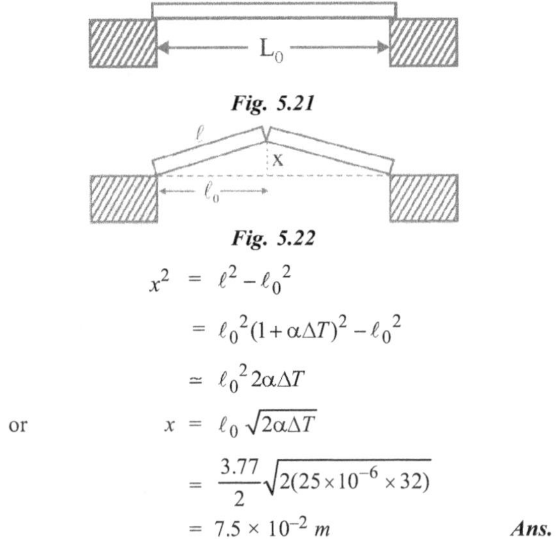

Fig. 5.21

Fig. 5.22

$$x^2 = \ell^2 - \ell_0^2$$

$$= \ell_0^2(1+\alpha\Delta T)^2 - \ell_0^2$$

$$\simeq \ell_0^2\, 2\alpha\Delta T$$

$$\text{or} \qquad x = \ell_0\sqrt{2\alpha\Delta T}$$

$$= \frac{3.77}{2}\sqrt{2(25\times10^{-6}\times32)}$$

$$= 7.5 \times 10^{-2}\,\text{m} \qquad\qquad \textit{Ans.}$$

Ex. 12

The temperature compensated pendulum is designed to compensate for the change in length due to temperature rise. *Fig. 5.23* shows one such pendulum. It consists of an isosceles triangular frame as shown in the figure. The pendulum is supported at mid-point of side AB, and it remains horizontal. Determine the ratio ℓ_1/ℓ_2, so that the length of the pendulum remain same at all temperatures.

Sol.

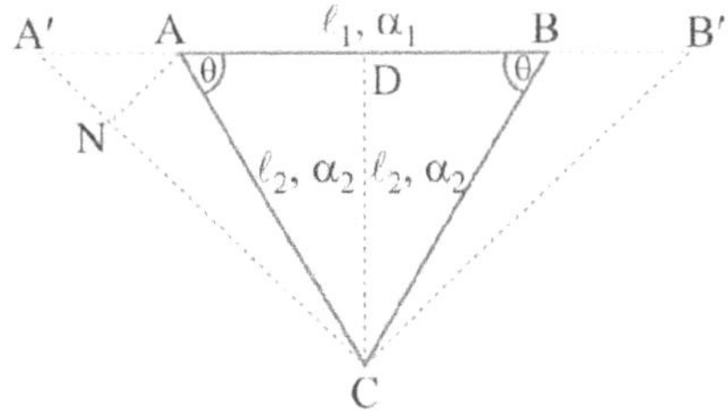

Fig. 5.23

The dotted line shows configuration after rise in temperature. As the height of the pendulum remain same, so end C remain at its position.

The increase in length of the rod AB

$$\Delta\ell_1 = \ell_1\alpha_1\Delta T$$

As the length increases equally on both sides of AB, so

$$AA' = \frac{1}{2}\ell_1\alpha_1\Delta T \qquad\qquad \ldots\text{(i)}$$

Draw normal from A to $A'C$, the increase in length of AC

$$A'N = \ell_2 \alpha_2 \Delta T \qquad \text{... (ii)}$$

From the $\Delta AA'N$,

$$A'N = AA'\cos\theta, \text{ as } \theta \text{ is small}$$

Here $$\cos\theta = \frac{\ell_1}{2\ell_2} \qquad \text{... (iii)}$$

From equations (i), (ii) and (iii), we get

$$\ell_2 \alpha_2 \Delta T = \left(\frac{1}{2}\ell_1 \alpha_1 \Delta T\right)\left(\frac{\ell_1}{2\ell_2}\right)$$

$$\therefore \quad \frac{\ell_1}{\ell_2} = 2\sqrt{\frac{\alpha_2}{\alpha_1}} \qquad \textit{Ans.}$$

5.6 Heat and Calorimetry

Heat is the energy in transit

When two bodies at different temperature make in contact, something is transferred between them . The word heat is meaningful only when energy is being transferred. The expressions like, heat of a body or heat in a body are meaningless. So the heat can be defined as the energy in transit that flows from one body to another due to difference of temperature between them. Once heat is transferred to a body, it becomes the part of its internal energy.

Unit of heat

CGS unit of heat : The CGS unit of heat is calorie.

Definition of calorie : It is the amount of heat energy required to raise the temperature of one gram of water through 1 °C (from 14.5 °C to 15.5 °C).

SI unit of heat : The SI unit of heat is joule (J).

Joule's mechanical equivalent of heat

James Precott Joule (1818 – 1889) performed a series of experiments and proved that heat is a form of energy. He showed that if an amount of work W (or any other form of energy) is converted into heat, the equal amount of heat is produced. Thus

$$W \propto Q$$

or $$W = JQ$$

or $$J = \frac{W}{Q}$$

If $Q = 1$, then $J = W$

The proportionality constant J is called Joule's mechanical equivalent of heat.

The value of J: $\qquad J = 4.186 \text{ J/cal}$

Note: J is not a physical quantity. It just a conversion factor.

British thermal unit : It is the amount of heat required to raise the temperature of 1 pound of water through 1 °F.

$$1 \text{ BTU} = 252 \text{ calorie}$$

5.7 Special Heat

It is defined as the amount of heat required to raise the temperature of unit mass of a substance through 1 K (1 °C). Suppose Q amount of heat is supplied to m amount of substance, the rise in temperature of substance is ΔT, then specific heat is given by

$$c = \frac{Q}{m\Delta T}$$

or we can write, $\qquad Q = mc\Delta T$

Units of specific heat

(i)   In CGS system, the unit of Q is calorie, m is gram and ΔT in °C. Therefore unit of c in this system becomes

$$c = \text{cal/g–°C}$$

(ii) In SI system, the unit of Q is Joule, m in kg and ΔT in kelvin. Therefore in this system unit of specific heat becomes $J/kg\text{-}K$.

1.   Specific heat of water is 1cal/g-°C or $4200\ J/kg\text{-}K$.
2.   Specific heat of ice is 0.5 cal/g-°C or $2100\ J/kg\text{-}K$.
3.   The maximum value of specific heat is 3.5 cal/g°C for hydrogen.
4.   The minimum value of specific heat is 0.022 cal/g°C for radon.

The specific heat of a substance is not constant at all temperature. Therefore specific heat used in the above formula is the mean value of specific heats. When c varies considerably with temperature, then for small change in temperature dT, we can write

$$dQ = mcdT$$

$$\therefore \qquad Q = \int_{T_1}^{T_2} mcdT$$

Here T_1 and T_2 are the initial and final temperatures.

Dulong and Petit's Law (1819)

"At near about room temperature the molar specific heat of most of the solids is equal to $3R$ or 6 cal/mol-K at constant volume".

In case of solids, the significant motion of atoms are vibratory motion. During vibration, the kinetic energy (E_k) of an atom changes periodically into potential energy (E_p) and vice-versa. So the average values of E_k and E_p are equal.

For each form of energy there are three degrees of freedom. Therefore a molecule has six degrees of freedom (3 for kinetic + 3 for potential). According to law of equi-partition of energy, each degree of freedom possesses energy $\dfrac{kT}{2}$ per atom. Therefore total energy associated with one mole of a substance at a temperature T is given by;

$$E_k = 3 \times \frac{kT}{2} = \frac{3}{2}kT$$

$$E_P = 3 \times \frac{kT}{2} = \frac{3}{2}kT$$

$\therefore$ Average vibrational energy per atom

$$= E_k + E_p = 3kT$$

The internal energy (due to vibration) of one mole of an atom of the solid is given by

$$
\begin{aligned}
U &= (3kT) \times N \\
&= 3(kN)T \\
&= 3RT \qquad\qquad (kN = R)
\end{aligned}
$$

Also, we have

$$C_V = \frac{dU}{dT}$$

$$= \frac{d(3RT)}{dT}$$

or

$$C_V = 3R$$

Proof of formula $C_V = \dfrac{dU}{dT}$, will be discussed in the next chapter.

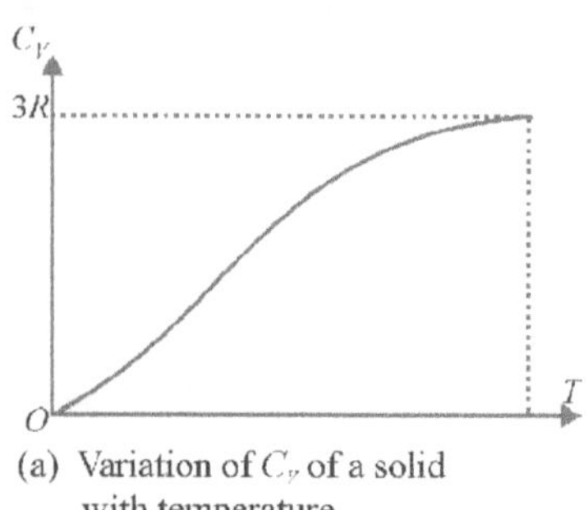

(a) Variation of C_v of a solid with temperature

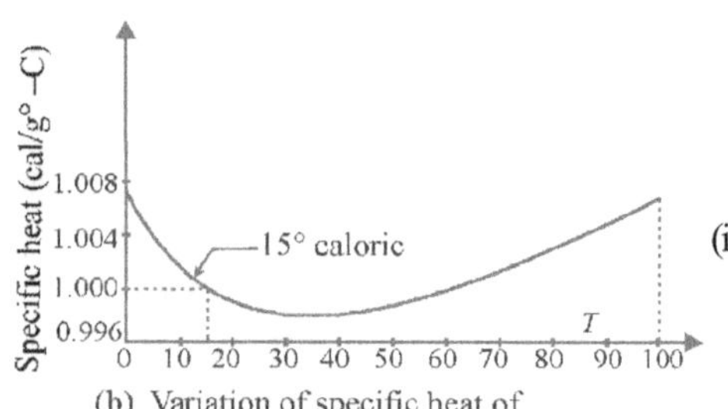

(b) Variation of specific heat of water with temperature

Fig. 5.24

Variation of specific heat of solid with temperature

The figure shows the variation of molar specific heat (C_V) as a function of temperature. It can be easily understand that at higher temperature the molar specific heat of all solids is close a value $3R$.

Specific heat of gas

Limit of specific heat of gas : Consider a gas of mass m and volume V at a pressure P.

(i)   Suppose gas is compressed suddenly without supplying heat :

Let the temperature of the gas rises by ΔT .

$$\therefore \qquad c = \frac{\Delta Q}{m \Delta T}$$

But $\Delta Q = 0$, $\therefore c = 0$.

(ii)   Heat is supplied to the gas and it is allowed to expand in such a way that there is no rise in temperature. i.e., $\Delta T = 0$

$$\therefore \qquad c = \frac{\Delta Q}{m \Delta T}$$

$$= \frac{\Delta Q}{m \times 0} = \infty$$

Thus the specific heat of a gas may varies from zero to infinity. It may have any positive or negative value. The exact value depends on the conditions of pressure and volume when heat is being supplied. Out of the many specific heats of a gas, two are of prime significance.

1.   **Molar specific heat at constant volume C_V**

It is the amount of heat required to raise the temperature of 1 mole of a gas through $1\,K\,(1\,°C)$ at constant volume. If Q_V is the heat given to n moles of a gas at constant volume and change in temperature be ΔT , then

$$C_V = \frac{Q_v}{n \Delta T}$$

or $$Q_V = nC_v \Delta T$$

2.   **Molar specific heat at constant pressure C_P**

It is the amount of heat required to raise the temperature of 1 mole of a gas through $1K\,(1°C)$ at constant pressure. If Q_P is the heat given to n moles of a gas at constant pressure and change in temperature be ΔT , then

$$C_P = \frac{Q_P}{n \Delta T}$$

or $$Q_P = nC_P \Delta T$$

Relation between C_V and C_P : Mayer's formula

Heat supplied to a gas at constant volume entirely used to raise its temperature. When a gas is heated at constant pressure, it expand to keep pressure constant and therefore some mechanical work is to be done in addition to raise the temperature of the gas. Hence more heat is required at constant pressure than that at constant volume. Thus for one mole of a gas, we have

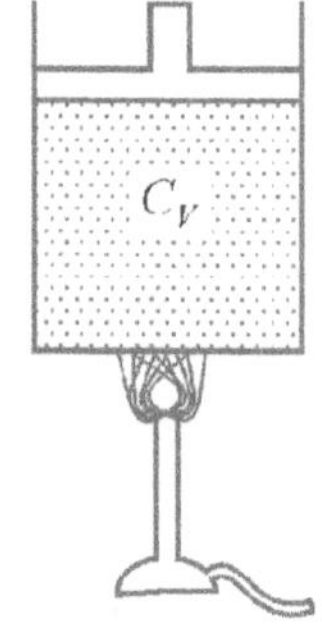

(a) Heat is supplied at constant volume

$$C_P - C_V \;=\; \text{Work done}$$
$$=\; P\Delta V \qquad \ldots(1)$$

At constant pressure, we have

$$PV_1 \;=\; RT \qquad \ldots(2)$$
$$\text{and} \qquad PV_2 \;=\; R(T+1) \qquad \ldots(3)$$

where V_1 is the volume of gas at temperature T and V_2 is the volume of gas at temperature $(T+1)$. Subtracting equation (2) from (3), we get

$$P(V_2 - V_1) \;=\; R$$
$$\text{or} \qquad P\Delta V \;=\; R$$

Substituting this value in equation (1), we get

$$C_P - C_V \;=\; R \qquad \textbf{Mayer's formula}$$

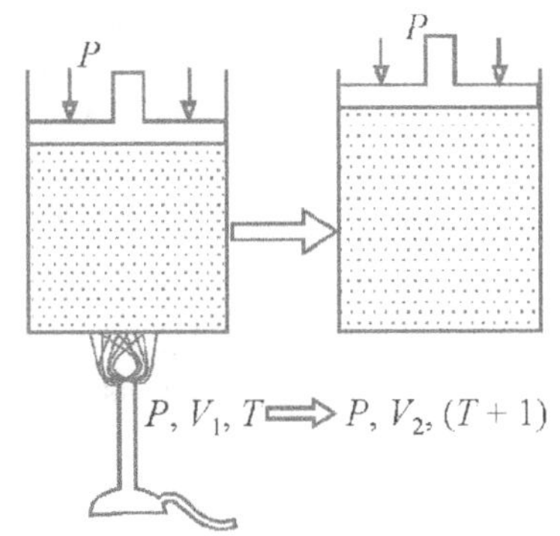

(b) Heat is supplied at constant pressure

Fig. 5.25

Note:

1. Substance which expand on heating, $P\Delta V$ is positive and therefore, $C_P - C_V = +ve$ or $C_P > C_V$. If any substance contracts on heating, $P\Delta V$ will be negative and therefore, $C_P - C_V = -ve$ or $C_P < C_V$.

2. $C_P - C_V = R$ holds good for all ideal gases.

3. For one gram of a gas, we have c_V and c_P and we can write $C_V = Mc_V$ and $C_P = Mc_P$. Also, $\qquad c_P - c_V \;=\; r$

   Here $\quad r = \dfrac{R}{M}$ which is different for different gases.

5.8 Heat capacity or thermal capacity

It is the amount of heat required to raise the temperature of whole amount of substance through 1K (1°C). By definition, we have

$$\text{Heat capacity} \;=\; \text{mass} \times \text{specific heat}$$
$$\text{or} \qquad S \;=\; mc$$

The CGS unit of heat capacity is cal/°C and SI unit is J/K.

5.9 Water Equivalent

The water equivalent of a body is defined as the mass of water which requires the same amount of heat as is required by the given body for the equal rise of temperature. Let the mass of substance be m, specific heat c and rise in temperature is ΔT, then

$$Q \;=\; mc\Delta T \qquad \ldots(i)$$

If water equivalent is w, then

$$Q \;=\; w \times 1 \times \Delta T \qquad (c \text{ of water is 1 cal/g-}°C)$$
$$\therefore \qquad w \times 1 \times \Delta T \;=\; mc\Delta T$$
$$\text{or} \qquad w \;=\; mc$$

Note: Water equivalent numerically equal to the heat capacity but the unit of water equivalent is gm or kg and that of heat capacity is cal/°C or J/°C.

Ex. 13 70 cal of heat is required to raise the temperature of 2 mole of an ideal gas at constant pressure from 30 °C to 35 °C. What is the amount of heat required to raise the temperature of same gas through the same range (30 °C to 35 °C) at constant volume? ($R = 2$ cal/mol-K)

Sol.   Heat required at constant pressure

$$Q_P = nC_P\Delta T$$

or $$70 = 2\,C_P\,(35 - 30)$$

$\therefore$ $$C_P = 7 \text{ cal/mol-K}$$

As $$C_P - C_V = R$$

$\therefore$ $$C_V = C_P - R = 7 - 2$$
$$= 5 \text{ cal/ mol - K}$$

Heat required at constant volume

$$Q_V = nC_V\Delta T$$
$$= 2 \times 5 \times (35 - 30)$$
$$= 50 \text{ cal} \hspace{3cm} \textit{Ans.}$$

Ex. 14 The specific heat of a substance varies as $(3t^2 + t) \times 10^{-3}$ cal/g-°C. What is the amount of heat required to raise the temperature of 1 kg of substance through 10°C to 20 °C?

Sol.   For small change in temperature dt, heat required,

$$dQ = mcdt$$

$\therefore$ $$Q = \int_{t_1}^{t_2} mcdt$$

Given; $$m = 1000\,g, \; c = (3t^2 + t)$$

$\therefore$ $$Q = \int_{10}^{20} 1000(3t^2 + t) \times 10^{-3}\,dt$$

$$= \left| t^3 + \frac{t^2}{2} \right|_{10}^{20}$$

$$= \left(20^3 + \frac{20^2}{2} \right) - \left(10^3 + \frac{10^2}{2} \right)$$

$$= 8200 - 1050$$

$$= 7150 \text{ cal} \hspace{2cm} \textit{Ans.}$$

Ex. 15 A metal sphere of radius R and specific heat C is rotated about an axis passing through its centre at a speed n rotation / second. It is suddenly stopped and 50% of its energy is used in increasing its temperature, then find the rise in temperature of the sphere.

Sol.   The rotation K.E. of the sphere

$$K = \frac{1}{2} I\omega^2$$

$$= \frac{1}{2}\left(\frac{2}{5} MR^2 \right)(2\pi n)^2 = \left(\frac{4\pi^2}{5} n^2 \right) MR^2$$

Kinetic energy used to raise the temperature

$$= \frac{50}{100}\left[\frac{4\pi^2 n^2}{5} MR^2 \right]$$

$$= \frac{2\pi^2 n^2}{5} MR^2$$

Let ΔT be the rise in temperature, then

$$MC\Delta T = \frac{2\pi^2 n^2}{5} MR^2$$

$\therefore$ $$\Delta T = \frac{2\pi^2 n^2 R^2}{5C} \hspace{2cm} \textit{Ans.}$$

5.10 CHANGE IN PHASE

A substance can exist in three possible phases *viz.*, solid, liquid and gas. Transition from one phase to another are accompanied by the absorption or liberation of heat and usually by change in volume, even when the transition occurs at constant temperature. As an example take small piece of ice in a container at –20 °C, and heat is supplied to the container at a uniform rate. The temperature starts increasing steadily, as shown by the segment *a* to *b* in *Fig. 5.26*, until the temperature rises to 0 °C. Thereafter ice starts melting.

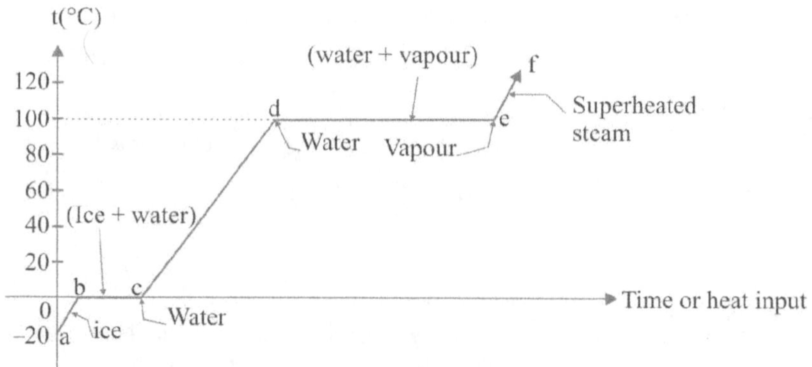

Fig. 5.26

The melting process is a change in phase, from the solid phase to the liquid phase. But the thermometer does not show any rise in temperature. When the whole ice has melted (point c) the temperature of water now rises at a uniform rate (from c to d) although this rate is slower than that from a to b. When temperature of water reaches 100 °C, it begins to boil. The temperature remains constant until whole water has converted into water vapour. Another change of phase has therefore taken place from liquid phase to the gaseous phase. If heating is still continue (from e to f), the temperature of vapour starts rising. The gaseous state would now be called **superheated steam**.

5.11 LATENT HEAT

The heat which is used to change the phase of substance at constant temperature is called latent heat or hidden heat.

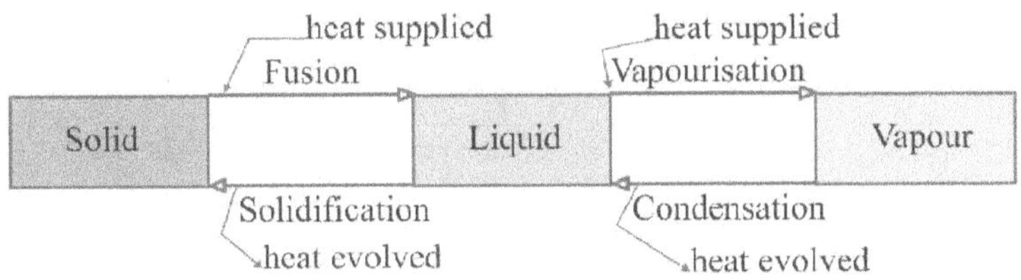

Fig. 5.27

Latent heat of fusion : The amount of heat required to convert unit mass of solid into liquid at its melting point is called latent heat of fusion.

Latent heat of vapourisation : The amount of heat required to convert unit mass of liquid into vapour at its boiling point is called latent heat of vapourisation.

The term heat of transformation is better used to both heats of fusion and heats of vapourisation, and let both are denoted by L. If Q is the amount of heat absorbed or liberated by m amount of substance, then L is defined as ;

$$L = \frac{Q}{m}$$

or
$$Q = mL$$

Unit of L

The CGS unit of L is cal/g.
The SI unit of L is J/kg.

Some values

Latent heat of fusion of ice is 80 cal/g or 336 kJ/kg.
Latent heat of vapourisation of water is 540 cal/g or 2259 kJ/kg at one atmospheric pressure.

IMPORTANT POINTS
1. Melting and freezing occur at the same temperature and therefore melting point and freezing point are equal.
2. As long as the change of phase (state) takes place, the temperature remains constant.
3. Some substances show increase in volume on melting. e.g., wax, ghee etc while some other substances show decrease in volume on melting e.g., ice.
4. The melting point of those substances (water, antimony) which contracts on melting, decreases with increase in pressure. The melting point of ice is 0°C at 1 atm and – 1°C at 133 atm, –2°C at 265 atm.
5. The melting point of those substances which expand on melting increases with increase in pressure.
6. Impurities lower freezing point. When salt is mixed with ice, the temperature of the mixture decreases.

About boiling

1. Boiling and condensing occur at the same temperature.
2. As long as the change of phase takes place, the temperature remains constant.
3. All liquids show increase in volume on vapourisation.
4. The boiling point of liquid increases with increase in pressure. The boiling point of water is 100°C at 1 atm and 130 °C at 2 atm.
5. In pressure cooker, the cooking occurs at 2 atm pressure.

The change in M.P. or B.P. with pressure can be calculate by using Clausius Clapeyron's equation (which is out of syllabus). The equation is ; $\dfrac{\Delta P}{\Delta T} = \dfrac{L}{T(V_2 - V_1)}$.

Ex. 16 The melting point of ice is 0°C at 1 atm. At what pressure it will be –1°C?

Sol. Here $\Delta T = (-1 - 0) = -1$, $T = 273 + 0 = 273\ K$

and $V_2 - V_1 = \left(1 - \dfrac{1}{0.9}\right) \times 10^{-3}\ m^3$

(given)

$\qquad\qquad L = 80\ \text{cal/g}$

We have, $\dfrac{\Delta P}{\Delta T} = \dfrac{L}{T(V_2 - V_1)}$

or $\dfrac{\Delta P}{(-1)} = \dfrac{80 \times 4.2 \times 10^3}{273\left(1 - \dfrac{1}{0.9}\right) \times 10^{-3}}$

$\therefore \qquad \Delta P = 132 \times 10^5\ \text{N/m}^2$

$\qquad\qquad\quad \simeq 132\ \text{atm}$

or $P_2 - P_1 = 132\ \text{atm}$

$\therefore \qquad P_2 = 132 + P_1 = 133\ \text{atm}$ ***Ans.***

Ice slab

Wire

Fig. 5.28

Regelation : Take an ice slab and place it on two supports. The weights are suspended on the ice slab with the help of wire. The wire will pass through the slab without spliting it. Just below the wire, ice melts at a lower temperature due to increase in pressure. When wire has moved down, the water above the wire freezes again. The phenomenon of melting of ice and its resolidification is called regelation.

FACTS TO KNOW

1. **Supercooled water :** Water below 0 °C is known as supercooled water. But this can be possible at a pressure greater than atmospheric pressure.
2. **Superheated steam :** Steam at a temperature greater than 100°C is known as superheated steam.
3. **Dry ice :** Solid carbon dioxide is called dry ice. Carbon dioxide at –78 °C remains in solid state. Solid carbon dioxide does not melt when exposed to air. It directly evaporates and forms its vapours.
4. **Vapour and gas :** These are the gaseous states of the substance. These two states have distinct boundary which is governed by a particular temperature called critical temperature. The gaseous state of substance below the critical temperature is called vapour and above critical temperature is called gas. A gas cannot be liquefied by mere application of pressure, however high it may be . A vapour can be liquefied by applying pressure. Thus to liquefy a gas, first it bring below critical temperature.

Critical temperature	
Substance	**Critical temperatrue °C**
Water	374
Ammonia	132
Carbon dioxide	31
Oxygen	–119
Hydrogen	–240
Helium	–268

Ex. 17 A solid material is supplied heat at a constant rate. The temperature of the material is changing with the heat input as shown in *Fig. 5.28*. Study the graph carefully and answer the following questions :

(i) What do the horizontal regions *AB* and *CD* represent?

(ii) If *CD = 2AB*, what do you infer ?

(iii) The slope of *OA* > the slope of *BC*. What does this indicate?

(iv) What does the slope *DE* represent?

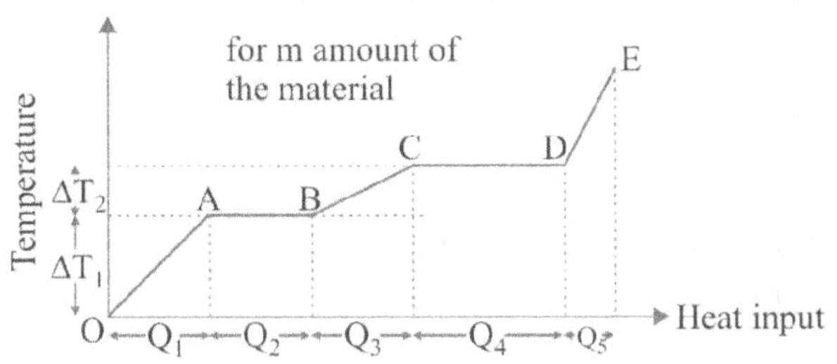

Fig. 5.29

Sol.

(i) In the regions *AB* and *CD* the temperature of the material remain constant. So *AB* represents fusion and *CD* represents vaporisation.

(ii) $CD = 2AB$ or $Q_4 = 2Q_2$, it shows that latent heat of vaporisation is twice than that of latent heat of fusion.

(iii) Let C_1 and C_2 are the specific heats of solid and liquid states respectively, then

$$Q_1 = mC_1\Delta T_1$$

or $$C_1 = \frac{1}{m\left(\dfrac{\Delta T_1}{Q_1}\right)} = \frac{1}{m \times \text{slope of } OA}$$

Similarly $$C_2 = \frac{1}{m \times \text{slope of } BC}$$

Since slope of OA > slope of BC, $\therefore\ C_1 < C_2$.

(iv) If C_3 is the specific heat of vapour state (region *DE*), then

$$C_3 = \frac{1}{m \times \text{slope of } DE}$$

or Slope of $DE = \dfrac{1}{mC_3} = \dfrac{1}{\text{heat capacity}}$

5.12 LAW OF MIXTURE OR LAW OF CALORIMETRY

When two or more non reacting substances are placed in contact, the heat lost by the hot substance is equal to the heat gained by cold substances. That is ;

Heat lost = Heat gained

Two substances at temperatures T_1 and T_2 are taken together in a calorimeter. Let T is the equilibrium temperature of the system.

(i) When substances of same phase are taken together

$$T_1 < T < T_2, \text{if } T_1 < T_2$$

(ii) When substances of different phases are taken together,

  (a) $T_1 < T < T_2$ or

  (b) $T = T_1$ or $T = T_2$.

Ex. 18 1g ice at 0°C is placed in a calorimeter having 1g water at 40 °C. Find equilibrium temperature and final contents. Assuming heat capacity of calorimeter is negligibly small.

Sol.

The heat required to melt the ice completely

$$= mL = 1 \times 80 = 80 \text{ cal}$$

The heat available on water

$$= mc\Delta T = 1 \times 1 \times (40 - 0)$$

$$= 40 \text{ cal.}$$

$\therefore$ Entire heat of water is utilised to melt the ice and its temperature falls to 0°C. Ice still at 0°C. So equilibrium temperature of contents remain 0°C. Let m is the amount of ice melt due to 40 cal heat, then

$$m \times 80 = 40$$

or $$m = \frac{1}{2}g$$

Final contents : ice $= 1 - \dfrac{1}{2} = \dfrac{1}{2}g$

water $= 1 + \dfrac{1}{2} = \dfrac{3}{2}g$ *Ans.*

Ex. 19 1g ice at – 40°C is placed in a container having 1g water at 10°C. Find equilibrium temperature. Assume heat capacity of container is negligibly small.

Sol.

The heat available on water to cool from 10°C to 0°C

$$= mc\Delta T = 1\times 1\times (10-0) = 10 \text{ cal}$$

Let temperature of ice becomes T after taking this heat

$$\therefore \qquad m_{ice}c\Delta T \;=\; 10$$

or $\quad 1\times 0.5 \times [T-(-40)] = 10$

$$T+40 \;=\; 20$$

$$T \;=\; -20°C$$

Now the system have $1g$ ice at $-20°C$ and $1g$ water at $0°C$. Let m gram water get freezed to bring the ice from $-20°C$ to $0°C$,

heat gained by ice = heat lost by water

$$\therefore \qquad m_{ice}c\,[0-(-20)] \;=\; m\times 80$$

or $\qquad 1\times 0.5 \times 20 = m\times 80$

$$m \;=\; \frac{1}{8}g$$

Thus equilibrium temperature becomes $0°C$, as both ice and water change into $0°C$.

Final contents :

$$ice \;=\; 1g + \frac{1}{8}g = \frac{9}{8}g$$

$$water \;=\; 1-\frac{1}{8} = \frac{7}{8}g \qquad\qquad \textit{Ans.}$$

Ex. 20 $1g$ steam at 100°C is passed in a insulating vessel having $1g$ ice at 0°C. Find the equilibrium temperature of the mixture. Neglecting heat capacity of the vessel.

Sol.

Heat available on steam (changes into steam to water)

$$= mL = 1\times 540 = 540 \text{ cal}$$

Heat gained by ice to change into water and then rise its temperature to 100°C

$$= m_{ice}L + m_{wat}c\Delta T$$

$$= 1\times 80 + 1\times 1\times (100-0)$$

$$= 180 \text{ cal.}$$

The above calculations show that some part of steam will condense to change the ice into water of 100°C. Let m is the mass of steam condensed, then

$$m\times 540 \;=\; 180$$

or $\qquad m \;=\; \dfrac{180}{540} = \dfrac{1}{3}g$

Final contents: $\quad$ ice $= 0g$

$$water \;=\; 1+\frac{1}{3} = \frac{4}{3}g$$

$$steam \;=\; 1-\frac{1}{3} = \frac{2}{3}g \qquad\qquad \textit{Ans.}$$

Ex. 21 The temperature of equal masses of three different liquids A, B and C are 12 °C, 19 °C and 28°C respectively. The temperature when A and B are mixed in 16 °C and when B and C are mixed it is 23 °C. What should be the temperature when A and C are mixed?

Sol.

Given $T_A = 12°C$, $T_B = 19°C$ and $T_C = 28°C$. Let C_A, C_B and C_C are the specific heats of respective liquids.

When liquid A and B are mixed, the temperature of mixture becomes 16 °C, then

$$mC_A(16-12) \;=\; mC_B(19-16)$$

or $\qquad\qquad C_B \;=\; \dfrac{4}{3}C_A \qquad\qquad\qquad …\text{ (i)}$

When liquid B and C are mixed, the temperature of mixture becomes 23 °C, then

$$mC_B(23-19) \;=\; mC_C(28-23)$$

or $\qquad\qquad C_B \;=\; \dfrac{5}{4}C_C \qquad\qquad\qquad …\text{ (ii)}$

From (i) and (ii), we get

$$C_A \;=\; \frac{15}{16}C_C$$

Now when A and C are mixed, let equilibrium temperature of mixture is T, then

$$mC_A(T-12) \;=\; mC_C(28-T)$$

or $\qquad \dfrac{15}{16}C_C(T-12) \;=\; C_C(28-T)$

$$31T \;=\; 628$$

or $\qquad\qquad T \;=\; 20.26\ °C \qquad\qquad \textit{Ans.}$

Ex. 22 A 10 kW drilling machine is used to drill a bore in a small aluminium block of mass 8.0 kg. How much is the rise in temperature of the block in 2.5 minute? Assuming 50% of power is used up in heating the machine itself or lost the surroundings specific heat of aluminium = 0.91 J/g- °C.

Sol.

Total energy used by drilling machine

$$= Pt$$

$$= (10 \times 10^3) \times (2.5 \times 60)$$

$$= 1.5 \times 10^6 \, J$$

The energy absorbed by the aluminium block

$$= \frac{50}{100} \times 1.5 \times 10^6$$

$$= 0.75 \times 10^6 \, J$$

Let ΔT be the rise in temperature of the aluminium block, then

$$mC\Delta T = 0.75 \times 10^6$$

$$(8 \times 10^3) \times 0.91 \times \Delta T = 0.75 \times 10^6$$

$$\therefore \qquad \Delta T = 103.02\,°C \qquad\qquad \textit{Ans.}$$

Ex. 23 In an experiment on the specific heat of a metal a 0.20 kg block of the metal at 150 °C is dropped in a copper calorimeter (of water equivalent 0.025 kg) containing 150 cm^3 of water at 27 °C. The final temperature is 40 °C. Compute the specific heat of the metal.

Sol.

Let specific heat of the metal is C, the heat lost by metal block $= mC\Delta T$

$$= 0.20\,C\,(150 - 40)$$

$$= 22\,C$$

Mass of water in the calorimeter

$$= \rho V = 1000 \times (150 \times 10^{-6}) = 0.15\,\text{kg}$$

Heat gained by water and calorimeter

$$= m_w C\Delta T + C\Delta T$$

$$= (0.15 \times 4200 + 0.025 \times 4200) \times (40 - 27)$$

$$= 735 \times 13$$

$$= 9555 \, J$$

By principle of calorimetry, we have

$$22C = 9555$$

$$\therefore \qquad C = \frac{9555}{22}$$

$$= 434.3 \ \text{J/kg-}°C \qquad\qquad \textit{Ans.}$$

Ex. 24 A child running a temperature of 101°F is given an antipyrine (i.e. a medicine that lowers fever) which causes an increase in the rate of evaporation of sweat from his body. If the fever is brought down to 98°F in 20 min, what is the average rate of extra evaporation caused by the drug? Assume the evaporation mechanism to be the only way by which heat is lost. The mass of the child is 30 kg. The specific heat of human body is approximately the same as that of water, and latent heat of evaporation of water at that temperature is about 580 cal /g.

Sol.

Mass of the child, $\quad M = 30\,\text{kg}$

The fall in temperature of body of child,

$$\Delta T = 101 - 98 = 3°F$$

$$= 3 \times \frac{5}{9} = \frac{5}{3}°C$$

Specific heat of human body

$$C = 1\ \text{cal/g}\,°C$$

The heat lost by the body of child

$$= MC\Delta T = 30 \times 10^3 \times 1 \times \frac{5}{3}$$

$$= 5 \times 10^4 \, \text{cal}$$

If M' gram of sweat evaporate from the body of the child, then heat absorbed by sweat

$$= M'L = M' \times 580 \, \text{cal}$$

Heat gained = Heat lost

or $\qquad\qquad M \times 580 = 5 \times 10^4$

$$\therefore \qquad\qquad M' = 86.2 \, g$$

Time taken by sweat to evaporate = 20 min

$\therefore \quad$ Rate of evaporation of sweat

$$= \frac{\text{Mass of sweat}}{\text{time of evaporation}}$$

$$= \frac{86.2}{20}$$

$$= 4.31 \ \text{g/min} \qquad\qquad \textit{Ans.}$$

Review of formulae & Important points

1. **Thermometer :** If X is the property which varies linearly, then temperature

$$t = \left(\frac{X_t - X_0}{X_{100} - X_0}\right) \times 100 \, \text{degree}$$

Here property X may be length of mercury column, resistance of metal etc.

2. **Temperature scales :**

$$\frac{C}{5} = \frac{F - 32}{9} = \frac{K - 273.15}{5}$$

1 div of C = 1.8 div of F = 1 div of K.

3. Triple point of water is 273.16 K at 4 mm of mercury.

4. $$T = T_{tr}\frac{P}{P_{tr}}$$

5. **Radiation pyrometer :** It is based on Stefan's law.

$$T = \left[\frac{E}{\sigma}\right]^{\frac{1}{4}} kelvin$$

6. **Expansion of solids :**

   (i) Coefficient of linear expansion

$$\alpha = \frac{\Delta L}{L_0 \Delta t}$$

   (ii) Coefficient of superficial expansion

$$\beta = \frac{\Delta A}{A_0 \Delta t}$$

   (iii) Coefficient of volume expansion

$$\gamma = \frac{\Delta V}{V_0 \Delta t}$$

   (iv) $\beta \simeq 2\alpha$; $\gamma \simeq 3\alpha$

7. **Density of material at any temperature**

$$\rho_t = \frac{\rho_0}{(1 + \gamma t)}$$

8. If ρ_1 and ρ_2 are the densities at t_1 and t_2 respectively, then coefficient of volume expansion

$$\gamma = \frac{\rho_1 - \rho_2}{\rho_2(t_2 - t_1)}$$

9. **Expansion of liquids :**
   If γ_a and γ_g are the apparent coefficient of expansion of liquid and volume coefficient of expansion of container, then

$$\gamma_r = \gamma_a + \gamma_g$$

   (i) $$\gamma_a = \frac{V_t - V_0}{V_0 t}$$

   (ii) $$\gamma_a = \frac{M_0 - M}{Mt}$$

10. **Expansion of gases :**

$$\gamma_v = \frac{1}{273}\Big/{}^{\circ}C$$

$$\gamma_p = \frac{1}{273}\Big/{}^{\circ}C$$

11. Fractional charge of M.I. of the rod due to small change in temperature ΔT

$$\frac{\Delta I}{I} = 2\alpha\Delta T$$

12. Mechanical equivalent of heat

$$J = \frac{W}{Q}$$

   1 cal = 4.2 J

13. If c is the specific heat of substance, then
$$Q = mc\Delta T$$
   If c is the function of temperature, then

$$Q = \int_{T_1}^{T_2} mc\, dT$$

14. **Specific heat of gas :**
   (i) If C_v is the specific heat of gas at constant volume, then
$$Q_v = nC_v\Delta T$$
   (ii) If C_p is the specific heat at constant pressure
$$Q = nC_p\Delta T$$

15. $C_p - C_v = R$

$$C_v = \frac{R}{\gamma - 1} \text{ and } C_p = \frac{\gamma R}{\gamma - 1}$$

16. Latent heat : $Q = mL$
   Latent heat of fusion of ice = 80 cal/g or 336 kJ/kg.
   Latent heat of vapourisation of water 540 cal/g or 2259 kJ/kg at one atmospheric pressure.

17. **Law of mixture :**
$$\text{Heat lost = heat gained}$$

TEC

MCQ Type 1

Exercise 5.1

LEVEL - 1

Only one option correct

1. A beaker is filled with water at 4°C. At one time the temperature is increased by few degrees above 4°C and at another time it is decreased by a few degrees below 4°C. One shall observe that:
   (a) The level remains constant in each case
   (b) In first case water flows while in second case its level comes down
   (c) In second case water over flows while in first case its comes down
   (d) Water overflows in both the cases

2. The coefficient of apparent expansion of a liquid is C when heated in a copper vessel and it is S when heated in a silver vessel. If A is the coefficient of linear expansion of copper, then that of silver is:
   (a) $\dfrac{C + S - 3A}{3}$
   (b) $\dfrac{C + 3A - S}{3}$
   (c) $\dfrac{S + 3A - C}{3}$
   (d) $\dfrac{C + S + 3A}{3}$

3. Liquid oxygen at 50 K is heated to 300 K at constant pressure of 1 atm. The rate of heating is constant. Which of the following graphs represents the variation of temperature with time?

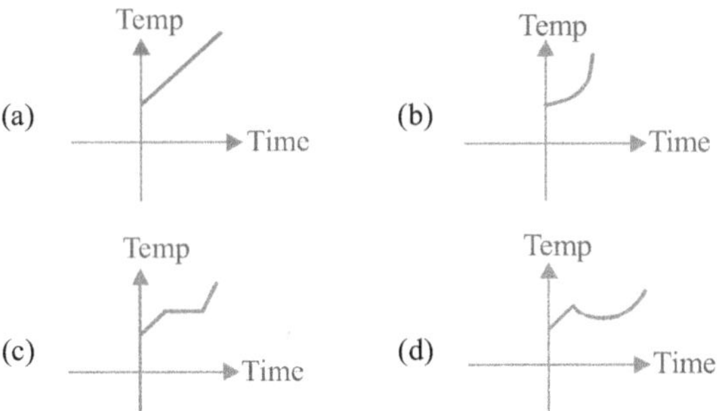

   (a)   (b)   (c)   (d)

4. A block of ice at −10°C is slowly heated and converted to steam at 100°C. Which of the following curves represents the phenomenon qualitatively :

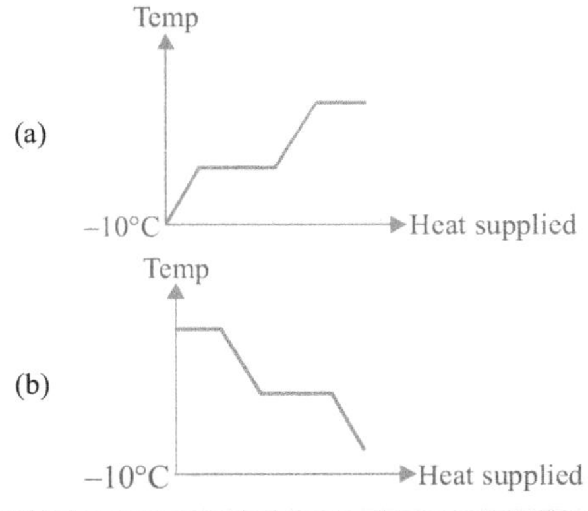

   (a)

   (b)

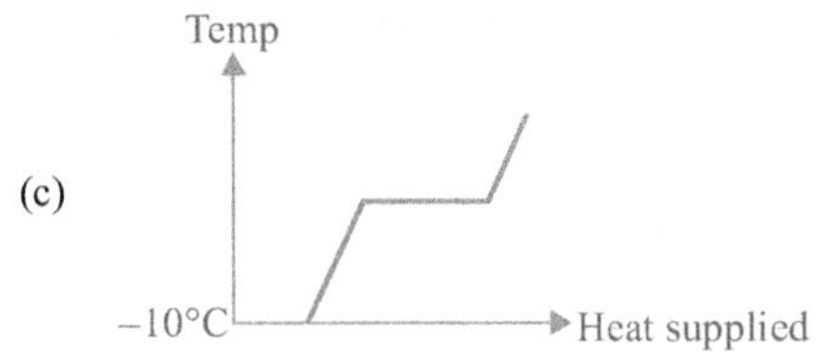

   (c)

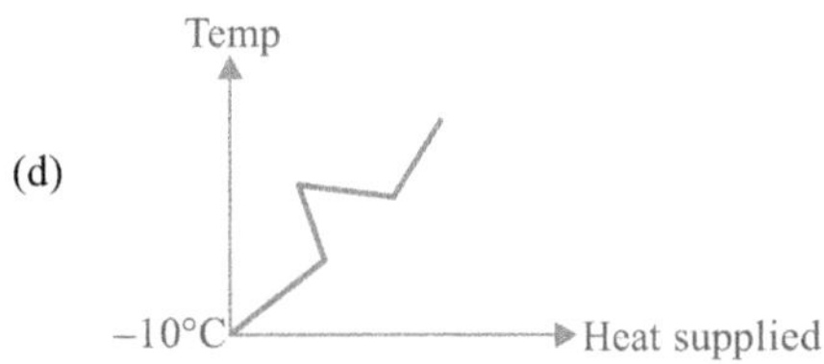

   (d)

5. 1 calorie is the heat required to increase the temperature of 1g of water by 1°C from :
   (a) 13.5°C to 14.5°C at 76 mm of Hg
   (b) 14.5°C to 15.5°C at 760 mm of Hg
   (c) 13.5°C to 15.5°C at 76 mm of Hg
   (d) 15.5°C to 16.5°C at 700 mm of Hg

6. Assuming no heat losses, the heat released by the condensation of x g of steam at 100°C can be used to convert y g of ice at 0°C into water at 100°C, the ratio $x : y$ is :
   (a) 1 : 1   (b) 1 : 2
   (c) 1 : 3   (d) 3 : 1

7. A solid substance is supplied heat at a constant rate and the variation of temperature with heat input is shown in the figure. Choose the correct statement :

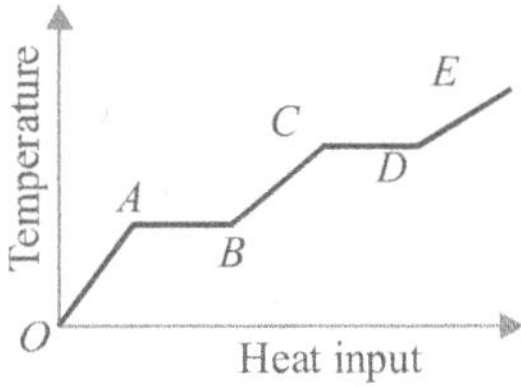

   (a) AB and CD represent changes of phase from liquid to vapour and from solid to liquid respectively.
   (b) The latent heat of vaporization is half the latent heat of fusion.
   (c) The specific heat in the solid state is less than that in the liquid state.
   (d) The specific heat in the solid state is more than that in the liquid state.

Answer Key		1	(d)	3	(c)	5	(b)	7	(c)
Sol. from page 405		2	(b)	4	(a)	6	(c)		

8. A spherical shell of copper is completely filled with a liquid at a temperature $t°C$. The bulk modulus of the liquid is K and coefficient of volume expansion is γ. If the temperature of the liquid and the shell is increased by ΔT, then the outward pressure Δp on the shell that results from the temperature increase is given by (α is the coefficient of linear expansion of the material of the shell):
   (a) $K(\gamma - 3\alpha)\,\Delta T$
   (b) $K(3\alpha - \gamma)\,\Delta T$
   (c) $3\alpha(K - \gamma)\,\Delta T$
   (d) $\gamma(3\alpha - K)\,\Delta T$

9. Three different materials of indentical masses are placed, in turn, in a special freezer that can extract energy from a material at a certain constant rate. During the cooling process, each material begins in the liquid state and ends in the solid state : Figure shows graphs of the temperature T versus time t for the three materials. The material which has the greatest heat of fusion is :

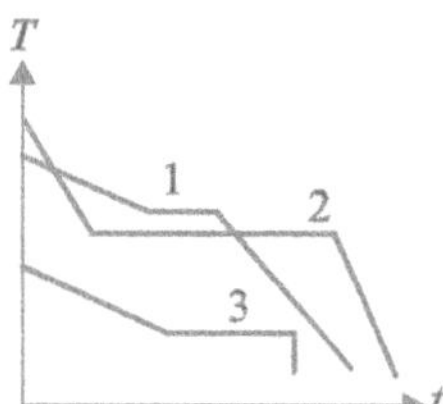

   (a) 1
   (b) 2
   (c) 3
   (d) Informations are not sufficient

10. A cylindrical metal rod is shaped into a ring with a small gap as shown. On heating the system :

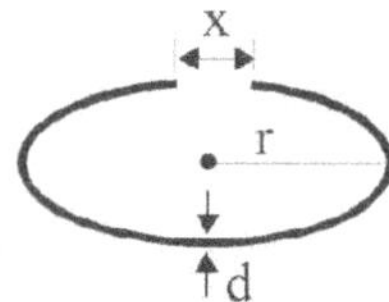

   (a) x decreases, r and d increase
   (b) x and r increase, d decreases
   (c) x, r and d all increase
   (d) x and r decreased, d remains constant

11. At what temperature the centigrade (Celsius) and Fahrenheit, readings are the same
   (a) $-40°$
   (b) $+40°$
   (c) $36.6°$
   (d) $-37°$

12. A constant volume gas thermometer shows pressure reading of 50cm and 90cm of mercury at 0°C and 100°C respectively. When the pressure reading is 60cm of mercury, the temperature is
   (a) 25°C
   (b) 40°C
   (c) 15°C
   (d) 12.5°C

13. Mercury boils at 367°C. However, mercury thermometers are made such that they can measure temperature up to 500°C. This is done by

(a) Maintaining vacuum above mercury column in the stem of the thermometer
(b) Filling nitrogen gas at high pressure above the mercury column
(c) Filling nitrogen gas at low pressure above the mercury level
(d) Filling oxygen gas at high pressure above the mercury column

14. A uniform metal rod is used as a bar pendulum. If the room temperature rises by 10°C, and the coefficient of linear expansion of the metal of the rod is 2×10^{-6} per °C, the period of the pendulum will have percentage increase of
   (a) -2×10^{-3}
   (b) -1×10^{-3}
   (c) 2×10^{-3}
   (d) 1×10^{-3}

15. When a rod is heated but prevented from expanding, the stress developed is independent of
   (a) material of the rod
   (b) rise in temperature
   (c) length of rod
   (d) none of above

16. At some temperature T, a bronze pin is a little large to fit into a hole drilled in a steel block. The change in temperature required for an exact fit is minimum when
   (a) Only the block is heated
   (b) Both block and pin are heated together
   (c) Both block and pin are cooled together
   (d) Only the pin is cooled

17. Density of substance at 0°C is 10 gm/cc and at 100°C, its density is 9.7 gm/cc. The coefficient of linear expansion of the substance will be
   (a) 10^{2}
   (b) 10^{-2}
   (c) 10^{-3}
   (d) 10^{-4}

18. Two uniform brass rods A and B of length l and $2l$ and radii $2r$ and r respectively are heated to the same temperature. The ratio of the increase in the volume of A to that of B is
   (a) $1:1$
   (b) $1:2$
   (c) $2:1$
   (d) $1:4$

19. The coefficient of apparent expansion of a liquid when determined using two different vessels A and B are γ_1 and γ_2 respectively. If the coefficient of linear expansion of the vessel A is α, the coefficient of linear expansion of the vessel B is.
   (a) $\dfrac{\alpha\gamma_1\gamma_2}{\gamma_1 + \gamma_2}$
   (b) $\dfrac{\gamma_1 - \gamma_2}{2\alpha}$
   (c) $\dfrac{\gamma_1 - \gamma_2 + \alpha}{3}$
   (d) $\dfrac{\gamma_1 - \gamma_2}{3} + \alpha$

20. Melting point of ice
   (a) increases with increasing pressure
   (b) decreases with increasing pressure
   (c) is independent of pressure
   (d) is proportional to pressure

21. Work done in converting one gram of ice at $-10°C$ into steam at 100°C is
   (a) 3045 J
   (b) 6056 J
   (c) 721 J
   (d) 616 J

Answer Key													
8	(a)	**10**	(c)	**12**	(a)	**14**	(d)	**16**	(a)	**18**	(c)	**20**	(b)
Sol. from page 405 **9**	(b)	**11**	(a)	**13**	(b)	**15**	(c)	**17**	(d)	**19**	(d)	**21**	(a)

22. In a water-fall the water falls from a height of 100 m. If the entire K.E. of water is converted into heat, the rise in temperature of water will be
(a) 0.23°C (b) 0.46°C
(c) 2.3°C (d) 0.023°C

23. Two metal strips that constitute a thermostat must necessarily differ in their
(a) Mass (b) Length
(c) Resistivity
(d) Coefficient of linear expansion

24. Steam is passed into 22g of water at 20°C. The mass of water that will be present when the water acquires a temperature of 90°C (Latent heat of steam is 540 cal/g) is
(a) 24.8 g (b) 24 g
(c) 36.6 g (d) 30 g

25. The graph AB shown in figure is a plot of temperature of a body in degree celsius and degree Fahrenheit. Then

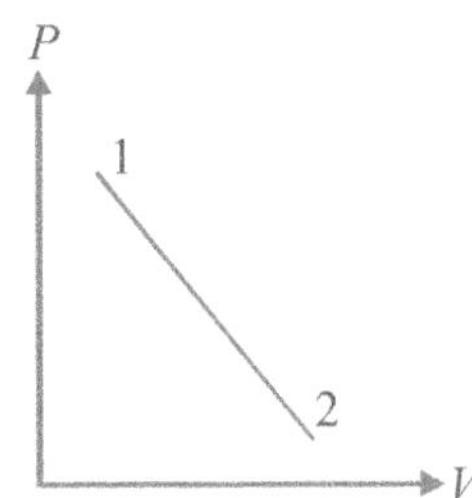

(a) Slope of line AB is 9/5 (b) Slope of line AB is 5/9
(c) Slope of line AB is 1/9 (d) Slope of line AB is 3/9

26. 1 gm of ice is passed into a container having 2gm water at 35°C. The equilibrium temperature of the mixture is :
(a) 0 °C (b) 12 °C
(c) 10 °C (d) 35 °C

27. A solid substance is at 30°C. To this substance heat energy is supplied at a constant rate. Then temperature versus time graph is as shown in the figure. The substance is in liquid state for the portion (of the graph)

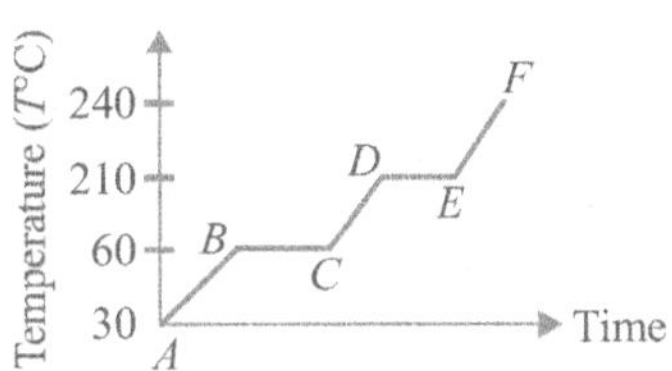

(a) BC (b) CD
(c) ED (d) EF

Answer Key						
Sol. from page 405	22	(d)	24	(a)	26	(a)
	23	(d)	25	(b)	27	(b)

LEVEL - 2

1. A volume V pressure P graph was obtained from state 1 to state 2 when a given mass of a gas is subjected to temperature changes. During the process the gas is :

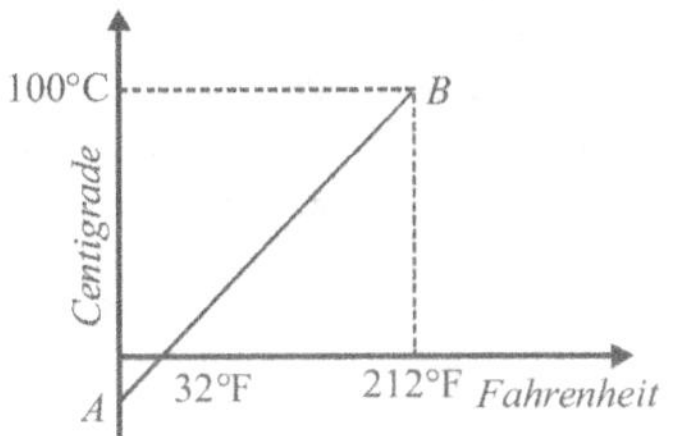

(a) Heated continuously
(b) Cooled continuously
(c) Heated in the beginning and cooled towards end
(d) Cooled in the beginning and heated towards end

2. A metallic solid sphere is rotating about its diameter as axis of rotation. If the temperature is increased by 20 °C, the percentage increase in its moment of inertia is (coefficient of linear expansion of metal = 10^{-5} per °C) :
(a) 0.1 (b) 0.2
(c) 0.03 (d) 0.04

3. When a block of iron floats in mercury at 0°C, a fraction k_1 of its volume is submerged , with at a temperature 60°C, a fraction k_2 is seen to be submerged. If the coefficient of volume expansion of iron is γ_{Fe} and that of mercury is γ_{Hg}, then the ratio k_1 / k_2 can be expressed as :

(a) $\dfrac{1+60\,\gamma_{Fe}}{1+60\,\gamma_{Hg}}$ (b) $\dfrac{1-60\,\gamma_{Fe}}{1+60\,\gamma_{Hg}}$

(c) $\dfrac{1-60\,\gamma_{Fe}}{1-60\,\gamma_{Hg}}$ (d) $\dfrac{1+60\,\gamma_{Hg}}{1+60\,\gamma_{Fe}}$

Answer Key						
Sol. from page 406	1	(c)	2	(d)	3	(a)

4. Two rods one of aluminium and the other of steel, having initial length l_1 and l_2 are connected together to form a single rod of length $(l_1 + l_2)$. The coefficients of linear expansion for aluminium and steel are α_{Al} and α_S respectively. If the length of each rod increases by the same amount when their temperature are raised by $t°C$, then the ratio $\dfrac{\ell_1}{\ell_1 + \ell_2}$ is :

(a) $\dfrac{\gamma_s}{\gamma_{Al}}$ (b) $\dfrac{\gamma_{Al}}{\gamma_s}$

(c) $\dfrac{\gamma_s}{(\gamma_{Al} + \gamma_s)}$ (d) $\dfrac{\gamma_{Al}}{(\gamma_{Al} + \gamma_s)}$

5. An ideal gas is initially at temperature T and volume V. Its volume is increased by ΔV due to an increase in temperature ΔT, pressure remaining constant. The quantity $\delta = \Delta V / V \Delta T$ varies with temperature (in kelvin) as :

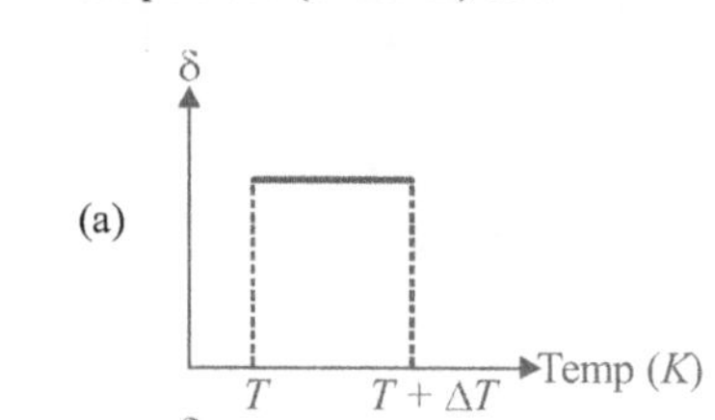
(a)

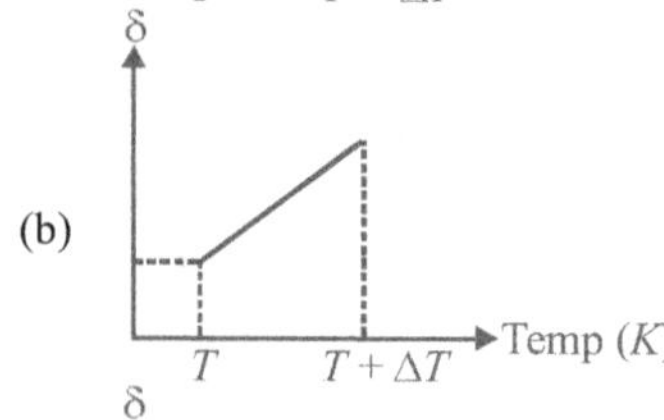
(b)

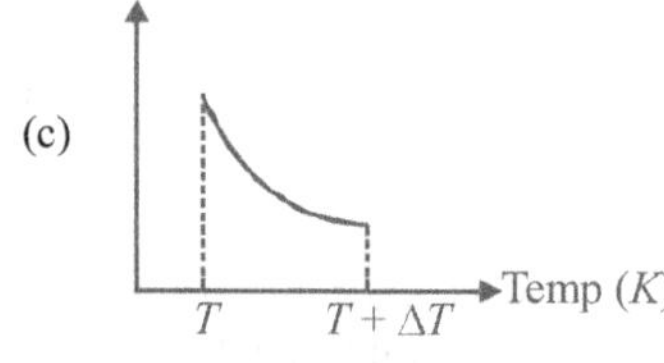
(c)

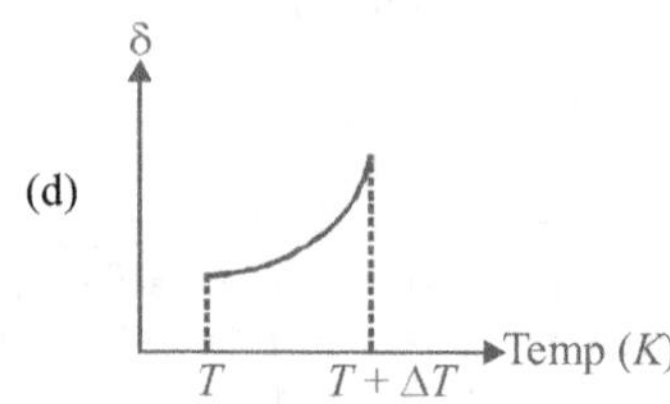
(d)

6. Which of the following graphs correctly represents the variation of $\beta = (dV/dP) / V$ with P for an ideal gas of constant temperature:

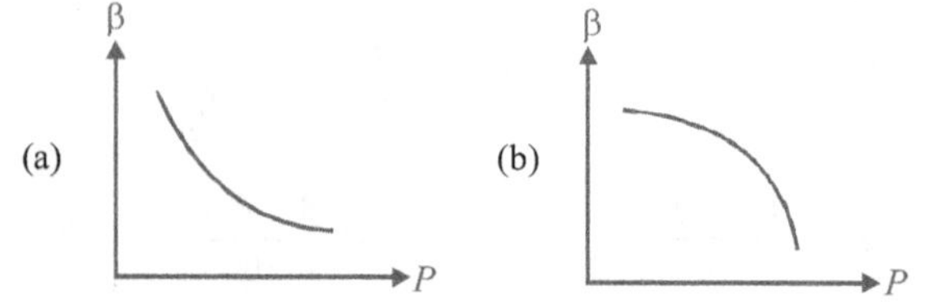
(a)   (b)

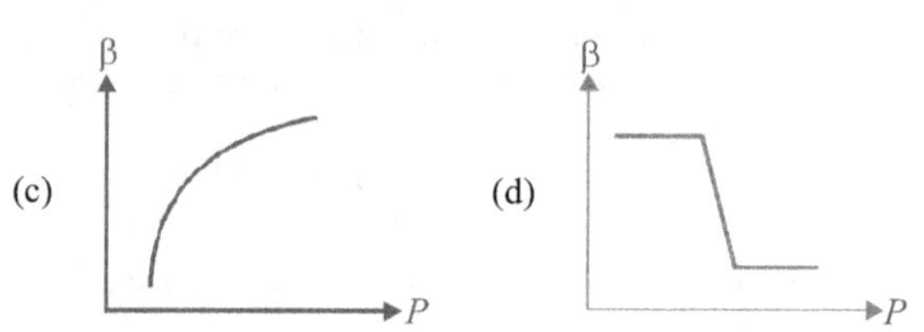
(c)   (d)

7. Two litre of water at $27°C$ is heated by $1\ kW$ heater in an open container. On an average heat is lost to surroundings at the rate 160 J/s. The time required for the temperature to reach $77°C$ is :

(a) 8 min 20 s   (b) 10 min
(c) 14 min   (d) 7 min

8. A steel rod of diameter 1.0 cm is clamped firmly at each end when its temperature is 25°C so that it can not contract on cooling. The tension in the rod at 0°C is ($\alpha = 1 \times 10^{-5}$/°C, Y = 2×10^{11} N/m²):

(a) $3925\ N$ (b) $7000\ N$
(c) $7400\ N$ (d) $4700\ N$

9. A glass bottle of capacity 50 cc at 0°C is filled with paraffin at 15°C. Given that the density of paraffin at 0°C is 0.82 g/cc, coefficient of expansion of paraffin for the range 0 to 15°C is 0.0009/°C and coefficient of linear expansion of glass is 0.000009/°C, the mass of paraffin in the bottle is :

(a) 40.5 g   (b) 54.0 g
(c) 50.4 g   (d) 5.04 g

10. A block of ice of mass $m = 10$ kg is moved back and forth over the flat horizontal surface of a large block of ice. Both blocks are at 0°C and the force that produces the back and forth motion acts only horizontally. The coefficient of friction between the two surfaces is 0.060. If 15.2 g of water is produced, the total distance travelled by the upper block relative to the lower is

$$(L_{ice} = 3.34 \times 10^5 \text{ J/kg})$$

(a) 432 m   (b) 863 m
(c) 368 m   (d) 216 m

11. A glass sinker has a mass M in air. When weighed in a liquid at temperature t_1, the apparent mass is M_1 and when weighed in the same liquid at temperature t_2, the apparent mass is M_2. If the coefficient of cubical expansion of the glass is γ_g, then the real coefficient of expansion of the liquid is :

(a) $\gamma_g + \left(\dfrac{M_2 - M_1}{M - M_2}\right) \cdot \dfrac{1}{(t_2 - t_1)}$ (b) $\gamma_g - \left(\dfrac{M_2 - M_1}{M - M_2}\right) \cdot \dfrac{1}{(t_2 - t_1)}$

(c) $\gamma_g - \left(\dfrac{M - M_2}{M_2 - M_1}\right) \cdot \dfrac{1}{(t_2 - t_1)}$ (d)

$\gamma_g + \left(\dfrac{M_2 - M_1}{M_2 + M_1}\right) \cdot \dfrac{1}{(t_2 - t_1)}$

12. A mercury thermometer is to be made with glass tubing of internal bore 0.5 mm and the distance between the fixed points is to be 20 cm. The coefficient of expansion of mercury is 0.000180/°C and the coefficient of linear expansion of glass is 0.000009/°C. The internal volume of the bulb and stem below the lower fixed point is :

(a) 0.527 cc   (b) 5.27 cc
(c) 2.57 cc   (d) 3.27 cc

Answer Key		4	(c)	6	(a)	8	(a)	10	(b)	12	(c)
Sol. from page 406		5	(c)	7	(a)	9	(a)	11	(a)		

13. A 5.0 g bullet (specific heat of material of bullet = 128 J/kg°C) moving with a velocity of 200 m/s enters a sand bag and stops. If the entire kinetic energy of the bullet is changed into heat energy that is added to the bullet, then the rise in the temperature of the bullet is:

(a) 312.5°C   (b) 156°C
(c) 500°C   (d) 624°C

14. A calorimeter (of water equivalent 50 g) contains 250 g of water and 50 g of ice at 0°C. 30 g of water at 80°C is added to it. The final condition of the system will be :

(a) the temperature of the system will be 4.2°C.
(b) the temperature of the system will still be 0°C and the entire ice will melt.
(c) the temperature will be 0°C and half of the ice will melt.
(d) the temperature will be 0°C and 20 g of ice will left.

15. 100 g of steam at 100°C is passed into 200 g of water and 20 g of ice at 0°C in a calorimeter whose water equivalent is 50 g. (L_{steam} = 540 cal/g and L_{ice} = 80 cal/g). The observed result is

(a) the temperature of the system becomes 169°C.
(b) half of the ice is melted and the temperature of the system remains 0°C.
(c) the temperature remains 100°C and 53 g of steam condenses.
(d) the temperature remains 100°C and the entire steam condenses.

16. The coefficients of linear expansion of steel and brass are $11 \times 10^{-6}/°C$ and $19 \times 10^{-6}/°C$ respectively. If their difference in lengths at all temperatures has to be kept constant is 30 cm, their lengths at 0°C should be

(a) 71.25 cm and 41.25 cm
(b) 82 cm and 52 cm
(c) 92 cm and 62 cm
(d) 62.25 cm and 32.25 cm

17. Two vertical glass tubes filled with a liquid are connected by a capillary tube as shown in the figure. The tube on the left is put in an ice bath at 0°C while the one on the right is kept at 30°C in a water bath. The difference in the levels of the liquid in the two tubes is 4.0 cm while the height of the liquid column at 0°C is 120 cm. The coefficient of volume expansion of the liquid is

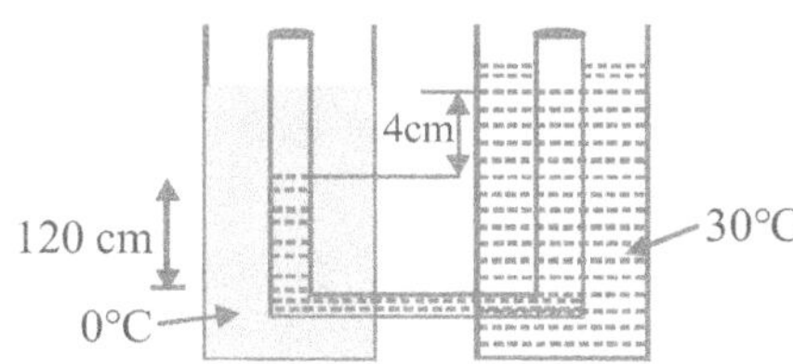

(a) $22 \times 10^{-4}/°C$ (b) $1.1 \times 10^{-4}/°C$
(c) $11 \times 10^{-4}/°C$ (d) $2.2 \times 10^{-4}/°C$

18. A brass scale of a barometer gives correct reading at 0°C. $\alpha_{Hg} = 0.6 \times 10^{-4}/°C$ $\alpha_{Brass} = 0.00002/°C$. The barometer reads 75 cm at 27°C. The atmospheric pressure at 0°C is

(a) 74.20 cm   (b) 74.62 cm
(c) 74.92 cm   (d) 75.04 cm

19. A metal block of mass 2 kg ($\rho = 5 \times 10^3$ kg/m³) is suspended from an ideal spring of force constant 25 N/m. The spring block system is immersed in 500 g of water contained in a vessel such that the block is at a height h from the bottom of the vessel. The system is released so as to sink to the bottom, resulting in a rise of temperature of 0.004°C of water. The height h through which the block went down is (Given : specific heat of the block = 250 J/kg °K and that of water = 4200 J/kg °K, heat capacity of vessel and spring are negligible. Take g = 10 m/s²)

(a) 0.35 m (b) 0.16 m
(c) 1.60 m (d) 0.26 m

20. A tungsten wire with a diameter of 0.20 mm is stretched until the tension is 50 N. The wire is then clamped to a stout aluminium rod when both are at a temperature of 20°C. The tension in the wire when both are brought to a temperature of 150°C is ($Y_{Tungsten} = 34 \times 10^{10}$ N/m², $\alpha_T = 4.5 \times 10^{-6}/°C$)

(a) 85.0 N (b) 57.5 N
(c) 100 N (d) 56.2 N

21. The table gives the initial length L, change in temperature ΔT and change in length ΔL of four rods. The rod, which has greatest coefficient of expansion

Rod	L(m)	ΔT(°C)	ΔL(m)
a	2	10	4×10^{-4}
b	1	20	4×10^{-4}
c	2	10	8×10^{-4}
d	4	5	4×10^{-4}

(a) a   (b) b
(c) c   (d) d

22. An ideal gas is expanding such that PT^2 = constant. The coefficient of volume expansion of the gas is

(a) $\dfrac{1}{T}$ (b) $\dfrac{2}{T}$
(c) $\dfrac{3}{T}$ (d) $\dfrac{4}{T}$

23. A piece of metal weighs 45g in air and 25g in a liquid of density 1.5×10^3 kg – m⁻³ kept at 30°C. When the temperature of the liquid is raised to 40°C, the metal piece weighs 27g. The density of liquid at 40°C, is 1.25×10^3 kg –m⁻³. The coefficient of linear expansion of metal is

(a) $1.3 \times 10^{-3}/°C$ (b) $5.2 \times 10^{-3}/°C$
(c) $2.6 \times 10^{-3}/°C$ (d) $0.26 \times 10^{-3}/°C$

24. Two rigid boxes containing different ideal gases are placed on a table. Box A contains one mole of nitrogen at temperature T_0, while Box B contains one mole of helium at temperature (7/3) T_0. The boxes are then put into thermal contact with each other and heat flows between them until the gases reach a common final temperature (Ignore the heat capacity of boxes). Then, the final temperature of the gases T_f in terms of T_0 is

(a) $T_f = \dfrac{7}{3}T_0$ (b) $T_f = \dfrac{3}{2}T_0$
(c) $T_f = \dfrac{5}{2}T_0$ (d) $T_f = \dfrac{3}{7}T_0$

25. A substance of mass m kg requires a power input of P watts to remain in the molten state at its melting point. When the power is turned off, the sample completely solidifies in time t sec. What is the latent heat of fusion of the substance ?

(a) $\dfrac{Pm}{t}$ (b) $\dfrac{Pt}{m}$

(c) $\dfrac{m}{Pt}$ (d) $\dfrac{t}{Pm}$

26. 2 kg of ice at $-20°C$ is mixed with 5 kg of water at $20°C$ in an insulating vessel having a negligible heat capacity. Calculate the final mass of water remaining in the container. It is given that the specific heats of water and ice are 1 kcal/kg per °C and 0.5 kcal/kg/°C while the latent heat of fusion of ice is 80 kcal/kg

(a) 7 kg   (b) 6 kg

(c) 4 kg   (d) 2 kg

27. In a vertical U-tube containing a liquid, the two arms are maintained at different temperatures t_1 and t_2. The liquid columns in the two arms have heights l_1 and l_2 respectively. The coefficient of volume expansion of the liquid is equal to

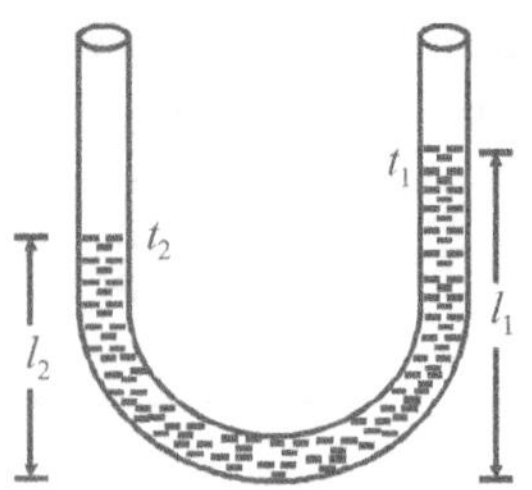

(a) $\dfrac{l_1 - l_2}{l_2 t_1 - l_1 t_2}$ (b) $\dfrac{l_1 - l_2}{l_1 t_1 - l_2 t_2}$

(c) $\dfrac{l_1 + l_2}{l_2 t_1 + l_1 t_2}$ (d) $\dfrac{l_1 + l_2}{l_1 t_1 + l_2 t_2}$

28. Three rods of equal length ℓ are joined to form an equilateral triangle PQR. O is the mid point of PQ. Distance OR remains same for small change in temperature. Coefficient of linear expansion for PR and RQ is same, *i.e.*, α_2 but that for PQ is α_1. Then

(a) $\alpha_2 = 3\alpha_1$

(b) $\alpha_2 = 4\alpha_1$

(c) $\alpha_1 = 3\alpha_2$

(d) $\alpha_1 = 4\alpha_2$

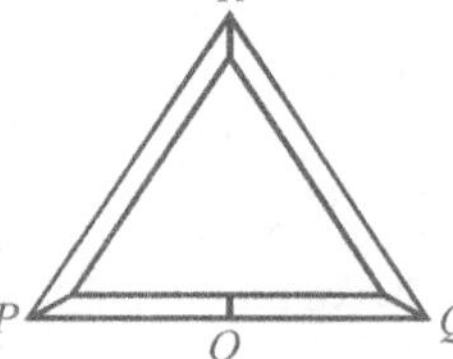

29. A horizontal tube open at both ends contains a column of liquid. The length of this liquid column does not change with temperature. Let γ = coefficient of volume expansion of the liquid and α = coefficient of linear expansion of the material of the tube

(a) $\gamma = \alpha$ (b) $\gamma = 2\alpha$

(c) $\gamma = 3\alpha$ (d) $\gamma = 0$

30. A cylindrical steel llay is inserted into a circular hole of diameter 2.60 m is a brass plate. When the plug and the plante are at a temperature 20 °C, the diameter of the plug is 0.010 mm smaller than that of the hole. The temperature at which the plug will just fit in is (given $\alpha_{steel} = 11 \times 10^{-6} /°C$ and $\alpha_{brass} = 19 \times 10^{-6} /°C$)

(a) $-20° C$ (b) $-48 °C$

(c) 10 °C   (d) none of these.

31. In two experiments with a continuous flow calorimeter to determine the specific heat capacity of a liquid , an input power of 60 W produced a rise of 10 K in the liquid. When the power was doubled, the same temperature rise was achieved by making the rate of flow of liquid three times faster. The power lost to the surrounding in each case was

(a) 20 W   (b) 30 W

(c) 40 W   (d) 120 W

Answer Key	**25**	(b)	**27**	(a)	**29**	(b)	**31**	(b)
Sol. from page 406	**26**	(b)	**28**	(d)	**30**	(b)		

Multiple correct options

1. A bimetallic strip is formed out of two identical strips, one of copper and other of brass. The coefficients of linear expansion of the two metals are α_C and α_B. On heating, the temperature of the strip goes up by ΔT and the strip bends to form an arc of radius of curvature R. Then R is
   (a) Proportional to ΔT
   (b) Inversely proportion a to ΔT
   (c) Proportional to $|\alpha_B - \alpha_C|$
   (d) Inversely proportional to $|\alpha_B - \alpha_C|$

2. Heat is supplied to a certain homogeneous sample of matter, at a uniform rate. Its temperature is plotted against time, as shown. Which of the following conclusions can be drawn ?

   (a) Its specific heat capacity is greater in the solid state than in the liquid state
   (b) Its specific heat capacity is greater in the liquid state than in the solid state
   (c) Its latent heat of vaporization is greater than its latent heat of fusion
   (d) Its latent heat of vaporization is smaller than its latent of fusion

3. When the temperature of a copper coin is raised by 80°C, its diameter increases by 0.2%, then
   (a) percentage rise in the area of a face is 0.4%
   (b) percentage rise in the thickness is 0.4%
   (c) percentage rise in the volume is 0.6%
   (d) coefficient of linear expansion of copper is $0.25 \times 10^{-4}/°C$

4. A vessel is partly filled with liquid. When the vessel is cooled to a lower temperature, the space in the vessel unoccupied by the liquid remains constant. Then the volume of the liquid (V_L), volume of the vessel (V_v), the coefficients of cubical expansion of the material of the vessel (γ_v) and of the liquid (γ_L) are related as
   (a) $\gamma_L > \gamma_v$
   (b) $\gamma_L < \gamma_v$
   (c) $\gamma_v / \gamma_L = V_v / V_L$
   (d) $\gamma_v / \gamma_L = V_L / V_v$

5. If α, β and γ are coefficients of linear, superficial and volume expansion respectively, then
   (a) $\dfrac{\beta}{\alpha} = \dfrac{1}{2}$
   (b) $\dfrac{\beta}{\gamma} = \dfrac{2}{3}$
   (c) $\dfrac{\gamma}{\alpha} = \dfrac{3}{1}$
   (d) $\dfrac{\beta}{\alpha} = \dfrac{\gamma}{\beta}$

6. A metal sphere of radius R and specific heat C is rotated about an axis passing through its centre at a speed n rotation /second. It is suddenly stopped and 50% of its energy is used in increasing its temperature, then choose the correct statement(s) from the following
   (a) Kinetic energy used to raise the temperature of the sphere is
   $$\frac{2\pi^2 n^2}{5} MR^2$$
   (b) Kinetic energy used to raise the temperature of the sphere is
   $$\frac{5\pi^2 n}{3} MR$$
   (c) The rise in the temperature of the sphere is $\dfrac{4\pi^2 n^2 R^2}{7C}$
   (d) The rise in the temperature of the sphere is $\dfrac{2\pi^2 n^2 R^2}{5C}$

Answer Key	1	(b, d)	3	(a, c, d)	5	(b, c)
Sol. from page 408	2	(b, c)	4	(a, d)	6	(a, d)

Read the two statements carefully to mark the correct option out of the options given below:
(a) If both the statements are true and the *statement - 2* is the correct explanation of *statement - 1*.
(b) If both the statements are true but *statement - 2* is not the correct explanation of the *statement - 1*.
(c) If *statement - 1* true but *statement - 2* is false.
(d) If *statement - 1* is false but *statement - 2* is true.

1. *Statement - 1*
    A body is in equilibrium in an inertial frame but not be equilibrium in an non-inertial frame.
    Statement - 2
    The body can be in thermal equilibrium in both the frames.
2. *Statement - 1*
    For the thermal equilibrium of two bodies, they must be in contact.
    Statement - 2
    Two bodies in contact must be in thermal equilibrium.
3. *Statement - 1*
    A tightly closed metal lid of a glass bottle can be opened more easily if it is put in hot water for some time.
    Statement - 2
    The coefficent of expansion of metal lid is greater than that of glass.
4. *Statement - 1*
    The coefficient of linear expansion has dimension K^{-1}.
    Statement - 2
    The coefficient of volume expansion has dimension K^{-1}.
5. *Statement - 1*
    The melting point of ice decreases with increase of pressure.
    Statement - 2
    Ice contracts on melting.
6. *Statement - 1*
    Fahrenheit is the smallest unit measuring temperature.
    Statement - 2
    Fahrenheit was the first temperature scale used for measuring temperature.
7. *Statement - 1*
    The temperature at which Centrigrade and Fahrenheit thermometers read the same is $-40°$.

Statement - 2

$$F = \frac{9}{5} C + 32.$$

8. *Statement - 1*
    Specific heat capacity is the cause of formation of land and sea breeze.
    Statement - 2
    The specific heat of water is more than land.
9. *Statement - 1*
    Water kept in an open vessel will quickly evaporate on the surface of the moon.
    Statement - 2
    The temperature at the surface of the moon is much higher than boiling point of the water.
10. *Statement - 1*
    Two bodies at different temperatures, if brought in contact do not necessary settle to the mean temperature.
    Statement - 2
    The two bodies may have different thermal capacites.
11. *Statement - 1*
    Heat is a conserved quantity.
    Statement - 2
    Energy of an isolated system remain conserved.
12. *Statement - 1*
    When solid melts or a liquid boils, the temperature does not increase when heat is supplied.
    Statement - 2
    The heat supplied is used to increase internal potential energy.

Answer Key	**1**	(b)	**3**	(a)	**5**	(a)	**7**	(a)	**9**	(a)	**11**	(d)
Sol. from page 409	**2**	(d)	**4**	(b)	**6**	(c)	**8**	(a)	**10**	(a)	**12**	(a)

Passage & Matrix

Exercise 3.4

Passage for (Q. 1 - 3) :

At very low temperatures, the molar heat capacity of rock salt varies with temperature according to Debye's law; thus

$$C = K \frac{T^3}{\theta^3}$$

where $K = 1940 J/mol\text{--}K$ and $\theta = 281 K$

1. The heat required to raise the temperature of 2 moles of rock salt from 10K to 50K is

(a) 240J   (b) 273J

(c) 348J   (d) 472J

2. The mean molar heat capacity in this range is

(a) 3.42 J/mol–K   (b) 4.12 J/mol–K

(c) 4.82 J/mol–K   (d) 5.08 J/mol–K

3. The true molar heat capacity at $50K$ is

(a) 8.3 J/mol–K   (b) 9.6 J/mol–K

(c) 10.3 J/mol–K   (d) 10.9 J/mol–K

Passage for (Q. 4 - 5) :

A uniform solid brass cylinder of mass M = 0.50 kg and radius R = 0.030 m is placed in frictionless bearings and set to rotate about its geometrical axis with an angular velocity of 60 rad/s.

4. The angular momentum of cylinder and required to reach this state of rotation, starting from rest is

(a) 0.75×10^{-2} J–s   (b) 1.35×10^{-2} J–s

(c) 2.25×10^{-2} J–s   (d) 2.70×10^{-1} J–s

5. After the cylinder has reached the specified state of rotation, it is heated without any mechanical contact from room temperature 20°C to 100°C, the fractional change in angular velocity of cylinder is (Take $\alpha = 2.0 \times 10^{-5}/\,^0C$)

(a) -3.2×10^{-3}.   (b) -6.4×10^{-3}

(c) 1.6×10^{-3} (d) 4.8×10^{-3}

Passage for (Q. 6 - 8) :

When a solid is heated, its length changes according to the relation $\ell = \ell_0(1 + \alpha\Delta T)$ where ℓ = final length, ℓ_0 = initial length, ΔT = change in temperature and α = coefficient of linear expansion.

The change in area of solid upon heating is called superficial expansion.

The area changes according to the following relation $A = A_0 (1 + \beta \Delta T)$ where A = final area, A_0 = initial area and β = coefficient of superficial expansion.

6. A metal disc having circular hole at its centre is heated. If the metal expands on heating, the diameter of the hole will

(a) increase

(b) decrease

(c) remain unchanged

(d) increases or decreases depending upon the metal

7. On heating a liquid of coefficient of cubical expansion γ in a container having coefficient of linear expansion $\gamma/3$, the level of liquid in the container will

(a) rise

(b) fall

(c) remain almost stationary

(d) none of these

8. The coefficient of linear expansion of brass and steel are α_1 and α_2. If we take a brass rod of length ℓ_1 and a steel rod of length ℓ_2 at 0°C, their difference in length will remain the same at any temperature if

(a) $\alpha_1 \ell_2 = \alpha_2 \ell_1$ (b) $\alpha_1 \ell_2^{\,2} = \alpha_2 \ell_1^{\,2}$

(c) $\alpha_1^{\,2} \ell_2 = \alpha_2^{\,2} \ell_1$ (d) $\alpha_1 \ell_1 = \alpha_2 \ell_2$

Passage for (Q. 9 - 11) :

A uniform disc is spinning about geometric axis in free space. Its temperature is increased by ΔT. The coefficient of linear expansion is α.

9. The fractional change in its angular velocity is

(a) $\alpha\Delta T$ (b) $-\alpha\Delta T$

(c) $2\alpha\Delta T$ (d) $-2\alpha\Delta T$

10. The fractional change in speed of rim is

(a) $\alpha\Delta T$ (b) $2\alpha\Delta T$

(c) $-\alpha\Delta T$ (d) $-2\alpha\Delta T$

11. The fractional change in its rotational kinetic energy is

(a) $\alpha\Delta T$ (b) $-\alpha\Delta T$

(c) $2\alpha\Delta T$ (d) $-2\alpha\Delta T$

Answer Key	1	(b)	3	(d)	5	(a)	7	(c)	9	(d)	11	(d)
Sol. from page 409	2	(a)	4	(b)	6	(a)	8	(d)	10	(c)		

12. Three liquids A, B and C having same specific heat and mass m, 2m and 3m have temperatures 20°C, 40°C and 60°C respectively. Temperature of the mixture when

Column -I		Column -II
(A) A and B are mixed	p.	33.3°C
(B) A and C are mixed	q.	52°C
(C) B and C are mixed	r.	50°C
(D) A, B and C all three are mixed	s.	46.67°C

13. A sphere is spinning about its diameter. Its temperature is gradually increased by ΔT. The coefficient of linear expansion of sphere is α. Match the columns :

Column - I		Column - II
(A) Fractional change in angular momentum	p.	$\alpha\Delta T$
(B) Fractional change in moment of inertia	q.	$-2\alpha\Delta T$
(C) Fractional change in angular velocity	r.	$2\alpha\Delta T$
(D) Fractional change in kinetic energy	s.	zero

14.

Column - I		Column - II
(A) Bimetalic strip	p.	Radiation from a body
(B) Steam engine	q.	Energy conversion
(C) Incondescent lamp	r.	Melting
(D) Electric fuse	s.	Thermal expansion

Answer Key	**12**	A → (p); B → (r); C → (q); D → (s)	**13**	A → (s); B → (r); C → (q); D → (q)
Sol. from page 409	**14**	A → (s, q); B → (q); C → (p, q); D → (q, r)		

TEC   Subjective Integer Type *Exercise 5.5*

Solution from page 410

1. A faulty thermometer reads 5°C in melting ice and 99°C in steam. Find the correct temperature in °F when the faulty thermometer reads 52°C. **Ans.** 122°F.

2. The pressure of air in the bulb of constant volume air thermometer is 75 cm of mercury at 0°C, 100 cm at 100°C and 80 cm at the room temperature. Calculate the room temperature. **Ans.** 20°C.

3. A one litre flask contains some mercury. It is found that at different temperatures, the volume of air inside the flask remains the same. What is the volume of mercury in this flask ? Given α for glass $9.0 \times 10^{-6}/$ °C and γ for mercury = $1.8 \times 10^{-4}/$ °C. **Ans.** 150 cm^3.

4. Three equal length straight rods of aluminium, Invar and steel all at 20°C, form an equilateral triangle with hinge pins at the vertices. At what temperature will the angle opposite the Invar rod be 59.95° ? **Ans.** 66 ° C.

5. A railway track (made of iron) is laid in winter when the average temperature is 18°C. The track consists of sections of 12.0 m placed one after the other. How much gap should be left between two such sections so that there is no compression during summer when the maximum temperature goes to 48°C ? Coefficient of linear expansion of iron = $11 \times 10^{-6}/$ °C. **Ans :** 0.4 cm.

6. The volume of a glass vessel is 1000 cc at 20°C. What volume of mercury should be poured into it at this temperature so that the volume of the remaining space does not change with temperature? Coefficients of cubical expansion of mercury and glass are $1.8 \times 10^{-4}/$°C and $9.0 \times 10^{-6}/$°C respectively. **Ans.** 50 cc.

7. How many grams of ice at −14°C are needed to cool 200 g of water from 25°C to 10°C ? Take specific heat of ice = 0.5 cal/g/°C and latent heat of ice = 80 cal/g. **Ans.** 31 g.

8. The internal energy of a monoatomic gas is 1.5 nRT. One mole of helium is kept in a cylinder of cross–section 8.5 cm^2. The cylinder is closed by a light frictionless piston. The gas is heated slowly in a process during which a total of 42 J heat is given to the gas. If the temperature rises through 2°C, find the distance moved by the piston. Atmospheric pressure = 100 kPa. **Ans.** 20 cm.

TEC

Subjective

Exercise 5.6

Solution from page 411

1. A constant volume gas thermometer using helium records a pressure of 20.0 kPa at the triple–point of water and pressure of 14.3 Pa at the temperature of 'dry ice' (solid CO_2). What is the temperature of 'dry ice' ? **Ans.** 195.30 K.

2. An ungraduated thermometer of uniform bore is attached to a centimeter scale and is found to read 10.3 cm in melting ice, 26.8 cm in boiling water and 6.5 cm in freezing mixture. Calculate the temperature of the freezing mixture. **Ans.** –23.03°C.

3. A hole is drilled in a copper sheet. The diameter of the hole is 4.24 cm at 27.0°C. What is the change in the diameter of the hole when the sheet is heated to 227°C ? Coefficient of linear expansion of copper = 1.70 x 10^{-5}/°C. **Ans.** 1.44×10^{-2} cm.

4. A steel tape 1 m long is correctly calibrated for a temperature of 27.0°C. The length of a steel rod measured by this tape is found to be 63.0 cm on a hot day when the temperature is 45.0°C. What is the actual length of the steel rod on that day ? What is the length of the same steel rod on a day when the temperature is 27.0°C ? Coefficient of linear–expansion of steel = 1.20×10^{-5}/°C ?

   Ans. 63.0136 cm.

5. A large steel wheel is to be fitted on to a shaft of the same material. At 27°C, the outer diameter of the shaft is 8.70 cm and the diameter of the central hole in the wheel is 8.69 cm. The shaft is cooled using 'dry ice' (solid carbon dioxide). At what temperature of the shaft does the wheel slip on the shaft ? Assume coefficient of linear expansion of the steel to be constant over the required temperature range. $\alpha_{steel} = 1.20 \times 10^{-5}$ / K. **Ans.** – 68.8°C.

6. A brass rod of length 50 cm and diameter 3.0 mm is joined to a steel rod of the same length and diameter. What is the change in length of the combined rod at 250°C, if the original lengths are at 40.0°C ? Is there a 'thermal stress' developed at the junction ? The ends of the rod are free to expand. Coefficient of linear expansion of brass = 2.0×10^{-5}/°C and that of steel = 1.2×10^{-5}/ °C.

   Ans. 0.34 cm, No.

7. A brass wire 1.8 m long at 27°C is held taut with little tension between two rigid supports. If the wire is cooled to a temperature of – 39°C, what is the tension developed in the wire, if its diameter is 2.0 mm ? Coefficient of linear expansion of brass =2.0×10^{-5}/°C, Young's modulus of brass = 0.91×10^{11} Pa.

   Ans. 3.77×10^2 N.

8. Density ρ, mass m and volume V are related as $\rho = m/V$. Prove that

   $$\gamma = -\frac{1}{\rho}\frac{d\rho}{dT}.$$

9. What should be the lengths of steel and copper rods at 0°C that the length of steel rod is 5 cm longer than copper at all temperatures? Given α for copper = 1.7×10^{-5}/°C and α for steel = 1.1×10^{-5}/°C. **Ans.** 9.17 cm, 14.17 cm.

10. Suppose that one early morning when the temperature is 10°C, a driver of an automobile gets his gasoline tank which is made of steel, filled with 75 litre of gasoline, which is also at 10°C. During the day, the temperature rises to 30°C. How much gasoline will overflow ? Given α for steel = 1.2×10^{-5}/ °C and γ for gasoline = 9.5×10^{-4}/ °C. **Ans.** 1.37 litre.

11. If coefficient of linear expansion α is treated as variable, dependent on temperature T, then show that the length L at temperature T,

    $$L = L_0\left[1 + \int_{T_0}^{T} \alpha(T)dt\right]$$

    where L_0 is length at reference temperature T_0.

12. A 1.28 m long vertical glass tube is half filled with a liquid at 20°C. How much will the height of the liquid column change when the tube is heated to 30°C ? Take $\alpha_{glass} = 1.0 \times 10^{-5}$/°C and $\beta_{liquid} = 4.0 \times 10^{-5}$/°C. **Ans.** 1.3×10^{-4} m.

13. In figure shown, left arm of a U–tube is immersed in a hot water bath at temperature T, and right arm is immersed in a bath of melting ice; the height of manometric liquid in respective columns is h_t and h_0. Determine the coefficient of expansion of the liquid.

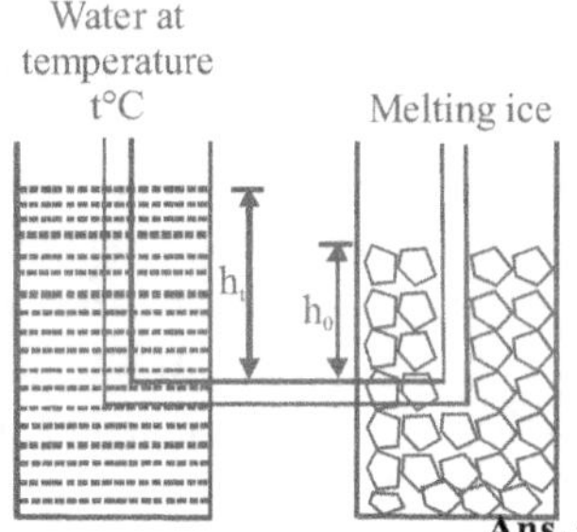

   Ans. $\gamma = [(h_t - h_0)/h_0 t]$.

14. Three rods A, B and C for an equilateral triangle at 0°C. Rods AB and BC have same coefficient of expansion α_1 and rod AC has α_2. If temperature of the system is increased by ΔT°C, what is the change in angle θ formed by rods AB and BC ?

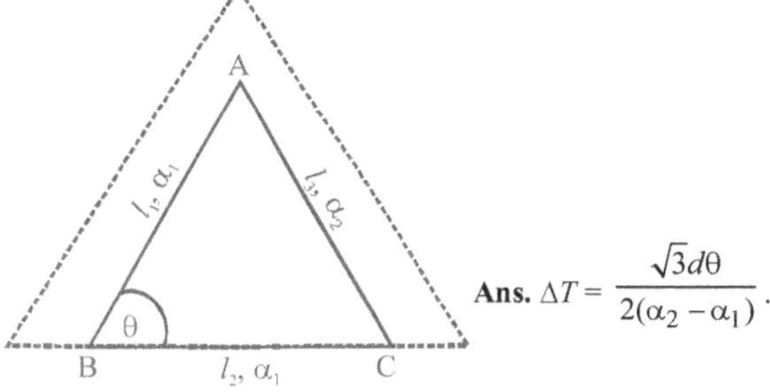

   Ans. $\Delta T = \dfrac{\sqrt{3}d\theta}{2(\alpha_2 - \alpha_1)}$.

15. A metre scale made of steel reads accurately at 20°C. In a sensitive experiment, distances accurate upto 0.055 mm in 1 m are required. Find the range of temperature in which the experiment can be performed with this metre scale. Coefficient of linear expansion of steel = 11×10^{-6}/ °C. **Ans :** 15°C to 25°C.

16. Two steel rods and an aluminium rod of equal length l_0 and equal cross–section are joined rigidly at their ends as shown in the figure below. All the rods are in a state of zero tension at 0°C. Find the length of the system when the temperature is raised to θ. Coefficient of linear expansion of aluminium and steel are α_a and α_s respectively. Young's modulus of aluminium is Y_a and of steel is Y_s.

Steel
Aluminium
Steel

$$\text{Ans : } l_0\left[1+\frac{\alpha_a Y_a + 2\alpha_s Y_s}{Y_a + 2Y_s}\theta\right].$$

17. A torsional pendulum consists of a solid disc connected to a thin wire ($\alpha = 2.4 \times 10^{-5}/°C$) at its centre. Find the percentage change in the time period between peak winter (5°C) and peak summer (45°C). **Ans :** 9.6×10^{-2}.

18. A circular disc made of iron is rotated about its axis at a constant velocity ω. Calculate the percentage change in the linear speed of a particle of the rim as the disc is slowly heated from 20°C to 50°C keeping the angular velocity constant. Coefficient of linear expansion of iron = $1.2 \times 10^{-5}/°C$. **Ans :** 3.6×10^{-2}.

19. A glass window is to fit in an aluminium frame. The temperature on the working day is 40°C and the glass window measures exactly 20 cm × 30 cm. What should be the size of the aluminium frame so that there is no stress on the glass in winter even if the temperature drops to 0°C ? Coefficient of linear expansion for glass and aluminium are $9.0 \times 10^{-6}/°C$ and $24 \times 10^{-6}/°C$ respectively.

Ans. 20.012 cm × 30.018 cm.

20. The apparatus shown in the figure consists of four glass columns connected by horizontal sections. The height of two central columns B and C are 49 cm each. The two outer columns A and D are open to atmosphere. A and C are maintained at a temperature of 95°C while the columns B and D are maintained at 5°C. The height of the liquid in A and D measured from the base line are 52.8 cm and 51 cm respectively. Determine the coefficient of thermal expansion of the liquid.

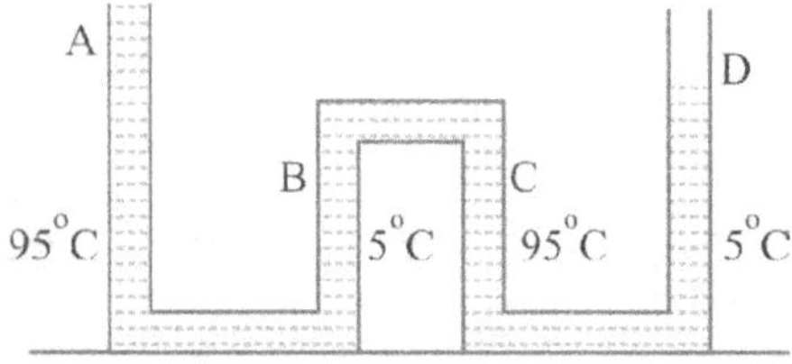

Ans. $2 \times 10^{-4}/°C$.

21. 0.05 kg steam at 373 K is mixed with 0.45 kg of ice at 253 K. Find the temperature of the mixture. Latent heat of vaporization for steam = 540 cal/g, latent heat of fusion of ice = 80 cal/g and specific heat of ice = 0.5 cal/g°C **Ans :** 0°C.

22. In an industrial process 10 kg of water per hour is to be heated from 20°C is passed from a boiler into a copper coil immersed in water. The steam condenses in the coil and is returned to the boiler as water at 90°C. How many kg of steam are reqiured per hour ? **Ans :** 1.27 kg.

23. An ice cube of mass 0.1 kg at 0°C is placed in an isolated container which is at 227°C. The specific heat 'S' of the container varies with temperature T according to empirical relation S = $A + BT$, where A = 100 cal/kg and $B = 2 \times 10^{-2}$ cal/kg–K². If the final temperature of the container is 27°C, determine the mass of the container. **Ans :** 0.495 kg.

24. The specific heat of substance varies with temperature according to equation c = $(2t^2 + t) \times 10^{-3}$ cal/g°C. Calculate the amount of heat required to raise the temperature of 100 g of substance from 20°C to 40°C. **Ans :** 37.9 kcal.

25. A fat man is used to consuming about 3000 k–cal worth of food everyday. His food contains 50 g of butter plus a plate of sweets everyday, besides items which provide him with other nutrients (proteins, vitamins, minerals, etc.) in addition to fats and carbohydrates. The caloric value of 10 g of butter is 60 kcal and that of a plate of sweets is of average 700 kcal. What dietary strategy should he adopt to cut down his calories to about 2100 kcal per day ? Assume the man cannot resist eating the full plate of sweets once it is offered to him.

Ans. The man intends to cut down 3000 – 2100 = 900 kcal. But avoiding sweets completely, he will cut down 700 kcal. To cut down another 200 kcal, he should cut down butter by (10/60) × 200 = 33 g per day. He should not cut down consumption of food, that provides him with vitamins and other vital nutrients.

26. A geyser heats water flowing at the rate of 30 l / min from 27°C to 77°C. If the geyser operates on a gas burner, what is the rate of consumption of the fuel if its heat of combustion is 4.0×10^4 J/g? **Ans :** 157.5 g/min.

27. Steam at 100°C is allowed to pass into a vessel containing 10 g of ice, 100 g of water at 0°C, until all the ice is melted and the temperature is raised to 5°C. Neglecting water equivalent of the vessel and the loss due to radiation etc. Calculate how much steam is condensed. The latent heat of steam is 536 cal/g and latent heat of ice is 80 cal/g. **Ans :** 2.13 g.

28. A copper block of mass 2.5 kg is heated in a furnace to a temperature of 500°C and then placed on a large ice block. What is the maximum amount of ice that can melt ? (specific heat of copper = 0.39 J/g–°C and heat of fussion of water = 335 J/g). **Ans :** 1.45 kg.

29. A 0.1 kg steel ball falls from a height of 10 m and bounces to a height 7 m.

(a) Why does it not bounce back to its original height ?

(b) If all the dissipated energy were absorbed by the ball as heat, how much will its temperature rise ? (specific heat of steel = 0.11 k cal/kg°C, 1 cal = 4.2 J) **Ans :** 0.064°C.

30. A lead bullet just melts when stopped by an obstacle. Assuming that 25 percent of the heat is absorbed by the obstacle, find the velocity of the bullet if its initial temperature is 27°C. (Melting point of lead = 327°C, specific heat of lead = 0.03 cal/g°C, latent heat of fusion of lead = 6 cal/g°C, J = 4.2 J/cal)

Ans : v = 409.9 m/s.

Hints & Solutions

1. (d) Water expands on both sides of 4 °C.

2. (b)
$$C = \gamma_\ell - 3A \text{ and } S = \gamma_\ell - \gamma_{silver}$$
After solving above equations, we get
$$\gamma_{silver} = C + 3A - S$$

3. (c) First the temperature of liquid oxygen increases thereafter it comes in gaseous state.

4. (b) First ice comes from -10 °C to 0 °C. Then it melts and its temperature rises to boiling point. Thereafter it will convert into steam.

5. (b) It is the definition of calorie.

6. (c) The heat lost in condensation $= x \times 540$ cal.
$$\therefore \quad x \times 540 = y \times 80 + y \times 1 \times (100 - 0)$$
$$\text{or} \quad \frac{x}{y} = \frac{1}{3}.$$

7. (c) As
$$dQ = mCdT$$
$$\therefore \quad C = \frac{1}{m}\left(\frac{dQ}{dT}\right) = \frac{1}{m} \times \frac{1}{(dT/dQ)}$$
The slope of $BC < OA$, $\therefore C_{solid} < C_{liquid}$.

8. (a)
$$\Delta V = V\gamma_{apparent}\Delta T$$
$$\text{or} \quad \frac{\Delta V}{V} = (\gamma - 3\alpha)\Delta T$$
Bulk modulus, $K = \dfrac{\Delta P}{\left(\dfrac{\Delta V}{V}\right)}$
$$\therefore \quad \Delta P = K\left(\frac{\Delta V}{V}\right) = K(\gamma - 3\alpha)\Delta T$$

9. (b) The change of state occurs at constant temperature, so material graph 2 will have greatest heat of fusion
i.e., $Q = H\Delta t$; Δt is largest for 2

10. (b) Material expands outward and so x, r increases. Due to linear expansion diameter of rod will increase.

11. (a) $\dfrac{x}{5} = \dfrac{x - 32}{9}, \therefore x = -40$

12. (a) $t = \left[\dfrac{P_t - P_0}{P_{100} - P_0}\right] \times 100 = \left[\dfrac{60 - 50}{90 - 50}\right] \times 100 = 25°C$

13. (b) By increasing pressure above mercury column, the boiling point can be increased.

14. (d)
$$\frac{\Delta T}{T} \times 100 = \left(\frac{\alpha\Delta T}{2}\right) \times 100$$
$$= \frac{2 \times 10^{-6} \times 10 \times 100}{2}$$
$$= 10^{-3}.$$

15. (c) The thermal stress, $f = Y\alpha\Delta T$; Clearly f does not depend on length of the rod.

16. (a) On heating the block, the hole size will increase.

17. (d)
$$\rho_t = \frac{\rho_0}{1 + \gamma t}$$
$$9.7 = \left[\frac{10}{1 + \gamma \times 100}\right], \therefore \gamma = 10^{-4}/°C$$

18. (c)
$$\Delta V = V\gamma\Delta T$$
$$\therefore \quad \frac{\Delta V_1}{\Delta V_2} = \frac{\pi(2r)^2 \ell\gamma\Delta T}{\pi r^2 \times 2\ell \times \gamma\Delta T} = \frac{2}{1} = 2:1$$

19. (d)
$$\gamma_1 = \gamma_\ell - 3\alpha \text{ and } \gamma_2 = \gamma_\ell - 3\alpha'$$
After solving, we get
$$\alpha' = \left(\frac{\gamma_1 - \gamma_2}{3}\right) + \alpha.$$

20. (b) Melting point of ice decreases with increase in pressure (experimentally).

21. (a) Heat needed,
$$Q = 1 \times 0.5 \times 10 + 1 \times 80 + 1 \times 1 \times 100 + 1 \times 540$$
$$= 3045 \text{ J}.$$

22. (d) $mg \times 100 = m \times 4200 \times \Delta T$
$$\therefore \Delta T = 0.023 \text{ °C}$$

23. (d) The rod should be expanded differently.

24. (a) $22 \times 1 \times (90 - 20) = m \times 540 + m \times 1 \times (100 - 90)$
$$\therefore \quad m = 2.8 \text{ g}$$
The total mass of water $= 22 + 2.8 = 24.8$ g.

25. (b) $\dfrac{C}{5} = \dfrac{F - 32}{9}$; or $C = \dfrac{5}{9}F - \dfrac{160}{9}$.
Thus the slope of line AB is 5/9.

26. (a) The amount of heat available in water $= 2 \times 1 \times (35 - 0) = 70$ cal. The heat needed to melt the ice completely is $1 \times 80 = 80$ cal. So ice will not melt completely and temperature of water falls to 0°C.

27. (b) At C, solid completely will convert into liquid.

1. (c)

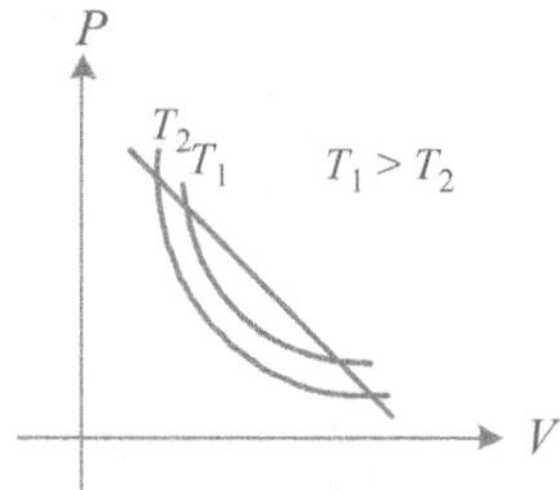

Figure shows two isotherms in which $T_1 > T_2$. Clearly gas is heated in the beginning and cool at the end.

2. (d)
$$\frac{\Delta I}{I} = 2\alpha \Delta T$$

or
$$\frac{\Delta I}{I} \times 100 = [2 \times 10^{-5} \times 20] \times 100$$
$$= 0.04$$

3. (a)
$$mg = F_b$$
$$(\rho_{Fe})V_0 g = (k_1 V_0)(\rho_{Hg})_0 g \qquad \dots (i)$$

and $(\rho_{Fe})_{60} V_t g = (k_2 V_t)(\rho_{Hg})_{60} g$

or $\left[\dfrac{(\rho_{Fe})_0}{1 + \gamma_{Fe} \times 60}\right] g = k_2 \left[\dfrac{(\rho_{Hg})_0}{1 + \gamma_{Hg} \times 60}\right] g \quad \dots (ii)$

From above equations, we get
$$\frac{k_1}{k_2} = \left[\frac{1 + 60\gamma_{Fe}}{1 + 60\gamma_{Hg}}\right]$$

4. (c)
$$\Delta \ell_1 = \ell_1 \alpha_{A\ell} t \text{ and } \Delta \ell_2 = \ell_2 \alpha_s t$$

As $\ell_1 \alpha_{A\ell} t = \ell_2 \alpha_s t$, $\therefore$ $\ell_1 \alpha_{Al} = \ell_2 \alpha_s$

$$\frac{\ell_1}{\ell_1 + \ell_2} = \frac{\ell_1}{\ell_1 + \dfrac{\ell_1 \alpha_{A\ell}}{\alpha_s}} = \frac{\alpha_s}{\alpha_{A\ell} + \alpha_s} = \frac{\gamma_s}{\gamma_{Al} + \gamma_s}.$$

5. (c) $PV = nRT$ and $P\Delta V = nR\Delta T$

$\therefore$ $\dfrac{\Delta V}{V \Delta T} = \dfrac{1}{T}$; It is like $y \propto \dfrac{1}{x}$.

6. (a) $PV = $ constant

or $PdV + VdP = 0$

$\therefore$ $\dfrac{dV}{V(dP)} = -\dfrac{1}{P}$; it is like $y \propto \dfrac{1}{x}$.

7. (a)
$$Pt = 160t + mC\Delta T$$

or $1000t = 160t + 2 \times 4200 \times (77 - 27)$

$\therefore$ $t = 500s$ or $8\min 20s$

8. (a) Tension, $F = (Y\alpha \Delta T)A$
$$= (2 \times 10^{11}) \times (10^{-5}) \times (25 - 0) \times \pi(0.5 \times 10^{-2})^2$$
$$= 3925 \text{ N}.$$

9. (a) The density of the paraffin
$$\rho = \left[\frac{\rho_0}{1 + \gamma \Delta t}\right] = \frac{0.82}{1 + 0.0009 \times 15} = 0.809 \text{ g/cm}^3$$

The mass of the paraffin at this temperature
$$m = \rho V = 0.809 \times 50 = 40.5 \text{ g}.$$

10. (b) The heat consumed in melting 15.2 g of ice
$$Q = mL = (15.2 \times 10^{-3}) \times 3.34 \times 10^5$$
$$= 5.07 \times 10^3 \text{J}$$

Thus $(\mu m g) \times x = 5.07 \times 10^3$

or $0.060 \times 10 \times 9.8 x = 5.07 \times 10^3$

$\therefore$ $x = 863 \text{ m}$

11. (a)
$$M_1 g = Mg - V_1 \rho_{\ell_1} g$$

or
$$M_1 g = Mg - V_1 \rho_1 g \qquad \dots (i)$$

and $M_2 g = Mg - V_1[1 + \gamma_g(t_2 - t_1)]\dfrac{\rho_1}{[1 + \gamma_\ell(t_2 - t_1)]} g$

$\hspace{10cm} \dots (ii)$

After simplifying, we get
$$\gamma_\ell = \gamma_g + \left(\frac{M_2 - M_1}{M - M_2}\right)\frac{1}{(t_2 - t_1)}.$$

12. (c)

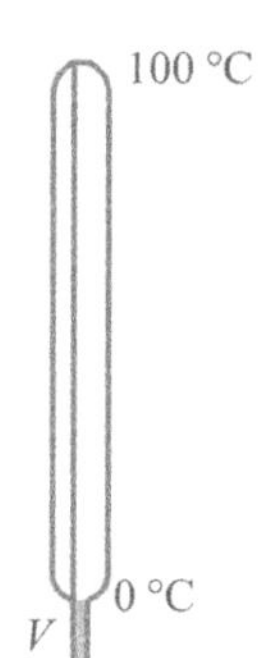

$$\Delta V = V\alpha \Delta T$$

or $(\ell A) = V(\alpha_{Hg} - \alpha_g)\Delta T$

or $20 \times \pi(0.25 \times 10^{-1})^2 = V(0.000180 - 0.000009) \times (100)$

$\therefore$ $V = 2.57 \text{ cm}^3$

13. (b)
$$\frac{1}{2}mv^2 = mC\Delta T$$

$\therefore$
$$\Delta T = \frac{v^2}{2C} = \frac{200^2}{2 \times 128}$$
$$= 156°C$$

14. (d) The heat available on water $= 30 \times 1 \times (80 - 0) = 2400$ cal.
To melt the ice, it need $= mL = 50 \times 80 = 4000$ cal
So if m amount of ice is melt, then
$$m \times 80 = 2400$$
or $m = 30 \text{ g}$
The ice left $= 20$ g

15. (c) If m is the mass of steam condenses, then
$$m \times 540 = (250) \times 1 \times (100 - 0) + 20 \times 80$$
$$+ 20 \times 1 \times (10000)$$
$\therefore$ $m = 53 \text{ g}$
The entire contents will reach the temperature 100°C.

16. (a)
$$\ell_s - \ell_b = 30 \qquad \dots (i)$$

Also $\Delta \ell_b - \Delta \ell_s = 0$

or $\ell_b \alpha_b \Delta T = \ell_s \alpha_s \Delta T$

or $\ell_b \times 19 \times 10^{-6} = \ell_s \times 11 \times 10^{-6} \qquad \dots (ii)$

or $\quad \ell_b = \dfrac{11}{19}\ell_s \qquad \qquad ...(iii)$

From above equations, we get

$\ell_s = 71.25$ cm and $\ell_b = 41.25$ cm

17. (c) The pressure at the bottom of both the limbs must be same, so

$$\rho_0 g h_0 = \rho_t g h_t$$

or $\quad \rho_0 h_0 = \left[\dfrac{\rho_0}{1+\gamma_\ell \times 30}\right] h_t$

or $\quad 120 = \left[\dfrac{124}{1+\gamma_\ell \times 30}\right]$

$\therefore \quad \gamma_\ell = 11\times 10^{-4}/°C$

18. (c) Suppose the correct barometer height at 0°C is ℓ_0, then

$$\ell_0 + \Delta \ell = 75$$

or $\ell_0 + 75\times(\alpha_{Hg}-\alpha_b)\times 27 = 75$

or $\ell_0 + 75\times(0.6\times 10^{-4}-0.2\times 10^{-4})\times 27 = 75$

$\therefore \quad \ell_0 = 74.92$ cm

19. (d) If y be the extension of the spring, then

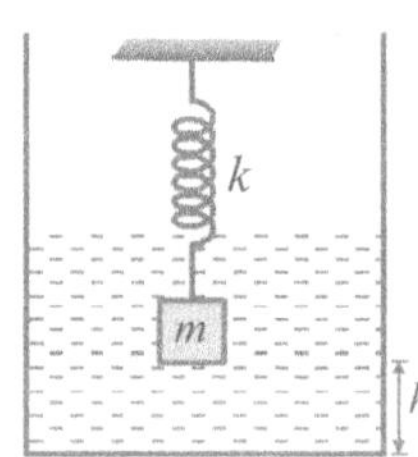

$$mg = ky + V\rho_w g$$

or $\quad 2g = 25\times y + \dfrac{2}{5\times 10^3}\times 10^3 \times g$

$\therefore \quad y = 0.64$ m

The energy of the spring block-spring system

$$= \dfrac{1}{2}ky^2 + mgh$$

Thus $m_w C_w \Delta T + m_b C_b \Delta T = \dfrac{1}{2}ky^2 + mgh$

$(0.5\times 4200 + 2\times 250)\times 0.004 = \dfrac{1}{2}\times 25 \times 0.64^2 + 2\times 10\times h$

$\therefore \quad h = 0.26$ m

20. (d) $\quad F = F_0 + Y\alpha \Delta T \times A$

$\quad = 50 + (34\times 10^{10})\times(4.5\times 10^{-6})\times$

$\quad (150-20)\times \pi\,(0.1\times 10^{-3})^2$

$\quad = 56.2$ N.

21. (c) $\alpha = \dfrac{\Delta L}{L\Delta T}$; It found greatest for rod (c).

22. (c) Given $PT^2 = $ constant ; $PV = nRT$ or $P = \dfrac{nRT}{V}$

$\therefore \quad \dfrac{nRT}{V}\times T^2 = $ constant

or $\quad T^3 = CV$

23. (c) $V_1 = \dfrac{(45-25)g}{d_1}$ and $V_2 = \dfrac{(45-27)g}{d_2}$

$\therefore \quad \dfrac{V_1}{V_2} = \dfrac{20}{18}\times\dfrac{d_2}{d_1}$

or $\dfrac{V_1}{V_1(1+r_{metal}\times 10)} = \dfrac{20}{18}\times\left[\dfrac{d_1}{(1+r_\ell \times 10)d_1}\right]$

After simplifying, we get $\alpha = \dfrac{\gamma_{metal}}{3} = 2.6\times 10^{-3}/°C$

24. (b) $1\times \dfrac{5R}{2}\times(T_f - T_0) = 1\times \dfrac{3R}{2}\times\left(\dfrac{7T_0}{3}-T_f\right)$

$\therefore \quad T_f = \dfrac{3T_0}{2}.$

25. (b) $Pt = mL$; $\therefore \quad L = \dfrac{Pt}{m}.$

26. (b) $2\times 0.5\times(20-0)+m\times 80 = 5\times 1\times 20$

$\therefore \quad m = 1$ kg

The total mass of water = 5kg + 1 kg = 6 kg.

27. (a) $\quad P_1 = P_2$

or $\quad \rho_1 g \ell_1 = \rho_2 g \ell_2$

or $\quad \dfrac{\rho_0}{1+\gamma_\ell t_1}\ell_1 = \dfrac{\rho_0}{1+\gamma_\ell t_2}\ell_2$

$\therefore \quad \gamma_\ell = \left[\dfrac{\ell_1 - \ell_2}{\ell_2 t_1 - \ell_1 t_2}\right].$

28. (d) $\quad (OR)^2 = (PR)^2 - (PO)^2 = \ell^2 - (\ell/2)^2$

$\quad = [\ell(1+\alpha_2 t)]^2 - \left[\dfrac{\ell}{2}(1+\alpha_1 t)\right]^2$

After simplifying and neglecting $\alpha_2^2 t^2$ and $\alpha_1^2 t^2$, we get

$$\alpha_1 = 4\alpha_2$$

29. (b) Let A_0 and A_t be the areas of cross-section of the tube at temperature 0 °C and t °C respectively,

l = length of the liquid column (constant)

V_0 and V_t be the volumes of the liquid at temperature 0 °C and t °C respectively,

$V_0 = \ell A_0 \qquad V_t = \ell A_t$

$V_t = V_0(1+\gamma t) \qquad A_t = A_0(1+2\alpha t)$

$\therefore V_t = \ell A_0(1+2\alpha t) = V_0(1+\gamma t) = \ell A_0(1+\gamma t)$ or $\gamma = 2\alpha.$

30. (b) $2.60 + 2.60\times \alpha_{steel}\,\Delta T = 2.60\,\alpha_{brass}\Delta T$

31. (b) $\quad 60 = mC\Delta T + W' \qquad ... (i)$

and $\quad 120 = (3m)C\Delta T + W' \qquad ... (ii)$

After solving above equations, we get

$W' = 30\,W.$

1.   **(b, d)**   Let ℓ_0 be the length and t the thickness of each strip. On heating, length of brass rod

$$\ell_1 = \ell_0(1+\alpha_B \Delta T)$$

By the geometry of the figure, we have

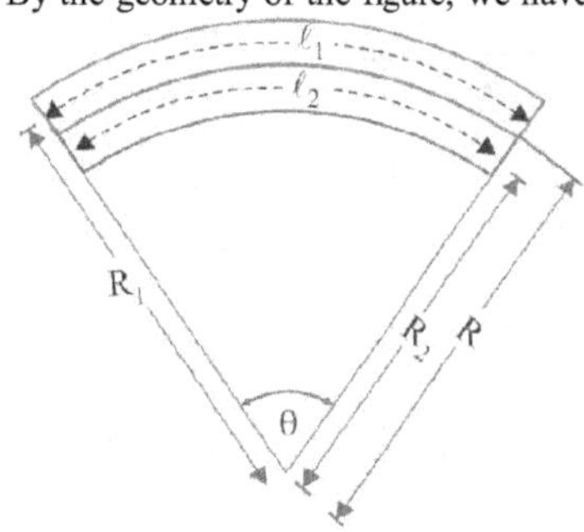

Fig. 5.18

$$\ell_1 = R_1\theta$$

$$= \left(R+\frac{t}{2}\right)\theta$$

$$\therefore \left(R+\frac{t}{2}\right)\theta = \ell_0(1+\alpha_B\Delta T) \qquad \ldots (i)$$

Similarly for copper strip, $\ell_2 = \ell_0(1+\alpha_C t) = R_2\theta$

$$\text{or} \quad \left(R-\frac{t}{2}\right)\theta = \ell_0(1+\alpha_C\Delta T) \qquad \ldots (ii)$$

Dividing equation (i) by (ii), we get

$$\Rightarrow \frac{\left(R+\dfrac{t}{2}\right)}{\left(R-\dfrac{t}{2}\right)} = \frac{1+\alpha_B\Delta T}{1+\alpha_C\Delta T}$$

$$\Rightarrow \left(R+\frac{t}{2}\right)(1+\alpha_C\Delta T) = \left(R-\frac{t}{2}\right)(1+\alpha_B\Delta T)$$

$$\Rightarrow R+R\alpha_C\Delta T +\frac{t}{2}+\frac{t}{2}\alpha_C\Delta T$$

$$= R+R\alpha_B\Delta T -\frac{t}{2}-\frac{t}{2}\alpha_B\Delta T$$

If ΔT is small, α is still small, so we can neglect their product. And, therefore, we have

$$R\alpha_B\Delta T - R\alpha_C\Delta T = t$$

$$\text{or} \qquad R = \frac{t}{(\alpha_B-\alpha_C)\Delta T} \qquad \textbf{\textit{Ans.}}$$

2.   **(b, c)**

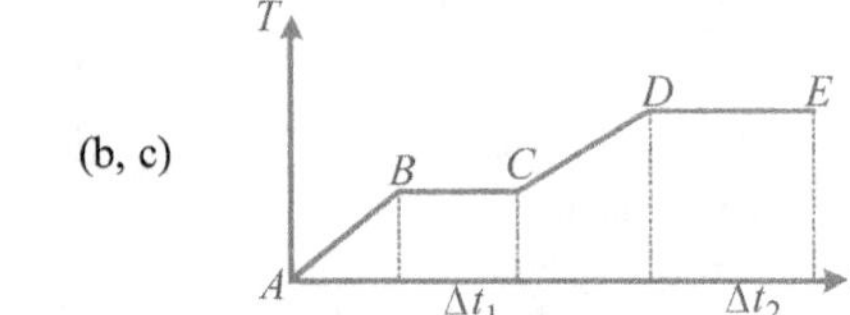

$$dQ = mCdT$$

$$\text{or} \qquad Hdt = mCdT$$

$$\therefore \qquad C = \left(\frac{H}{m}\right)\frac{1}{(dT/dt)}$$

As $\dfrac{dT}{dt}$ of CD is smaller, so $C_{liquid} > C_{solid}$

$$Q_1 = H(\Delta t_1) \text{ and } Q_2 = H(\Delta t_2)$$

As $\Delta t_2 > \Delta t_1$, $\therefore Q_2 > Q_1$.

3.   **(a, c, d)**   Given,

$$\frac{\Delta D}{D}\times 100 = 0.2\% \text{ or } \frac{\Delta R}{R}\times 100 = 0.2\%$$

$$\therefore \frac{\Delta V}{V}\times 100 = \left[2\frac{\Delta R}{R}+\frac{\Delta t}{t}\right]\times 100 = 2\times 0.2 + 0.2$$

$$= 0.6\ \%$$

Also $$\frac{\Delta D}{D} = \frac{0.2}{100}$$

$$\text{or} \qquad \frac{D\alpha\times 80}{D} = \frac{0.2}{100}$$

$$\therefore \quad \alpha = 0.25\times 10^{-4}/°C\ .$$

4.   **(a, d)**   Obviously $\gamma_L > \gamma_v$.

$$\Delta V_L = \Delta V_v$$

$$\text{or} \quad V_L\gamma_L\Delta T = V_v\gamma_v\Delta T$$

$$\therefore \qquad V_L\gamma_L = V_v\gamma_v .$$

5.   **(b, c)** $\beta = 2\alpha$ and $\gamma = 3\alpha$

$$\therefore \frac{\beta}{\gamma} = \frac{2}{3} \text{ and } \frac{\gamma}{\alpha} = 3$$

6.   **(a, d)**   Kinetic energy of the sphere,

$$K = \frac{1}{2}I\omega^2$$

$$= \frac{1}{2}\times\frac{2}{5}MR^2(2\pi n)^2$$

$$= \frac{4}{5}\pi^2 n^2 MR^2 .$$

Kinetic energy used to raise, the temperature

$$= 0.5\left(\frac{4}{5}\pi^2 n^2 MR^2\right)$$

$$= \frac{2}{5}\pi^2 n^2 mR^2$$

If ΔT be the raise in temperature of the sphere, then

$$MC\Delta T = \frac{2}{5}\pi^2 n^2 MR^2$$

$$\therefore \qquad \Delta T = \frac{2\pi^2 n^2 R^2}{5C} .$$

Solutions EXERCISE-5.3

1. (b) In non-inertial frame, there is a pseudo force, which disturb the equilibrium. Thermal equilibrium has no effect of force.
2. (d) Without contact the heat can be transfer due to radiation.
3. (a) correctly explained
4. (b) Coefficient of linear expansion and coefficient of volume expansion both have same unit, i.e., $1°$ C or / K.
5. (a) Correctly explained
6. (c) In Fahrenheit, the fixed points are equally divided into 180 division instead of 100 division.

7. (a)
$$F = \frac{9}{5}C + 32$$

or
$$x = \frac{9}{5}x + 32$$

$$\therefore \quad x = -40°$$

8. (a) The specific heat of water is greater than specific heat of land. Because of this water looses heat slowly in comparision to land, which causes temperature difference between two and so land and sea breeze.

9. (a) Correctly explained

10. (a) $m_1 C_1 (T_1 - T) = m_2 C_2 (T - T_2)$

$$\therefore \quad T = \left[\frac{m_1 C_1 T_1 + m_2 C_2 T_2}{m_1 C_1 + m_2 C_2} \right]$$

11. (d) Heat is not a conserved quantity because it is the moving energy.

12. (a) At the change of state, the internal potential energy increases.

Solutions EXERCISE-5.4

Passage (Q.1 - 3)

1. (b)
$$Q = \int_{10}^{50} nCdT = \int_{10}^{50} 2\left[k \frac{T^3}{\theta^3} \right] dT$$

$$= \frac{2 \times 1940}{(281)^3} \int_{10}^{50} T^3 dT$$

$$= \frac{2 \times 1940}{(281)^3} \times \frac{|T^4|_{10}^{50}}{4}$$

$$= 273 \text{ J.}$$

2. (a)
$$C_{mean} = \frac{\int_{10}^{50} CdT}{(50-10)} = \frac{1}{40} \int_{10}^{50} K \frac{T^3}{\theta^3} dT$$

$$= 3.42 \text{ J/mol - K.}$$

3. (d)
$$C = K \frac{T^3}{\theta^3} = 1940 \times \frac{50^3}{281^3} = 10.9 \text{ J/mol-K}$$

Passage (Q.4 - 5)

4. (b)
$$L = I\omega = \frac{MR^2}{2} \times \omega = \frac{0.50(0.030)^2}{2} \times 60$$

$$= 1.35 \times 10^{-2} \text{ J-s}$$

5. (a) In the process $\vec{L}$, remains constant.

$$\Delta R = R\alpha\Delta T$$

Also $\dfrac{2\Delta R}{R} + \dfrac{\Delta\omega}{\omega} = 0$

$$\therefore \quad \frac{\Delta\omega}{\omega} = -\frac{2\Delta R}{R} = -2\alpha\Delta T$$

$$= -2 \times 2 \times 10^{-5} \times 80$$

$$= -3.2 \times 10^{-3}.$$

Passage (Q.6 - 8)

6. (a) Due to expansion of material, the diameter of hole will increase.

7. (c) $\gamma_{apparent} = \gamma_{liquid} - \gamma_{cont} = \gamma - 3 \times \dfrac{\gamma}{3} = 0$

So $\Delta V = V \times \gamma_{apparent} \times \Delta T = 0$.

8. (d) For lengths of the rods to be constant

$$\Delta\ell_1 = \Delta\ell_2$$

or $\ell_1\alpha_1\Delta T = \ell_2\alpha_2\Delta T$

$$\therefore \quad \ell_1\alpha_1 = \ell_2\alpha_2$$

Passage (Q.9 - 11)

9. (d) $\Delta R = R\alpha\Delta T$.

In the process, the angular momentum of the disc remains constant, so

$$L = I\omega = \frac{MR^2}{2}\omega$$

or $\dfrac{\Delta L}{L} = \dfrac{2\Delta R}{R} + \dfrac{\Delta\omega}{\omega}$

or $0 = 2\alpha\Delta T + \dfrac{\Delta\omega}{\omega}$

$$\therefore \quad \frac{\Delta\omega}{\omega} = -2\alpha\Delta T$$

10. (c) The angular momentum can also be written as
$$L = mvR$$

or $$\frac{\Delta L}{L} = \frac{\Delta v}{v} + \frac{\Delta R}{R}$$

or $$0 = \frac{\Delta v}{v} + \alpha\Delta T \;;\; \therefore \; \frac{\Delta v}{v} = -\alpha\Delta T$$

11. (d) As, $$K = \frac{L^2}{2I},$$

$$\therefore \quad \frac{\Delta k}{k} = \frac{2\Delta L}{L} - \frac{\Delta I}{I}$$
$$= 0 - 2\alpha\Delta T\,.$$
$$= -2\alpha\Delta T,$$

12. **A→ p; B→ r; C→ q; D→ s**

A and B: $(m)(s)(\theta - 20) = (2m)(s)(40 - \theta)$

or $$\theta = \frac{100}{3} = 33.3°C$$

A and C : $(m)(s)(\theta - 20) = (3m)(s)(60 - \theta)$
$$\theta = 50°C$$
B and C : $(2m)(s)(\theta - 40) = (3m)(s)(60 - \theta)$
$$\theta = 52\ °C$$
A, B and C : $(m)(s)(\theta - 20) + (2m)(s)(60 - \theta)$
$$= (3m)(s)(60 - \theta)$$
$$\theta = 46.67°C$$

13. **A→ s; B→ r; C→ q; D→ q**

$$I = \frac{2}{5}mR^2$$

$$\therefore \quad \frac{\Delta I}{I} = \frac{\Delta M}{M} + \frac{2\Delta R}{R}$$
$$= 0 + 2\alpha\Delta T = 2\alpha\Delta T$$

In the process, angular momentum is constant and so,

$$\frac{\Delta L}{L} = 0.$$

As $$L = I\omega$$

$$\therefore \quad \frac{\Delta L}{L} = \frac{\Delta I}{I} + \frac{\Delta\omega}{\omega}$$

or $$0 = 2\alpha\Delta T + \frac{\Delta\omega}{\omega}$$

or $$\frac{\Delta\omega}{\omega} = -2\alpha\Delta T.$$

Also $$\frac{\Delta k}{k} = -2\alpha\Delta T.$$

14. **A→ s, q; B→ q ; C→ p, q; D→ q, r**
Theoritical.

1. If x is the temperature on faulty thermometer, then

$$\frac{X - FP}{BP - FP} = \frac{C - 0}{100 - 0}$$

or $$\frac{52 - 5}{99 - 5} = \frac{C}{100}$$

$$\therefore \quad C = 50°\ C$$
$$= 122°\ F \qquad \textbf{Ans.}$$

2. Temperature $$t = \left[\frac{P_t - P_0}{P_{100} - P_0}\right] \times 100$$

$$= \left[\frac{80 - 75}{100 - 75}\right] \times 100$$

$$= 20°\ C \qquad \textbf{Ans.}$$

3. Suppose V be the volume of the mercury in the flask. For volume of air in the flask to be constant, increase in volume of mercury
$$= \text{increase in volume of flask}$$

or $$V\gamma_{Hg}\,\Delta t = (10^3)\gamma_g\,\Delta t$$

or $$V = \frac{10^3 \times (3 \times 9 \times 10^{-6})}{1.8 \times 10^{-4}}$$

$$= 150\ cm^3 \qquad \textbf{Ans.}$$

4. See the solution of problem 14 from exercise 5.6.

5. The expansion of each rail
$$\Delta \ell = \ell\alpha\,\Delta t$$
$$= 12 \times 11 \times 10^{-6} \times (48 - 18)$$
$$= 0.4 \times 10^{-2}\ m \qquad \textbf{Ans.}$$

6. Suppose V be the volume of mercury. For the volume of empty space to be constant,
$$\Delta V_{mercury} = \Delta V_{glass}$$

or $$V\gamma_{mercury}\,\Delta t = 1000\gamma_{glass}\,\Delta t$$

$$\therefore \quad V = \frac{1000 \times 9 \times 10^{-6}}{1.8 \times 10^{-4}}$$

$$= 50\ cm^3 \qquad \textbf{Ans.}$$

7. If m be the required mass of the ice, then
$$m \times 0.5 \times [0 - (-14)] + m \times 80 + m \times 1 \times (10 - 0)$$
$$= 200 \times 1 \times (25 - 10)$$
$$\therefore \quad m = 31\ g. \qquad \textbf{Ans.}$$

8. Given, $$U = 1.5\ nRT$$
$$\therefore \quad dU = 1.5\ nR(dT)$$
$$= 1.5 \times 1 \times 8.3 \times 2$$
$$= 24.9\ J$$

We know that, $$Q = dU + W$$
$$\therefore \quad W = Q - dU$$
$$= 42 - 24.9$$
$$= 17.1\ J$$

As $$W = P\Delta V$$
$$= P\Delta(Ax)$$
$$= PA(\Delta x)$$

$$\therefore \quad \Delta x = \frac{W}{PA}$$

$$= \frac{17.1}{100 \times 10^3 \times 8.5 \times 10^{-4}}$$

$$= 20 \times 10^{-2}\ m \qquad \textbf{Ans.}$$

1. We know that

$$\frac{P}{P_{tr}} = \frac{T}{T_{tr}}$$

$$\therefore \quad T = \frac{T_{tr}}{P_{tr}} \times P$$

$$= \frac{274.16}{20} \times 14.3$$

$$= 195.30 \text{ k} \qquad \textbf{\textit{Ans.}}$$

2. The temperature

$$t = \left[\frac{\ell_t - \ell_0}{\ell_{100} - \ell_0}\right] \times 100$$

$$= \left[\frac{6.5 - 10.3}{26.8 - 10.3}\right] \times 100$$

$$= -23.03° \text{ C.} \qquad \textbf{\textit{Ans.}}$$

3. The change in diameter is given by

$$\Delta D = D \, \alpha \, \Delta t$$

$$= 4.24 \times (1.70 \times 10^{-5}) \times (227 - 27)$$

$$= 1.44 \times 10^{-2} \text{ cm} \qquad \textbf{\textit{Ans.}}$$

4. The length of the rod at hot day

$$\ell_2 = \ell_1 [\, 1 + \alpha \, (t_2 - t_1)\,]$$

$$= 63 \,[\, 1 + 1.2\,0 \times 10^{-5}\,(45 - 27)\,]$$

$$= 63.013 \text{ cm} \qquad \textbf{\textit{Ans.}}$$

5. For the slip of the wheel on the shaft

$$\Delta D = D \, \alpha \, \Delta t$$

or

$$-0.01 = 8.70 \times 1.20 \times 10^{-5} \times \Delta t$$

$$\therefore \quad \Delta t = -95.78° \text{ C}$$

$$\therefore \quad \text{Final temperature } t = 27 + (-95.78)$$

$$= -68.78° \text{ C}$$

$$= -68.8° \text{ C} \qquad \textbf{\textit{Ans.}}$$

6. The change in length in brass rod

$$\Delta \ell_b = \ell \, \alpha \, \Delta t$$

$$= 50 \times 2.0 \times 10^{-5} \times (250 - 40)$$

$$= 0.21 \text{ cm}$$

For steel rod

$$\Delta \ell_s = \ell \, \alpha \, \Delta t$$

$$= 50 \times 1.2 \times 10^{-5} \times (250 - 40)$$

$$= 0.13 \text{ cm}$$

The total change

$$\Delta \ell = \Delta \ell_b + \Delta \ell_s$$

$$= 0.21 + 0.13$$

$$= 0.34 \text{ cm}$$

As the rods are free to expand, so no stress will developed anywhere.

7. The thermal stress in the wire

$$f_{th} = Y \alpha \, \Delta t$$

$$= 0.91 \times 10^{11} \times 2.0 \times 10^{-5} \times |-39 - 27|$$

$$= 1.20 \times 10^8 \text{ N/m}^2$$

The tension in the wire

$$F = F_{th} \, A$$

$$= f \times \pi \, r^2$$

$$= 1.20 \times 10^8 \times \pi \, (10^{-3})^2$$

$$= 3.77 \times 10^2 \text{ N.} \qquad \textbf{\textit{Ans.}}$$

8. Given

$$\rho = \frac{m}{V}$$

$$= mV^{-1}$$

Differentiating both sides w.r.t. temperature we have

$$\frac{d\rho}{dt} = -mV^{-2} \frac{dV}{dt} \qquad [m = \text{constant}]$$

$$= -\frac{m}{V}\left(\frac{dV}{Vdt}\right)$$

As

$$\frac{dV}{Vdt} = \gamma$$

$$\therefore \quad \frac{d\rho}{dT} = -\rho \, \gamma$$

or

$$\gamma = -\frac{1}{\rho} \frac{d\rho}{dt} \qquad \textbf{Proved}$$

9. Suppose ℓ_{0_1}, and ℓ_{0_2} be the lengths of steel and copper rods at 0° C respectively.

Their lengths at temperature t are given by

$$\ell_1 = \ell_{0_1} (\, 1 + \alpha_1 t)$$

and

$$\ell_2 = \ell_{0_2} (\, 1 + \alpha_2 t)$$

Given

$$\ell_1 - \ell_2 = 5 \text{ cm}$$

or

$$\ell_{0_1} (\, 1 + \alpha_1 t) - \ell_{0_2} (\, 1 + \alpha_2 t) = 5 \qquad \text{.......(i)}$$

Differentiating equation (i) w.r.t.t, we have

$$\ell_{0_1} \alpha_1 - \ell_{0_2} \alpha_2 = 0$$

$$\therefore \quad \ell_{0_1} = \frac{\alpha_2}{\alpha_1} \ell_{0_2}$$

$$= \left(\frac{1.7 \times 10^{-5}}{1.1 \times 10^{-5}}\right) \ell_{0_2}$$

or $\qquad \ell_{0_1} = 1.545\, \ell_{0_2} \qquad$ ......(i)

At $\qquad t = 0$

$$\ell_{0_1} - \ell_{0_2} = 5 \qquad ......(ii)$$

After solving equations (i) and (ii), we get

$$\ell_{0_1} = 14.17\,\text{cm},$$

$$\ell_{0_2} = 9.17\,\text{cm} \qquad \textbf{\textit{Ans.}}$$

10. The volume of overflow gasoline

$$\begin{aligned}
\Delta V &= V\,\alpha_{app}\,\Delta t \\
&= V\,[\alpha_{gas} - \alpha_{st}]\,\Delta t \\
&= 75\,[\,9.5 \times 10^{-4} - 0.12 \times 10^{-4}\,] \\
&\qquad\qquad\qquad\qquad \times (30 - 10) \\
&= 1.37\ \text{litre.} \qquad \textbf{\textit{Ans.}}
\end{aligned}$$

11. If α is the function of temperature, then with small change in temperature (dT), the length

$$L_0 = L_0\,\alpha\,dT$$

Thus $\qquad L = L_0 + \displaystyle\int_0^T L_0 \alpha dT \qquad \textbf{\textit{Ans.}}$

12. The change in height of liquid column

$$\Delta h = \frac{1.28}{2}\alpha_{liquid}\Delta t - 1.28\,\alpha_{glass}\Delta t$$

$$= \frac{1.28}{2} \times (4 \times 10^{-5}) \times 10 - 1.28 \times 1 \times 10^{-5} \times 10$$

$$= 1.3 \times 10^{-5}\ \text{m.} \qquad \textbf{\textit{Ans.}}$$

13. By Pascal's law the pressure intensity at the bottom of left arm is equal to the pressure intensity at the bottom of right arm. Thus

$$h_t\,\rho_t\,g = h_0\,\rho_0\,g$$

or $\quad h_0\,(\,1 + \gamma\,t\,) \times \dfrac{\rho_0}{(1 + \gamma t)} = h_0\,\rho_0$

After simplifying, we get

$$\gamma = \left[\frac{h_t - h_0}{h_0 t}\right] \qquad \textbf{\textit{Ans.}}$$

14. Suppose the length of the rods becomes ℓ_1, ℓ_2 and ℓ_3 when they heat. If θ is the angle between A and B, then

$$\cos\theta = \frac{\ell_1^2 + \ell_2^2 - \ell_3^2}{2\ell_1\ell_2}$$

or $\quad 2\ell_1\ell_2 \cos\theta = \ell_1^2 + \ell_2^2 - \ell_3^2 \qquad$ ....(i)

On differentiating equation (i), we get

$$(2\,\ell_1 \cos\theta)\, d\ell_2 + (2\ell_2 \cos\theta)\, d\ell_1 - (2\,\ell_1\ell_2)\sin\theta\, d\theta$$
$$= 2\,\ell_1\,(d\ell_1) + 2\ell_2\,(d\ell_2) - 2\ell_3\,(d\ell_3) \ .....(ii)$$

When temperature of the system is increased by ΔT,

$$d\ell_1 = \ell_1\,\alpha_1\,\Delta T;\ \ d\ell_2 = \ell_2\,\alpha_1\,\Delta T;\ \ and$$

$$d\ell_3 = \ell_3\,\alpha_2\,\Delta T\,;$$

If ΔT is small, then $\ell_1 = \ell_2$
$$= \ell_3$$

and $\qquad \theta = 60°.$

Putting these values in above equations and simplifying, we get

$$\Delta T = \frac{\sqrt{3}\,d\theta}{2(\alpha_2 - \alpha_1)} \qquad \textbf{\textit{Ans.}}$$

15. The change in length, $\Delta\ell = \ell\alpha\,\Delta t$

$$0.055 \times 10^{-3} = 1 \times 11 \times 10^{-6} \times \Delta t$$

$\therefore \qquad \Delta t = 5°\,C$

Thus the range of temperature $= 20°C \pm 5°C$

$$= 15°\,C\ \text{to}\ 25°\,C \qquad \textbf{\textit{Ans.}}$$

16. Suppose A be the cross – section of the each rod.

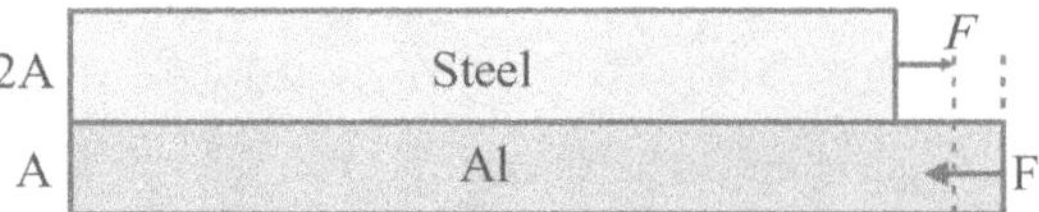

Change in length of steel rod

$$\begin{aligned}
\Delta_{st} &= \Delta_t + \Delta_F \\
&= \ell_0 \alpha_s\,\theta + \frac{F\ell_0}{AY_a} \qquad ......(i)
\end{aligned}$$

Change in length of aluminium rod

$$\begin{aligned}
\Delta_{A\ell} &= \Delta_t - \Delta_F \\
&= \ell_0 \alpha_a\,\theta - \frac{F\ell_0}{AY_a} \qquad .....(ii)
\end{aligned}$$

At equilibrium, $\qquad \Delta_{st} = \Delta_{A\ell}$

or $\quad \ell_0\alpha_s\,\theta + \dfrac{F\ell_0}{2AY_s} = \ell_0\alpha_a\,\theta - \dfrac{F\ell_0}{AY_a}$

or $\quad F\left[\dfrac{1}{2Y_s} + \dfrac{1}{Y_a}\right] = A\,(\alpha_a - \alpha_s)\,\theta$

$\therefore \qquad F = \dfrac{A(\alpha_a - \alpha_s)\theta}{\left[\dfrac{1}{2Y_s} + \dfrac{1}{Y_a}\right]}$

From equation (i),

$$\Delta_{st} = \ell_0 \alpha_s \theta + \frac{A(\alpha_a - \alpha_s)\theta \ell_0}{2A\left[\dfrac{1}{2Y_s} + \dfrac{1}{Y_a}\right]Y_s}$$

$$= \left[\frac{\alpha_a Y_a + 2\alpha_s Y_s}{Y_a + 2Y_s}\right]\ell_0\theta$$

The length of the system $= \ell_0 + \Delta_{st}$

$$= \ell_0 + \left[\frac{\alpha_a Y_a + 2\alpha_s Y_s}{Y_a + 2Y_s}\right]\ell_0\theta$$

$$= \ell_0\left[1 + \frac{\alpha_a Y_a + 2\alpha_s Y_s}{Y_a + 2Y_s}\theta\right] \quad \textbf{\textit{Ans.}}$$

17. Time period of torsional pendulum

$$T = 2\pi\sqrt{\frac{I}{C}}$$

$$\therefore \qquad \frac{\Delta T}{T} = \frac{1}{2}\frac{\Delta I}{I}$$

As $\qquad I = kL^2$

$$\therefore \qquad \frac{\Delta I}{I} = \frac{2\Delta L}{L}$$

Due to small change in temperature ΔT,

$$\Delta L = L\alpha\,\Delta T$$

$$\therefore \qquad \frac{\Delta I}{I} = 2\alpha\,\Delta T$$

and $\qquad \dfrac{\Delta T}{T} = \dfrac{1}{2} \times 2\alpha\Delta T$

$$= \alpha\,\Delta T$$

$$= 2.4 \times 10^{-5} \times (45 - 5)$$

$$= 9.60 \times 10^{-4}$$

$$= 9.6 \times 10^{-2}\,\% \quad \textbf{\textit{Ans.}}$$

18. We know that $\qquad v = \omega\,r \qquad (\omega\ \text{constant})$

$$\therefore \qquad \frac{\Delta v}{v} = \frac{\Delta r}{r}$$

With small change in temperature ΔT,

$$\Delta r = r\alpha\,\Delta t$$

$$\therefore \qquad \frac{\Delta v}{v} = \frac{r\alpha\,\Delta t}{r}$$

$$= \alpha\,\Delta t$$

$$= 1.2 \times 10^{-5} \times (50 - 20)$$

$$= 3.6 \times 10^{-4}$$

$$= 3.6 \times 10^{-2}\,\% \quad \textbf{\textit{Ans.}}$$

19. Suppose size of the aluminium from on the worky day be $\ell \times b$
At $0°$ C, the length of aluminium frame

$$= \ell\,(1 - \alpha \times 40\,)$$

$$= \ell\,(1 - 24 \times 10^{-6} \times 40\,)$$

The length of glass window at the same temperature

$$= 30\,(1 - \alpha \times 40)$$

$$= 30\,(1 - 9 \times 10^{-6} \times 40)$$

For no stress, their sizes must be equal and so

$$\ell\,(1 - 24 \times 10^{-6} \times 40) = 30\,(1 - 9 \times 10^{-6} \times 40)$$

$$\therefore \qquad \ell = 30.018\ \text{cm.}$$

Similarly $\qquad b = 20.012\ \text{cm} \qquad \textbf{\textit{Ans.}}$

20. Using Pascal's law, we have

$$P_a + \rho_A\,gh_A - \rho_B\,gh_B + \rho_c\,gh_c - \rho_D gh_D = P_a$$

Here $\qquad \rho_A = \rho_c$

$$= \rho_{95}$$

and $\qquad \rho_B = \rho_D$

$$= \rho_5$$

$$\therefore \qquad \rho_{95}\,(h_A + h_c) = \rho_5\,(h_B + h_D)$$

or $\qquad \left[\dfrac{\rho_0}{1 + \gamma \times 95}\right](52.8 + 49) = \left[\dfrac{\rho_0}{1 + \gamma \times 5}\right](49 + 51)$

After simplifying, we get

$$\gamma = 2 \times 10^{-4}\,/°C$$

\textit{Ans.}

21. Heat required to melt the ice completely

$$= 450 \times 0.5 \times (20) + 450 \times 80$$

$$= 40500\ \text{cal}$$

The heat available on stream

$$= 50 \times 540 + 50 \times 1 \times (100 - 0)$$

$$= 32000\ \text{cal.}$$

It shows that steam will loose its entire heat and comes down to $0°C$. The ice will not melt completely and so equilibrium temperature is $0°C$. If m amount of ice, is melted, then

$$450 \times 0.5 \times 20 + m \times 80 = 32000$$

$$m = 343.75\ \text{g} \qquad \textbf{\textit{Ans.}}$$

22. If m amount steam is needed per hour, then

$$10 \times 1 \times (90 - 20) = m \times 540 + m \times 1 \times (100 - 90)$$

$$\therefore \qquad m = 1.27\ \text{kg} \qquad \textbf{\textit{Ans.}}$$

23. The heat gained by ice $H = 0.1 \times 80 + 0.1 \times 1 \times (27 - 0)$

$$= 10.7\ \text{kcal}$$

$$= 10.7 \times 10^3\ \text{cal}$$

If m be the mass of the contains, then heat lost by it

$$= \int_{300}^{500} ms\,dT = m\int_{300}^{500} (A + BT)\,dT$$

$$= m\left|AT + \frac{BT^2}{2}\right|_{300}^{500}$$

$$= m\left[\left(100 \times 500 + \frac{2 \times 10^{-2} \times 500}{2}\right) - \left(100 \times 300 + \frac{2 \times 10^{-2} \times 300^2}{2}\right)\right]$$

$$= 21600\,m$$

Thus $\quad 21600\,m = 10.7 \times 10^3$

$\therefore \qquad\qquad m = 0.495$ kg.   ***Ans.***

24. Given, $\quad C = (2t^2 + t) \times 10^{-3}$ Cal/g°C.

The heat required $\quad H = \displaystyle\int_{t_1}^{t_2} mC\,dt$

$$= 100 \int_{20}^{40} (2t^2 + t) \times 10^{-3}\,dt$$

$$= 0.1\left|\frac{2t^3}{3} + \frac{t^2}{2}\right|_{20}^{40}$$

$$= 3790 \text{ Cal} = 3.79 \text{ K cal. } \textbf{\textit{Ans.}}$$

25. Answer is the solution

26. The heat required to raise the temperature of water.

$$H = 30 \times 1 \times (77 - 27)$$
$$= 1500 \text{ k cal / min}$$
$$= 1500 \times 10^3 \times 4.2 = 63 \times 10^5 \text{ J/min.}$$

Thus fuel needed per minutes

$$= \frac{63 \times 10^5}{4 \times 10^4} = 157.5 \text{ g/ min } \textbf{\textit{Ans.}}$$

27. The heat required

$$H = [10 \times 80 + 10 \times 1 \times (5 - 0)]$$
$$+ [100 \times 1 \times (5 - 0)]$$
$$= 1350 \text{ cal.}$$

If m amount of steam condenses, then

$$m \times 536 + m \times 1 \times (100 - 5) = 1350$$

$\therefore \qquad\qquad m = 2.13$ g.   ***Ans.***

28. The heat available

$$H = mC\Delta T$$
$$= 2.5 \times 0.39 \times (500 - 0)$$
$$= 487.5 \text{ k cal}$$

If m amount of ice is melted due to this heat, then

$$m = \frac{487.5}{335} = 1.45 \text{ kg.} \quad \textbf{\textit{Ans.}}$$

29.   (a)   The ball does not bounce back to the same height because some of its kinetic energy is lost in collision, which will convert into heat.

    (b)   The loss in kinetic energy

$$= mg(h_1 - h_2)$$
$$= 0.1 \times 9.8 \times (10 - 7)$$
$$= 2.94 \text{ J.}$$

If ΔT be the rise in temperature of the ball, then

$$0.1 \times (0.11 \times 10^3 \times 4.2)\,\Delta T = 2.94$$

$\therefore \qquad \Delta T = 0.064°C$ ***Ans.***

30. If v be the speed of the bullet, then

$$0.75 \times \left(\frac{1}{2}mv^2\right) = mC\Delta T + mL$$

$$0.75 \times \frac{v^2}{2} = (0.03 \times 4.2 \times 10^3) \times (327 - 27) + 6 \times 4.2 \times 10^3$$

$\therefore \qquad\qquad v = 409.9 \text{ m/s}$ ***Ans.***

Kinetic Theory of Gases

(415 - 456)

6.1 Introduction

It can be simply understand that any gas occupies the volume of its container due to the freedom of motion of its molecules. Pressure exerted by a gas is due to collisions of gas molecules on the walls of its container. And temperature of a gas can be related to the kinetic energy of these molecules. In the present chapter we shall relate volume, pressure and temperature to the microscopic properties like speed and kinetic energy of gas molecules.

6.2 Gas laws

Boyle's law (1660)

It states that the volume of a given mass of a gas is inversely proportional to its pressure, provided the temperature remain constant. That is

$$V \propto \frac{1}{P}$$

or

$$V = \frac{k}{P} \Rightarrow PV = k$$

If P_i and V_i are the initial values of pressure and volume and P_f and V_f are the final values, then

$$P_iV_i = P_fV_f$$

Boyle's law is true for an ideal gas, it is obeyed approximately by real gases and is not a fundamental law like Newton's laws.

The following graphs shows the variation of P with V and P with $\frac{1}{V}$ for a given mass of a gas at constant temperature.

Charle's law (1787)

It states that at constant pressure, the volume of a given mass of a gas increases or decreases by $\frac{1}{273.15}$ of volume at 0°C for each 1°C rise or fall of temperature.

If V_0 is the volume of gas at 0 °C, then volume of the gas at t °C,

$$V_t = V_0\left(1+\frac{t}{273.15}\right) = V_0\left(\frac{273.15+t}{273.15}\right)$$

As $273.15+0 = T_0$ and $273.15+t = T$

$$\therefore \qquad V_t = V_0\frac{T}{T_0}$$

or

$$\frac{V_t}{T} = \frac{V_0}{T_0}$$

or

$$\frac{V}{T} = \text{Constant} \quad \text{or} \quad V \propto T$$

Thus Charle's law can be started in another way that at constant pressure, the volume of given mass of a gas is directly proportional to its absolute temperature. The following graph shows the variation of volume of given mass of a gas with temperature.

Gay-Lussac's law or Pressure law

It states that if the volume remains constant, the pressure of a given mass of a gas increases or decreases by $\frac{1}{273.15}$ of its pressure at 0°C for each 1°C rise or fall in the temperature.

If P_0 is the pressure of a given mass of gas at 0°C, then its pressure at t°C

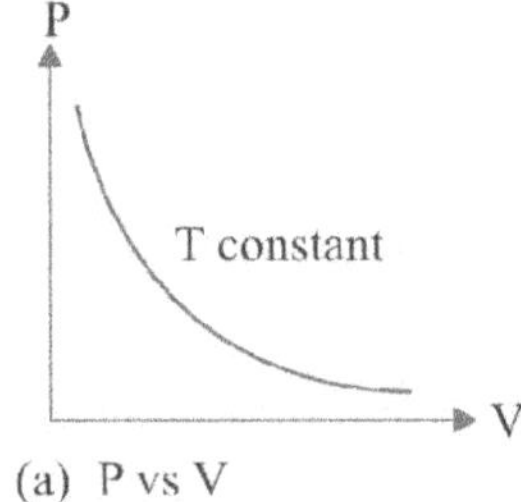

(a) P vs V

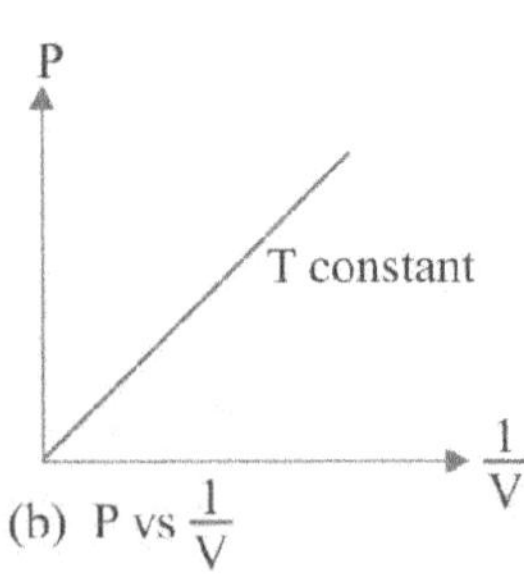

(b) P vs $\frac{1}{V}$

Fig. 6.1

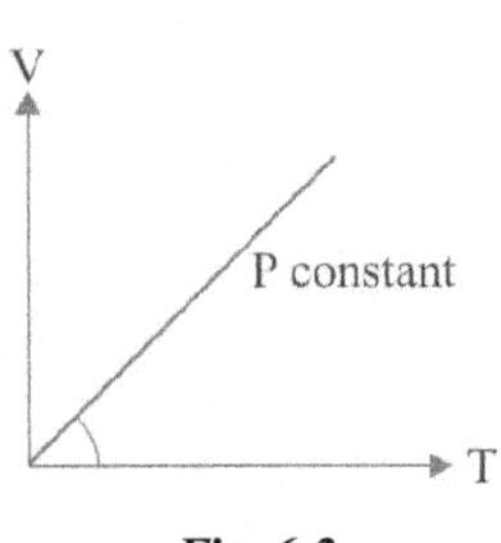

Fig. 6.2

$$P_t = P_0\left(1+\frac{t}{273.15}\right) = P_0\frac{(273.15+t)}{273.15}$$

$$= P_0\frac{T}{T_0}$$

or
$$\frac{P_t}{T} = \frac{P_0}{T_0}$$

or
$$\frac{P}{T} = \text{Constant or } P \propto T$$

Thus Gay-Lussac's law can be stated in another form that at constant volume, the pressure of a given mass of a gas is directly proportional to the absolute temperature. The following figure shows the variation of pressure of a given mass of a gas with temperature.

Ideal / perfect gas equation

If we relate P, V and T all together by gas laws, we will get

$$PV = nRT$$

where n is the number of moles and R is called universal gas constant. This equation is called ideal gas equation.

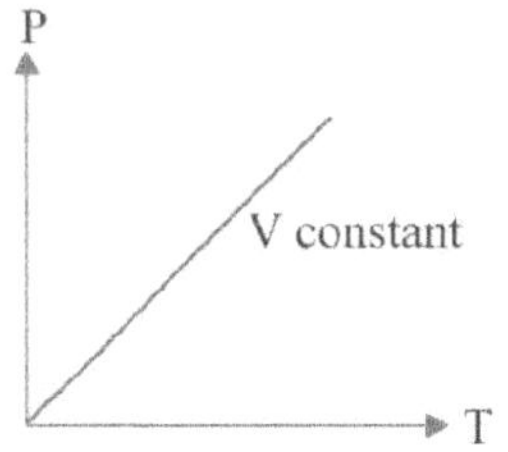

Fig. 6.3

More about ideal gas equation

1. In deriving ideal gas equation the following assumptions are used :
    (i) The size of molecules are negligibly small in comparison to the size of the container.
    (ii) Intermolecular forces are negligibly small.

2. If m is the mass and M is the molecular mass of the gas, then, $n = \dfrac{m}{M}$

    $$\therefore \quad PV = \left(\frac{m}{M}\right)RT$$

3. For 1 mole of a gas, $n = 1$

    $$\therefore \quad PV = RT$$

4. If ΔV is the volume of gas of mass Δm, then

    $$P\Delta V = \frac{\Delta m}{M}RT$$

    or
    $$P = \frac{(\Delta m/\Delta V)}{M}RT$$

    $$= \frac{\rho RT}{M} \qquad \left(\frac{\Delta m}{\Delta V} = \rho\right)$$

5. If μ is the number of molecules and N is the Avogadro number, then $n = \dfrac{\mu}{N}$

    $$\therefore \quad PV = \frac{\mu}{N}RT$$

    $$= \mu\left(\frac{R}{N}\right)T$$

Here $\dfrac{R}{N} = k$, is called Boltzmann's constant. Thus we can write

$$PV = \mu kT$$

6. For one molecule , $\mu = 1$, $PV = kT$

Universal gas constant R

From ideal gas equation, we can write

$$R = \frac{PV}{nT}$$

$$= \frac{\text{Work}}{\text{number of moles} \times \text{temperature}}$$

SI unit of $R = J$/mol-K

Numerical value of R

For one mole of a gas at STP,

$$R = \frac{P_0 V_0}{T_0}$$

Here $P_0 = 1.013 \times 10^5$ N/m^2, $V_0 = 22.4$ litre $= 22.4 \times 10^{-3}$ m^3 and $T_0 = 273 + 0 = 273$ K

$$\therefore \qquad R = \frac{(1.013 \times 10^5) \times (22.4 \times 10^{-3})}{273}$$

$$= 8.31 \text{ J/mol-K}$$

$$= \frac{4.31}{4.2}$$

$$= 1.98 \text{ cal/mol-K}$$

Numerical value of k

We know that,

$$k = \frac{R}{N}$$

$$= \frac{8.31}{6.02 \times 10^{23}}$$

$$= 1.38 \times 10^{-23} \text{ J/K}$$

6.3 IDEAL GAS

We have already used the phrase 'ideal or perfect gas'. The question arises that; what is an ideal gas ? The gas law $PV = nRT$ that governs macroscopic properties gives the answer. Although there is no such thing in nature which is truely ideal gas, all gases approach the ideal state at low pressure and high temperature.

Note:

For practical purposes, real gases below a pressure of two atmosphere can be considered as ideal gases. A saturated vapour in equilibrium with own liquid can be considered to have the properties of an ideal gas.

Deviation from ideal behaviour

(i)   The ratio $\dfrac{PV}{nT}$ is plotted as a function of P and T. For an ideal gas this quantity is constant and equal to R, but for real gases it varies with temperature. At high temperature and low pressure this quantity approaches the value R.

(ii)   Figure shows the comparison between the theoretical curves predicated by Boyle's law and experimental curve at two different temperatures.

(iii)   Figure shows the comparison between the theoretical curve predicted by Charle's law and the experimental curve at two different temperature.

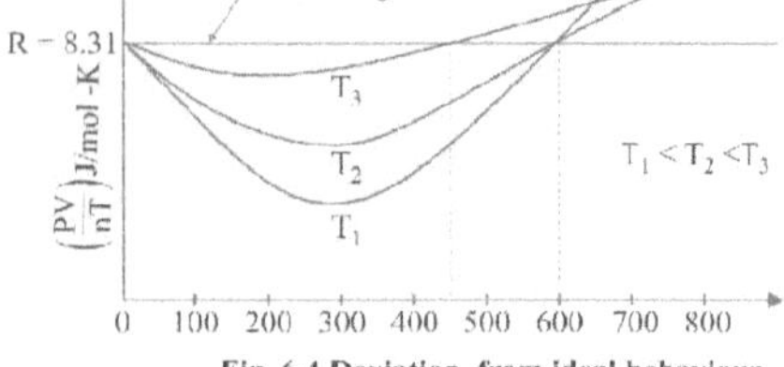

Fig. 6.4 Deviation from ideal behaviour.

Fig. 6.4

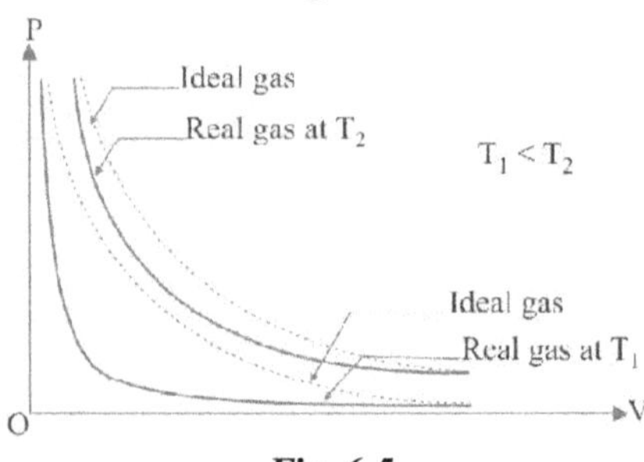

Fig. 6.5

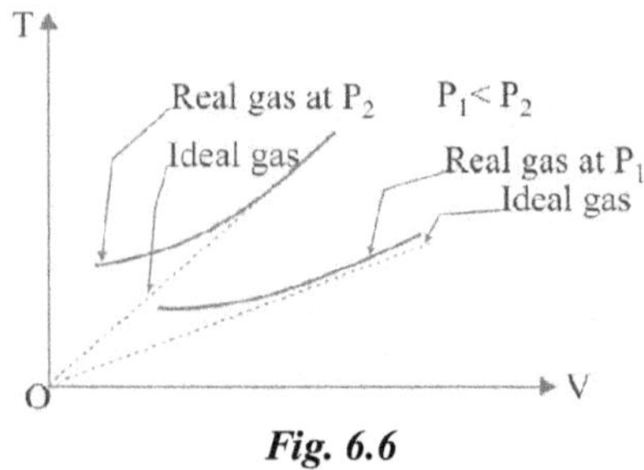

Fig. 6.6

Vander Waal's equation

The ideal gas equation $PV = nRT$, can be used for real gases at high temperature and low pressure at which intermolecular forces are negligibly small. Vander waal modified this equation so that it can be used for real gases at a wide range of temperature and pressure. He made following corrections :

(i)   **Volume correction :** Due to finite size of molecule, some part of volume of gas is occupied by the molecules. So the space available for the motion of molecules of gas will be slightly less (b) than the volume of gas. Hence effective volume becomes $(V - b)$.

(ii)   **Pressure correction :** Due to intermolecular forces, molecules do not exert that force on the walls of the container as they would have exerted in absence of intermolecular forces. The effective pressure as calculated is ; $P + \dfrac{a}{V^2}$.

Vander Waal's equation for 1 mole of a gas,

$$\left(P + \frac{a}{V^2}\right)(V - b) = RT$$

for n moles of a gas,

$$\left(P + \frac{an^2}{V^2}\right)(V - nb) = nRT$$

Critical constants

The critical temperature and the corresponding values of pressure and volume at the critical point are called the critical constants. At the critical point, the rate of change of pressure with volume (dP/dV) is zero. This point is called the point of inflexion.
According to Vander Waal's equation

$$\left(P + \frac{a}{V^2}\right)(V - b) = RT$$

$$\therefore \qquad P = \left(\frac{RT}{V - b}\right) - \frac{a}{V^2} \qquad \qquad ...(1)$$

Differentiating equation (1) w.r.t. V, we have

$$\frac{dP}{dV} = -\frac{RT}{(V - b)^2} + \frac{2a}{V^3} \qquad \qquad ...(2)$$

At the critical point $\dfrac{dP}{dV} = 0$, $T = T_c$ and $V = V_c$

$$\therefore \qquad \frac{-RT_c}{(V_c - b)^2} + \frac{2a}{V_c^3} = 0$$

$$\text{or} \qquad \frac{2a}{V_c^3} = \frac{RT_c}{(V_c - b)^2} \qquad \qquad ...(3)$$

Differentiating equation (2), we have

$$\frac{d^2P}{dV^2} = \frac{2RT}{(V - b)^3} - \frac{6a}{V^4}$$

At the critical point $\dfrac{d^2P}{dV^2}$ is also zero. Putting

$T = T_c$ and $V = V_c$

$$\therefore \qquad \frac{2RT_c}{(V_c - b)^3} - \frac{6a}{V_c^4} = 0 \qquad \qquad ...(4)$$

Solving equations (3) and (4), we get

$$V_c = 3b$$

Substituting the value of V_c in equation (3), we have

$$\frac{2a}{27b^3} = \frac{RT_c}{4b^2}$$

or

$$T_c = \frac{8a}{27bR}$$

Substituting values of V_c and T_c in equation (1), we have

$$P_c = \frac{R \times 8a}{27Rb(2b)} - \frac{a}{9b^2}$$

or

$$P_c = \frac{a}{27b^2}$$

Variation of atmospheric pressure with height

Suppose P and $(P + dP)$ are the pressures at h and $h + dh$ respectively, then

$$-dP = \rho g dh \qquad \ldots(i)$$

Let ΔV be the volume of Δm mass of the gas, then density of gas

$$\rho = \frac{\Delta m}{\Delta V}$$

Also

$$P\Delta V = \frac{\Delta m}{M} RT$$

or

$$P = \frac{(\Delta m / \Delta V)RT}{M}$$

$\therefore$

$$P = \frac{\rho RT}{M}$$

or

$$\rho = \frac{PM}{RT}$$

Substituting value of P in equation (i), we get

$$dP = -\frac{PM}{RT} g dh$$

or

$$\frac{dP}{P} = -\left(\frac{Mg}{RT}\right)dh \qquad \ldots(ii)$$

Integrating both sides of equation (ii), we get

$$\int_{P_0}^{P} \frac{dP}{P} = -\left(\frac{Mg}{RT}\right)\int_{0}^{h} dh$$

or

$$\left| \ln P \right|_{P_0}^{P} = -\frac{Mg}{RT} \left| h \right|_{0}^{h}$$

or

$$\ln \frac{P}{P_0} = -\frac{Mgh}{RT}$$

$\therefore$

$$P = P_0 e^{-\frac{Mgh}{RT}}$$

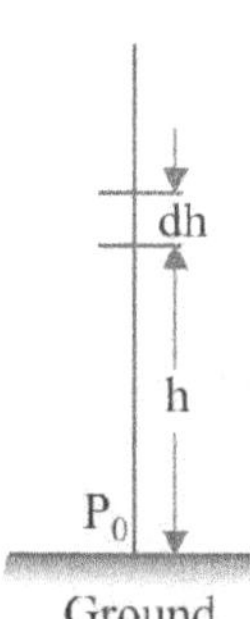

Fig. 6.7

Here P_0 is the pressure at the ground level, $h = 0$. Also we have assume that the temperature of the atmosphere does not change with height.

Ex. 1 A closed container of volume 0.02 m^3 contains a mixture of neon and argon gases at 27 °C temperature and $1.0 \times 10^5\ N/m^2$ pressure. If the gram-molecular weight of neon and argon are 20 and 40 respectively, find the masses of the individual gases in the container. Assuming them to be ideal ($R = 8.314$ J/mol-K). Total mass of the mixture is 28 g.

Sol.

Let m be the mass of the neon gas, then mass of argon will be $28 - m$.

Number of moles of neon,

$$n_1 = \frac{m}{20}$$

Number of moles of argon,

$$n_2 = \frac{28 - m}{40}$$

Now by ideal gas equation, we have

$$PV = nRT$$

Here $\quad n = n_1 + n_2 = \dfrac{m}{20} + \dfrac{28 - m}{40}, P = 1.0 \times 10^5\ N/m^2$

$$T = 273 + 27 = 300\ K,\ V = 0.02\ m^3$$

$$\therefore\quad (1.0 \times 10^5) \times 0.02 = \left[\frac{m}{20} + \frac{(28 - m)}{40}\right] \times 8.314 \times 300$$

After solving, we get, $m = 4.07\ g$

$\therefore\quad$ Mass of neon gas $= 4.07\ g$

$\quad\quad$ Mass of argon gas $= 28 - m$

$$= 28 - 4.07 = 23.93\ g \qquad \textbf{\textit{Ans.}}$$

Ex. 2 A narrow uniform glass tube 80 cm long and open at both ends is half immersed in mercury. Then, the top of the tube is closed and it is taken out of mercury. A column of mercury 22 cm long then remains in the tube. What is the atmospheric pressure?

Sol.

Suppose A is the area of cross-section of the tube and P is the atmospheric pressure. When half tube is inside mercury then volume of air in the tube.

$$V_1 = A \times 40 = 40\,A\ cm^3$$
$$P_1 = P$$

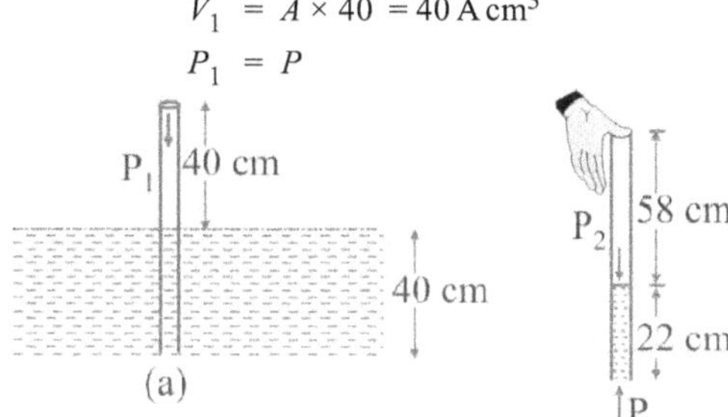

Fig. 6.8

When the tube is taken out of mercury, the volume of air,

$$V_2 = A \times 58 = 58A$$

If P_2 is the pressure of air in the tube, then

$$P_2 + 22 = P$$
or $\quad\quad P_2 = P - 22$

Now by Boyle's law, we have

$$P_1 V_1 = P_2 V_2$$
$$P \times 40\,A = (P - 22) \times 58\,A$$
or $\quad\quad 18\,P = 22 \times 58$
$\therefore\quad\quad P = 70.9\ cm$ $\qquad\qquad$ **_Ans._**

Ex. 3 An ideal monoatomic gas is confined in a cylinder by a spring-loaded piston of cross-section 8.0×10^{-3} m². Initially the gas is at 300 K and occupies a volume of 2.4×10^{-3} m³ and the spring is in the relaxed state (fig. 6.9). The gas is heated by a small heater untill the piston moves out slowly by 0.1 m. Calculate the final temperature of the gas. The force constant of the spring is 8000 N/m, and the atmospheric pressure is 1.0×10^5 N/m². The cylinder and the piston are thermally insulated. The piston and the spring are massless and there is no friction between the piston and the cylinder. Neglect any heat-loss through the lead wires of the heater. The heat capacity of the heater coil is negligible.

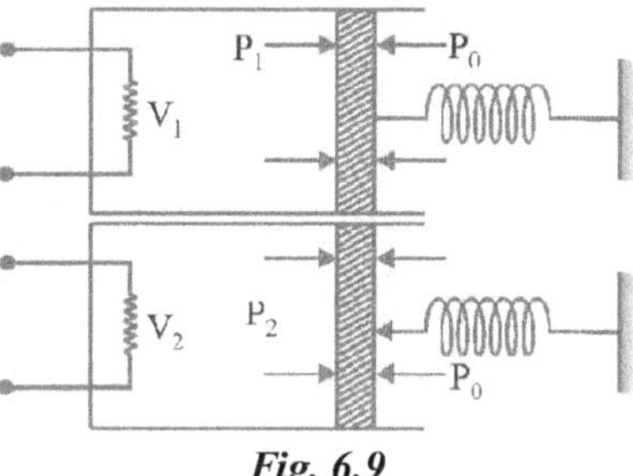

Fig. 6.9

Sol.

Given; initial volume of the gas,

$$V_1 = 2.4 \times 10^{-3}\ m^3$$

The spring is in relaxed state, so,

$$P_1 = \text{atmospheric pressure}$$
$$= 1.0 \times 10^5\ N/m^2$$
$$T_1 = 300\ K$$

When piston moves by 0.1 m, the final volume of gas becomes,

$$V_2 = V_1 + Ax$$
$$= 2.4 \times 10^{-3} + 8.0 \times 10^{-3} \times 0.1$$
$$= 3.2 \times 10^{-3}\ m^3$$

Final pressure, $\quad P_2 = P_1 + \dfrac{kx}{A}$

$$= 1.0 \times 10^5 + \frac{8000 \times 0.1}{8.0 \times 10^{-3}}$$
$$= 2.0 \times 10^5\ N/m^2$$

Let T_2 be the final temperature of the gas, then by gas law, we have

$$\frac{P_1 V_1}{T_1} = \frac{P_2 V_2}{T_2}$$

or $\quad\quad T_2 = \left(\dfrac{P_2 V_2}{P_1 V_1}\right) T_1$

$$= \frac{(2.0 \times 10^5) \times (3.2 \times 10^{-3})}{(1.0 \times 10^5) \times (2.4 \times 10^{-3})} \times 300$$

$$T_2 = 800\ K. \qquad\qquad \textbf{\textit{Ans.}}$$

Ex. 4 A mercury manometer consists of two unequal arms of equal cross-section and length 100 cm and 50 cm. The two open ends are sealed with air in the tube at a pressure of 80 cm of mercury. Some amount of mercury is now introduced in the manometer through the stopcock connected to it. If mercury rises in the shorter tube to a length 10 cm in steady state, find the length of the mercury column risen in the longer tube.

Sol.

For shorter arm;

Initial volume of air $= A \times 50$ cm^3

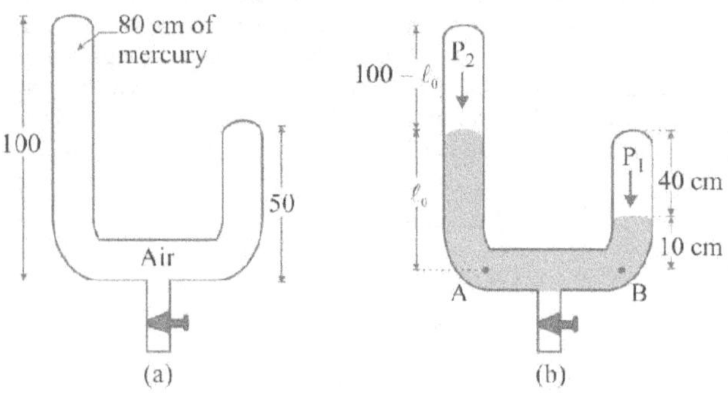

Fig. 6.10

When mercury is introduced in the tube, the volume of air remains
$$= A \times 40 \text{ cm}^3$$

Let P_1 be the pressure of the air in shorter arm, then by $PV =$ constant, we have

$$80 \times (A \times 50) = P_1 \times (A \times 40)$$
$$\therefore \qquad P_1 = 100 \text{ cm}$$

For longer arm;

Initial volume of air $= A \times 100$ cm^3

Let ℓ_0 be the length of mercury, then volume of air remains

$$= A \times (100 - \ell_0)$$

Let P_2 be the pressure of the air in the longer air, then by Pascal's law

$$P_A = P_B$$
$$\ell_0 + P_2 = 10 + P_1$$
$$\therefore \qquad P_2 = (10 + P_1) - \ell_0 = (10 + 100) - \ell_0$$
$$= (110 - \ell_0) \text{ cm}$$

Now by $\qquad PV =$ constant, we have

$$(110 - \ell_0) \times A(100 - \ell_0)$$
$$= 80 \times (A \times 100)$$

or $\qquad (110 - \ell_0)(100 - \ell_0)$
$$= 8000$$
$$\ell_0{}^2 - 210\ell_0 + 3000 = 0$$
$$\ell_0 = 15.5 \quad \ell_0 = 15.5 \text{ cm} \qquad \textbf{\textit{Ans.}}$$

Ex. 5 A vessel of volume $V = 5.0$ litre contains 1.4 g of nitrogen at temperature, $T = 1800$ K. Find the pressure of the gas if 30% of its molecules are dissociated into atoms at this temperature.

Sol.

Mass of molecular nitrogen

$$= \frac{70}{100} \times 1.4 = 0.98 \text{ g}$$

Mass of atomic nitrogen $= \dfrac{30}{100} \times 1.4 = 0.42$ g

Number of moles of molecular nitrogen,

$$n_1 = \frac{0.98}{28} = 0.035$$

Number of moles of atomic nitrogen

$$n_2 = \frac{0.42}{14} = 0.03$$

The pressure of the gas = pressure exerted by molecular nitrogen + pressure exerted by atomic nitrogen

i.e., $\qquad P = P_1 + P_2$

$$= \frac{n_1 RT}{V} + \frac{n_2 RT}{V} = \frac{(n_1 + n_2)RT}{V}$$

$$= \frac{(0.035 + 0.03) \times 8.31 \times 1800}{5 \times 10^{-3}}$$

$$= 1.94 \times 10^5 \text{ N/m}^2 \qquad \textbf{\textit{Ans.}}$$

Ex. 6 A horizontal tube of length ℓ closed at both ends contains an ideal gas of molecular weight M. The tube is rotated at a constant angular velocity ω about a vertical axis passing through an end. Assuming the temperature to be uniform and constant, show that

$$P_2 = P_1 e^{\frac{M\omega^2 \ell^2}{2RT}}$$

where P_2 and P_1 denote the pressures at the free end and the fixed end respectively.

Sol.

Consider an element of the gas of thickness dx at a distance x from the axis of rotation. Let P and $P + dP$ are the pressures on left and right side of the element, then net force acting on the element of gas of mass dm

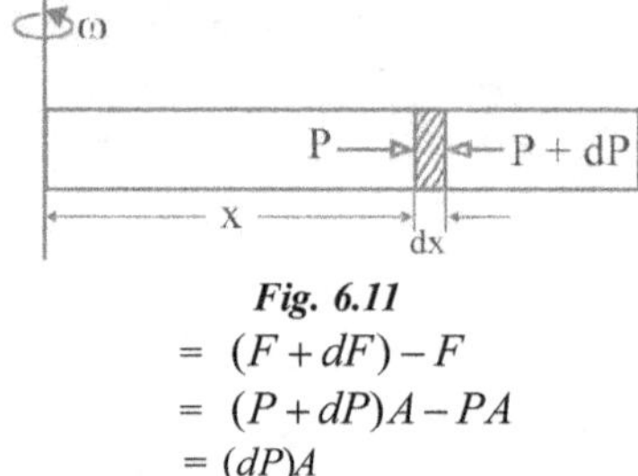

Fig. 6.11

$$= (F + dF) - F$$
$$= (P + dP)A - PA$$
$$= (dP)A$$

As the element is moving in a circle so by Newton's second law

$$(dP)A = (dm)\omega^2 x \qquad \dots \text{(i)}$$

Using $PV = nRT$ for the element, we have

$$P(A\,dx) = \frac{dm}{M} RT$$

or $\qquad dm = \left(\frac{MPA}{RT}\right) dx$

Substituting the value of dm in equation (i), we get

$$(dP)A = \left(\frac{MPA}{RT}\right)\omega^2 x\,dx$$

or

$$dP = \left(\frac{MP\omega^2}{RT}\right)x\,dx$$

or

$$\frac{dP}{P} = \left(\frac{M\omega^2}{RT}\right)x\,dx \qquad \ldots \text{(ii)}$$

Integrating both sides of equation (ii), we have

$$\int_{P_1}^{P_2}\frac{dP}{P} = \left(\frac{M\omega^2}{RT}\right)\int_0^{\ell} x\,dx$$

$$\left|\ln P\right|_{P_1}^{P_2} = \left(\frac{M\omega^2}{RT}\right)\left|\frac{x^2}{2}\right|_0^{\ell}$$

or

$$\ln\frac{P_2}{P_1} = \frac{M\omega^2\ell^2}{2RT}$$

$$\therefore \qquad P_2 = P_1 e^{\frac{M\omega^2\ell^2}{2RT}}$$

6.4 KINETIC THEORY OF GASES

Kinetic theory of gases was developed by Maxwell. He made the following assumptions:
1. The gas is composed of small indivisible large number of particles called molecules. The properties of the individual molecules are same as that of the gas as a whole.
2. The size of molecule is negligibly small in comparison to the average distance between the molecules.
3. Intermolecular forces between the molecules are negligibly small. Thus all internal energy of the gas is kinetic.
4. Effect of gravity on them is negligibly small and Newton laws are valid for their motion.
5. The molecules are in a state of continuous random motion, moving in all directions with all possible velocities.
6. The collision between the molecules and with the walls of the container are perfectly elastic. Between two collision a molecule moves in a straight path with a uniform velocity. The average distance moved by a molecule between two successive collisions is called mean free path.
7. The time of collision is negligibly small in comparison to the time of the free path between the molecules.

Note:

It is not possible to define macro property like pressure by taking small number of molecules (say two) in the container.

Pressure and temperature : A molecular view

Pressure exerted by a gas

The molecules of a gas are in a state of continuous random motion. They collide with one another and also with the walls of the container. Due to collisions with the walls, the momentum of molecules will change. As collisions of molecules with the walls of the container are elastic, so an equal amount of momentum is transferred to the walls of the container. According to Newton's second law of motion, the rate of transfer of momentum to the wall is equal to the force exerted on the wall. The force exerted per unit area of the wall is the pressure of the gas.

Expression of pressure

Consider an ideal gas enclosed in a cubical container of volume V. Suppose the sides of the container are parallel to the co-ordinate axes and held at temperature T.

Now consider a typical molecule of mass m, moving with velocity $\vec{v}(v_x, v_y, v_z)$ which is about to collide with the wall (see figure 6.12). As the collision is elastic, the molecule will rebound with the same speed. The velocity of molecule after collision become $(-v_x, v_y, v_z)$. This means that the only change in the momentum is then along the x-axis, and that change is

$$-mv_x - mv_x = -2mv_x$$

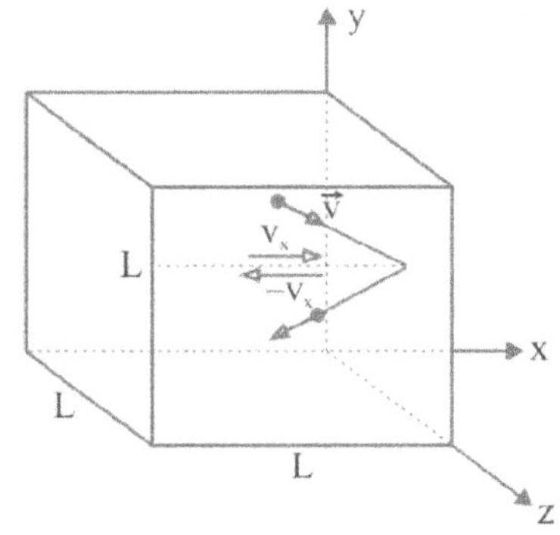

Fig. 6.12

By the conservation of momentum, the momentum delivered ΔP to the wall by the molecules is $2mv_x$.

If Δt be the time, the molecule takes to travel between the parallel walls at speed v_x, then

$$\Delta t \;=\; \frac{2L}{v_x}.$$

The rate at which momentum is delivered to the wall by the single molecule is

$$\frac{\Delta P}{\Delta t} \;=\; \frac{2mv_x}{\dfrac{2L}{v_x}} = \frac{mv_x^{\,2}}{L}$$

If n be the total number of molecules is the container then total force exerted on the wall

$$F \;=\; \frac{mv_{x_1}^2}{L} + \frac{mv_{x_2}^2}{L} + \dots\dots + \frac{mv_{x_n}^2}{L}$$

$$=\; \frac{nm}{L}\left[\frac{v_{x_1}^2 + v_{x_2}^2 + \dots + v_{x_n}^2}{n}\right]$$

Here $\left[\dfrac{v_{x_1}^2 + v_{x_2}^2 + \dots + v_{x_n}^2}{n}\right]$ is the average value of the square of the x-components, which can be written as $\overline{v}_x^{\,2}$.

$$\therefore \qquad F \;=\; \frac{nm}{L}\,\overline{v}_x^{\,2} \qquad\qquad \dots(1)$$

The pressure of the gas

$$P \;=\; \frac{F}{A} = \frac{(nm\overline{v}_x^{\,2})/L}{L^2}$$

$$=\; \frac{nm\overline{v}_x^{\,2}}{L^3} = \frac{nm\overline{v}_x^{\,2}}{V} \qquad\qquad \dots(2)$$

For any molecule, $v^2 = v_x^2 + v_y^2 + v_z^2$. As there are many molecules and they are moving in random directions, so the average values of the squares of their velocity components are equal. Thus we have $v^2 = 3v_x^2$ or $v_x^2 = \dfrac{v^2}{3}$. Equation (2) becomes

$$P \;=\; \frac{nm\overline{v}^{\,2}}{3V} \qquad\qquad \dots(3)$$

The square root of $\overline{v}^{\,2}$ is called the root-mean square speed of the molecules and can be denoted by v_{rms}. Thus we can write

$$P \;=\; \frac{nmv_{rms}^2}{3V} \qquad\qquad \dots(4)$$

As nm = mass of the gas, so $\dfrac{nm}{V} = \rho$ = density of gas. Thus equation (4) becomes

$$P \;=\; \frac{1}{3}\rho v_{rms}^2 \qquad\qquad \dots(5)$$

6.5 Translational Kinetic Energy

Kinetic interpretation of temperature

Consider one mole of a gas, and let P, V, T and M be the pressure, volume, temperature and molecular mass of the gas respectively, then

$$P = \frac{Nm}{3V} v_{rms}^2 \quad (n = N)$$

$$= \frac{Mv_{rms}^2}{3V} \quad (Nm = M) \qquad \dots(1)$$

or $$PV = \frac{2}{3} \times \left(\frac{1}{2} Mv_{rms}^2 \right)$$

But $\frac{1}{2} Mv_{rms}^2$ is the average translational kinetic energy E of one mole of the gas

$$\therefore \quad PV = \frac{2E}{3}$$

For one mole of an ideal gas, we have $PV = RT$

$$\therefore \quad RT = \frac{2E}{3}$$

or $$E = \frac{3}{2} RT \text{ per mole} \qquad \dots(2)$$

If N is the Avogadro's number, then average kinetic energy per molecule is given by

$$e = \frac{3}{2} \frac{RT}{N}$$

As $\frac{R}{N} = k$, Boltzmann's constant

$$\therefore \quad e = \frac{3}{2} kT \text{ per molecules} \qquad \dots(3)$$

Thus the mean kinetic energy is proportional to the absolute temperature of the gas. It does not depend on the pressure, volume and nature of the gas.

Again from equation (1)

$$v_{rms} = \sqrt{\frac{3PV}{M}}$$

or $$v_{rms} = \sqrt{\frac{3RT}{M}} \qquad \dots(4)$$

i.e., $$v_{rms} \propto \sqrt{T}$$

From above treatment, it can be concluded that the temperature of a gas is the measure of the average kinetic energy of its molecules. This is what we mean by the kinetic interpretation of temperature.

Also, at $T = 0$, $v_{rms} = 0$, so we can define the absolute zero is the temperature at which motion of all the molecules stop.

6.6 Graham's Law of Diffusion

Let us consider two gases of densities ρ_1 and ρ_2 and their respective rms speeds are v_1 and v_2.

Pressure exerted by gas 1, $$P_1 = \frac{1}{3} \rho_1 v_1^2$$

and pressure exerted by gas 2, $$P_2 = \frac{1}{3} \rho_2 v_2^2$$

When gases diffuse one another and steady condition is reached, we have

$$P_1 = P_2$$

or

$$\frac{1}{3}\rho_1 v_1^2 = \frac{1}{3}\rho_2 v_2^2$$

$\therefore$

$$\frac{v_1}{v_2} = \sqrt{\frac{\rho_2}{\rho_1}}$$

As we know that rate of diffusion is directly proportional to its rms speed. Thus if r_1 and r_2 be the respective rates of diffusion, then

$$\frac{r_1}{r_2} = \frac{v_1}{v_2} = \sqrt{\frac{\rho_2}{\rho_1}}$$

Thus the rate of diffusion of a gas is inversely proportional to the square root of its density.

6.7 DALTON'S LAW OF PARTIAL PRESSURE

Consider number of gases in a container of volume V. The pressure exerted by gases when taken in the container separately are ;

$$P_1 = \frac{1}{3}\frac{n_1 m_1 v_1^2}{V}, \ P_2 =, \ \frac{1}{3}\frac{n_2 m_2 v_2^2}{V}, \ldots\ldots$$

When gases are taken together in the container, the total pressure

$$= P_1 + P_2 + \ldots$$

$$= \frac{1}{3}\frac{n_1 m_1 v_1^2}{V} + \frac{1}{3}\frac{n_2 m_2 v_2^2}{V} + \ldots\ldots$$

As the temperature of all the gases in the mixture is the same, therefore

$$\frac{1}{2}m_1 v_1^2 = \frac{1}{2}m_2 v_2^2 \ldots\ldots\ldots = \frac{1}{2}mv^2 \text{ (say)}$$

or

$$m_1 v_1^2 = m_2 v_2^2 \ldots\ldots\ldots = mv^2$$

$\therefore$

$$P_1 + P_2 + \ldots = \frac{1}{3V}(n_1 + n_2 + \ldots)mv^2$$

where $n_1 + n_2 + = n,$, is the total number of molecules in the container.

$\therefore$

$$P_1 + P_2 + \ldots\ldots = \frac{nmv^2}{3V}$$

or

$$P_1 + P_2 + \ldots\ldots = P$$

Thus the total pressure exerted by number of nonreacting gases when taken together in a container is equal to the sum of their partial pressure.

6.8 THE DISTRIBUTION OF MOLECULAR SPEED

The root-mean-square speed v_{rms} gives a general idea of the molecular speed for a gas at a given temperature. This does not mean that speed of each molecule is v_{rms}. Many of the molecules have speed less than v_{rms} and many have speed greater than v_{rms}. Maxwell derived an equation giving the distribution of molecules in different speed. If dN represents the number of molecules with speeds between v and $v + dv$, then

$$dN = 4\pi N \left(\frac{m}{2\pi kT}\right)^{3/2} v^2 e^{-\frac{mv^2}{2kT}} dv$$

Figure shows the plot of $\dfrac{dN}{dv}$ against v at any temperature T.

The important features of the speed distribution curve are as follows :

(i) At any temperature, the speed of molecules varies from zero to infinity.

(ii) The number of molecules with speeds v to $v + dv$ is equal to the area of the strip shown.

(iii) The speed at which $\dfrac{dN}{dv}$ is maximum, is called most probable speed v_{mp}. Its value is given by

$$v_{mp} = \sqrt{\dfrac{2kT}{m}}$$

Different types of speeds of gas molecules

1. **Root mean square speed** . It is defined as the square root of mean of squares of the speed of different molecules, i.e.,

$$v_{rms} = \sqrt{\dfrac{v_1^2 + v_2^2 + \ldots\ldots + v_n^2}{n}}$$

According to kinetic theory of gases,

$$v_{rms} = \sqrt{\dfrac{3RT}{M}} = \sqrt{\dfrac{3kT}{m}}$$

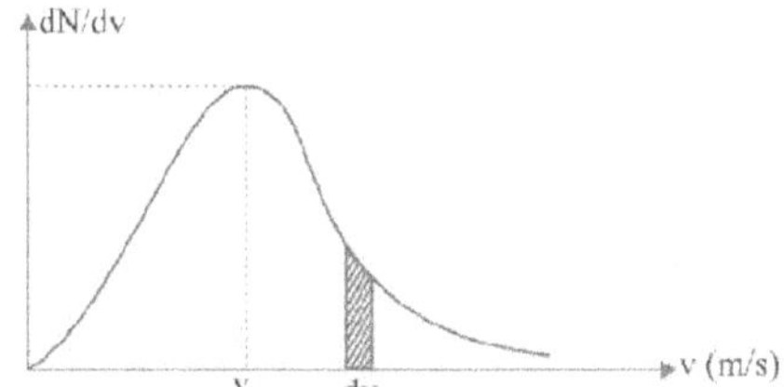

Fig. 6.13

when M is the mass of one mole while m is the mass of one molecule.

(i) At room temperature the rms speed of hydrogen gas will be

$$v_H = \sqrt{\dfrac{3RT}{M}} = \sqrt{\dfrac{3 \times 8.31 \times 300}{2 \times 10^{-3}}} = 1920 \ m/s$$

(ii) As speed of sound in a gas $v = \sqrt{\dfrac{\gamma RT}{M}}$

$$\therefore \qquad \dfrac{v}{v_{rms}} = \sqrt{\dfrac{\gamma}{3}}$$

$$v = \sqrt{\dfrac{\gamma}{3}} v_{rms}$$

2. **Average speed**. It is defined as the arithmetic mean of the speeds of the molecules of a gas at a given temperature. If v_1, v_2, ..., v_n are the speeds of the n gas molecules, then the average speed v is given by

$$v_{av} = \dfrac{v_1 + v_2 + \ldots.. + v_n}{n}$$

By Maxwell speed distribution law, it can be shown that

$$v_{av} = \sqrt{\dfrac{8RT}{\pi M}} = \sqrt{\dfrac{8kT}{\pi m}} = 0.92 \, v_{rms}$$

3. **Most probable speed** It is the speed with which the largest number of molecules in a gas are moving. At any temperature it is given by

$$v_{mp} = \sqrt{\dfrac{2RT}{M}}$$

$$= 0.816 \, v_{rms}$$

It can be seen from above that

$$v_{rms} > v_{av} > v_{mp}$$

Ex. 7 At what temperature will the average velocity of oxygen molecule be sufficient so as to escape from the earth? Escape velocity from earth is 11.0 km/s and mass of one molecule of oxygen is 5.34×10^{-26} kg. Boltzmann constant $k = 1.38 \times 10^{23}$ J/molecule - K

Sol.

The average velocity of molecule at any temperature is given by

$$v_{av} = \sqrt{\frac{2kT}{m}}$$

For the molecule to just escape from the earth

$$v_{av} = v_e$$

or

$$\sqrt{\frac{2kT}{m}} = v_e$$

$\therefore$

$$T = \frac{mv_e^2}{2k}$$

$$= \frac{5.34 \times 10^{-26} \times (11.0 \times 10^3)^2}{2 \times 1.38 \times 10^{-23}}$$

$$= 2.34 \times 10^5 \text{ K} \qquad\qquad \textit{Ans.}$$

Ex. 8 N molecules each of mass m of gas A and $2N$ molecules each of mass $2m$ of gas B are contained in the same vessel which is maintained at a temperature T. The mean square of the velocity of the molecules of B type is denoted by v^2 and the mean square of the x-component of the velocity of A type is denoted by ω^2, then what is the ratio of $\dfrac{\omega^2}{v^2}$ =?

Sol.

The mean square velocity of gas molecule is given by $v^2 = \dfrac{3kT}{m}$.

For gas A, $\qquad v_A^2 = \dfrac{3kT}{m}$ $\qquad\qquad$ ...(i)

For a gas molecule, $\quad v^2 = v_x^2 + v_y^2 + v_z^2$

$$= 3v_x^2 \quad (v_x^2 = v_y^2 = v_z^2)$$

or $\qquad v_x^2 = \dfrac{v^2}{3}$

From equation (i), we get

$$v_x^2 = \frac{v_A^2}{3} = \frac{3kT/m}{3} = \frac{kT}{m} \qquad\qquad \text{...(ii)}$$

For gas B, $\qquad v_B^2 = v^2 = \dfrac{3kT}{m_B} = \dfrac{3kT}{2m}$ $\qquad$ ...(iii)

Dividing equation (ii) by (iii), we get

$$\frac{\omega^2}{v^2} = \frac{kT/m}{3kT/2m} = \frac{2}{3} \qquad\qquad \textit{Ans.}$$

Ex. 9 The mass of hydrogen molecules is 3.32×10^{-27} kg. If 10^{23} hydrogen molecules strike a fixed wall of area 2 cm^2 per second at an angle of 45° to the normal and rebound elastically with a speed of 10^3m/s, calculate the pressure on the wall.

Sol.

As the collision of molecule with the wall is elastic, so the magnitude of momentum of molecule before collision will equal to after collision.

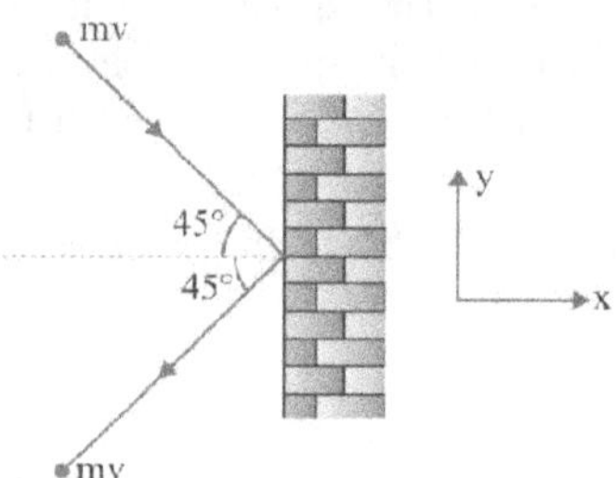

Fig. 6.14

Let x-axis indicates the direction of normal then change in momentum

$$\Delta P_x = -mv\cos 45° - mv\cos 45°$$

$$= -2mv\cos 45°$$

$$= -\frac{2mv}{\sqrt{2}} = -\sqrt{2}mv$$

and $\qquad \Delta P_y = -mv\sin 45° - (-mv\sin 45°) = 0$

$\therefore$ The momentum delivered to the wall $= \sqrt{2}mv$

Thus pressure exerted,

$$P = \frac{F}{A} = \frac{\Delta P_x / \Delta t}{A} = \frac{\Delta P_x \times n}{A} = \frac{\sqrt{2}mnv}{A}$$

where, $n = 10^{23}$ per second, $A = 2 \times 10^{-4}$cm^2, $v = 10^3$ m/s

$\therefore$

$$P = \frac{\sqrt{2} \times (3.32 \times 10^{-27}) \times (10^{23}) \times 10^3}{2 \times 10^{-4}}$$

$$= 2.347 \times 10^3 \text{ N/m}^2 \qquad\qquad \textit{Ans.}$$

Ex. 10 16g of oxygen and 14 g of nitrogen are mixed in an enclosure of volume 10 litre and temperature 27°C. Calculate the pressure exerted by the mixture.

Sol. We know that

$$PV = nRT$$

or $\qquad PV = \dfrac{m}{M}RT$

$\therefore \qquad P = \dfrac{mRT}{MV}$

Pressure exerted by oxygen;

$$P_{oxygen} = \frac{mRT}{MV} = \frac{16 \times 8.31 \times 300}{32 \times 10 \times 10^{-3}}$$

$$= 1.246 \times 10^4 \text{ N/m}^2$$

Pressure exerted by nitrogen;

$$P_{nitrogen} = \frac{mRT}{MV} = \frac{14 \times 8.31 \times 300}{28 \times 10 \times 10^{-3}}$$

$$= 1.246 \times 10^5 \text{ N/m}^2$$

Now by Dalton's law of partial pressure, the total pressure

$$P = P_{oxygen} + P_{nitrogen}$$

$$= 1.246 \times 10^5 + 1.246 \times 10^5$$

$$= 2.493 \times 10^5 \text{ N/m}^2 \qquad\qquad \textit{Ans.}$$

Ex. 11 Two perfect gases at absolute temperatures T_1 and T_2 are mixed. There is no loss of energy. Find the temperature of mixture if masses of molecules are m_1 and m_2 and the number of molecules in the gases are n_1 and n_2 respectively.

Sol.

The average kinetic energy of a gas molecule $= \dfrac{3}{2}kT$.

The total kinetic energy before mixing the two gases

$$= n_1 \times \dfrac{3}{2}kT_1 + n_2 \times \dfrac{3}{2}kT_2$$

If T is the temperature of the mixture, then the mean kinetic energy after mixing

$$= (n_1 + n_2) \times \dfrac{3}{2}kT$$

As there is no loss of energy, so

$$(n_1 + n_2) \times \dfrac{3}{2}kT \ = \ n_1 \times \dfrac{3}{2}kT_1 + n_2 \times \dfrac{3}{2}kT_2$$

$$\therefore \qquad T \ = \ \dfrac{n_1 T_1 + n_2 T_2}{n_1 + n_2}$$

Ex. 12 You are given the following group of particles, n_i representing the number of molecules with speed v_i

n_i	v_i (m/s)
2	1.0
4	2.0
9	3.0
5	4.0
3	5.0

Calculate (i) most probable speed (ii) average speed (iii) root-mean-square speed.

Sol.

(i) The most probable speed is 3.0 m/s, by which the largest molecules are moving at any time.

(ii) The average speed is given by

$$v_{av} \ = \ \dfrac{n_1 v_1 + n_2 v_2 + n_3 v_3 + n_4 v_4 + n_5 v_5}{n_1 + n_2 + n_3 + n_4 + n_5}$$

$$= \ \dfrac{2 \times 1 + 4 \times 2 + 9 \times 3 + 5 \times 4 + 3 \times 5}{2 + 4 + 9 + 5 + 3}$$

$$= \ \dfrac{72}{23} = 3.13 \text{ m/s}$$

(iii) The root-mean square speed is given by

$$v_{rms} \ = \ \left[\dfrac{n_1 v_1^2 + n_2 v_2^2 + n_3 v_3^2 + n_4 v_4^2 + n_5 v_5^2}{n_1 + n_2 + n_3 + n_4 + n_5} \right]^{1/2}$$

$$= \left[\dfrac{2 \times 1^2 + 4 \times 2^2 + 9 \times 3^2 + 5 \times 4^2 + 3 \times 5^2}{2 + 4 + 9 + 5 + 3} \right]^{1/2}$$

$$= \left[\dfrac{254}{23} \right]^{1/2} = 3.32 \text{ m/s}$$

Ex. 13 During an experiment an ideal gas is found to obey an additional law $VP^2 =$ constant. The gas is initially at temperature T and volume V. When it expands to a volume $2V$, calculate the resulting temperature.

Sol.

The ideal gas equation

$$PV \ = \ nRT \qquad\qquad \text{... (i)}$$

The gas obeys an additional law

$$VP^2 \ = \ C \ \text{(constant)} \qquad\qquad \text{... (ii)}$$

From equation (i),

$$P \ = \ \dfrac{nRT}{V}$$

Substituting this value in equation (ii), we get

$$V \left(\dfrac{nRT}{V} \right)^2 \ = \ C$$

$$\text{or} \qquad \dfrac{T^2}{V} \ = \ \dfrac{C}{n^2 R^2} = k \text{ (new constant)}$$

If T' is the temperature corresponding to volume $2V$, then

$$\dfrac{T^2}{V} \ = \ \dfrac{T'^2}{2V}$$

After simplifying, we get

$$T' \ = \ \sqrt{2}\,T \qquad\qquad\qquad \textit{Ans.}$$

6.9 DEGREES OF FREEDOM

The degrees of freedom are the minimum number of informations required to know about the system.

For thermodynamic system (moving particles), these are the total number of independent terms of energy. These are :

The independent possible motions are translational, rotational and vibrational, so there are three types of degrees of freedom. These are :

(i) Translational degrees of freedom : The maximum number of translational degrees of freedom can be three. These are $\dfrac{1}{2}mv_x^2$, $\dfrac{1}{2}mv_y^2$, $\dfrac{1}{2}mv_z^2$.

(ii) Rotational degrees of freedom : The maximum number of rotational degrees of freedom can be three . These are $\dfrac{1}{2}I_x \omega_x^2$, $\dfrac{1}{2}I_y \omega_y^2$, $\dfrac{1}{2}I_z \omega_z^2$.

(iii) Vibrational degrees of freedom : Their numbers depend on atoms in the molecule and their arrangement. These degrees of freedom are consider at a very high temperature.

At room temperature only translational and rotational degrees of freedom are taken into account.

General expression of degrees of freedom f

$$f = 3N - k$$

where, N = number of particles in the system (number of atoms in a molecule)

k = number of independent relations between the particles.

1. **Monoatomic gas :** It has assumed that the molecules of a gas are negligible in size, so moment of inertia and hence rotational kinetic energy of monoatomic gas molecules about the axis passes through itself will be zero.

   The degrees of freedom of monoatomic gas molecules are due to three independent translational motions along x, y, and z-axis. The degree of freedoms are $\frac{1}{2}mv_x^2$, $\frac{1}{2}mv_y^2$, $\frac{1}{2}mv_z^2$.

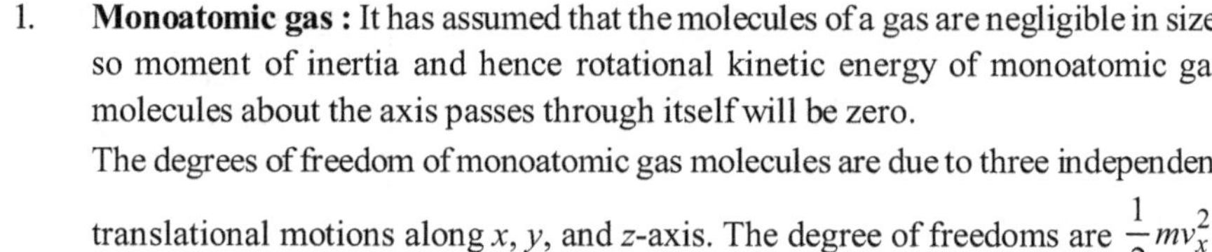

2. **Diatomic gas :** In diatomic gases the molecules are assumed to be in the shape of dumbbells; two atoms of negligible size at some separation. In addition to translational motion, the molecule, can rotate about an axis, so the degrees of freedom of diatomic gas molecules are due to translation and due to rotation both. If the line joining the two atoms (particles) is taken as the z-axis, then moment of inertia and hence rotational kinetic energy about z-axis becomes zero. The molecule has three degrees of freedom of translation and two degrees of freedom of rotation.

   These are : $\frac{1}{2}mv_x^2, \frac{1}{2}mv_y^2, \frac{1}{2}mv_z^2, \frac{1}{2}I_x\omega_x^2, \frac{1}{2}I_y\omega_y^2$

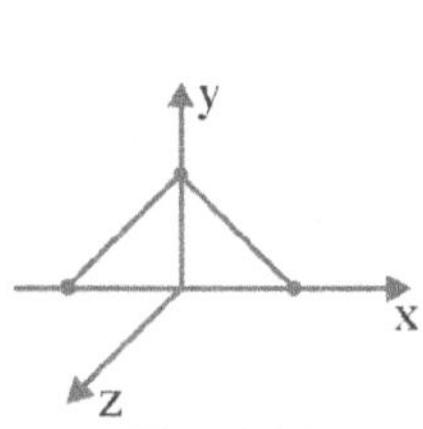
Fig. 6.15

If vibrational degrees of freedom are taken into account, then total number of degrees of freedom of diatomic molecule becomes seven. These are :

$$\frac{1}{2}mv_x^2, \frac{1}{2}mv_y^2, \frac{1}{2}mv_z^2, \frac{1}{2}I_x\omega_x^2, \frac{1}{2}I_y\omega_y^2, \frac{1}{2}\mu v^2, \frac{1}{2}kr^2.$$

Here $\frac{1}{2}\mu v^2$ corresponds to kinetic energy of vibration (μ is the reduced mass) and $\frac{1}{2}kr^2$ corresponds to potential energy of vibration (k is the force constant, r is the separation between the atoms).

3. **Triatomic or polyatomic gas :** A non-linear molecule has non zero moment of inertia about any axis, so there are three translational and three rotational degrees of freedom. Total number of degrees of freedom are six. These are :

$$\frac{1}{2}mv_x^2, \frac{1}{2}mv_y^2, \frac{1}{2}mv_z^2, \frac{1}{2}I_x\omega_x^2, \frac{1}{2}I_y\omega_y^2, \frac{1}{2}I_z\omega_z^2.$$

Fig. 6.16

Degrees of freedom of different gases

Atomicity of gas	Example	Figure	Degrees of freedom f
Monoatomic	He, Ne, Ar	•	3 translational
Diatomic	H_2, N_2, O_2, Co	•——•	3 translational + 2 rotational = 5
Triatomic (non-linear)	H_2O, SO_2	△	3 translational + 3 rotational = 6

Ex. 14 What are the degrees of freedom in the following cases.

(i) A particle moves along a straight line.

(ii) A particle is projected in space.

(iii) Motion of fan.

(iv) Motion of ant.

(v) Motion of mosquito or fly (no rotation).

Sol.

(i) One, translational.

(ii) Two, translational

(iii) One, rotational.

(iv) Two, translational.

(v) Three, translational.

6.10 LAW OF EQUIPARTITION OF ENERGY

According to this law, for a system in thermal equilibrium, the total energy of a dynamic system is equally distributed among its various degrees of freedom. The energy associated with each degree of freedom is $\dfrac{kT}{2}$ per molecule or $\dfrac{RT}{2}$ per mole.

C_V, C_P and γ for different gases

1. **Monoatomic gas**

   Degrees of freedom $\quad f = 3$

   Kinetic energy per mole $\quad E = U = 3 \times \dfrac{RT}{2} = \dfrac{3RT}{2}$

   Molar specific heat at constant volume

   $$C_V = \frac{\partial U}{\partial T} = \frac{3R}{2}$$

   Molar specific heat at constant pressure

   $$C_P = C_V + R = \frac{5R}{2}$$

   Ratio of specific heats $\quad \gamma = \dfrac{C_P}{C_V} = \dfrac{5R/2}{3R/2}$

   $$= \frac{5}{3} = 1.67$$

2. **Diatomic Gas**

   Degree of freedom $\quad f = 5$

   Kinetic energy per mole $\quad U = 5 \times \dfrac{RT}{2} = \dfrac{5RT}{2}$

   Molar specific heat at constant volume

   $$C_V = \frac{\partial U}{\partial T} = \frac{5R}{2}$$

   Molar specific heat at constant pressure

   $$C_P = C_V + R = \frac{7R}{2}$$

   Ratio of specific heats $\quad \gamma = \dfrac{C_P}{C_V} = \dfrac{7R/2}{5R/2}$

   $$= \frac{7}{5} = 1.4$$

3. **Triatomic or polyatomic**

Degrees of freedom $\qquad f = 6$

Kinetic energy per mole $\qquad U = 6 \times \dfrac{RT}{2} = 3RT$

Molar specific heat at constant volume

$$C_V = \frac{\partial U}{\partial T} = 3R$$

Molar specific heat at constant pressure
$$C_P = C_V + R = 4R$$

Ratio of specific heats $\qquad \gamma = \dfrac{C_P}{C_V} = \dfrac{4R}{3R}$

$$= \frac{4}{3} = 1.33$$

For a molecule with f degrees of freedom

Kinetic energy per mole $\qquad U = f \times \dfrac{RT}{2} = \dfrac{fRT}{2}$

Molar specific heat at constant volume

$$C_V = \frac{\partial U}{\partial T} = \frac{fR}{2}$$

Molar specific heat at constant pressure

$$C_P = C_V + R = \frac{fR}{2} + R$$

$$= R\left(\frac{f}{2} + 1\right)$$

Ratio of specific heats $\qquad \gamma = \dfrac{C_P}{C_V} = \dfrac{R(f/2 + 1)}{\dfrac{fR}{2}}$

or $\qquad \gamma = 1 + \dfrac{2}{f}$

6.11 MEAN FREE PATH

The mean free path of a gas molecule may be defined as the average distance travelled by the molecule between two successive collisions.

Let $\lambda_1, \lambda_2, \ldots, \lambda_n$ be the distances travelled by a gas molecule during n collisions, then the mean free path of gas molecule is given by

$$\lambda = \frac{\lambda_1 + \lambda_2 + \ldots + \lambda_n}{n}$$

During the collision, a molecule of a gas moves in a straight line with constant velocity. The statistical study of heat gives the mean free path as following :

$$\lambda = \frac{1}{\sqrt{2}\,\pi n d^2}$$

where d is the diameter of molecule, n is the number molecules per unit volume
If we take one mole of a gas, then

$$n = \frac{N}{V} = \frac{N}{\left(\dfrac{RT}{P}\right)} = \frac{P}{\left(\dfrac{R}{N}\right)T} = \frac{P}{kT}$$

$$\therefore \qquad \lambda = \frac{kT}{\sqrt{2}\,\pi d^2 P}$$

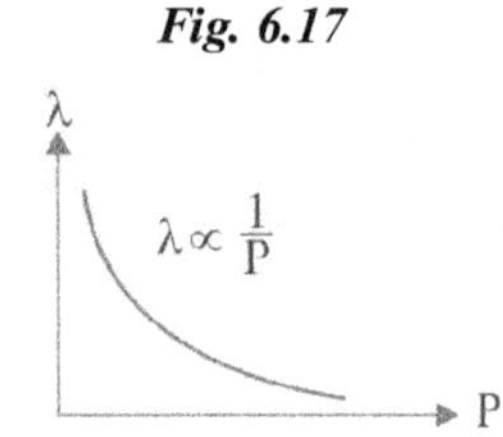

Fig. 6.17

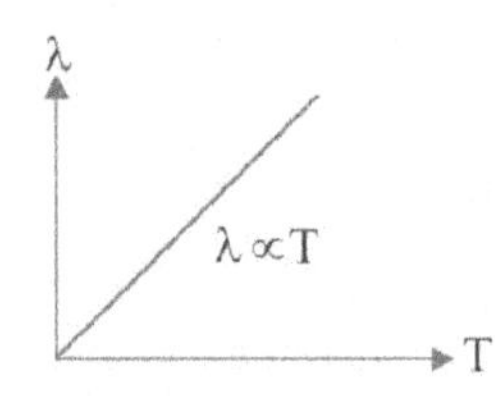

(a) Variation of λ with P

(b) Variation of λ with T

Fig. 6.18

Ex. 15 The temperature of the walls of a vessel containing a gas at a temperature T is T_{wall}. In which case is the pressure exerted by the gas on the vessel walls higher : when the vessel walls are colder than the gas ($T_{wall} < T$) or when they are warmer than the gas ($T_{wall} > T$)?

Sol.

If the temperature of walls of the vessel T_{wall} is equal to the temperature T of the gas, then a molecule striking the wall changes the normal component P_x to its momentum by $-P_x$. So the change in the momentum will be $2P_x$. When $T_{wall} > T$, the gas is heated. This means that gas molecules bounce off the wall at a higher velocity than that at which they impinge the wall, and hence a higher momentum. As a result, the change in momentum will be larger than $2P_x$. If, however, $T_{wall} < T$, the gas is cooled, i.e., gas molecules bounce off the wall with a smaller momentum and hence change in momentum will be smaller than $2P_x$. Thus the pressure exerted by the gas on the walls is higher when the walls are warmer.

Ex. 16 Estimate the mean free path and collision frequency of nitrogen molecule in a cylinder containing nitrogen at 2.0 atm and temperature 17°C. Take the radius of a nitrogen molecule to be roughly 1.0° Å. Compare the collision time with the time the molecule moves freely between two successive collisions. (Molecular mass of N_2 = 28.0g)

Sol.

Here
$$T = 273 + 17 = 290 \text{ K}$$
$$d = 2 \times 1.0 \times 10^{-10} \text{ m}$$
$$P = 2.0 \text{ atm} = 2 \times 1.013 \times 10^5 \text{ N/m}^2$$
$$k = 1.37 \times 10^{-23} \text{ J/K}$$

Mean free path, $\lambda = \dfrac{kT}{\sqrt{2}\pi d^2 P}$

$$= \frac{1.37 \times 10^{-23} \times 290}{\sqrt{2}\pi \times (2 \times 10^{-10})^2 \times (2 \times 1.013 \times 10^5)}$$

$$= 1.1 \times 10^{-7} \text{ m}$$

Root mean square speed of nitrogen molecules

$$v_{rms} = \sqrt{\frac{3RT}{M}}$$

$$= \sqrt{\frac{3 \times 8.31 \times 290}{28 \times 10^{-3}}} = 5.1 \times 10^2 \text{ m/s}$$

The time interval between two successive collisions

$$\Delta t = \frac{\lambda}{v_{rms}} = \frac{1.1 \times 10^{-7}}{5.1 \times 10^2} = 2.2 \times 10^{-10} \text{ s}$$

The frequency of collision

$$n = \frac{1}{\Delta t} = \frac{1}{(\lambda / v_{rms})} = \frac{v_{rms}}{\lambda}$$

$$= \frac{5.1 \times 10^2}{1.1 \times 10^{-7}} = 4.6 \times 10^9 \text{ Hz}$$

Time taken for the collision

$$= \frac{\text{diameter of molecule}}{v_{rms}}$$

$$= \frac{2.0 \times 10^{-10}}{5.1 \times 10^2} = 4 \times 10^{-13} \text{ s}$$

The time between two successive collisions is nearly 500 times the time taken for a collision.

6.12 PHASES AND PHASE DIAGRAMS

Isotherm of water : A graph plotted between the pressure and volume of a system at constant temperature is called an isotherm. Figure 6.19 shows isotherms for water in the temperature range 350°C to 380°C.

From the figure it can be concluded that :

(i) At 350°C, part AB of isotherm represents vapour phase of water. In this region Boyle's law is obeyed (PV = constant). With increase in pressure some part of vapour condenses into water, so part BC represents the transition phase. When entire vapour changes into water, there is no appreciable change in volume with pressure (part CD).

(ii) With the increase in temperature, liquification becomes difficult, and so liquid-vapour region becomes shorter. At 374.1°C, it reduces to point H, called critical point and the corresponding temperature is called **critical temperature**.

(iii) The state above critical temperature is called gaseous phase.

Pressure-temperature phase diagram for water

(i) In the space above the steam-line and right of ice-line, water exists in liquid phase.

(ii) In the space below the steam line and right of hoar frost line, water exists in gaseous phase (steam).

(iii) In the space above the hoar-frost line and on left of ice-line, water exists in solid phase as ice.

Triple point : It is the point on P-T diagram at which all the three phases of a substance can co-exist in equilibrium with each other. For water it is 273.16 K at 4.6 mm of Hg.

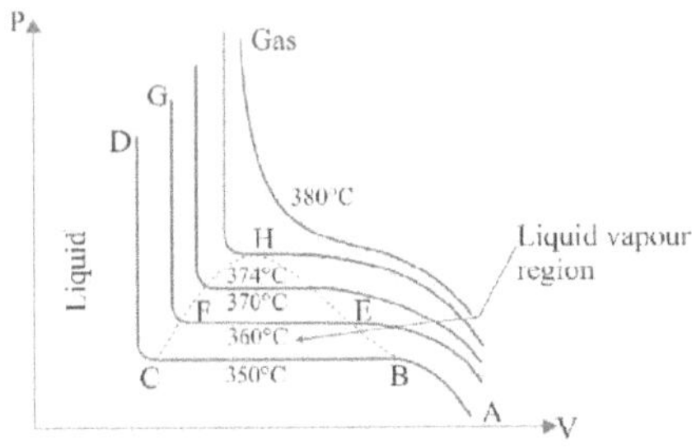

Fig. 6.19

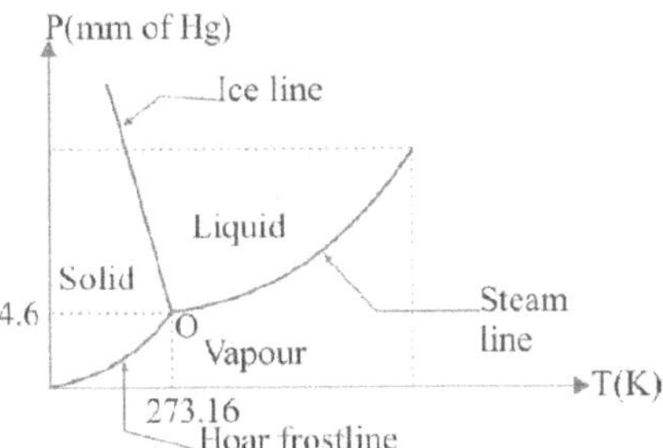

Fig. 6.20

Fig. 6.20 shows the P-T phase diagram for water. From the graph it can be concluded that ;

Ex. 17 The volume vs. temperature T graphs for a certain amount of a perfect gas are at two pressures P_1 and P_2 are shown in figure 6.21. Which one is greater P_1 or P_2?

Sol. For a perfect gas

$$PV = nRT$$

$$\therefore \quad \frac{V}{T} = \frac{nR}{P} = \frac{\text{constant}}{P}$$

Thus slope of V–T is inversely proportional to pressure.

As slope of 1 is smaller, so $P_1 > P_2$.

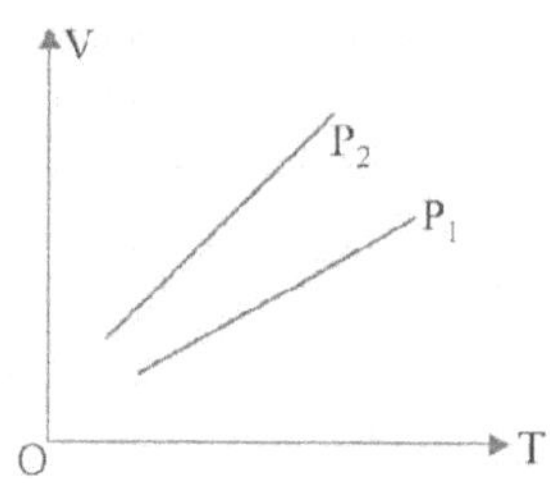

Fig. 6.21

Ex. 18 From the graph for a perfect gas state whether m_1 or m_2 is greater.

Sol. For a perfect gas

$$PV = nRT$$

$$= \frac{m}{M}RT$$

$$\therefore \quad \frac{T}{P} = \frac{MV}{mR} = \frac{\text{constant}}{m}$$

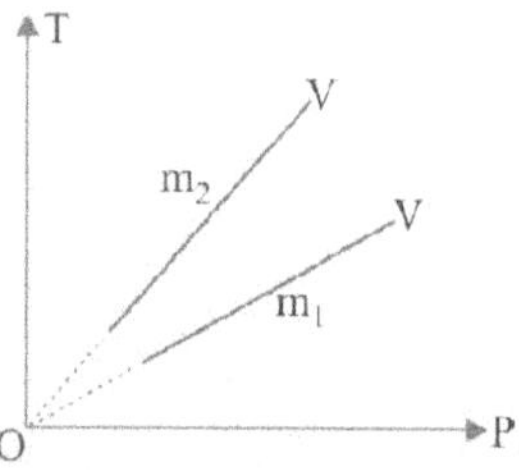

Fig. 6.22

Thus slope of T–P is inversely proportional to mass of the gas. As slope of 1 is smaller, so $m_1 > m_2$.

Ex. 19 The P–T graph for the given mass of a perfect gas is shown in figure. What inference can be drawn regarding the change in volume.

Sol.

For a perfect gas

$$PV = nRT$$

$$\therefore \quad \frac{P}{T} = \frac{nR}{V} = \frac{\text{constant}}{V}$$

or $$V \propto \frac{1}{\left(\dfrac{P}{T}\right)}$$

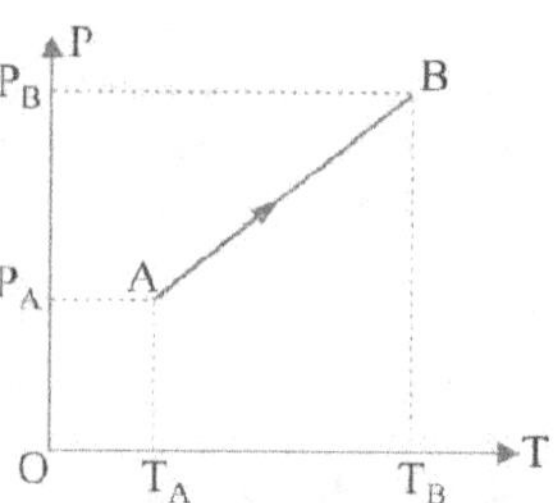

Fig. 6.23

From the figure, it is clear that $\left(\dfrac{P_B}{T_B}\right) < \left(\dfrac{P_A}{T_A}\right)$

$$\therefore \qquad V_A < V_B.$$

Ex. 20 An electric bulb of volume 250 cm³ was sealed off during manufacture at a pressure of 10^{-3}mm of mercury at 27°C. Compute the number of air molecules contained in the bulb. Given that $R = 8.31\ J/mol - K$ and $N = 6.02 \times 10^{23}/\text{mol}$.

Sol.

Pressure inside bulb $\quad P = h\rho g = 10^{-6} \times (13.6 \times 10^3) \times 9.8$

$$= 0.13\ \text{N/m}^2$$

Assuming air as an ideal gas, we can use

$$PV = nRT$$

or $$n = \frac{PV}{RT} = \frac{0.13 \times 250 \times 10^{-6}}{8.31 \times 300}$$

$$= 1.3 \times 10^{-8}\ \text{mole.}$$

$\therefore$ Number of molecules $= (1.3 \times 10^{-8}) \times (6.02 \times 10^{23})$

$$= 7.83 \times 10^{15} \qquad\qquad \textit{Ans.}$$

Ex. 21 A vertical hollow cylinder of height 1.52 m is fitted with a movable piston of negligible mass and thickness. The lower half portion of the cylinder contains an ideal gas and the upper half is filled with mercury. The cylinder is initially at 300 K. When the temperature is raised half of the mercury comes out of the cylinder. Find the temperature assuming the thermal expansion of mercury to be negligible.

Sol.

Let A be the area of cross-section of the piston.

Initially, $\qquad V_1 = 76A, P_1 = p_a + 76$ cm of Hg

$$= 2p_a \qquad\qquad (p_a = 76\ \text{cm})$$

$$T_1 = 300\ K$$

Finally, $\qquad V_2 = 114\,A,$

$$P_2 = p_a + 38\ \text{cm of Hg}$$

$$= p_a + \frac{p_a}{2} = \frac{3p_a}{2}$$

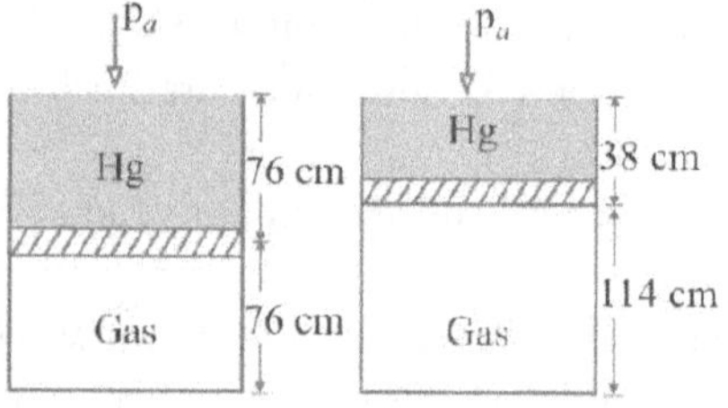

Fig. 6.24

If T_2 is the final temperature then by ideal gas equation

$$\frac{P_1 V_1}{T_1} = \frac{P_2 V_2}{T_2}$$

$$\therefore \quad T_2 = \frac{P_2 V_2 T_1}{P_1 V_1}$$

$$= \frac{\left(\frac{3p_a}{2}\right) \times (114A) \times 300}{(2p_a) \times (76A)}$$

$$= 337.5 \ K \qquad\qquad \textbf{Ans.}$$

Ex. 22 One gram mole of oxygen at 27°C and 1 atmospheric pressure is enclosed in a vessel. **(a) Assuming the molecules to the moving with v_{rms}, find the number of collisions per second which the molecules make with one square meter area of the vessel wall. (b) the vessel is next thermally insulated and moved with a constant speed v_0. It is then suddenly stopped. The process results in a rise of temperature of the gas by 1°C. Calculate speed v_0.** $(k = 1.38 \times 10^{-23} \text{ J/K and } N = 6.02 \times 10^{23} \text{ /mol.}).$

Sol.

Mass of one molecule of oxygen

$$= \frac{\text{mass of one mole}}{\text{no. of molecules in one mole}}$$

$$= \frac{32 \times 10^{-3}}{6.02 \times 10^{23}} = 5.316 \times 10^{-26} \text{ kg}$$

(a) The speed of the oxygen molecule

$$v_{rms} = \sqrt{\frac{3kT}{m}}$$

Momentum of the oxygen molecule

$$p = mv$$

$$= m\sqrt{\frac{3kT}{m}} = \sqrt{3mkT}$$

According to kinetic theory of gases, the molecule makes elastic collision with the wall, so momentum after collision becomes $-p$. The change in momentum

$$\Delta p = 2p = 2\sqrt{3mkT}$$

$$= 2\sqrt{3 \times 5.316 \times 10^{-26} \times 1.38 \times 10^{-23} \times 300}$$

$$= 5.139 \times 10^{-23} \text{ N} - \text{s}$$

If there are n collisions per second, then force exerted

$$F = \frac{\Delta p}{\Delta t} = n\Delta p \qquad \left(\frac{1}{\Delta t} = n\right)$$

Pressure, $\quad P = \dfrac{F}{A} = \dfrac{n\Delta p}{1} = n\Delta p$

or $\quad 1.01 \times 10^5 = n \times 5.139 \times 10^{-23}$

$$\therefore \quad n = 1.965 \times 10^{27} \qquad\qquad \textbf{Ans.}$$

(b) When the vessel is stopped, its K.E. will be converted into internal energy, so we have

$$\frac{1}{2}mv_0^2 = nC_V\Delta T$$

$$= n\left(\frac{5}{2}R\right)\Delta T$$

or $\quad \dfrac{1}{2} \times (32 \times 10^{-3}) \times v_0^2$

$$= 1 \times \left(\frac{5}{2} \times 8.31\right) \times 1$$

After solving , we get $v_0 = 36$ m/s $\qquad\qquad$ **Ans.**

Ex. 23 Two closed vessels of equal volume contain air at 105 k Pa, 300 K and are connected throw a narrow tube. If one of the vessels is now maintained at 300 K and the other at 400 K, what will be the pressure in the vessels?

Sol.

Initially, pressure, volume and temperature of each vessel be P_0, V_0 and T_0. Let n be the number of moles in each vessel, then $n = \dfrac{P_0 V_0}{R T_0}$. When other vessel is kept at temperature $T = 400 \ K$, the pressure of the system changes. Let new pressure becomes P. If n_1 and n_2 are the number of moles of air in first and second vessel respectively, then

$$n_1 = \frac{PV_0}{RT_0}, \quad n_2 = \frac{PV_0}{RT} .$$

For an isolated system

$$n + n = n_1 + n_2$$
$$\text{or} \qquad 2n = n_1 + n_2$$

$$2\frac{P_0 V_0}{RT_0} = \frac{PV_0}{RT_0} + \frac{PV_0}{RT}$$

$$\frac{2P_0}{T_0} = P\left[\frac{1}{T_0} + \frac{1}{T}\right]$$

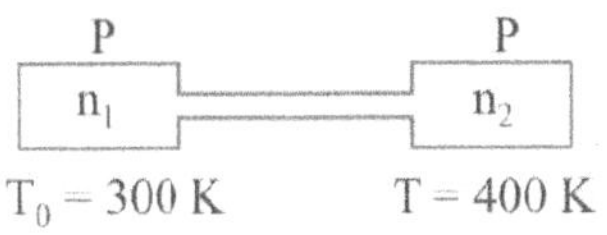

P   n₁   n₂   P

$T_0 = 300$ K $\qquad$ $T = 400$ K

Fig. 6.25

$$\therefore \quad P = \frac{2P_0 T}{T + T_0}$$

$$= \frac{2 \times 10^5 \times 400}{400 + 300} = 120 \text{ kPa} \qquad \textbf{Ans}$$

C_V and C_P :

We have, $\quad C_P - C_V = R$ and $\dfrac{C_P}{C_V} = \gamma$

$$\therefore \quad C_V = \frac{R}{\gamma - 1} \text{ and } C_P = \frac{\gamma R}{\gamma - 1}$$

γ of the mixture :

(i) If n_1 moles of C_{V_1}, n_2 moles of C_{V_2}, ______ are mixed, then by conservation of energy, we have

$$U_1 + U_2 + \ldots\ldots\ldots = U$$

or $\quad n_1 C_{V_1} \Delta T + n_2 C_{V_2} \Delta T + \ldots\ldots = (n_1 + n_2 + \ldots)(C_V)_{mix} \Delta T$

Here $(C_V)_{mix}$ is the specific heat of the mixture at constant volume

After solving above equation, we get

$$(C_V)_{mix} = \frac{n_1 C_{V_1} + n_2 C_{V_2} + \ldots}{n_1 + n_2 + \ldots}$$

and $\quad (C_P)_{mix} = (C_V) + R$

$$\gamma_{mix} = \frac{(C_P)_{mix}}{(C_V)_{mix}}$$

(ii) If n_1 moles of γ_1 and n_2 moles of γ_2, ... are mixed, then by conservation of energy, we have

$$U_1 + U_2 + \ldots\ldots = U$$

or $\quad n_1 C_{V_1} \Delta T + n_2 C_{V_2} \Delta T + \ldots\ldots = (n_1 + n_2 + \ldots)(C_V)_{mix} \Delta T$

or $\quad n_1\left(\dfrac{R}{\gamma_1 - 1}\right) + n_2\left(\dfrac{R}{\gamma_2 - 1}\right) + \ldots\ldots = (n_1 + n_2 + \ldots)\left(\dfrac{R}{\gamma - 1}\right)$

or $\quad \dfrac{n_1}{\gamma_1 - 1} + \dfrac{n_2}{\gamma_2 - 1} + \ldots\ldots = \dfrac{(n_1 + n_2 + \ldots\ldots)}{\gamma_{mix} - 1}$

Note:

It is not correct to get γ of the mixture by using a formula

$$\gamma_{mix} = \left[\frac{n_1 \gamma_1 + n_2 \gamma_2}{n_1 + n_2}\right] \text{ for mixture of two gases.}$$

Ex. 24 A gaseous mixture enclosed in a vessel consists of one gm mole of a gas A with ($\gamma = 5/3$) and another B with ($\gamma = 7/5$) at a temperature T. The gases A and B do not react with each other and assumed to be ideal. Find the number of gm moles of the gas if γ of the gaseous mixture is 19/13.

Sol. For two gases, we can write

$$\frac{n_1}{\gamma_1 - 1} + \frac{n_2}{\gamma_2 - 1} = \frac{n_1 + n_2}{\gamma_{mean} - 1}$$

Here, $\qquad n_1 = 1$ and $n_2 = ?$

$\qquad\qquad \gamma_1 = 5/3$ and $\gamma_2 = 7/5$

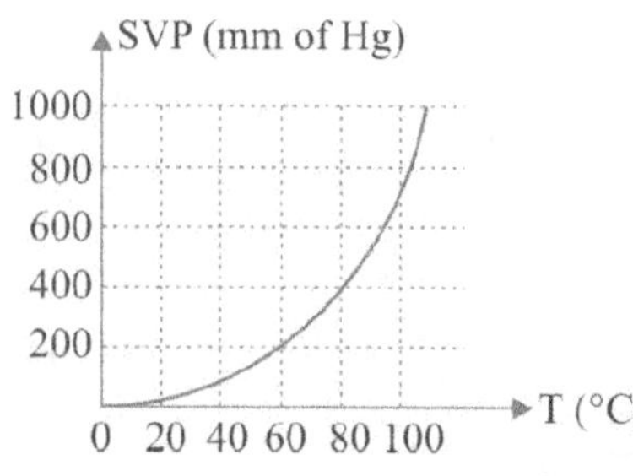

Fig. 6.27

Substituting these values in above equation, we get

$$\frac{1}{\dfrac{5}{3} - 1} + \frac{n_2}{\dfrac{7}{5} - 1} = \frac{1 + n_2}{\dfrac{19}{13} - 1}$$

or $\qquad \dfrac{3}{2} + \dfrac{5 n_2}{2} = \dfrac{13(1 + n_2)}{6}$

or $\qquad 3(3 + 5 n_2) = 13(1 + n_2)$

$\qquad\qquad 9 + 15 n_2 = 13 + 13 n_2$

$\qquad\qquad\qquad n_2 = 2 \text{ gm mole} \qquad\qquad$ **Ans.**

Ex. 25 A gas is enclosed in a vessel of volume V at a pressure P. It is being pumped out of the vessel by means of a piston pump with a stroke volume v. What is the final pressure in the vessel after n strokes of the pump? Assume temperature remains constant.

Sol.

When v volume of a gas is pumped out from the vessel, the remaining gas will occupy the volume of the container. The total volume of gas thus becomes $(V + v)$, let P_1 be the pressure of the gas of volume $(V + v)$, then by Boyle's law

$$PV = P_1(V + v)$$

$\therefore \qquad\qquad P_1 = P\left(\dfrac{V}{V + v}\right) \qquad\qquad \ldots \text{(i)}$

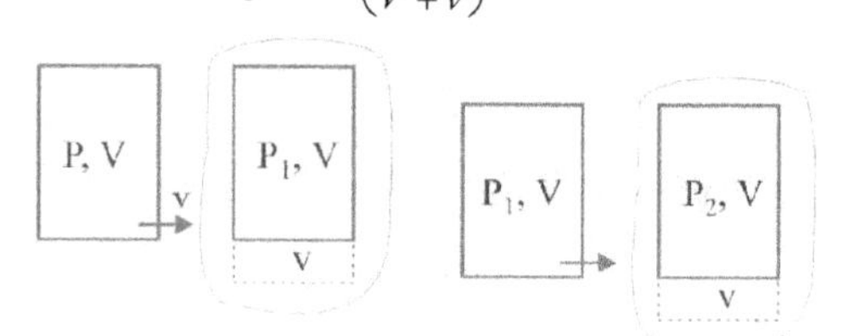

Fig. 6.26

Similar treatment after second stroke gives

$$P_1 V = P_2(V + v)$$

$\therefore \qquad\qquad P_2 = P_1\left(\dfrac{V}{V + v}\right) \qquad\qquad \ldots \text{(ii)}$

Substituting the value of P_1 from (i) in (ii), we get

$$P_2 = P\left(\frac{V}{V + v}\right)^2$$

After n strokes, let P_n be the pressure of the gas in the vessel, then

$$P_n = P\left(\frac{V}{V + v}\right)^n \qquad\qquad \textbf{Ans.}$$

6.13 VAPOUR PRESSURE

Consider a closed vessel having some water. Due to evaporation some water transforms into vapour and adjusted between the air molecules in the space above water. This vapour exerted pressure on the water, which is called **vapour pressure.** After some time the volume of water becomes constant and the vapour above it becomes saturated. When space above water contains the maximum possible amount of vapour, the vapour is called saturated, and the corresponding vapour pressure is called **saturation vapour pressure (SVP).** The saturation vapour pressure of a substance is constant at a given temperature. It increases with increase in temperature. Figure (6.27) shows the saturation vapour pressure of water, as a function of temperature.

Saturation vapour pressure of water

T (°C)	Vapour pressure (mm of Hg)	T (°C)	Vapour pressure (mm of Hg)
0	4.58	100	760
5	6.51	120	1490
10	8.94	140	2710
15	12.67	160	4630
20	17.5	180	7510
40	55.1	200	11650
60	149	220	17390
80	355		

6.14 DEW POINT

The temperature at which the saturation vapour pressure becomes equal to the existing vapour pressure is called due point. If the temperature is decreased below the dew point, some of the vapour condenses.

6.15 HUMIDITY

The amount of water vapour present in unit volume of air is called absolute humidity. Its SI unit is kg/m^3

Relative humidity: $RH = \dfrac{\left[\begin{array}{l}\text{Amount of water vapour present in a given} \\ \text{volume of air at a given temperature}\end{array}\right]}{\left[\begin{array}{l}\text{Amount of water vapour required to saturated} \\ \text{the same volume of air at the same temperature}\end{array}\right]}$

As the pressure exerted by vapour is directly proportional to the amount of vapour present in a given volume $PV = \dfrac{m}{M}RT$, so relative humidity can also be defined as

$$RH = \frac{\text{Vapour pressure of air}}{\text{SVP at the same temperature}}$$

or $$RH = \frac{\text{SVP at dew point}}{\text{SVP at the existing temperature}}$$

Ex. 26 The relative humidity in a closed room at 15°C is 60%. If the temperature rises to 20°C what will be the relative humidity? SVP at 15°C and 20°C are 12.67 and 17.36 mm of Hg respectively.

Sol.   The SVP at 15°C = 12.67 mm of Hg

$$RH = \frac{\text{Vapour pressure at 15°C } (P_{15})}{\text{SVP at 15°C}}$$

or $$0.60 = \frac{P_{15}}{16.67} \Rightarrow P_{15} = 7.6 \text{ mm of Hg}$$

From P_{15} , we have to find the vapour pressure at 20°C (P_{20}) . By gas equation $PV = nRT$, we have

$$\frac{P_{15}}{P_{20}} = \frac{273+15}{273+20} = \frac{288}{293}$$

or $$P_{20} = \frac{293}{288} \times P_{15} = \frac{293}{288} \times 7.6$$

$$= 7.73 \text{ mm of Hg}$$

$$\text{RH at 20°C} = \frac{P_{20}}{\text{SVP at 20°C}} = \frac{7.73}{17.36}$$

$$= 0.445 = 44.5\% \qquad \textit{Ans}$$

Ex. 27 A jar contains a gas and a few drops of water at TK. The pressure in the jar is 830 mm of Hg. The temperature of the jar is reduced by 1%. The saturated vapour pressures of water at the two temperatures are 30 and 25 mm of Hg. Calculate the new pressure in the jar.

Sol.   The pressure in the jar due to gas and due to water vapours = 830 mm of Hg.

Saturated vapour pressure at temperature $T = 30$ mm of Hg.

So pressure of the gas at temperature $T, P_1 = 830 - 30 = 800$ mm of Hg.

The final temperature of the jar $T_2 = T - 0.01T = 0.99T$

Let P_2 be the final pressure of the gas, then by gas law

$$\frac{P_1 V_1}{T_1} = \frac{P_2 V_2}{T_2}$$

or $$\frac{800V}{T} = \frac{P_2 V}{0.99T}$$

or $$P_2 = 792 \text{ mm of Hg}$$

The saturated vapour pressure at

$$T_2 = 25 \text{ mm of Hg}$$

The final total pressure in the jar

$$= 792 + 25 = 817 \text{ mm of Hg} \qquad \textit{Ans.}$$

Review of formulae & Important Points

1. **Boyle's law**
$$PV = \text{constant}$$

2. **Charle's law**
$$\frac{V}{T} = \text{constant}$$

3. **Lay-Lussac's law**
$$\frac{P}{T} = \text{constant}$$

4. **Perfect gas equation**
$$PV = nRT$$

5. **Vander Waal's equation for real gases**
$$\left(P + \frac{an^2}{V^2}\right)(V - nb) = nRT$$

6. **Pressure,** $\quad P = \dfrac{nmv_{rms}^2}{3V}$

7. **Kinetic energy of gas**

   (i) Translational K.E. $= \dfrac{3}{2}RT$ per mole for each gas

   (ii) For diatomic gas

   Translational + rotational K.E. $= \dfrac{5}{2}RT$ per mole

8. **Root mean square velocity** $\quad v_{rms} = \sqrt{\dfrac{3RT}{M}}$

9. **Dalton's law of partial pressure**
$$P = P_1 + P_2 + \dots$$

10. **Degrees of freedom :**
   (i) Manoatomic gas
   Degrees of freedom $f = 3$ translational

   Kinetic energy per mole $= \dfrac{3}{2}RT$

$$C_v = \frac{\partial U}{\partial T} = \frac{3}{2}R$$

$$C_p = C_v + R = \frac{5}{2}R$$

$$\gamma = \frac{C_p}{C_v} = \frac{5}{3}$$

(ii) Diatomic gas
Degree of freedom $= 5$ (3 translational + 2 rotational)

Kinetic energy per mole $= \dfrac{5RT}{2}$

$$C_v = \frac{5R}{2}$$

$$C_p = \frac{7R}{2}$$

$$\gamma = \frac{7}{5}$$

(iii) Triatomic or polyatomic gas
Degrees of freedom $= 6$

(3 translational + 3 rotational)

Kinetic energy per mole $= 3RT$
$$C_v = 3RT$$
$$C_p = 4R$$

$$\gamma = \frac{4}{3}$$

11. **In general,** $\quad \gamma = 1 + \dfrac{2}{f}$

12. **Mean free path,** $\quad \lambda = \dfrac{kT}{\sqrt{2}\pi d^2 P}$

13. **γ of the mixture :**
   (i) When C_v and C_p are given : For two gases with n_1 and n_2 moles

$$[C_v]_{mix} = \frac{n_1 C_{v_1} + n_2 C_{v_2}}{n_1 + n_2}$$

$$[C_p]_{mix} = \frac{n_1 C_{p_1} + n_2 C_{p_2}}{n_1 + n_2}$$

$$\gamma_{mix} = \frac{[C_p]_{mix}}{[C_v]_{mix}}$$

(ii) For two gases of γ_1 and γ_2 with n_1 and n_2 moles

$$\frac{(n_1 + n_2)}{\gamma_{mix} - 1} = \frac{n_1}{\gamma_1 - 1} + \frac{n_2}{\gamma_2 - 1}$$

KTG

MCQ Type 1

Exercise 6.1

LEVEL - 1

Only one correct option

1. Two identical cylinders contain helium at 2.5 atmosphere and argon at 1 atmosphere respectively. If both the gases are filled in one of the cylinders, the pressure would be
(a)   3.5 atmosphere
(b)   1.75 atmosphere
(c)   1.5 atmosphere
(d)   1 atmosphere

2. The air density at Mount Everest is less than that at the sea level. It is found by mountaineers that for one trip lasting a few hours, the extra oxygen needed by them corresponds to 30,000 cc at sea level (pressure 1 atmosphere, temperature 27°C). Assuming that the temperature around Mount Everest is − 73°C and that the oxygen cylinder has capacity of 5.2 liters, the pressure at which oxygen be filled (at site) in the cylinder is
(a)   3.86 atmospheres
(b)   5.00 atmospheres
(c)   5.77 atmospheres
(d)   1 atmospheres

3. We have a jar A filled with gas characterised by parameters P, V and T and another jar B filled with a gas with parameters $2P$, $V/4$ and $2T$, where the symbols have the usual meanings. The ratio of the number of molecules of jar A to those of jar B is
(a)   1 : 1
(b)   1 : 2
(c)   2 : 1
(d)   4 : 1

4. At room temperature the r.m.s. speed of the molecules of a certain diatomic gas is found to be 1920 m/s. The gas is:
(a) H_2
(b) F_2
(c) O_2
(d) Cl_2

5. Three closed vessels A, B and C are at the same temperature T and contain gases which obey the Maxwellian distribution of velocities. Vessel A contains only O_2, B only N_2 and C a mixture of equal quantities of O_2 and N_2. If the average speed of the O_2 molecules in vessel A is v_1, that of the N_2 molecules in vessel B is v_2, the average speed of the O_2 molecules in vessel C is

(a) $\dfrac{v_1 + v_2}{2}$

(b) v_1
(c) $(v_1 v_2)^{1/2}$

(d) $\sqrt{\dfrac{3kT}{m}}$ where m is the mass of an oxygen molecule

6. A vessel contains a mixture of 1 mole of oxygen and two moles of nitrogen at 300 K. The ratio of the average rotational kinetic energy per O_2 molecule to that per N_2 molecule is
(a)   1 : 1
(b)   1 : 2
(c)   2 : 1
(d)   depends on the moment of inertia of the two molecules

7. The average transitional energy and the rms speed of molecules in a sample of oxygen gas at 300 K are 6.21×10^{-21} J and 484 m/s respectively. The corresponding values at 600 K are nearly (assuming ideal gas behaviour)
(a) 12.42×10^{-21} J, 968 m/s
(b) 8.78×10^{-21} J, 684 m/s
(c) 6.21×10^{-21} J, 968 m/s
(d) 12.42×10^{-21} J, 684 m/s

8. The average transitional kinetic energy of O_2 (molar mass 32) molecules at a particular temperature is 0.048 eV. The transitional kinetic energy of N_2 (molar mass 28) molecules in eV at the same temperature is
(a)   0.0015
(b)   0.003
(c)   0.048
(d)   0.768

9. A vessel contains 1 mole of O_2 gas (molar mass 32) at a temperature T. The pressure of the gas is P. An identical vessel containing one mole of He gas (Molar mass 4) at a temperature $2T$, has a pressure of

(a) $\dfrac{P}{8}$
(b) P

(c) $2P$
(d) $8P$

10. Which of the following molecular properties is the same for all ideal gases at a given temperature are
(a)   rms momentum
(b)   rms velocity
(c)   mean kinetic energy
(d)   mean free path

11. The temperature of an ideal gas is increased from 120 K is 480 K. If at 120 K, the root mean square velocity of the gas molecules is v, then at 480 K, it will be
(a) $4v$
(b) $2v$

(c) $\dfrac{v}{2}$
(d) $\dfrac{v}{4}$

12. The plot of isotherms will not be a straight line when it is a plot between
(a) p and T
(b) V and p
(c) S (entropy) and T
(d) pV and V

13. The internal energy of an ideal gas decreases by the same amount as the work done by the system
(a)   the process must isothermal
(b)   the process must be adiabatic
(c)   the process must isobaric
(d)   the temperature of the system must increase

Answer Key	1	(a)	3	(d)	5	(b)	7	(d)	9	(c)	11	(b)	13	(b)
Sol. from page 449	2	(a)	4	(a)	6	(a)	8	(c)	10	(c)	12	(b)		

14. Figure shows two flasks connected to each other. The volume of the flask 1 is twice that of flask 2. The system is filled with an ideal gas at temperature $100\,K$ and $200\,K$ respectively. If the mass of the gas in 1 be m, then what is the mass of the gas in flask 2

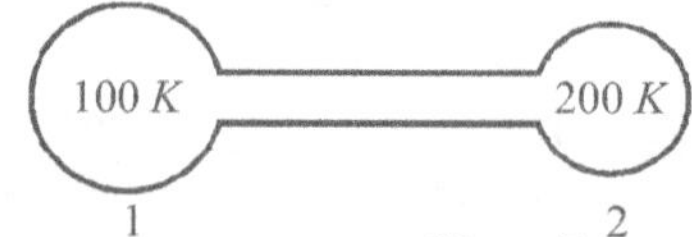

   (a) m (b) $m/2$
   (c) $m/4$ (d) $m/8$

15. If pressure of a gas contained in a closed vessel is increased by 0.4% when heated by 1°C, the initial temperature must be
   (a) 250 K   (b) 250°C
   (c) 2500 K   (d) 25°C

16. To double the volume of a given mass of an ideal gas at 27°C keeping the pressure constant, one must raise the temperature in degree centigrade to
   (a) 54°   (b) 270°
   (c) 327°   (d) 600°

17. Air is pumped into an automobile tube upto a pressure of 200 kPa in the morning when the air temperature is 22°C. During the day, temperature rises to 42°C and the tube expands by 2%. The pressure of the air in the tube at this temperature, will be approximately
   (a) 212 kPa (b) 209 kPa
   (c) 206 kPa (d) 200 kPa

18. The gas in vessel is subjected to a pressure of 20 atmosphere at a temperature 27°C. The pressure of the gas in a vessel after one half of the gas is released from the vessel and the temperature of the remainder is raised by 50°C is
   (a) 8.5 atm (b) 10.8 atm
   (c) 11.7 atm (d) 17 atm

19. In Vander Waal's equation a and b represent
$$\left(P+\frac{a}{V^2}\right)(V-b)=RT$$
   (a) Both a and b represent correction in volume
   (b) Both a and b represent adhesive force between molecules
   (c) a represents adhesive force between molecules and b correction in volume
   (d) a represents correction in volume and b represents adhesive force between molecules

20. Which of the following statements is true?
   (a) Absolute zero temperature is zero energy temperature.
   (b) Two different gases at the same temperature pressure have equal root mean square velocities.
   (c) The root mean square speed of the molecules of different ideal gases, maintained at the same temperature are the same.
   (d) Given sample of 1cc of hydrogen and 1 cc of oxygen both at NTP; oxygen sample has a large number of molecules.

21. According to the kinetic theory of gases, at absolute temperature
   (a) water freezes   (b) liquid helium freezes
   (c) molecular motion stops   (d) liquid hydrogen freezes

22. The speeds of 5 molecules of a gas (in arbitrary units) are as follows : 2, 3, 4, 5, 6. The root mean square speed for these molecules is
   (a) 2.91   (b) 3.52
   (c) 4.00   (d) 4.24

23. For a gas $\dfrac{R}{C_V}=0.67$. This gas is made up of molecules which are
   (a) diatomic
   (b) mixture of diatomic and polyatomic molecules
   (c) monoatomic
   (d) polyatomic

24. If c_p and c_v denote the specific heats of nitrogen per unit mass at constant pressure and constant volume respectively, then
   (a) $c_p-c_v=R/28$ (b) $c_p-c_v=R/14$
   (c) $c_p-c_v=R$ (d) $c_p-c_v=28R$

25. The specific heats at constant pressure is greater than that of the same gas at constant volume because
   (a) At constant pressure work is done in expanding the gas
   (b) At constant volume work is done in expanding the gas
   (c) The molecular attraction increases more at constant pressure
   (d) The molecular vibration increases more at constant pressure

26. The specific heat of a gas
   (a) has only two values c_p and c_v
   (b) has a unique value at a given temperature
   (c) can have any value between 0 and ∞
   (d) depends upon the mass of the gas

27. Gas at a pressure P_0 is contained in a vessel. If the masses of all the molecules are halved and their speeds are doubled, the resulting pressure P will be equal to
   (a) $4P_0$ (b) $2P_0$
   (c) P_0 (d) $\dfrac{P_0}{2}$

28. One kg of a diatomic gas is at a pressure of 8×10^4 N/m². The density of the gas is 4 kg/m³. What is the energy of the gas due to its thermal motion
   (a) 3×10^4 J   (b) 5×10^4 J
   (c) 6×10^4 J   (d) 7×10^4 J

29. At 0 K which of the following properties of a gas will be zero
   (a) Kinetic energy   (b) Potential energy
   (c) Vibrational energy   (d) Density

30. A closed compartment containing gas is moving with some acceleration in horizontal direction. Neglect effect of gravity. Then the pressure in the compartment is
   (a) same everywhere   (b) lower in the front side
   (c) lower in the rear side   (d) lower in the upper side

31. A gas is filled in the cylinder shown in the figure. The two pistons are joined by a string. If the gas is heated, the pistons will
   (a) move towards left
   (b) move towards right
   (c) remain stationary
   (d) none of these

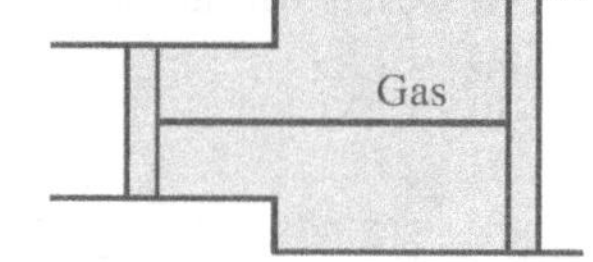

32. An experiment is carried on a fixed amount of gas at different temperatures and at high pressure such that it deviates from the ideal gas behaviour. The variation of $\dfrac{PV}{RT}$ with P is shown in the diagram. The correct variation will correspond to

(a)   Curve A

(b)   Curve B

(c)   Curve C

(d)   Curve D

33. The change in volume V with respect to an increase in pressure P has been shown in the figure for a non-ideal gas at four different temperatures T_1, T_2, T_3 and T_4. The critical temperature of the gas is

(a) T_1

(b) T_2

(c) T_3

(d) T_4

34. From the following $P\text{-}T$ graph what inference can be drawn

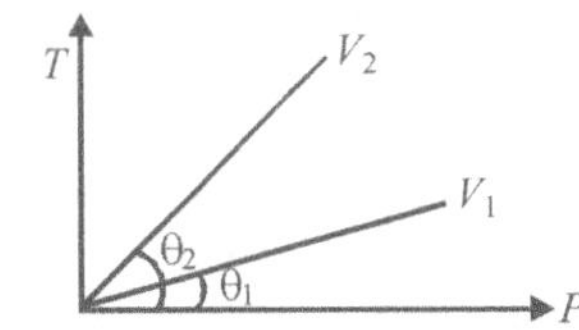

(a) $V_2 > V_1$

(b) $V_2 < V_1$

(c) $V_2 = V_1$

(d)   None of the above

35. Which one the following graphs represents the behaviour of an ideal gas?

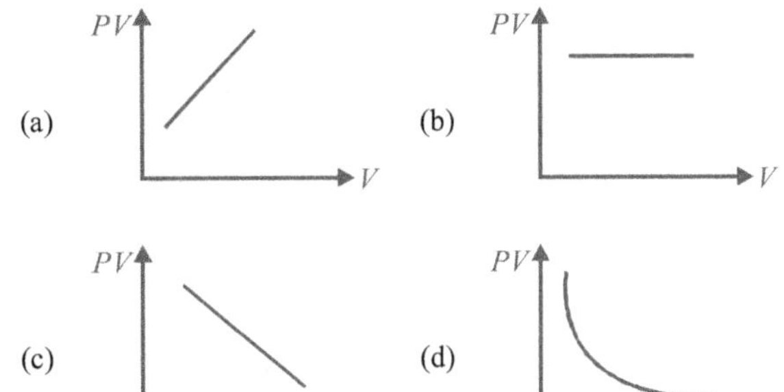

Answer Key
Sol. from page 449

32	(b)	33	(b)	34	(a)	35	(b)

LEVEL - 2

1. If one mole of monoatomic gas $\left(\gamma = \dfrac{5}{3}\right)$ is mixed with one mole of diatomic gas $\left(\gamma = \dfrac{7}{5}\right)$, the value of γ for the mixture is

(a)   1.40   (b)   1.50

(c)   1.53   (d)   3.07

2. The temperature at which the average transitional kinetic energy of a molecule is equal to the energy gained by an electron in accelerating from rest through a potential difference of 1 volt is

(a) 4.6×10^3 K   (b) 11.6×10^3 K

(c) 23.2×10^3 K   (d) 7.7×10^3 K

3. A diatomic gas is heated at constant pressure. The fraction of the heat energy is used to increase the internal energy is

(a) $\dfrac{3}{5}$ (b) $\dfrac{3}{7}$

(c) $\dfrac{5}{7}$ (d) $\dfrac{5}{9}$

4. For a gas if ratio of specific heat at constant pressure and volume is γ then the value of degree of freedom is

(a) $\dfrac{3\gamma - 1}{2\gamma - 1}$ (b) $\dfrac{2}{\gamma - 1}$

(c) $\dfrac{9}{2}(\gamma - 1)$ (d) $\dfrac{25}{2}(\gamma - 1)$

5. Two ideal gas at absolute temperature T_1 and T_2 are mixed. There is no loss of energy. The masses of the molecules are m_1 and m_2 and the number of molecules in the gases are n_1 and n_2 respectively. The temperature of the mixture is

(a) $\dfrac{T_1 + T_2}{2}$ (b) $\dfrac{T_1 + T_2}{n_1 n_2}$

(c) $T_1 + T_2$ (d) $\dfrac{n_1 T_1 + n_2 T_2}{n_1 + n_2}$

6. Half mole of helium gas is contained at STP. The heat energy needed to double the pressure of the gas keeping the volume constant (specific heat of the gas = 3J/g –K) is

(a)   3276 J   (b)   1638 J

(c)   819 J   (d)   409.5 J

Answer Key
Sol. from page 450

1	(b)	2	(d)	3	(c)	4	(b)	5	(d)	6	(b)

7. Two thermally insulated vessels 1 and 2 are filled with air at temperatures (T_1, T_2), volume (V_1, V_2) and pressure (P_1, P_2) respectively. If the valve joining the two vessels is opened, the temperature inside the vessel at equilibrium will be

(a) $T_1 + T_2$

(b) $(T_1 + T_2)/2$

(c) $\dfrac{T_1 T_2 (P_1 V_1 + P_2 V_2)}{P_1 V_1 T_2 + P_2 V_2 T_1}$

(d) $\dfrac{T_1 T_2 (P_1 V_1 + P_2 V_2)}{P_1 V_1 T_1 + P_2 V_2 T_2}$

8. The adjoining figure shows graph of pressure and volume of a gas at two different temperatures T_1 and T_2. Which of the following inferences is correct?

(a) $T_1 > T_2$

(b) $T_1 = T_2$

(c) $T_1 < T_2$

(d) none of these

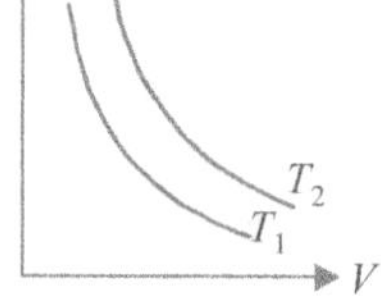

9. The root mean square of the molecules of a diatomic gas is v. When the temperature is double, the molecules dissociate into two atoms. The new root mean square speed of the atom is

(a) v

(b) $2v$

(c) $\sqrt{2}v$

(d) $4v$

10. The equation of state of a gas is given by $\left(P + \dfrac{aT^2}{V}\right)V^c = (RT + b)$, where a, b, c and R are constants.

The isotherms can be represented by $P = AV^m - BV^n$, where A and B depend only on temperature and

(a) $m = -c$ and $n = -1$

(b) $m = c$ and $n = -1$

(c) $m = -c$ and $n = 1$

(d) $m = c$ and $n = -1$

11. A horizontal uniform glass tube of 100 cm, length sealed at both ends contain 10 cm mercury column in the middle. The temperature and pressure of air on either side of mercury column are respectively 81°C and 76 cm of mercury. If the air column at one end is kept at 0°C and the other end at 273°C, the pressure of air which is at 0°C is (in cm of Hg)

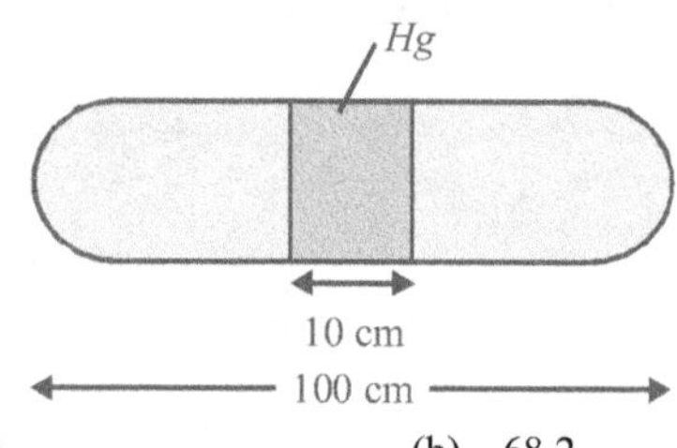

(a) 76

(b) 68.2

(c) 102.4

(d) 122

12. A gas mixture consists of 2 moles of oxygen and 4 moles of argon at temperature T. Neglecting all vibrational modes, the total internal energy of the system is

(a) $4\,RT$

(b) $15\,RT$

(c) $9\,RT$

(d) $11\,RT$

13. Two different masses m and $3m$ of an ideal gas are heated separately in a vessel of constant volume, the pressure P and absolute temperature T, graphs for these two cases are shown in the figure as A and B. The ratio of slopes of curves B to A is

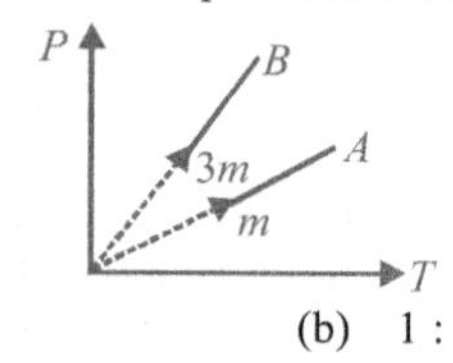

(a) $3:1$

(b) $1:3$

(c) $9:1$

(d) $1:9$

14. One gram mole of nitrogen at 27°C and 1 atm pressure is contained in a vessel and the molecules are moving with their rms speed. The number of collisions per second which the molecules make with an area of $1\,\text{m}^2$ on the vessel's wall is

(a) 2×10^{27}

(b) 2×10^{20}

(c) 2×10^{10}

(d) 2×10^{24}

15. Consider the following statements :

A gas can be liquefied by increasing the pressure

1. above the critical pressure only

2. Only when the temperature of the enclosed gas is below the critical temperature

3. Only when the volume of the enclosed gas is below the critical volume

Which of the statements given above is / are correct :

(a) 1 and 2

(b) 2 only

(c) 3 only

(d) 2 and 3

16. One mole of an ideal gas is taken from an initial state (p, v, T) to a final state $(2p, 2V, 4T)$ by two different paths as shown in the figures 1 and 2 given. If the changes in internal energy between the final and the initial states of the gas along the paths I and II are denoted by ΔU_I and ΔU_II respectively, then :

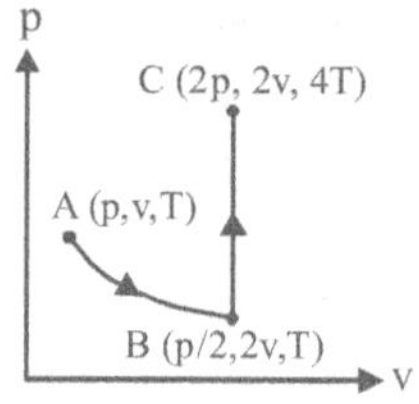 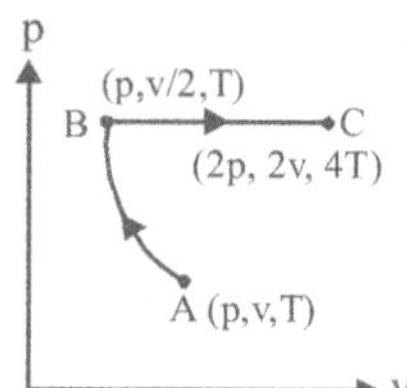

(a) $\Delta U_\text{I} = \Delta U_\text{II}$

(b) $\Delta U_\text{I} > \Delta U_\text{II}$

(c) $\Delta U_\text{I} < \Delta U_\text{II}$

(d) $\Delta U_\text{I} = 0.66\,\Delta U_\text{II}$

17. Five gas molecules chosen at random are found to have speeds of 500, 600, 700, 800 and 900 m/s:
    (a) The root mean square speed and the average speed are the same.
    (b) The root mean square speed is 14 m/s higher than the average speed.
    (c) The root mean square speed is 14 m/s lower than the average speed.
    (d) The root mean square speed is $\sqrt{14}$ m/s higher than the average speed.

18. A nitrogen molecule has some rms speed at 0°C on the surface of the earth. With this speed, it goes straight up. If therei is no collisions with other molecules, the molecule will rise up to a height of
    (a) 8.2 km
    (b) 12.4 km
    (c) 10.6 km
    (d) 15.2 km

19. A vessel containing one gram mole of oxygen at 27°C and 1 atm pressure is thermally insulated and moles with a constant speed v_0. It is then suddenly stopped and this results in a rise of temperature of the gas by 1°C the speed v_0 is
    (a) 63.03 m/s
    (b) 30.63 m/s
    (c) 36.03 m/s
    (d) 33.06 m/s

20. A tube closed at one end is lowered, with the open end down, into a fresh water lake. If one third of the tube is filled with water, the distance between the surface of the lake and level of water in the tube is
    (a) 6.41 m
    (b) 5.82 m
    (c) 5.10 m
    (d) 4.20 m

Answer Key								
Sol. from page 450	**17**	(b)	**18**	(b)	**19**	(c)	**20**	(c)

KTG — MCQ Type 2 — *Exercise 6.2*

Multiple correct options

1. C_v and C_p denote the molar specific heat capacities of a gas at constant volume and constant pressure, respectively. Then
   (a) $C_p - C_v$ is larger for a diatomic ideal gas than for a monoatomic ideal gas
   (b) $C_p + C_v$ is larger for a diatomic ideal gas than for a monoatomic ideal gas
   (c) C_p / C_v is larger for a diatomic ideal gas than for a monoatomic ideal gas
   (d) $C_p . C_v$ is larger for a diatomic ideal gas than for a monoatomic ideal gas

2. A box contains a mixture of H_2 and He gases. Which of the following statements are corrects?
   (a) The average translational kinetic energies of H_2 molecules and He atoms are same
   (b) The average energies of H_2 molecules and He atoms are same
   (c) H_2 molecules have greater average energy than that of He atoms
   (d) The average speed of H_2 molecules and He atoms are same

3. From the following statements, concerning ideal gas at any given temperature T, select the correct one(s)
   (a) The coefficient of volume expansion at constant pressure is same for all ideal gases
   (b) The average translational kinetic energy per molecule of oxygen gas is $3KT$ (K being Boltzmann constant)
   (c) In a gaseous mixture, the average translational kinetic energy of the molecules of each component is same
   (d) The mean free path of molecules increases with the decrease in pressure

4. A gas in container A is in thermal equilibrium with another gas in container B. Both contain equal masses of the two gases in the respective containers. Which of the following can be true?
   (a) $P_A V_A = P_B V_B$
   (b) $P_A = P_B, V_A \neq V_B$
   (c) $P_A \neq P_B, V_A = V_B$
   (d) $\dfrac{P_A}{V_A} = \dfrac{P_B}{V_B}$

5. Graph shows a hypothetical speed distribution for a sample of N gas particle (for $v > v_0$; $\dfrac{dN}{dv} = 0$)

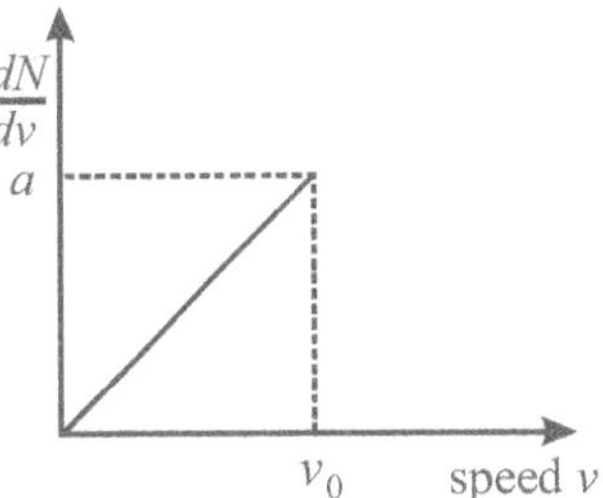

   (a) The value of v_0 is 2N
   (b) The ratio v_{avg}/v_0 is equal to 2/3
   (c) The ratio v_{rms}/v_0 is equal to $1/\sqrt{2}$
   (d) Three fourth of the total particle has a speed between $0.5 v_0$ and v_0

Answer Key						
Sol. from page 451	**1**	(b, d)	**3**	(a, c, d)	**5**	(a, b, c, d)
	2	(a, c)	**4**	(b, c)		

6. Let $\bar{v}$, v_{rms} and v_p respectively denote the mean speed, the root-mean-square speed and the most probable speed of the molecules in an ideal monoatomic gas at absolute temperature T. The mass of a molecule is m. Then

   (a) No molecule can have speed greater than v_{rms}

   (b) No molecule can have speed less than $\dfrac{v_p}{\sqrt{2}}$

   (c) $v_p < \bar{v} < v_{rms}$

   (d) The average kinetic energy of a molecule is $\dfrac{3}{4}mv_p^2$

7. Hydrogen gas and oxygen gas have volume 1 cm^3 each at NTP

   (a) Number of molecules is same in both the gases

   (b) The rms velocity of molecules of both the gases is the same

   (c) The internal energy of each gas is the same

   (d) The average velocity of molecules of each gas is the same

8. Velocities of four gas molecules are $2, 3, -4, -1$ m/sec respectively. Then

   (a) the mean velocity of molecules is zero

   (b) the mean speed of molecules is 2.5 m/s

   (c) the mean square velocity of molecules is 7.5 m^2/s^2

   (d) the root mean square velocity of molecules is 2.74 m/s

9. Choose the correct statement(s)?

   (a) In an adiabatic expansion the product of pressure and volume decreases.

   (b) The rms translational speed for all ideal gas molecules at the same temperature is not the same but it depends on the mass.

   (c) Temperature of an ideal gas is doubled from 100°C to 200°C. The average kinetic energy of each particle is also doubled.

   (d) The *rms* translational speed for all ideal gas molecules at the same temperature is not the same and does not depend on the mass.

10. A gas expands such that its initial and final temperature are equal. Also, the process followed by the gas traces a straight line on the P-V diagram :

   (a) The temperature of the gas remains constant throughout

   (b) The temperature of the gas first increases and then decreases

   (c) The temperature of the gas first decreases and then increases

   (d) The straight line has a negative slope

11. Two vessels of the same volume contain the same gas at same temperature. If the pressure in the vessels be in the ratio of $1 : 2$, then

   (a) the ratio of the average kinetic energy is $1 : 2$

   (b) the ratio of the root mean square velocity is $1 : 1$

   (c) the ratio of the average velocity is $1 : 2$

   (d) the ratio of number of molecules is $1 : 2$

12. The total kinetic energy of translatory motion of all the molecules of 5 litres of nitrogen exerting a pressure P is 3000 J.

   (a) the total K.E. of 10 litres of N_2 at a pressure of $2P$ is 3000J

   (b) the total K.E. of 10 litres of He at a pressure of $2P$ is 3000 J

   (c) the total K.E. of 10 litres of O_2 at a pressure of $2P$ is 12000 J

   (d) the total K.E. of 10 litres of Ne at a pressure of $2P$ is 12000 J

13. A mixture of ideal gases 7 kg of nitrogen and 11 kg of CO_2. Then

   (a) equivalent molecular weight of the mixture is 36

   (b) equivalent molecular weight of the mixture is 18

   (c) γ for the mixture is 5/2

   (d) γ for the mixture is 47/35

   (Take γ for nitrogen and CO_2 as 1.4 and 1.3 respectively)

14. Hydrogen gas and oxygen gas have volume 1cm^3 each at N.T.P., Then

   (a) number of molecules is same in both the gases.

   (b) the rms velocity of molecules of both the gases is the same.

   (c) the internal energy of each gases is the same.

   (d) the average velocity of molecules of each gas is the same.

15. In case of hydrogen and oxygen at N.T.P., which of the following quantities is/are the same?

   (a) average momentum per molecule

   (b) average kinetic energy per molecule

   (c) kinetic energy per unit volume

   (d) kinetic energy per unit mass

16. For two different gases X and Y, having degrees of freedom f_1 and f_2 and molar heat capacities at constant volume Cv_1 and Cv_2 respectively, the lnP versus lnV graph is plotted for adiabatic process, as shown

   (a) $f_1 > f_2$

   (b) $f_2 > f_1$

   (c) $Cv_2 > Cv_1$

   (d) $Cv_1 > Cv_2$

17. The volume of a gas and the number of gas molecules within that volume for four situations are (1) $2V_0$ and N_0, (2) $3V_0$ and $3N_0$, (3) $8V_0$ and $4N_0$ (4) $3V_0$ and $9N_0$. Which of them has mean free path greatest :

   (a) 1   (b) 2

   (c) 3   (d) 4

Answer Key		6	(c, d)	8	(a, b, c, d)	10	(b, d)	12	(c, d)	14	(a, c, d)	16	(b, c)
Sol. from page 451		7	(a, c, d)	9	(a, b)	11	(b, d)	13	(a, d)	15	(a, b, c)	17	(a, c)

Statement Questions — *Exercise 6.3*

Read the two statements carefully to mark the correct option out of the options given below:
(a) If both the statements are true and the *statement - 2* is the correct explanation of *statement - 1*.
(b) If both the statements are true but *statement - 2* is not the correct explanation of the *statement - 1*.
(c) If *statement - 1* true but *statement - 2* is false.
(d) If *statement - 1* is false but *statement - 2* is true.

1. *Statement - 1*

Consider a gas of neutrons, it to behave much better as an ideal gas as compared to hydrogen gas at the same pressure and temperature.

Statement - 2

Internal potential energy of gas of neutrons is zero.

2. *Statement - 1*

When we place a gas cylinder on a moving train, its internal kinetic energy increases.

Statement - 2

Its temperature remains constant.

3. *Statement - 1*

When you come out of a river after a dip, you feel cold.

Statement - 2

The temperature of atmosphere is less than that of river water.

4. *Statement - 1*

Cooking is faster in pressure cooker.

Statement - 2

Aluminium is good conductor of heat.

5. *Statement - 1*

In pressure temperature (*P-T*) phase diagram of water, the slope of the melting curve is found to be negative.

Statement - 2

Ice contracts on melting.

6. *Statement - 1*

For an atom the number of degrees of freedom is 3.

Statement - 2

The ratio of specific heats at constant pressure and volume is a constant. i.e.,

$$\frac{C_p}{C_v} = \gamma \ .$$

7. *Statement - 1*

A gas has unique value of specific heat.

Statement - 2

Specific heat is defined as the amount of heat required to raise the temperature of unit mass of the substance through one degree centigrade.

8. *Statement - 1*

Absolute zero is the temperature corresponding to zero energy.

Statement - 2

The temperature at which no molecular motion cease is called absolute zero temperature.

9. *Statement - 1*

At low density, variable of gases P, V and T follows the equation $PV = \mu RT$.

Statement - 2

At low density real gases are more closely to ideal gases.

10. *Statement - 1*

For an ideal gas, at constant temperature, the product of pressure and volume is constant.

Statement - 2

The mean square velocity of the molecules is inversely proportional to mass.

11. *Statement - 1*

For an ideal gas (in mole)

$$C_p - C_v = R.$$

Statement - 2

At constant pressure, some heat is spent in expansion of the gas.

Answer Key	1	(a)	3	(c)	5	(a)	7	(d)	9	(a)	11	(a)
Sol. from page 452	2	(d)	4	(b)	6	(b)	8	(d)	10	(b)		

Passage & Matrix

PASSAGES

Passage for (Q. 1 - 3) :

A balloon whose volume is $500 m^3$ is to be filled with hydrogen at atmospheric pressure.

1. If hydrogen is stored in cylinders of volume $0.05 m^3$ at an atmospheric pressure of 15×10^5 Pa. Then number of cylinders required are

  (a)   425   (b)   570

  (c)   675   (d)   690

2. The total weight can be supported by the balloon in air at standard condition is

  (a)   3775 N   (b)   4500 N

  (c)   5934 N   (d)   6231 N

3. The weight supported by the balloon, if filled with helium instead of hydrogen is

  (a)   5498 N   (b)   3212 N

  (c)   2000 N   (d)   1825 N

Passage for (Q. 4 - 6) :

A gaseous mixture enclosed in a volume V consists of one gram mole of a gas A with $\gamma \, (C_p / C_v) = 5 / 3$ and another has B with $\gamma = 7/5$ at a certain temperature T. The gram molecular weights of the gases A and B are 4 and 32 respectively. The gases A and B do not react with each other and are assumed to be ideal. The gaseous mixture follows the equation $PV^{19/13} =$ constant, in adiabatic processes.

4. The number of gram moles of the gas B in the gaseous mixture is

  (a)   2 g mole   (b)   1 gm mole

  (c)   3g mole   (d)   4 gm mole

5. The speed of the sound in the gaseous mixture at $T = 300$ K is

  (a)   300.0 m/s   (b)   400.7 m/s

  (c)   480 m/s   (d)   512 m/s

6. If T is raised by 1 K from 300 K, the percentage change in the speed of sound in the gaseous mixture is

  (a)   0.10 %   (b)   0.20 %

  (c)   0.17 %   (d)   none of these

Passage for (Q. 7 - 9) :

A cubical box of side 1 m contains helium gas (atomic weight 4) at a pressure of $100 \, N/m^2$. During an observation time of 1 s , an atom travelling with the root mean square speed parallel to one of its edges of the cube, was found to make 500 collisions with a particular wall, without any collision with other atoms. Taking $R = (25/3)$ J/mol–K and $k = 1.38 \times 10^{-23} \, J/K$. Evaluate

7. The temperature of the gas is

  (a)   160 K   (b)   210 K

  (c)   280 K   (d)   320 K

8. The average kinetic energy per atom is

  (a) 1.612×10^{-21} J   (b) 3.312×10^{-21} J

  (c) 3.521×10^{-21} J   (d) 4.20×10^{-21} J

9. The total mass of helium gas in the box is

  (a)   0.1 g   (b)   0.2 g

  (c)   0.3 g   (d)   0.4 g

Passage for (Q. 10 - 12) :

A cylinder contains nitrogen gas at 2.0 atm pressure and temperature 17°C. Take the radius of a nitrogen molecule to be roughly 1.0° Å. (Molecular mass of $N_2 = 28.0$ g)

10. The mean free path of nitrogen molecules is

  (a) 1.1×10^{-7} m   (b) 1.1×10^{-6} m

  (c) 2.3×10^{-5} m   (d) 4.5×10^{-8} m

11. The collision frequency of nitrogen molecules is

  (a) 4.6×10^{7} Hz   (b) 4.6×10^{9} Hz

  (c) 5.6×10^{8} Hz   (d) 5.5×10^{9} Hz

12. The time taken for a collision is

  (a) 5×10^{-9} s   (b) 6×10^{-12} s

  (c) 4×10^{-13} s   (d) 4×10^{-14} s

Answer Key	1	(c)	3	(a)	5	(b)	7	(a)	9	(c)	11	(b)
Sol. from page 452	2	(c)	4	(a)	6	(c)	8	(b)	10	(a)	12	(c)

13. X and Y are two equal size containers. X contains 5 mole of H_2 and Y has 10 mole of O_2 at the same temperature. Assuming that the gases are ideal, match columns

Column I		Column II
A.	In the container X	(p) pressure of the gas is more
B.	In the container Y	(q) rms speed of gas molecules is more
C.	Since the number of molecules is more	(r) average thermal energy of a molecule is the same as that of a molecule in the other container
D.	Since the gas has a smaller molecular mass	(s) internal energy of the system is more than that of the system in the other container

14.

Column I		Column II
A.	An ideal gas obeys gas equation	(p) with decrease in pressure
B.	A real gas behaves as an ideal gas at low pressure	(q) at all temperature
C.	Mean free path of molecules increases	(r) same for all gases
		(s) at high temperature

15. Match **Column I** (Physical Variables) with **Column II** (Expressions) and select the correct answer using the codes given below (n = number of gas molecules present per unit volume, k = Boltzmann constant, T = absolute temperature, m = mass of the particle) :

Column I		Column II
A.	Most probable velocity	(p) nkT
B.	Energy per degree of freedom	(q) $\sqrt{3kT/m}$
C.	Pressure	(r) $\sqrt{2kT/m}$
D.	R.M.S. velocity	(s) $kT/2$

16.

Column I		Column II
A.	v_{av}	(p) $\sqrt{\dfrac{3RT}{M}}$
B.	v_{rms}	(q) $\sqrt{\dfrac{8RT}{\pi M}}$
C.	v_{mp}	(r) $\dfrac{\sqrt{\gamma Rt}}{M}$
D.	v_{sound}	(s) $\sqrt{\dfrac{2RT}{M}}$

Answer Key	13	A → (q, r); B → (p, r, s); C → (p, s); D → (q)	15	A → (r); B → (s); C → (p); D → (q)
Sol. from page 452	14	A → (r, s); B → (r, s); C → (p)	16	A → (q); B → (s); C → (p); D → (q)

TEC Subjective Integer Type Exercise 5.5

Solution from page 454

1. An ideal gas is kept in a long cylindrical vessel fitted with a frictionless piston of cross–sectional area 10 cm^2 and weight 1 kg. The vessel itself is kept in a big chamber containing air at atmospheric pressure 100 kPa.

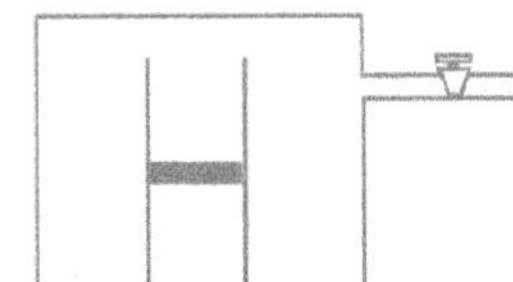

The length of the gas column is 20 cm. If the chamber is now completely evacuated by an exhaust pump, what will be the length of the gas column? Assume the temperature to remain constant throughout the process. **Ans :** 2.2 m.

2. A gas consisting of rigid diatomic molecules is expanded adiabatically. How many time has the gas to be expanded to reduce the root mean square velocity of the molecules $\eta = 1.50$ times. **Ans :** 7.6 times.

3. 0.014 kg of nitrogen is enclosed in a vessel at a temperature of 27°C. How much heat has to be transferred to the gas to double the r.m.s. velocity of its molecules ? **Ans :** 9315 J.

4. A jar contains a gas and a few drops of water at TK. The pressure in the jar is 830 mm of mercury. The temperature in the jar is reduced by 1%. The saturated vapour pressure at the two temperatures are 30 mm and 25 mm of mercury. Calculate the new pressure in the jar. **Ans.** 817 mm of mercury.

Solution from page 454

1. A metre long narrow bore held horizontally (and closed at one end) contains a 76 cm long mercury thread, which traps a 15 cm column of air. What happens if the tube is held vertically with the open end at the bottom ?

   Ans. The mercury thread will decrease in length by 23.8 cm.

2. An air bubble of volume 1.0 cm^3 rises from the bottom of a lake 40 m deep at a temperature of 12°C. To what volume does it grow, when it reaches the surface which is at a temperature of 35°C ?

   Ans. 5.275×10^{-6} m^3 .

3. An oxygen cylinder of volume 30 litre has an initial gauge pressure of 15 atm and a temperature of 27°C. After some oxygen is withdrawn from the cylinder, the gauge pressure drops to 11 atm and its temperature drop to 17°C. Estimate the mass of oxygen taken out of the cylinder, $R = 8.3$ J mol^{-1} K^{-1}, molecule weight of oxygen = 32.   **Ans :** 0.141 kg.

4. Figure shows plot of PV/T versus P for 1.00×10^{-3} kg of oxygen gas at two different temperatures.

   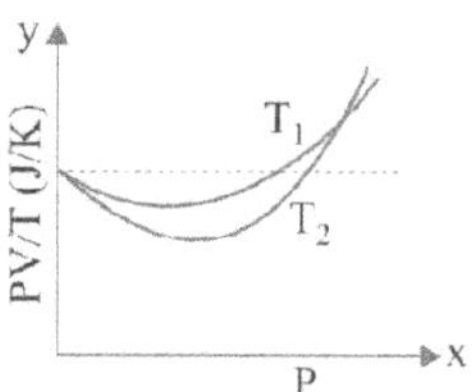

   (a) What does the dotted plot signify ?
   (b) Which is true : $T_1 > T_2$ or $T_1 < T_2$?
   (c) What is the value of PV/T where the curves meet on the $y-$axis ?
   (d) If we obtained similar plots for 1.00×10^{-3} kg of hydrogen, would we get the same value of PV/T at the point where the curves meet on the $y-$axis ? If not what mass of hydrogen yields the same value of PV/T (for low pressure high temperature region of the plot) ?
   (Molecular mass of H$_2$ = 2.02 u, of
   $\qquad$ O$_2$ = 32.0 u, R = 8.31 J /mol–K)
   $\qquad\qquad$ **Ans :** (a) Ideal behaviour of the gas
   $\qquad$ (b) $T_1 > T_2$ (c) 0.26 J/K (d) 6.3×10^{-5} kg.

5. Figure shows a cylindrical tube of radius 5 cm and length 20 cm. It is closed by a tight –fitting cork. The friction coefficient between the cork and the tube is 0.20.

   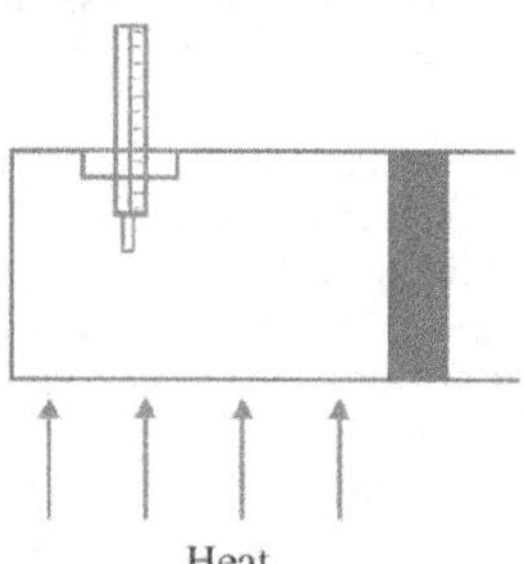

   The tube contains an ideal gas at a pressure of 1 atm and a

temperature of 300 K. The tube is slowly heated and it is found that the cork pops out when the temperature reaches 600 K. Let dN denotes the magnitude of the normal contact force exerted by a small length dl of the cork along the periphery (see the figure). Assuming that the temperature of the gas is uniform at any instant,

calculate $\dfrac{dN}{d\ell}$.   **Ans :** 1.25×10^4 N/m.

6. In a certain region of space there are 5 molecules/cm^3 on an average. The temperature there is 3 K. What is the average pressure of this very dilute gas ?   **Ans :** 2.07×10^{-16} N/m^2.

7. How will the rate of collision of rigid diatomic molecules against the vessel's wall will change, if the gas expanded adiabatically η times ?   **Ans :** rate decreases by $\eta^{(1+i)/i}$.

8. Two glass bulbs of equal volume are connected by a narrow tube and are filled with a gas at 0°C and a pressure of 76 cm of mercury. One of the bulbs is then placed in melting ice and the other is placed in water bath maintained at 62°C. What is the new value of the pressure inside the bulbs ? The volume of the connecting tube is negligible.   **Ans :** 83.75 cm of mercury.

9. Calculate the ratio of the speed of sound in neon to that in water vapour at any temperature (molar weight of neon = 2.02×10^{-2} kg / mole and molar weight of water vapour = 1.8×10^{-2} kg/ mole).

   $\qquad\qquad\qquad\qquad\qquad$ **Ans :** 1.06.

10. A monoatomic ideal gas expanded adiabatically to η times of its initial volume. Calculate ratio of final rate of collisions of molecules with unit area of container's walls to the initial rate.

    $\qquad\qquad\qquad\qquad\qquad$ **Ans :** $1/\eta^{4/3}$.

11. The piston cylinder arrangement shown contains a diatomic gas at temperature 300 K. The cross–sectional area of the cylinder is 1 m^2. Initially the height of the piston above the base of the cylinder is 1 m. The temperature is now raised to 400 K at constant pressure.

    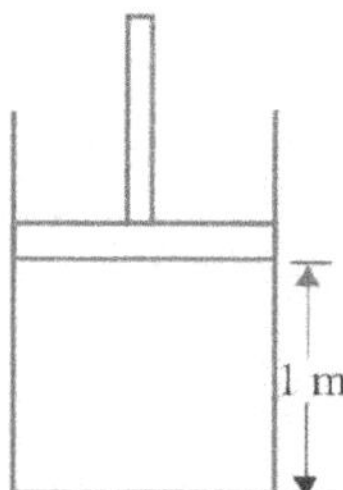

    Find the new height of the piston above the base of the cylinder. If the piston is now brought back to its original height without any heat loss, find the new equilibrium temperature of the gas. You can leave the answer in fraction.

    $\qquad\qquad\qquad\qquad$ **Ans.** $\dfrac{4}{3}$ m, 488.8 K.

12. The pressure of an ideal gas varies according to the law $P = P_0 - AV^2$, where P_0 and A are positive constants. Find the highest temperature that can be attained by the gas.

    $\qquad\qquad\qquad$ **Ans.** $T_{\max} = \dfrac{2P_0}{3nR}\sqrt{\dfrac{P_0}{3A}}$

Hints & Solutions

1. (a) By Dalton's law
$$P = P_1 + P_2 = 2.5 + 1 = 3.5 \text{ atmosphere}$$

2. (a) $P_1 = 1 \text{ atm}, V_1 = 30 \text{ litre}, T_1 = 273 + 27 = 300 \text{ K}$

$P_2 = ?, V_2 = 5.2 \text{ litre}, T_2 = 273 - 73 = 200 \text{ K}$

Using $\dfrac{P_1 V_1}{T_1} = \dfrac{P_2 V_2}{T_2}$, $\therefore P_2 = \dfrac{P_1 V_1}{T_1} \times \dfrac{T_2}{V_2} = \dfrac{1 \times 30 \times 200}{300 \times 5.2}$

$= 3.85 \text{ atmosphere.}$

3. (d) $\eta = \dfrac{PV}{RT}$, $\therefore \dfrac{n_1}{n_2} = \dfrac{PV/T}{2P \times \dfrac{V}{4}} = 4:1$

$\qquad\qquad\qquad \dfrac{}{2T}$

4. (a) $v_{rms} = 1920 = \sqrt{\dfrac{3RT}{M}} = \sqrt{\dfrac{3 \times 8.31 \times 300}{M}}$

$\therefore M = 2 \times 10^{-3} \, kg = 2g$

It is hydrogen.

5. (b) The average speed; $v = \sqrt{\dfrac{8RT}{\pi M}}$; $v \propto \sqrt{T}$.

6. (a) Each degree of rotation of diatomic molecule has energy

$\dfrac{RT}{2}$ per mole.

7. (d) $E = \dfrac{3}{2} \times 300$; $E' = \dfrac{3}{2} R(600) = 2E = 2 \times 6.21 \times 10^{-21}$

$= 12.42 \times 10^{-21} \text{ J.}$

$v_{rms} = \sqrt{\dfrac{3R \times 300}{M}}$; $v'_{rms} = \sqrt{\dfrac{3R \times 600}{M}} = \sqrt{2} \, v_{rms}$

$= 682.44 \text{ m/s}$

8. (c) The average translational energy depends only on temperature.

9. (c) $PV = 1 \times RT$ and $P'V = 1 \times R \times 2T$

$\therefore P' = 2P$

10. (c) $E = \dfrac{3}{2} RT$, so it is same for all ideal gases at same temperature.

11. (b) $\dfrac{v_1}{v_2} = \sqrt{\dfrac{T_1}{T_2}} = \sqrt{\dfrac{120}{480}} = \sqrt{\dfrac{1}{4}}$

or $v_2 = 2v_1$

12. (b) $PV = $ constant; so graph between P and V will be a rectangular hyperbola.

13. (b) $Q = \Delta U + W$

or $Q = \Delta U - \Delta U = 0$; It is an adiabatic process.

14. (c) $P(2V) = \left(\dfrac{m}{M}\right) R \times 100$ and $PV = \left(\dfrac{m'}{M}\right) R \times 200$

$\therefore m' = \dfrac{M}{4}$.

15. (a) $P = kT$

$\therefore \dfrac{\Delta P}{P} = \dfrac{\Delta T}{T}$

or $\dfrac{0.4}{100} = \dfrac{1}{T}$

$\therefore T = 250 \text{ K}$

16. (c) $\dfrac{V}{T} = \dfrac{2V}{T'}$

$\therefore T' = 2T = 2(273 + 27) = 600 \, K$

$= 600 - 273 = 327 \, °C$

17. (b) $V_1 = A\ell, T_1 = 273 + 22 = 295 \text{ K}, P_1 = 200 \text{ kPa}$

$V_2 = A(1.02 \, \ell) \; T_2 = 273 + 42 = 315 \, K$,

$P_2 = \dfrac{P_1 V_1}{T_1} \dfrac{T_2}{V_2} = \dfrac{200 \times A\ell \times 315}{295 \times 1.02 \, A\ell}$

$= 209 \text{ kPa}$

18. (b) $20 \times V = \dfrac{m}{M} R \times 300$

and $PV = \dfrac{m/2}{M} R \times (273 + 50)$

$\therefore P = 10.8 \text{ atm}$

19. (c) a represents correction for intermolecular forces and b for finite size of molecule.

20. (a) $E = \dfrac{3}{2} RT$; $T = 0$, $E = 0$.

21. (c) $v_{rms} = \sqrt{\dfrac{3RT}{M}}$; $T = 0$, $v_{rms} = 0$.

22. (d) $v_{rms} = \sqrt{\dfrac{2^2 + 3^2 + 4^2 + 5^2 + 6^2}{5}} = 4.24$

23. (c) $\dfrac{R}{C_v} = 0.67 \Rightarrow C_v = \dfrac{R}{0.67} = \dfrac{3R}{2}$.

Thus gas is monoatomic.

24. (a) $c_p - c_v = R$

or $Mc_p - Mc_v = R$

$\therefore c_p - c_v = \dfrac{R}{M} = \dfrac{R}{28}$

25. (a) Work done is to be done in expanding the gas at constant pressure.

26. (c) $C = \dfrac{Q}{m\Delta T}$; If $\Delta T = 0$, $C = \infty$ and if $Q = 0$, then $C = 0$

27. (b) $P_0 = \dfrac{1}{3} \dfrac{mnc^2}{V}$ and $P' = \dfrac{1}{3}\left(\dfrac{m}{2}\right) \times n \times (2c)^2 = 2 P_0$.

28. (a) $P = \dfrac{1}{3}\rho c^2$ or $c^2 = \dfrac{3P}{\rho}$

$\therefore E = \dfrac{1}{2} mc^2 = \dfrac{1}{2} \times 1 \times 3 \times \dfrac{8 \times 10^4}{4} = 3 \times 10^4 \text{ J}$

29. (a) $v_{rms} = \sqrt{\dfrac{3RT}{M}} = \sqrt{\dfrac{3R \times 0}{M}} = 0$

     $\therefore$ K.E is zero at zero Kelvin.

30. (b) Due to pseudo force the pressure at backside becomes greater and at front side becomes smaller.

31. (b) The force on the larger piston $F = PA$ will be greater because A is layer. So piston will move towards right.

32. (b) With the increase in pressure, the gas deviates from its ideal behaviour.

33. (b) Critical temperature is the temperature above which real gas can not be liquify by applying pressure.

34. (a) $$PV = nRT$$

     or $$V = nR\left(\dfrac{T}{P}\right) = nR\tan\theta$$

     As $\theta_2 > \theta_1$; $\therefore$ $V_2 > V_1$

35. (b) $PV = nRT$; $\therefore$ PV = constant at constant temperature.

1. (b) $$\dfrac{n_1 + n_2}{\gamma - 1} = \dfrac{n_1}{\gamma_1 - 1} + \dfrac{n_2}{\gamma_2 - 1}$$

     or $$\dfrac{2}{\gamma - 1} = \dfrac{1}{\dfrac{5}{3} - 1} + \dfrac{1}{\dfrac{7}{5} - 1}$$

     $\therefore$ $r = \dfrac{3}{2}$.

2. (d) $$1\,\text{eV} = \dfrac{3}{2}kT$$

     or $$1.6 \times 10^{-19} = \dfrac{3}{2} \times 1.38 \times 10^{-23} T$$

     $\therefore$ $T = 7.7 \times 10^3$ K.

3. (c) Friction is given by,

$$F = \dfrac{1}{\gamma} = \dfrac{1}{7/5} = \dfrac{5}{7}.$$

4. (b) $$\gamma = 1 + \dfrac{2}{f} \; ; \therefore \; f = \left[\dfrac{2}{\gamma - 1}\right]$$

5. (d) From conservation of energy,
$$E = E_1 + E_2$$

$$(n_1 + n_2)\dfrac{3}{2}kT = n_1 \times \dfrac{3}{2}kT_1 + n_2 \times \dfrac{3}{2}kT_2$$

     $\therefore$ $$T = \left[\dfrac{n_1 T_1 + n_2 T_2}{n_1 + n_2}\right]$$

6. (b) $C_v = M c_v = 4 \times 3 = 12$ J/mol-K
To doubling the pressure, the temperature will be doubled, so
$$\Delta T = T_2 - T_1 = 273\,K$$

Thus $Q = nC_v\Delta T = \dfrac{1}{2} \times 12 \times 273 = 1638$ J

7. (c) $$\dfrac{P(V_1 + V_2)}{T} = \dfrac{P_1 V_1}{T_1} + \dfrac{P_2 V_2}{T_2} \quad \dots \text{(i)}$$

     Also $P(V_1 + V_2) = P_1 V_1 + P_2 V_2 \quad \dots \text{(ii)}$
After solving above equations, we get

$$T = \left[\dfrac{(P_1 V_1 + P_2 V_2)T_1 T_2}{P_1 V_1 T_2 + P_2 V_2 T_1}\right]$$

8. (c) With increase in temperature, the product (PV) increases.

9. (b) $v_{rms} = \sqrt{\dfrac{3RT}{M}}$; and $v_{rms} = \sqrt{\dfrac{3R(2T)}{M/2}} = 2v_{rms}$.

10. (a) $$\left(P + \dfrac{aT^2}{V}\right)V^c = (RT + b) \Rightarrow P = (RT + b)V^{-c} - (aT^2)V^{-1}$$

     On comparing with equation, $P = AV^m - BV^n$,
$m = -c$ and $n = -1$.

11. (c) $\ell_1 = \ell_2 = 45$ cm
The pressure must be same on both sides. Hence

$$\dfrac{\ell_1}{T_1} = \dfrac{\ell_2}{T_2} \Rightarrow \dfrac{\ell_1}{273} = \dfrac{\ell_2}{273 + 273} \Rightarrow \ell_1 = \dfrac{\ell_2}{2}$$

     Also $\ell_1 + \ell_2 = 90$; $\therefore$ $\ell_1 = 30$cm and $\ell_2 = 60$cm

     Now $$\dfrac{P_1(\ell_1 A)}{T_1} = \dfrac{P(\ell A)}{T}$$

     or $$\dfrac{P_1 \times 30}{273} = \dfrac{76 \times 45}{273 \times 81} \Rightarrow P_1 = 102.4 \text{ cm}.$$

12. (d) $E = 2 \times \dfrac{5}{2}RT + 4 \times \dfrac{3}{2}RT = 11\,RT.$

13. (a) $PV = \dfrac{m}{M}RT$; $\therefore$ $\dfrac{P}{T} = Cm$

     or $$\dfrac{\text{slope of } B}{\text{slope of } A} = \dfrac{m_B}{m_A} = \dfrac{3m}{m} = 3$$

14. (a) Number of collisions can be calculated as
$$n(2mv_{rms}) = PA$$

     $\therefore$ $n = \left[\dfrac{PA}{2mv_{rms}}\right]$; $v_{rms} = \sqrt{\dfrac{3kT}{m}}$

15. (d) The real gas cannot be liquified above critical temperature by applying pressure.

16. (a) The change in internal energy depends only on initial and final state, so $\Delta U_I = \Delta U_{II}$.

17. (b) $$v_{av} = \left[\dfrac{500 + 600 + 700 + 800 + 900}{5}\right] = 700\,\text{m/s}$$

     and

$$v_{rms} = \sqrt{\dfrac{500^2 + 600^2 + 700^2 + 800^2 + 900^2}{5}} = 714\,\text{m/s}$$

     Thus v_{rms} is greater than average speed by 14 m/s.

18. (b) $v_{rms} = \sqrt{\dfrac{3RT}{M}} = \sqrt{\dfrac{3 \times 8.31 \times 273}{28 \times 10^{-3}}} = 493$ m/s

Thus $\dfrac{1}{2}mv_{rms}^2 = \dfrac{mgh}{1 + \dfrac{h}{R}}$. After substituting the values and

simplifying, we get $h = 12.4$ km

19. (c) $\Delta U = \dfrac{5}{2}R\Delta T = \dfrac{1}{2}mv_0^2$;

$m = 32 \times 10^{-3}$ kg

After substituting values and simplifying, we get

$v_0 = 36.03$ m/s

20. (c) $(y\rho g + P_a) \times \dfrac{2v}{3} = P_a V$

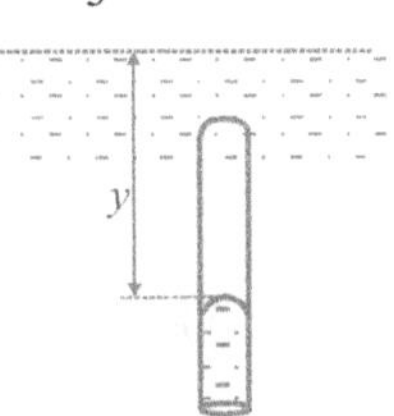

After substituting values and simplifying, we get $y = 5.10$ m

Solutions EXERCISE 6.2

1. (b, d) $C_P + C_v = \dfrac{5R}{2} + \dfrac{3R}{2} = 4R$ for monoatomic gas

and $C_P + C_v = \dfrac{7R}{2} + \dfrac{5R}{2} = 6R$ for diatomic gas

Similarly $C_P C_v$ is larger for diatomic gas.

2. (a, c) Average translational energy of any ideal gas is

$E_{\text{translational}} = \dfrac{3}{2}RT$

While total energy of diatomic molecule will be greater than that of monoatomic.

$E_{\text{diatomic}} = \dfrac{5RT}{2}, \quad E_{\text{monoatomic}} = \dfrac{3}{2}RT$

3. (a, c, d) $\gamma_v = \gamma_p = \dfrac{1}{273}/K$

$E = \dfrac{3}{2}RT$ is same for all ideal gases at same temperature. The mean free path, $\lambda = \dfrac{kT}{\sqrt{2}\pi d^2 P}$; so it increases with decrease in pressure.

4. (b, c) $P_A V_A = nRT = \dfrac{m}{M_A}RT$ and $P_B V_B = \dfrac{m}{M_B}RT$

So if $P_A = P_B$, $V_A M_A = V_B M_B$.

5. (a,b,c,d) Area under the curve is equal to number of molecules of the gas sample.

Hence $N = \dfrac{1}{2}av_0 \Rightarrow av_0 = 2N$

$v_{avg} = \dfrac{1}{N}\int_0^\infty v\, N(v)dv = \dfrac{1}{N}\int_0^{v_0} C\left(\dfrac{a}{v_0}v\right)dv = \dfrac{2}{3}v_0$

$\Rightarrow \dfrac{v_{avg}}{v_0} = \dfrac{2}{3}$

$v_{rms}^2 = \dfrac{1}{N}\int_0^\infty v^2\, N(v)dv = \dfrac{1}{N}\int_0^{v_0} v^2\left(\dfrac{a}{v_0}v\right)dv = \dfrac{v_0^2}{2}$

$\Rightarrow \dfrac{v_{rms}}{v_0} = \dfrac{1}{\sqrt{2}}$

Area under the curve from $0.5\, v_0$ to v_0 is $\dfrac{3}{4}$ of total area.

6. (c,d) $v_{rms} = \sqrt{\dfrac{3RT}{M}}$; $\bar{v} = \sqrt{\dfrac{8RT}{\pi M}} = \sqrt{2.55\dfrac{RT}{M}}$

$v_p = \sqrt{\dfrac{2RT}{M}}$

7. (a,c,d) Same volume means same molecules, same temperature means same internal energy $\left(U = \dfrac{f}{2}nRT\right)$.

Average velocity is zero.

8. (a,b,c,d) Mean velocity $= \dfrac{2+3-4-1}{4} = 0$;

Mean speed $= \dfrac{2+3+4+1}{4} = 2.5$ m/sec

Mean square velocity $\overline{v^2} = \dfrac{2^2 + 3^2 + (-4)^2 + (-1)^2}{4}$

$= \dfrac{4+9+16+1}{4} = 7.5$ m²/sec²

Root mean square velocity $v_{rms} = \sqrt{\overline{v^2}} = \sqrt{7.5}$

$= 2.7386$ m/sec.

9. (a, b)

(a) In an adiabatic expansion, internal energy decreases and hence temperature decreases.

$\therefore$ From equation of state of ideal gas $PV = nRT$,
The product of P and V decreases.

(b) $v_{rms} = \sqrt{\dfrac{3kT}{m}}$

(c) The temperature in kelvin scale is not doubled.

10. (b, d) $T_1 > T_2$; So on expansion the temperature first increases, then decreases.

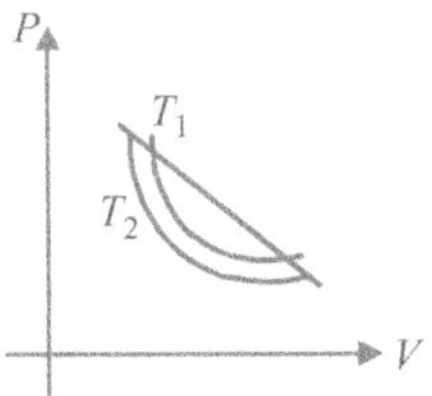

11. (b, d) As the temperature is same so v_{rms} must be same. As

$$P = \frac{1}{3}mnC^2\ ;$$ so number of molecules are in the ratio of their pressure.

12. (c, d) $$v_{rms} = \sqrt{\frac{3PV}{M}}$$

$$\therefore\ K = \frac{1}{2}Mv_{rms}^2 = \frac{3}{2}PV$$

$$K' = \frac{3}{2}(2P \times 2V) = 4K = 4 \times 3000 = 12000\ \text{J}\ .$$

13. (a, d)
$$M = \frac{M_1 + M_2}{1+1} = \frac{28 + 44}{2} = 36$$

$$\frac{n_1 + n_2}{\gamma_{mix} - 1} = \frac{n_1}{\gamma_1 - 1} + \frac{n_2}{\gamma_2 - 1}$$

$$\therefore\ \frac{\frac{1}{4} + \frac{1}{4}}{\gamma_{mix} - 1} = \frac{1/4}{1.4 - 1} + \frac{1/4}{1.3 - 1}$$

or
$$\left[\frac{2}{\gamma_{mix} - 1}\right] = \frac{1}{0.4} + \frac{1}{0.3}$$

$$\therefore\qquad \gamma_{mix} \simeq 1.343$$

14. (a, c, d) $PV = nRT\ ;\ \therefore\ n = \dfrac{PV}{RT}\ ;$ As P, V and T are same, so n must be same.
Both the gases are diatomic, so their internal energy is equal.

15. (b, c) $K_1 = \dfrac{3}{2}kT$ per molecule and $K_2 = \dfrac{3}{2}PV$

Clearly both K_1 and K_2 are equal for hydrogen and oxygen.

16. (b, c) For adiabatic process, $PV^\gamma = \text{constant}\,(k)$

Also $\ell n\,P + \gamma\ell n\,V\ =\ \ell n\,k$

$\therefore\qquad\qquad \ell n\,P\ =\ -\gamma\ell n\,V + \ell n\,k$

As slope of x is greater than y, so

$$\gamma_x\ >\ \gamma_y$$

As $\qquad C_v\ =\ \dfrac{R}{\gamma - 1}\ ;$ so $C_{v_1} < C_{v_2}$

Also $\qquad \gamma\ =\ 1 + \dfrac{2}{f}$

or $\qquad f\ =\ \left(\dfrac{2}{\gamma - 1}\right)\ ;\ \therefore\ f_1 < f_2\ .$

17. (a, c) Mean free path, $\lambda\ =\ \dfrac{1}{\sqrt{2}\pi d^2 n}$

$n = \dfrac{N}{V}\ ;$ which greatest for least value of n. n is least in case (a) and (c).

1. (a) Neutron is chargeless particle, so intermolecular force between them is neglegible small.
2. (d) Internal energy can be increased when molecules of gas will get greater velocity w.r.t. container.
3. (c) The heat will be extracted from body in evaporation of water.
4. (b) In pressure cooker, boiling point is increased due to increased pressure. Aluminium is a good conductor of heat.
5. (a) The P-T diagram is shown in figure.

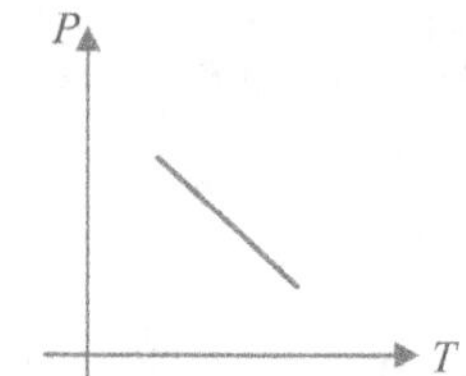

6. (b) An atom can have only translatory motion, so its degrees of freedom can be $\dfrac{1}{2}mv_x^2$, $\dfrac{1}{2}mv_y^2$, $\dfrac{1}{2}mv_z^2$.
7. (d) The specific heat of a gas can be from 0 to ∞.
8. (d) At absolute zero temperature, K.E. of the gas becomes zero. But internal energy may be due to its internal potential energy.
9. (a) At high temperature and low pressure (low density), real gas behaves like an ideal gas.
10. (b) $PV = \text{constant}$ and $v_{rms} = \sqrt{\dfrac{3kT}{m}}$
11. (a) $\qquad C_P - C_v\ =\ \text{Work done}$

$$=\ P\Delta V = R\Delta T = R \times 1 = R\ .$$

Passage (Q.1– 3)

1. (c) If n be the number of cylinders then
$$PV\ =\ n\,P'V'$$
or $\quad 1.013 \times 10^5 \times 500\ =\ n \times 15 \times 10^5 \times 0.05$
$$\therefore\qquad\qquad n\ =\ 675.$$

2. (c) $PV = nRT \Rightarrow PV = \left(\dfrac{m}{M}\right)RT$

$$\therefore\ m = \frac{PVM}{RT} = \frac{1.013 \times 10^5 \times 500 \times 2 \times 10^{-3}}{8.31 \times 273} = 44.5\ \text{kg}$$

The total weight supported

$$=\ F_b - mg = V\rho_{air}g - mg$$
$$=\ 500 \times 1.3 \times 9.8 - 44.5 \times 9.8$$
$$=\ 5934\ \text{N}$$

3. (a) $PV = \dfrac{m}{M}RT \Rightarrow m = \dfrac{PVM}{RT}$

$$= \dfrac{1.013 \times 10^5 \times 500 \times 4 \times 10^{-3}}{8.31 \times 273} = 89 \text{ kg}$$

The total weight supported by helium balloon
$$= 500 \times 1.3 \times 9.8 - 89 \times 9.8$$
$$= 5498 \text{ N}.$$

Passage (Q. 4 - 6) :

4. (a) γ of the mixture is given by

$$\dfrac{n_1 + n_2}{\gamma - 1} = \dfrac{n_1}{\gamma_1 - 1} + \dfrac{n_2}{\gamma_2 - 1}$$

or $\quad \dfrac{1 + n_2}{\gamma - 1} = \dfrac{1}{\dfrac{5}{3} - 1} + \dfrac{n_2}{\dfrac{7}{5} - 1}$

$\therefore \qquad n_2 = 2 \text{ g mole} \qquad$ *Ans.*

5. (b) $\qquad V = \sqrt{\dfrac{rRT}{M}}$

Here, $\qquad M = \dfrac{n_1 M_1 + n_2 M_2}{n_1 + n_2}$

$$= \dfrac{1 \times 4 + 2 \times 32}{1 + 2} = \dfrac{68}{3}$$

$\therefore \qquad v = \sqrt{\dfrac{(19/13) \times 8.31 \times 300}{(68/3) \times 10^{-3}}}$

$$= 400.7 \text{ m/s} \qquad \textit{Ans.}$$

6. (c) As $\qquad v = \sqrt{\dfrac{\gamma RT}{M}}$

$\therefore \qquad \dfrac{\Delta v}{v} = \dfrac{1}{2} \times \dfrac{\Delta T}{T}$

$$= \dfrac{1}{2} \times \dfrac{1}{300}$$
$$= 0.17\%$$

Passage (Q. 7 - 9) :

7. (a) The time between successive collisions,

$$t = \dfrac{1}{500} s$$

The root mean square speed

$$v_{rms} = \dfrac{2\ell}{t}$$

$$= \dfrac{2 \times 1}{1/500}$$

$$= 1000 \ m/s.$$

By the definition of rms speed,

$$v_{rms} = \sqrt{\dfrac{3RT}{M}}$$

or $\qquad 100 = \sqrt{\dfrac{3RT}{M}}$

or $\qquad 100 = \sqrt{\dfrac{3 \times 25/3 \times T}{4 \times 10^{-3}}}$

$\therefore \qquad T = 160 \ K$

8. (b) Mean kinetic energy per atom

$$= \dfrac{3}{2}kT$$
$$= \dfrac{3}{2} \times 1.38 \times 10^{-23} \times 160$$
$$= 3.312 \times 10^{-21} \text{ J}.$$

9. (c) We know that $\quad PV = \dfrac{m}{M}RT$

$\therefore \qquad m = \dfrac{PVM}{RT}$

$$= \dfrac{100 \times 1 \times 4}{\left(\dfrac{25}{3}\right) \times 160}$$

$$= 0.3 \ g \qquad \textit{Ans.}$$

Passage (Q. 10 - 12) :

10. (a) Here $\quad T = 273 + 17 = 290$ K
$\qquad d = 2 \times 1.0 \times 10^{-10}$ m
$\qquad P = 2.0 \text{ atm} = 2 \times 1.013 \times 10^5 \text{ N/m}^2$
$\qquad k = 1.37 \times 10^{-23} \text{ J/K}$

Mean free path, $\lambda = \dfrac{kT}{\sqrt{2}\pi d^2 P}$

$$= \dfrac{1.37 \times 10^{-23} \times 290}{\sqrt{2}\pi \times (2 \times 10^{-10})^2 \times (2 \times 1.013 \times 10^5)}$$

$$= 1.1 \times 10^{-7} \text{ m}$$

11. (b) Root mean square speed of nitrogen molecules

$$v_{rms} = \sqrt{\dfrac{3RT}{M}} = \sqrt{\dfrac{3 \times 8.31 \times 290}{28 \times 10^{-3}}} = 5.1 \times 10^2 \, m/s$$

The frequency of collision $\quad n = \dfrac{1}{\Delta t} = \dfrac{1}{(\lambda / v_{rms})} = \dfrac{v_{rms}}{\lambda}$

$$= \dfrac{5.1 \times 10^2}{1.1 \times 10^{-7}} = 4.6 \times 10^9 \, Hz$$

12. (c) Time taken for the collision $= \dfrac{\text{diameter of molecule}}{v_{rms}}$

$$= \dfrac{2.0 \times 10^{-10}}{5.1 \times 10^2} = 4 \times 10^{-13} s$$

13. **(A) $\rightarrow$ q, r; (B) $\rightarrow$ p, r, s; (C) $\rightarrow$ p, s; (D) $\rightarrow$ q**
14. **(A) $\rightarrow$ r, q ; (B) $\rightarrow$ r,s; (C) $\rightarrow$ p**
    (A) All ideal gases obey gas equation at all temperature.
    (B) All real gases obey gas equation at high temperature, at which intermolecular forces are zero.

    (C) Mean free path, $\lambda = \dfrac{kT}{\sqrt{2}\pi d^2 P}$; so it decreases with increase in pressure.

15. **(A) $\rightarrow$ r; (B) $\rightarrow$ s; (C) $\rightarrow$ p ; (D) $\rightarrow$ q**
16. **(A) $\rightarrow$ q; (B) $\rightarrow$ p; (C) $\rightarrow$ s ; (D) $\rightarrow$ r**

Solutions EXERCISE-6.5

1. The pressure exerted by the weight of the piston

$$= \frac{mg}{A}$$

$$= \frac{1 \times 10}{10 \times 10^{-4}}$$

$$= 1 \times 10^4 \text{ N/m}^2$$

Thus initial pressure of the gas

$$P_1 = 100 \times 10^{-3} + 10^4$$
$$= 110 \times 10^3 \text{ N/m}^2$$
$$V_1 = A \ell_1$$
$$= A \times 0.20$$
$$P_2 = 10^4 \text{ N/m}^2$$

Using $P_1 V_1 = P_2 V_2$

or $P_1 (A \ell_1) = P_2 (A \ell_2)$

$$\therefore \quad \ell_2 = \frac{P_1 \ell_1}{P_2}$$

$$= \frac{110 \times 10^3}{1 \times 10^4} \times 0.20$$
$$= 2.2 \text{ m} \qquad \textbf{Ans.}$$

2. v_1 and v_2 are the rms velocities at temperatures T_1 and T_2 respectively, then

$$\frac{v_1}{v_2} = \sqrt{\frac{T_1}{T_2}}$$

or $$\eta = \sqrt{\frac{T_1}{T_2}}$$

$$\therefore \quad T_2 = \frac{T_1}{\eta^2}$$

For the adiabatic process,

$$\left(\frac{V_2}{V_1}\right)^{\gamma - 1} = \frac{T_1}{T_2}$$

$$= \eta^2$$

For diatomic gas, $\gamma = 5$

and $\eta = 1.5$

After simplifying, we get

$$V_2 = 7.6 V_1 \qquad \textbf{Ans.}$$

3. We have $$\frac{v_1}{v_2} = \sqrt{\frac{T_1}{T_2}}$$

$$\therefore \quad \frac{1}{2} = \sqrt{\frac{T_1}{T_2}}$$

or $$T_2 = 4 T_1$$

$$\therefore \quad \Delta T = T_2 - T_1$$

or $$3 T_1 = 3 \times (273 + 27)$$
$$= 900 \text{ K}$$

The heat required $Q = \mu C_v \Delta T$

$$= \left[\frac{14}{28}\right] \times \frac{5}{2} \times 8.31 \times 900$$

$$= 9315 \text{ J} \qquad \textbf{Ans.}$$

4. The initial pressure of gas

$$P_1 = 830 \text{ mm} - 30 \text{ mm}$$
$$= 800 \text{ mm}$$

and $$T_1 = T$$

If P is now pressure in the jar, then final pressure of the gas

$$P_2 = (P - 25)$$

and $$T_2 = \left(T - \frac{T}{100}\right)$$

We know that $$\frac{P_1}{T_1} = \frac{P_2}{T_2}$$

or $$\frac{800}{T} = \frac{P - 25}{\left(T - \dfrac{T}{100}\right)}$$

$$\therefore \quad P = 817 \text{ mm of } Hg \qquad \textbf{Ans.}$$

Solutions EXERCISE-6.6

1. Suppose the air column in the tube becomes $(15 + x)$, then

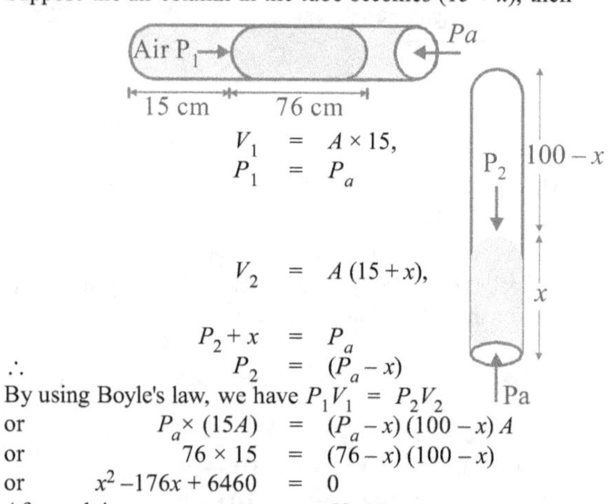

$$V_1 = A \times 15,$$
$$P_1 = P_a$$

$$V_2 = A (15 + x),$$

$$P_2 + x = P_a$$

$$\therefore \quad P_2 = (P_a - x)$$

By using Boyle's law, we have $P_1 V_1 = P_2 V_2$

or $$P_a \times (15A) = (P_a - x)(100 - x) A$$

or $$76 \times 15 = (76 - x)(100 - x)$$

or $$x^2 - 176x + 6460 = 0$$

After solving, $x = 52.17$ cm

Thus mercury thread will decrease in length by 23.8 cm.

2. At the bottom of the lake, $V_1 = 1 \text{ cm}^3,$

$$P_1 = P_a + 40 \, m$$
$$= 10.3 + 40$$
$$= 50.3 \, m \text{ of water.}$$
$$T_1 = 273 + 12$$
$$= 285K.$$

At the surface, $$P_2 = P_a$$
$$= 10.3 \, m \text{ of water.}$$
$$T_2 = 273 + 35$$
$$= 308 \text{ K.}$$

Using $$\frac{P_1 V_1}{T_1} = \frac{P_2 V_2}{T_2}$$

or $$V_2 = \frac{P_1 V_1 T_2}{P_2 T_1}$$

$$= \frac{50.3 \times 1 \times 10^{-6} \times 308}{10.3 \times 285}$$

$$= 5.275 \times 10^{-6} \text{ m}^3 \qquad \textbf{Ans.}$$

3. Given,

$$P_1 = 15 + 1$$
$$= 16 \text{ atm (absolute)}$$
$$V_1 = 30 \times 10^{-3} \text{ m}^3,$$
$$T_1 = 273 + 27$$
$$= 300 \ K.$$
$$P_2 = 12 \text{ atm},$$
$$T_2 = 273 + 17$$
$$= 290 \ K.$$

We have

$$PV = \frac{m}{M}RT$$

$$\therefore \quad m = \frac{P_1 VM}{RT_1}$$

$$= \left[\frac{(16 \times 1.013 \times 10^5) \times (30 \times 10^{-3}) \times (32 \times 10^{-3})}{8.31 \times 300}\right]$$

$$= 0.624 \text{ kg}.$$

Finally

$$m' = \frac{P_2 VM}{RT_2}$$

$$= \left[\frac{(12 \times 1.013 \times 10^5) \times (30 \times 10^{-3}) \times (32 \times 10^{-3})}{8.31 \times 290}\right]$$

$$= 0.484 \text{ kg}$$

The mass of the oxygen taken out

$$= m - m'$$
$$= 0.624 - 0.484$$
$$= 0.141 \text{ kg}. \qquad \textbf{Ans.}$$

4. (c) The value,

$$\frac{PV}{T} = \mu R$$

$$= \left(\frac{1}{32}\right) \times 8.31$$

$$= 0.26 \text{ J/K} \qquad \textbf{Ans.}$$

(d) For hydrogen, $\dfrac{PV}{T} = \mu R$

$$= \left(\frac{1}{2}\right) \times 8.31$$

$$= 4.15 \text{ J/K} \qquad \textbf{Ans.}$$

For the same value as in case (c), we have

$$0.26 = \left[\frac{m}{M_H}\right] \times 8.31$$

$$\therefore \quad m = 6.3 \times 10^{-2} \text{ g}$$
$$= 6.3 \times 10^{-5} \text{ kg} \qquad \textbf{Ans.}$$

5. By gas law,

$$\frac{P_1}{T_1} = \frac{P_2}{T_2}$$

$$\therefore \quad P_2 = \frac{T_2}{T_1} P_1$$

$$= \frac{600}{300} \times 1$$

$$= 2 \text{ atm}$$

For the equilibrium of the cork, we have

$$P_2 A = f_r + P_a A$$

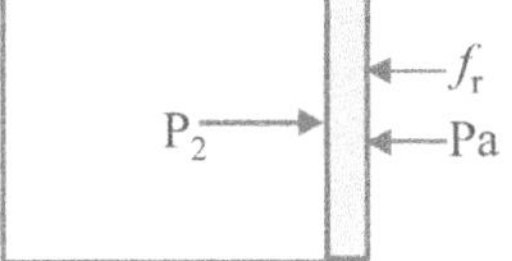

$$\therefore \quad f_r = (P_2 - P_a) A$$
$$= 1 \text{ atm} \times A$$
$$= (1.013 \times 10^5) \times \pi r^2$$

If normal reaction N is distributed uniform over the perimeter, then

$$f_r = \mu\left[\left(\frac{dN}{dl}\right) \times 2\pi r\right]$$

$$\therefore \quad \frac{dN}{dl} = \frac{f_r}{\mu \times 2\pi r}$$

$$= \frac{1.013 \times 10^5 \times \pi r^2}{0.2 \times 2\pi r}$$

$$= \frac{1.013 \times 10^5 \times 0.05}{0.2 \times 2}$$

$$= 1.25 \times 10^4 \ N/m \qquad \textbf{Ans.}$$

6. We know that, for n molecules
$$PV = nkT$$

$$\therefore \quad P = \left(\frac{n}{V}\right)kT$$

$$= (5 \times 10^6) \times (1.38 \times 10^{-23}) \times 3$$
$$= 2.07 \times 10^{-16} \ N/m^2 \quad \textbf{Ans.}$$

7. In adiabatic process,

$$V_2^{\gamma-1} T_2 = V_1^{\gamma-1} T_1$$

$$\therefore \quad \frac{T_2}{T_1} = \left[\frac{V_1}{V_2}\right]^{\gamma-1}$$

$$= \left[\frac{1}{\eta}\right]^{\gamma-1} \qquad \text{...(i)}$$

The number of molecules in unit volume

$$n = \frac{\mu N}{V}$$

$$= \frac{\mu V}{\dfrac{\mu RT}{P}}$$

$$= \frac{P}{\left(\dfrac{R}{N}\right)T}$$

$$= \frac{P}{kT}$$

The volume swept by the molecules in 1 second
$$= A \times \text{distance travelled in 1 sec.}$$
$$= A \times v_{\text{rms}}$$

These molecules move along six possible directions : $\pm x$, $\pm y$ and $\pm z$.

Thus in any direction, the numbers are $= \dfrac{1}{6} nA v_{\text{rms}}$

These are the number of collisions per second

As

$$v_{\text{rms}} = \sqrt{\frac{3RT}{M}}$$

$$\therefore \quad A = \frac{1}{6} \times \frac{P}{kT} \times \sqrt{\frac{3RT}{M}}$$

Also
$$A = \frac{1}{6} \times \frac{\mu N}{V} \times \sqrt{\frac{3RT}{M}}$$

$\therefore$
$$A \propto \sqrt{\frac{T}{V^2}}$$

Thus
$$\frac{A_1}{A_2} = \sqrt{\frac{T_1}{T^2} \times \frac{V_2^2}{V_1^2}} \qquad \ldots(ii)$$

From equations (i) and (ii), we get
$$\frac{A_1}{A_2} = \sqrt{\eta^{\gamma-1} \times \eta^2}$$
$$= \eta^{\frac{\gamma+1}{2}} \qquad \textit{Ans.}$$

In the answer given in exercise, i used for number of degrees of freedom.

8. By conservation of matter, we have
$$\mu + \mu = \mu_1 + \mu_2$$
or
$$2\frac{PV}{RT} = \frac{P'V}{RT_1} + \frac{P'V}{RT_2}$$
or
$$\frac{2P}{T} = P'\left[\frac{1}{T_1} + \frac{1}{T_2}\right]$$
$\therefore$
$$P' = \frac{2P}{T}\left[\frac{T_1 T_2}{T_1 + T_2}\right]$$
$$= \frac{2 \times 76}{273}\left[\frac{273 \times (273 + 62)}{273 + (273 + 62)}\right]$$
$$= 83.75 \text{ cm of mercury.} \qquad \textit{Ans.}$$

9. The speed of sound in any gas is given by
$$v = \sqrt{\frac{\gamma RT}{M}}.$$

Thus for neon and water vapour, we have
$$\frac{v_{neon}}{v_{water\,vap}} = \sqrt{\frac{\gamma_{neon}}{\gamma_{water\,vap}} \times \frac{M_{water\,vap}}{M_{neon}}}$$
$$= \sqrt{\frac{1.67}{1.33} \times \frac{1.8}{2.02}}$$
$$= 1.06 \qquad \textit{Ans.}$$

10. See the solution of quesion 7.

11. At constant pressure $\dfrac{V_1}{T_1} = \dfrac{V_2}{T_2}$

or
$$\frac{A\ell_1}{T_1} = \frac{A\ell_2}{T_2}$$
$\therefore$
$$\ell_2 = \frac{T_2}{T_1}\ell_1$$
$$= \frac{400}{300} \times 1$$
$$= \frac{4}{3}m \qquad \textit{Ans.}$$

Again by $TV^{\gamma-1} = $ constant, we have
$$T_3 = T_2\left(\frac{V_2}{V_3}\right)^{\gamma-1}$$
$$= 400 \times (4/3)^{1.4-1}$$
$$= 488.8\ K. \qquad \textit{Ans.}$$

12. The ideal gas equation
$$PV = nRT$$
Given
$$P = P_0 - AV^2,$$
$\therefore$
$$(P_0 - AV^2)V = nRT$$
or
$$P_0 V - AV^3 = nRT \qquad \ldots(i)$$
Differentiating above equation w.r.t. V, we have
$$P_0 - 3AV^2 = nR\left(\frac{dT}{dV}\right).$$

For highest value of $T, dT/dV = 0$
or
$$P_0 - 3AV^2 = 0$$
$\therefore$
$$V = \sqrt{\frac{P_0}{3A}}$$

Now from equation (i), we have
$$\left(P_0 - A \times \frac{P_0}{3A}\right)\left(\sqrt{\frac{P_0}{3A}}\right) = nRT_{max}$$
$\therefore$
$$T_{max} = \frac{2P_0}{3nR}\sqrt{\frac{P_0}{3A}} \qquad \textit{Ans.}$$

Laws of Thermodynamics
(457-526)

Fig. 7.1

Thermodynamics versus mechanics

Mechanics deals with motion of the body (system) as a whole and its external K.E. and P.E. Thermodynamics deals with the motion of particles of the body and its internal K.E. and P.E.

7.1 Thermodynamical Terms

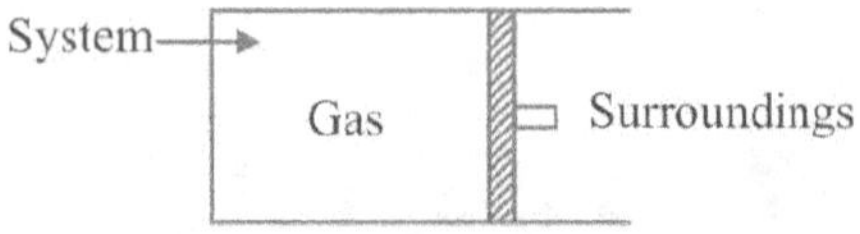

(i)   **Thermodynamical system:** A thermodynamical system is an assembly of large number of particles which can be described by thermodynamic variables like pressure (P), volume (V), temperature (T).

(ii)   **Surroundings:** Everything outside the system which can have a direct effect on the system is called surroundings. The gas cylinder in the kitchen is the thermodynamic system and the relevant part of the kitchen is the surroundings.

(iii)   **An adiabatic wall:** The wall which prevent the passage of matter and energy.

(iv)   **Diathermic wall:** It prevent the passage of matter but allow the passage of energy. An aluminium can is an example of a container whose walls are diathermic.

(v)   **An isolated system:** In this type of system neither the mass nor the energy can be exchanged with the surroundings.

(vi)   **Equation of state:** The relationship between the pressure, volume and temperature of the thermodynamical system is called equation of state.
For example: $PV = nRT$.

7.2 Internal energy

There are intermolecular forces in real gases, so they possess internal potential energy (U_p). If the volume of the gas increases, work is to be done by the gas against intermolecular attraction and so its potential energy increases $\left(U_p = -\dfrac{k}{r}\right)$. The molecules of a gas are always in motion. The motion may be translational, rotational or vibrational. Hence molecules of gas possess internal kinetic energy (U_k). With increase in temperature the average kinetic energy of the gas molecules also increases.

$$[U_k = \frac{3}{2}RT \text{ (monoatomic gas)}].$$

Thus internal energy of a system is the sum of its internal kinetic and internal potential energy. The internal energy (U) can be written as:

$$U = U_k + U_P.$$

7.3 Internal Energy of An ideal Gas

In ideal gases there are no intermolecular forces, so internal potential energy of an ideal gas is zero. The internal energy of an ideal gas is only due to its internal kinetic energy, so we can write $U = U_k$. As internal kinetic energy is the function of temperature, so internal energy of an ideal gas depends only on temperature.

More about internal energy

1.   Internal energy of an ideal gas;

$$U = \frac{3}{2}RT \qquad \text{for monoatomic gas}$$

$$U = \frac{5}{2}RT \qquad \text{for diatomic gas}$$

2. If the temperature of the gas changes by ΔT, then change in internal energy of the gas

$$\Delta U = nC_V\Delta T.$$

For one mole

$$\Delta U = C_V\Delta T$$

$$\therefore \quad C_V = \frac{\Delta U}{\Delta T} \quad \text{or} \quad C_V = \frac{dU}{dT}$$

3. In isothermal process, $\Delta U = 0$ and hence $\Delta U = 0$.
4. In cyclic process, $\Delta U = 0$ and hence $\Delta U = 0$.
5. For an isolated system, $\Delta Q = 0$, $\Delta W = 0$ and hence $\Delta U = 0$.
6. The change in internal energy depends only on the initial and final states of the system.

7.4 Work in Volume Change

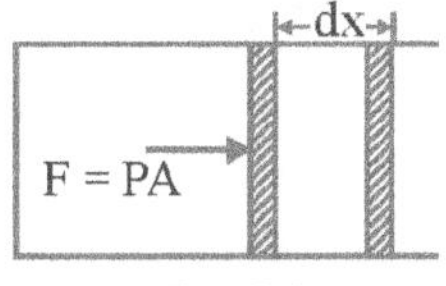

Fig. 7.2

Let us consider a gas or liquid contained in a cylinder equipped with a movable piston, as shown in *Fig. 7.2*. Suppose that the cylinder has a cross-sectional area A and the pressure exerted by the gas at the piston is P.

The force exerted by gas on the piston

$$F = PA$$

If the piston moves out a small distance dx, the work done

$$dW = Fdx = PAdx$$
$$= PdV$$

where $dV = Adx$, is the change in volume of the gas.

The total work done by the gas when its volume changes from V_i to V_f

$$W = \int_{V_i}^{V_f} PdV$$

If the pressure remain constant while volume changes, then the work done

$$W = P(V_f - V_i) = P\Delta V$$

Indicator diagram

The state of a thermodynamical system can be understand completely if only two thermodynamical variables are known because the third variable gets automatically fixed by $PV = nRT$. The graphical representation of the state of system with the help of two variables is called an **indicator diagram**.

Cyclic process and non - cyclic process

If a system having gone through a change, returns to its initial state then process is called a cyclic process. If system does not return to its initial state, the process is called non-cyclic process.

Work done from P - V diagram

Fig. 7.5 shows a P - V diagram for a system under going expansion from the state A (P_i,V_i) to B (P_f,V_f). Suppose that the volume increases by small amount dV in which pressure assumed to be constant (P).

The work done in small change in volume

$$dW = PdV$$
$$= \text{area of the shaded strip}$$

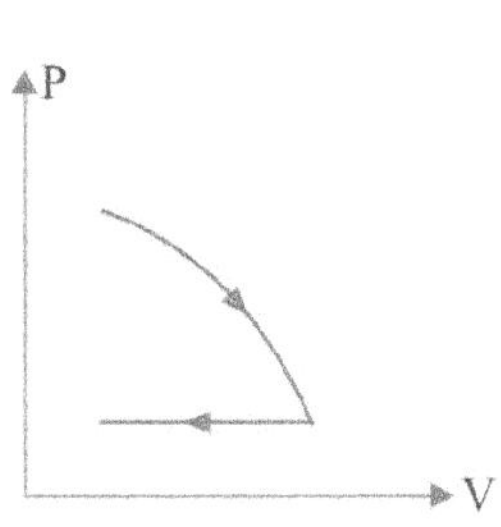

(a) cyclic process

Fig. 7.3

(b) Non-cyclic process

Fig. 7.4

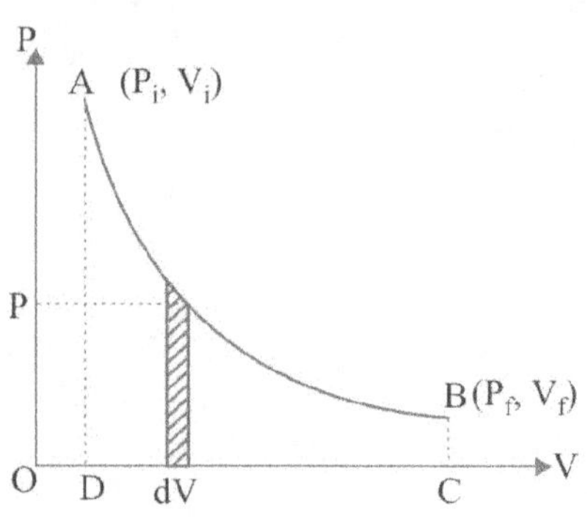

Fig. 7.5

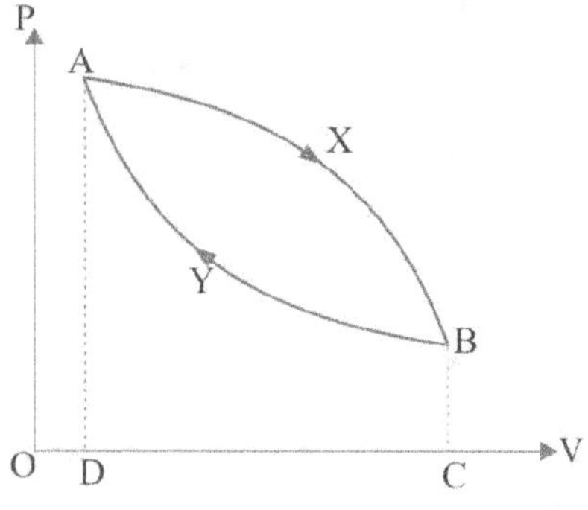

Fig. 7.6

The total work done can be obtained by adding the areas of all such strips between C and D.

Thus work done

$$W = \text{area } ABCD$$

Sign conventions

Work done by the system (expansion) taken as position. Work done on the system (compression) taken as negative.

7.5 Work Done in Cyclic Process

Suppose gas expands from initial state A to final state B via the path AXB.
The work done in this expansion

$$W_X = +\text{area } AXBCDA$$

Now gas returns to its initial state B via path BYA.
Work done during this compression

$$W_Y = -\text{area } BYADCB$$

The net work done

$$
\begin{aligned}
W &= W_X + W_Y \\
&= \text{area } AXBCDA - \text{area } BYADCB \\
&= +\text{area } AXBYA
\end{aligned}
$$

Thus for a cyclic process

(i)   Work done in complete cycle is equal to the area of the loop representing the cycle.

(ii)   If the closed loop is traced in the clockwise direction, the expansion curve lies above the compression curve. ($W_X > W_Y$), the area of loop is positive.

(iii) If the closed loop is traced in the anticlockwise direction, the expansion curve lies below the compression curve ($W_X < W_Y$), the area of the loop is negative.

More cyclic processes

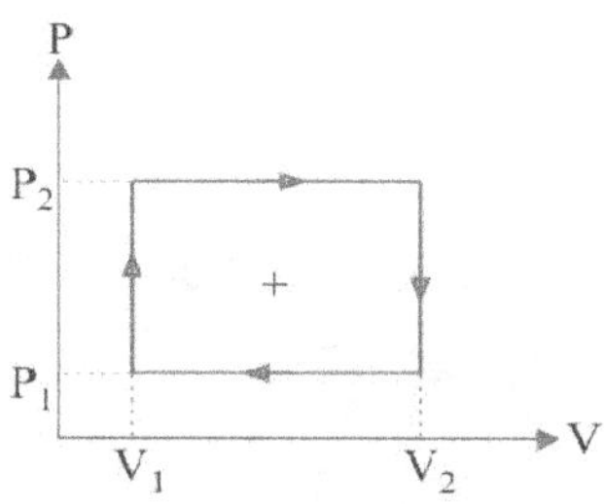

$$W = \text{area of rectangle}$$
$$= (P_2 - P_1) \times (V_2 - V_1)$$

Fig. 7.7

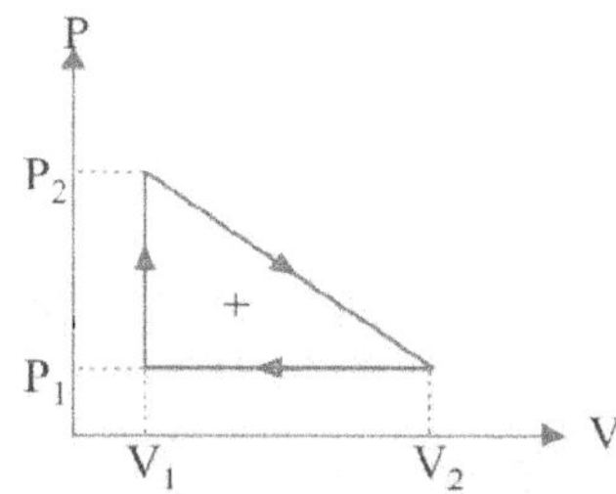

$$W = \text{area of rectangle}$$
$$= \frac{1}{2}(P_2 - P_1) \times (V_2 - V_1)$$

Fig. 7.8

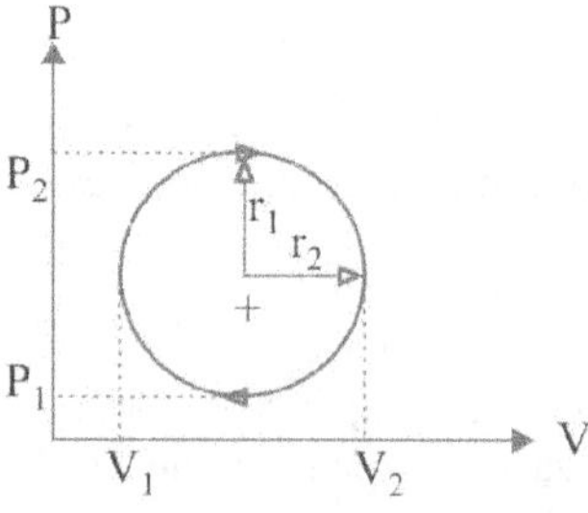

$$W = \text{area of the circle}$$
$$= \pi\, r_1 r_2 = \pi \frac{(P_2 - P_1)}{2} \times \frac{(V_2 - V_1)}{2}$$

Fig. 7.9

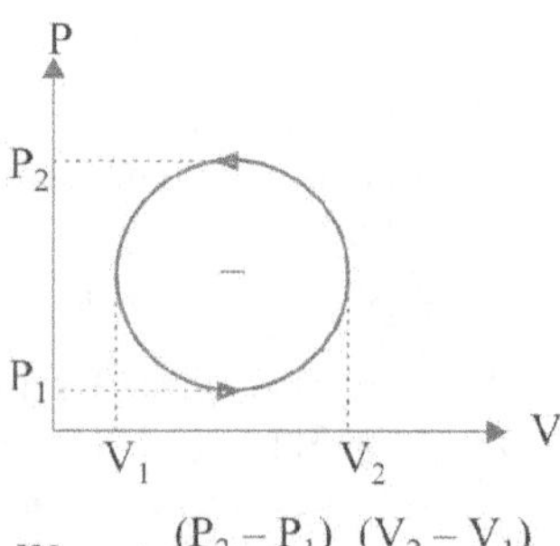

$$W = -\pi \frac{(P_2 - P_1)}{2} \times \frac{(V_2 - V_1)}{2}$$

Fig. 7.10

Work done in non-cyclic process

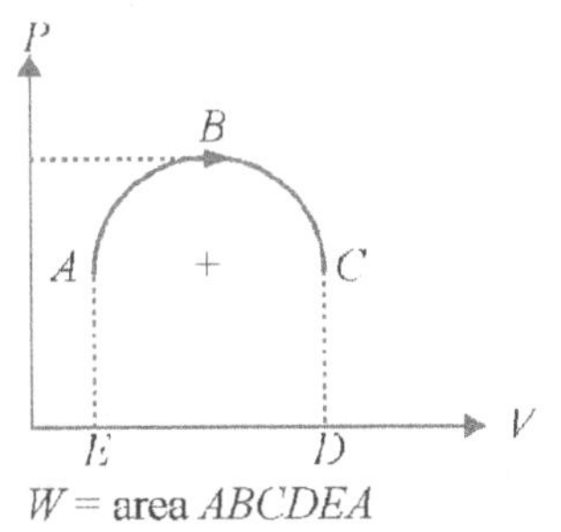

W = area $ABCDEA$

Fig. 7.11

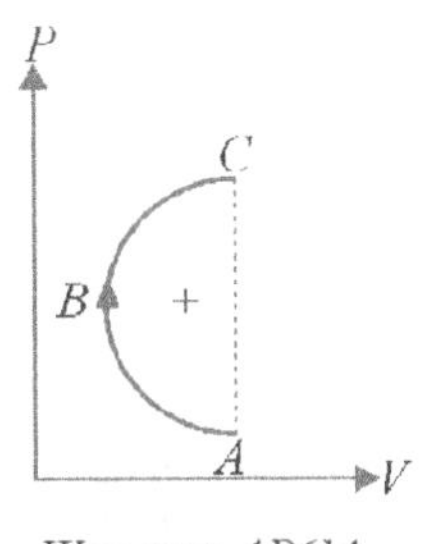

W = area $ABCA$

Fig. 7.12

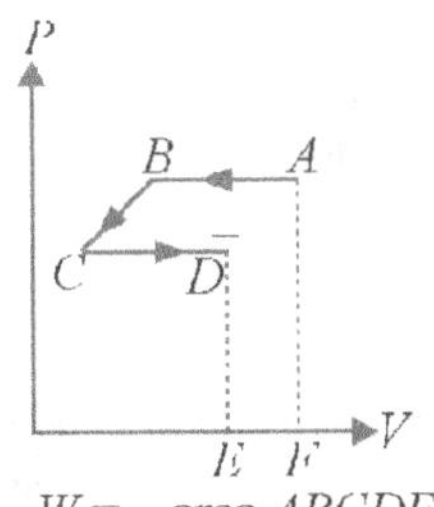

W = – area $ABCDEFA$

Fig. 7.13

Ex. 1 A gas expands in a piston - cylinder device from volume V_1 to V_2, the process being described by $P = \dfrac{a}{V} + b$, a and b are constants. Find work done in the process.

Sol.

Work done

$$W = \int_{V_1}^{V_2} P\,dV$$

$$= \int_{V_1}^{V_2} \left(\frac{a}{V} + b\right) dV$$

$$= \left| a\ell n V + bV \right|_{V_1}^{V_2}$$

$$= (a\ell n V_2 + bV_2) - (a\ell n V_1 + bV_1)$$

$$= a\ell n\left(\frac{V_2}{V_1}\right) + b(V_2 - V_1) \qquad \textit{Ans.}$$

Ex. 2 Find the minimum attainable pressure of ideal gas in the process $T = T_0 + \alpha V^2$, where T_0 and α are positive constants and V is the volume of one mole of gas. Draw the approximate P vs V plot of this process.

Sol.

Given , $\qquad T = T_0 + \alpha V^2 \qquad$ ...(i)

For one mole of a gas $PV = RT$

or $\qquad V = \dfrac{RT}{P}$

Substituting this value in equation (i), we get

$$T = T_0 + \alpha\left(\frac{RT}{P}\right)^2 = T_0 + \alpha\frac{R^2 T^2}{P^2}$$

or $\qquad TP^2 = T_0 P^2 + \alpha R^2 T^2$

or $\qquad P = \sqrt{\alpha}\, RT(T - T_0)^{-1/2} \qquad$ ...(ii)

After differentiating , we get

$$\frac{dP}{dT} = \sqrt{\alpha}\, R\left[(T - T_0)^{-1/2} - \frac{1}{2}T(T - T_0)^{-3/2}\right]$$

For minimum pressure,

$$\frac{dP}{dT} = 0$$

$$\therefore \qquad 0 = \sqrt{\alpha}\, R\left[(T - T_0)^{-1/2} - \frac{1}{2}T(T - T_0)^{-3/2}\right]$$

After solving , $\qquad T = 2T_0$

From equation (ii)

$$P_{min} = \sqrt{\alpha}\, R.2T_0(2T_0 - T_0)^{-1/2}$$

$$= 2R\sqrt{\alpha T_0}$$

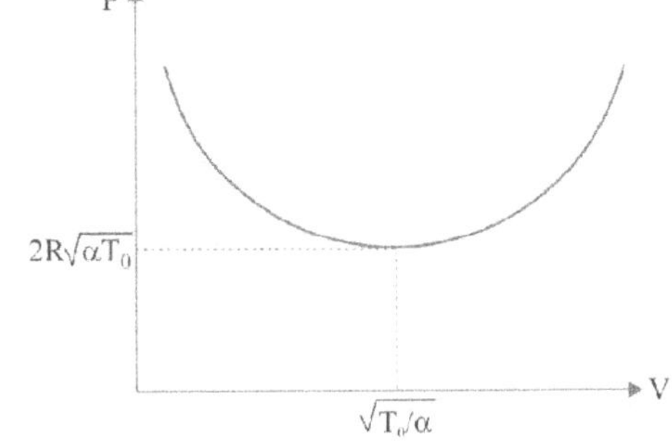

Fig. 7.14

7.6 First Law of Thermodynamics

The first law of thermodynamics is based on conservation of energy. According to this law heat Q supplied to a system is equal to the sum of the change in internal energy (ΔU) and work done by the system (W). Thus we can write

$$Q = \Delta U + W$$

More about first law of thermodynamics :

1.   Heat supplied to the system taken as positive and heat given by the system taken as negative.

2.   It makes no different between heat and work. It does not indicate that why the whole of heat energy cannot be converted into work.

3. Heat and work depend on the initial and final states but on the path also. The change in internal energy depends only on initial and final states of the system.

4. The work done by the system against constant pressure P is $W = P\Delta V$. So the first law of thermodynamics can be written as $Q = \Delta U + P\Delta V$.

5. Differential form of the first law;

$$dQ = dU + dW$$
or
$$dQ = dU + PdV.$$

Ex. 3 **1.0 m³ of water is converted into 1671m³ of steam at atmospheric pressure and 100°C temperature. The latent heat of vapourisation of water is 2.3×10^6 J/ kg. If 2.0 kg of water be converted into steam at atmospheric pressure and 100°C temperature, then how much will be the increase in its internal energy? Density of water is 1.0×10^3 kg/m³, atmospheric pressure = 1.01×10^5 N/m².**

Sol.

Heat given to water to change into steam

$$Q = ML = 2.0 \times 2.3 \times 10^6$$
$$= 4.6 \times 10^6 \text{J}$$

Volume of water $\quad V = \dfrac{\text{Mass}}{\text{density}} = \dfrac{2.0}{10^3}$

$$= 2.0 \times 10^{-3} \text{ m}^3$$

Volume of steam formed will be
$$= 2.0 \times 10^{-3} \times 1671$$
$$= 3342 \times 10^{-3} \text{m}^3$$

The change in volume in the process
$$\Delta V = V = 3342 \times 10^{-3} - 2.0 \times 10^{-3}$$
$$= 3340 \times 10^{-3} \text{m}^3$$

The work done against the atmospheric pressure
$$W = P\Delta V$$
$$= (1.01 \times 10^5) \times (3340 \times 10^{-3})$$
$$= 0.337 \times 10^6 \text{J}$$

By first law of thermodynamics
$$Q = \Delta U + W$$
$$\therefore \quad \Delta U = Q - W$$
$$= 4.6 \times 10^6 - 0.337 \times 10^6$$
$$= 4.263 \times 10^6 \text{ J`} \qquad \textit{Ans.}$$

Here positive value of ΔU indicates that internal energy in the process increases.

Ex. 4 **At 0°C and normal atmospheric pressure, the volume of 1g of water increases from 1cm³ to 1.091 cm³ on freezing. What will be the change in its internal energy? Normal atmospheric pressure is 1.013×10^5 N/m² and latent heat of fusion of ice = 80 cal/ g.**

Sol.

Heat released by water on freezing
$$Q = -mL$$
$$= -1 \times 80 = -80 \text{ cal} = -336 \text{ J}$$

During freezing water expands against the atmospheric pressure. Hence work done in the process
$$W = P\Delta V = (1.013 \times 10^5) \times (1.091 - 1) \times 10^{-6}$$
$$= 0.092 \text{ J}$$

By first law of thermodynamics
$$Q = \Delta U + W$$
or
$$-336 = \Delta U + 0.092$$
$$\therefore \quad \Delta U = -336.092 \text{ J} \qquad \textit{Ans.}$$

Ex. 5 **A system is taken from an initial state i to a final state f as shown in the *Fig. 7.15*. When it goes from i to f via iaf it is found that $Q = 70$ cal and $W = 40$ cal, and along the path ibf, $Q = 40$ cal.**

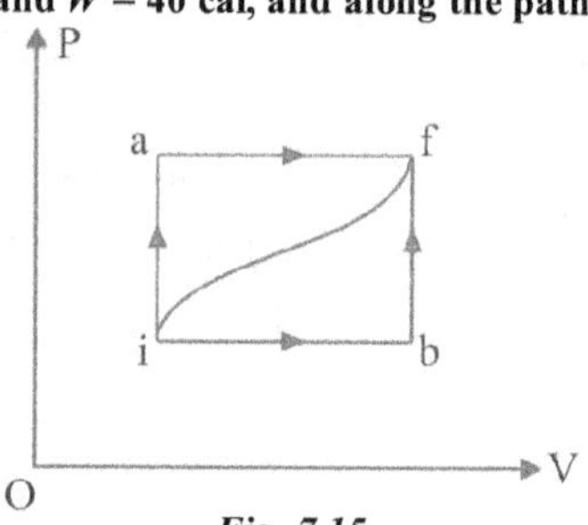

Fig. 7.15

(a) What is W along the path ibf ?

(b) If $W = -15$ cal for the curved path *fi*, what is Q for the path?

(c) If internal energy at *i* (U_i) =20 cal, what is U_f

(d) If $U_b = 25$ cal, what is Q for the process *ib*?

Sol.

From first law of thermodynamics
$$\Delta U = Q - W$$
or
$$U_f - U_i = 70 - 40 = 30 \text{ cal}$$

As ΔU is independent of path, so it remain same for *ibf* or if.

(a) Along path *ibf*, $Q = +40$ cal, ΔU +30 cal

As $\quad Q = \Delta U + W$
$$\therefore \quad W = Q - \Delta U = +40 - 30 = 10 \text{ cal}$$

(b) For the return path *fi*,
$$\Delta U = U_i - U_f = -(U_f - U_i) = -30 \text{ cal}$$
and
$$W = -15 \text{ cal}$$
$$\therefore \quad Q = W + \Delta U$$
$$= -15 - 30 = -45 \text{ cal}$$

(c)
$$U_i = 20 \text{ cal}$$

We have, $U_f - U_i = +30$
$$\therefore \quad U_f = 30 + U_i = 30 + 20 = 50 \text{ cal}$$

(d) $U_i = 20$ cal and $U_b = 25$ cal
$$\therefore \quad \Delta U = U_b - U_i = 25 - 20 = 5 \text{ cal}$$
$$W_{ib} = W_{ibf} = 10 \text{ cal}$$
$$Q = \Delta U + W$$
$$= 5 + 10 = 15 \text{ cal}$$

Ex. 6 **Air is contained in a piston - cylinder arrangement as shown in *Fig. 7.16* with a cross - sectional area of 4 cm² and an initial volume of 20 cc. The air is initially at a pressure of 1 atm and temperature of 20°C. The piston is connected to a spring whose spring constant is $k = 10^4$ N/m, and the spring is initially undeformed. How much heat must be added to the air to increase the pressure to 3 atm. (For air, $C_V = 718$ J/kg°C, molecular mass of air 28.97)**

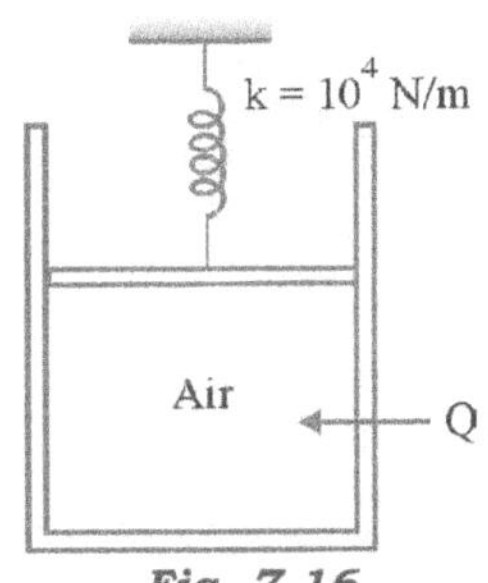

Fig. 7.16

Sol.

When pressure changes from 1 atm to 3 atm , the change in pressure
$$P = 2 \text{ atm}$$
$$= 2 \times 1 \times 10^5 \text{ N/m}^2$$
The force exerted on the piston
$$F = PA = 2 \times 10^5 \times 4 \times 10^{-4}$$
$$= 80 \text{ N}$$
The compression of the spring
$$x = \frac{F}{k} = \frac{80}{10^4} = 0.008 \text{m}$$
The change in volume of the air due to displacement of piston by x
$$\Delta V = Ax = 4 \times 10^{-4} \times 0.008$$
$$= 3.2 \times 10^{-6} \text{m}^3$$
$\therefore$ Final volume $V_2 = V_1 + \Delta V$
$$= 20 \times 10^{-6} + 3.2 \times 10^{-6}$$
$$= 23.2 \times 10^{-6} \text{ m}^3$$
By equation of state
$$\frac{P_1 V_1}{T_1} = \frac{P_2 V_2}{T_2}$$
$$T_2 = \frac{P_2 V_2 T_1}{P_1 V_1}$$
$$= \left(\frac{3}{1}\right) \times \frac{(23.2 \times 10^{-6})}{(20 \times 10^{-6})} \times (273 + 20)$$
$$= 1020 \text{ K}$$
The change in internal energy of air
$$\Delta U = m C_V \Delta T$$
$$= (2.38 \times 10^{-5}) \times 718 \times (1020 - 293)$$
$$= 12.42 \text{ J}$$
Work done in compressing the spring by x
$$W = \frac{1}{2} k x^2 = \frac{10^4}{2} \times (0.008)^2 = 0.32 \text{ J}$$
From first law of thermodynamics
$$Q = \Delta U + W = 12.42 + 0.32 = 12.74 \text{ J } \textbf{\textit{Ans.}}$$

Ex. 7 Consider the cyclic process *ABCA*, shown in *Fig. 7.17* performed on a sample of 2.0 mole of an ideal gas. A total of 1200 J of heat is withdrawn from the sample in the process. Find the work done by the gas during the part *BC*.

Sol.

In the cyclic process
$$\Delta U = 0$$
From first law of thermodynamics for the cyclic process
$$Q = \Delta U + W$$
$\therefore$
$$W = Q - \Delta U = -1200 - 0$$
$$= -1200 \text{ J}$$

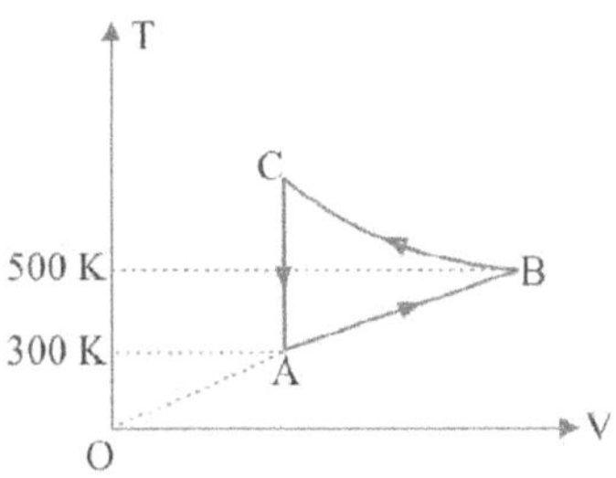

Fig. 7.17

From C to A, $\Delta V = 0$ $\therefore$ $W_{CA} = 0$
For the whole cycle
$$W_{AB} + W_{BC} + W_{CA} = W$$
$$= -1200$$
As $W_{CA} = 0, \therefore$ $W_{AB} + W_{BC} = -1200 \text{ J}$ ...(i)
Work done from A to B :

In the process $V \propto T$, so pressure remains constant.
We know that $PV = nRT$
or $P\Delta V = nR\Delta T$
$\therefore$ $W_{AB} = P\Delta V = nR\Delta T = 2 \times 8.31 \times (500 - 300)$
$$= 3324 \text{ J}$$
Substituting this value in equation (i), we get
$$3324 + W_{BC} = -1200$$
$\therefore$ $W_{BC} = -4524 \text{ J}$ *Ans.*

Ex. 8 *Fig.7.18* **shows the variation in the internal energy U with the volume V of 2.0 mole of an ideal gas in a cyclic process abcda. The temperature of the gas at b and c are 500 K and 300 K respectively. Calculate the heat absorbed by the gas during the process.**

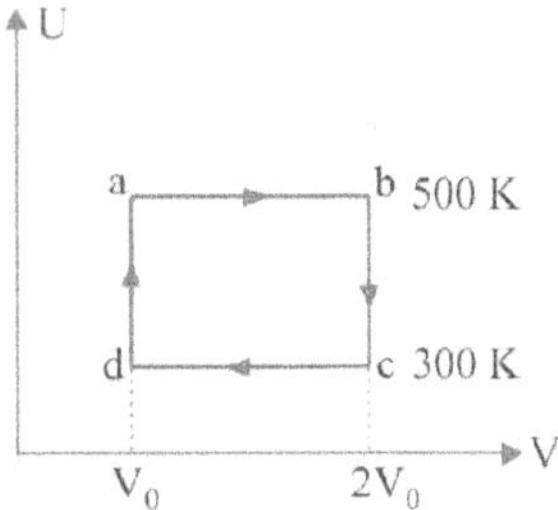

Fig. 7.18

Sol.

In the process a to b and c to d
As $\Delta U = 0$, $\therefore$ $\Delta T = 0$ or T constant
$$W = \int_{V_i}^{V_f} P \, dV$$
We have $PV = nRT \Rightarrow P = \frac{nRT}{V}$
$\therefore$
$$W = \int_{V_i}^{V_f} (nRT) \frac{dV}{V}$$

$$= nRT \mid \ell nV \mid_{V_i}^{V_f} = nRT\ell n\frac{V_f}{V_i}$$

$$W_{ab} = nRT_b\ell n\frac{2V_0}{V_0} = 2R \times 500\,\ell n\,2 = 1000\,R\ell n2$$

and $\quad\quad W_{cd} = nRT_c\ell n\frac{V_0}{2V_0} = 2R \times 300\,\ell n\frac{1}{2} = -600\,R\ell n2$

There is no volume changes from b to c and from d to a, so

$$W_{bc} = W_{da} = 0$$

The work done in complete cycle

$$\begin{aligned} W &= W_{ab} + W_{bc} + W_{cd} + W_{da} \\ &= 1000\,R\,\ell n2 + 0 - 600\,R\,\ell n2 + 0 \\ &= 400\,R\,\ell n2 \end{aligned}$$

From first law of thermodynamics

$$\begin{aligned} Q &= \Delta U + W \\ &= 0 + 400\,R\,\ell n2 \\ &= 400\,R\,\ell n2 \end{aligned}$$
Ans.

Fig. 7.19

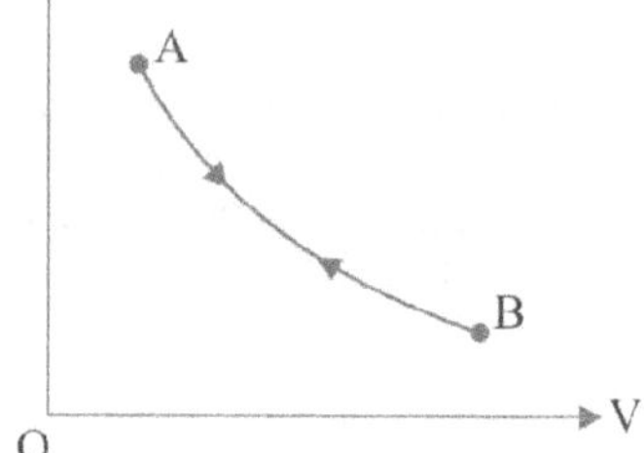

Fig. 7.20 **Reversible process**

Quasi-static process

Quasi-static process is the nearly static process. At every state, the temperature and pressure of the system differ only infinitesimally from those of the surroundings. A quasistatic process is an ideal concept that is applicable to all thermodynamic systems including electric and magnetic systems.

Consider the expansion of a gas in a closed cylinder fitted with a piston. Initially weights are put on the piston and the pressure of the gas inside the cylinder is higher than the atmospheric pressure. If the weight are small and are taken off slowly one by one, the process can be considered quasistatic. If, however, all the weights are removed at once, the expansion takes place suddenly and it will be a non-equilibrium process (non quasi-static).

7.7 REVERSIBLE PROCESS

Any process which return to its initial state of thermodynamical variables at each stage of variation as it proceed in direct process is called reversible process. A complete reversible process is an ideal concept as it can never be realised in practice because dissipative forces cannot be completely eliminated.

(i)   The process must be quasi - static.

(ii)   The dissipative forces such as viscosity, friction etc. must be absent.

(iii)   The work done in complete cycle will be zero.

Examples:

(i)   The gradual extension and compression of an elastic spring is approximately reversible.

(ii)   The electrolysis process is reversible if internal resistance is negligibly small.

(iii)   Slow compression and expansion of an ideal gas at constant temperature.

Irreversible process

A process is said to be irreversible if it cannot be retraced back exactly in the opposite direction. During an irreversible process, work is always done to overcome friction. Energy is also dissipated in the form of conduction and radiation. Most of the process occurring in nature are irreversible.

Examples :

(i)   Dissolution of salt in water.

(ii)   Diffusion of gases.

(iii)   Sudden expansion or compression of gas.

(iv)   Passage of an electric current through a resistance.

(v)   Rain fall.

(vi)   Rusting of iron.

7.8 THERMODYNAMICAL PROCESSES

Any process may have own equation of state, but each thermodynamical process must obey $PV = nRT$.

1. Isobaric process

If a thermodynamic system undergoes physical change at constant pressure, then the process is called isobaric.

(i) Isobaric process obeys Charle's law, $V \propto T$

(ii) Slope of $P \sim V$ curve, $\dfrac{dP}{dV} = 0$.

(ii) Specific heat at constant pressure

$$C_P = \frac{5R}{2} \text{ for monoatomic and } C_P = \frac{7R}{2} \text{ for diatomic}$$

(iv) Bulk modulus of elasticity: As P is constant, $\Delta P = 0$

and $$B \;=\; \frac{\Delta P}{\left(-\dfrac{\Delta V}{V}\right)} = 0$$

(v) Work done: $\qquad W \;=\; P\Delta V = nR\Delta T$

(vi) First law of thermodynamics in isobaric process

$$\begin{aligned} Q &= \Delta U + W = \Delta U + P\Delta V = \Delta U + nR\Delta T \\ &= nC_V\Delta T + nR\Delta T = n(C_V + R)\Delta T \\ &= nC_P\Delta T \end{aligned}$$

(vii) Examples: Boiling of water and freezing of water at constant pressure etc.

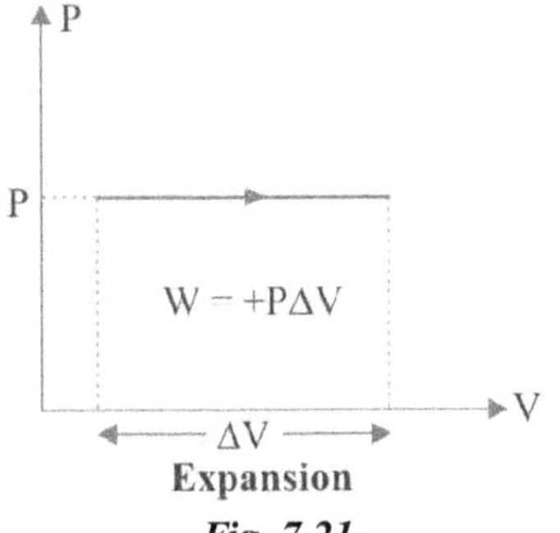

Expansion
Fig. 7.21

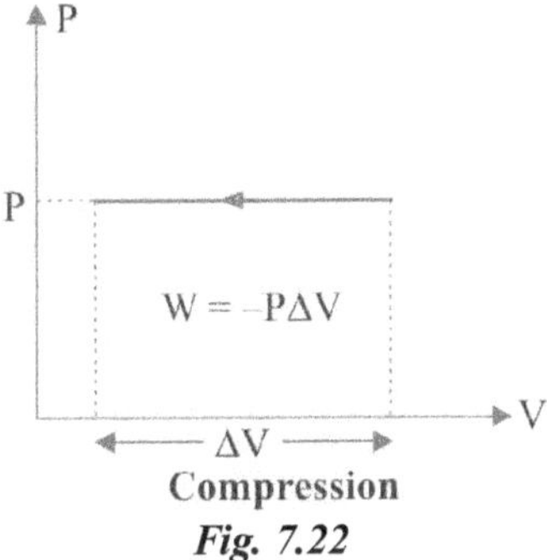

Compression
Fig. 7.22

2. Isochoric or isometric process

A thermodynamical process in which volume of the system remain constant, is called isochoric process.

(i) An isochoric process obeys Gay - Lussac's Law, $P \propto T$

(ii) Slope of $P - V$ curve, $\dfrac{dP}{dV} = \infty$

(ii) Specific heat at constant volume

$$C_V = \frac{3R}{2} \text{ for monoatomic and } C_V = \frac{5R}{2} \text{ for diatomic}$$

(iv) Bulk modulus of elasticity : As V is constant, $\Delta V = 0$

$\therefore \qquad B \;=\; \dfrac{\Delta P}{\left(\dfrac{-\Delta V}{V}\right)} = \infty$

(v) Work done : $\qquad W \;=\; P\Delta V = 0$

(vi) First law of thermodynamics in ischoric process

$$\begin{aligned} Q &= \Delta U + W = \Delta U + 0 \\ \text{or} \quad Q &= \Delta U \\ &= nC_V\Delta T \end{aligned}$$

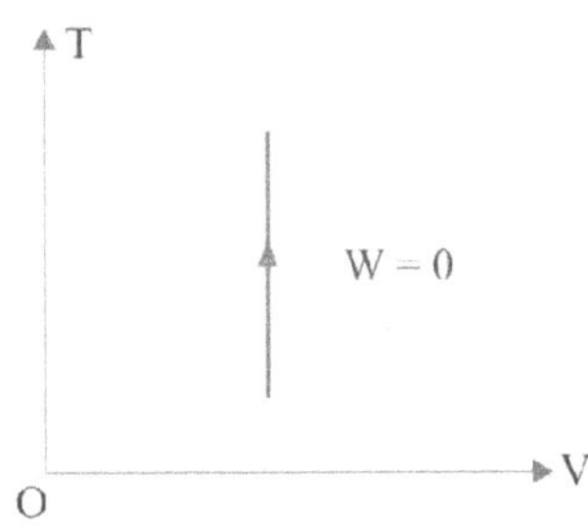

Fig. 7.23

3. Isothermal process

A thermodynamical process in which pressure and volume of the system change at constant temperature, is called isothermal process.

(i) An isothermal process obeys Boyle's law $PV =$ Constant.

(ii) The wall of the container must be perfectly conducting so that free exchange of heat between the system and surroundings can take place.

(iii) The process must be very slow, so as to provide sufficient time for the exchange of heat.

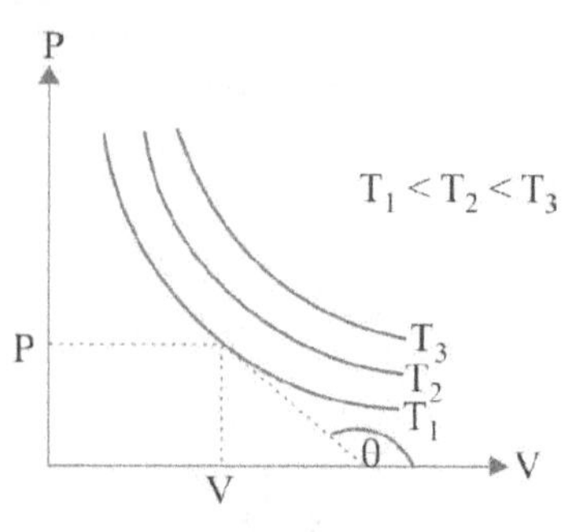

Fig. 7.24

(iv) Slope of $P - V$ curve:

For isothermal process

$$PV = \text{Constant}$$

After differentiating w.r.t. volume, we get

$$P + V\frac{dP}{dV} = 0$$

or

$$\frac{dP}{dV} = \frac{-P}{V} \quad \text{or} \quad \tan\theta = \frac{-P}{V}$$

(v) Specific heat at constant temperature:

As $\Delta T = 0$,

$$\therefore \quad C = \frac{\Delta Q}{n\Delta T} = \infty$$

(vi) Isothermal elasticity: Bulk modulus at constant temperature is called isothermal elasticity. It can be defined as

$$E_{iso} = B = \frac{\Delta P}{\dfrac{-\Delta V}{V}} = \frac{dP}{\left(\dfrac{-dV}{V}\right)}$$

From above

$$\frac{dP}{\left(\dfrac{-dV}{V}\right)} = P$$

$$\therefore \quad E_{iso} = P$$

(vi) Work done :

$$W = \int_{V_i}^{V_f} PdV$$

By

$$PV = nRT \Rightarrow P = \frac{nRT}{V}$$

$$\therefore \quad W = \int_{V_i}^{V_f} nRT\left(\frac{dV}{V}\right)$$

$$= nRT\left|\ell nV\right|_{V_i}^{V_f}$$

or

$$W = nRT\ell n\left(\frac{V_f}{V_i}\right)$$

Here $\left(\dfrac{V_f}{V_i}\right)$ is called expansion ratio.

Also $P_iV_i = P_fV_f$, $\quad \therefore \quad \dfrac{V_f}{V_i} = \dfrac{P_i}{P_f}$

$$\therefore \quad W = nRT\ell n\left(\frac{V_f}{V_i}\right) = nRT\ell n\left(\frac{P_i}{P_f}\right)$$

(viii) First law of thermodynamics in isothermal process.

As

$$\Delta T = 0, \quad \therefore \quad \Delta U = 0$$
$$Q = \Delta U + W = 0 + W$$

or

$$Q = W$$

4. Adiabatic process

An adiabatic process is one in which pressure, volume and temperature of the system change but heat will not exchange between system and surroundings.

(i) Adiabatic process must be sudden, so that heat does not get time to exchange between system and surroundings.

(ii) The walls of the container must be perfectly insulated.

(iii) **Adiabatic relation between *P* and *V***

According to first law of thermodynamics

$$dQ = dU + dW$$

For adiabatic process, $dQ = 0$, $\therefore dU + dW = 0$ ...(1)

For one mole of gas

$$dU = C_V dT \text{ and } dW = PdV$$

Substituting these values in equation (1), we have

$$C_V dT + PdV = 0 \qquad \text{...(2)}$$

For one mole of an idea gas,

$$PV = RT \qquad \text{...(3)}$$

After differentiating equation (3), we get

$$PdV + VdP = RdT$$

or

$$dT = \frac{PdV + VdP}{R}$$

From equation (2)

$$C_V\left(\frac{PdV + VdP}{R}\right) + PdV = 0$$

or $C_V PdV + C_V VdP + RPdV = 0$

or $(C_V + R)\,PdV + C_V VdP = 0$

or $C_P PdV + C_V VdP = 0$

After rearranging, we get

$$\frac{C_P}{C_V}\frac{dV}{V} + \frac{dP}{P} = 0$$

Substituting $\dfrac{C_P}{C_V} = \gamma$, we have

or

$$\gamma\frac{dV}{V} + \frac{dP}{P} = 0 \qquad \text{...(4)}$$

Integrating equation (4), we get

$$\gamma\int\frac{dV}{V} + \int\frac{dP}{P} = C$$

or $\gamma \ell n V + \ell n\, P = C$

or $\ell n V^\gamma + \ell n P = C$

or $\ell n (PV^\gamma) = C$

or $PV^\gamma = e^C$

or $PV^\gamma = k$

Adiabatic relation between *V* and *T* & *P* and *T*

For one mole of gas

$$PV = RT, \text{ or } P = \frac{RT}{V}$$

Substituting in $PV^\gamma = k$, we get

$$\left(\frac{RT}{V}\right)V^{\gamma} = k$$

or

$$V^{\gamma-1}T = \frac{k}{R} = \text{new constant}$$

Also

$$V = \frac{RT}{P}$$

$$\therefore \quad P\left(\frac{RT}{P}\right)^{\gamma} = k$$

or

$$P^{1-\gamma}T^{\gamma} = \frac{k}{R^{\gamma}} = \text{another constant}$$

(iv) **Slope of $P-V$ curve :** We have $PV^{\gamma} = k$. On differentiating,

we have $\quad P\gamma V^{\gamma-1} + V^{\gamma}\dfrac{dP}{dV} = 0$

or

$$\frac{dP}{dV} = -\gamma\frac{P}{V}$$

or

$$\tan\theta = -\gamma\frac{P}{V}$$

As slope of isothermal curve $= -\dfrac{P}{V}$

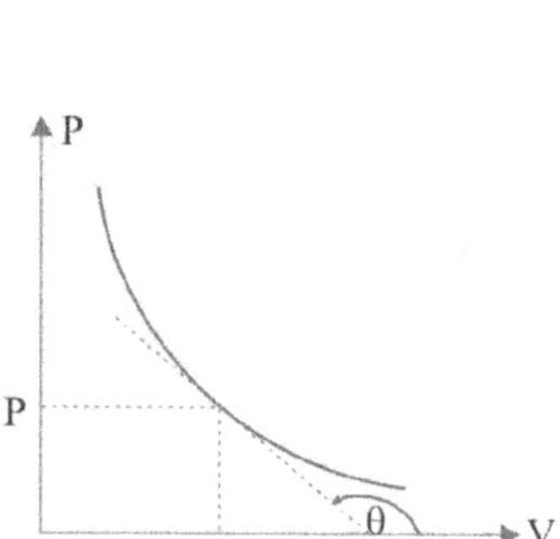

Fig. 7.25

$\therefore$ Slope of adiabatic curve $= \gamma \times$ slope of isothermal curve.
Since $\gamma > 1$, so slope of adiabatic always be greater than slope of isothermal curve.

(v) **Specific heat :** $\qquad C = \dfrac{Q}{n\Delta T} = \dfrac{0}{n\Delta T} = 0$

(vi) **Adiabatic elasticity:** Bulk modulus of gas at constant heat is called adiabatic elasticity. If can be defined as

$$E_{ad} = B = \frac{\Delta P}{\left(\dfrac{-\Delta V}{V}\right)} = \frac{dP}{\left(\dfrac{-dV}{V}\right)}$$

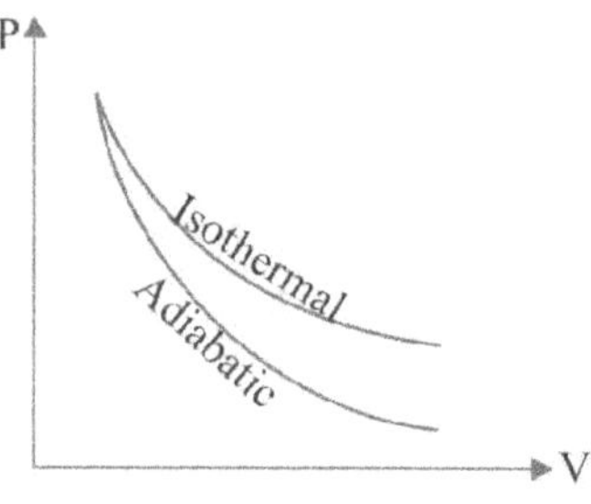

Fig. 7.26

As

$$\frac{dp}{\left(-\dfrac{dV}{V}\right)} = \gamma P$$

$$\therefore \qquad E_{ad} = \gamma P$$

As $\;E_{iso} = P,\qquad \therefore E_{ad} = \gamma E_{iso}$

(vii) **Work done :** $\qquad W = \displaystyle\int_{V_i}^{V_f} PdV$

For adiabatic process $\quad PV^{\gamma} = P_iV_i^{\gamma} = P_fV_f^{\gamma} = k$

or $\qquad\qquad\qquad\quad P = kV^{-\gamma}$

$$\therefore \qquad W = \int_{V_i}^{V_f} kV^{-\gamma}dV$$

$$= k\left|\frac{V^{1-\gamma}}{(1-\gamma)}\right|_{V_i}^{V_f}$$

$$= \frac{1}{(1-\gamma)}[kV_f^{1-\gamma} - kV_i^{1-\gamma}]$$

$$= \frac{1}{(1-\gamma)}[(P_fV_f^{\gamma})V_f^{1-\gamma} - (P_iV_i^{\gamma})V_i^{1-\gamma}]$$

$$= \frac{1}{(1-\gamma)}\left[P_fV_f - P_iV_i\right]$$

or
$$W = \frac{(P_iV_i - P_fV_f)}{(\gamma-1)}$$

Also
$$P_iV_i = nRT_i \text{ and } P_fV_f = nRT_f$$

$\therefore$
$$W = \frac{nR}{\gamma-1}[T_i - T_f]$$

(viii) First law of thermodynamics in adiabatic process

$$Q = \Delta U + W$$

As
$$Q = 0, \qquad \therefore \ \Delta U = -W$$

or
$$U_f - U_i = -W$$

$\therefore$
$$U_f = U_i - W$$

Summary of four gas processes :

Fig. 7.28 shows four different processes : Isobaric, isothermal, adiabatic and isochoric.

Path	Constant quantity	Process type	Some results $\Delta U = Q - W$ and $\Delta U = nC_V\Delta T$ for all paths
1	P	Isobaric	$Q = nC_\mathrm{P}\Delta T;\ \ W = P\Delta V$
2	T	Isothermal	$Q = W = nRT\ell n(V_f/V_i);\ \ \Delta U = 0$
3	$PV^\gamma,\ TV^{\gamma-1}$	Adiabatic	$Q = 0;\ \ W = -\Delta U$
4	V	Isochoric	$Q = \Delta U = nC_V\Delta T;\ \ W = 0$

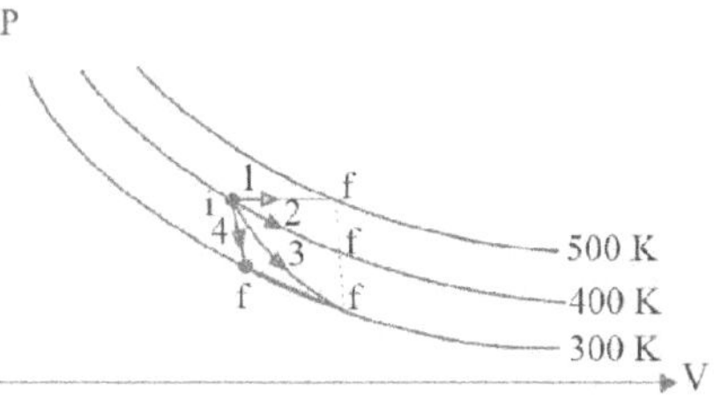

Fig. 7.28 **P – V diagram representing four different processes for an ideal gas**

7.9 CHANGE IN INTERNAL ENERGY

1. **In boiling :** Suppose m mass of liquid transforms into vapour at boiling point. Its volume changes from V_i to V_f. Thus work done by the liquid

$$W = P\Delta V = P(V_f - V_i)$$

If L be the latent heat of vapourisation of liquid, then amount of heat required, $Q = mL$.

Now from first law of thermodynamics

$$Q = \Delta U + W$$

or
$$mL = \Delta U + P(V_f - V_i)$$

$\therefore$
$$\Delta U = mL - P(V_f - V_i)$$

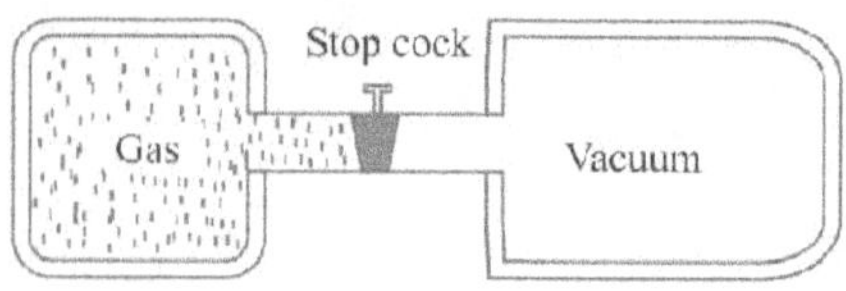

Fig. 7.27

2. **In melting** : Suppose m mass of solid transforms into liquid at melting point. In this process change in volume is negligibly small, $\Delta V \simeq 0$, so $W = 0$.

If L be the latent heat of fusion of solid, then amount of heat required, $Q = mL$.

Now from first law of thermodynamics

$$Q = \Delta U + W$$

or $$mL = \Delta U + 0$$

$$\therefore \quad \Delta U = mL$$

3. **In free expansion** : Consider two insulated vessels, one contains a gas and other is evacuated (see *Fig. 7.27*). When stop-cock is opened, the gas rushes into the evacuated vessel and expand freely. As process is sudden (adiabatic) so $Q = 0$, also gas expands freely, so

$$W = P\Delta V = 0 \times \Delta V = 0.$$

From first law of thermodynamics

$$Q = \Delta U + W$$

or $$0 = \Delta U + 0$$

$$\therefore \quad \Delta U = 0$$

Thus in free expansion internal energy of the gas will not change.

7.10 POLYTROPIC PROCESS

A process $PV^r = $ constant is called polytropic process, in which $r \neq 1$ or γ.

(i) **Work done in polytropic process:** As we have calculated in adiabatic process, here also work done

$$W = \frac{nR}{r-1}\left[T_i - T_f\right]$$

$$= \frac{-nR}{r-1}\left[T_f - T_i\right]$$

or $$W = -\frac{nR\Delta T}{r-1}$$

For one mole of a gas $n = 1$

$$\therefore \quad W = \frac{-R\Delta T}{r-1}$$

(ii) **Specific heat :** If C is the molar specific heat, then heat required to increase the temperature of one mole of a gas by ΔT

$$Q = C\Delta T$$

Form first law of thermodynamics

$$Q = \Delta U + W$$

or $$C\Delta T = C_V\Delta T - \frac{R\Delta T}{r-1}$$

$$\therefore \quad C = C_V - \frac{R}{r-1} = \frac{R}{\gamma-1} - \frac{R}{r-1}$$

Ex. 9 An ideal gas expands according to law $PV^2 = $ constant. What is the value of molar heat capacity?

Sol.

Compare the given process $PV^2 = $ constant with $PV^r = $ constant, we have $r = 2$.

We know that $$C = C_V - \frac{R}{r-1}$$

$$= C_V - \frac{R}{2-1} = C_V - R \qquad \textbf{\textit{Ans.}}$$

Ex. 10 An ideal gas $(C_p/C_v = \gamma)$ is taken through a process in which the pressure and the volume vary as $P = aV^b$. Find the value of b for which the specific heat capacity in the process is zero.

Sol.

Given, $$P = aV^b$$

or $$PV^{-b} = a$$

Compare with $PV^r = $ Constant, we have

$$r = -b$$

We know that, $$C = C_V - \frac{R}{r-1}$$

Here, $C = 0$, $C_V = \dfrac{R}{\gamma - 1}$

$\therefore$ $0 = \dfrac{R}{\gamma - 1} - \dfrac{R}{-b - 1}$

or $b = -\gamma$ *Ans.*

Ex. 11 A certain amount of gas occupies volume V_0 at pressure P_0 and temperature T_0. It is allowed to expand (i) isobarically, (ii) adiabatically and (iii) isothermally . In which case the work done is maximum and in which case it is minimum?

Sol.

Work done by all the processes given are shown in *Fig. 7.29.*

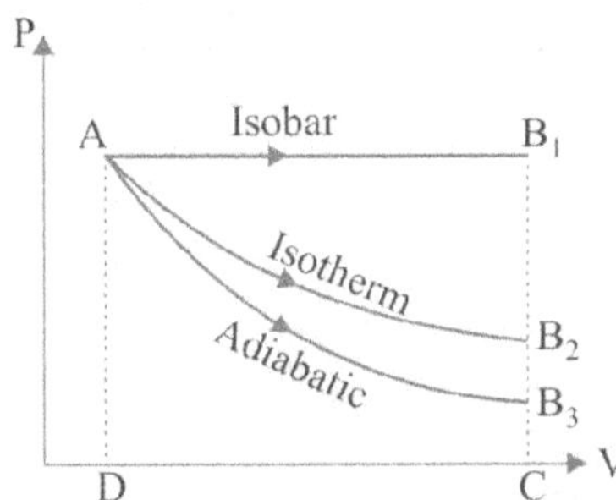

Fig. 7.29

It is clear from the figure that area AB_1CD is the largest and area AB_3CD is the least one. If W_{isob}, W_{iso} and W_{ad} represent work done in isobaric, isothermal and adiabatic processes respectively, then $W_{isob} > W_{iso} > W_{ad}$.

Ex. 12 The volume of an ideal gas is V at pressure P. On increasing the pressure by ΔP, the change in volume of the gas is ΔV_1 under isothermal conditions and ΔV_2 under adiabatic conditions. Under which of the two conditions, will the change in volume be more?

Sol.

Under isothermal conditions, the isothermal elasticity

$$E_{iso} = \frac{\Delta P}{\left(\dfrac{\Delta V_1}{V}\right)} = P$$

$\therefore$ $\Delta V_1 = \dfrac{\Delta P V}{P}$

Under adiabatic conditions, the adiabatic elasticity

$$E_{ad} = \frac{\Delta P}{\left(\dfrac{\Delta V_2}{V}\right)} = \gamma P$$

$\therefore$ $\Delta V_2 = \dfrac{\Delta P V}{\gamma P} = \dfrac{\Delta V_1}{\gamma}$

As $\gamma > 1$, $\therefore$ $\Delta V_2 < \Delta V_1$ *Ans.*

Ex. 13 A motor car tyre has a pressure of 2 atmosphere at room temperature of 27°C. If the tyre suddenly bursts, find the resulting temperature.

Sol.

Here, $P_1 = 2$ atm, $T_1 = 273 + 27 = 300$ K

When tyre burst, $P_2 = 1$ atm, $T_2 = ?$

For air $\gamma = 7/5$.

As the process is sudden, so we have

$$\frac{P_1^{\gamma-1}}{T_1^{\gamma}} = \frac{P_2^{\gamma-1}}{T_2^{\gamma}}$$

or $$\left(\frac{P_2}{P_1}\right)^{\gamma-1} = \left(\frac{T_2}{T_1}\right)^{\gamma}$$

$$\left(\frac{1}{2}\right)^{(7/5)-1} = \left(\frac{T_2}{300}\right)^{7/5}$$

After solving, we get $T_2 = 246.1$ K   *Ans.*

Ex. 14 Two samples of a gas initially at same temperature and pressure are compressed from a volume V to $\dfrac{V}{2}$. One sample is compressed isothermally and the other adiabatically. In which sample is the pressure greater?

Sol.

Here $V_i = V$, $V_f = \dfrac{V}{2}$, $\therefore \dfrac{V_i}{V_f} = 2$

In isothermal process

$$P_i V_i = P_f V_f$$

$\therefore$ $P_f = \dfrac{P_i V_i}{V_f} = P_i \times 2 = 2P_1$

In adiabatic process

$$P_i V_i^{\gamma} = P_f V_f^{\gamma}$$

$\therefore$ $P_f = P_i \left(\dfrac{V_i}{V_f}\right)^{\gamma} = P_i (2)^{\gamma}$

As $\gamma > 1$, so $2^{\gamma} > 2$ and hence the pressure in adiabatic pressure will be greater.

Ex. 15 One mole of a gas is carried through the cycle shown in the *Fig. 7.30*. The gas expands at constant temperature T from volume V to $2V$. It is then compressed to the initial volume at constant pressure and is finally brought back to its original state by heating at constant volume. Calculate the work done by the gas in complete cycle.

Sol.

Work done in isothermal process A to B

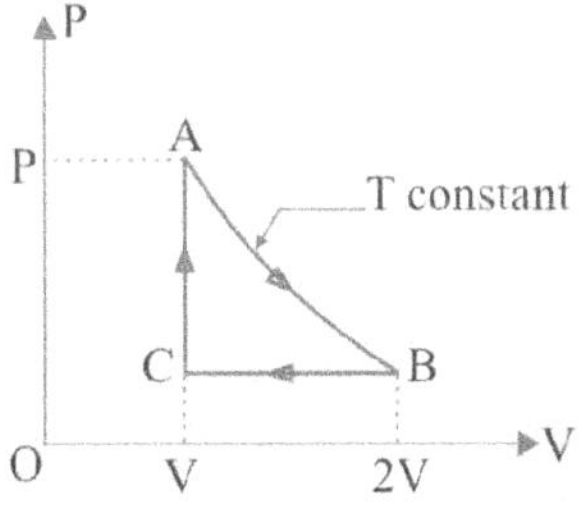

Fig. 7.30

$$W_{AB} = nRT\ell n\frac{V_f}{V_i} = 1RT\ell n\frac{2V}{V}$$

$$= RT\ell n2$$

If pressure at B is P_B, then

$$P_A V_A = P_B V_B$$

or $$PV = P_B \times 2V \Rightarrow P_B = P/2$$

Work done in isobaric process from B to C at constant pressure $P/2$

$$W_{BC} = P_B(V_f - V_i)$$

$$= \frac{P}{2}(V - 2V) = -\frac{PV}{2}$$

$$= \frac{-RT}{2}$$

Work done in isochoric process C to A, $W_{CA} = 0$

$\therefore$ Work done in whole cycle

$$W = W_{AB} + W_{BC} + W_{CA}$$

$$= RT\ell n2 - \frac{RT}{2} + 0$$

$$= RT\left(\ell n2 - \frac{1}{2}\right) \qquad \textit{Ans.}$$

Ex. 16 1 mole of a monoatomic gas is taken from a point A to another point B along the path ACB. The initial temperature at A is T_0. Calculate the heat absorbed by the gas in the process $A \to C \to B$.

Sol.

If T_B be the temperature at B, then by gas law

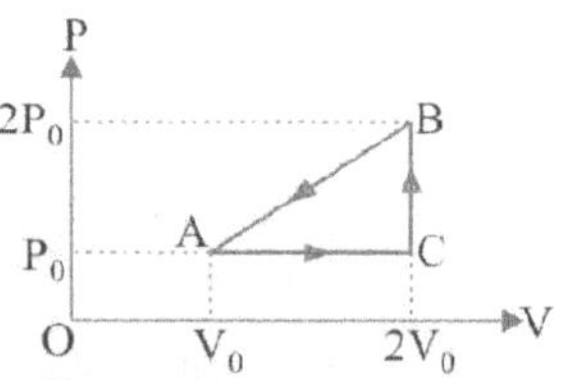

Fig. 7.31

$$\frac{P_A V_A}{T_A} = \frac{P_B V_B}{T_B}$$

$\therefore$ $$T_B = \frac{P_B V_B}{P_A V_A}T_A = \frac{(2P_0)(2V_0)}{P_0 V_0}T_0$$

The change in internal energy from A to B

$$\Delta U = nC_V\Delta T = 1\times\frac{3R}{2}\times(4T_0 - T_0)$$

$$= \frac{9RT_0}{2}$$

Work done in the process A to C

$$W_{AC} = P\Delta V = P_0(2V_0 - V_0)$$
$$= P_0 V_0 = RT_0$$

and $$W_{CB} = 0$$

$\therefore$ Total work done from $A \to C \to B$

$$W_{AC} + W_{CB} = RT_0 + 0 = RT_0$$

From first law of thermodynamics
$$Q = \Delta U + W$$

$$= \frac{9RT_0}{2} + RT_0$$

$$= \frac{11RT_0}{2}$$

Thus heat absorbed by the gas from $A \to C \to B$ is $\dfrac{11RT_0}{2}$. **Ans.**

Ex. 17 A vessel of volume V_0 contains an ideal gas at pressure P_0 and temperature T. Gas is continuously pumped out of this vessel at a constant volume- rate $\dfrac{dV}{dT} = r$, keeping the temperature constant. The pressure of the gas being taken out equals the pressure inside the vessel. Find (a) the pressure of the gas as a function of time, (b) the time taken before half the original gas is pumped out.

Sol.

(a) As the temperature in the process is constant, so we have
$$PV = k$$
Differentiating w.r.t. time, we get

$$P\frac{dV}{dt} + V\frac{dP}{dt} = 0$$

Upon substituting $\dfrac{dV}{dt} = r$ and $V = V_0$ (which is constant) and rearranging, we get

$$\frac{dP}{P} = \frac{-r}{V_0}dt$$

Integrating above equation

$$\int_{P_0}^{P}\frac{dP}{P} = -\frac{r}{V_0}\int_0^t dt$$

$$|\ell nP|_{P_0}^{P} = \frac{-rt}{V_0}$$

$$\ell nP - \ell nP_0 = \frac{-rt}{V_0}$$

or $$\ell n\left(\frac{P}{P_0}\right) = -\frac{rt}{V_0}$$

or $$\frac{P}{P_0} = e^{\frac{-rt}{V_0}}$$

or $$P = P_0 e^{\frac{-rt}{V_0}} \qquad \textit{Ans.}$$

(b) If t is the time in which pressure reduces to $\dfrac{P_0}{2}$, then

$$\frac{P_0}{2} = P_0 e^{\frac{-rt}{V_0}}$$

or $$e^{rt/V_0} = 2$$

or $$\frac{rt}{V_0} = \ell n2$$

$\therefore$ $$t = \frac{V_0\ell n2}{r} \qquad \textit{Ans.}$$

Ex. 18 Two moles of monoatomic gas occupy two chambers of a cylinder - piston system in which the piston is free to move and the walls of the cylinder and the piston are made of insulating material. The initial volumes, pressures and temperatures of the two chambers are the same- P_0, V_0 and T_0. The chamber in the left is heated internally by some device resulting in expansion of the gas pushing the piston to the right. The gas in the right chamber is compressed until the pressure becomes 32 times the initial pressure. Calculate:

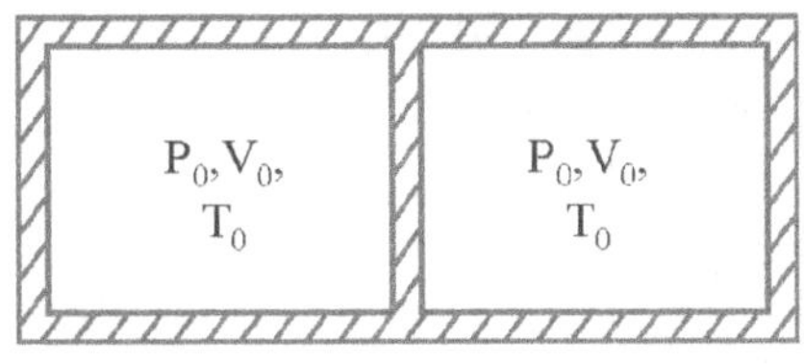

Fig. 7.32

(a)   the work done in compression,
(b)   the final temperatures of the two chambers,
(c)   the change in internal energy of the left chamber, and
(d)   the heat absorbed by the left chamber.

Sol.

(a)   As the system is made of insulating material so process between the chambers will be adiabatic.

When pressure in the right chamber becomes 32 times initial, let its volume becomes V_R. Then

$$P_0 V_0^\gamma = (32 P_0) V_R^\gamma$$

or $\qquad V_R = \left(\dfrac{1}{32}\right)^{\frac{1}{\gamma}} V_0$

For monoatomic gas

$$\gamma = \dfrac{5}{3}$$

$\therefore \qquad V_R = \left(\dfrac{1}{32}\right)^{\frac{3}{5}} V_0 = \dfrac{V_0}{8}$

If T_R is the corresponding temperature of the right chamber, then

$$\dfrac{P_0 V_0}{T_0} = \dfrac{(32 P_0)(V_0/8)}{T_R}$$

or $\qquad T_R = 4 T_0$

The work done on the gas in right chamber

$$W = \dfrac{-(P_i V_i - P_f V_f)}{(\gamma - 1)}$$

$$= \dfrac{-\left(P_0 V_0 - 32 P_0 \times \dfrac{V_0}{8}\right)}{\left(\dfrac{5}{3} - 1\right)}$$

$$= \dfrac{9 P_0 V_0}{2} = \dfrac{9 R T_0}{2}$$

(b)   Total volume of the two chambers $= 2 V_0$.   *Ans.*

Finally when volume of right chamber becomes $\dfrac{V_0}{8}$, the volume of left chamber will be

$$= 2V_0 - \dfrac{V_0}{8} = \dfrac{15 V_0}{8}$$

The pressure of the left chamber is also $P_L = 32 \, P_0$.
If T_L is the final temperature of the left chamber, then

$$\dfrac{P_0 V_0}{T_0} = \dfrac{(32 P_0)\left(\dfrac{15 V_0}{8}\right)}{T_L} \Rightarrow T = 60 T_0 \quad \textit{Ans.}$$

(c)   The change in internal energy of the gas in left chamber,

$$\Delta U = n C_V \Delta T = 1 \times \dfrac{3R}{2} \times (60 T_0 - T_0)$$

$$= 88.5 T_0 \qquad \textit{Ans.}$$

(d)   The heat absorbed by the left chamber = heat absorbed by right chamber

$$Q = \Delta U + W$$

$$= 88.5 R T_0 + \dfrac{9}{2} R T_0$$

$$= 93.0 \, R T_0 \qquad \textit{Ans.}$$

Ex. 19 *Fig. 7.33* shows an adiabatic cylindrical tube of volume V_0, divided in two parts by a frictionless adiabatic separator. Initially, the separator is kept in the middle, an ideal gas at pressure P_1 and temperature T_1 is injected into the left part and another ideal gas at pressure P_2 and temperature T_2 is injected into the right part. $\dfrac{C_p}{C_v} = \gamma$ is the same for both the gases. The separator is slid slowly and is released at a position where it can stay in equilibrium. Find

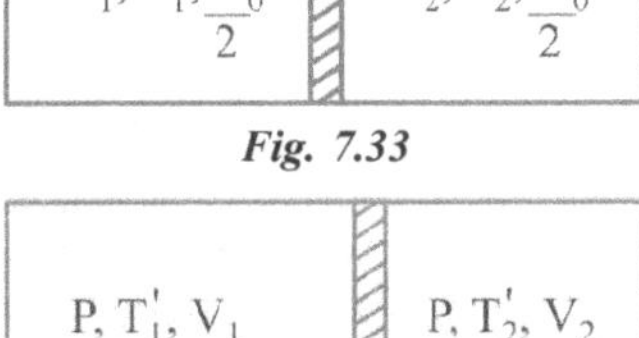

Fig. 7.33

Fig. 7.34

(a)   the volumes of the two parts,
(b)   the heat given to the gas in the left part and
(c)   the final common pressure of the gases.

Sol.

The separator will stop in the position when pressure of both the parts of the tube become equal. Let it is P.
If V_1 and V_2 are the volumes of two parts, then

$$V_1 + V_2 = V_0 \qquad \qquad \text{...(i)}$$

(a)   The process in each part is adiabatic, so

$$P_1 \left(\dfrac{V_0}{2}\right)^\gamma = P V_1^\gamma \qquad \qquad \text{...(ii)}$$

and $\qquad P_2 \left(\dfrac{V_0}{2}\right)^\gamma = P V_2^\gamma \qquad \qquad \text{...(iii)}$

Dividing equation (ii) by (iii), we have

$$\dfrac{P_1}{P_2} = \dfrac{V_1^\gamma}{V_2^\gamma}$$

or $\qquad V_1 = \left(\dfrac{P_1}{P_2}\right)^{1/\gamma} V_2 \qquad \qquad \text{...(iv)}$

Substituting this value in equation (i), we get

$$V_2 = \left[\frac{V_0\, P_2^{1/\gamma}}{P_1^{1/\gamma}+P_2^{1/\gamma}}\right] \text{ and } V_1 = \left[\frac{V_0\, P_1^{1/\gamma}}{P_1^{1/\gamma}+P_2^{1/\gamma}}\right]$$

Ans.

(b)   As cylindrical tube and separator both are adiabatic, so no heat is given in the process.   **Ans.**

(c)   Substituting value of V_1 in equation (ii), we get

$$P = \left[\frac{P_1^{1/\gamma}+P_2^{1/\gamma}}{2^{\gamma}}\right]$$ **Ans.**

Ex. 20 A smooth vertical tube having two different sections is open from both ends and equipped with two pistons of different areas (see *Fig. 7.35*). Each piston slides within a respective tube section. One mole of ideal gas is enclosed between the pistons tied with a non-stretchable thread.

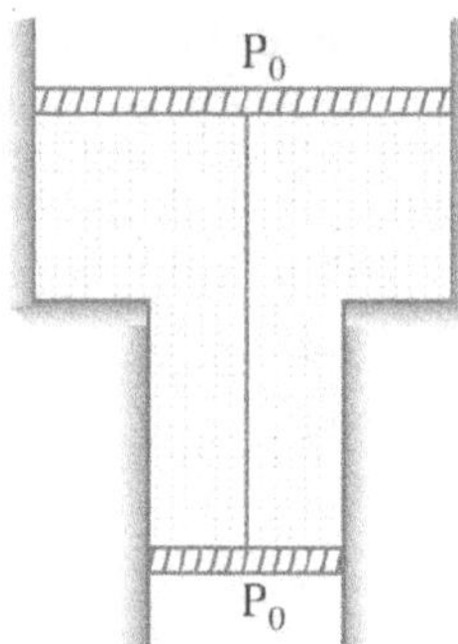

Fig. 7.35

The cross - sectional area of upper piston is ΔS greater than that of the lower one. The combined mass of two pistons is equal to m. The outside air pressure is P_0. By how much temperature must the gas between the pistons be heated to shift the piston through a distance ℓ?

Sol.

One mole of the gas is confined between upper and lower pistons. Let m_1 and m_2 be their masses and S_1 and S_2 respective areas. If P is the pressure of the gas inside and F is the tension in the string, then for upper piston

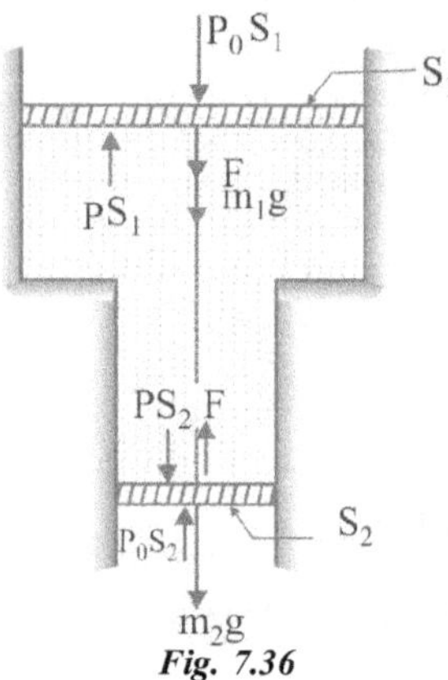

Fig. 7.36

$$P_0 S_1 + F + m_1 g = P\, S_1$$

or $$F = (P - P_0)\, S_1 - m_1\, g$$ ...(i)

For lower piston

$$P_0 S_2 + F = PS_2 + m_2 g$$

or $$F = (P - P_0)S_2 + m_2 g$$ ...(ii)

Equating equations (i) and (ii)

$$(P - P_0)\, S_1 - m_1 g = (P - P_0)\, S_2 + m_2 g$$

or $$(P - P_0)\, (S_1 - S_2) = (m_1 + m_2)g$$

Given, $$S_1 - S_2 = \Delta S \text{ and } m_1 + m_2 = m$$

$$\therefore \quad (P - P_0)\Delta S = mg$$

or $$P = P_0 + \frac{mg}{\Delta S}$$ ...(iii)

Now from equation of state, $PV = nRT$, we can write

$$P\Delta V = nR\Delta T$$

or $$\left(P_0 + \frac{mg}{\Delta S}\right)(\ell\Delta S) = 1\times R\times \Delta T$$ $\left[\begin{array}{l}\Delta V = \ell\Delta S\\ n = 1\end{array}\right]$

After simplifying, we get

$$\Delta T = \frac{\ell}{R}(P_0\Delta S + mg)$$ **Ans.**

Ex. 21 An ideal gas has a molar heat capacity C_V at constant volume. Find the molar heat capacity of this gas as a function of its volume V, if the gas under goes the following process:

(a) $T = T_0 e^{\alpha V}$ (b) $P = P_0 e^{\alpha V}$

Sol.

If C be the molar heat capacity of the gas, then first law of thermodynamics, $Q = \Delta U + W$ can be written as

$$C\Delta T = C_V\Delta T + P\Delta V$$

or $$C = C_V + P\frac{\Delta V}{\Delta T}$$

For the ideal gas $$PV = RT \text{ or } P = R\frac{T}{V}$$

$$\therefore \quad C = C_V + \frac{RT}{V}\left(\frac{dV}{dT}\right)$$ ...(i)

(a)   For the given process $T = T_0 e^{\alpha V}$

Differentiating w.r.t. volume, we get

$$\frac{dT}{dV} = \frac{d}{dV}\left(T_0 e^{\alpha V}\right)$$

$$= \alpha\left(T_0 e^{\alpha V}\right) = \alpha T$$

or $$\frac{dV}{dT} = \frac{1}{\alpha T}$$ ...(ii)

Now from equation (i) and (ii), we get

$$C = C_V + \frac{RT}{V}\times\frac{1}{\alpha T}$$

$$= C_V + \frac{R}{\alpha V}$$ **Ans.**

(b)   For the process $P = P_0 e^{\alpha V}$, we have

$$\frac{RT}{V} = P_0 e^{\alpha V}$$

Differentiating w.r.t. volume, we get

$$\frac{-RT}{V^2}+\frac{R}{V}\frac{dT}{dV} = P_0\alpha e^{\alpha V}$$

or $$\frac{R}{V}\left(\frac{dT}{dV}\right) = \frac{P_0}{V}e^{\alpha V} + P_0\alpha e^{\alpha V}$$

or $\quad \dfrac{R}{V}\left(\dfrac{dT}{dV}\right) = P_0 e^{\alpha V}\left(\dfrac{1+\alpha V}{V}\right)$

or $\quad \dfrac{dT}{dV} = \dfrac{P_0 e^{\alpha V}}{R}(1+\alpha V)$

or $\quad \dfrac{dV}{dT} = \dfrac{R}{P_0 e^{\alpha V}(1+\alpha V)}$

$$= \dfrac{R}{P(1+\alpha V)} = \dfrac{R}{\dfrac{RT}{V}(1+\alpha V)}$$

$$= \dfrac{V}{T(1+\alpha V)} \qquad \text{...(iii)}$$

From equations (i) and (iii), we get

$$C = C_V + \dfrac{RT}{V} \times \dfrac{V}{T(1+\alpha V)}$$

$$= C_V + \dfrac{R}{1+\alpha V} \qquad \textbf{\textit{Ans.}}$$

Ex. 22 **A mass of air is initially at 260°C and 700 $k\,P_a$ and occupies 0.028 m^3. The air is expanded at constant pressure to 0.084m^3. A polytropic process with r = 1.5 is then carried out followed by a constant temperature process which completes a cycle. All the processes are reversible. Sketch the cycle in the PV diagram. Find (a) the heat required, (b) the heat rejected in the cycle, and (c) the efficiency of the cycle.**
$$C_V = 0.718 \text{ kJ/kgK}, \ R_{air} = 0.287 \text{ kJ/ kgK}$$

Sol.

The complete cycle is shown in *Fig. 7.37*. For m kg of the air we can write

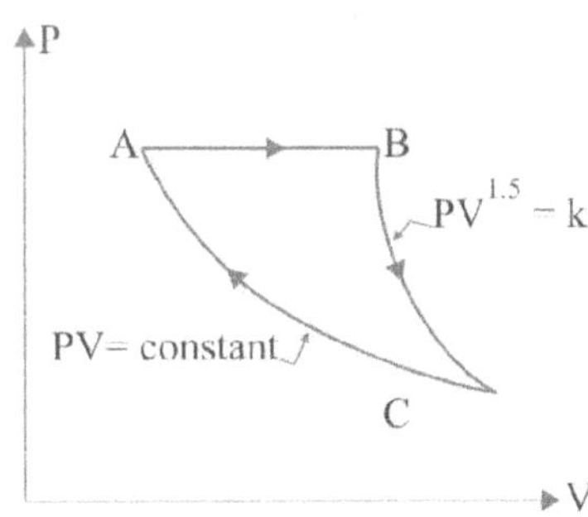

Fig. 7.37

$$m = \dfrac{P V_1}{R_{air} T_1} = \dfrac{700 \times 0.028}{0.287 \times 533} = 0.128 \text{ kg}$$

At A :

$$P_A = 700 \, kPa$$
$$V_A = 0.028 \text{ m}^3$$
$$T_A = 273 + 260 = 533 \, K$$

At B : $P_B = 700 \, kPa \qquad$ (As process is isobaric from A to B)
$$V_B = 0.084 \text{ m}^3$$
$$T_B = ?$$

By equation of state

$$\dfrac{P_A V_A}{T_A} = \dfrac{P_B V_B}{T_B}$$

or $\quad T_B = \dfrac{P_B V_B T_A}{P_A V_A} = \dfrac{V_B T_A}{V_A} \quad (P_A = P_B)$

$$= \dfrac{0.084}{0.028} \times T_A = 3T_A = 3 \times 533 = 1599\text{K}$$

At C : As process $C \to A$ is isothermal , so
$$T_C = 533 \text{ K}$$
$$V_C = V_A$$

In the process B to C,
$$PV^{1.5} = k$$

By equation of state, $\quad V = \dfrac{nRT}{P}$

$$P\left(\dfrac{nRT}{P}\right)^{1.5} = k$$

or $\quad \dfrac{T^{1.5}}{P^{0.5}} = k'$

Thus we have

$$\left(\dfrac{T_B}{T_C}\right)^{1.5} = \left(\dfrac{P_B}{P_C}\right)^{0.5}$$

$$\therefore \ P_C = P_B\left(\dfrac{T_C}{T_B}\right)^{1.5/0.5} = P_B\left(\dfrac{1}{3}\right)^3 = \dfrac{P_B}{27}$$

For the process $A \to B$:
$$C_P = C_V + R_{air} = 0.718 + 0.287 = 1.005 \text{ kJ/ kg K.}$$

$$Q_{AB} = mC_P(T_B - T_A) = 0.128 \times 1.005 \times (1599 - 533)$$

$$= 137.13 \text{ kJ}$$

For the process $B \to C$:

$$W_{BC} = mR_{air}\left(\dfrac{T_B - T_C}{r-1}\right)$$

and $\quad \Delta U = U_C - U_B = mC_V(T_C - T_B)$

$\therefore \qquad Q_{BC} = \Delta U + W_{BC}$

$$= mC_V(T_C - T_B) + mR_{air}\left(\dfrac{T_B - T_C}{r-1}\right)$$

$$= m(T_C - T_B)\left[C_V - \dfrac{R_{air}}{r-1}\right]$$

$$= 0.128[533 - 1599]\left[0.718 - \dfrac{0.287}{1.5 - 1}\right]$$

$$= 0.128 \times (-1066) \times 0.144$$

$$= -19.65 \text{ k J}$$

For process $C \to A$: As

$$T_C = T_A = 0, \qquad \therefore \ \Delta U = U_A - U_C = 0$$

$$W_{CA} = mR_{air}T_A \ell n \frac{V_A}{V_C} = mR_{air}T_A \ell n \frac{P_C}{P_A}$$

$$= 0.128 \times 0.287 \times 533 \times \ell n \left(\frac{1}{27}\right)$$

$$= -64.53 \text{ k J}$$

(a) Heat received in the cycle,
$$Q_{AB} = 137.13 \text{ kJ}$$

(b) Heat rejected in the cycle,
$$Q = 19.59 + 64.53$$
$$= 84.12 \text{ kJ}$$

(c) The efficiency of the cycle,

$$\eta = 1 - \frac{Q}{Q_{AB}}$$

$$= 1 - \frac{84.12}{137.13}$$

$$= 0.39 \text{ or } 39\%$$

Ex. 23 One mole of an ideal monoatomic gas is taken round the cyclic process *ABCA* as shown in *Fig. 7.38*. Calculate

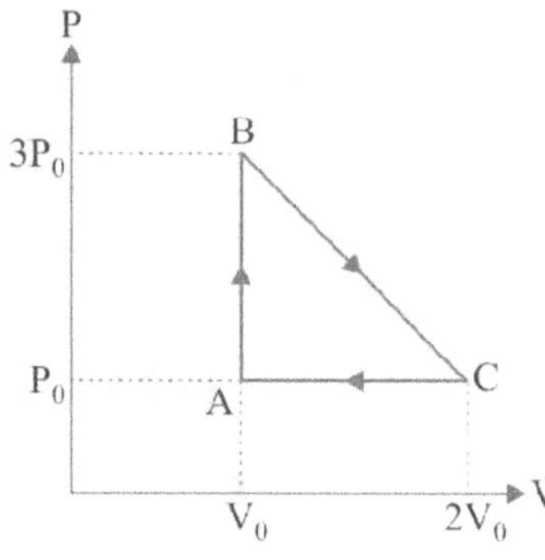

Fig. 7.38

(a) the work done by the gas
(b) the heat rejected by the gas in the path *CA* and the heat absorbed by the gas in the path *AB*
(c) the net heat absorbed by the gas in the path *BC*
(d) the maximum temperature attained by the gas during the cycle.

Sol.

(a) The work done by the gas in entire cycle
$$W = \text{area of ABCA}$$

$$= \frac{1}{2}(2V_0 - V_0) \times (3P_0 - P_0)$$

$$= \frac{1}{2}V_0 \times 2P_0 = P_0V_0$$

(b) For one mole of a gas, we have $T = \dfrac{PV}{R}$

$$\therefore \quad T_A = \frac{P_0V_0}{R}, \quad T_B = \frac{(3P_0)V_0}{R} = \frac{3P_0V_0}{R}$$

and $$T_C = \frac{P_0(2V_0)}{R} = \frac{2P_0V_0}{R}$$

As path CA is isobaric, so heat rejected

$$Q_{CA} = nC_P(T_A - T_C)$$

$$= 1 \times \frac{5R}{2} \times \left[\frac{P_0V_0}{R} - \frac{2P_0V_0}{R}\right]$$

$$= -\frac{5P_0V_0}{2}$$

As path *AB* is isochoric, so heat absorbed

$$Q_{AB} = nC_V(T_B - T_A)$$

$$= 1 \times \frac{3R}{2} \times \left[\frac{3P_0V_0}{R} - \frac{P_0V_0}{R}\right]$$

$$= 3P_0V_0$$

(c) For the complete cycle *ABCA*, $\Delta U = 0$.
From first law of thermodynamics, we have
$$Q = \Delta U + W$$
$$= 0 + W$$
or $$Q = W$$
or $$Q_{AB} + Q_{BC} + Q_{CA} = W$$
$$\therefore \quad Q_{AB} = W - (Q_{AB} + Q_{CA})$$

$$= P_0V_0 - \left(3P_0V_0 - \frac{5}{2}P_0V_0\right)$$

$$= \frac{P_0V_0}{2}$$

(d) We know that $PV = RT$. For T to be maximum, PV must be maximum.

$P - V$ relation for the process *BC*:
$$P = kV + k' \qquad \text{...(i)}$$

For point B, $3P_0 = kV_0 + k'$ $\qquad$ ...(ii)

For point C, $P_0 = k(2V_0) + k'$ $\qquad$ ...(iii)

After solving equations (i) and (ii), we get

$$k = -\frac{2P_0}{V_0} \text{ and } k' = 5P_0$$

Substituting these values in equation (i), we have

$$P = -\frac{2P_0V}{V_0} + 5P_0 \qquad \text{...(iv)}$$

Substituting this value of P in $PV = RT$, we have

$$\left(\frac{-2P_0V}{V_0} + 5P_0\right)V = RT$$

or $$T = \frac{P_0}{R}\left(5V - \frac{2V^2}{V_0}\right) \qquad \text{...(v)}$$

For maximum value, $\dfrac{dT}{dV} = 0$,

So $$\frac{dT}{dV} = \frac{P_0}{R}\left[5 - \frac{4V}{V_0}\right] = 0$$

which gives $$V = \frac{5V_0}{4}$$

Putting this value of V in equation (v), we get

$$T_{\max} = \frac{P_0}{R}\left[5\left(\frac{5V_0}{4}\right) - 2\left(\frac{5V_0}{4}\right)^2\left(\frac{1}{V_0}\right)\right]$$

$$= \frac{P_0}{R}\left[\frac{25V_0}{4} - \frac{25V_0}{8}\right]$$

$$= \frac{25P_0V_0}{8R}$$

Ex. 24 Two moles of an ideal monoatomic gas is taken through a cycle *ABCA* as shown in the *P – T* diagram. During the process *AB*, pressure and temperature of the gas vary such that *PT* = Constant . If T_1=300 K, calculate

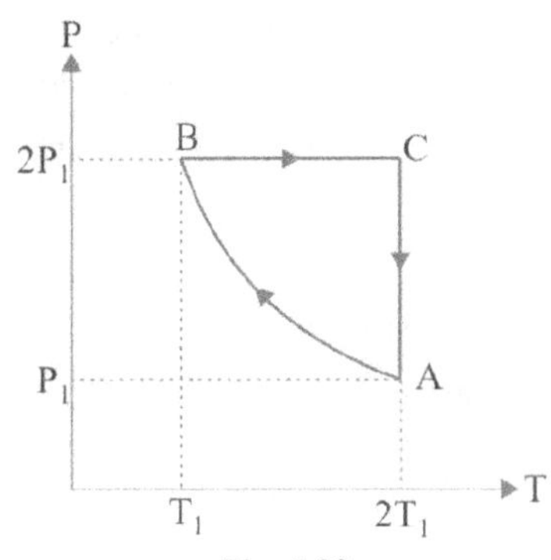

Fig. 7.39

(a) the work done of the gas in the process *AB* and

(b) the heat absorbed or released by the gas in each of the processes. Give answers in terms of the gas constant *R*.

Sol.

For the process $A - B$, it is given that

$$PT = \text{constant}$$

Differentiating above equation partially, we have

$$PdT + TdP = 0 \qquad \text{...(i)}$$

Equation of state for two moles of a gas

$$PV = 2RT \text{ or } P = \frac{2RT}{V} \qquad \text{...(ii)}$$

After differentiating equation (ii) partially, we get

$$PdV + VdP = 2R\,dT \qquad \text{...(iii)}$$

From equations (i) and (ii), we have

$$\left(\frac{2RT}{V}\right)dT + T\,dP = 0$$

or $\qquad 2RT\,dT + VT\,dP = 0$

$\therefore \qquad\qquad V\,dP = -2R\,dT \qquad \text{...(iv)}$

Now from equations (iii) and (iv), we have

$$-2RdT + VdP = 2RdT$$

or $\qquad\qquad PdV = 4R\,dT \qquad \text{...(v)}$

(a) The work done in the process *AB*

$$W_{AB} = \int PdV = \int_{600}^{300} 4R\,dT$$

$$= 4R\,|\,T\,|_{600}^{300} = 4R(300 - 600)$$

$$= -1200\,R \qquad\qquad \textit{Ans.}$$

(b) (i) As process $B \rightarrow C$ is isobaric, so

$$Q_{BC} = nC_P\Delta T = 2\times\frac{5R}{2}\times(600 - 300)$$

$$= 1500\,R \qquad\qquad \textit{Ans.}$$

(ii) Process $C \rightarrow A$ is isothermal, so $\Delta U = 0$

$$Q_{CA} = \Delta U + W_{CA} = W_{CA}$$

$$W_{CA} = nRT\ell n\left(\frac{P_1}{P_2}\right)$$

$$= 2R\times 600\ell n\left(\frac{2P_1}{P_1}\right)$$

$$= 1200\,R\,\ell n\,2$$

$\therefore \qquad Q_{CA} = 1200\,R\ell n2$

Again for the process $A \rightarrow B$

$$Q_{AB} = \Delta U + W_{AB}$$

$$= nC_V\Delta T + W_{AB}$$

$$= 2\times\frac{3R}{2}\times(300 - 600) - 1200R$$

$$= -900\,R - 1200\,R$$

$$= -2100\,R$$

7.11 WEAKNESS OF FIRST LAW AND NEED OF SECOND LAW

(i) **It does not tell about direction of flow of heat:**
Heat always flows from hot body to a cold body. But first law has no explanation why heat cannot flow from cold body to hot body.

(ii) **In which conditions heat can be converted into work:**
A revolving wheel stops due to friction.
According to first law, kinetic energy of wheel is converted into heat. But it fails to explain why heat energy cannot be converted into kinetic energy of the wheel.

(iii) **Amount of heat can be converted into work:**
No practical device converts entire heat into work. First law has no explanation of this fact.
Second law of thermodynamics provides answers of these questions.

7.12 Second Law of Thermodynamics

(i) **Kelvin - Plank statement**

It is impossible to construct an engine that can convert heat completely into work without producing any other effect. According to the statement the efficiency of any heat engine always be less than 100%.

(ii) **Clausius statement**

For a self acting machine, it is impossible to transfer heat from a colder body to a hotter body without the aid of external agency.

7.13 Entropy

Entropy is the another thermodynamical variable which many times very useful to understand the system. Entropy is related to the disorder or randomness in the system. To understand this, let us consider two systems as shown in *Fig. 7.40*:

If S_1 and S_2 are the entropies of the system 1 and 2 respectively at any temperature, then $S_1 < S_2$.

(i) Entropy is not a conserved quantity.

(ii) Entropy can be created but cannot be destroyed.

(iii) Entropy of the universe always increases.

If a system at temperature T is supplied a small amount of heat ΔQ, then change in entropy of the system can be defined as

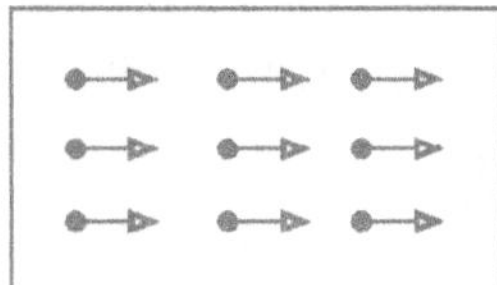

System 1

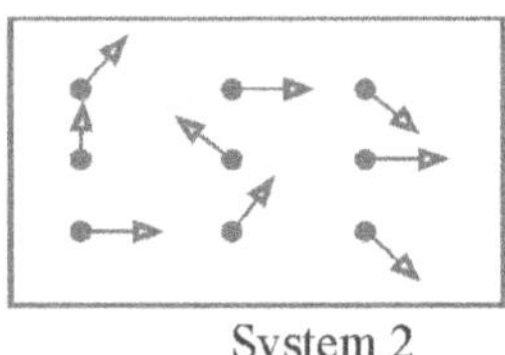

System 2

Fig. 7.40

$$\Delta S = \frac{\Delta Q}{T} \qquad \text{for constant } T$$

For a system with variable T, we have

$$\Delta S = S_f - S_i = \int_{S_i}^{S_f} \frac{dQ}{T}$$

The second law of thermodynamics may be stated in terms of entropy as:

It is impossible to have a process in which the entropy of an isolated system is decreased.

Ex. 25 One kilogram of ice at 0°C is melted and converted to water at 0°C. Compute the change in entropy.

Sol.

As the temperature in the process remain constant, so change in entropy,

$$\Delta S = \frac{\Delta Q}{T}$$

Here $\qquad \Delta Q = mL = 1 \times 334 \times 10^3 = 334 \times 10^3 \, J$

and $\qquad T = 273 + 0 = 273$ K

$$\therefore \qquad \Delta S = \frac{334 \times 10^3}{273} = 1223 \, J/K \qquad \textbf{Ans.}$$

Ex. 26 One kilogram of water at 0°C is heated to 100°C. Compute its change in entropy.

Sol.

As temperature in the process is not constant, so

$$\Delta S = \int_{T_1}^{T_2} \frac{dQ}{T}$$

For small change in temperature dT of the water of specific heat C, we have

$$dQ = mCdT$$

$$\therefore \qquad \Delta S = \int_{T_1}^{T_2} mC\frac{dT}{T} = mC\,|\,\ell nT\,|_{T_1}^{T_2}$$

$$= mC\ell n\left(\frac{T_2}{T_1}\right)$$

$$= 1000 \times 4.2 \times \ell n\left(\frac{273+100}{273+0}\right)$$

$$= 1000 \times 4.2 \times \ell n\frac{373}{273}$$

$$= 1308 \, J/K \qquad \textbf{Ans.}$$

7.14 HEAT ENGINE

It is a device which is used to convert heat energy into mechanical energy in a cyclic process.

There are two types of heat engine.

(i) External combustion engine: In this type of engine, heat needed for the engine is produced by the burning of the fuel outside the cylinder.

Example: steam engine.

(ii) Internal combustion engine: In this type of heat engine, heat needed for the engine is produced by the burning of the fuels inside the cylinder.

Example: diesel engines, petrol engines etc.

The efficiency of the steam engine is less than 20%.

The efficiency of petrol engine is about 25%.

The efficiency of diesel engine is about 40%.

Parts of a heat engine

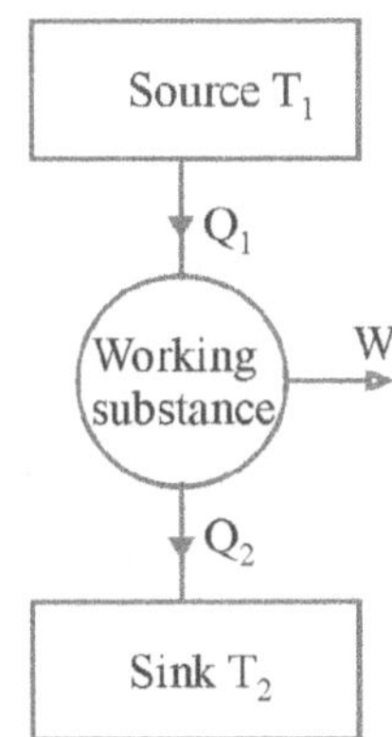

Fig. 7.41

(i) **Source:** It is a heat reservoir at higher temperature T_1. Its thermal capacity should be very large so that any amount of heat can be drawn from it without appreciable change in temperature of source.

(ii) **Sink:** It is a heat reservoir at a lower temperature T_2. Its thermal capacity is also very large so that any amount of heat can be added without appreciable change in temperature.

(iii) **Working substance:** Working substance is the material which performs mechanical work. It may be solid, liquid or gas.

In heat engine, the engine draws heat from the source Q_1 and after doing some mechanical work W, it rejects the remaining heat to the sink. Thus conservation of energy gives

$$Q_1 = W + Q_2$$

or

$$W = Q_1 - Q_2$$

Efficiency of heat engine is given by

$$\eta = \frac{\text{Output}}{\text{Input}}$$

$$= \frac{\text{Work done by engine}}{\text{Heat absorbed by engine from source}} = \frac{W}{Q_1}$$

$$= \frac{Q_1 - Q_2}{Q_1} = 1 - \frac{Q_2}{Q_1}$$

Note:

The practical value of η is always be less than 1 or 100%.

If engines of efficiencies η_1, η_2, ... are put in series, then output efficiency of the system of engines will be $\eta = \eta_1 \times \eta_2 \times ....$

7.15 CARNOT REVERSIBLE HEAT ENGINE

Sadi Carnot in 1824 conceived a theoretical engine which is free from all the defects of practical engines. It has the maximum efficiency and it is an ideal heat engine. It is based on four operations, which constitutes a Carnot cycle. These are: Isothermal expansion, adiabatic expansion, isothermal compression and adiabatic compression.

Carnot heat engine has three main parts:

(i)   Source, T_1 (ii)   Sink, T_2 (iii)   Working substance, W

A perfectly insulating stand is also provided so that the working substance can undergo adiabatic operation.

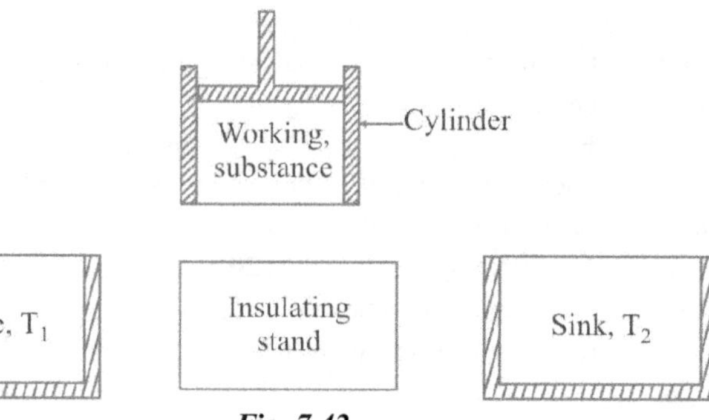

Fig. 7.42

Carnot cycle

Carnot cycle has four operations. Thermodynamic coordinates after each operation are shown in *Fig. 7.44*. Initially at A coordinates are P_1, V_1, T_1.

1.   **Isothermal expansion:** If Q_1 is the heat absorbed from the source and W_1 is the work done, then,

$$Q_1 \;=\; W_1 = nRT_1 \ell n \left(\frac{V_f}{V_i} \right) \qquad (\text{As } \Delta U = 0)$$

$$= \; nRT_1 \ell n \left(\frac{V_2}{V_1} \right)$$

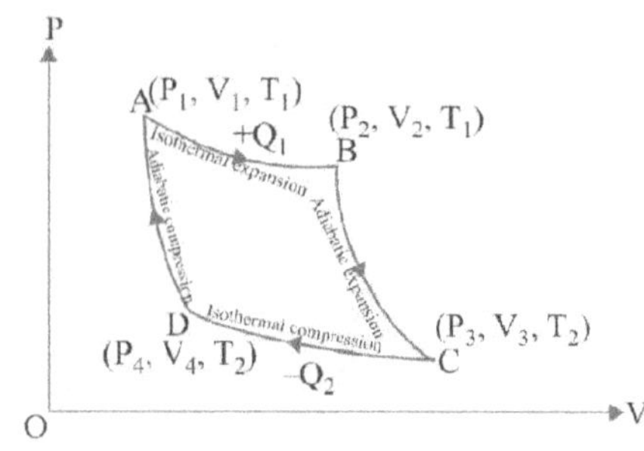

Fig. 7.43

2.   **Adiabatic expansion:** If W_2 is the work done during the adiabatic expansion, then

$$W_2 \;=\; \frac{nR(T_i - T_f)}{\gamma - 1} = \frac{nR(T_1 - T_2)}{\gamma - 1}$$

3.   **Isothermal compression:** If Q_2 is the heat reject to the sink and W_3 is the work done during the process, then

$$Q_2 \;=\; W_3 = nRT_2 \ell n \left(\frac{V_f}{V_i} \right) = nRT_2 \ell n \left(\frac{V_4}{V_3} \right)$$

$$(\text{As } \Delta U = 0)$$

$$= \; -nRT_2 \ell n \left(\frac{V_3}{V_4} \right)$$

4.   **Adiabatic compression:** If W_4 is the work done during the adiabatic compression, then

$$W_4 \;=\; \frac{nR(T_i - T_f)}{\gamma - 1} = \frac{nR(T_2 - T_1)}{\gamma - 1}$$

$$= \; -nR \frac{(T_1 - T_2)}{\gamma - 1}$$

Net work done in the whole cycle

$$W \;=\; W_1 + W_2 + W_3 + W_4$$

$$= nRT_1 \ell n\left(\frac{V_2}{V_1}\right) + \frac{nR(T_1 - T_2)}{\gamma - 1} - nRT_2 \ell n\left(\frac{V_3}{V_4}\right) - nR\frac{(T_1 - T_2)}{\gamma - 1}$$

$$= nR\left[T_1 \ell n\left(\frac{V_2}{V_1}\right) - T_2 \ell n\left(\frac{V_3}{V_4}\right)\right] \qquad \ldots(i)$$

In the adiabatic expansion $B \to C$

$$T_1 V_2^{\gamma - 1} = T_2 V_3^{\gamma - 1}$$

or
$$\left(\frac{V_2}{V_3}\right)^{\gamma - 1} = \frac{T_2}{T_1} \qquad \ldots(ii)$$

Similarly in the adiabatic compression $D \to A$

$$T_2 V_4^{\gamma - 1} = T_1 V_1^{\gamma - 1}$$

or
$$\left(\frac{V_1}{V_4}\right)^{\gamma - 1} = \frac{T_2}{T_1} \qquad \ldots(iii)$$

From equations (ii) and (iii), we have

$$\frac{V_2}{V_3} = \frac{V_1}{V_4}$$

or
$$V_1 V_3 = V_2 V_4 \qquad \ldots(iv)$$

Also
$$\frac{V_2}{V_1} = \frac{V_3}{V_4}$$

Efficiency of carnot engine

$$\eta = \frac{\text{Work done by engine}\,(W)}{\text{Heat absorbed by engine from source}\,(Q_1)}$$

$$= \frac{nR\left[T_1 \ell n\left(\frac{V_2}{V_1}\right) - T_2 \ell n\left(\frac{V_3}{V_4}\right)\right]}{nRT_1 \ell n\left(\frac{V_2}{V_1}\right)}$$

As
$$\frac{V_2}{V_1} = \frac{V_3}{V_4}$$

$\therefore$
$$\eta = \frac{T_1 - T_2}{T_1} = 1 - \frac{T_2}{T_1}.$$

Note:

1. The isothermal process will take place only when the piston moves very slowly to give enough time for the heat transfer between source and working substance. The adiabatic process will take place when the piston moves extremely fast to avoid heat transfer. Any practical engine can not satisfy these conditions.

2. All practical engines have an efficiency less than the carnot engine (Carnot theorem).

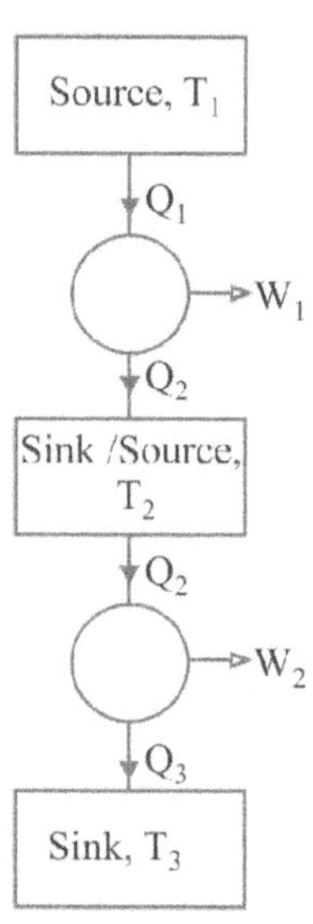

Fig. 7.44

More about η

1. For η to be unity or 100%, $\left(\dfrac{T_2}{T_1}\right) \to 0$. It can be possible if either $T_2 = 0$ K or $T_1 = \infty$. Practically these are not possible (till now), so Carnot engine cannot have efficiency 100%.

2.
$$\eta = 1 - \frac{T_2}{T_1} = \frac{T_1 - T_2}{T_1},$$

with decrease in temperature difference $(T_1 - T_2)$ between source and sink will decrease the efficiency of the engine.

If $\qquad T_1 - T_2 = 0 \quad$ or $\quad T_1 = T_2,\ \eta = 0$

3. As
$$\eta = 1 - \frac{Q_2}{Q_1} \quad \text{and} \quad \eta = 1 - \frac{T_2}{T_1}$$

$$\therefore \qquad \frac{Q_2}{Q_1} = \frac{T_2}{T_1} \quad \text{or} \quad \frac{Q_1}{T_1} = \frac{Q_2}{T_2} = \frac{Q}{T}\ \text{Constant}$$

4. When two engines are put in series, the net work done,
$$W = W_1 + W_2$$
By conservation of energy, we have
$$Q_1 = Q_3 + (W_1 + W_2)$$
$$= Q_3 + W$$
or $\qquad W = Q_1 - Q_3$

$$\therefore \qquad \eta = \frac{W}{Q_1} = \frac{Q_1 - Q_3}{Q_1}$$

$$= 1 - \frac{Q_3}{Q_1} = 1 - \frac{T_3}{T_1}$$

7.16 REFRIGERATOR OR HEAT - PUMP

Carnot cycle is reversible cycle. It can work as a heat engine and also as a refrigerator. In a refrigerator, the working substance absorbs an amount of heat Q_2 from the sink (cold reservoir) at temperature T_2. W is the work done by external agency and it rejects a larger quantity of heat Q_1 to the source (hot reservoir). By conservation of energy, we have,
$$Q_1 = Q_2 + W$$
or $\qquad W = Q_1 - Q_2$
Coefficient of performance of a refrigerator is defined as:

$$\beta = \frac{\text{Heat absorbed from sink}}{\text{Work done}}$$

$$= \frac{Q_2}{W}$$

$$= \frac{Q_2}{Q_1 - Q_2} = \frac{1}{\left(\dfrac{Q_1}{Q_2} - 1\right)}$$

or $$\beta = \frac{1}{\dfrac{T_1}{T_2} - 1} = \frac{1 - \eta}{\eta}$$

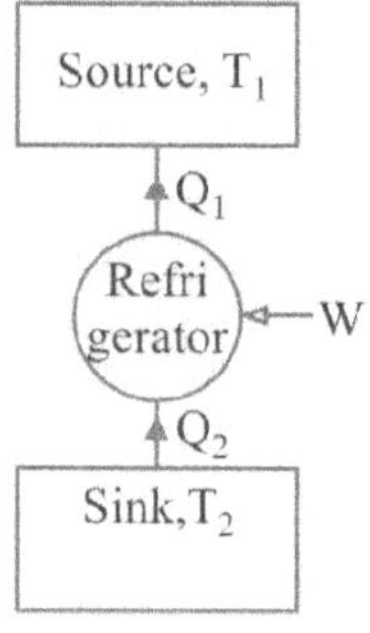

Fig. 7.45

In domestic refrigerator, the interior of it acts as the sink and the room (surroundings) acts as the source. Work is done by the electrical energy and frown CCl_2F_2 is used as a working substance.

More about β

1. Coefficient of performance β always be greater than 1. Practical refrigerators have a coefficient of performance close to 10.

2. As $\beta = \dfrac{T_2}{T_1 - T_2}$, so lesser the temperature difference $T_1 - T_2$, higher is the value of β.

3. When refrigerator works, the temperature of sink T_2 decreases due to formation of ice and $T_1 - T_2$ increases. This decrease the value of β. So defrosting is necessary to increase the performance of the refrigerator.

4. If the door of the refrigerator is opened, it rejects Q_1 amount of heat which is greater than heat absorbed from the room Q_2, so the temperature of the room will increase.

Ex. 27 One of the most efficient engines ever developed operated between 2100 K and 700 K. Its actual efficiency is 40%. What percentage of its maximum possible efficiency is this?

Sol.

Here $\qquad T_1 = 2100 \text{ K and } T_2 = 700 \text{ K}$

$\therefore \qquad \eta_{max} = 1 - \dfrac{T_2}{T_1} = 1 - \dfrac{700}{2100}$

$$= 1 - \dfrac{1}{3} = \dfrac{2}{3} = 66.6\%$$

Given, $\qquad \eta_{actual} = 40\%$

The % of maximum efficiency

$$= \dfrac{\eta_{actual}}{\eta_{max}} \times 100$$

$$= \dfrac{40}{66.6} \times 100 \approx 60\% \qquad \textit{Ans.}$$

Ex. 28 The efficiency of a Carnot cycle is $\dfrac{1}{6}$. If on reducing the temperature of the sink by 65°C, the efficiency becomes $\dfrac{1}{3}$, find the initial and final temperatures between which the cycle is working.

Sol.

If T_1 and T_2 are the temperatures of source and sink respectively, then

$$\eta_1 = 1 - \dfrac{T_2}{T_1}$$

or $\qquad \dfrac{1}{6} = 1 - \dfrac{T_2}{T_1} \qquad\qquad ...(i)$

When temperature of sink reduces by 65°C, then $\eta_2 = \dfrac{1}{3}$

$\therefore \qquad \dfrac{1}{3} = 1 - \dfrac{T_2 - 65}{T_1} \qquad\qquad ...(ii)$

Solving equations (i) and (ii), we get

$$T_1 = 390\ K \text{ and } T_2 = 325\ K \qquad \textit{Ans.}$$

Ex. 29 A Carnot engine whose heat sink is at 27°C has an efficiency of 40%. By how many degrees should the temperature of the source be changed to increase the efficiency by 10% of the original efficiency?

Sol.

Here, $\qquad T_2 = 273 + 27 = 300 \text{ K}$

We know that $\qquad \eta = 1 - \dfrac{T_2}{T_1}$

or $\qquad 0.40 = 1 - \dfrac{300}{T_1}$

or $\qquad T_1 = 500 \text{ K}$

Increase in efficiency of engine = 10% of 40 = 4%
Thus new efficiency of the engine becomes = 40 + 4 = 44%

Let T_1' is the new temperature of the source, then

$$0.44 = 1 - \dfrac{T_2}{T_1'}$$

or $\qquad 0.44 = 1 - \dfrac{300}{T_1'}$

or $\qquad T_1' = 535.7\ K$

Increase in temperature of the source

$$= T_1' - T_1 = 535.7 - 500$$

$$= 35.7\ K \qquad \textit{Ans.}$$

Ex. 30 Five moles of an ideal gas taken in a Carnot engine working between 100°C and 30°C. The useful work done in one cycle is 420 joule. Calculate the ratio of the volume of the gas at the end and beginning of the isothermal expansion.

$$R = 8.4 \text{ J/mol. K}$$

Sol.

Here,
$$T_1 = 273 + 100 = 373 \, K \text{ and}$$
$$T_2 = 273 + 30 = 303 \, K$$

We know that
$$\frac{Q_1}{Q_2} = \frac{T_1}{T_2} = \frac{373}{303}$$

or
$$Q_1 = \frac{373}{303} Q_2 \qquad ...(i)$$

Work done in the cycle $W = Q_1 - Q_2 = 420$ J $\qquad ...(ii)$

From equations (i) and (ii), we have

$$\frac{373}{303} Q_2 - Q_2 = 420$$

or
$$Q_2 = 1818 \text{ J}$$
and
$$Q_1 = Q_2 + 420$$
$$= 1818 + 420 = 2238 \text{ J}$$

When the gas is carried through Carnot cycle, the heat absorbed Q_1 during isothermal expansion will equal to the work done by the gas. If V_1 and V_2 are the volumes of the gas at the beginning and at the end of the isothermal expansion, then

$$Q_1 = W = nRT \ell n \left(\frac{V_2}{V_1} \right)$$

or
$$2238 = 5 \times 8.4 \times 373 \, \ell n \left(\frac{V_2}{V_1} \right)$$

or
$$\ell n \left(\frac{V_2}{V_1} \right) = 0.1428$$

or
$$\frac{V_1}{V_2} = 1.153 \qquad \textbf{\textit{Ans.}}$$

Ex. 31 Two Carnot engines A and B are operated in series. The first one A receives heat at 800 K and rejects to a reservoir at temperature T K. The second engine B receives the heat rejected by the first engine and in turn rejects to a heat reservoir at 300 K. Calculate the temperature TK for the following cases:

(i) When the outputs of the two engines are equal.

(ii) When the efficiencies of the two engines are equal.

Sol.

For engine A: $T_1 = 800$ K and $T_2 = TK$

We know that,
$$\frac{Q_2}{Q_1} = \frac{T_2}{T_1} = \frac{T}{800} \qquad ...(i)$$

Efficiency of the engine
$$\eta_A = \frac{W_A}{Q_1}$$

or
$$1 - \frac{T_2}{T_1} = \frac{W_A}{Q_1}$$

$$\therefore \qquad W_A = Q_1 \left(1 - \frac{T_2}{T_1} \right) = Q_1 \left(1 - \frac{T}{800} \right) \qquad ...(ii)$$

For engine B: $T_1' = TK$ and $T_2' = 300 \, K$

Efficiency of the engine
$$\eta_B = \frac{W_B}{Q_1'}$$

or
$$1 - \frac{T_2'}{T_1'} = \frac{W_B}{Q_1'}$$

$$\therefore \qquad W_B = Q_1' \left(1 - \frac{T_2'}{T_1'} \right) = Q_1' \left(1 - \frac{300}{T} \right) \qquad ...(iii)$$

Since the engine B absorbs the heat rejected by the engine A.

So
$$Q_1' = Q_2$$

Now equation (ii) becomes
$$W_B = Q_2 \left(1 - \frac{300}{T} \right) \qquad ...(iv)$$

Case (i) When outputs of the two engines are equal
$$W_A = W_B$$
$$Q_1 \left(1 - \frac{T}{800} \right) = Q_2 \left(1 - \frac{300}{T} \right)$$

or
$$1 - \frac{T}{800} = \frac{Q_2}{Q_1} \left(1 - \frac{300}{T} \right)$$

From (i)
$$\frac{Q_2}{Q_1} = \frac{T}{800}$$

$$\therefore \qquad 1 - \frac{T}{800} = \frac{T}{800} \left(1 - \frac{300}{T} \right)$$

After solving, we get , $T = 550 \, K$ $\qquad \textbf{\textit{Ans.}}$

Case (ii) When the efficiencies are equal
$$\eta_A = \eta_B$$

or
$$1 - \frac{T}{800} = 1 - \frac{300}{T}$$

After solving, we get
$$T = 489.9 \, K \qquad \textbf{\textit{Ans.}}$$

Ex. 32 How much energy in watt hour may be required to convert 2 kg of water into ice at 0°C, assuming that the refrigerator is ideal? Given temperature of freezer is –15°C, room temperature is 25°C and initial temperature of water is 25°C.

Sol.

Here
$$T_1 = 273 + 25 = 298 \, K \text{ and}$$
$$T_2 = 273 - 15 = 258 \, K$$

Specific heat of water,
$$C = 4.2 \times 10^3 \text{ J/kg K}$$

Latent heat of fusion of ice,

$$L = 3.36 \times 10^5 \, J/kg$$

The amount of heat required to transform water of 25°C into ice of 0°C

$$Q_2 = mC\Delta T + mL$$
$$= 2 \times 4.2 \times 10^3 \times (25 - 0) + 2 \times 3.36 \times 10^5$$
$$= 2.1 \times 10^5 + 6.72 \times 10^5$$
$$= 8.82 \times 10^5 J$$

Heat rejected to the surroundings;

We have $\quad \dfrac{Q_1}{Q_2} = \dfrac{T_1}{T_2}$

$\therefore \qquad Q_1 = Q_2 \left(\dfrac{T_1}{T_2}\right)$

$$= 8.82 \times 10^5 \left(\dfrac{298}{258}\right) = 10.19 \times 10^5 \, J$$

Energy supplied to convert water into ice,

$$W = Q_1 - Q_2$$
$$= 10.15 \times 10^5 - 8.82 \times 10^5$$
$$= 1.33 \times 10^5 \, J$$
$$= \dfrac{1.33 \times 10^5}{3600} = 36.96 \; Wh \qquad \textbf{\textit{Ans.}}$$

Review of formulae & Important Points

1. **Internal energy** of an ideal gas is due to its kinetic energy, which is the function of temperature.

$$U = \frac{3}{2} RT \text{ for monoatomic gas}$$
$$= \frac{5}{2} RT \text{ for diatomic gas}$$

Also $\qquad \Delta U = nC_v\Delta T$

If $\qquad \Delta T = 0, \Delta U = 0.$

In cyclic process,
$$\Delta U = 0.$$

2. **Work done,** $\quad W = \displaystyle\int_{V_i}^{V_f} P dV$

3. **First law of thermodynamics**
$$Q = \Delta U + W$$
In diferential form, it can be written as
$$dQ = dU + W$$

4. **Thermodynamic processes :**
$PV = $ const for isothermal; $PV^r = $ constant for adiabatic.
(i) Work done in isobaric process,
$$W = P\Delta V = nR\Delta T$$
(ii) Work done in isochoic process
$$W = 0$$
Also $\quad Q = \Delta U + W = \Delta U + 0 = nC_V\Delta T$
(iii) Work done in isothermal process
$$W = nRT\ell n\frac{V_f}{V_i} = nRT\ell n\frac{P_i}{P_f}$$
$$E_{iso} = P$$
(iv) Work done in adiabatic process
$$W = \frac{(P_iV_i - P_fV_f)}{(\gamma - 1)}$$
or $\qquad W = \dfrac{nR}{\gamma - 1} = (T_i - T_f)$
$$E_{ad} = \gamma P$$
$$E_{ad} = \gamma E_{iso}$$

5. **Polytropic process :**
$$PV^r = 1, \; r \neq 1 \text{ or } \gamma.$$
Work done, $\quad W = \dfrac{nR}{r - 1}[T_i - T_f]$

Specific heat, $\quad C = C_V - \dfrac{R}{r - 1}$

6. **Second law of thermodynamics**
(i) **Kelvin-Plank statement :** It is impossible to construct an engine that can convert heat completely into work.
(ii) **Clausius statement :** For a self acting machine, it is impossible to transfer heat from a colder body to a hotter body without the aid of external agency.

7. **The change in entropy,**
$$\Delta S = \frac{\Delta Q}{T}.$$
For a system with variable T
$$\Delta S = \int_{S_i}^{S_f} \frac{dQ}{T}$$

8. **Efficiency of heat engine**
$$\eta = \frac{W}{Q_1} = \frac{Q_1 - Q_2}{Q_1} = 1 - \frac{Q_2}{Q_1}$$

9. **Carnot heat engine :**
$$V_1 V_3 = V_2 V_4$$
$$\eta = 1 - \frac{T_2}{T_1}$$

10. **Regrigerator or heat pump:** Coefficient of performance
$$\beta = \frac{Q_2}{W} = \frac{Q_2}{Q_1 - Q_2} = \frac{1}{\dfrac{Q_1}{Q_2} - 1}$$
$$= \frac{1}{\dfrac{T_1}{T_2} - 1} = \frac{\eta}{1 - \eta}$$

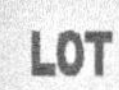

LOT | MCQ Type 1 | *Exercise 7.1*

LEVEL - 1

Only one option correct

1. An ideal monoatomic gas is taken round the cycle $ABCDA$ as shown in figure. The work done during the cycle is

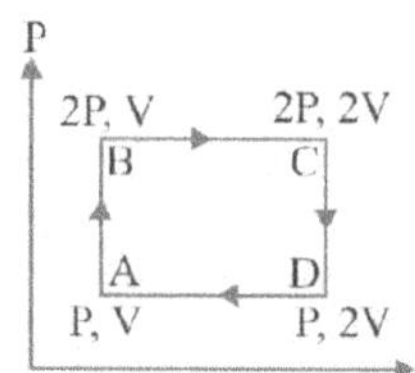

   (a) PV
   (b) $2PV$
   (c) $PV/2$
   (d) Zero

2. Two identical containers A and B with frictionless pistons contain the same ideal gas at the same temperature and the same volume V. The mass of the gas in A is m_A and that in B is m_B. The gas in each cylinder is now allowed to expand isothermally to the same final volume $2V$. The changes in pressure in A and B are found to be ΔP and $1.5\ \Delta P$ respectively. Then
   (a) $4\ m_A = 9\ m_B$
   (b) $2m_A = 3m_B$
   (c) $3m_A = 2m_B$
   (d) $9m_A = 4m_B$

3. The specific heat of a gas at constant pressure is greater than the specific heat of the same gas at constant volume because :
   (a) work is done in the expansion of the gas at constant pressure.
   (b) work is done in the expansion of the gas at constant volume.
   (c) the attraction between the molecules increases at constant pressure.
   (d) the molecular attraction increases at constant volume.

4. One mole of a monoatomic gas is heated at constant pressure of 1 atmosphere from 0 K to 100 K. If the gas constant R is taken as 8.32 J/mol-K, the change in the internal energy of the gas is approximately
   (a) 2.3 J
   (b) 46 J
   (c) 1.25×10^3 J
   (d) 8.67×10^4 J

5. The P-V diagram of process on a system is shown in figure. During the process, the work done by the system

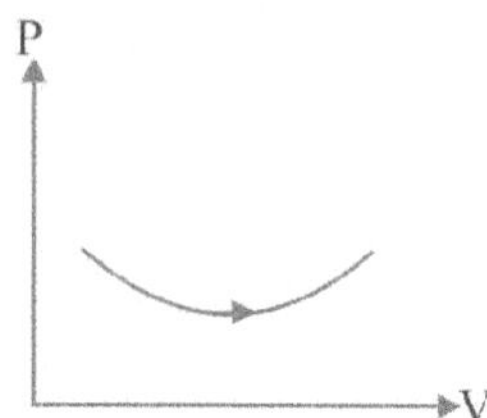

   (a) increases continuously
   (b) decreases continuously
   (c) first increases, becomes maximum and then decreases
   (d) first decreases, becomes minimum and then increases

6. When an ideal diatomic gas is heated at constant pressure. The fraction of heat energy supplied which increases the internal energy of the gas is
   (a) $\dfrac{2}{5}$
   (b) $\dfrac{3}{5}$
   (c) $\dfrac{3}{7}$
   (d) $\dfrac{5}{7}$

7. In a given process on an ideal gas, $dW = 0$ and $dQ < 0$, then for the gas
   (a) the temperature will decrease.
   (b) the volume will increase.
   (c) the pressure will remain constant.
   (d) the temperature will increase.

8. Choose the correct statement from among the following?
   (a) A monoatomic gas has three degrees of freedom because it undergoes translational as well as rotational motion.
   (b) A diatomic molecule undergoes both translational and rotational motion and has six degrees of freedom.
   (c) A diatomic molecule is capable of rotating energetically about each of three mutually perpendicular axes.
   (d) The molecule of a polyatomic gas is capable of rotating energetically about each of three mutually perpendicular axes and undergoes both translational and rotational motion.

9. In figure, three isothermal processes are shown for the same gas and for same change in volume $(V_i - V_f)$ but at different temperature. If ΔQ_1, ΔQ_2, and ΔQ_3 are the heat transferred in the respective process, then :

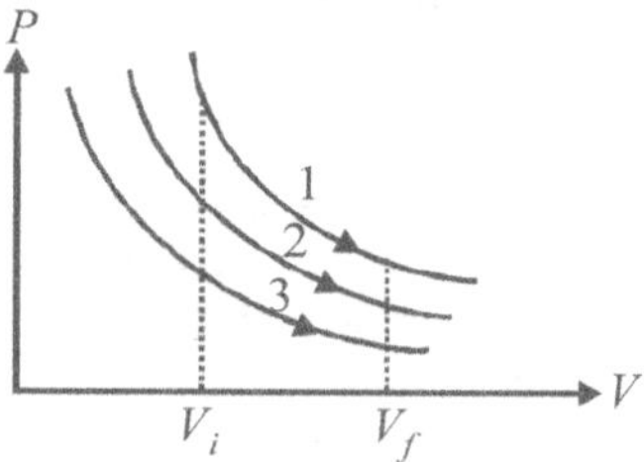

   (a) $\Delta Q_1 = \Delta Q_2 = \Delta Q_3$
   (b) $\Delta Q_1 > \Delta Q_2 > \Delta Q_3$
   (c) $\Delta Q_1 < \Delta Q_2 < \Delta Q_3$
   (d) $\Delta Q_1 = \Delta Q_2 = \Delta Q_3 = 0$

10. A gas, confined to an isolated cylinder, is compressed adiabatically to half its volume. The entropy of the gas :
    (a) increases
    (b) decreases
    (c) remains same
    (d) none of the above

Answer Key	1	(a)	3	(a)	5	(a)	7	(a)	9	(b)
Sol. from page 509	2	(c)	4	(c)	6	(d)	8	(d)	10	(c)

11. An ideal gas is made to go through a cyclic thermodynamical process in four steps. The amount of heat involved are $Q_1 = 600J$, $Q_2 = -400J$, $Q_3 = -300J$ and $Q_4 = 200J$ respectively. The corresponding work involved are $W_1 = 300J$, $W_2 = -200J$, $W_3 = -150J$ and W_4. The value of W_4 is
(a) $-50J$
(b) $100J$
(c) $150J$
(d) $50J$

12. A container of volume $1m^3$ is divided into two equal compartments by a partition. One of these compartments contains an ideal gas at 300 K. The other compartment is vacuum. The whole system is thermally isolated from its surroundings. The partition is removed and the gas expands to occupy the whole volume of the container. Its temperature now would be
(a)   300 K
(b)   239 K
(c)   200 K
(d)   100 K

13. For free expansion of the gas which of the following is true
(a) $Q = W = 0$ and $\Delta E_{int} = 0$
(b) $Q = 0$, $W > 0$ and $\Delta E_{int} = -W$
(c) $W = 0$, $Q > 0$ and $\Delta E_{int} = Q$
(d) $W > 0$, $Q < 0$ and $\Delta E_{int} = 0$

14. Which of the following parameters does not characterize the thermodynamic state of matter
(a)   Volume
(b)   Temperature
(c)   Pressure
(d)   Work

15. Which of the following statements is correct for any thermodynamic system
(a)   The internal energy changes in all processes
(b)   Internal energy and entropy are state functions
(c)   The change in entropy can never be zero
(d)   The work done in an adiabatic process is always zero

16. The gas law $\dfrac{PV}{T}$ = constant is true for
(a)   Isothermal changes only
(b)   Adiabatic changes only
(c)   Both isothermal and adiabatic changes
(d)   Neither isothermal nor adiabatic changes

17. One mole of an ideal gas expands at a constant temperature of 300 K from an initial volume of 10 litres to a final volume of 20 litres. The work done in expanding the gas is
($R = 8.31$ J/mole-K)
(a)   750 J
(b)   1728 J
(c)   1500 J
(d)   3456 J

18. During an adiabatic process, the pressure of a gas is found to be proportional to the cube of its absolute temperature. The ratio C_p/C_v for the gas is
(a) $\dfrac{3}{2}$
(b) $\dfrac{4}{3}$
(c) 2
(d) $\dfrac{5}{3}$

19. In a reversible isochoric change
(a) $\Delta W = 0$
(b) $\Delta Q = 0$
(c) $\Delta U = 0$
(d)   all

20. If the door of a running refrigerator is kept open, then which of the following is true
(a)   Room is cooled
(b)   Room is heated
(c)   Room is either cooled or heated
(d)   Room is neither cooled nor heated

21. If we consider solar system consisting of the earth and sun only as one of the ideal thermodynamic system. The sun works as source of energy having temperature 6000 K and the earth as sink having temperature 300 K, the efficiency of solar system would be on the basis of exchange of radiations
(a)   30%
(b)   65%
(c)   75%
(d)   95%

22. A carnot engine, having an efficiency of $\eta = \dfrac{1}{10}$ as heat engine, is used as a refrigerator. If the work done on the system is 10 J, the amount of energy absorbed from the reservoir at lower temperature is
(a)   99 J
(b)   90 J
(c)   1 J
(d)   100 J

23. In the following indicator diagram, the net amount of work done will be

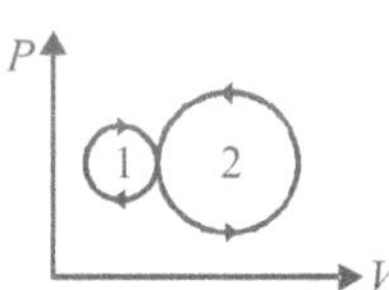

(a)   Positive
(b)   Negative
(c)   Zero
(d)   Infinity

24. The temperature-entropy diagram of a reversible engine cycle is given in the figure. Its efficiency is

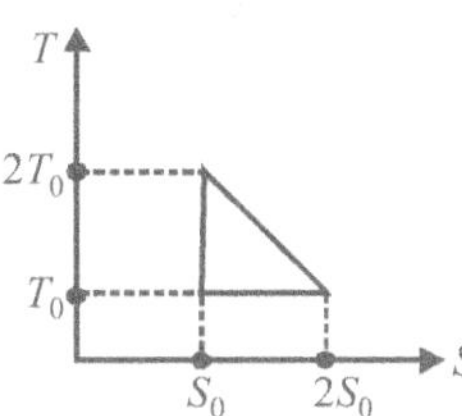

(a)   1/3
(b)   2/3
(c)   1/2
(d)   1/4

Answer Key	11	(c)	13	(a)	15	(b)	17	(b)	19	(d)	21	(d)	23	(b)
Sol. from page 509	12	(a)	14	(d)	16	(c)	18	(a)	20	(b)	22	(b)	24	(a)

25. A thermodynamic system undergoes cyclic process $ABCDA$ as shown in figure. The work done by the system is

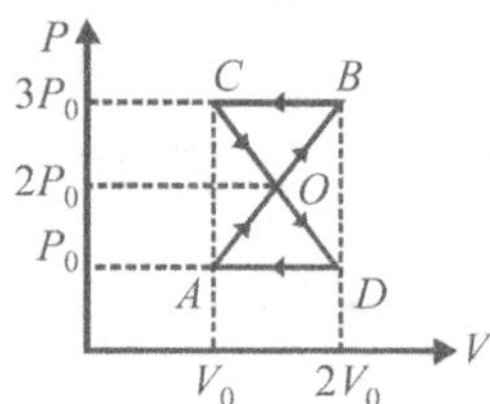

(a) $P_0 V_0$

(b) $2 P_0 V_0$

(c) $\dfrac{P_0 V_0}{2}$

(d) Zero

26. The P-V diagram of a system undergoing thermodynamic transformation is shown in figure. The work done by the system in going from $A \to B \to C$ is 30J and 40J heat is given to the system. The change in internal energy between A and C is

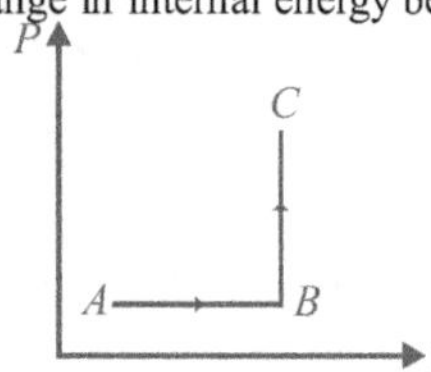

(a) 10 J

(b) 70 J

(c) 84 J

(d) 134 J

27. In the following figure, four curves A, B, C and D are shown. The curves are

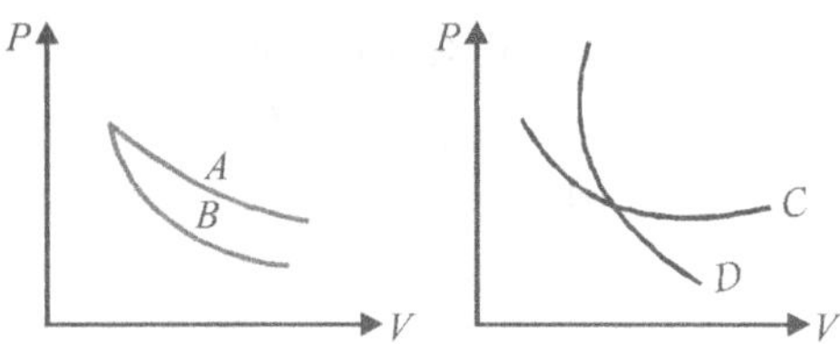

(a) Isothermal for A and D while adiabatic for B and C

(b) Adiabatic for A and C while isothermal for B and D

(c) Isothermal for A and B while adiabatic for C and D

(d) Isothermal for A and C while adiabatic for B and D

28. The equation of state of a gas is given as $P(V - b) = nRT$ where b is a constant, n is the number of moles and R is the universal gas constant. When 2 moles of this gas undergo reversible isothermal expansion from volume V to volume $2V$, what is the work done by the gas

(a) $2RT \ln\left[\dfrac{V - b}{2V - b}\right]$

(b) $2RT \ln\left[\dfrac{2V - b}{V - b}\right]$

(c) $2RT \ln\left[\dfrac{V - b}{2V}\right]$

(d) $2RT \ln\left[\dfrac{2V}{V - b}\right]$

29. For an ideal gas the equation of a process for which the heat capacity of the gas varies with temperature as $C = \alpha/T$ (α is a constant is given by)

(a) $V\ln T$ = constant

(b) $VT^{1/(\gamma - 1)}e^{\alpha/RT}$ = constant

(c) $V^{\frac{1}{\gamma - 1}}Te^{\alpha/RT}$ = constant

(d) $V^{\gamma - 1}$ = constant

30. 5 g of a gas is carried through a cycle $ABCDA$ in a piston cylinder assembly as shown. If in the portion from A to B, 5.5 kcal of heat flows into the gas and the temperature of the gas at A is 427°C, C_v for the gas is

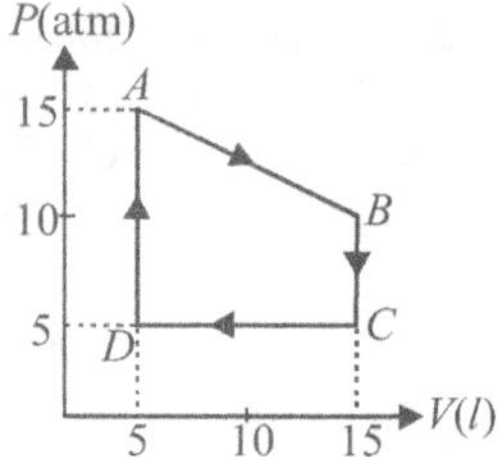

(a) 0.49 kJ/kg°C

(b) 0.298 kJ/kg°C

(c) 3.03 kJ/kg°C

(d) 0.98 kJ/kg°C

31. 2 k mol of hydrogen at NTP expands isobarically to twice its initial volume. The change in its internal energy is ($C_v = 10$ kJ/kg.K and atm pressure = 1×10^5 N/m²)

(a) 10.9 MJ

(b) 9.10 MJ

(c) 109 MJ

(d) 1.09 MJ

32. A thermodynamic process is shown in the figure. In the process AB 500 J of heat are added and in process BD, 150 J of heat are added. The change in the internal energy in the process ABD is :

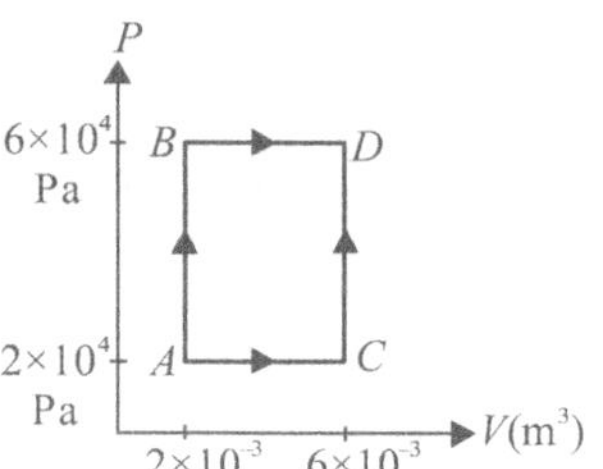

(a) 890 J

(b) 410 J

(c) 650 J

(d) 240 J

33. One mole of a monoatomic ideal gas is taken through a reversible cycle ABC as shown in the figure. The process BC is adiabatic. The work done per cycle is (given that temperatures of A, B and C are 300, 600 and 450 K) :

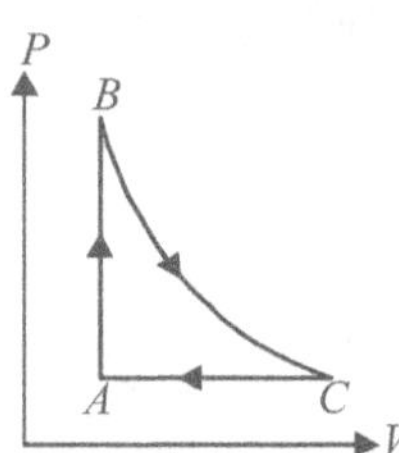

(a) 75 R

(b) 150 R

(c) 112.5 R

(d) 45 R

Answer Key	25	(d)	27	(d)	29	(d)	31	(a)	33	(a)
Sol. from page 509	26	(a)	28	(b)	30	(c)	32	(b)		

LEVEL - 2

Only one option correct

1. $\frac{1}{2}$ mole of helium gas is contained in a container at STP. The heat energy needed to double the pressure of the gas, keeping the volume constant (heat capacity of the gas = 3 J/g K) is
(a) 3276 J
(b) 1638 J
(c) 819 J
(d) 409.5 J

2. A monoatomic ideal gas initially at temperature T_1 is enclosed in a cylinder fitted with a frictionless piston. The gas is allowed to expand adiabatically to a temperature T_2 by releasing the piston suddenly. If L_1 and L_2 are the lengths of gas column before and after expansion respectively, then $\frac{T_1}{T_2}$ is

(a) $\left(\dfrac{L_1}{L_2}\right)^{2/3}$
(b) $\dfrac{L_1}{L_2}$
(c) $\dfrac{L_2}{L_1}$
(d) $\left(\dfrac{L_2}{L_1}\right)^{2/3}$

3. A gas mixture consists of 2 moles of oxygen and 4 moles of argon at temperature T. Neglecting all vibrational modes, the total internal energy of the system is
(a) $4\,RT$
(b) $15\,RT$
(c) $9\,RT$
(d) $11\,RT$

4. P-V plots of two gases during adiabatic processes are shown in figure. Plots 1 and 2 should correspond respectively to

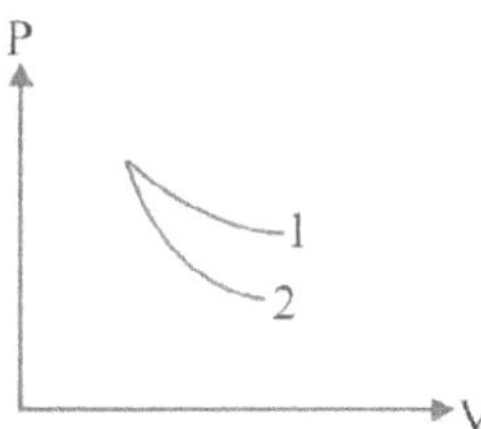

(a) He and O_2
(b) O_2 and He
(c) He and Ar
(d) O_2 and N_2

5. An ideal gas expands isothermally from a volume V_1 to V_2 and then compressed adiabatically to original volume V, initial pressure is P_1 and final pressure is P_2. If the total work done is W, then
(a) $P_2 > P_1,\ W > 0$
(b) $P_2 < P_1,\ W < 0$
(c) $P_2 > P_1,\ W < 0$
(d) $P_2 = P_1,\ W = 0$

6. An ideal gas is taken through the cycle $A \to B \to C \to A$ as shown in figure. If the net heat supplied to the gas in the cycle is 5 J, the work done the gas in the process $C \to A$ is

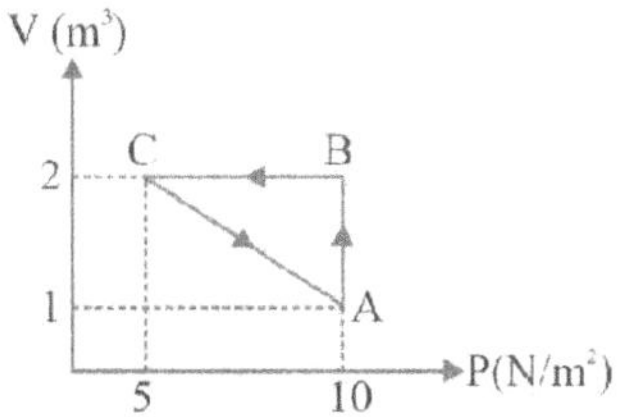

7. An ideal gas heat engine operates in a Carnot cycle between 227°C and 127°C. It absorbes 6.0×10^4 cal at the higher temperature. The amount of heat converted into work is equal to
(a) 4.8×10^4 cal
(b) 3.5×10^5 cal
(c) 1.6×10^4 cal
(d) 1.2×10^4 cal

(a) -5 J
(b) -10 J
(c) -15 J
(d) -20 J

8. A carnot engine takes in 3000 kcal of heat from a reservoir at 627°C and gives it to a sink at 27°C. The work done by the engine is
(a) 4.2×10^6 J
(b) 8.4×10^6 J
(c) 16.8×10^6 J
(d) zero

9. The specific heat at constant pressure of an ideal gas, $C_p = \dfrac{5R}{2}$. The gas is kept in a closed vessel of volume 0.0083 m^3 at 300 K and a pressure of 1.6×10^6 N/m^2. 2.49×10^4 J of heat energy is supplied to the gas. The final temperature and the pressure respectively are
(a) 567.2 K and 6.3×10^6 N/m^2
(b) 675.2 K and 3.6×10^6 N/m^2
(c) 275.2 K and 2.3×10^6 N/m^2
(d) 465.6 K and 4.2×10^6 N/m^2

10. A bubble has a volume of 3 mm^3 at a depth of 20 m in a lake of pure water. If the bubble slowly rises upto the surface of the lake, its volume will be (atmospheric pressure is 100 kPa)
(a) 7.24 mm^3
(b) 4.44 mm^3
(c) 8.88 mm^3
(d) 6.66 mm^3

11. A 0.5 hp motor is stirring 4 kg of water. Assuming there is no heat loss except in heating the water, the time it will take to raise the temperature of the water by 5°C is
(a) 4.73 min
(b) 3.75 min
(c) 5 min
(d) none of these

12. A 500 ml sealed cylinder contains nitrogen at a pressure of 1 atm. A tiny glass tube lies at the bottom of the cylinder. Its volume is 0.50 ml and it contains hydrogen at a pressure of 4.5 atm. The glass tube is broken so that hydrogen also fills the cylinder. The new pressure in the cylinder is (1 atm = 1×10^5 N/m^2)
(a) 76.34 cm Hg
(b) 82.40 cm Hg
(c) 94.24 cm Hg
(d) 104.34 cm Hg

13. 4 kg of oxygen gas is heated so as to raise its temperature from 20 to 120°C. If the heating is done at constant pressure, the external work done by the gas is ($C_p = 0.219$ cal/g°C and $C_v = 0.157$ cal/g°C)
(a) 628 kJ
(b) 104 kJ
(c) 366 kJ
(d) 206 kJ

14. On P-V coordinates, the slope of an isothermal curve of a gas at a pressure $P = 1$MPa and volume $V = 0.0025$ m^3 is equal to -400 MPa/m^3. If $C_p / C_v = 1.4$, the slope of the adiabatic curve passing through this point is :
(a) -56 MPa/m^3
(b) -400 MPa/m^3
(c) -560 MPa/m^3
(d) none of these

Answer Key	1	(b)	3	(d)	5	(c)	7	(d)	9	(b)	11	(c)	13	(b)
Sol. from page 510	2	(d)	4	(b)	6	(a)	8	(b)	10	(c)	12	(a)	14	(c)

15. The *P-V* diagram here shows six curved paths (connected by vertical paths) that can be followed by a gas. Which two of them should be part of a closed cycle if the network done by the gas is to be at its maximum positive value?

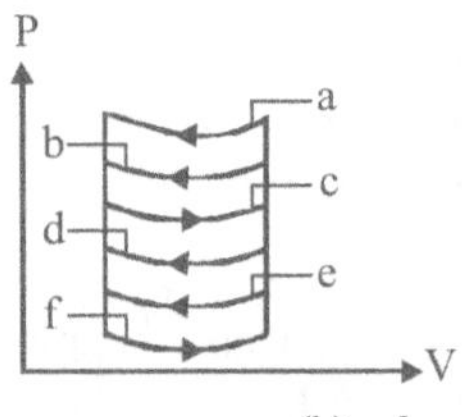

(a) a, f

(b) b, c

(c) b, e

(d) c, e

16. In the *P-V* diagram of figure shown, the gas does 5J of work along isotherm ab and 4J along adiabat bc. What is the change in the internal energy of the gas if the gas traverse the straight path from a to c?

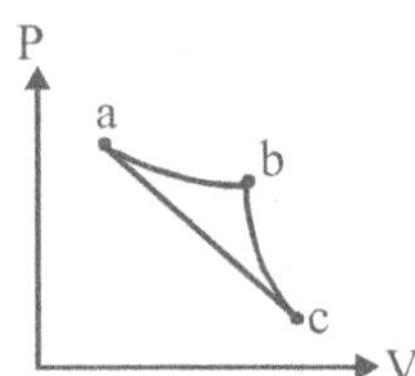

(a) 1J

(b) -4J

(c) 5J

(d) 9J

17. Water is heat on a stove. The temperature of the water rises (i) from 20°C to 30°C (ii) from 30°C to 40°C (iii) from 80°C to 90°C. In which case the change in entropy is greatest

(a) (i)

(b) (ii)

(c) (iii)

(d) (ii) and (iii)

18. An ideal gas has temperature T_1 at the initial state i shown in the *P-V* diagram. The gas has a higher temperature T_2 at the final states a and b, which it can reach the paths shown. The change in entropy:

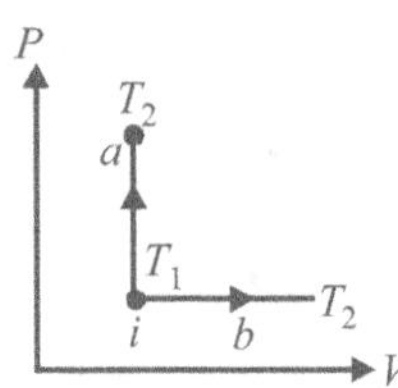

(a) greatest in a

(b) greatest in b

(c) same in a and b

(d) nothing can be said

19. Unit mass of a liquid with volume V_1 is completely changed into a gas of volume V_2 at a constant external pressure P and temperature T. If the latent heat of evaporation for the given mass is L, then the increase in the internal energy of the system is

(a) Zero

(b) $P(V_2 - V_1)$

(c) $L - P(V_2 - V_1)$

(d) L

20. Two kg of water is converted into steam by boiling at atmospheric pressure. The volume changes from $2 \times 10^{-3} m^3$ to 3.34 m^3. The work done by the system is about

(a) -340 kJ

(b) -170 kJ

(c) 170 kJ

(d) 340 kJ

21. A closed system undergoes a process $1 \rightarrow 2$ for which the values W_{1-2} and Q_{1-2} are 50 kJ and -20 kJ respectively. If the system is returned to state 1 and $Q_{2 \rightarrow 1}$ is $+$ 10 kJ the work done $W_{2 \rightarrow 1}$ is

(a) 40 kJ

(b) 50 kJ

(c) -60 kJ

(d) -50 kJ

22. A cylindrical tube of uniform cross-sectional area A is fitted with two air tight frictionless pistons. The pistons are connected to each other by a metallic wire. Initially the pressure of the gas is P_0 and temperature is T_0, atmospheric pressure is also P_0. Now the temperature of the gas is increased to $2T_0$, the tension in the wire will be

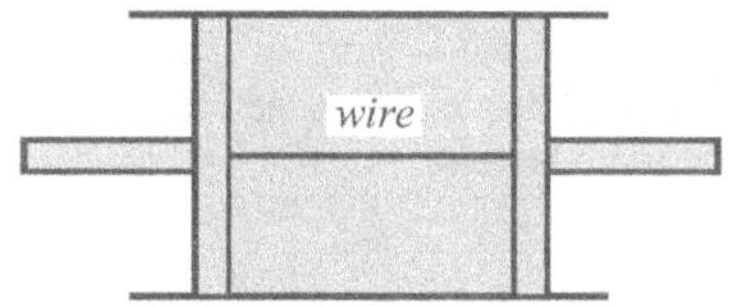

(a) $2 P_0 A$

(b) $P_0 A$

(c) $\dfrac{P_0 A}{2}$

(d) $4 P_0 A$

23. An ideal gas is subjected to cyclic process involving four thermodynamic states, the amounts of heat (Q) and work (W) involved in each of these states

$Q_1 = 6000$ J; $Q_2 = -5500$ J; $Q_3 = -3000$ J; $Q_4 = +3500$ J

$W_1 = 2500$ J; $W_2 = -1000$ J; $W_3 = -1200$ J; $W_4 = x$J

The ratio of the net work done by the gas to the total heat absorbed by the gas is η. The values of x and η respectively are

(a) $500; 7.5\%$

(b) $700; 10.5\%$

(c) $1000; 21\%$

(d) $1500; 15\%$

24. A thermally insulated rigid container contains an ideal gas heated by a filament of resistance 100 Ω through a current of $1A$ for 5 min then change in internal energy is

(a) 0 kJ

(b) 10 kJ

(c) 20 kJ

(d) 30 kJ

25. Two cylinders A and B fitted with pistons contain equal amounts of an ideal diatomic gas at 300 K. The piston of A is free to move while that of B is held fixed. The same amount of heat is given to the gas in each cylinder. If the rise in temperature of the gas in A is 30 K, then the rise in temperature of the gas in B is

(a) 30 K

(b) 18 K

(c) 50 K

(d) 42 K

<table>
<tr><td rowspan="2">Answer Key</td><td>15</td><td>(d)</td><td>17</td><td>(a)</td><td>19</td><td>(c)</td><td>21</td><td>(c)</td><td>23</td><td>(b)</td><td>25</td><td>(d)</td></tr>
<tr><td colspan="14"></td></tr>
<tr><td>Sol. from page 510</td><td>16</td><td>(b)</td><td>18</td><td>(b)</td><td>20</td><td>(d)</td><td>22</td><td>(b)</td><td>24</td><td>(d)</td><td></td><td></td></tr>
</table>

26. 1 k mol of a monoatomic gas is taken from a point A to another point B along the path ACB. The initial temperature at A is T_0. The heat absorbed by the gas in the process $A \to C \to B$ is

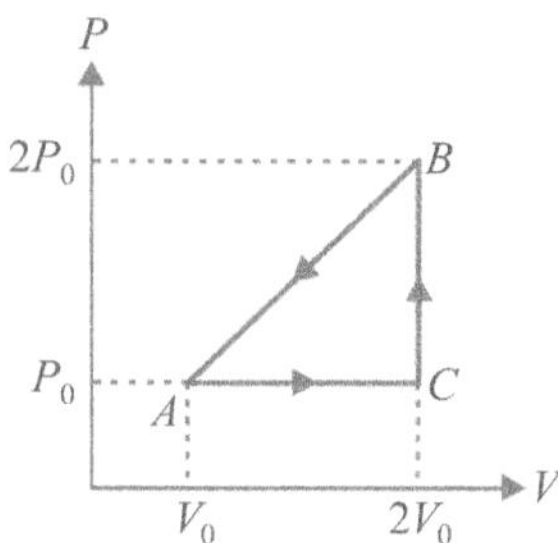

(a) $\dfrac{11}{2}RT_0$

(b) $\dfrac{9RT_0}{2}$

(c) $\dfrac{15RT_0}{2}$

(d) $\dfrac{5RT_0}{2}$

27. A cyclic process $ABCD$ is shown in the figure P-V diagram. Which of the following curves represent the same process

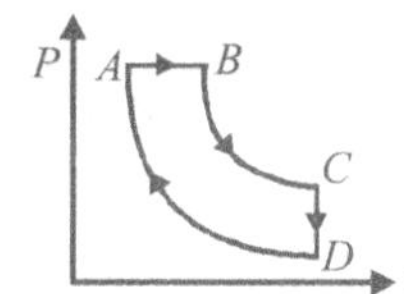

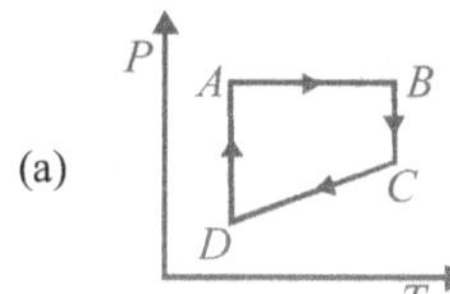

(a)

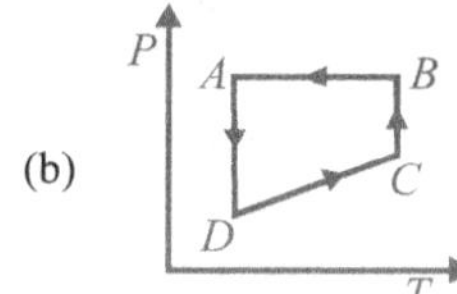

(b)

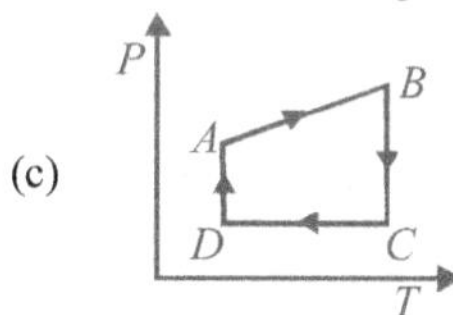

(c)

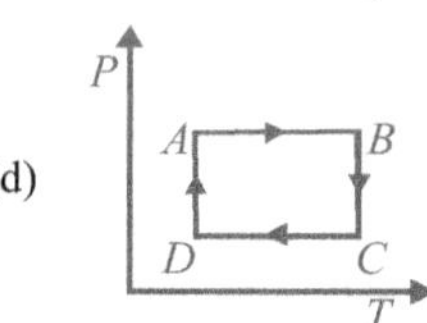

(d)

28. A cyclic process $ABCA$ is shown in the V-T diagram. Process on the P-V diagram is

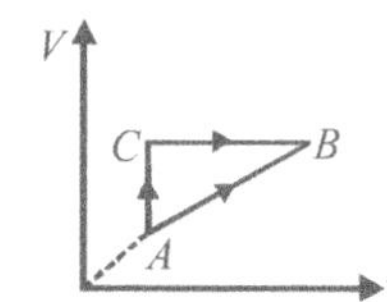

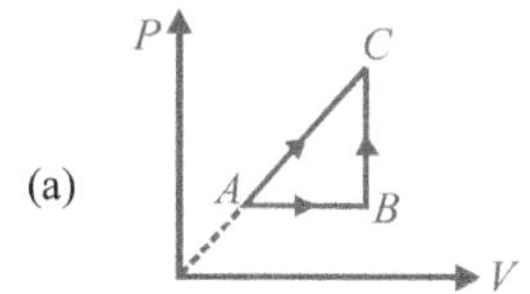

(a)

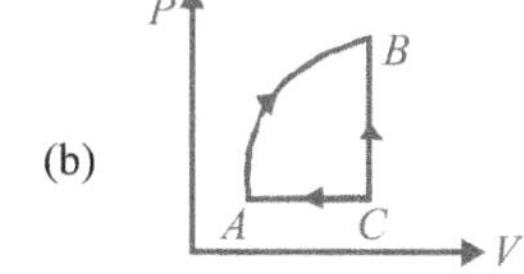

(b)

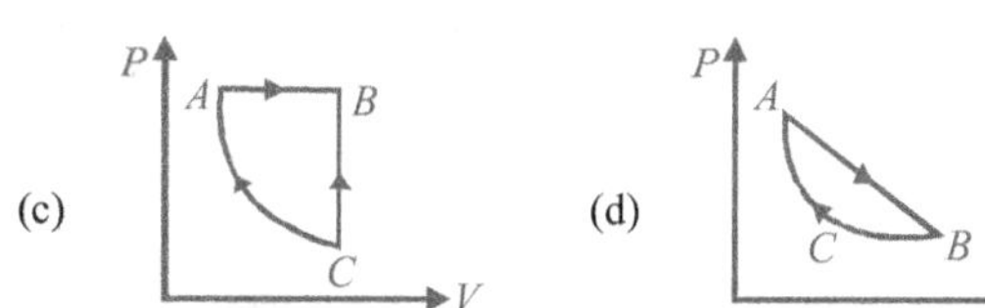

(c)

(d)

29. Carbon monoxide is carried around a closed cycle abc in which bc is an isothermal process as shown in the figure. The gas absorbs 7000 J of heat as its temperature increases from 300 K to 1000 K in going from a to b. The quantity of heat rejected by the gas during the process ca is

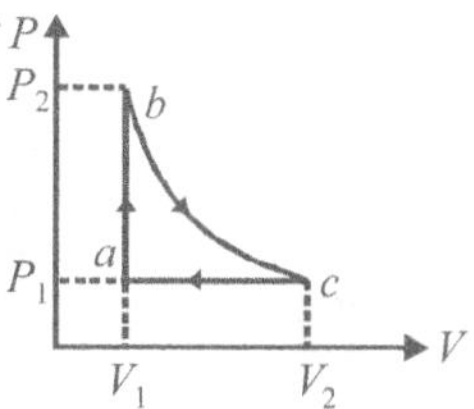

(a) 4200 J

(b) 5000 J

(c) 9000 J

(d) 9800 J

30. Six moles of an ideal gas performs a cycle shown in figure. If the temperature are $T_A = 600\ K$, $T_B = 800\ K$, $T_C = 2200\ K$ and $T_D = 1200\ K$ the work done per cycle is

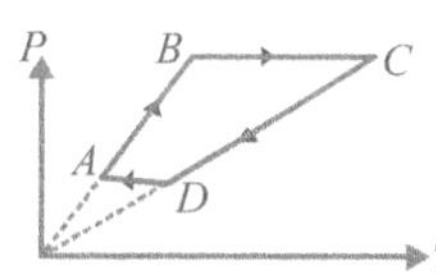

(a) 20 kJ

(b) 30 kJ

(c) 40 kJ

(d) 60 kJ

31. In the following P-V diagram two adiabatics cut two isothermals at temperatures T_1 and T_2 (fig). The value of $\dfrac{V_a}{V_d}$ will be

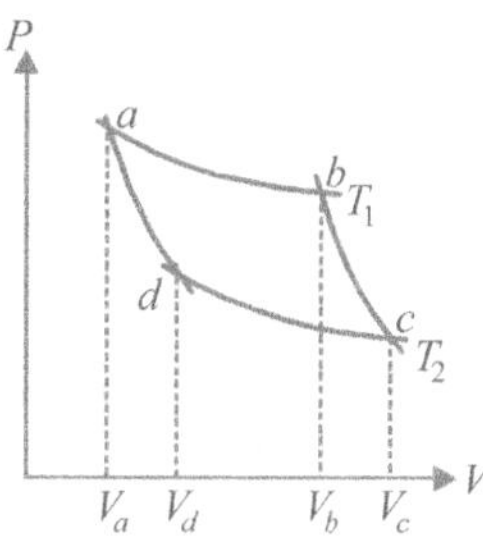

(a) $\dfrac{V_b}{V_c}$

(b) $\dfrac{V_c}{V_b}$

(c) $\dfrac{V_d}{V_a}$

(d) $V_b V_c$

32. One mole of an ideal gas having initial volume V, pressure $2P$ and temperature T undergoes a cyclic process $ABCDA$ as shown below

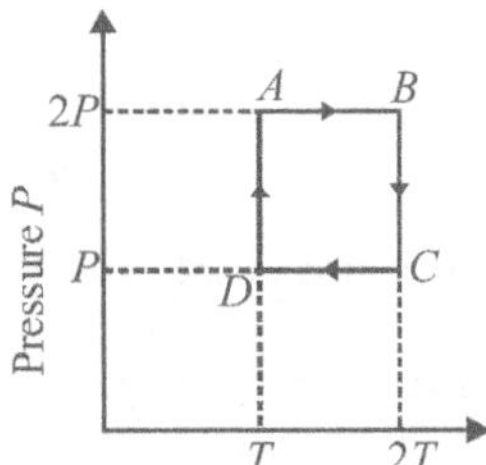

The net work done in the complete cycle is

(a) Zero

(b) $RT \ln 2$

(c) $RT \ln 2$

(d) $\dfrac{3}{2} RT \ln 2$

33. In P-V diagram shown in figure ABC is a semicircle. The work done in the process ABC is

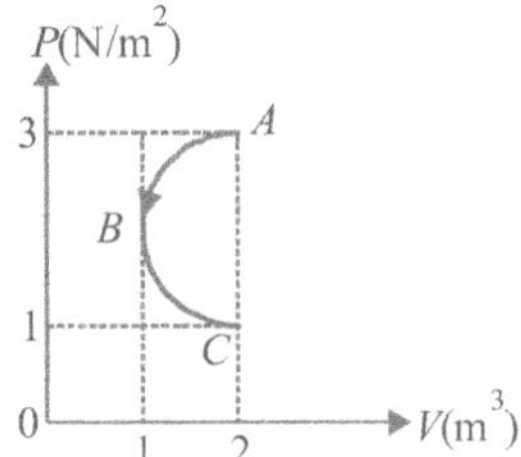

(a) 4 J

(b) $\dfrac{-\pi}{2}$ J

(c) $\dfrac{\pi}{2}$ J

(d) zero

34. One mole of an ideal gas is taken from state A to state B by three different processes,

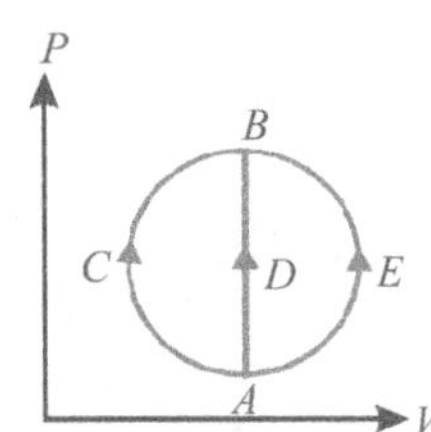

(i) ACB (ii) ADB (iii) AEB as shown in the P-V diagram. The heat absorbed by the gas is

(a) greater in process (ii) than in (i)

(b) the least in process (ii)

(c) the same in (i) and (iii)

(d) less in (iii) than in (ii)

35. The efficiency of an ideal gas with adiabatic exponent 'γ' for the shown cyclic process would be

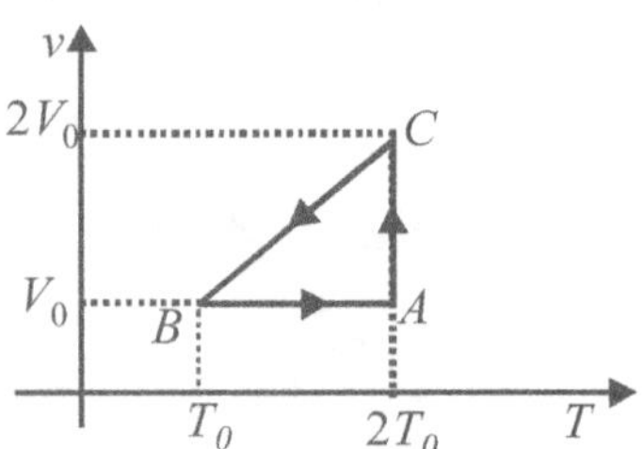

(a) $\dfrac{(2\ln 2 - 1)}{\gamma/(\gamma - 1)}$

(b) $\dfrac{(1 - 2\ln 2)}{\gamma/(\gamma - 1)}$

(c) $\dfrac{(2\ln 2 + 1)}{\gamma/(\gamma - 1)}$

(d) $\dfrac{(2\ln 2 - 1)}{\gamma/(\gamma + 1)}$

36. The specific heat capacity of a monoatomic gas for the process $TV^2 = $ constant is (where R is gas constant)

(a) R

(b) 2 R

(c) $\dfrac{R}{3}$

(d) $\dfrac{R}{4}$

37. An ideal gas can be expanded from an initial state to a certain volume through two different processes,

(i) $PV^2 = K$ and (ii) $P = KV^2$, where K is a positive constant. Then, choose the correct option from the following

(a) Final temperature in (i) will be greater than in (ii)

(b) Final temperature in (ii) will be greater than in (i)

(c) Work done by the gas in both the processes would be equal

(d) Total heat given to the gas in (i) is greater than in (ii)

38. The molar heat capacity C for an ideal gas going through a given process is given by $C = a/T$, where a is a constant. If $\gamma = C_p/C_V$, the work done by one mole of gas during heating from T_0 to $\eta\, T_0$ through the given process will be

(a) $\dfrac{1}{a} \ln \eta$

(b) $a \ln \eta - \left(\dfrac{\eta - 1}{\gamma - 1}\right) RT_0$

(c) $a \ln \eta - (\gamma - 1) RT_0$

(d) none of these

39. In an H_2 gas process, $PV^2 = $ constant. The ratio of work done by gas to change in internal energy is

(a) 2/3

(b) 0.4

(c) – 0.4

(d) – 2/3

40. In a process the pressure of a gas is inversely proportional to the square of the volume. If temperature of the gas is increased, then work done by the gas

(a) is positive

(b) is negative

(c) is zero

(d) may be positive

Answer Key	32	(c)	34	(d)	36	(a)	38	(b)	40	(c)
Sol. from page 510	33	(c)	35	(a)	37	(b)	39	(c)		

41. A system consists of a cylinder, piston and a spring as shown. The initial volume of the cylinder is 100 l and its pressure is 100 kPa so that it just balances the atmosphere pressure plus the piston weight. In this position, the spring connected to the piston exerts no force on it. Heat is now transferred to the system so as to expand air to double its volume, at which the pressure in the cylinder is 300 kPa. The work done by the system is (in case of a spring $F = -kx$) :

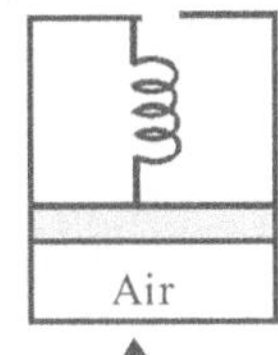

(a) 200 J   (b) 2×10^6 J

(c) 20 kJ   (d) 2 kJ

42. A one mol sample of an ideal gas is carried around the thermodynamics cycle shown in the figure. The cycle consists of three steps : (i) an isothermal expansion (a → b), (ii) an isobaric compression (b → c), and (iii) a constant volume increases in pressure (c → a). If $T_a = 400$ K, $P_a = 4$ atm and $P_b = P_c = 1$ atm, the work done by the gas per cycle is

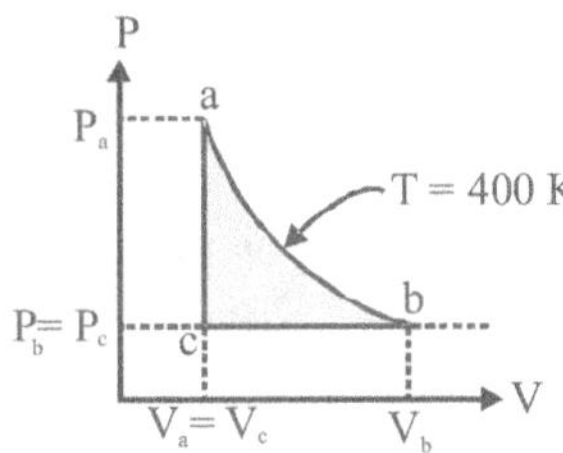

(a) 211.6 J   (b) 1158 J

(c) 705.3 J   (d) 2116 J

43. A closed system undergoes a change of state by process 1 → 2 for which $Q_{12} = 10$ J and $W_{12} = -5$ J. The system is now returned to its initial state by a different path 2 → 1 for which Q_{21} is -3J. The total energy change for the cycle is

(a) -8J   (b) zero

(c) -2J   (d) $+5$J

44. Relation between U, P, V for an ideal gas is U = 3 + 2PV then gas is

(a) monoatomic   (b) diatomic

(c) triatomic

(d) mixture of monoatomic and diatomic

45. 1 mole of a monoatomic gas at temperature T_0 expand slowly according to the law $P^2 = T$. Its final temperature is $2T_0$, then heat supplies to the gas is

(a) $\dfrac{R}{T_0 / 2}$ (b) RT_0

(c) $\dfrac{3}{2}RT_0$ (d) $2RT_0$

46. An exhausted chamber with nonconducting walls is connected through a valve to the atmosphere where the pressure is p_0 and the temperature is T_0. The valve is opened slightly and air flows into the chamber until the pressure within the chamber is p_0. Assuming the air to behave like an ideal gas with constant heat capacities, the final temperature of the air in the chamber is

(a) $\gamma \, T_0$ (b) (T_0 / γ)

(c) $(1 / \gamma - 1)T_0$ (d) $(\gamma / 1 - \gamma) \, T_0$

47. A cube of side 5 cm made of iron and having a mass of 1500 g is heated from 25° C to 400°C. The specific heat for iron is 0.12 cal/g°C and the coefficient of volume expansion is $3.5 \times 10^{-5}/°$C, the change in the internal energy of the cube is (atm pressure = 1×10^5 N/m^2)

(a) 320 kJ   (b) 282 kJ

(c) 141 kJ   (d) 423 kJ

48. During the charging of a storage battery, the current is 22 A and the voltage is 12 V. The rate of heat transfer from the battery is 12 W. The rate of change of internal energy is

(a) 504 J/s   (b) 252 J/s

(c) 25.2 J/s   (d) 126 J/s

49. A vertical cylinder closed from both ends is equipped with an easily moving piston dividing the volumes into two parts, each containing one mole of air. In equilibrium at $T_0 = 300$ K, the ratio of the volume of the upper and lower parts is 4. The temperature at which this ratio will be 3 is

(a) 320 K   (b) 420 K

(c) 480 K   (d) 500 K

50. A vessel of volume V is evacuated by means of a piston air pump. One piston stroke captures the volume v_0. The pressure in the vessel is to be reduced to $\left(\dfrac{1}{n}\right)$ of its original pressure P_0. If the process is assumed to be isothermal and air is considered an ideal gas, the number of strokes needed in the process is

(a) $\left[\dfrac{\ell n \, n}{\ell n\left(1 - \dfrac{v_0}{V}\right)}\right]$ (b) $\left[\dfrac{\ell n \, n}{\ell n\left(1 + \dfrac{v_0}{V}\right)}\right]$

(c) $\left[\dfrac{\ell n\left(1 - \dfrac{v_0}{V}\right)}{\ell n}\right]$ (d) none of these

Answer Key										
Sol. from page 510	**41**	(c)	**43**	(a)	**45**	(d)	**47**	(b)	**49**	(b)
	42	(d)	**44**	(d)	**46**	(a)	**48**	(b)	**50**	(b)

Multiple options correct

1. The figure shows four path on P-V diagram along which a gas can be taken from state i to f. The path according to the greatest change in internal energy is :

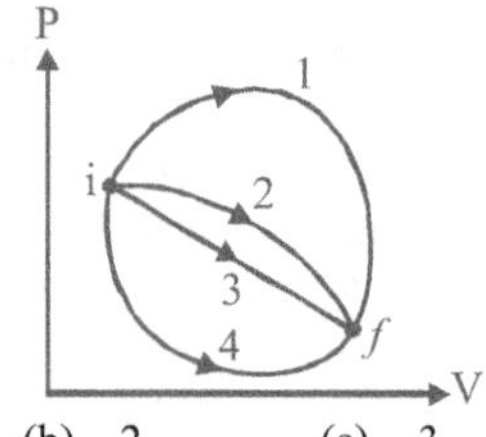

   (a)   1   (b)   2   (c)   3   (d)   4

2. In figure here shows four paths traversed by a gas on a P-V diagram. If ΔU_1, ΔU_2, ΔU_3 and ΔU_4 are the change in internal energies in their respective paths, then :

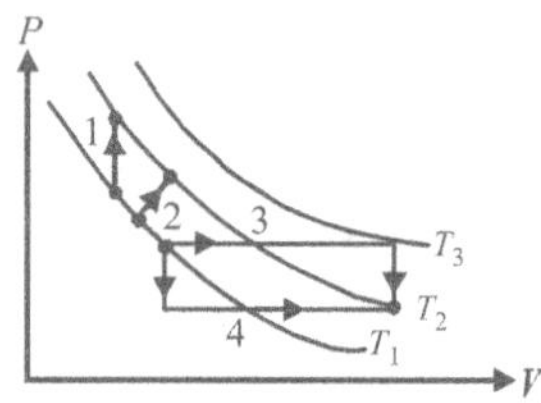

   (a) $\Delta U_1 = \Delta U_2 = \Delta U_3 = \Delta U_4$ (b) $\Delta U_1 + \Delta U_2 = \Delta U_3 + \Delta U_4$
   (c) $\Delta U_1 > \Delta U_2 > \Delta U_3 > \Delta U_4$ (d)   None of these

3. During the melting of a slab of ice at 273 K at atmospheric pressure

   (a)   Positive work is done by ice-water system on the atmosphere

   (b)   Positive work is done on the ice-water system by the atmosphere

   (c)   The internal energy of the ice-water system increases

   (d)   the internal energy of the ice-water system decreases

4. The figure shows the P-V plot of an ideal gas taken through a cycle $ABCDA$. The part ABC is a semi-circle and CDA is half of an ellipse. Then,

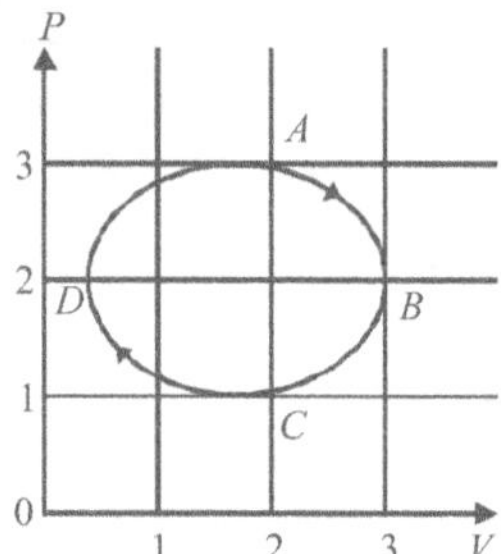

   (a)   The process during the path $A \rightarrow B$ is isothermal

   (b)   Heat flows out of the gas during the path $B \rightarrow C \rightarrow D$

   (c)   Work done during the path $A \rightarrow B \rightarrow C$ is zero

   (d)   Positive work is done by the gas in the cycle $ABCDA$

5. For any monoatomic gas the quantity/quantities independent of the nature of the gas at the same temperature is/are

   (a)   the number of molecules in one mole

   (b)   the number of molecules in equal volume and pressure

   (c)   the translational kinetic energy of one mole

   (d)   the kinetic energy of unit mass

6. Temperature versus pressure graph of an ideal gas is shown in figure. During the process AB

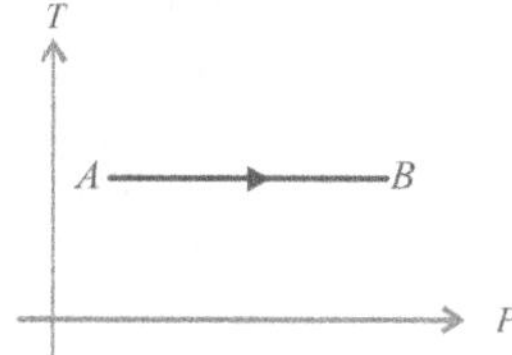

   (a)   internal energy of the gas remains constant

   (b)   volume of the gas is increased

   (c)   work done by the atmosphere on the gas is positive

   (d)   pressure is inversely proportional to volume

7. One mole of a gas is subjected to two processes AB and BC, one after the other as shown in the figure. BC is represented by PV^n = constant. We can conclude that (where T = temperature, W = work done by gas, V = volume and U = internal energy).

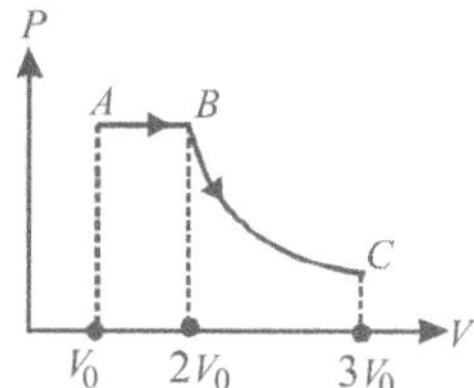

   (a) $T_A = T_B = T_C$ (b) $V_A < V_B, P_B < P_C$
   (c) $W_{AB} > W_{BC}$ (d) $T_A < T_B$

8. One mole of an ideal gas is taken through the cyclic process shown in the V-T diagram, where V = volume and T = absolute temperature of gas. Which of the following statements is/are correct?

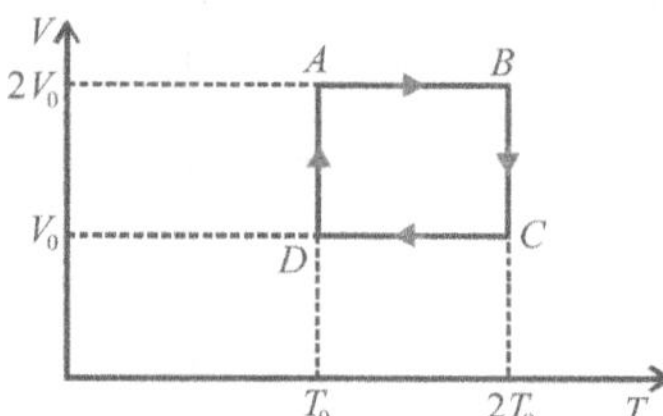

   (a)   Heat is given out by the gas in the whole process

   (b)   Heat is absorbed by the gas in the complete cycle

   (c)   The magnitude of the work by the gas is $RT_0 \ln 2$

   (d)   The magnitude of the work done by the gas is $V_0 T_0$

Answer Key	1	(a, b, c, d)	3	(b, c)	5	(a, b, c)	7	(c, d)
Sol. from page 514	2	(a, b)	4	(b, d)	6	(a, d)	8	(a, c)

9. Heat is supplied to a certain homogeneous sample of matter at a uniform rate.

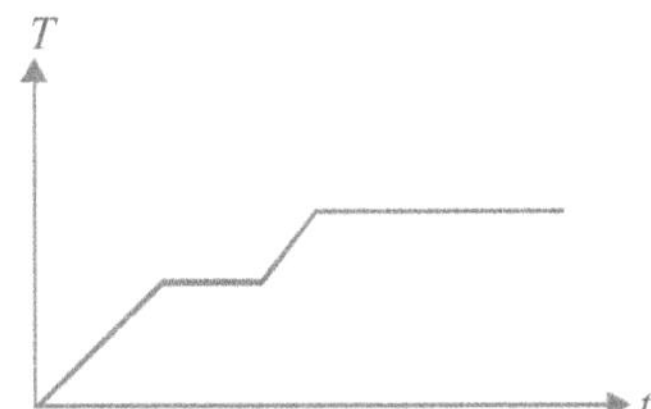

Its temperature is plotted against time as shown in the figure. Which of the following conclusions can be drawn ?

(a) its specific heat capacity is greater in the solid state than in the liquid state

(b) its specific heat capacity is greater in the liquid state than in the solid state

(c) its latent heat of vaporization is greater than its latent heat of fusion

(d) its latent heat of vaporization is smaller than its latent heat of fusion

10. An ideal gas is taken from the state A (pressure P, volume V) to the state B (pressure $P/2$, volume $2V$) along a straight line path in the P-V diagram. Select the correct statement (s) from the following

(a) The work done by the gas in the process A to B exceeds the work that would be done by it if the system were taken from A to B along the isotherm.

(b) In the T-V diagram, the path AB becomes a part of a parabola

(c) In the P-T diagram, the path AB becomes a part of a hyperbola

(d) In going from A to B, the temperature T of the gas first increases to a maximum value and then decreases

11. During an experiment, an ideal gas is found to obey a condition VP^2 = constant. The gas is initially at a temperature T, pressure P and volume V. The gas expands to volume $4V$.

(a) The pressure of gas changes to $\dfrac{P}{2}$

(b) The temperature of gas changes to $4T$

(c) The graph of above process on the P-T diagram is parabola

(d) The graph of above process of the P-T diagram is hyperbola

12. During an experiment, an ideal gas is found to obey a condition $\dfrac{P^2}{\rho}$ = constant [ρ = density of the gas]. The gas is initially at temperature T, pressure P and density ρ. The gas expands such that density changes to $\rho/2$.

(a) The pressure of gas changes to $\sqrt{2}\,P$

(b) The temperature of gas changes to $\sqrt{2}\,T$

(c) The graph of above process on the P-T diagram is parabola

(d) The graph of above process of the P-T diagram is hyperbola

13. An idea gas is taken from state 1 to state 2 through optional path A, B, C & D as shown in P-V diagram. Let Q, W and U represent the heat supplied, work done & internal energy of the gas respectively. Then

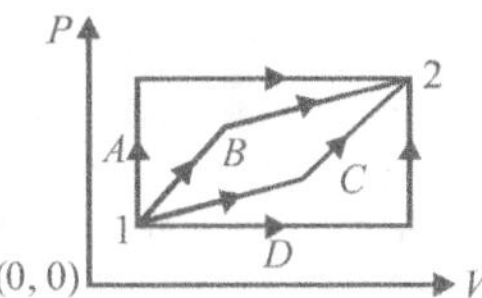

(a) $Q_B - W_B > Q_C - W_C$ (b) $Q_A - Q_D = W_A - W_D$

(c) $W_A < W_B < W_C < W_D$ (d) $Q_A > Q_B > Q_C > Q_D$

14. Two gases have the same initial pressure, volume and temperature. They expand to the same final volume, one adiabatically and the other isothermally

(a) The final temperature is greater for the isothermal process

(b) The final pressure is greater for the isothermal process

(c) The work done by the gas is greater for the isothermal process

(d) All the above options are incorrect

15. A cyclic process $ABCD$ is shown in the P-V diagram. Which of the following curves represents the same process if BC & DA are isothermal processes

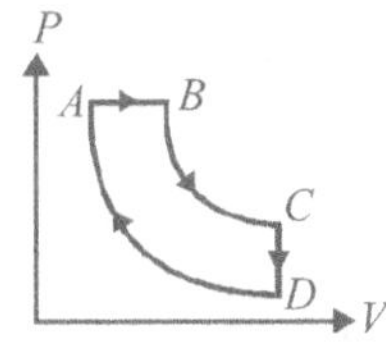

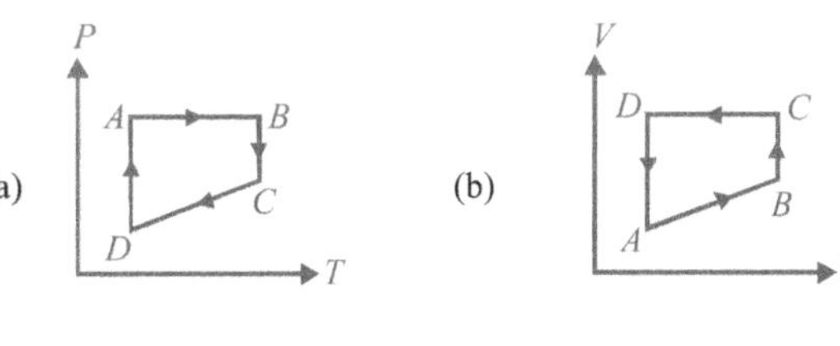

(a)   (b)

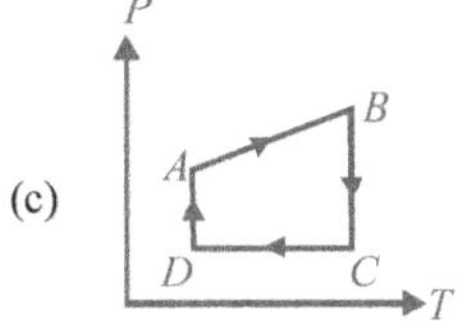 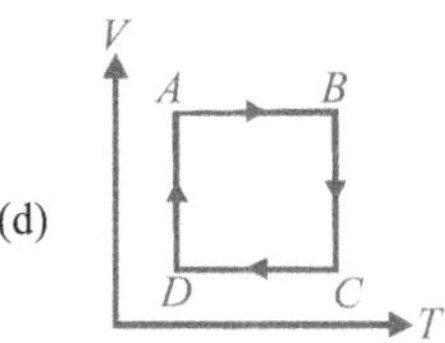

(c)   (d)

16. Four Carnot engines operate between reservoir temperature of (i) 300 K and 400 K (ii) 400 K and 500 K (iii) 500 K and 600 K (iv) 600 K and 800 K. Which engines has greatest thermal efficiency?

(a) (i)   (b) (ii)

(c) (iii)   (d) (iv)

Answer Key	9	(a, c)	11	(a, d)	13	(b, d)	15	(a, b)
Sol. from page 514	10	(a, b, d)	12	(b, d)	14	(a, b, c)	16	(a, d)

Read the two statements carefully to mark the correct option out of the options given below:
(a) If both the statements are true and the *statement - 2* is the correct explanation of *statement - 1*.
(b) If both the statements are true but *statement - 2* is not the correct explanation of the *statement - 1*.
(c) If *statement - 1* true but *statement - 2* is false.
(d) If *statement - 1* is false but *statement - 2* is true.

1. **Statement - 1** Zeroth law of thermodynamics explain the concept of energy.

   Statement - 2

   Energy depends on temperature.

2. **Statement - 1**

   Work and heat are two equivalent forms of energy.

   Statement - 2

   Work is the transfer of mechanical energy irrespective of temperature difference, whereas heat is the transfer of thermal energy because of temperature difference only.

3. **Statement - 1**

   Reversible systems are difficult to find in real world.

   Statement - 2

   Most processes are dissipative in nature.

4. **Statement - 1**

   Thermodynamic processes in nature are irreversible

   Statement - 2

   Dissipative effects can not be eliminated.

5. **Statement - 1**

   In isothermal process whole of the heat energy supplied to the body is converted into internal energy.

   Statement - 2

   According to the first law of thermodynamics
   $\Delta Q = \Delta U + W.$

6. **Statement - 1**

   When a bottle of cold carbonated drink is opened a slight fog forms around the opening.

   Statement - 2

   Adiabatic expansion of the gas causes lowering of temperature and condensation of water vapours.

7. **Statement - 1**

   Air quickly leaking out of a balloon becomes cooler.

   Statement - 2

   The leaking air undergoes adiabatic expansion.

8. **Statement - 1**

   In an electric fan be switched on in a closed room, the air of the room will be heated.

   Statement - 2

   Electrical energy is converted into heat.

9. **Statement - 1**

   In an adiabatic process, change in internal energy of a gas is equal to work done on or by the gas in the process.

   Statement - 2

   Temperature of gas remains constant in an adiabatic process.

10. **Statement - 1**

    An adiabatic process is an isoentropic process.

    Statement - 2

    Change in entropy is zero in case of adiabatic process.

11. **Statement - 1**

    Efficiency of a Carnot engine increase on reducing the temperature of sink.

    Statement - 2

    Efficiency of a Carnot engine is defined as the ratio of net mechanical work done per cycle by the gas to the amount of heat energy absorbed per cycle from the source.

Answer Key	**1**	(d)	**3**	(a)	**5**	(d)	**7**	(a)	**9**	(c)	**11**	(a)
Sol. from page 515	**2**	(a)	**4**	(a)	**6**	(a)	**8**	(a)	**10**	(b)		

LOT   Passage & Matrix   *Exercise 7.4*

Passage for (Q. 1 - 3) :

Two moles of helium gas are taken over the cycle *ABCDA*, as shown in the *P – T* diagram.

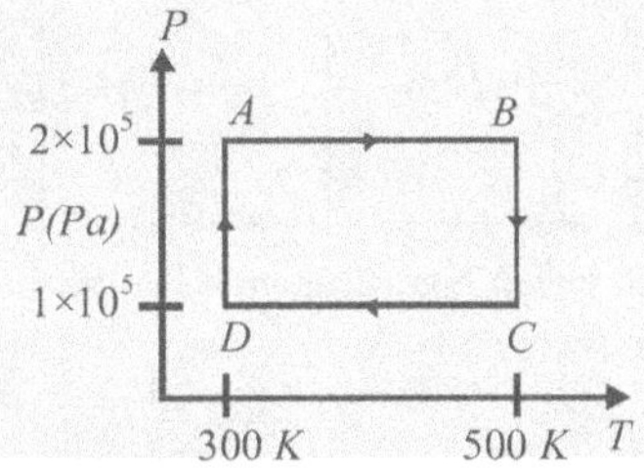

1. Assuming the gas to be ideal the work done on the gas in taking it from *A* to *B* is

(a) $200\,R$ (b) $300\,R$

(c) $400\,R$ (d) $500\,R$

2. The work done on the gas in taking it from *D* to *A* is

(a) $-414\,R$ (b) $+414\,R$

(c) $-690\,R$ (d) $+690\,R$

3. The net work done on the gas in the cycle *ABCDA* is

(a) zero   (b) $276\,R$

(c) $1076\,R$ (d) $1904\,R$

Passage for (Q. 4 -6) :

A small spherical monoatomic ideal gas bubble $\left(\gamma = \dfrac{5}{3}\right)$ is trapped inside a liquid of density ρ_1 (see figure). Assume that the bubble does not exchange any heat with the liquid. The bubble contains n moles of gas. The temperature of the gas when the bubble is at the bottom is T_0, the height of the liquid is H and the atmospheric pressure is P_0 (Neglect surface tension)

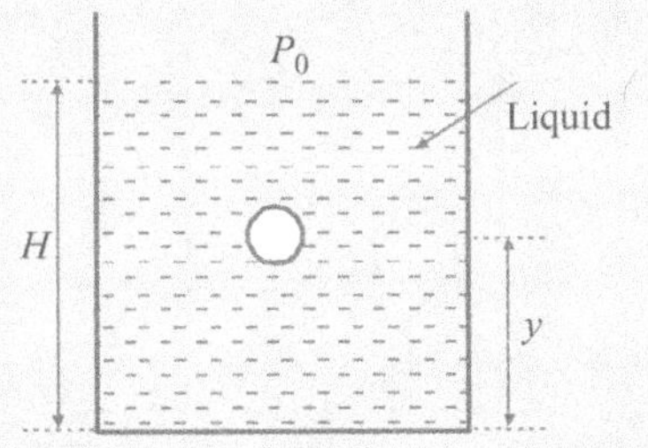

4. As the bubble moves upwards, besides the buoyancy force the following forces are acting on it

(a) Only the force of gravity

(b) The force due to gravity and the force due to the pressure of the liquid

(c) The force due to gravity, the force due to the pressure of the liquid and force due to viscosity of liquid

(d) The force due to the gravity and the force due to viscosity of the liquid

5. When the gas bubble is at height y from the bottom, its temperature is

(a) $T_0\left(\dfrac{P_0 + \rho\ell\,g\,h}{P_0 + \rho\ell\,g\,y}\right)^{2/5}$

(b) $T_0\left(\dfrac{P_0 + \rho\ell\,g(H - y)}{P_0 + \rho\ell\,g\,H}\right)^{2/5}$

(c) $T_0\left(\dfrac{P_0 + \rho\ell\,g\,H}{P_0 + \rho\ell\,g\,H}\right)^{3/5}$

(d) $T_0\left(\dfrac{P_0 + \rho\ell\,g(H - y)}{P_0 + \rho\ell\,g\,H}\right)^{3/5}$

6. The buoyancy force acting on the gas bubble is (Assume R is the universal gas constant)

(a) $\rho\ell nRgT_0\,\dfrac{(P_0 + \rho\ell gH)^{2/5}}{(P_0 + \rho\ell gy)^{7/5}}$

(b) $\dfrac{\rho\ell nRgT_0}{(P_0 + \rho\ell gH)^{2/5}[P_0 + \rho\ell g(H - y)]^{3/5}}$

(c) $\rho_\ell nRgT_0\,\dfrac{(P_0 + \rho\ell gH)^{3/5}}{(P_0 + \rho\ell gy)^{8/5}}$

(d) $\dfrac{\rho\ell nRgT_0}{(P_0 + \rho\ell gH)^{3/5}[P_0 + \rho\ell g(H - y)]^{2/5}}$

Answer Key	1	(c)	3	(b)	5	(b)
Sol. from page 515	2	(a)	4	(d)	6	(b)

Passage for (Q. 7 - 9) :

When a system is taken from state a to state b in figure along the path acb, 80 J of heat flow into the system and 30 J of work are done.

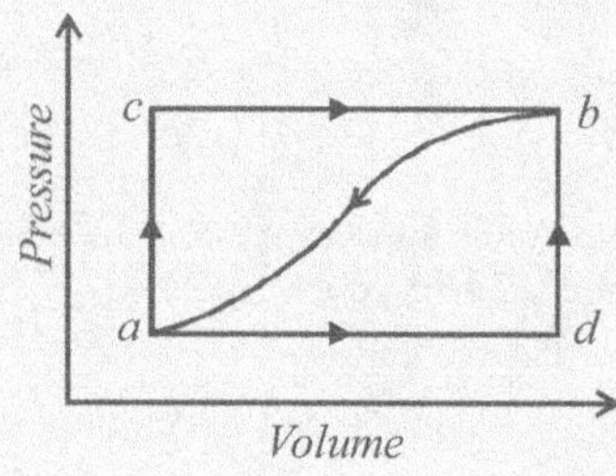

7. The heat flows into the system along path adb if the work is 10J.
   (a) 40 J
   (b) 50 J
   (c) 60 J
   (d) 70 J
8. When the system is returned from b to a along the curved path, the work done by the system is $-20J$. The heat liberate is
   (a) 40 J
   (b) 50 J
   (c) 60J
   (d) 70 J
9. If $U_a = 0$ and $U_d = 40J$, the heat absorbed in the process ad is
   (a) 20 J
   (b) 30 J
   (c) 40 J
   (d) 50 J

Passage for (Q. 10 - 12) :

Consider the isothermal compression of 0.10 mole of an ideal gas at $T = 0°C$. The initial pressure is 1 atm and the final volume is 1/5 the initial volume.

10. The work done in the process is
    (a) 242 J
    (b) -366 J
    (c) -432 J
    (d) 512 J
11. The heat exchange in the process is
    (a) -312 J
    (b) -366 J
    (c) $+332$ J
    (d) $+432$ J
12. The change in internal energy in the process is
    (a) 72 J
    (b) 212 J
    (c) 302 J
    (d) Zero

Passage for (Q. 13 - 15) :

A carnot engine is operated between two reservoirs at temperatures of 400 K and 300 K.

13. If the engine receives 1200 cal from the reservoir at 400 K in each cycle, how many calories per cycle does it reject to the reservoir at 300 K?
    (a) 400 cal
    (b) 650 cal
    (c) 750 cal
    (d) 900 cal
14. If the engine is operated in reverse, as a refrigerator and receives 1200 cal from the reservoir at 300 K, how many calories does it deliver to the reservoir at 400 K?
    (a) 400 cal
    (b) 800 cal
    (c) 1200 cal
    (d) 1600 cal

15. How many calories would be produced if the mechanical work required to operate the refrigerator in previous question were converted directly to heat?
    (a) 400 cal
    (b) 800 cal
    (c) 1200 cal
    (d) 1600 cal

Passage for (Q. 16 -18) :

A diathermic piston divides adiabatic cylinder of volume V_0 into two equal parts as shown in the figure. Both parts contain ideal monoatomic gases. The initial pressure and temperature of gas in left compartment are P_0 and T_0 while that in right compartment are $2P_0$ and $2T_0$. Initially the piston is kept fixed and the system is allowed to acquire a state of thermal equilibrium.

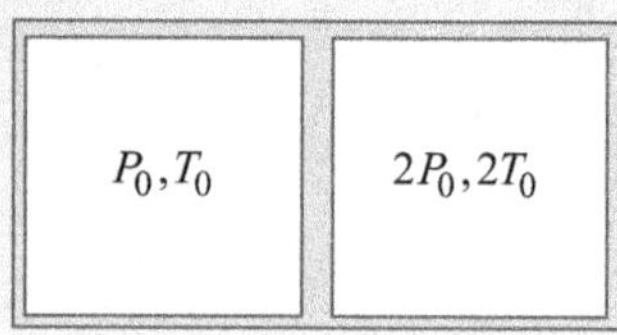

16. The pressure in left compartment after thermal equilibrium is achieved is
    (a) P_0
    (b) $\dfrac{3}{2}P_0$
    (c) $\dfrac{4}{3}P_0$
    (d) none of these
17. The heat that flown from right compartment to left compartment before thermal equilibrium is achieved is
    (a) $P_0 V_0$
    (b) $\dfrac{3}{4}P_0 V_0$
    (c) $\dfrac{3}{8}P_0 V_0$
    (d) $\dfrac{2}{3}P_0 V_0$
18. If the pin which was keeping the piston fixed in removed and the pisiton is allowed to slide slowly such that a state of mechanical equilibrium is achieved. The volume of left compartment when pistion is in equilibrium is
    (a) $\dfrac{3}{4}V_0$
    (b) $\dfrac{V_0}{4}$
    (c) $\dfrac{V_0}{2}$
    (d) $\dfrac{2}{3}V_0$

Passage for (Q. 19 - 21) :

Figure shows the variation of the internal energy U with the density ρ of one mole of ideal monoatomic gas for a thermodynamic cycle $ABCA$. Here process AB is a part of rectangular hyperbola.

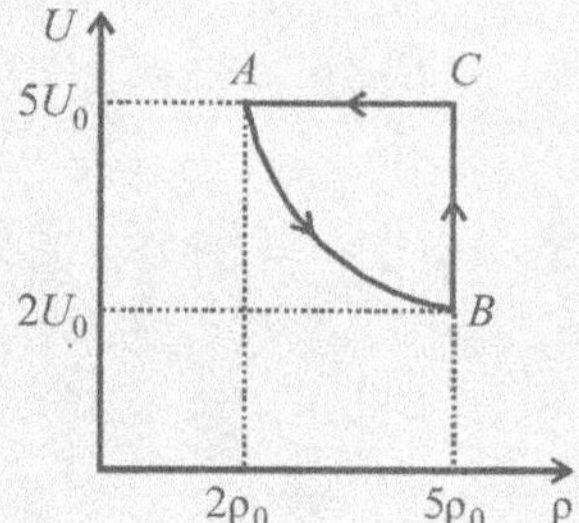

Answer Key		7	(c)	9	(d)	11	(b)	13	(d)	15	(a)	17	(c)
Sol. from page 515		8	(d)	10	(b)	12	(d)	14	(d)	16	(b)	18	(c)

19. The *P-V* diagram of above process is

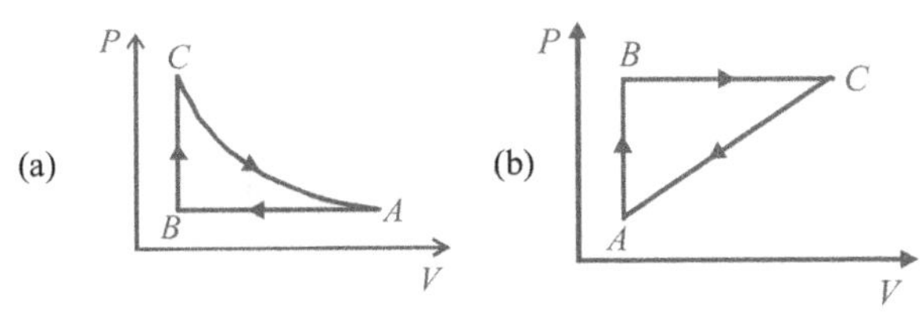

(a)   (b)

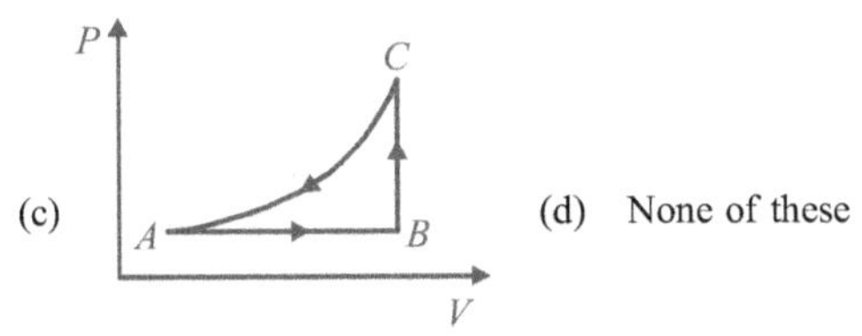

(c)   (d) None of these

20. The total amount of heat absorbed by the system for cyclic process is

(a) $\left(\dfrac{10}{3}\ln 2.5 - 2\right)U_0$ (b) $\left(\dfrac{10}{5}\ln 0.4 - 2\right)U_0$

(c) $50\,U_0$ (d) None of these

21. The work done in process AB is

(a) $-U_0$ (b) $-2U_0$

(c) $-5U_0$ (d) None of these

Passage for (Q. 22 -24) :

Two moles of helium gas undergo a cyclic process as shown in figure. Assuming the gas to be ideal, calculate the following quantities in this process.

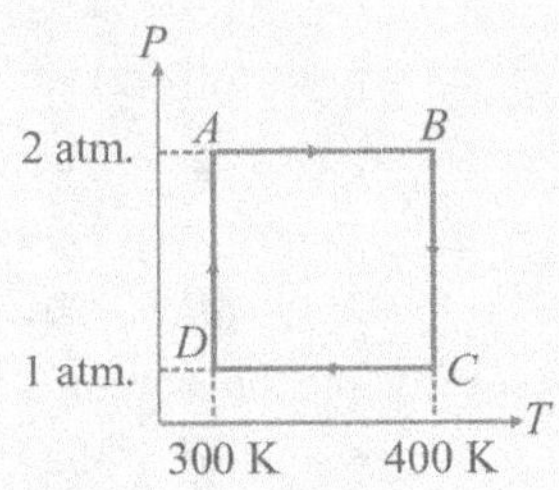

22. The net change in the heat energy is

(a) 1050 J   (b) 1150.7 J

(c) 1225 J   (d) 1260.3 J

23. The net work done is

(a) 1150.7 J   (b) 1260.3 J

(c) 625 J   (d) none of these

24. The net change in internal energy is

(a) 1150. 7 J   (b) 625 J

(c) 550 J   (d) zero

Passage for (Q. 25 -27) :

In the given figure an ideal gas changes its state from state A to state C by two paths ABC and AC

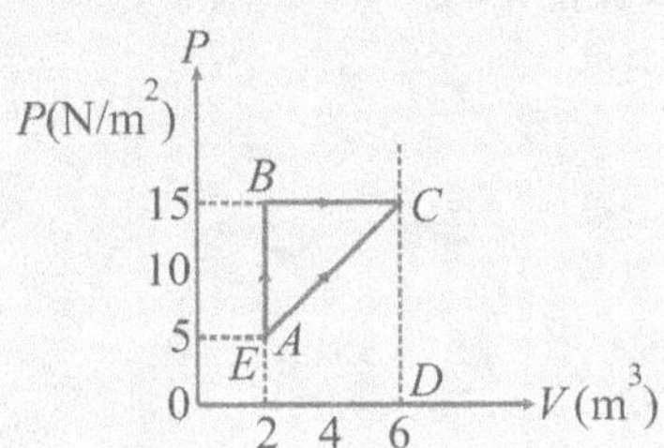

25. The paths along which work done is least

(a) AB (b) AC

(c) BC (d) all are equal

26. The internal energy of gas at A is 10 J and amount of heat supplied to change its state to C through the path AC is 200 J

Calculate the internal energy at C

(a) 100 J   (b) 120 J

(c) 170 J   (d) 220 J

27. The internal energy of gas at state B is 20 J. Find the amount of heat supplied to the gas to go from A to B.

(a) 5 J   (b) 8 J

(c) 12 J   (d) 10 J

Passage for (Q. 28 -30) :

20,000 J of heat energy is supplied to a metallic object of mass 1 kg at atmospheric pressure at 20°C.

Given specific heat of metal = 400 J/kg/°C. Density of metal = 9000 kg/m^3, coefficient of expansion = 9×10^{-5}/°C. Atmospheric pressure = 10^5 N/m^2.

28. The final temperature of metal

(a) 50°C   (b) 70°C

(c) 90°C   (d) 95°C

29. The work done by the metal

(a) 0.01 J   (b) 0.04

(c) 0.05 J   (d) zero

30. The change in internal energy of the metal

(a) 10000 J   (b) 14500 J

(c) 17550 J   (d) 19999.95 J.

Answer Key	19	(a)	21	(b)	23	(a)	25	(b)	27	(d)	29	(c)
Sol. from page 515	20	(a)	22	(b)	24	(d)	26	(c)	28	(b)	30	(d)

Passage for (Q. 31 -33) :

A fixed thermally conducting cylinder has a radius R and height L_0. The cylinder is open at its bottom and has small hole at its top . A piston of mass M is held at a distance L from the top surface. as shown in the figure. The atmospheric pressure is P_0.

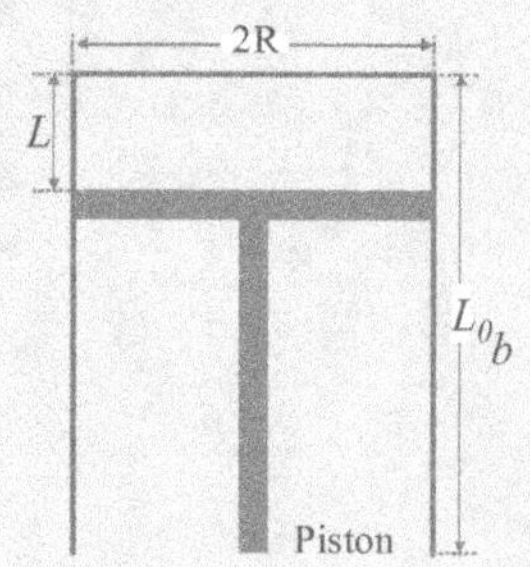

31. The piston is now pulled out slowly and held at a distance $2L$ from the top. The pressure in the cylinder between its top and the pistom will then be

(a) P_0

(b) $\dfrac{P_0}{2}$

(c) $\dfrac{P_0}{2} + \dfrac{Mg}{\pi R^2}$

(d) $\dfrac{P_0}{2} - \dfrac{Mg}{\pi R^2}$

32. While the piston is at a distance 2L from the top, the hole at the top is sealed. The piston is then released, to a position where it can stay in equilibrium. In this condition, the distance of the piston from the top is

(a) $\left(\dfrac{2P_0\pi R^2}{\pi R^2 P_0 + Mg}\right)(2L)$

(b) $\left(\dfrac{P_0\pi R^2 - Mg}{\pi R^2 P_0}\right)(2L)$

(c) $\left(\dfrac{P_0\pi R^2 + Mg}{\pi R^2 P_0}\right)(2L)$

(d) $\left(\dfrac{P_0\pi R^2}{\pi R^2 P_0 - Mg}\right)(2L)$

33. The piston is taken completely out of the cylinder. The hole at the top is sealed. A water tanks is brought below the cylinder and put in a position so that thewater surface in the tank is at the same level as the top of the cylinder as shown in the figure. The density of the water is r. In equilibrium, the height H of the water column in the cylinder satisfies

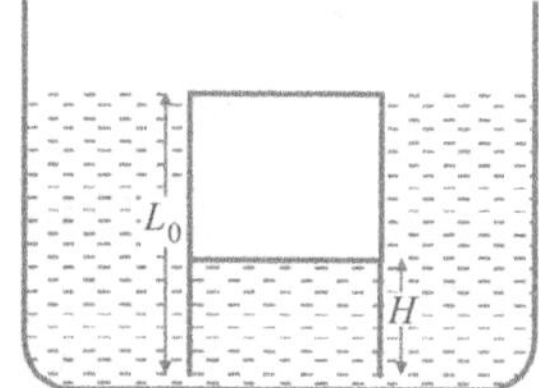

(a) $\rho g(L_0 - H)^2 + P_0(L_0 - H) + L_0 P_0 = 0$

(b) $\rho g(L_0 - H)^2 - P_0(L_0 - H) - L_0 P_0 = 0$

(c) $\rho g(L_0 - H)^2 + P_0(L_0 - H) - L_0 P_0 = 0$

(d) $\rho g(L_0 - H)^2 - P_0(L_0 - H) + L_0 P_0 = 0$

Passage for (Q. 34 -36) :

Two cylinder A and B having pistons (massless) of cross sectional area $100\ cm^2$ and $200\ cm^2$ respectively. The pistons are connected by massless rod. The pistons can move freely without friction. The cylinder A contains 100 gm of an ideal gas ($\gamma = 1.5$) at pressure 10^5 N/m^2 and temperature T_0. The cylinder B contains identical gas at same temperature T_0 but has different mass. The pistons are held at the state such that volume of gas in cylinder A and cylinder B are same and is equal to 10^{-2} m^3. The walls and piston of cylinder A are thermally insulated where as gas in cylinder B is maintained at temperature T_0. The whole system is in vacuum. Now the temperature T_0. The whole system is in vacuum. Now the piston is slowly released and its moves towards left and mechanical equilibrium is reached at the state when the volume of gas in cylinder A beocmes 25×10^{-4} m^3.

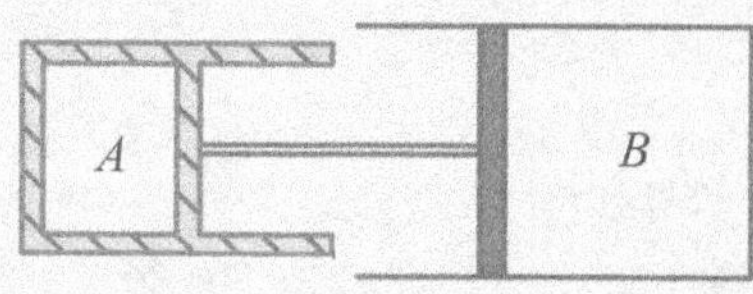

34. The mass of gas in cylinder B is

(a) 200 gm

(b) 600 gm

(c) 500 gm

(d) 1 kg

35. The change in internal energy of gas in cylinder A is

(a) 2000 J

(b) 1000 J

(c) 500 J

(d) 3000 J

36. The compressive force in the connecting rod at equilibrium is

(a) 2000 N

(b) 4000 N

(c) 8000 N

(d) 10000 N

Answer Key	**31**	(a)	**33**	(c)	**35**	(a)
Sol. from page 515	**32**	(d)	**34**	(d)	**36**	(c)

37. **Column I** contains a list of processes involving expansion of an ideal gas. Match this with **Column II** describing the thermodynamic change during this process.

Column - I

A. An insulated container has two chambers separated by a valve. Chamber I contains an ideal gas and the Chamber II has vacuum. the valve is opened.

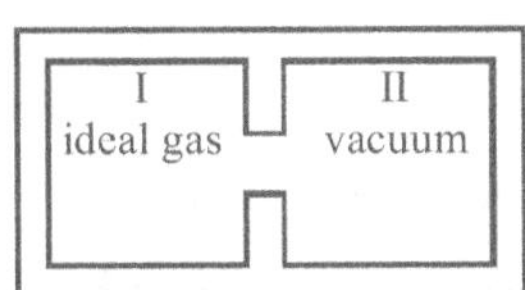

B. An ideal monoatomic gas expands to twice its original volume such that its pressure $P \propto \dfrac{1}{V^2}$ where V is the volume of the gas

C. An ideal monoatomic gas expands to twice its original volume such that its pressure $P \propto \dfrac{1}{V^{4/3}}$ where V, is its volume

D. An ideal monoatomic gas expands such that its pressure P and volume V follows the behaviour

shown in the graph

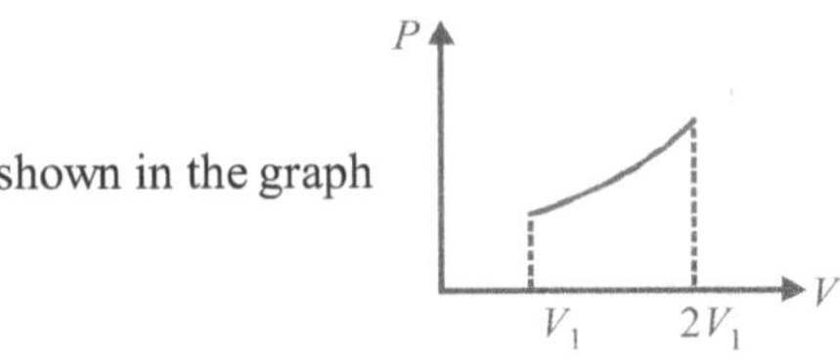

Column - II

(p) The temperature of the gas decreases

(q) The temperature of the gas increases or remains constant

(r) The gas loses heat

(s) The gas gains heat

38. One end of a copper rod is immersed in boiling water at 100°C, the other end in ice water mixture at 0°C. The sides of the rod are insulated. During a certain time interval, 0.5 kg of ice melts. Match the following columns:

Column - I

A. The entropy change of the boiling water

B. The entropy change of the ice-water mixture

C. The entropy change of the copper rod

D. The total entropy change of the entire system

Column - II

(p) 610 J/K

(q) zero

(r) – 446 J/K

(s) 164 J/K

39. **Column-I**

A. The coefficient of volume expansion at constant pressure

B. At constant temperature, an increase in volume results in

C. An ideal gas obeys Boyle's and Charle's law

D. A real gas behaves as an ideal gas at low pressure

Column-II

(p) decrease in pressure

(q) at all temperature

(r) same for all gases

(s) at high temperature

Answer Key	**37**	(A) → q; (B) → p, r; (C) → p, s; (D) → q, s	**39**	(A) → r; (B) → p; (C) → q; (D) → s
Sol. from page 515	**38**	(A) → r; (B) → p; (C) → q; (D) → s		

40. The P-V diagram of 0.2 mol of a diatomic ideal gas is shown in figure. Process BC is adiabatic, $\gamma = 1.4$.

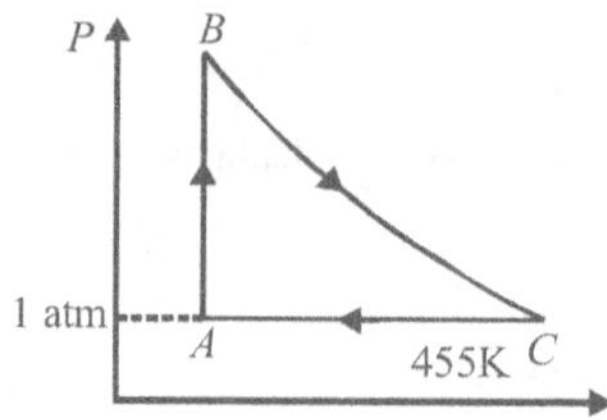

Column I		Column II	
A.	ΔQ_{AB} (J)	(p)	602
B.	ΔW_{BC} (J)	(q)	-644
C.	ΔU_{CA} (J)	(r)	1246
D.	ΔU_{BC} (J)	(s)	-602

41. A gas undergoes a process according to the graph. P is pressure, V is volume, W is work done by the gas, ΔU is change in internal energy of the gas and ΔQ is heat given to the system.

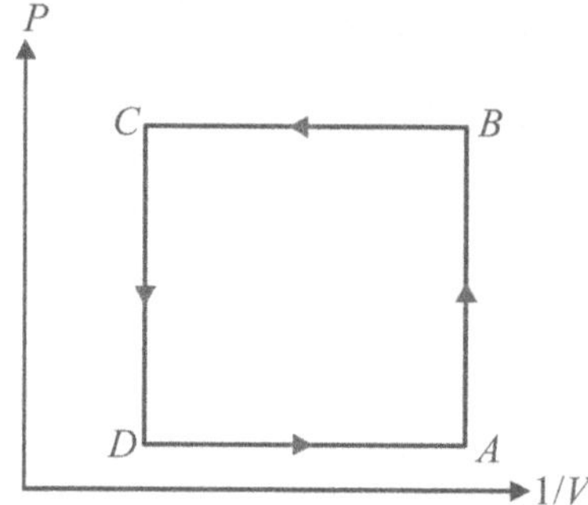

Column-I		Column-II	
A.	For process AB	(p)	$\Delta U > 0, \Delta Q > 0$
B.	For process BC	(q)	$\Delta U < 0, \Delta Q < 0$
C.	For process CD	(r)	$\Delta Q \times \Delta U \times W = 0$
D.	For process DA	(s)	$\Delta Q \times \Delta U < 0$

42. Match the column

Column I		Column II	
(Processes for ideal gases)		**(Symbols have usual meaning)**	
A.	Isothermal	(p)	$\Delta U = 0$
B.	Isobaric	(q)	$Q = 0$
C.	Isochoric	(r)	$W = 0$
D.	Adiabatic free expansions	(s)	$\Delta U = nC_V\Delta T$

43. There is an ideal gas sample. The ratio of C_P and C_V for gas sample is γ. In initial state its pressure is P_1 and volume is V_1. Now it is expanded isothermally from volume V_1 to V_2. Then it is compressed adiabatically from volume V_2 to V_1 again.

Regarding the above situation, match the following

Column I		Column II	
A.	Heat given to system (i.e. ideal gas sample) during isothermal expansion.	(p)	Positive
B.	Work done by gas during adiabatic compression	(q)	$\dfrac{P_1 V_1}{(\gamma-1)}\left[\left(\dfrac{V_2}{V_1}\right)^{\gamma-1} - 1\right]$
C.	Change in internal energy of gas sample during adiabatic process.	(r)	$\dfrac{P_1 V_1}{(1-\gamma)}\left[\left(\dfrac{V_2}{V_1}\right)^{\gamma-1} - 1\right]$
D.	Change in internal energy of gas sample from most initial state to the final state.	(s)	Negative.

Answer Key	**40**	(A) → r; (B) → p; (C) → q; (D) → s.	**42**	(A) → p, s; (B) → s; (C) → r, s; (D) → p, q, r, s
Sol. from page 515	**41**	(A) → p, r; (B) → p; (C) → q, r; (D) → q	**43**	(A) → p; (B) → r, s; (C) → p, q; (D) → p, q

44. Match **Column I** with **Column II** and select the correct answer :

A. Isothermal process

B. Isentropic process

C. Isochoric process

D. Isobaric process

(p) No heat exchange

(q) Constant temperature

(r) Constant pressure

(s) Constant volume

(t) Constant enthalpy

45. Match **Column I** with **Column II** and select the correct answer using the codes given below the lists :

A. Absolute zero

B. Triple point

C. Critical temperature

D. Adiabatic work

(p) Gaseous state

(q) Entropy of the universe

(r) Third law of thermodynamics

(s) Sublimation

(t) First law of thermodynamics

46. Match **Diagram I** with **Diagram II** and select the correct answer using the codes given below the Diagrams.

A. 1

B. 2

C. 3

D. 4

(p)

(q)

(r)

(s)

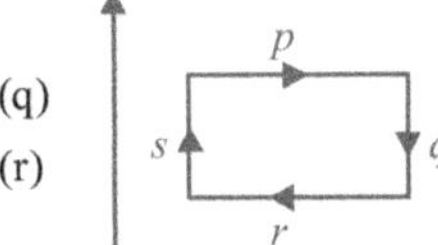

47. $V - T$ graph of a thermodynamic process is shown in figure. If heat given to process is taken to be positive. (ΔQ is heat given to the process, ΔU is change in internal energy in the process, ΔW is the work doen in the process)

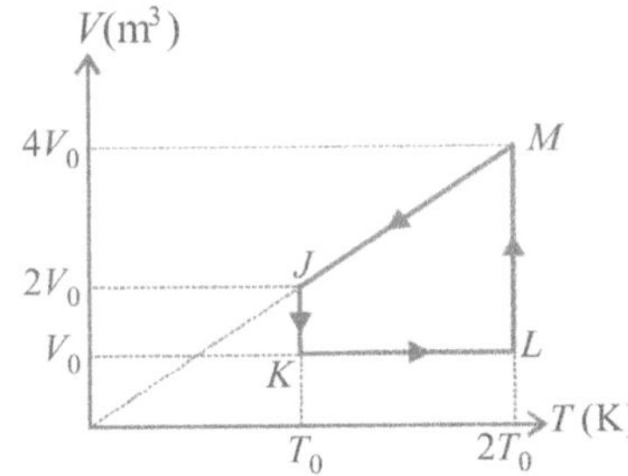

Column I		Column II
A. JK		(p) $\Delta W \geq 0$
B. KL		(q) $\Delta Q < 0$
C. LM		(r) $\Delta W < 0$
D. MJ		(s) $\Delta Q > 0$
		(t) $\Delta U = 0$

Answer Key

Sol. from page 515

44	(A) → q; (B) → p; (C) → s; (D) → r	**46** (A) → p; (B) → s; (C) → r; (D) → q
45	(A) → r; (B) → s; (C) → p; (D) → t	**47** (A) → (q, r, t) ; (B) → s; (C) → (p, s, t) ; (D) → (q, r)

48. A sample of gas goes from state A to state B in four different manners, as shown by the graphs. Let W be the work done by the gas and ΔU be change in internal energy along the path AB. Correctly match the graphs with the statements provided.

Column I

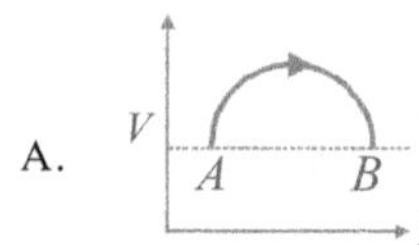

A.

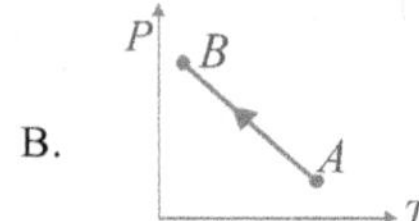

B.

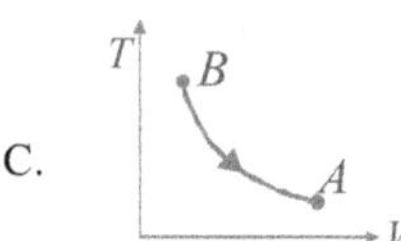

C.

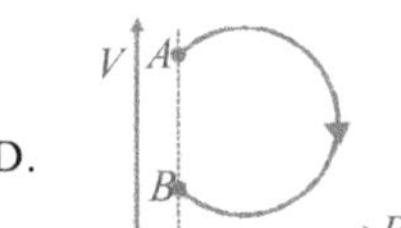

D.

Column II

(p)   Both W and ΔU are positive

(q)   Both W and ΔU are negative

(r) W is positive whereas ΔU is negative

(s)   W is negative whereas ΔU is positive

Answer Key

Sol. from page 515   **48**   (A) → s;   (B) → q;   (C) → r;   (D) → q

LOT   Subjective Integer Type   *Exercise 7.5*

Solution from page 519

1. An ideal gas having initial pressure P, volume V and temperature T is allowed to expand adiabatically until its volume becomes $5.66\,V$ while its temperature fall to $\dfrac{T}{2}$.

(i)   How many degrees of freedom do the gas molecules have ?

(ii)   Obtain the work done by the gas during the expansion as a function of the initial pressure P and volume V.

Ans : (i) 5;   (ii) $1.25\,PV$.

2. Two Carnot engines A and B are operated in series. The first one A receives heat at $900\,K$ and rejects to a reservoir at temperature T K. The second engine B receives the heat rejected by the first engine and in turn rejects to a heat reservoir at 400 K. Calculate the temperature T for the situation when (i) the efficiencies of the two engines are equal   (ii) the work outputs of the two engines are equal.

Ans. (i) 600 K, (ii) 650 K.

3. Two moles of an ideal monoatomic gas are confined within a cylinder by a massless and frictionless spring loaded piston of cross–sectional area $4 \times 10^{-3}\ m^2$. The spring is initially, in its relaxed state. Now the gas is heated by an electric heater, placed inside the cylinder, for some time. During this time, the gas expands and does 50 J of work in moving the piston through a distance 0.10 m. The temperature of the gas increases by 50 K. Calculate the spring constant and the heat supplied by the heater.

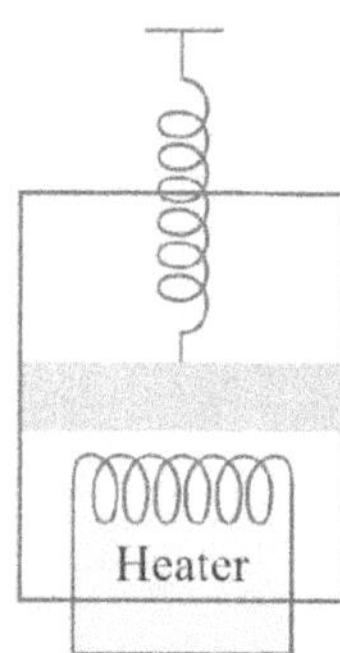

Ans : 2000 N/m, 1295 J.

4. A weightless piston divides a thermally insulated cylinder into two parts of volumes V and $3V$. 2 moles of an ideal gas at pressure $P = 2$ atmosphere are confined to the part with volume $V = 1$ litre. The remainder of the cylinder is evacuated. Initially the gas is at room temperature. The piston is now released and the gas expands to fill the entirespace of the cylinder. The piston is then pressed back to the initial position. Find the increase of internal energy in the process . The ratio of the specific heat of the gas $\gamma = 1.5$.

Ans : 400 J.

5. Calculate the work done when one mole of a perfect gas is compressed adiabatically. The initial pressure and volume of the gas are 10^5 N/m^2 and 6 litre respectively. The final volume of the gas is 2 litre. Molar specific heat of the gas at constant volume is $\dfrac{3R}{2}$.

Ans : 957 J.

6. Find the amount of workdone to increase the temperature of one mole of an ideal gas by 30°C if it is expanding under the condition $V \propto T^{2/3}$. (R = 1.99 cal / mol–K)

Ans : 167 J

7. Three moles of an ideal monoatomic gas perform a cycle shown in figure. The gas temperatures in different states are $T_1 = 400\ K$, $T_2 = 800\ K$, $T_3 = 2400\ K$, and $T_4 = 1200\ K$. Determine the work done by the gas during the cycle.

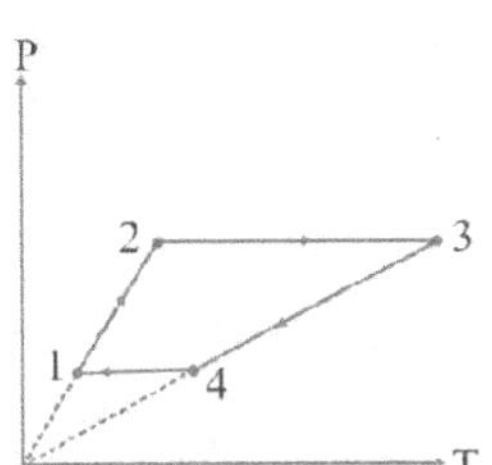

Ans. $W = 3R\ (T_1 + T_3 - T_2 - T_4) = 20$ kJ.

8. Determine the work done by an ideal gas during a closed cycle $1 \rightarrow 4 \rightarrow 3 \rightarrow 2 \rightarrow 1$ shown in figure if $P_1 = 10^5$ Pa, $P_0 = 3 \times 10^5$ Pa, $P_2 = 4 \times 10^5\ Pa$, $V_2 - V_1 = 10$ litre, and segments 4–3 and 2–1 of the cycle are parallel to the V–axis.

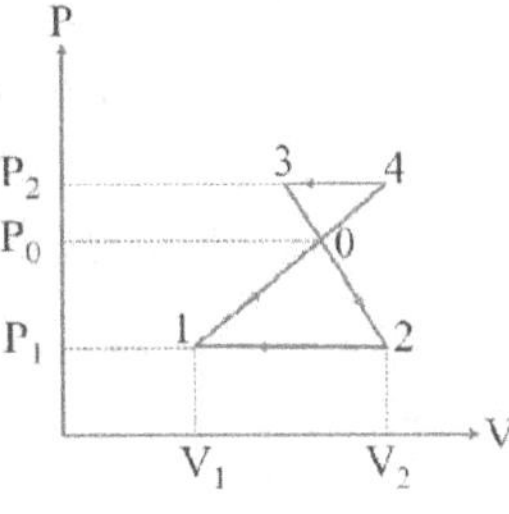

Ans. ≈ 750 J.

LOT — Subjective — *Exercise 7.6*

Solution from page 520

1. Answer the following questions :

(a) A vessel with a movable piston maintained at a constant temperature by a thermostat contains a certain amount of liquid in equilibrium with its vapour. Does this vapour obey Boyle's law ? In other words, what happens when the volume of vapour is decreased ? Does the vapour pressure increase ?

(b) What is meant by 'superheated water' and 'supercooled vapour' ? Do these states of water lie on its $P–V–T$ surface? Give some practical applications of these states of water.

Ans.

(a) No, the vapour is equilibrium with its liquid does not obey Boyle's law. When the volume of the vapour is decreased by applying pressure, some of the vapours condense into liquid, maintaining the same pressure of the vapour at the given temperature i.e., vapour pressure does not increase when the volume of vapours is decreased.

(b) **Superheated water :** Water in liquid phase having temperature above the boiling point of water at the given pressure is called superheated water. It is highly unstable stage.

Suppercooled vapour : Water in vapour phase having temperature below its boiling point at the given pressure is called supercooled vapour. It is also highly unstable stage.

2. An ideal gas has a specific heat at a constant pressure, $C_p = (5/2)R$. The gas is kept in a closed vessel of volume 0.0083 m^3 at a temperature of 300 K and a pressure of 1.6×10^6 N/m^2. An amount of 2.49×10^4 J of heat energy is supplied to the gas. Calculate the final temperature and pressure of the gas.

Ans : 675 K, 3.6×10^6 N/m^2.

3. One mole of a monoatomic gas is mixed with three moles of a diatomic gas. What is the molecular specific heat of the mixture at constant volume? Take $R = 8.31$ J mol^{-1} K^{-1} ?

Ans : 18.7 J mole^{-1} K^{-1}.

4. A sample of gas ($\gamma = 1.5$) is compressed adiabatically from a volume of 1600 cm^3 to 400 cm^3. If the initial pressure is 150 kPa, what is the final pressure and how much work is done on the gas in the process ?

Ans : 1200 kPa, $- 480$ J.

5. Two gases have the same initial pressure P_0, volume V_0 and temperature T_0. They expand to the same volume, one adiabatically and the other isothermally.

(i) In which case is the final pressure greater ?

(ii) In which case is the work done greater ?

(iii) In which case is the final temperature greater ?

Ans : (i) Final pressure is greater for the isothermal expansion.

(ii) More work is done in the isothermal expansion.

(iii) Final temperature is greater for the isothermal expansion.

6. One mole of an ideal gas whose pressure changes with volume as $P = \alpha V$, where α is a constant, is expanded so that its volume increases η times. Find the change in internal energy and heat capacity of the gas.

Ans : $\dfrac{\alpha V^2}{\gamma - 1}[\eta^2 - 1],\ \dfrac{R}{2}\left(\dfrac{\gamma + 1}{\gamma - 1}\right)$.

7. Two rectangular boxes shown in figure has a partition which can slide without friction along the length of the box has one mole of a monoatomic ideal gas $\left(\gamma = \dfrac{5}{3}\right)$ at a pressure P_0 , volume V_0 and temperature T_0. The chamber on the left is slowly heated by an electric heater.

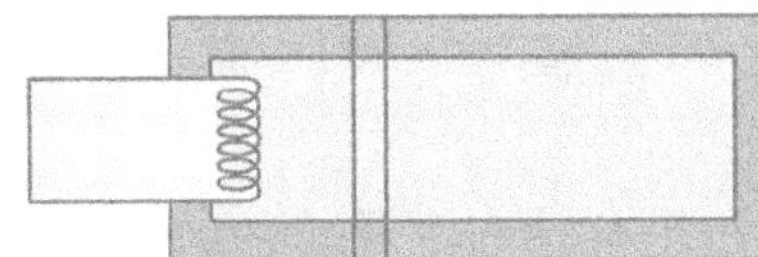

The walls of the box and the partitions are thermally insulated. Heat loss through the lead wires of the heater is negligible. The gas in the left chamber expands, pushing the partition until the final pressure in both chambers becomes $\dfrac{243P_0}{32}$. Determine

(i) the final temperature of the gas in each chamber and

(ii) the work done by the gas in the right chamber.

Ans : (i) $\dfrac{9}{4}\,T_0$ (ii) $-\dfrac{15}{8}\,P_0V_0$

8. Two moles of helium gas ($\gamma = \dfrac{5}{3}$) are initially at temperature 27 °C and occupy a volume of 20 litre. The gas is first expanded at constant pressure until the volume is doubled. Then it undergoes an adiabatic change until the temperature returns to its initial value.

(i) Sketch the process on a P–V diagram.

(ii) What are the final volume and pressure of the gas ?

(iii) What is the work done by the gas ?

Ans. (i)

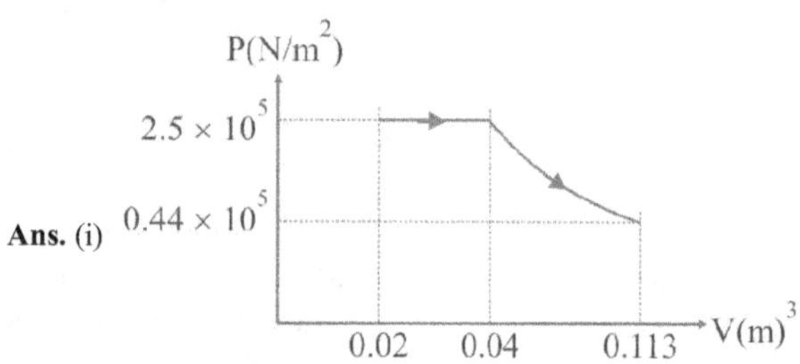

(ii) volume = 113.14 x 10^{-3} m^3, pressure = 0.88 x 10^5 N/ m^2

(iii) 5000 J, 12450 J.

9. One mole of an ideal monoatomic gas undergoes the process $P = \alpha\, T^{1/2}$ where α is a constant. (i) Find the work done by the gas if its temperature increases by 50 K. (ii) Find the molar specific heat of the gas.

Ans : (i) 207.7 J (ii) $\dfrac{R}{2}\left(\dfrac{\gamma+1}{\gamma-1}\right)$.

10. One mole of an ideal gas with heat capacity at constant pressure C_p undergoes the process $T = T_0 + \alpha\, V$, where T_0 and α are constants. Find

(a) heat capacity of the gas as a function of its volume,

(b) the amount of heat transferred to the gas, if its volume increased from V_1 to V_2.

Ans : (a) $C_p + \dfrac{RT_0}{\alpha V}$ (b) $\alpha\,(V_2 - V_1)\,C_p + RT_0 \log_e \dfrac{V_2}{V_1}$.

11. A piston divides a closed gas cylinder into two parts. Initially the piston is kept pressed such that one part has a pressure P and volume $5\,V$ and the other part has pressure $8\,P$ and volume V. The piston is now left free. Find the new pressure and volume for the adiabatic and isothermal processes. For this gas $\gamma = 1.5$.

Ans : $\dfrac{13P}{6}$, $\dfrac{30}{13}V$, $\dfrac{48V}{13}$; 1.84 P, $\dfrac{10V}{3}$, $\dfrac{8V}{3}$.

12. Three moles of an ideal gas ($C_p = \dfrac{7}{2}\,R$) at pressure P_A and temperature T_A is isothermally expanded to twice its initial volume. It is then compressed at constant pressure to its original volume. Finally the gas is compressed at constant volume to its original pressure P_A.

(a) Sketch P-V and P-T diagrams for the complete process.

(b) Calculate the new work done by the gas and net heat supplied to the gas during the complete process.

Ans : (a)

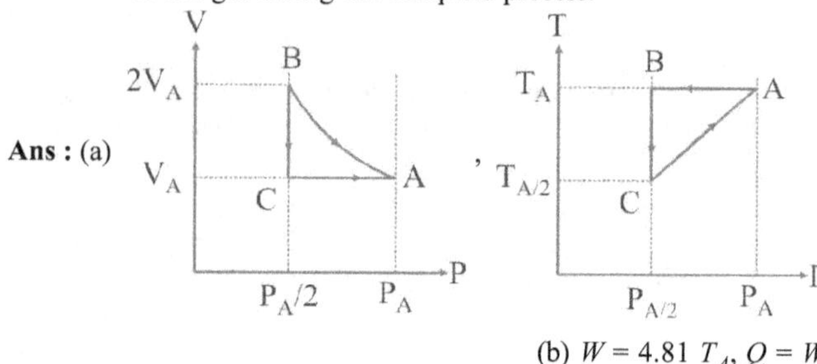

(b) $W = 4.81\,T_A$, $Q = W$

13. Calculate the difference in efficiencies of a Carnot engine working between

(i) 400 K and 350 K and (ii) between 350 K and 300 K.

Ans. 1.8 %.

14. An ideal engine operates by taking in steam from a boiler at a temperature of 327°C and rejecting heat to the sink at a temperature of 27°C. The engine runs at 500 rpm and the heat taken is 600 k-cal in each revolution. Calculate

(i) The Carnot efficiency of the engine (ii) the work done in each cycle

(iii) the heat rejected in each revolution and

(iv) the power output of this engine.

Ans : (i) 50 % (ii) 1.26×10^6 J (iii) 300 kcal (iv) 1.05×10^7 W.

15. A Carnot cycle is performed by air initially at 327°C. Each stage represents a compression or expansion in the ratio 1 : 6. Calculate

(i) the lowest temperature and (ii) efficiency of the cycle. (Given $\gamma = 1.4$).

Ans : (i) 293 K or 20°C (ii) 51.2 %.

16. A Carnot engine having a perfect gas as the working substance is driven backward and is used for freezing water already at 0°C. If the engine is driven by a 500 W electric motor having a efficiency of 60 %, how long will it take to freeze 15 kg of water. Take 15°C and 0°C as the working temperatures of the engine and assume there are no heat losses in the refrigerating system. Latent heat of ice = 333×10^3 J/kg.

Ans : 914.8 s.

17 If you are asked to increase the efficiency of a Carnot engine by increasing the temperature of the source or by decreasing the temperature of the sink by 10 K, which method would you prefer and why ?

Ans : The efficiency of a Carnot engine can be increased by a greater amount by decreasing the temperature of the sink.

18. A perfect Carnot engine utilises an ideal gas as the working substance. The source temperature is 227°C and the sink temperature is 127°C. Find the efficiency of this engine, and find the heat received from the source and the heat released to the sink when 10,000 J of external work is done.

Ans. 20%, 5×10^4 J, 4×10^4 J.

19. An ideal gas is taken through a cyclic thermodynamic process through four steps. The amount of heat involved in these steps are $Q_1 = 5960$ J, $Q_2 = -5585$ J, $Q_3 = -2980$ J and $Q_4 = 3645$ J respectively. The corresponding works involved are $W_1 = 2200$ J, $W_2 = -825$ J, $W_3 = -1100$ J and W_4 respectively.

(i) Find the value of W_4.

(ii) What is the efficiency of the cycle ?

Ans : (a) 765 J (b) 10.82 %

20. One mole of a monoatomic ideal gas is taken through the cycle shown in figure.

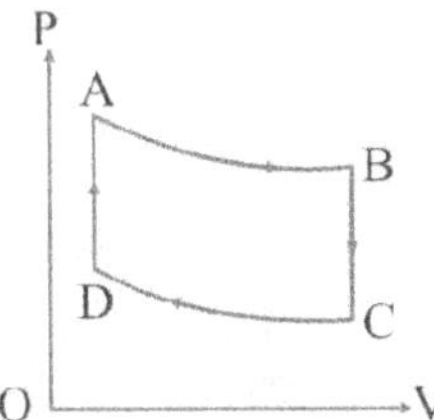

$A \rightarrow B$ adiabatic expansion

$B \rightarrow C$ cooling at constant volume

$C \rightarrow D$ adiabatic compression

$D \rightarrow A$ heating at constant volume

The pressure and temperature at A, B etc. are denoted by P_A, P_B, ...; T_A, T_B, ..., etc. respectively.

Given that $T_A = 1000\,K$, $P_B = \dfrac{2}{3}\,P_A$ and $P_C = \dfrac{1}{3}\,P_A$.

Calculate the following quantities :

(i) The work done by the gas in process $A \rightarrow B$

(ii) The heat lost by the gas in process $B \rightarrow C$

(iii) The temperature T_D.

Given that $\left(\dfrac{2}{3}\right)^{2/5} = 0.85$

Ans : (i) 1869.83 J (ii) 5297.63 J (iii) $T_D = 500$ K

21. There are two vessels. Each of then contains one mole of a monoatomic ideal gas. Initial volume of the gas in each vessel is 8.3×10^{-3} m^3 at 27°C. Equal amount of heat is supplied to each vessel. In one of the vessels, the volume of the gas is doubled without change in its internal energy, where as the volume of the gas is held constant in the second vessel. The vessels are now connected to allow free mixing of the gas. Find the final temperature and pressure of the combined gas system.

Ans : 369.3 K, 2.46×10^5 N/ m^2.

22. The pressure in monoatomic gas increases linearly from 4×10^5 N/m^2 to 8×10^5 N/m^2, when its volume increases from 0.2 m^3 to 0.5 m^3. Calculate the following :

(i)   Work done by the gas,

(ii) Increase in the internal energy,

(iii) Amount of heat supplied,

(iv) Molar heat capacity of the gas.

Ans : (i) 1.8×10^5 J (ii) 4.8×10^5 J
(iii) 6.6×10^5 J (iv) 17 J.

23. One mole of a diatomic ideal gas ($\gamma = 1.4$) is taken through a cyclic process starting from point A. The process $A \rightarrow$ B is an adiabatic compression, $B \rightarrow C$ is isobaric, $C \rightarrow D$ an adiabatic expansion and $D \rightarrow A$ is isochoric. The volume ratios are $V_A / V_B = 16$ and $V_C / V_B = 2$ and the temperature at A is $T_A = 300°K$. Calculate the temperature of the gas at the points B and D and find the efficiency of the cycle.

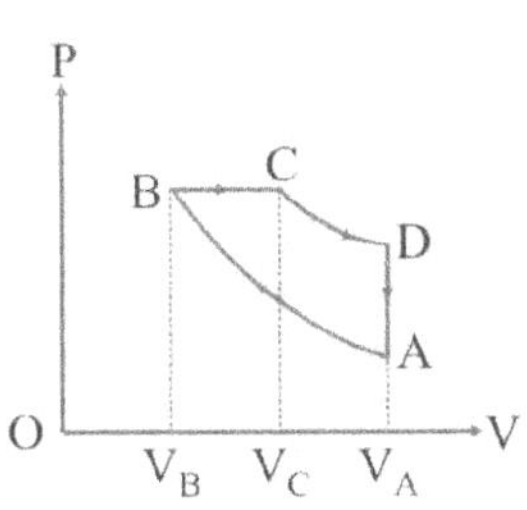

Ans : 909 K, 791.3 K, 61.4 %.

24. Two moles of an ideal monoatomic gas, initially at pressure P_1 and volume V_1 undergo an adiabatic compression until its volume is V_2. Then the gas is given heat Q at constant volume V_2.

(a) Sketch the complete process on a $P - V$ diagram.

(b) Find the total work done by the gas, the total change in its internal energy and the final temperature of the gas. (Given your answers in terms of P_1, V_1, V_2, Q and R).

Ans : (a) 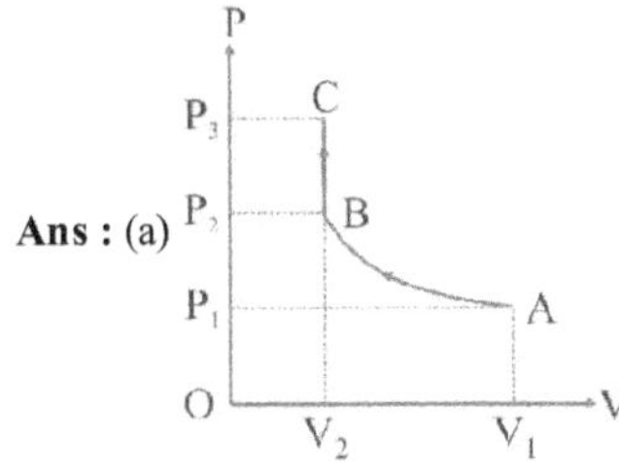

(b) $W = \dfrac{3}{2}\,P_1 V_1 \left[1 - \left(\dfrac{V_1}{V_2}\right)^{2/3} \right]$,

$\Delta U = Q + \dfrac{3}{2}\,P_1 V_1 \left[\left(\dfrac{V_1}{V_2}\right)^{2/3} - 1 \right]$, $T = \left[\dfrac{Q}{3R} + \dfrac{P_1 V_1^{5/3}}{2R V_2^{2/3}} \right]$

25. Two vessels of volumes V_1 and V_2 contain the same ideal gas. The pressures in the vessels are P_1 and P_2 and the temperatures are T_1 and T_2 respectively. The two vessels are now connected to each other through a narrow tube. Assuming that no heat is exchanged between the surrounding and the vessels, find the common pressure and temperature attained after the connection.

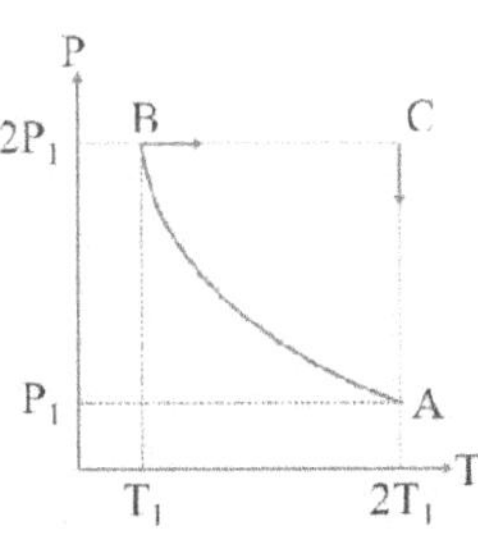

Ans. $\dfrac{P_1 V_1 + P_2 V_2}{V_1 + V_2}$, $\dfrac{T_1 T_2 (P_1 V_1 + P_2 V_2)}{P_1 V_1 T_2 + P_2 V_2 T_1}$

26. Two moles of an ideal monoatomic gas is taken through a cycle $ABCA$ as shown in the P–T diagram. During the process AB, pressure and temperature of the gas vary such that PT = constant. If $T_1 = 300\,K$. Calculate

(a) the work done on the gas in the process AB and

(b) the heat absorbed or released by the gas in each of the processes. Give answers in terms of the gas constant R.

Ans. (a) $-1200\,R$ (b) $-2100\,R$, $1500\,R$, $831.7\,R$.

27. A cyclic process (cycle) 1–2–3–4–1 consisting of two isobars 2–3 and 4–1, isochor 1–2, and a certain process 3–4 represented by a straight line on the P–V diagram involves n moles of an ideal gas. The gas temperatures in states 1, 2 and 3 are T_1, T_2 and T_3 respectively, and points 2 and 4 lie on the same isotherm. Determine the work done by the gas during the cycle.

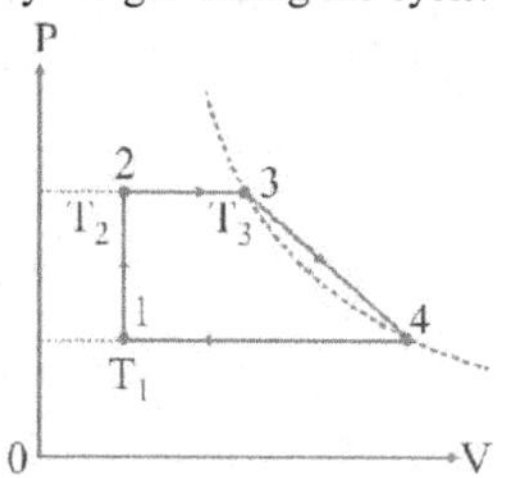

$$\textbf{Ans. } W = nR\,(T_2 - T_1)\left(\frac{T_2}{T_1} + \frac{T_3}{T_2} - 2\right)$$

28. A vessel of volume $V = 30\ l$ is separated into three equal parts by stationary semipermeable thin particles. The left middle and right parts are filled with $m_{H_2} = 30$ g of hydrogen , $m_{O_2} = 160$ g of oxygen and $m_{N_2} = 70$ g of nitrogen respectively. The left partition lets through only hydrogen, while the right partition lets through hydrogen and nitrogen. What will be the pressure in each part of the vessel after the equilibrium has been set in if the vessel is kept at a constant temperature $T = 300$ K ?

H_2	O_2	N_2

$$\textbf{Ans. } P_1 = 1.3\ GPa\ ,\ P_2 = 4.5\ G\,Pa,\ P_3 = 2.0\ G\,Pa.$$

29. A sample of 2 kg of monoatomic helium (assumed ideal) is taken through the process ABC and another sample of 2 kg of the same gas is taken through the process ADC . Given molecular mass of helium = 4

(i) What is the temperature of helium in each of the states A, B, C and D ?

(ii) Is there any way of telling afterwards which sample of helium went through the process ABC and which went through the process ADC ? Write yes or no.

(iii) How much is the heat involved in each of the processes ABC and ADC ?

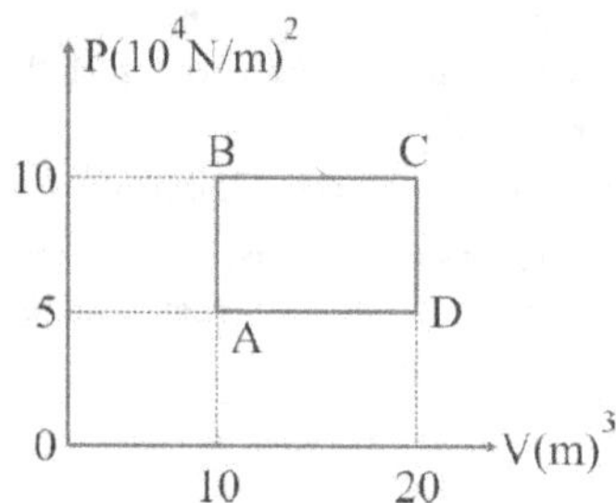

Ans : (i) 120.33 K, 240.66 K, 481.32 K, 240.66 K (ii) No
(iii) $3.25 \times 10^6\ J$, $2.75 \times 10^6\ J$

30. A horizontal cylindrical vessel of length 2 l is separated by a thin heat – insulating piston into two equal parts each of which contains n moles of an ideal monoatomic gas at a temperature T. The piston is connected to the end faces of the vessel by undeformed spings of rigidity k each. When an amount of heat Q is supplied to the gas in the right part, the piston is displaced to the left by a distance $x = l/2$.

Determine the amount of heat Q' given away at the temperature T to a thermostat with which the gas in the left part is in thermal contact all the time.

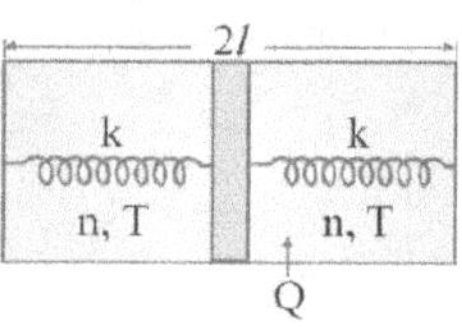

$$\textbf{Ans. } Q\,' = Q - 3\,nRT - \frac{5}{2}\,kl^2\,.$$

31. A thermally insulated vessel is divided into two parts by a heat–insulating piston which can move in the vessel without friction. The left part of the vessel contains one mole of an ideal monoatomic gas, and the right part is empty. The piston is connected to the right wall of the vessel through a spring whose length in free state is equal to the length of the vessel.

Determine the heat capacity C of the system, neglecting the heat capacities of the vessel, piston and spring.

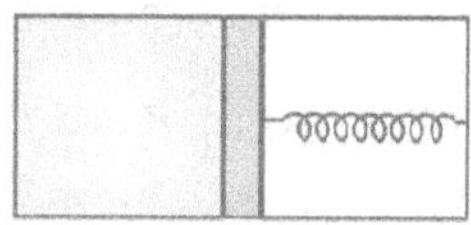

$$\textbf{Ans. } C = 2R.$$

32. A thin U–tube sealed at one end consists of three bends of length $l = 250$ mm each, forming right angles. The vertical parts of the tube are filled with mercury to half the height.

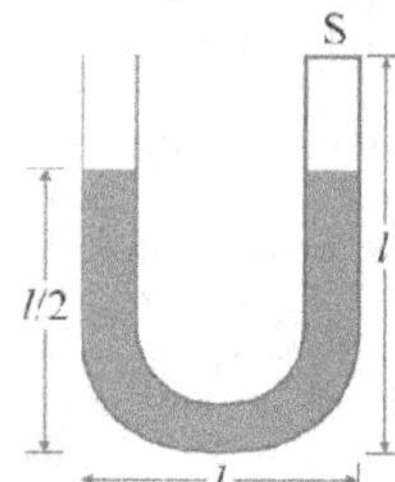

All of mercury can be displaced from the tube by heating slowly the gas in the sealed end of the tube, which is separated from the atmospheric air by mercury. Determine the work done by the gas there by if the atmospheric pressure is $P_0 = 10^5$ Pa, the density of mercury is $\rho_{mer} = 13.6 \times 10^3$ kg/m^3, and the cross–sectional area of the tube is $S = 1$ cm^2.

$$\textbf{Ans. } W = \frac{5}{2}\,P_0 Sl + \frac{7}{4}\,\rho_{Hg}\,gSl^2 \approx 7.7\ J.$$

33. A monoatomic ideal gas of two moles is taken through a cyclic process starting from A as shown in figure. The volume ratios are $V_B/V_A = 2$ and $V_D/V_A = 4$. If the temperature T_A at A is 27°C, calculate

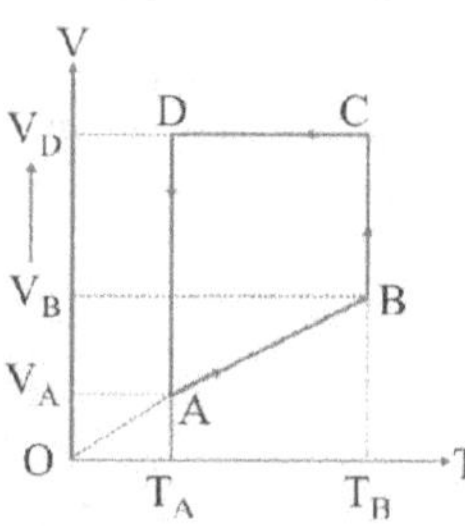

(a) the temperature of the gas at point B,

(b) heat absorbed or released by the gas in each process,

(c) the total work done by the gas during the complete cycle. Express your answer in terms of gas constant R.

Ans : (a) 327°C
(b) 1500 R, 831.6 R, $-$ 900 R, $-831.6\ R$ (c) 600 R

Hints & Solutions

1. (a) W = area enclosed = $P \times V = PV$

2. (c) $\Delta P = \dfrac{n_A RT}{V} - \dfrac{n_A RT}{2V} = \dfrac{n_A RT}{2V}$ ...(i)

   and $1.5\Delta P = \dfrac{n_B RT}{V} - \dfrac{n_B RT}{2V} = \dfrac{n_B RT}{2V}$ ...(ii)

   From above equations

   $$\dfrac{\Delta P}{1.5\Delta P} = \dfrac{n_A}{n_B}$$

   $$= \dfrac{m_A}{m_B}$$

   $$m_B = 1.5\, m_A$$

3. (a) $C_p - C_v$ = work done

4. (c) $\Delta U = nC_v \Delta T = n \times \dfrac{3R}{2} \times \Delta T$

   $$= 1 \times \dfrac{3}{2} \times 8.32 \times (100 - 0)$$

   $$= 1248 \text{ J}$$

5. (a) During the process,
   $W = P\Delta V$; ΔV increasing,
   so work done increases.

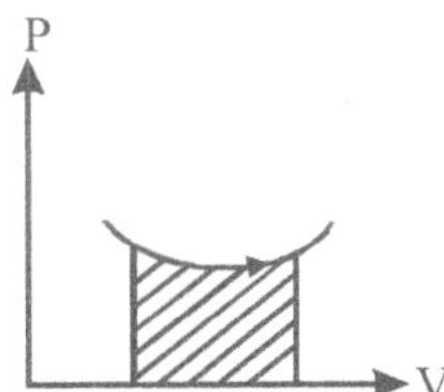

6. (d) The required fraction,

   $$F = \dfrac{C_v}{C_p} = \dfrac{1}{\gamma} = \dfrac{1}{7/5} = \dfrac{5}{7}$$

7. (a) $dQ = dU + dW$
   As $dW = 0$ and $dQ < 0$, $\therefore dU < 0$, so internal energy and hence temperature decreases.

8. (d) Polyatomic gas has non-zero moment of inertia so there are rotational degrees of freedom in addition to translation.

9. (b) In isothermal process,
   $$\Delta U = 0,$$
   $\therefore \qquad Q = 0 + W$
   Area of $P - V$ is greater for 1, so W and hence Q_1 is greatest.

10. (c) Change in entropy,
   $$\Delta S = \dfrac{\Delta Q}{T}.$$
   For adiabatic process
   $$\Delta Q = 0, \text{ and}$$
   so $\qquad \Delta S = 0$

11. (c) For cyclic process,
   $$\Delta U = 0,$$
   $\therefore \qquad Q = \Delta U + W$

   or $600 - 400 - 300 + 200 = 300 - 200 - 150 + W_4$
   $\therefore \qquad W_4 = 150$ J

12. (a) For the container, $Q = 0$;
   $$W = P\Delta V = 0$$
   Now $\qquad Q = \Delta U + W$
   or $\qquad 0 = \Delta U + 0 \implies \Delta U = 0$
   So, $\qquad \Delta T = 0$.

13. (a) In free expansion,
   $$W = P\Delta V = 0 \times \Delta V = 0.$$
   Also $\qquad Q = 0$
   So, $\qquad Q = \Delta U + W \implies \Delta U = 0$

14. (d) P, V and T are the parameter to characterize the thermodynamic state of matter.

15. (b) Change in internal energy and entropy depends on initial and final state.

16. (c) $PV = nRT$, is equation of ideal gas, so it true of any process.

17. (b) $$W = nRT \ln \dfrac{V_f}{V_i}$$

   $$= 1 \times 8.31 \times 300 \ln\left(\dfrac{20}{10}\right)$$

   $$= 1728 \text{ J}$$

18. (a) $P = KT^3$; and

   $$PV = nRT \implies T = \dfrac{PV}{nR}$$

   So $\qquad P = k\left(\dfrac{PV}{nR}\right)^3$

   or $\qquad PV^{3/2}$ = constant

   $\therefore \qquad \gamma = 3/2$.

19. (d) In reversible isochoric process, $\Delta v = 0$; so
   $W = 0$. Also $\Delta U = 0$.
   $\therefore \qquad Q = 0 + 0 = 0$

20. (b) The heat reject by the refrigerator to source (room)
   $$Q_1 = Q_2 + W,$$
   So room will be heated.

21. (d) $\eta = 1 - \dfrac{T_2}{T_1} = 1 - \dfrac{300}{6000} = 0.95$.

22. (b) $$\beta = \dfrac{Q_2}{W} = \dfrac{1}{\dfrac{T_1}{T_2} - 1} = \dfrac{1 - \eta}{\eta}$$

   or $\qquad \dfrac{Q_2}{10} = \dfrac{1 - \frac{1}{10}}{\frac{1}{10}}$

   $\therefore \qquad Q_2 = 90$ J

23. **(b)** The area of 2 is larger than 1, so work done will be negative.

24. **(a)**

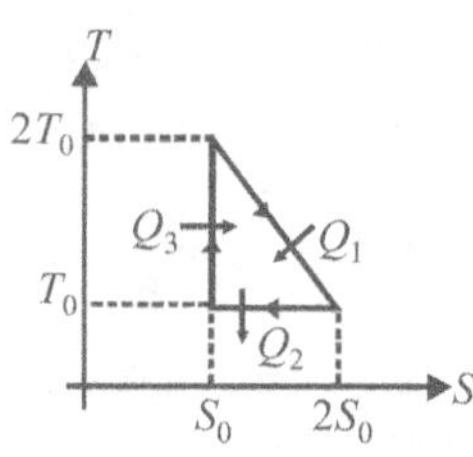

$$Q_1 = \frac{2T_0 + T_0}{2} \times S_0 = \frac{3}{2}T_0 S_0$$

$$Q_2 = T_0 S_0 \text{ and } Q_3 = 0$$

$$\therefore \quad \eta = \frac{Q_1 - Q_2}{Q_1} = 1 - \frac{2}{3} = \frac{1}{3}$$

25. **(d)**

$$W = W_{AODA} + W_{OBCO}$$
$$= + W - W = 0$$

26. **(a)**

$$Q = \Delta U + W$$

or $\quad 40 = \Delta U + 30, \therefore \Delta U = 10 \text{ J.}$

27. **(d)** The slope of adiabatic curve will be greater than slope of isothermal curve.

28. **(b)**

$$P(V - b) = nRT, \therefore P = \frac{nRT}{(V - b)}.$$

Thus

$$W = \int_V^{2V} P dV = nRT \int_V^{2V} \frac{dV}{V - b}$$

$$= nRT \left| \ell n(V - b) \right|_V^{2V}$$

$$= nRT \ell n \left[\frac{2V - b}{V - b} \right]$$

$$= 2RT \ell n \left[\frac{2V - b}{V - b} \right]$$

29. **(b)** $\quad dQ = dU + PdV \Rightarrow \dfrac{\alpha}{T} dT = C_V dT + PdV$

$$\Rightarrow \frac{\alpha}{T} dT = C_v dT + \frac{RT}{V} dV$$

$$\Rightarrow C = VT^{\frac{1}{\gamma - 1}} e^{\alpha / RT}$$

30. **(c)**

$$\frac{P_A V_A}{T_A} = \frac{P_B V_B}{T_B}$$

$$\Rightarrow \quad \frac{15 \times 5}{(273 + 427)} = \frac{10 \times 15}{T_2}$$

$$\therefore \quad T_2 = 1400 \text{ K}$$

$$W_{AB} = \left(\frac{15 + 10}{2} \right) \times 10 = 125 \text{ atm-}\ell$$

$$= 125 \times 10^5 \times 10^{-3}$$
$$= 12500 \text{ J}$$

Thus $\quad Q = \Delta U + W$

or $\quad 5500 \times 4.2 = \Delta U + 12500$

$\Rightarrow \quad \Delta U = 10600 \text{ J.}$

$\therefore \quad \Delta U = 10600 = m\, C_v \Delta T$

$$= \frac{5}{1000} \times C_v \times (700)$$

or $\quad C_v = 3.03 \text{ kJ/kg} - °C$

31. **(a)**

$$\Delta U = n\, C_v \Delta T$$
$$= 2 \times 10^3 \times 20 \times 273$$
$$= 10.9 \text{ MJ.}$$

32. **(b)**

$$W_{ABD} = W_{AB} + W_{BD}$$
$$= 0 + 6 \times 10^4 \times 4 \times 10^{-3}$$
$$= 240 \text{ J.}$$

Now, $\quad Q = \Delta U + W$

or $\quad 500 + 150 = \Delta U + 240$

$\therefore \quad \Delta U = 410 \text{ J.}$

33. **(a)**

$$W_{AB} = 0,$$

$$W_{BC} = \frac{R}{\gamma - 1}\left(T_i - T_f\right)$$

$$= \frac{R}{\gamma - 1}\left(T_2 - T_3\right),$$

$$W_{CA} = P\Delta V = R\Delta T = -R(T_3 - T_1)$$

$$\therefore \quad W = W_{AB} + W_{BC} + W_{CA}$$

$$= \frac{R}{\gamma - 1}\left(T_2 - T_3\right) - R\left(T_3 - T_1\right)$$

After substituting values, we get
$$W = 75\ R.$$

Solutions **EXERCISE 7.1 LEVEL -2**

1. **(b)** The double the volume, the temperature will also be doubled.

So, $\quad \Delta T = 2T - T = T = 273 \text{ K}$

$\therefore \quad Q = nC\Delta T$

$$= \frac{1}{2} \times (3 \times 4) \times 273$$

$$= 1638 \text{ J.}$$

2. **(d)** Using, $\quad T_1 V_1^{\gamma - 1} = T_2 V_2^{\gamma - 1}$

or $\quad T_1\left(AL_1\right)^{\gamma - 1} = T_2\left(AL_2\right)^{\gamma - 1}$

$$\therefore \quad \frac{T_1}{T_2} = \left(\frac{L_2}{L_1}\right)^{\gamma - 1} = \left(\frac{L_2}{L_1}\right)^{\frac{5}{3} - 1}$$

$$= \left(\frac{L_2}{L_1}\right)^{\frac{2}{3}}$$

3. **(d)**

$$U = 2 \times \frac{5}{2} RT + 4 \times \frac{3R}{2}$$

$$= 11\ RT$$

4. **(b)** The slope of adiabatic curve $= \gamma\left(-\dfrac{P}{V}\right)$

   The r for monoatomic gas is greater, so 1 for O_2 and 2 for He.

5. **(c)** The given processes are shown in figure. Clearly $P_2 > P_1$ and work done is negative.

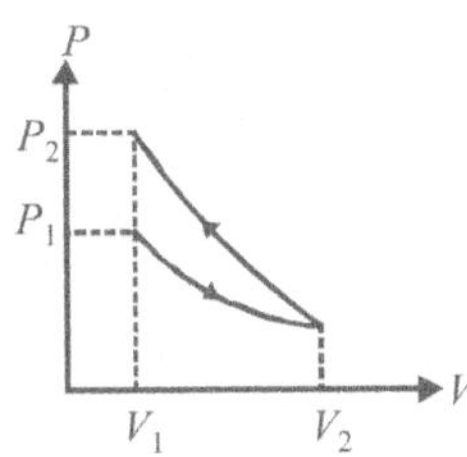

6. **(a)**
$$W = W_{AB} + W_{BC} + W_{CA}$$
$$= W_{AB} + 0 + W_{CA}$$
$$W_{AB} = P(\Delta V) = 10 \times (2-1) = 10 \text{ J.}$$

   Now, $\quad Q = \Delta U + W$
   or $\quad 5 = 0 + (10 + W_{CA})$
   $\therefore \quad W_{CA} = -5 \text{ J.}$

7. **(d)**
$$\frac{Q_1}{Q_2} = \frac{T_1}{T_2} = \left[\frac{273+227}{273+127}\right]$$
$$= \frac{500}{400} = \frac{5}{4}$$

   $\therefore \quad Q_2 = \dfrac{5}{4}Q_1 = \dfrac{4}{5} \times 6 \times 10^4 = 4.8 \times 10^4 \text{ cal}$

   $\therefore \quad W = Q_1 - Q_2 = 1.2 \times 10^4 \text{ cal.}$

8. **(b)**
$$\frac{W}{Q_1} = 1 - \frac{T_2}{T_1} = 1 - \left[\frac{273+27}{273+627}\right] = \frac{2}{3}$$

   $\therefore \quad W = \dfrac{2}{3}Q_1 = \dfrac{2}{3} \times 3000 = 2000 \text{ kcal.}$
   $$= 8.4 \times 10^6 \text{ J}$$

9. **(b)**
$$n = \frac{PV}{RT}$$
$$= \left[\frac{1.6 \times 10^6 \times 0.0083}{8.31 \times 300}\right] = 5.33$$
$$Q = nC_v\Delta T$$

   or $\quad 2.49 \times 10^4 = 5.33 \times \left(\dfrac{3 \times 8.31}{2}\right) \times \Delta T$

   or $\quad \Delta T = 375 \text{ K}$
   $\therefore \quad T_f = T_i + 375 = 675 \text{ K.}$

10. **(c)** Using, $\quad P_1 V_1 = P_2 V_2$
$$(100 \times 10^3 + 1000g \times 20) \times 3 = (100 \times 10^3) \times V_2$$
   $\therefore \quad V_2 = 8.88 \text{ mm}^3$

11. **(b)** $\quad Pt = mC\Delta T$

   $\therefore \quad t = \dfrac{mC\Delta T}{P} = \dfrac{4 \times 4200 \times 5}{0.5 \times 746}$

   $= 3.75 \text{ min.}$

12. **(a)** For tiny glass tube,
$$P_1 V_1 = P_2 V_2$$
   $\therefore \quad P_2 = \dfrac{P_1 V_1}{V_2} = \dfrac{4.5 \times 0.50}{500}$
   $$= 0.0045 \text{ atm.}$$
   Thus $\quad P = 1\text{atm} + 0.0045 \text{ atm}$
   $$= 1.0045 \text{ atm} = 76.34 \text{ cm of Hg.}$$

13. **(b)**
$$W = P(\Delta V) = m\left(C_p - C_v\right)\Delta T$$
$$= 4(0.219 - 0.157) \times 4200 \times (120 - 20)$$
$$\simeq 104 \times 10^3 \text{J}$$

14. **(c)** Slope of adiabatic curve
$$= \gamma \times \text{slope of isothermal curve}$$
$$= 1.4 \times (-400) = -560 \text{ MPa/m}^3$$

15. **(d)** For maximum positive work, the area enclosed in $P - V$ diagram should be maximum. By observation it will be between the curves c and e.

16. **(b)** Along ab, $Q = 0 + 5 = 5$. $\Delta U_{ab} = 0$

   Along bc, $0 = \Delta U_{bc} + 4$, $\quad \therefore \quad \Delta U_{bc} = -4$J

   In cyclic process $abca$,
   $$\Delta U_{ab} + \Delta U_{bc} + \Delta U_{ca} = 0$$
   or, $\quad 0 - 4 + \Delta U_{ca} = 0$
   $\therefore \quad \Delta U_{ca} = +4$J
   Thus $\quad \Delta U_{ac} = -4$ J

17. **(a)** $\Delta S = \int\left(\dfrac{dQ}{T}\right)$; As T is smaller for (i), so

   change in entropy is greatest in case (i)

18. **(b)**
$$Q_a = \Delta U + 0 = \Delta U$$
   and $\quad Q_b = \Delta U + P\Delta V$

   As $Q_b > Q_a$, $\quad \therefore$ Change in entropy is greater in case(b).

19. **(c)** $Q = mL = 1 \times L = L$; $W = P(V_2 - V_1)$
   Now $\quad Q = \Delta U + W$
   or $\quad L = \Delta U + P(V_2 - V_1)$
   $\therefore \quad \Delta U = L - P(V_2 - V_1)$

20. **(d)** $W = P(\Delta V) = 1 \times 10^5 \times (3.34 - 2 \times 10^{-3}) = 340 \times 10^3$J.

21. **(c)**
$$-20 = \Delta U + 50 \Rightarrow \Delta U = -70.$$
   From $2 \to 1$, $\Delta U = 70$ kJ.
   Now $\quad 10 = 70 + W \Rightarrow W = -60$ kJ.

22. **(b)** $\dfrac{P_0}{T_0} = \dfrac{P_2}{2T_0} \Rightarrow P_2 = 2P_0$

   Now tension $\quad F = (\Delta P)A = P_0 A.$

23. **(b)**
$$Q = Q_1 + Q_2 + Q_3 + Q_4$$
$$= 6000 - 5500 - 3000 + 3500$$

$$= +1000 \text{ J}$$
$$W = W_1 + W_2 + W_3 + W_4$$
$$= 2500 - 1000 - 1200 + x$$
$$= +300 + x$$

In cyclic process,

$$\Delta U = 0$$

Now, $\qquad Q = \Delta U + W$

or $\qquad 1000 = 0 + (300 + x)$

$\therefore \qquad x = 700 \text{ J}$

$$\eta = \frac{W}{Q_1 + Q_4}$$

$$= \frac{1000}{6000 + 3500} = 10.5\%$$

24. (d)
$$Q = \Delta U + 0$$
$$= i^2 RT = 1^2 \times 100 \times (5 \times 60)$$
$$= 3 \times 10^4 \text{ J.}$$

25. (d)
$$Q = nC_P \times 30 = n \times \frac{7R}{2} \times 30$$

and
$$Q = n \times \frac{5R}{2} \times \Delta T$$

$\therefore \qquad n \times \dfrac{7R}{2} \times 30 = n \times \dfrac{5R}{2} \times \Delta T$

or $\qquad \Delta T = 42 \text{ K.}$

26. (a) $A \to C \to B : \quad T_B = 4T_0$

Now, $\qquad Q = \Delta U + W = nC_v \Delta T + P\Delta V$

$$= \frac{3}{2}R \times 3T_0 + RT_0$$

$$= \frac{11RT_0}{2}$$

27. (a) Process AB is isobasic and BC is isothermal, CD isochoric and DA isothermic compression.

28. (c) Process AB is isobasic, AC isothermic and CB isochoric.

29. (d)
$$Q_{ab} = nC_v \Delta T$$

or $\qquad 7000 = n \times 5 \times \dfrac{8.31}{2} \times (1000 - 300)$

$\therefore \qquad n = 0.48$

Now, $\qquad Q_{ca} = nC_p \Delta T$

$$= 0.48 \times \frac{7 \times 8.31}{2} \times (1000 - 300)$$

$$\simeq 9800 \text{ J.}$$

30. (c) $W_{AB} = 0, \qquad W_{BC} = P(\Delta V)$

$$= nR\Delta T = 6 \times 8.31 \times (2200 - 800)$$
$$= 69.8 \text{ kJ.}$$

$W_{CD} = 0, \qquad W_{DA} = -P(\Delta V)$

$$= nR\Delta T = 6 \times 8.31 \times (600 - 1200)$$

$$= -29.9 \text{ kJ.}$$
$$W = W_{AB} + W_{BC} + W_{CA} + W_{DA}$$
$$\simeq 40 \text{ kJ.}$$

31. (a) We know that $\dfrac{V_a}{V_b} = \dfrac{V_d}{V_c} \Rightarrow \dfrac{V_a}{V_d} = \dfrac{V_b}{V_c}$

32. (c)
$$W_{AB} = P\Delta V$$
$$= 1 \times R(\Delta T) = RT.$$

$$W_{BC} = nR(2T)\ell n\frac{P_i}{P_f}$$

$$= 1 \times 2RT\ell n2 = 2RT\ell n2$$

$$W_{CD} = P\Delta V$$

$$= nR\Delta T = 1 \times R \times (T - 2T)$$
$$= -RT$$

$$W_{DA} = nRT\ell n\frac{P_i}{P_f} = 1 \times R \times T\ell n\left(\frac{1}{2}\right)$$

$$= -RT\ell n2$$
$$W = W_{AB} + W_{BC} + W_{CA} + W_{DA}$$
$$= RT\ell n2$$

33. (c)
$$W = \frac{\pi r_1 r_2}{2} = \frac{\pi \times 1 \times 1}{2}$$
$$= \pi/2 \text{ J}$$

34. (d) The change in internal energy ΔU is same in all process.

$$Q_{ACB} = \Delta U + W_{ACB},$$
$$Q_{ADB} = \Delta U,$$
$$Q_{AEB} = \Delta U + W_{AEB}$$

Here W_{ACB} is positive and W_{AEB} is negative.
Hence $Q_{ACB} > Q_{ADB} > Q_{AEB}$.

35. (a) $W_{AB} = 0, \qquad W_{BC} = P\Delta V = nR\Delta T = -nRT_0$

$$W_{CA} = nRT\ell n\frac{V_f}{V_i} = nR(2T_0)\ell n2$$

$$Q_{BC} = nC_p\Delta T = \left(\frac{nR\gamma}{\gamma - 1}\right)T_0$$

Efficiency, $\qquad \eta = \dfrac{W}{Q} = \left[\dfrac{2\ell n2 - 1}{\gamma/(\gamma - 1)}\right]$

36. (a)
$$dQ = dU + dW$$

or $\qquad nCdT = nC_v dT + PdV$

$\therefore \qquad C = C_v + \dfrac{P}{n}\left(\dfrac{dV}{dT}\right)$

Differentiating $TV^2 = $ constant, w.r.t. T, we get

$$\frac{dV}{dT} = -\frac{V}{2T}$$

Also, $\qquad PV = nRT \Rightarrow \dfrac{P}{n} = \dfrac{RT}{V}$

Now, $\qquad C = Cv + \dfrac{RT}{V} \times \left(-\dfrac{V}{2T}\right)$

$$= \dfrac{3R}{2} - \dfrac{R}{2} = R.$$

37. (b) $\qquad PV = nRT \text{ or } P = \dfrac{nRT}{V}$

(i) $\qquad \dfrac{nRT}{V} \times V^2 = K \text{ or } VT = C_1$

(ii) $\qquad \dfrac{nRT}{V} = KV^2 \text{ or } \dfrac{V^3}{T} = C_2$

Clearly final temperature in (ii) will be greater than (i).

38. (b) $\quad Q = \displaystyle\int_{T_0}^{\eta T_0} CdT = a\ln\dfrac{\eta T_0}{T_0} = a\ln\eta$

$\Delta U = C_V \Delta T = \dfrac{R}{\gamma - 1}(\eta - 1)T_0$

$W = Q - \Delta U = a\ln\eta - \left[\dfrac{\eta - 1}{\gamma - 1}\right]RT_0$

39. (c) $\quad W = \dfrac{P_1V_1 - P_2V_2}{2 - 1} = \dfrac{P_1V_1 - P_2V_2}{1}$

$\Delta U = \dfrac{nR}{(\gamma - 1)}\Delta T = \dfrac{nR\Delta T}{(\gamma - 1)} = \dfrac{P_2V_2 - P_1V_1}{\gamma - 1}$

$\dfrac{W}{\Delta U} = -0.4 \ (\because \gamma \text{ for diatomic gas} = 1.4)$

40. (b) $\quad P \propto \dfrac{1}{V^2} \Rightarrow P = \dfrac{k}{V^2} \Rightarrow PV^2 = k$

$PV.V = k \Rightarrow nRTV = k \Rightarrow TV = k_1$

Since temperature increases therefore volume decreases.

41. (c) $\quad P_{av} = \dfrac{P_i + P_f}{2} = \left[\dfrac{100 + 300}{2}\right] \times 10^3 Pa = 200 \times 10^3 \text{ Pa}$

and $\Delta V = 100 \times 10^{-3} \text{ m}^3$

$\therefore W = P_{av}\Delta V = 200 \times 10^3 \times 100 \times 10^{-3}$

$\qquad = 20 \text{ kJ}$

42. (d) $\quad W_{ab} = RT\ell n\left(\dfrac{V_b}{V_a}\right) = R \times 400\ell n\left(\dfrac{P_a}{P_b}\right)$

$W_{bc} = P_b\Delta V = P_b(V_c - V_b),$

and $W_{ca} = P\Delta V = 0$

$W = W_{ab} + W_{bc} + W_{ca}$

After substituting the values and simplifying, we get
$W = 2116 \text{ J}$

43. (d) From $1 \rightarrow 2$;

$Q_{12} = \Delta U_2 + W$

or $\quad 10 = \Delta U_{21} - 5$

$\therefore \Delta U_{21} = 15$

For $2 \rightarrow 1$:
$Q_{21} = \Delta U_{12} + W$
$\qquad = -15 - 3$
$\qquad = -18 \text{ J}$

Total energy change $= Q_{12} + Q_{21} = 10 - 18 = -8 \text{ J}$

44. (d) $\quad C_v = \dfrac{dU}{dT} = 2R$

also $C_v = \dfrac{1 \times \dfrac{3R}{2} + 1 \times \dfrac{5R}{2}}{2} = 2R$

45. (d) $\quad P^2 = T \text{ or } P = \sqrt{T}$

$W = \displaystyle\int_{T_0}^{2T_0} PdV = \int_{T_0}^{2T_0}\dfrac{RdT_0}{2} = \dfrac{RT_0}{2}$

$Q = \Delta U + W = PV\Delta T + W = \dfrac{3R}{2} \times T_0 + \dfrac{RT_0}{2} = 2RT_0$

46. (a) The work done of thermodynamics,

$Q = \Delta U + W$

or $\qquad 0 = nC_v(\Delta T) - P_0V_0$

or $\qquad 0 = n\dfrac{R}{\gamma - 1}(T - T_0) - nRT_0$

$\therefore \qquad T = \gamma T_0$

47. (b) $\quad Q = mC\Delta T = 1.5 \times 0.12 \times 4200 \times (400 - 25)$
$\qquad = 2.83 \times 10^5 \text{ J}$

$W = P(\Delta V) = P(V\gamma\Delta T)$
$\qquad = 10^5 \times (5 \times 10^{-2})^3 \times 3.5 \times 10^{-5} \times 375 = 0.164 \text{ J}$
Thus $\qquad Q = \Delta U + W$
or $\quad 2.83 \times 10^5 = \Delta U + 0.164 \ ; \ \Delta U = 282 \text{ kJ}$

48. (b) The power input $P = Vi = 12 \times 22$
$\qquad = 264 \ W.$
$\therefore \qquad \Delta U = 264 - 12 = 252 \ W.$

49. (b) $\quad V_0 + 4V_0 = (V + 3V) \Rightarrow V = \dfrac{5V_0}{4}$

$P_1 + P_1 = P_2 \Rightarrow P_1 + P_1 = P_2$

Here $\qquad P_1 = \dfrac{RT_0}{4V_0} \text{ and } P_2 = \dfrac{RT_0}{V_0}$

$\therefore \qquad P_P = \dfrac{RT_0}{V_0}\left(1 - \dfrac{1}{4}\right) \qquad \text{... (i)}$

Also $\qquad P_P = \dfrac{RT}{V}\left(1 - \dfrac{1}{3}\right) \qquad \text{...(ii)}$

From above equations, we get $T = 420$ K.

50. (b) $\qquad VP = (V + V_0)P_1$

$\Rightarrow \qquad P_1 = \left[\dfrac{VP}{V + V_0}\right]$

and $\qquad VP_1 = (V + V_0)P_2$

1. (a,b,c,d) The change in internal energy depend on initial and final state and so it is same in all.

2. (a,b) In each path, the change in temperature is
$$\Delta T = T_2 - T_1, \quad \therefore \quad \Delta U_1 = \Delta U_2 = \Delta U_3 = \Delta U_4.$$

3. (b,c) At 0°C, water contracts, so work is to be done by atmosphere.
As $\qquad Q = \Delta U - W$
$\therefore \qquad \Delta U = Q + W.$

4. (b,d) W_{DAB} is +ve and W_{BCD} is –ve. As $W_{DAB} > W_{BCD}$, so net work done is positive.
$Q = \Delta U + W_{BCD}$, as W_{BCD} is negative, so Q will decreases.

5. (a,b,c) $\qquad PV = nRT = \dfrac{n_0}{N} RT = n_0 KT$

or $\qquad n_0 = \dfrac{PV}{KT}.$

So n_0 is same for all at equal P, V and T.

Also $\qquad E = \dfrac{3}{2} kT.$

It is same for each gas.

6. (a, d) As $\Delta T = 0$, so $\Delta U = 0$
Pressure is increasing, so volume will decrease. The work done will be negative.
Also $PV =$ constant.

7. (c,d) $\Delta V_{AB} = \Delta V_{BC}$; So area under AB is greater than area under BC. So $W_{AB} > W_{BC}$.
For A to B, $V \propto T$.

8. (a,c) $\Delta U = 0$; $\therefore$ $Q = -W = -RT_0 \ell n2$
$W = W_{BC} + W_{DA} = -2RT_0 \ell n2 + RT_0 \ell n2 = -RT_0 \ell n2$

9. (a,c) If H is the rate of heat supplied, then
$Q_1 = H\Delta t_1$, $Q_2 = H\Delta t_2$,
$Q_3 = H\Delta t_3$, $Q_4 = H\Delta t_2$
As $\Delta t_1 > \Delta t_3$, so $Q_1 > Q_3$ and so $C_{solid} > C_{liquid}$
As $\Delta t_4 > \Delta t_2$, so $Q_4 > Q_2$ and so $L_{vapour} > L_{fusion}$

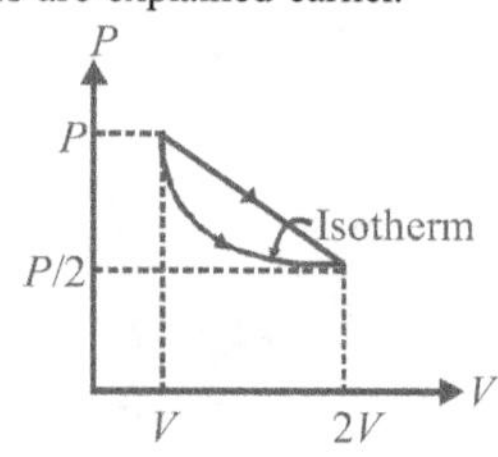

10. (a,b,d) The area under isotherm is smaller than area under straight line process.
Others are explained earlier.

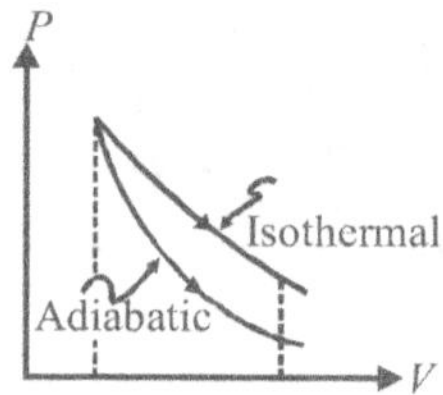

11. (a,d) $VP^2 = (4U) P_2^2 \Rightarrow P_2 = \dfrac{P}{2}$
We have, $\qquad PV = nRT$
or $\qquad V = \dfrac{nRT}{P}$,
$$\dfrac{nRT}{P} \times P^2 = K$$
or $\qquad PT =$ constant.
It represents hyperbola between P and T.

12. (b,d) $\dfrac{P^2}{\rho} = \dfrac{P_2^2}{\rho/2} \Rightarrow P_2 = \dfrac{P}{\sqrt{2}}$

As $PV = mRT$ or $P = \rho RT$; $\therefore$ $\rho = \dfrac{P}{RT}$.

Thus $\qquad \dfrac{P^2}{P/RT} = K$
or $\qquad PT =$ constant;
It represents hyperbola.

Also $\qquad PT = \dfrac{P}{\sqrt{2}} \times T_2$, $\therefore$ $T_2 = \sqrt{2}\, T$

13. (b,d) $\Delta U_A = \Delta U_B = \Delta U_C = \Delta U_D = \Delta U$
$Q_A = \Delta U + W_A$, and $Q_B = \Delta U + W_B$,
$Q_C = \Delta U + W_C$, and $Q_D = \Delta U + W_D$,
Also, $W_A > W_B > W_C > W_D$.
$\Rightarrow$ $Q_A - Q_D = W_A - W_D$,
and $Q_A > Q_B > Q_C > Q_D$.

14. (a,b,c) The area under isothermal is greater than area under adiabatic curve.
So $W_{isothermal} > W_{adiabatic}$.

In isothermal pressure, $P_2 = \dfrac{PV}{V_2}$

In adiabatic process, $P_2' = P\left(\dfrac{V}{V_2}\right)^\gamma$

For $V_2 > V$, $\gamma > 1$ so $P_2' < P_2$.

15. (a, b)

16. (a, d) $\eta_1 = 1 - \dfrac{300}{400} = \dfrac{1}{4}$; $\eta_2 = 1 - \dfrac{400}{500} = \dfrac{1}{5}$

$\eta_3 = 1 - \dfrac{500}{600} = \dfrac{1}{6}$; $\eta_4 = 1 - \dfrac{600}{800} = \dfrac{1}{4}$

Solutions **EXERCISE-7.3**

1. (d) Zeroth law of thermodynamics tells about thermal equilibrium.

2. (a) Explanation is in the statements.

3. (a) Explanation is in the statements.

4. (a)

5. (d) In isothermal process, $\Delta T = 0$ and so $\Delta U = 0$.

   Thus $Q = 0 + W = W$.

6. (a) The opening of bottle is the rapid or adiabatic process. In the process temperature falls.

7. (a) The quike process will be adiabatic process.

8. (a) The electrical energy first convert into kinetic energy of fan and then into heat energy due to collisions with air molecules.

9. (c) In adiabatic process, $Q = 0$

   $\therefore\quad 0 = \Delta U + W$ or $\Delta U = -W$.

   Temperature will change in adiabatic process.

10. (b) In adiabatic process, $\Delta Q = 0$.

    $\therefore\quad \Delta S = \dfrac{\Delta Q}{T} = 0$

11. (a) $\eta = 1 - \dfrac{T_2}{T_1}$; clearly when T_2 is decreases η will increase.

Solutions **EXERCISE-7.4**

Passage (Q1 – 3) :

1. (c)
$$\begin{aligned}W_{AB} &= P(\Delta V)_{AB} = nR\Delta T \\ &= 2R \times (500 - 300) \\ &= 400\,R.\end{aligned}$$

2. (a)
$$\begin{aligned}W_{DA} &= nRT\ln\frac{P_i}{P_f} = 2R \times 300\ln\frac{1}{2} \\ &= -600R\ln 2 \\ &= -414\,R\end{aligned}$$

3. (b)
$$\begin{aligned}W_{BC} &= nR(500)\ln 2 = 2R \times 500\ln 2 \\ &= 693\,R \\ W_{CD} &= P(\Delta V)_{CD} = nR\Delta T \\ &= 2R \times (300 - 500) \\ &= -400\,R.\end{aligned}$$

$$\therefore\quad \begin{aligned}W &= W_{AB} + W_{DA} + W_{BC} + W_{CD} \\ &= 276\,R\end{aligned}$$

Passage for (Q. 4 -6) :

4. (d) The correct choice is (d)

5. (b) For an adiabatic pressure $TP^{\frac{1-\gamma}{\gamma}}$ = constant.

$$T_0\left[P_0 + \rho\ell gH\right]^{-2/5} = T_0\left[P_0 + \rho\ell g(H - y)\right]^{-2/5}$$

Which gives $T = T_0\left[\dfrac{P_0 + \rho\ell g(H - y)}{(P_0 + \rho\ell gH)}\right]^{2/5}$

So the correct choice is (b).

6. (b) Buoyant force F = weight of liquid displaced = $\rho_\ell Vg$, V = volume of the bubble

From $PV = nRT$, we have $V = \dfrac{nRT}{P}$ Therefore,

$$F = \frac{nRT\rho_\ell g}{P}$$

$$= \frac{nR\rho_\ell g}{[P_0 + \rho_\ell g(H - y)]} \times T_0\left[\frac{P_0 + \rho_\ell g(H - y)}{P_0 + \rho_\ell gh}\right]^{2/3}$$

$$= \frac{mR\rho_\ell g}{(P_0 + \rho_\ell gH)^{2/5}[P_0 + \rho_\ell g(H - y)]^{3/5}}$$

Hence the correct choice is (b)

Passage (Q.7 – 9) :

7. (c) acb : $80 = \Delta U_{ab} + 30 = 50$ J.

   $\Rightarrow \qquad \Delta U_{ab} = 50$ J

   $\therefore \qquad \Delta U_{ba} = -50$ J

   In path adb, $Q = \Delta U + W = 50 + 10 = 60$ J.

8. (d) In path b to a : $Q = \Delta U_{ba} + W = -50 - 20 = -70$J

9. (d) $\Delta U_{ad} = 40 - 0 = 40$ J

   $\therefore \qquad Q = \Delta U + W = 40 + 10 = 50$ J.

Passage (Q.10 – 12) :

10. (b)
$$W = nRT\ln\frac{V_f}{V_i}$$

$$= 0.10R \times 273 \times \ln\frac{1}{5}$$

$$= -365\,\text{J}.$$

11. (b) $Q = \Delta U + W = 0 - 366 = -366$ J.

12. (d) As the process is isothermal, so $\Delta U = 0$,

Passage (Q.13 -15) :

13. (b)
$$\frac{Q_1}{Q_2} = \frac{T_1}{T_2} = \frac{400}{300}$$

$$\therefore \qquad Q_2 = \frac{3}{4}\,Q_1 = \frac{3}{4} \times 1200 = 900\ \text{cal.}$$

14. (d)
$$Q_1 = \frac{T_1}{T_2}\,Q_2 = \frac{4}{3} \times 1200 = 1600\ \text{cal.}$$

15. (a)
$$\beta = \frac{Q_2}{W} = \left[\frac{1}{\dfrac{T_1}{T_2} - 1}\right]$$

or $\qquad \dfrac{1200}{W} = \left[\dfrac{1}{\dfrac{400}{300} - 1}\right]$

$$\therefore \qquad W = 400\ \text{cal.}$$

Passage (Q.16 -18) :

16. (b) $n_1 C_v (T - T_0) + n_2 C_v (T - 2T_0) = 0$

$$T = \frac{3}{2}T_0$$

$$P_f = \frac{P_i T_f}{T_i} = \frac{3}{2}P_0$$

17. (c) $\Delta Q = n_1 C_v (T_f - T_0)$

$$= \frac{P_0 V_0}{2RT_0} \times \frac{3}{2} R \times \left(\frac{3}{2} T_0 - T_0\right) = \frac{3}{8} P_0 V_0$$

18. (c)   Let ΔV is change in volume in any compartment then

$$n_1 = \frac{P_0 V_0}{2RT_0} = \frac{P_f \left(\dfrac{V_0}{2} - \Delta V\right)}{RT_f} \quad \text{and}$$

$$n_2 = \frac{2P_0 V_0}{2RT_0} = \frac{P_f \left(\dfrac{V_0}{2} + \Delta V\right)}{RT_f} \Rightarrow \Delta V = 0$$

Passage (Q.19 -21) :

19. (a)   Process AB, U_P = constant

$$\frac{P}{\rho} = \frac{RT}{M} \text{ and } U \propto t$$

$\Rightarrow P = \text{const}$

Process $BC \rightarrow$ isochoric

Process $CA \rightarrow$ isothermal

20. (a) $Q = Q_{AB} + Q_{BC} + Q_{CA}$

$$Q = -5U_0 + 3U_0 + \frac{10U_0}{3} \ln 2.5$$

21. (b) $W_{AB} = \Delta Q_{AB} - \Delta U_{AB} = -5U_0 - (-3U_0) = -2U_0$

Passage (Q.22 - 24) :

22. (b)   23. (a)   24. (d)

Initial volume of the gas

$$V_A = \frac{nRT}{P}$$

$$= \frac{2 \times 8.31 \times 300}{2 \times 1.013 \times 10^5}$$

$$= 0.025 \text{ m}^3.$$

Volume at B $V_B = \dfrac{T_B}{T_A} V_A$

$$= \frac{400}{300} \times 0.025$$

$$= 0.003 \text{ m}^3$$

Work done: $W_{AB} = P_B (V_B - V_A)$

$$= 2 \times 1.013 \times 10^5 \, (0.033 - 0.025)$$

$$= 1620.8 \text{ J}$$

$$W_{BC} = nRT_B \ln \frac{P_B}{P_C}$$

$$= 2 \times 8.31 \times 400 \ln 2$$

$$= 4608.0 \text{ J}$$

$$W_{CD} = nR \, (T_D - T_C)$$

$$= 2 \times 8.31 \, (300 - 400)$$

$$= -1620.8 \text{ J}$$

$$W_{DA} = nRT_D \ln \frac{P_D}{P_A}$$

$$= 2 \times 8.31 \times 300 \ln 1/2$$

$$= -3456.0 \text{ J}$$

Total work done $W = W_{AB} + W_{BC} + W_{CD} + W_{DA}$

$$= 1150.7 \text{ J} \qquad \textit{Ans.}$$

In closed cycle, $\Delta U = 0.$

Now by first law of thermodynamics

$$Q = \Delta U + W$$

$$= 0 + 1150.7$$

$$= 1150.7 \text{ J.} \qquad \textit{Ans.}$$

Passage (Q.25 - 27) :

25. (b)   Work done for path $A - B - C$

$$W_{AB} = P\Delta V$$

$$= 0,$$

$$W_{BC} = P_B (V_C - V_B)$$

$$= 15 \, (6 - 2)$$

$$= 60 \text{ J},$$

$\therefore$ $W_{ABC} = W_{AB} + W_{BC}$

$$= 60 \text{ J}$$

Work done for the path $A - C$

$$W_{AC} = \frac{1}{2}[15 + 5] \times 4$$

$$= 40 \text{ J}$$

Clearly work done along path AC is minimum.

26. (c)   Along path $A - C$

$$Q = \Delta U + W$$

or $200 = (U_C - 10) + 40$

$\therefore$ $U_C = 170 \text{ J.}$

Ans.

27. (d)   Along path $A - B$

$$Q = \Delta U + W$$

$$= (20 - 10) + 0$$

$$= 10 \text{ J.}$$

Ans.

Passage (Q.28 - 30) :

28. (b)   If ΔT is the change in temperature of the metal object, then

$$Q = mc \, \Delta T$$

or $20000 = 1 \times 400 \times \Delta T$

$\therefore$ $\Delta T = 50°C.$

The final temprature $T_f = T_i + \Delta T$

$$= 20 + 50$$

$$= 70°C.$$

29. (c)   Volume of the object, $V = \dfrac{m}{\rho}$

$$= \frac{1}{9000} \text{ m}^3$$

If ΔV is the change in volume of the object, then

$$\Delta V = V\gamma \, \Delta T$$

$$= \frac{1}{900} \times 9 \times 10^{-5} \times 50$$

$$= 5 \times 10^{-7} \text{ m}^3.$$

Work done in expansion

$$W = P\Delta V$$

$$= 10^5 \times 5 \times 10^{-7}$$

$$= 0.05 \text{ J} \qquad \textit{Ans.}$$

30. (d)   Now, $Q = \Delta U + W$

$\therefore$ $\Delta U = Q - W$

$$= 2000 - 0.05$$
$$= 19999.95 \text{ J} \qquad \textbf{Ans.}$$

Passage for (Q. 31 -33) :

31. (a) Since the cylinder has a hole at the top, it is open to atmosphere. Hence the pressure in the cylinder = atmospheric pressure P_0, which is choice (a).

32. (d) Let $A = \pi R^2$ be the cross-sectional area of the cylinder. Let x be the distance of the piston from the top when equilibrium is attained. Since the process is slow, it is isothermal. Thus
$$P_1 V_1 = P_2 V_2$$
where $P_1 = P_0$, $V_1 = A \times (2L)$

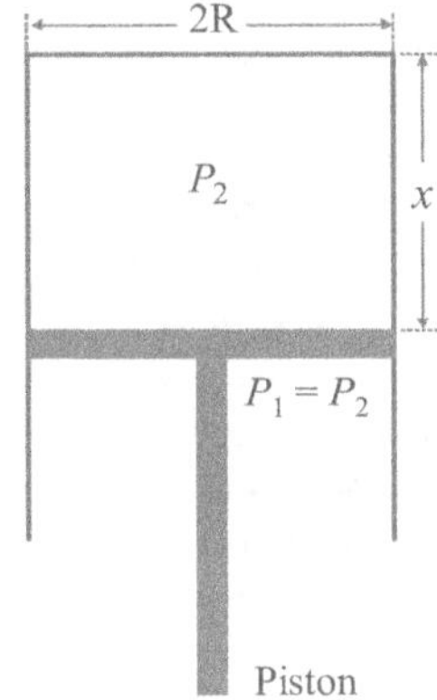

At equilibrium, the downward force equals the upward force
i.e. $\qquad Mg = (P_0 - P_2)A$

Which gives $\qquad P_2 = P_0 - \dfrac{Mg}{A}$, Also $V_2 = Ax$.

Substituting for P_1, V_1, P_2 and V_2 in Eq. (1) we have

$$P_0 \times A \times (2\,L) = \left(P_0 - \frac{Mg}{A} \right) Ax$$

$$\Rightarrow \qquad x = \frac{P_0(2L)}{\left(P_0 - \dfrac{Mg}{A} \right)} = \left[\frac{P_0 \pi R^2}{\pi R^2 P_0 - Mg} \right] (2L)$$

Hence the correct choice is (d)

33. Let A be the corss-sectional area of the cylinder. At equilibrium. Pressure at the top level of water inside the cylinder = pressure just below the level of water i.e.,
$$P_1 = P_2$$

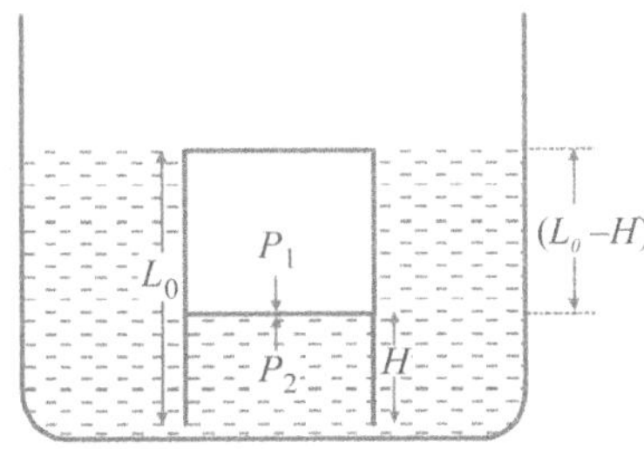

From Boyle's law, we have
$$P_t \times A(L_0 - H) = P_0 L_0 A$$

$$\Rightarrow \qquad P_1 = \frac{P_0 L_0}{(L_0 - H)} \qquad \qquad \ldots (1)$$

Also P_2 = atmospheric pressure + pressure due to a column of length $(L_0 - H)$ of water

$$= P_0 + \rho g (L_0 - H) \qquad \qquad \ldots (2)$$

$$\Rightarrow \quad \rho g (L_0 - H)^2 + P_0(L_0 - H) - P_0 L_0 = 0$$

Hence the correct choice is (c).

Passage (Q.34 - 36):
$$m_A = 100 \text{ gm} \,; \ V_A = V_B = 10^{-2} \text{ m}^3$$
$$P_A = 10^5 \text{ N/m}^2.$$

In cylinder A, the process is adiabatic, so
$$P_1 V_1^\gamma = P_2 V_2^\gamma$$
$$10^5 (10^{-2})^{1.5} = P_2\,(25 \times 10^{-4})^{1.5}$$
$$\therefore \qquad P_2 = 8 \times 10^5$$

34. (d) For cylinder B,
$$P_f = \frac{F}{A_2} = \frac{8000}{200 \times 10^{-4}}$$
$$= 4 \times 10^5 \text{ N/m}^2$$
$$W_B = fx = W_A$$
or $\qquad 8000x = 2000 \Rightarrow x = 0.25\text{m}$
$$\Delta V_B = Ax = 200 \times 10^{-4} \times 0.25$$
$$= 50 \times 10^{-4} \text{ m}^3$$
$$\therefore \qquad V_f = 10^{-2} + 50 \times 10^{-4} = 250 \times 10^{-4}\text{m}^3$$
For cylinder A,
$$10^5 \times 10^{-2} = \frac{100}{M} RT_0 \qquad \qquad \ldots(i)$$
For cylinder B,
$$\left(4 \times 10^5 \right) \times \left(250 \times 10^{-4} \right) = \frac{m_B}{M} RT_0 \qquad \ldots(ii)$$
After solving above equations, we get
$$m_B = 1000 \text{ gm.}$$

35. (a)
$$W_A = \frac{\left(P_1 V_1 - P_2 V_2 \right)}{\gamma - 1}$$
$$= \frac{10^5 \times 10^{-2} - 8 \times 10^5 \times 25 \times 10^{-4}}{1.5 - 1}$$
$$= -\,2000 \text{ J}$$
Now $\qquad Q_A = \Delta U + W_A$
or $\qquad 0 = \Delta U - 2000 \Rightarrow \Delta U = 2000 \text{ J.}$

36. (c) So at equilibrium, the force on the connecting rod
$$F = P_2 A_2 = 8 \times 10^5 \times 1000 \times 10^{-4}$$
$$= 8000\text{N}$$

37. **(A)→(q)**
As the ideal gas expands in vacuum, no work is done ($W = 0$). Also the container is insulated therefore no heat is lost or gained ($Q = 0$). According to first law of thermodynamics
$$\Delta U = Q + W$$
$$\therefore \quad \Delta U = 0$$
$\Rightarrow$ There is no change in the temperature of the gas

(B)→(p, r)
● Given $PV^2 = $ constant $\qquad \qquad \ldots$(i)

Also for an ideal gas $\dfrac{PV}{T} = $ constant $\qquad \ldots$(ii)

From (i) & (ii) $\quad V \times T = $ constant
As the gas expands its volume increases and temperature decreases
$\therefore$ (p) is the correct option.

- To find whether heat is released or absorbed let us find a relationship between Q and change in temperature ΔT.

We know that $Q = nC\Delta T$ ...(i)

where C = molar specific heat

Also for a polytropic process we have

$$C = C_v + \frac{R}{1-n} \quad \text{and} \quad PV^n = \text{constant}$$

Here PV^2 = Constant. Therefore $n = 2$

$$\therefore C = C_v + \frac{R}{1-2} = C_v - R$$

For monoatomic gas $C_v = \frac{3}{2}R$

$$\therefore C = \frac{3}{2}R - R = \frac{R}{2}$$

Substituting this value in (1), we get

$$Q = n \times \frac{R}{2} \times \Delta T.$$

In this case the temperature decreases i.e. ΔT is negative. Therefore Q is negative. This in turn means that heat is lost by the gas during the process. (r) is the correct option.

(C)→(p, s)

- Proceeding in the same way we get in this case

$$V^{1/3} \times T = \text{constant}$$

$\Rightarrow$ As the gas expands and volume increases, the temperature decreases. Therefore (p) is the correct option.

- In this process, $x = \frac{4}{3}$.

$$\therefore C = C_v + \frac{R}{1 - \frac{4}{3}} = \frac{3}{2}R + \frac{3R}{-1} = \frac{3}{2}R - 3R = \frac{-3R}{2}$$

$$\therefore Q = n\left(\frac{-3R}{2}\right)\Delta t$$

As ΔT is negative, Q is positive. This in turn means that heat is gained by the gas during the process (s) is the correct option.

(D)→(q, s)

- Also $\Delta T = \dfrac{\Delta(PV)}{nR}$

Here $\Delta(PV)$ is positive $\therefore \Delta T$ is positive $\therefore$ temperature increases. So, (q) is the correct option

- From the graph it is clear that during the process the pressure of the gas increases which shows that the internal energy of the gas has increased. Also the volume increases which means work is done by the system which needs energy. From these two interpretation we can comfortably conclude that the gas gains heat during the process. (s) is the correct option.

38. **(A) → r** $\qquad \Delta S = \dfrac{\Delta Q}{T} = \dfrac{-mL}{T}$

$$= \frac{-0.5 \times 4200 \times 80}{373}$$

$$\simeq -446 \text{ J/K}$$

(B) → p $\qquad \Delta S = \dfrac{\Delta Q}{T} = \dfrac{-mL}{T}$

$$= \frac{-0.5 \times 4200 \times 80}{273} \simeq 610 \text{ J/K}$$

(C) → q   As the sides of the rod are insulated, so

$$\Delta S = \frac{\Delta Q}{T} = 0.$$

(D) → s   The total change in entropy

$$\Delta S = 610 - 446 = 164 \text{ J/K}$$

39. **(A) → r** $\qquad C_v = \dfrac{1}{273} /\,°C$ same for all gases

(B) → p $\qquad PV = \cos A \Rightarrow P \propto \dfrac{1}{V}$

(C) → q   Ideal gas obey gas law at each range of temperature.

(D) → s

At high temperature, intermolecular forces become zero and so real gas behaves like ideal gas.

40. **A → r; B → p; C → q; D → s**
41. **A → p, r; B → p; C → q, r; D → q**
42. **A → p, s ; B → s ; C → r, s ; D → p,q,r,s**
43. **A → p; B → r, s; C → p, q; D → p,q**
44. **(A) → q**   Isothermal process occur at constant temperature.

(B) → p   For constant entropy, $\Delta Q = 0$.

(C) → s   Isochoric process is at constant volume.

(D) → r   Isobaric process is at constant pressure.

45. Explanation is given in theory of the chapter.
46. **(A) → p**

It is the isothermal expansion at T_1.

(B) → s

Adiabatic expansion in which temperature falls from T_1 to T_2.

(C) → r

Isothermal compression at T_2.

(D) → q

Adiabatic compression at T_2.

47. **(A) → (q,r,t)**

As temperature is constant, so $\Delta U = 0$. Volume is decreasing, $W = -$ve. Thus $Q = 0 - W = -W$.

(B) → s

$\Delta V = 0$, $\therefore W = 0$. Also $Q = \Delta U + 0 = \Delta U$. As temperature is increasing, so $\Delta U = +$ve and so $Q > W$.

(C) → (p,s,t)

As temperature is constant, so $\Delta U = 0$. Volume is increasing in the process, so $W = +$ve.

Now $Q = 0 + W = W$, $\therefore Q > 0$.

(D) → (q,r)

It is isobasic process in which volume is decreasing, so, $W = -$ve. $Q = \Delta U - W$.

48. **(A) → s**

In the process, pressure increasing which $\Delta V = 0$, so temperature will increase.

(B) → q

In the process, temperature and volume both decrease, and so $\Delta U = 0$ and $W = -$ve.

(C) → r

In the process temperature decreases and volume increases, so $\Delta U = -$ve and $W = +$ve.

(D) → q

In the process $V_B < V_A$, $\therefore \Delta V = -$ve and so $W = -$ve. P and V both decrease, so T must be decreased. Therefore $\Delta U = -$ve.

1. (i) We know that $V_1^{\gamma-1}T_1 = V_2^{\gamma-1}T_2$

or $\quad V^{\gamma-1}T = (5.66V)^{\gamma-1} \times \dfrac{T}{2}$

$\therefore \quad \gamma = 1.4$ (diatomic gas)

Thus degrees of freedom of the gas is 5.

Work done in the process

$$W = \left[\frac{P_1V_1 - P_2V_2}{\gamma - 1}\right]$$

Also $\quad \dfrac{PV}{T} = \dfrac{P_2V_2}{T_2}$

$\therefore \quad P_2 = \dfrac{P}{11.32}$

Now $\quad W = \left[\dfrac{PV - \dfrac{P}{11.32} \times 5.66V}{1.4 - 1}\right] = 1.25\,PV.$

Ans.

2. $\quad \eta_A = \dfrac{W_A}{Q_1} = \dfrac{T_1 - T_2}{T_1}$

and $\quad \eta_2 = \dfrac{W_B}{Q_1'}$

$\quad = \dfrac{T_1' - T_2'}{T_1'}$

(i) Putting $\quad W_A = W_B$ and known values, we get
$T = 600K$

(ii) Putting $\quad \eta_A = \eta_B$,
$T = 650\,K.$ **Ans.**

3. Work done in the process

$$W = (PA)x + \frac{1}{2}kx^2$$

or $\quad 50 = 10^5 \times 4 \times 10^{-3} \times 0.1 + \dfrac{1}{2}k \times (0.1)^2$

$\therefore \quad k = 2000$ N/m. **Ans.**

Also $\quad \Delta U = nC_V\Delta T$

$\quad = 2 \times \dfrac{3R}{2} \times 50 = 1245$ J

Thus $\quad Q = \Delta U + W = 1245 + 50 = 1295$ J.

Ans.

4. If P_1 be the pressure after expansion, then
$PV = P_1(3V + V)$

$\therefore \quad P_1 = \dfrac{P}{4}.$

For the adiabatic compression, let P_2 be the final pressure, then
$$P_1(4V)^\gamma = P_2V$$
$\therefore \quad P_2 = P_1(4)^{1.5}$
$\quad = 8\,P_1$

The change in internal energy,

$$\Delta U = nC_V\Delta T$$

$$= n\frac{R}{\gamma - 1}[T_2 - T_1]$$

$$= \frac{P_2V_2 - P_1V_1}{\gamma - 1} = 400 \text{ J}.$$

For adiabatic process, $T_2 = T_0\left(\dfrac{4V}{V}\right)^{\gamma-1} = 2\,T_0$ **Ans.**

5. For the gas $\quad \gamma = 5/3.$

Work done $\quad W = \left[\dfrac{P_1V_1 - P_2V_2}{\gamma - 1}\right]$

After substituting the values and simplifying, we get
$W = 957$ J **Ans.**

6. Given, $\quad V = kT^{2/3}$

$\therefore \quad dV = k \times \dfrac{2}{3}T^{-1/3}dT = \dfrac{2}{3}kT^{-1/3}dT$

Work done $\quad dW = PdV$

$$= \frac{RT}{V}dV$$

$$= \frac{RT}{kT^{2/3}} \times \frac{2}{3}kT^{-1/3}dT = \frac{2}{3}R(dT)$$

Total work done $\quad W = \dfrac{2}{3}R\displaystyle\int_{T_1}^{T_2} dT$

$$= \frac{2}{3}R[T_2 - T_1]$$

$$= 2 \times 1.99 \times 30 = 39.8 \text{ cal} = 167 \text{ J}.$$

Ans.

7. In the process 1 to 2 and 3 to 4,
$$P \propto T,$$
and so volume of the gas remains constant.

$\therefore \quad W_{12} = W_{34} = 0$
$\quad\quad W_{23} = P_2(V_3 - V_2)$

and $\quad W_{41} = P_1(V_1 - V_4)$

Thus total work $\quad W = P_2(V_3 - V_2) + P_1(V_1 - V_4)$

We have $\quad P_1V_1 = 3RT$
$\quad\quad P_1V_4 = 3RT_4$
$\quad\quad P_2V_2 = 3RT_2$

and $\quad\quad P_2V_3 = P_3V_3$
$\quad\quad\quad = 3RT_3$

Substituting these values into the expression, we get
$$W = 3R(T_1 + T_3 - T_2 - T_4)$$
$$= 2 \times 10^4 \text{ J}. \quad\quad \textbf{Ans.}$$

8. The work done in the complete cycle is equivalent to two cycles $1 \to 0 \to 2 \to 1$ and $0 \to 4 \to 3 \to 0$.

In the first cycle the work is positive while in the second cycle it is negative. The work done in the first cycle

$$W_1 = \frac{(P_0 - P_1)(V_2 - V_1)}{2}.$$

For the second cycle, the triangle on the $P\text{-}V$ diagram similar to the triangle corresponding to the first cycle. Therefore the work done in the second cycle

$$W_2 = -W_1 \frac{(P_2 - P_0)^2}{(P_0 - P_1)^2}$$

Total work done $W = W_1 + W_2$

$$= W_1 \left[\frac{1 - (P_2 - P_0)^2}{(P_0 - P_1)^2} \right]$$

$$\simeq 750 \text{ J.} \qquad \textbf{\textit{Ans.}}$$

1. Answer is the solution.

2. We know that $PV = nRT$

$$\therefore \qquad n = \frac{PV}{RT} = \frac{1.6 \times 10^6 \times 0.0083}{8.31 \times 300} = \frac{16}{3}$$

Given $C_p = \dfrac{5R}{2}$

$$\therefore \qquad C_v = \frac{3R}{2}$$

If ΔT be the change in temperature, then

$$Q = nC_v \Delta T$$

or $2.49 \times 10^4 = \dfrac{16}{3} \times \dfrac{3}{2} R \Delta T$

$$\therefore \qquad \Delta T = 375\,K$$

Final temperature $T' = T + \Delta T$
$$= 300 + 375 = 675\,K$$

At constant volume $\dfrac{P}{P'} = \dfrac{T}{T'}$

$$\therefore \qquad P' = \frac{T'}{T} \times P = \frac{675}{300} \times 1.6 \times 10^6$$
$$= 3.6 \times 10^6 \text{ N/m}^2 \qquad \textbf{\textit{Ans.}}$$

3. $$[C_v]_{mix} = \frac{n_1 C_{v_1} + n_2 C_{v_2}}{n_1 + n_2}$$

$$= \left[\frac{1 \times \dfrac{3R}{2} + 3 \times \dfrac{5R}{2}}{1 + 3} \right]$$

$$= \frac{9R}{4} = \frac{9}{4} \times 8.31 = 18.7 \text{ J/mol-K} \quad \textbf{\textit{Ans.}}$$

4. For adiabatic process

$$P_1 V_1^\gamma = P_2 V_2^\gamma$$

$$\therefore \qquad P_2 = \frac{P_1 V_1^\gamma}{V_2^\gamma} = 150 \left[\frac{1600}{400} \right]^{1.5} = 1200 \text{ kPa}$$

Work done

$$W = \frac{P_1 V_1 - P_2 V_2}{\gamma - 1}$$

$$= \frac{150 \times 10^3 \times 1600 \times 10^{-6} - 1200 \times 10^3 \times 400 \times 10^{-6}}{1.5 - 1} = -480 \text{ J.}$$
$$\textbf{\textit{Ans.}}$$

5. The two processes are shown in figure.

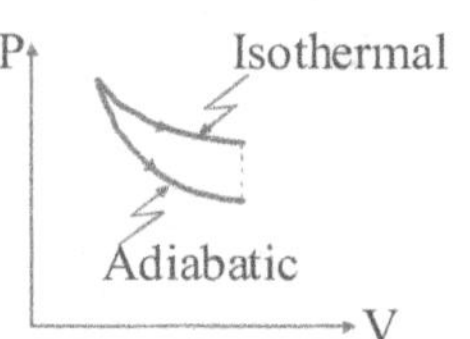

(i) From the $P\text{-}V$ diagram, it is clear that pressure in isothermal expansion is greater than adiabatic expansion.

(ii) Area under $P\text{-}V$ graph is greater for isothermal expansion, and so work done is greater in this case.

(iii) As T is proportional to P, so temperature is greater in case of isothermal expansion.

6. Given $P = \alpha V$ ....(i)

The work done in the process

$$W = \int_V^{\eta V} P dV = \int_V^{\eta V} \alpha V dV$$

$$= \frac{\alpha V^2}{2} \left(\eta^2 - 1 \right)$$

The change in internal energy

$$\Delta U = nC_v \Delta T = 1 \times \frac{R}{\gamma - 1} \left[T_f - T_i \right]$$

$$= \left[\frac{P_f V_f - P_i V_i}{\gamma - 1} \right]$$

$$= \left[\frac{\eta^2 \alpha V^2 - \alpha V^2}{\gamma - 1} \right] = \alpha V^2 \left[\frac{\eta^2 - 1}{\gamma - 1} \right]$$

The heat exchange in the process

$$Q = \Delta U + W$$

$$= \frac{\alpha V^2}{(\gamma - 1)} (\eta^2 - 1) + \frac{\alpha V^2}{2} [\eta^2 - 1]$$

$$= \frac{\alpha V^2}{2} (\eta^2 - 1) \left[\frac{\gamma + 1}{\gamma - 1} \right]$$

By $PV = nRT,$

$$T = \frac{PV}{R} \qquad (n = 1)$$

$$\therefore \qquad T_i = \frac{(\alpha V)V}{R} = \frac{\alpha V^2}{R}$$

and $T_f = \dfrac{\eta^2 \alpha V^2}{R}$

By the definition of heat capacity

$$C = \frac{Q}{T_f - T_i} = \frac{R}{2}\left[\frac{\gamma+1}{\gamma-1}\right] \qquad \textbf{\textit{Ans.}}$$

7. (i) Let P_1, V_1 and T_1 are the new pressure, volume and temperature of the right chamber. Then

$$P_0 V_0^\gamma = P_1 V_1^\gamma$$

or $$P_0 V_0^\gamma = \left(\frac{243}{32}P_0\right)V_1^\gamma$$

$\therefore$ $$V_1 = \frac{8}{27}V_0$$

Again $$V_0^{\gamma-1}T_0 = V_1^{\gamma-1}T_1$$

$\therefore$ $$T_1 = \left[\frac{V_0}{V_1}\right]^{\gamma-1}T_0 = \frac{9}{4}T_0 \qquad \textbf{\textit{Ans.}}$$

(ii) Work done by the gas in right chamber

$$W = \frac{P_0 V_0 - P_1 V_1}{\gamma-1}$$

$$= \frac{P_0 V_0 - \left[\frac{243 P_0}{32} \times \frac{8V_0}{27}\right]}{\left(\frac{5}{3}-1\right)} = -\frac{15}{8}P_0 V_0$$

$$\textbf{\textit{Ans.}}$$

8. For perfect gas $PV = nRT$

$\therefore$ $$P = \frac{nRT}{V}$$

$$= \frac{2 \times 8.3 \times 300}{20 \times 10^{-3}} = 2.5 \times 10^5 \text{ N/m}^2$$

(i)

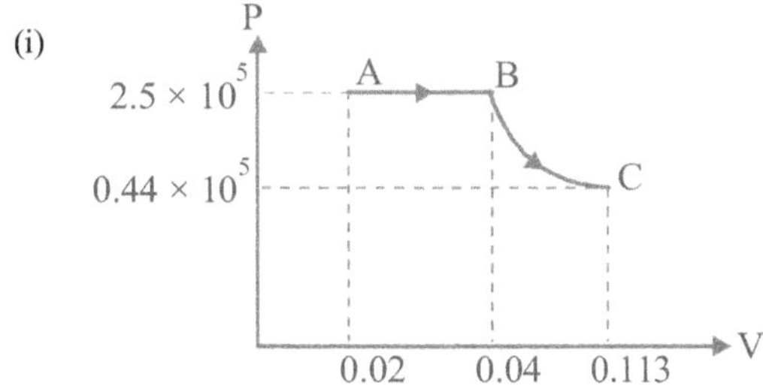

(ii) At B:
$$P_B = 2.5 \times 10^5 \text{ N/m}^2$$
$$V_B = 2V$$
$$= 2 \times 20 \times 10^{-3} = 0.04 \text{ m}^3$$
$$T_B = 600 \, K$$

Now $$V_B^{\gamma-1}T_B = V_C^{\gamma-1}T_C$$

$\therefore$ $$V_C = V_B\left[\frac{T_B}{T_C}\right]^{\frac{1}{\gamma-1}}$$

$$= 0.04 \times 2\sqrt{2} = 0.113 \text{ m}^3,$$

(iii) Work done $$W_{AB} = P\Delta V$$
$$= (2.5 \times 10^5) \times (40-20) \times 10^{-3}$$
$$= 5000 \text{ J}$$

$$W_{BC} = \frac{nR}{\gamma-1}[T_B - T_C]$$

$$= \frac{2 \times 8.3}{\left(\frac{5}{3}-1\right)}[600-300] = 7450 \text{ J}$$

Total work done $$W = W_{AB} + W_{BC}$$
$$= 12450 \text{ J.} \qquad \textbf{\textit{Ans.}}$$

9. (i) Given $$P = \alpha T^{1/2}$$

By ideal gas equation $PV = RT$

or $$\alpha T^{1/2} V = RT$$

or $$\alpha V = RT^{1/2}$$

or $$\alpha \, dV = \frac{R}{2}T^{-1/2}dT$$

or $$(\alpha T^{1/2})dV = \frac{R}{2}dT$$

or $$P(dV) = \frac{R}{2}dT$$

Work done $$W = \int_{T_1}^{T_2} P\,dV$$

$$= \int_{T_1}^{T_2} \frac{R}{2}dT = \frac{R}{2}[T_2 - T_1]$$

$$= \frac{8.31}{2} \times 50 = 207.7 \text{ J}$$

(ii) If C be the molar specific heat, then by first law of thermodynamics

$$Q = \Delta U + W$$

or $$C\Delta T = C_V \Delta T + \frac{R}{2}\Delta T$$

$\therefore$ $$C = \frac{R}{\gamma-1} + \frac{R}{2} = \frac{R}{2}\left[\frac{\gamma+1}{\gamma-1}\right]. \qquad \textbf{\textit{Ans.}}$$

10. (a) First law of thermodynamics
$$dQ = dU + dW$$
If C be the heat capacity of the gas, then
$$CdT = C_V dT + PdV$$

or $$C = C_V + P\left(\frac{dV}{dT}\right)$$

$$= C_V + \frac{RT}{V}\left(\frac{dV}{dT}\right)$$

Given $$T = T_0 + \alpha V$$
One differentiating w. r. t. T, we get

$$1 = 0 + \alpha\frac{dV}{dT}$$

$\therefore$ $$\frac{dV}{dT} = \frac{1}{\alpha}$$

Now $$C = C_V + \frac{R(T_0 + \alpha V)}{V} \times \frac{1}{\alpha}$$

$$= C_V + \frac{RT_0}{\alpha V} + R$$

$$= (C_V + R) + \frac{RT_0}{\alpha V}$$

$$= C_P + \frac{RT_0}{\alpha V}. \qquad \textbf{\textit{Ans.}}$$

(b) Given, $T = T_0 + \alpha V$

Also $PV = RT$ $(n = 1)$

From above $P = \left(\dfrac{RT_0}{V} + \alpha R \right)$

Work done $W = \displaystyle\int_{V_1}^{V_2} P.dV$

$$= \int_{V_1}^{V_2} \left(\frac{RT_0}{V} + \alpha R \right) dV$$

$$= RT_0 \ln(V_2/V_1) + \alpha R(V_2 - V_1)$$

The heat transferred

$$Q = \Delta U + W = C_V \Delta T + W$$

$$= C_V[\alpha \Delta V] + W$$

$$= \frac{R}{\gamma - 1}[\alpha(V_2 - V_1)] + W$$

$$= \alpha(V_2 - V_1)C_P + RT_0 \ln\frac{V_2}{V_1} \quad \textbf{\textit{Ans.}}$$

11. If V_1 and V_2 are the final volumes under isothermal condition and P' is the common pressure, then

$$P \times 5V = P'V_1 \qquad \text{........... (i)}$$
and $8P \times V = P'V_2 \qquad \text{........... (ii)}$
Also $V_1 + V_2 = 5V + V \qquad \text{............(iii)}$
After solving above equations, we get

$$V_1 = \frac{30}{13}V$$

$$V_2 = \frac{24}{13}V$$

$$P' = \frac{13P}{6} \qquad \textbf{\textit{Ans.}}$$

Under adiabatic condition: $P(5V)^\gamma = P''V_1^\gamma$

and $8PV^\gamma = P''V_2^\gamma$
Also $V_1 + V_2 = 5V + V$
After solving above equations, we get

$$V_1 = \frac{10V}{3}$$

$$V_2 = \frac{8V}{3}$$

$$P'' = 1.84\,P \qquad \textbf{\textit{Ans.}}$$

12. (a)

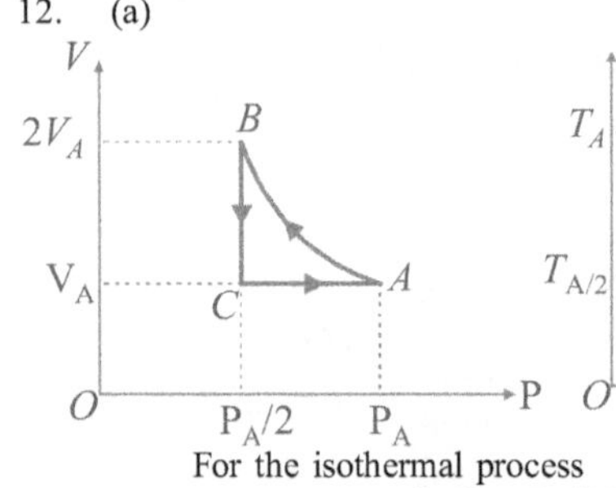

For the isothermal process
$$P_A V_A = P_B(2V_A)$$
$$\Rightarrow \qquad P_B = P_A/2.$$

(b) Work done $W_{AB} = nRT_A \ln\dfrac{V_B}{V_A}$

$$= 3 \times 8.3 \times T_A \ln 2 = 17.26\,T_A$$

$$W_{BC} = P(V_C - V_B)$$

$$= \frac{P_A}{2}(V_A - 2V_A)$$

$$= -P_A V_A/2 = -nRT_A/2$$

$$= \frac{-3 \times 8.3}{2}T_A = -12.45\,T_A$$

$$W_{CA} = 0$$

Total work done $W = W_{AB} + W_{BC} + W_{CA}$
$$= 4.81\,T_A$$

As $\Delta U = 0$
$\therefore$ $Q = W.$ $\qquad \textbf{\textit{Ans.}}$

13. $\eta = 1 - \dfrac{T_2}{T_1} = \left[1 - \dfrac{350}{400}\right] \times 100 = 12.50\%$

and $\eta' = 1 - \dfrac{T_2'}{T_1'} = \left[1 - \dfrac{300}{350}\right] \times 100 = 14.3\%$

Difference in efficiencies
$$\eta' - \eta = 1.8\%. \qquad \textbf{\textit{Ans.}}$$

14. (i) Efficiency $\eta = 1 - \dfrac{T_2}{T_1} = 1 - \dfrac{300}{600} = 50\%$

(ii) The heat taken in each revolution
$$Q = 600 \text{ kcal}$$

We know that $\eta = \dfrac{W}{Q}$

$\therefore$ $W = \eta\,Q$
$$= 0.5 \times (600 \times 10^3) \times 4.2$$
$$= 1.26 \times 10^6 \text{ J} \qquad \textbf{\textit{Ans.}}$$

(iii) Heat rejected $Q_2 = Q_1 - W$
$$= 600 - 300 = 300 \text{ kcal}$$

(iv) Power output $P = \dfrac{W}{t}$

$$= \frac{500 \times 1.26 \times 10^6}{60}$$

$$= 1.05 \times 10^4 \text{ kW} \qquad \textbf{\textit{Ans.}}$$

15. (i) We can write $V_1^{\gamma-1}T_1 = V_2^{\gamma-1}T_2$

$\therefore$ $T_2 = \left(\dfrac{V_1}{V_2}\right)^{\gamma-1}$

$$T_2 = \left(\frac{1}{2}\right)^{1.4-1} \times 600 = 293 \text{ K} \qquad \textbf{\textit{Ans.}}$$

(ii) Efficiency, $\eta = 1 - \dfrac{T_2}{T_1} = 1 - \dfrac{293}{600} = 51.2\% \qquad \textbf{\textit{Ans.}}$

16. Given, $T_1 = 273\,K,$
$$T_2 = 15 + 273 = 280\,K$$
Useful power $= \eta P$
$$= 0.6 \times 500 = 300 \text{ J/s}$$
We know that coefficient of performance

$$\beta = \frac{Q_2}{W} = \left(\frac{T_2}{T_1 - T_2}\right)$$

$$= 300 \times \left(\frac{273}{288 - 273}\right) = 5460 \text{ J/s}$$

Heat needed to melt the ice
$$Q = mL = 15 \times 333 \times 10^3 \text{ J}$$
Time taken in freezing water
$$t = \frac{Q}{Q_2} = \frac{15 \times 333 \times 10^3}{5640} = 914.8 \, s$$

Ans.

17. Suppose initially the engine is working between the temperatures $300 \, K$ and $600 \, K$. Thus
$$\eta = 1 - \frac{T_2}{T_1} = 1 - \frac{300}{600} = 0.50$$

Now temperature of source is increased by 10 K,
$$\eta_1 = 1 - \frac{300}{610} = 0.508.$$

When temperature of sink is decreased by $10K$
$$\eta_2 = 1 - \frac{290}{600}$$
$$= 0.517.$$
Clearly $\eta_2 > \eta_1$. **Ans.**

18. Efficiency of the engine $\eta = 1 - \dfrac{T_2}{T_1} = 1 - \dfrac{400}{500} = 20\%$

By the definition $\quad \eta = \dfrac{W}{Q_1}$

$\therefore \qquad Q_1 = \dfrac{W}{\eta} = \dfrac{10000}{0.20} = 5 \times 10^4 \text{ J},$

and $\qquad Q_2 = Q_1 - W = 4 \times 10^4 \text{ J}.$ **Ans.**

19. $$Q = Q_1 + Q_2 + Q_3 + Q_4$$
$$= 5960 - 5585 - 2980 + 3645$$
$$= 1040 \text{ J}$$
The total work done $\quad W = W_1 + W_2 + W_3 + W_4$
$$= 2200 - 825 - 1100 + W_4$$
$$= 275 + W_4$$
As the process is cyclic, so
$$\Delta U = 0.$$
Thus $\qquad Q = \Delta U + W$
or $\qquad 1040 = 0 + 275 + W_4$
$\therefore \qquad W_4 = 765 \text{ J}$
and $\qquad W = 275 + 765 = 1040$

$$\eta = \frac{\text{work done}}{\text{heat absorbed}}$$

$$= \frac{W}{Q_1 + Q_4} = \frac{1040}{5960 + 3645} = 10.82\%$$

Ans.

20. For the adiabatic process A to B:
$$\frac{P_A^{\gamma-1}}{T_A^{\gamma}} = \frac{P_B^{\gamma-1}}{T_B^{\gamma}}$$

$\therefore \quad T_B = T_A \left[\dfrac{P_B}{P_A}\right]^{\gamma-1} = 1000 \left(\dfrac{2}{3}\right)^{5/3-1} = 850 \, K.$

Work done $\quad W_{AB} = \dfrac{R[T_A - T_B]}{\gamma - 1}$

$$= \frac{8.31(1000 - 850)}{(5/3 - 1)} = 1869.83 \text{ J } \textbf{\textit{Ans.}}$$

(ii) In the process B to C: As volume is constant, so
$$\frac{P_B}{T_B} = \frac{P_C}{T_C}$$

$\therefore \qquad T_C = T_B \dfrac{P_C}{P_B} = 850 \times \dfrac{1/3}{2/3} = 425 \, K$

The change in internal energy
$$\Delta U = C_V \Delta T$$
$$= \frac{3R}{2}(T_C - T_B)$$
$$= \frac{3 \times 8.31}{2}(425 - 850) = -5297.63 \text{ J}.$$
Now by first law of thermodynamics, we have
$$Q = \Delta U + W$$
or $\qquad Q = -5297.63 + 0$
$$= -5297.63 \text{ J} \qquad \textbf{\textit{Ans.}}$$

(iii) For path A to B, $\dfrac{P_A^{\gamma-1}}{T^{\gamma}} = \dfrac{P_B^{\gamma-1}}{T^{\gamma}}$ ......(i)

For path B to C, $\dfrac{P_B}{T_B} = \dfrac{P_C}{T_C}$ .....(ii)

For path C to D, $\dfrac{P_C^{\gamma-1}}{T_C^{\gamma}} = \dfrac{P_D^{\gamma-1}}{T_D^{\gamma}}$ .....(iii)

For path A to D, $\dfrac{P_A}{T_A} = \dfrac{P_D}{T_D}$ .....(iv)

From these equations, we have
$$T_A T_C = T_D T_B$$

$\therefore \qquad T_D = \dfrac{T_A T_C}{T_B}$

$$= \frac{1000 \times 425}{850} = 500 \text{ K.} \qquad \textbf{\textit{Ans.}}$$

21. In the first case, $\quad \Delta U = 0$
$\therefore \qquad\qquad Q = 0 + W = W$
$$= nRT \ln\left(\frac{V_2}{V_1}\right)$$
$$= nR \times 300 \ln 2 \qquad .....(i)$$
In the second case, $\quad W = 0,$
and $\qquad\qquad \Delta U = nC_V \Delta T$
$$= n \times \frac{3R}{2} \times \Delta T$$
From (i) and (ii),
$$nR \times 300 \ln 2 = n \times \frac{3R}{2} \times \Delta T$$
$\therefore \qquad\qquad \Delta T = 138.6 \text{ K}$
The final temperature of the second vessel
$$T = T_i + \Delta T$$
$$= 300 + 138.6 = 438.6 \text{ K}$$
The temperature of the combined gas
$$T_f = \frac{n_1 T_1 + n_2 T_2}{n_1 + n_2}$$
$$= \frac{1 \times 300 + 1 \times 438.6}{1 + 1} = 369.3 \text{ K. } \textbf{\textit{Ans.}}$$

Now using $PV = nRT$, we get

$$P_f = 2.46 \times 10^5 \ \text{N/m}^2 \qquad \textbf{\textit{Ans.}}$$

22. (i)   Work done, $W = \dfrac{1}{2}[4 \times 10^5 + 8 \times 10^5](0.5 - 0.2)$

$$= 1.8 \times 10^5 \ \text{J}$$

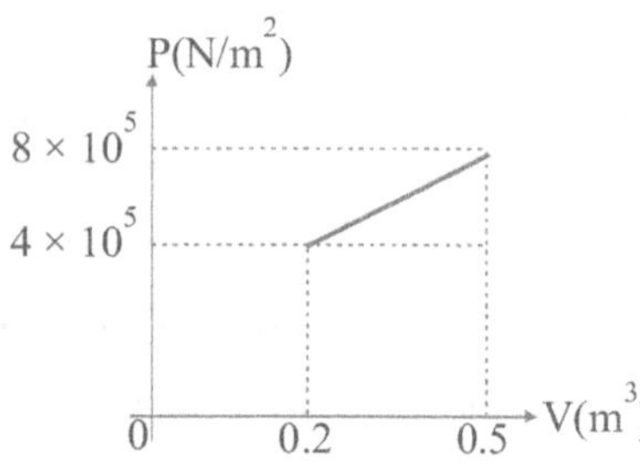

(ii)   The change in internal energy,

$$\Delta U = nC_V \Delta T$$

$$= n\left(\dfrac{3R}{2}\right)[T_2 - T_1]$$

$$= \dfrac{3}{2}[nRT_2 - nRT_1]$$

$$= \dfrac{3}{2}[P_2V_2 - P_1V_1]$$

$$= 4.8 \times 10^5 \ \text{J.} \qquad \textbf{\textit{Ans.}}$$

(iii)   Amount of heat supplied

$$Q = \Delta U + W$$
$$= 4.8 \times 10^5 + 1.8 \times 10^5$$
$$= 6.6 \times 10^5 \ \text{J.}$$

(iv) $C = \dfrac{Q}{\Delta T} = \dfrac{Q}{\left(\dfrac{P_2V_2}{R} - \dfrac{P_1V_1}{R}\right)} = 17 \ \text{J.} \quad \textbf{\textit{Ans.}}$

23.   For adiabatic process, we have

$$V^{\gamma-1} T = \text{constant},$$

or $V_A^{\gamma-1} T_A = V_B^{\gamma-1} T_B$

$\therefore$ $T_B = T_A \left[\dfrac{V_A}{V_B}\right]^{\gamma-1}$

$$= 300 \times (16)^{1.4-1} = 909 \ \text{K.}$$

At constant pressure, $T_C = T_B\left[\dfrac{V_C}{V_B}\right] = 909 \times 2 = 1818 \ \text{K.}$

Also $T_D = T_C \left[\dfrac{V_C}{V_D}\right]^{\gamma-a} = 1818\left(\dfrac{1}{8}\right)^{1.4-1}$

$$= 791.3 \ \text{K.}$$

Heat absorbed $Q_{BC} = nC_P(T_C - T_B)$

$$= 1 \times \dfrac{\gamma R}{(\gamma-1)}(T_C - T_B) = 3182 \ R$$

Heat released $Q_{DA} = nC_V(T_D - T_A)$

$$= 1 \times \dfrac{R}{(\gamma-1)}(T_D - T_A) = \dfrac{2455R}{2}.$$

Work done: $W_{AB} = \dfrac{nR}{\gamma-1}[T_A - T_B] = \dfrac{5R}{2} \times 609$

$$W_{BC} = nR[T_C - T_B] = 909 \ R$$

$$W_{CD} = \dfrac{nR}{\gamma-1}(T_C - T_D) = -\dfrac{5R}{2} \times 1027$$

$$W_{DA} = 0$$

$\therefore$ $W = W_{AB} + W_{BC} + W_{CD} + W_{DA}$

$$= 1954 \ R$$

Efficiencey $\eta = \dfrac{\text{work done}}{\text{heat absorbed}} = \dfrac{W}{Q_{AB}}$

$$= \dfrac{1954R}{3182R} = 61.4\% \qquad \textbf{\textit{Ans.}}$$

24. (a)   Sketch of the process is given in the answer.

(b)   Work done: $W_{AB} = \dfrac{[P_1V_1 - P_2V_2]}{(\gamma-1)}$ ... (i)

We have $P_1V_1^{\gamma} = P_2V_2^{\gamma}$

$$P_2 = \dfrac{P_1V_1^{\gamma}}{V_2^{\gamma}} \qquad \qquad \text{...(ii)}$$

From equations (i) and (ii), we have

$$W_{AB} = \dfrac{P_1V_1\left[1 - \left(\dfrac{V_1}{V_2}\right)^{\gamma-1}\right]}{(\gamma-1)}$$

$$= \dfrac{P_1V_1\left[1 - \left(\dfrac{V_1}{V_2}\right)^{5/3-1}\right]}{(5/3-1)}$$

$$= \dfrac{3}{2}P_1V_1\left[1 - \left(\dfrac{V_1}{V_2}\right)^{2/3}\right] \qquad \textbf{\textit{Ans.}}$$

Now by first law of thermodynamics

$$Q = \Delta U + W$$

$\therefore$ $\Delta U = Q - W$

$$= Q - \dfrac{3}{2}P_1V_1\left[1 - \left(\dfrac{V_1}{V_2}\right)^{2/3}\right] \quad \textbf{\textit{Ans.}}$$

25.   The number of moles of the gas is given by

$$n = \dfrac{PV}{RT}$$

$\therefore$ $n_1 = \dfrac{P_1V_1}{RT_1}$

and $n_2 = \dfrac{P_2V_2}{RT_2}$

If T is the final temperature, then

$$n = \dfrac{P(V_1 + V_2)}{RT}$$

For isolated system

$$n_1 + n_2 = n$$

or $\dfrac{P_1V_1}{RT_1} + \dfrac{P_2V_2}{RT_2} = \dfrac{P(V_1 + V_2)}{RT}$ .....(i)

Also by conservation of energy for isolated system

$$U_1 + U_2 = U$$

$$n_1 \times \dfrac{3}{2}kT_1 + n_2 \times \dfrac{3}{2}kT_2 = (n_1 + n_2) \times \dfrac{3}{2}kT$$

or $\dfrac{P_1V_1}{RT_1} \times T_1 + \dfrac{P_2V_2}{RT_2} \times T_2 = \left[\dfrac{P_1V_1}{RT_1} + \dfrac{P_2V_2}{RT_2}\right]^T$

$\therefore \qquad T = T_1T_2\left[\dfrac{P_1V_1 + P_2V_2}{P_1V_1T_2 + P_2V_2T_1}\right]$

From equation (i), $\qquad P = \left[\dfrac{P_1V_1 + P_2V_2}{V_1 + V_2}\right].$ **Ans.**

26. (a) Given $\qquad PT = k$ ...(i)
    Also $\qquad PV = nRT$ ...(ii)
    From equations (i) and (ii), we get

    $$V = \dfrac{nR}{k}T^2$$

    $\therefore \qquad dV = \dfrac{2nRT}{k}dT$

    Work done $\quad W_{AB} = \int PdV$

    $$= \int_{T_1}^{T_2}\left(\dfrac{k}{T}\right) \times \dfrac{2nRT}{k}dT$$

    $$= 2nR\int_{T_1}^{T_2}dT = 2nR\,[T_2 - T_1]$$

    $$= 2 \times 2R\,[300 - 600] = -1200\,R.\ \textbf{Ans.}$$

    (b) Change in internal energy

    $$\Delta U_{AB} = nC_V\Delta T$$

    $$= 2 \times \dfrac{3R}{2} \times (-300) = -900\,R$$

    Now $\qquad Q = \Delta U_{AB} + W_{AB}$

    $$= -900\,R - 1200R = -2100\,R \quad \textbf{Ans.}$$

27. Work done in the complete cycle,

    $$W = \text{Area of the trapezium}$$

    $$= (P_2 - P_1)\left[\dfrac{(V_4 - V_1) + (V_3 - V_2)}{2}\right]$$

    Here $\qquad V_3 = \dfrac{V_2T_3}{T_2} = \dfrac{V_1T_3}{T_2},$

    and $\qquad V_4 = \dfrac{V_1T_4}{T_1} = \dfrac{V_1T_2}{T_1},$

    $$P_2 = \dfrac{P_1T_2}{T_1},$$

    After substituting these values, we get

    $$W = P_1V_1\left(\dfrac{T_2 - T_1}{T_1}\right)\left(\dfrac{T_2}{T_1} + \dfrac{T_3}{T_2} - 2\right)$$

    For n-moles, $\qquad P_1V_1 = nRT_1$

    $\therefore \qquad W = nR(T_2 - T_1)\left(\dfrac{T_2}{T_1} + \dfrac{T_3}{T_2} - 2\right)$ **Ans.**

28. Pressure is given by $\quad P = \dfrac{mRT}{MV},$

    Partial pressures: $\quad P_{H_2} = \dfrac{m_{H_2}}{M_{H2}}\dfrac{RT}{V},$

$$P_{N_2} = \dfrac{m_{N_2}}{M_{N_2}}\dfrac{RT}{V},$$

and $\qquad P_{O_2} = \dfrac{m_{O_2}}{M_{O_2}}\dfrac{RT}{V}$

According to Dalton's law,

$$P_1 = P_{H_2}$$
$$\simeq 1.3 \times 10^9\,P_a$$
$$P_2 = P_{H_2} + P_{O_2}$$
$$\simeq 4.5 \times 10^9\,P_a$$

And $\qquad P_3 = P_{H_2} + P_{N_2}$

$$\simeq 2.0 \times 10^9\,P_a \qquad \textbf{Ans.}$$

29. (i) $\qquad n = \dfrac{m}{M} = \dfrac{2 \times 10^3}{4} = 500$

    By the equation, $PV = nRT$, we have

    $$T = \dfrac{PV}{nR}$$

    $\therefore \qquad T_A = \dfrac{(5 \times 10^4) \times 10}{500 \times 8.31}$

    $$= 120.33\text{ K}$$

    Similarly, $\quad T_B = 240.66\text{ K},$
    $$T_C = 481.32\text{ K},$$
    $$T_D = 240.66\text{ K}.$$

    (ii) No.

    (iii) The change in internal energy is given by

    $$\Delta U = nC_V\Delta T\,.$$

    Thus $\qquad [\Delta U]_{ABC} = nC_V\Delta T$

    $$= 500 \times \dfrac{3}{2}R \times [T_C - T_A]$$

    $$= 2.25 \times 10^6\text{ J}$$

    and $\qquad [\Delta U]_{ADC} = 2.25 \times 10^6\text{ J}$

    $$W_{ABC} = 10 \times (10 \times 10^4) = 10^6\text{ J}$$

    And $\qquad W_{ADC} = 5 \times 10^4(20 - 10)$

    $$= 0.5 \times 10^6\text{ J}$$

    Now $\qquad Q = \Delta U + W$

    $\therefore \qquad Q_{ABC} = 3.25 \times 10^6\text{ J}$

    and $\qquad Q_{ADC} = 2.75 \times 10^6\text{ J}.$ **Ans.**

30. As the piston does not conduct heat so the temperature of left part does not change. If ΔT is the change in temperature of right part, then

    $$\Delta U = nC_V\Delta T$$

    $$= n\dfrac{3R}{2}\Delta T$$

    By first law of thermodynamics, we have

    $$(Q - Q') = \Delta U + W$$

    Here work done, $\qquad W = 2\left(\dfrac{1}{2}kx^2\right)$

    $$= 2 \times \dfrac{1}{2} \times k(\ell/2)^2 = \dfrac{k\ell^2}{4}$$

    $\therefore \qquad Q - Q' = n\dfrac{3R}{2}\Delta T + \dfrac{k\ell^2}{4}$ ....(i)

    For the equilibrium of the piston

    $$P_2A = P_1A + 2\left(k\dfrac{\ell}{2}\right)$$

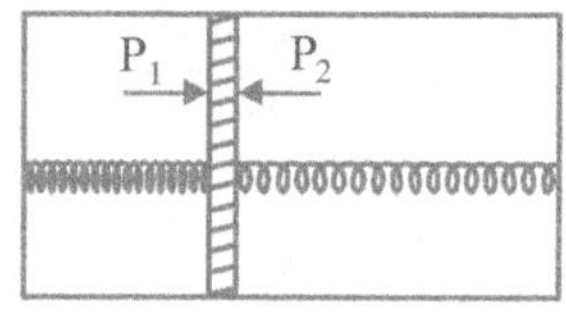

or
$$P_2 = P_1 + \frac{k\ell}{A}$$

or
$$\frac{2nR(T + \Delta T)}{(3A\ell)} = \frac{2nRT}{A\ell} + \frac{k\ell}{A} \qquad ......(ii)$$

From equations (i) and (ii), we get

$$Q' = Q - 3nRT - \frac{5}{2}k\ell^2 \qquad \textbf{\textit{Ans.}}$$

31. If ΔT is the increase in temperature of the gas, then increase in internal energy of the gas,

$$\Delta U_1 = nC_V \Delta T$$

$$= 1 \times \frac{3R}{2}\Delta T$$

$$= \frac{3R\Delta T}{2}$$

The energy stored in the spring in compressing from x_1 to x_2,

$$\Delta U_2 = \frac{1}{2}k(x_2^2 - x_1^2)$$

We know that for pressure P of the gas
$$PA = k\,x$$

$$\therefore \qquad x = \frac{PA}{k}$$

or
$$x^2 = \frac{P(Ax)}{k} = \frac{PV}{k} = \frac{RT}{k}$$

$$\therefore \qquad \Delta U_2 = \frac{R}{2}(T_2 - T_1) = \frac{R\Delta T}{2}$$

The total energy spend

$$\Delta U = \Delta U_1 + \Delta U_2 = 2R\Delta T$$

$$\therefore \qquad C = 2R. \qquad \textbf{\textit{Ans.}}$$

32. The work done by the gas is the sum of work done W_1 against the force of atmospheric pressure and the work done W_2 against the gravity. Thus total work done,
$$W = W_1 + W_2$$
The mercury-gas interface is shifted upon the complete displacement of mercury

$$s = 2\ell + \ell/2 = \frac{5\ell}{2},$$

and hence
$$W_1 = Fs$$

$$= P_0 S \times \frac{5\ell}{2} = \frac{5P_0 S\ell}{2}$$

The work done W_2 against the gravity is equal to the change in the potential energy of mercury as a result of its displacement. The whole of mercury rises as a result of displacement by l relative to the horizontal part of the tube. This quantity regarded as the final height of the centre of gravity of the whole mercury. The initial position of centre of gravity of murcury is $= \ell/8$.
Thus
$$W_2 = U_2 - U_1$$

$$Mg(\ell - \ell/8) = \frac{7}{8}Mg\ell.$$

where
$$M = 2\,\ell\,S\,\rho_{mer}$$
$$\therefore \qquad W = W_1 + W_2$$

$$= \frac{5}{2}P_0 S\ell + \frac{7}{4}\rho_{mer}\,gS\ell^2$$

$$\approx 7.7 \text{ J.} \qquad \textbf{\textit{Ans.}}$$

33. For the process A to B: $\dfrac{V_A}{T_A} = \dfrac{V_B}{T_B}$

$$\therefore \qquad T_B = T_A\left(\frac{V_B}{V_A}\right) = 300 \times 2$$

$$= 600 \text{ K} = 327^\circ C$$

$$\Delta U_{AB} = nC_V \Delta T$$

$$= 2 \times \frac{3R}{2} \times 300 = 900\,R$$

$$P_A = \frac{nRT_A}{V_A}$$

Work done, $\qquad W_{AB} = P_A(V_B - V_A)$

$$= \frac{nRT_A}{V_A}(V_B - V_A) = nRT_A\left[\frac{V_B}{V_A} - 1\right]$$

$$= 2\,R \times 300\,[2 - 1] = 600\,R$$

Thus heat absorbed $\quad Q = \Delta U + W = 600\,R + 900\,R = 1500\,R$
For the process B to C:

$$W_{BC} = nRT_B \ln\left(\frac{V_C}{V_B}\right)$$

$$= nRT_B \ln\left(\frac{V_D}{V_B}\right)$$

$$= 2R \times 600\,\ln 2 = 831.6\,R.$$

As the temperature is constant from B to C, so

$$\Delta U_{BC} = 0.$$

Heat absorbed in the process

$$Q = \Delta U_{BC} + W_{AB}$$
$$= 0 + 831.6\,R = 831.6\,R. \qquad \textbf{\textit{Ans.}}$$

For the process C to D :
$$W_{CD} = P(V_D - V_C) = 0$$
and
$$\Delta U_{CD} = nC_V \Delta T$$

$$= 2 \times \frac{3R}{2} \times (-300) = -900\,R.$$

Heat absorbed $\qquad Q = \Delta U + W_{CD}$
$$= -900\,R + 0 = -900\,R. \qquad \textbf{\textit{Ans.}}$$

For the process D to A :

$$W_{DA} = nRT_D \ln\left(\frac{V_A}{V_D}\right)$$

$$= 2R \times 300\ln\left(\frac{1}{4}\right) = -831.6\,R$$

$$\Delta U_{DA} = 0$$

Heat absorbed $\qquad Q = \Delta U_{DA} + W_{DA}$
$$= -831.6\,R. \qquad \textbf{\textit{Ans.}}$$

Total work done $\qquad W = W_{AB} + W_{BC} + W_{CD} + W_{DA}$
$$= 600\,R. \qquad \textbf{\textit{Ans.}}$$

Heat Transfer

(527 - 570)

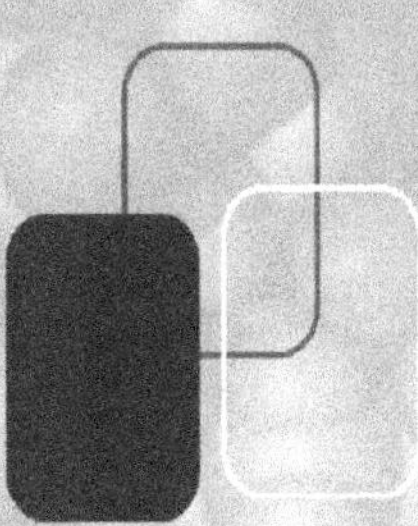

8.1 MODES OF HEAT TRANSFER

There are three modes of heat transfer. These are :

(i)   Conduction,   (ii)   convection and   (iii)   radiation.

Heat transfer by the process of conduction mainly occurs in solids. Liquid and gases heated by the process of convection. The heat transfer by radiation requires no intervening medium. The heat from sun to earth comes by radiation. Radiation is the fastest mode of heat transfer. Radiation is the universal mode of heat transfer which always occurs.

8.2 THERMAL CONDUCTION

Conduction is a process in which heat is transmitted from one part of a body to other part at a lower temperature by molecular collisions, without transfer of the material medium.

Molecular theory of thermal conduction

When one end of the rod is heated, the molecules at the hot end vibrate with larger amplitude and hence with greater kinetic energy. As these molecules collide with the neighbouring molecules, the energy being shared between them. So the kinetic energy of the neighbouring molecules increases. These molecules transfer the energy to the next molecules and so on. In this way, heat is transferred from hot to the colder end of the rod.

8.3 STEADY STATE AND TEMPERATURE GRADIENT

Consider a metal rod, whose sides are covered with an insulating material so that convection and radiation are prevented. When rod starts heating from its one end, the temperature of subsequent cross-sections of the rod starts increasing. The rod is said to be in the variable state of heat conduction. After some time, the temperature of every cross-section of the rod becomes constant and there is no further absorption of heat in any part of the rod. This is the steady state of the rod.

At steady state :

(i)   The temperature of two different cross-sections of the rod are different, but temperature of each cross-section remain constant.

(ii)   The temperature of the cross-section decreases when we move from hot end.

(iii)   The rate of flow of heat through every cross-section remain constant.

If T_1 and T_2 are the temperatures of two cross-sections separated by distance x, then temperature gradient is defined as :

$$\text{Temperature gradient} \quad = \quad \frac{T_1 - T_2}{x} = -\frac{\Delta T}{\Delta x}$$

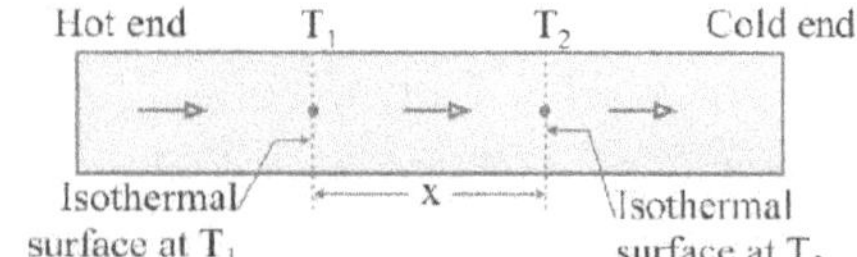

Fig. 8.1

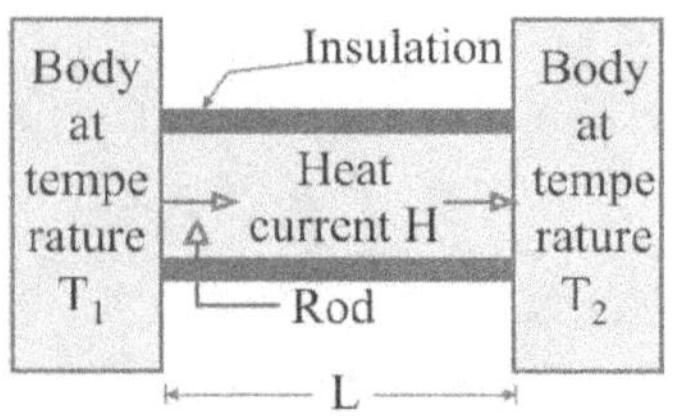

Fig. 8.2

Note:

(i)   If the temperature T_1 and T_2 are in kelvin or if they are $\theta_1\,°C$ and $\theta_2\,°C$, then

$$\frac{T_1 - T_2}{x} = \frac{\theta_1 - \theta_2}{x}$$

(ii)   For small x, temperature gradient $= \dfrac{-\Delta T}{\Delta x} = \dfrac{-dT}{dx} = \dfrac{-d\theta}{dx}$

8.4 RATE OF FLOW OF HEAT : HEAT CURRENT

Fig. 8.2 represents a rod of material of cross-sectional area A and length L.
Let the left end of the rod be kept at a temperature T_1 and the right end at a lower temperature T_2. The direction of flow of heat current is from left to the right through the rod.
Experiments shows that, the rate of flow of heat through the rod in the steady state is proportional to the area of cross-section of rod A, and the temperature difference $(T_1 - T_2)$, and inversely proportional to the length L. If Q is the heat flows in time t, then heat current.

$$H = \frac{Q}{t} = KA\frac{(T_1 - T_2)}{L} = -KA\frac{\Delta T}{L} \qquad \ldots (1)$$

The SI unit of H is J/s or W. Here K is called coefficient of thermal conductivity. It is a material property which does not depend on size and shape of the specimen. The SI unit of K is $W/m\text{-}K$.

> **Note :**
>
> Equation (1) may be used to compute rate of flow of heat through a homogeneous body of uniform cross-section perpendicular to the direction of flow of heat. In case of non-uniform cross-section, the temperature does not necessarily change uniformly along the direction of flow of heat. The equation (1) can be used as :
>
> $$H = -KA\frac{dT}{dx}$$
>
> when dT is the temperature difference across the distance dx. The negative sign indicates that temperature of the rod decreases with x.

8.5 THERMAL RESISTANCE

We know that heat current

$$H = KA\frac{(T_1 - T_2)}{L}$$

or

$$H = \frac{(T_1 - T_2)}{\left(\dfrac{L}{KA}\right)} \qquad \ldots (1)$$

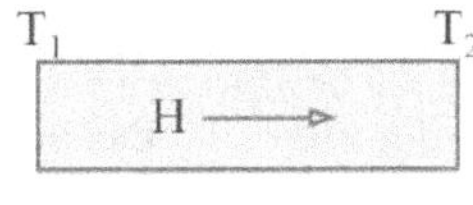

Fig. 8.3

In electricity, electric current is given by

$$i = \frac{(V_1 - V_2)}{R} \qquad \ldots (2)$$

where $V_1 - V_2$ is the potential difference across the resistor R.

If we compare equation (1) with equation (2), we find that $\dfrac{L}{KA}$ is a type of resistance, is called thermal resistance R_H.

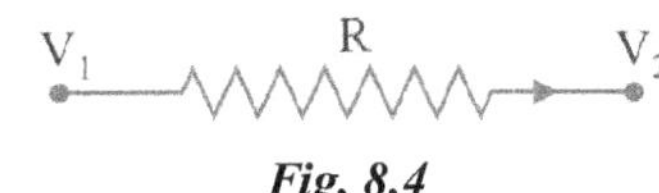

Fig. 8.4

So

$$R_H = \frac{L}{KA}$$

Temperature difference is analogous to the potential difference in electricity.

SI unit of $R_H = \dfrac{K}{J/s} = \dfrac{K}{W}$.

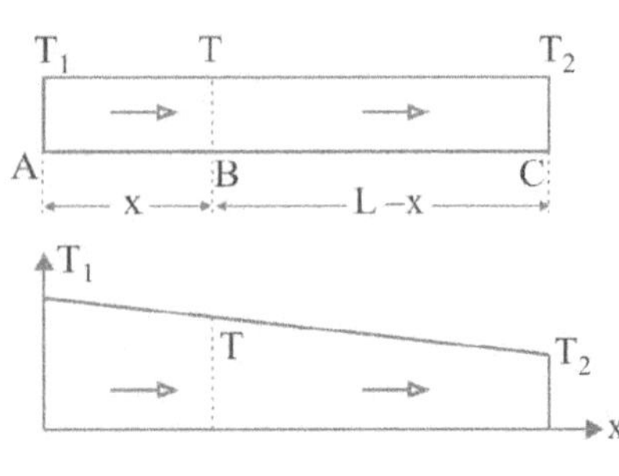

Fig. 8.5

Temperature of a section of rod at a distance x

Consider a rod of length L at steady state. Let T_1 is the temperature of left end and T_2 is the temperature of right end of the rod, with $T_1 > T_2$. If T is the temperature of the section under consideration, then heat current through AB will equal to heat current through BC, so we have

$$KA\frac{T_1 - T}{x} \;=\; KA\frac{T - T_2}{(L - x)}$$

After solving, we get

$$T \;=\; T_1 - \left(\frac{T_1 - T_2}{L}\right)x$$

Above equation represents a straight line between T and x with negative slope, so the temperature of the rod falls linearly from T_1 and T_2 in a distance L.

Ex. 1 Two metal cubes A and B of same size are arranged as shown in *Fig. 8.6* . The extreme ends of the combination are maintained at the identical temperatures. The arrangement is thermally insulated. The coefficient of thermal conductivity of A and B are 300 W/m – °C and 200 W/m – °C respectively. After steady state is reached, what will be the temperature T of the interface?

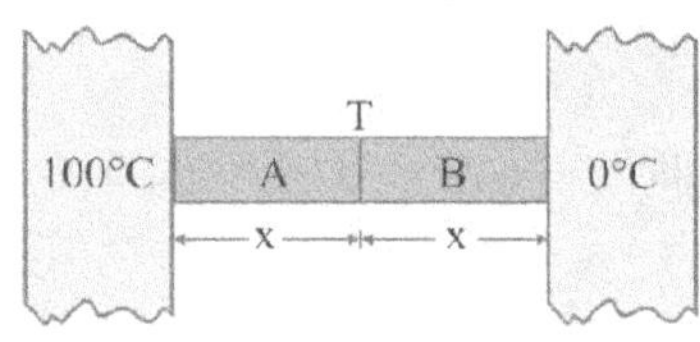

Fig. 8.6

Sol.
In steady state;
Rate of flow of heat through A = Rate of flow of heat through B

or $\qquad K_1 A\left(\dfrac{100 - T}{x}\right) \;=\; K_2 A\dfrac{(T - 0)}{x}$

or $\qquad 300 A\dfrac{(100 - T)}{x} \;=\; 200 A\dfrac{(T - 0)}{x}$

or $\qquad 300 - 3T \;=\; 2T$

$\therefore \qquad\qquad T \;=\; 60°C$ $\qquad\qquad$ *Ans.*

Ex. 2 A 'thermocole' cubical icebox of side 30 cm has a thickness of 5.0 cm. If 4.0 kg of ice are put in the box, estimate the amount of ice remaining after 6h. The outside temperature is 45°C and coefficient of thermal conductivity of thermocole = 0.01 J/ sm - °C. Given heat of fusion of water = 335 × 10³ J/kg.

Sol.
Area of six faces of the box

$$= 6\ell^2 = 6\times(0.30)^2$$
$$= 0.54 \text{ m}^2$$

and $\qquad L = 5.0 \text{ cm} = 0.05 \text{ m}$

time, $\qquad t = 6h = 6\times 3600 \text{ s}$

$$T_1 - T_2 = 45 - 0 = 45°C$$

Total heat entering into the box in $6h$

$$Q = \frac{KA(T_1 - T_2)}{L}.t$$

$$= \frac{0.01\times 0.54\times 45 \times 6\times 3600}{0.05}$$

$$= 104976 \text{ J}$$

If m be the amount of ice melted, then

$$Q = mL$$

or $\qquad m = \dfrac{Q}{L} = \dfrac{104976}{335\times 10^3}$

$$= 0.313 \text{ kg}$$

Mass of the ice left after

$$6h = 4 - 0.313 \text{ kg} = 3.687 \text{ kg} \qquad\quad \textit{Ans.}$$

Ex. 3 A brass boiler has a base area of 0.15 m² and thickness 1.0 cm. It boils water at the rate of 6.0 kg/min, when placed on a gas. Estimate the temperature of the part of the flame in contact with the boiler. Thermal conductivity of brass = 109 J/sm-°C and heat of vapourisation of water = 2256 J/g.

Sol.

Let T_1 be the temperature of the part of the flame in contact with boiler. The amount of heat flows into water in 1 minute

$$Q = KA\frac{T_1 - T_2}{L}t$$

$$= \frac{109 \times 0.15 \times (T_1 - 100)\times 60}{0.01} J$$

Mass of the water boiled in 1 minute = 6 kg = 6000 g
Heat required to boil the water $Q = mL = 6000 \times 2256$ J

$\therefore \quad \dfrac{109\times 0.15 \times (T_1 - 100)\times 60}{0.01} = 6000 \times 2256$

or $\qquad T_1 - 100 = 138$

or $\qquad\quad T_1 = 238° \text{C}$ $\qquad\qquad$ *Ans.*

8.6 DETERMINATION OF THERMAL CONDUCTIVITY

1. **Ingen-Hausz experiment**

    Ingen-Hausz devised an experiment to compare the thermal conductivities of the metals. If $\ell_1, \ell_2,.....$ are the lengths of wax melted on the metal rods, then the ratio of thermal conductivities is $K_1 : K_2 : K_3... = \ell_1^2 : \ell_2^2 : \ell_3^2 :.....$

2. Searle's method

Consider a rod XY whose thermal conductivity is to be determined. The left end X of the rod is placed in a steam jacket and steam is continuously passed through it. Heat is transferred along the rod and when steady state is reached, the thermometers T_1, T_2, T_3 and T_4 record constant temperatures. Let in time t, m be the mass of water collected.

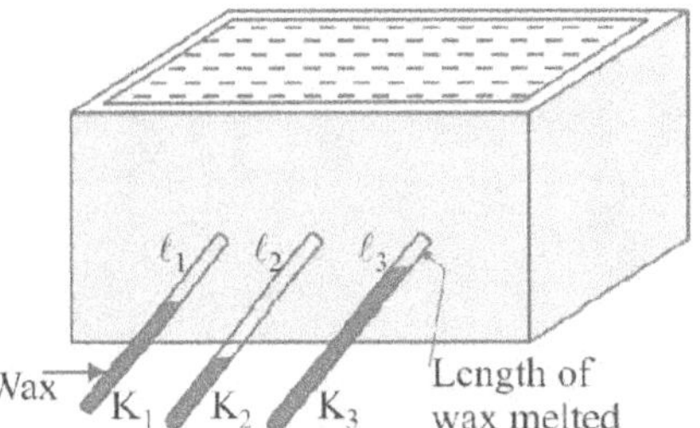

Fig. 8.7

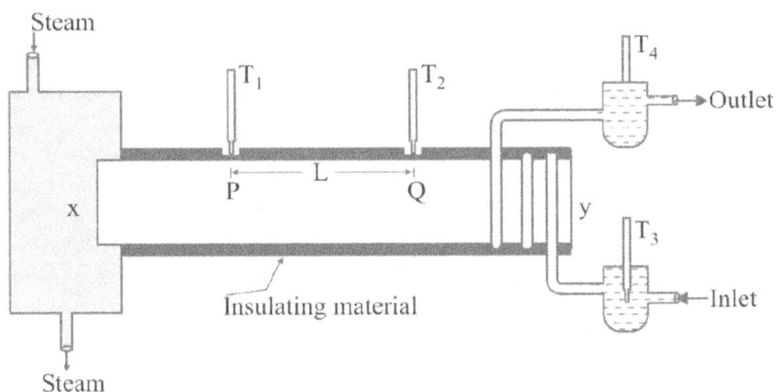

Fig. 8.8

Quantity of heat flows from the section at P and Q in one second,

$$Q = \frac{KA(T_1 - T_2)}{L} \times 1 \qquad \ldots (1)$$

where L is the distance between sections of the rod at temperatures T_1 and T_2.

Amount of heat gained by water in one second

$$= \text{mass of water collected in one second}$$
$$\times \text{ specific heat} \times \text{temperature rise}$$

$$= \frac{m}{t} \times c \times (T_4 - T_3) \qquad \ldots (2)$$

From equations (1) and (2)

$$KA\frac{(T_1 - T_2)}{L} = \frac{mc(T_4 - T_3)}{t}$$

or

$$K = \frac{mcL(T_4 - T_3)}{At(T_1 - T_2)}$$

Wiedemann - Franz law

The ratio of the thermal and electrical conductivities is the same for all metals at the same temperature. Moreover, the ratio is directly proportional to the absolute temperature of the metal. If K and σ are the thermal and electrical conductivities of a metal at a temperature T, then

$$\frac{K}{\sigma} \propto T$$

or

$$\frac{K}{\sigma T} = \text{constant}$$

At low temperatures the ratio K/σ decreases and its value becomes zero at absolute zero.

8.7 COMBINATION OF METALLIC RODS

1. **Series combination :** Suppose n number of rods each of cross-sectional area A and lengths $\ell_1, \ell_2, ...\ell_n$ and conductivities $K_1, K_2, ...,K_n$ are placed in series.

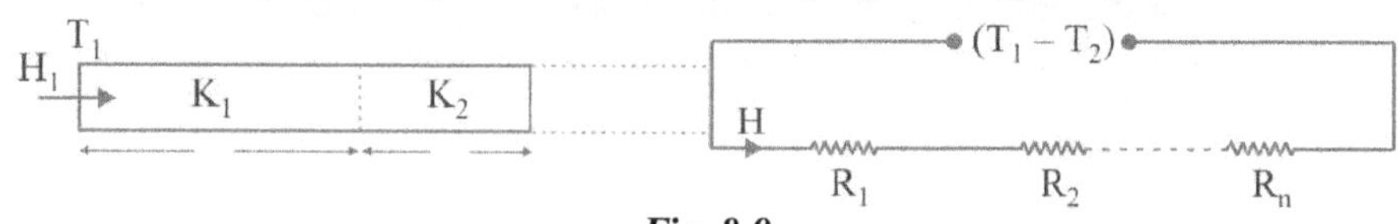

Fig. 8.9

(i) **Equivalent thermal resistance :** If $R_1, R_2, ...$ are the thermal resistances of the rods, then equivalent resistance

$$R_H = R_1 + R_2 + ... + R_n$$

(ii) **Heat current :** The heat current remains same for all rods.

$$\therefore \qquad H = \frac{Q}{t} = H_1 = H_2 = ... = \frac{(T_1 - T_2)}{R_H}$$

(iii) **Equivalent thermal conductivity :**

We know that $\qquad R_H = R_1 + R_2 + ... + R_n$

or $\qquad \dfrac{\ell_1 + \ell_2 + ... + \ell_n}{KA} = \dfrac{\ell_1}{K_1 A} + \dfrac{\ell_2}{K_2 A} + ... + \dfrac{\ell_n}{K_n A}$

or $\qquad K = \dfrac{\ell_1 + \ell_2 + ... + \ell_n}{\dfrac{\ell_1}{K_1} + \dfrac{\ell_2}{K_2} + ... + \dfrac{\ell_n}{K_n}} = \dfrac{\Sigma \ell}{\Sigma(\ell/K)}$

(iv) For two rods : $\qquad K = \dfrac{2 K_1 K_2}{K_1 + K_2}$

2. **Parallel combination :** Suppose n number of rods or slabs each of length ℓ and area of cross-sections $A_1, A_2, ..., A_n$ and thermal conductivities $K_1, K_2, ...,K_n$ are placed in contact.

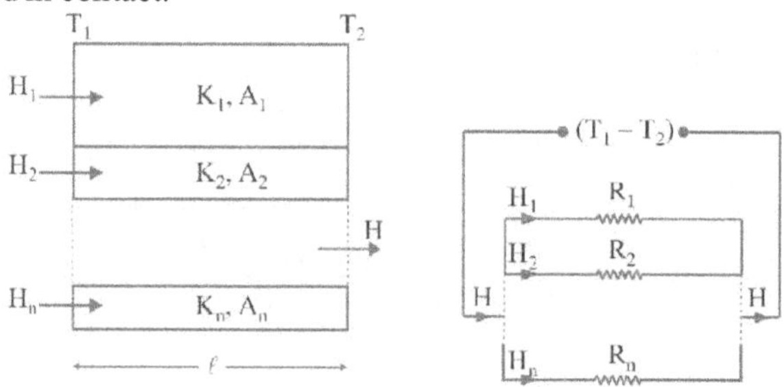

Fig. 8.10

(i) **Equivalent thermal resistance :** If $R_1, R_2, ..., R_n$ are the resistances of the rods, then equivalent resistance

$$\frac{1}{R_H} = \frac{1}{R_1} + \frac{1}{R_2} + ... + \frac{1}{R_n}$$

(ii) **Heat current :** $\qquad H_1 = \dfrac{(T_1 - T_2)}{R_1},$

$$H_2 = \frac{(T_1 - T_2)}{R_2}, ..., H_n = \frac{(T_1 - T_2)}{R_n}$$

and $\qquad H = H_1 + H_2 + ... + H_n = \dfrac{(T_1 - T_2)}{R_H}$

(iii) Equivalent thermal conductivity :

We know that

$$\frac{1}{R_H} = \frac{1}{R_1} + \frac{1}{R_2} + \dots\dots + \frac{1}{R_n}$$

or

$$\frac{1}{\dfrac{\ell}{K(A_1 + A_2 + \dots + A_n)}} = \frac{1}{\dfrac{\ell}{K_1 A_1}} + \frac{1}{\dfrac{\ell}{K_2 A_2}} + \dots + \frac{1}{\dfrac{\ell}{K_n A_n}}$$

or

$$K = \frac{K_1 A_1 + K_2 A_2 + \dots + K_n A_n}{A_1 + A_2 + \dots + A_n}$$

$$= \frac{\Sigma KA}{\Sigma A}$$

(iv) For two slabs :

$$K = \frac{K_1 A_1 + K_2 A_2}{A_1 + A_2}$$

Ex. 4 An electric heater is used in a room of total wall area 137 m² to maintain a temperature of +20°C inside it, when the outside temperature is –10°C. The walls have three different layers materials. The innermost layer of wood of thickness 2.5 cm, the middle layer is of cement of thickness 1.0 cm and the outermost layer is of brick of thickness 25.0 cm. Find the power of the electric heater. Assume that there is no heat loss through the floor and the ceiling. The thermal conductivities of wood, cement and brick are 0.125, 1.5 and 1.0 W/m –°C respectively.

Sol.

Equivalent thermal conductivity of the wall

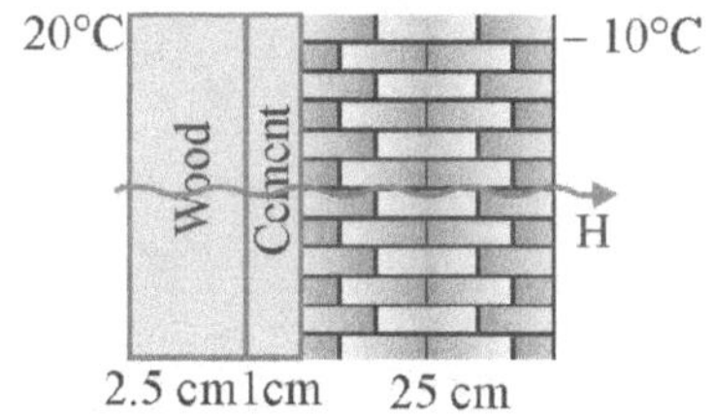

Fig. 8.11

$$K = \frac{\ell_1 + \ell_2 + \ell_3}{\dfrac{\ell_1}{K_1} + \dfrac{\ell_2}{K_2} + \dfrac{\ell_3}{K_3}}$$

$$= \frac{0.025 + 0.01 + 0.25}{\left(\dfrac{0.025}{0.125} + \dfrac{0.01}{1.5} + \dfrac{0.25}{1.0}\right)}$$

$$= \frac{0.285}{0.457} = 0.624 \text{ W/m-°C}$$

The rate of flow of heat is given by

$$H = KA\frac{T_1 - T_2}{L}$$

$$= 0.624 \times 137 \times \frac{[20 - (-10)]}{0.285}$$

$$= \frac{0.624 \times 137 \times 30}{0.285} = 9000 \ W \qquad \textit{Ans.}$$

8.8 REDIAL FLOW OF HEAT

Consider two thin spherical shells of radii r_1 and r_2. A medium of thermal conductivity K is contained between these shells. A heater is placed at the centre of the shells. Heat is conducted through the medium radially from inner to the outer shell. Let the temperatures of the inner and the outer shells be T_1 and T_2 at steady state.

Choose an element of radial thickness dr at a radial distance r from the centre of shells. Let dT is the temperature difference across it. The rate of flow of heat through the element

$$H = KA\left(-\frac{dT}{dx}\right)$$

Here

$$A = 4\pi r^2 \text{ are } dx = dr, H \text{ is constant}$$

$\therefore$

$$H = -K(4\pi r^2)\frac{dT}{dr}$$

or

$$\frac{dr}{r^2} = -\frac{4\pi K}{H}dT \qquad \dots (1)$$

Integrating equation (1), we have

$$\int_{r_1}^{r_2}\frac{dr}{r^2} = -\frac{4\pi K}{H}\int_{T_1}^{T_2} dT$$

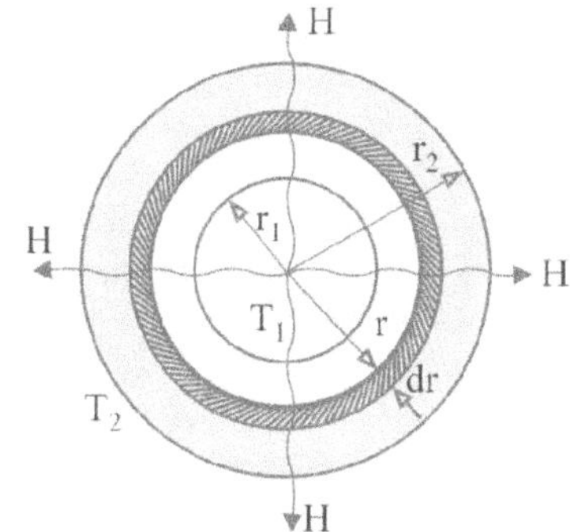

Fig. 8.12

$$\left|-\frac{1}{r}\right|_{r_1}^{r_2} = -\frac{4\pi K}{H}|T|_{T_1}^{T_2}$$

or

$$\frac{1}{r_1} - \frac{1}{r_2} = \frac{4\pi K}{H}(T_1 - T_2)$$

or

$$K = \frac{H(r_2 - r_1)}{4\pi r_1 r_2 (T_1 - T_2)} \qquad \ldots(2)$$

8.9 CYLINDRICAL FLOW OF HEAT

Consider a cylindrical tube of length ℓ, r_1 and r_2 are the inner and outer radius of the tube. The thermal conductivity of material of the tube is K. A heater is placed inside the tube. After steady state, let temperatures of inner and outer surfaces are T_1 and T_2 respectively. Heat is conducted radially across the tube.

Choose an elements of radial thickness dr at a distance of r from the axis of the tube. Let dT is the temperature difference across it. The rate of flow of heat through the element

$$H = KA\left(\frac{-dT}{dx}\right)$$

Here $A = 2\pi r \ell$ and $dx = dr$, H is constant

$$\therefore \qquad H = -K(2\pi r \ell)\frac{dT}{dr}$$

or

$$\frac{dr}{r} = \frac{-2\pi K \ell}{H}dT \qquad \ldots(1)$$

Integrating equation (1), we have

$$\int_{r_1}^{r_2} \frac{dr}{r} = -\frac{2\pi K \ell}{H}\int_{T_1}^{T_2} dT$$

or

$$\left|\ln r\right|_{r_1}^{r_2} = -\frac{2\pi K \ell}{H}|T|_{T_1}^{T_2}$$

or

$$\ln r_2 - \ln r_1 = \frac{2\pi K \ell}{H}(T_1 - T_2)$$

or

$$K = \frac{H \ln\left(\dfrac{r_2}{r_1}\right)}{2\pi \ell (T_1 - T_2)} \qquad \ldots(2)$$

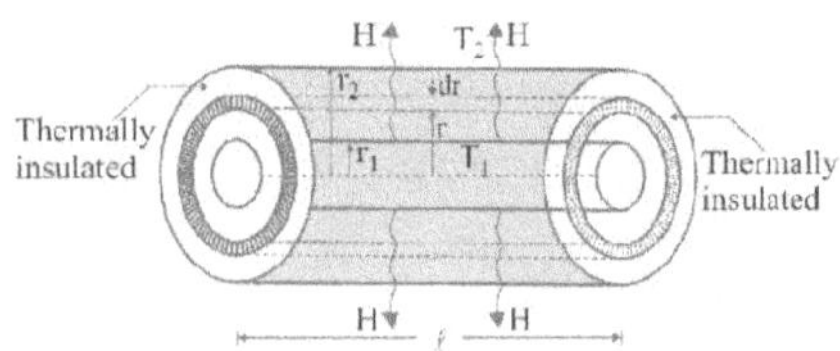

Fig. 8.13

8.10 FORMATION OF ICE ON PONDS

When temperature of the atmosphere falls below 0°C, the water in pond starts freezing from the uppermost layer.

Consider a layer of water of thickness y which has already frozen. Let dy thick layer of water is under process of freezing.

Let the temperature of air over the top face of ice be $-T$°C and that of water below ice 0°C. Suppose (dy) thick ice will form in time dt. If A is the area of the pond, then mass of ice formed, $m = (A dy)\rho$

Heat lost by water in process of formation of ice

$$= mL = (A dy)\rho L \qquad \ldots(1)$$

Fig. 8.14

where L is the latent heat of fusion of ice. This heat is conducted across y thick layer of ice into the atmosphere. If K is the thermal conductivity of ice, then heat conducted in time dt

$$= KA\frac{[0-(-T)]}{y}dt$$

$$= KA\frac{T(dt)}{y} \qquad \ldots(2)$$

Equating equations (1) and (2), we have

$$KAT\frac{(dt)}{y} = (Ady)\rho L$$

or

$$dt = \frac{\rho L}{KT}ydy \qquad \ldots(3)$$

If t is the time to form $y_2 - y_1$ thick ice, then

$$\int_0^t dt = \frac{\rho L}{KT}\int_{y_1}^{y_2} ydy$$

or

$$t = \frac{\rho L}{2KT}\left|y^2\right|_{y_1}^{y_2}$$

$$t = \frac{\rho L}{2KT}(y_2^2 - y_1^2)$$

If t_1 is the time to form top 1 m of ice and t_2 is time to form next 1 m of ice, then

$$t_1 = \frac{\rho L}{2KT}(1^2 - 0^2) = \frac{\rho L}{2KT}$$

and

$$t_2 = \frac{\rho L}{2KT}(2^2 - 1^2) = \frac{3\rho L}{2KT}$$

$\therefore$

$$t_2 = 3t_1$$

Ex. 5 *Fig. 8.15 shows a large tank of water at a constant temperature θ_0 and a small vessel containing a mass m of water at an initial temperature θ_1 $(<\theta_0)$. A metal rod of length L, area of cross-section A and thermal conductivity K connects the two vessels. Find the time taken for the temperature of the water in the smaller vessel to become θ_2 $(\theta_1 < \theta_2 < \theta_0)$. Specific heat capacity of water is c and all other heat capacities are negligible.*

Sol.

Let θ be the temperature of the water in the smaller vessel at any time t. In next time interval dt, the amount of heat flow

$$Q = KA\frac{(\theta_0 - \theta)}{L}dt \qquad \ldots(i)$$

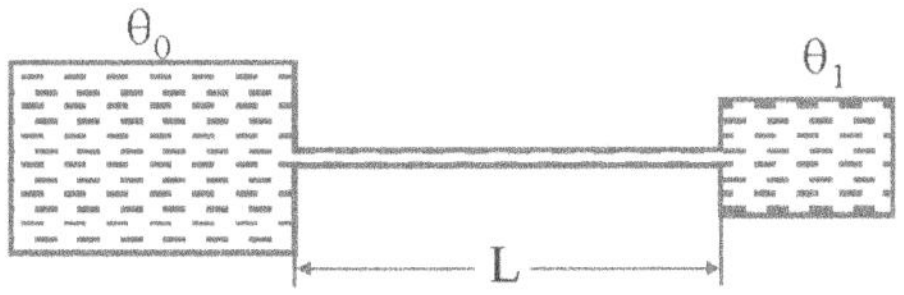

Fig. 8.15

This heat increases the temperature of the water by $d\theta$, then

$$Q = mc(d\theta) \qquad \ldots(ii)$$

Equating equations (i) and (ii), we have

$$\frac{KA(\theta_0 - \theta)}{L}dt = mcd\theta$$

or

$$dt = \frac{mcL}{KA}\frac{d\theta}{(\theta_0 - \theta)}$$

If t is the required time, then

$$\int_0^t dt = \frac{mcL}{KA}\int_{\theta_1}^{\theta_2}\frac{d\theta}{(\theta_0 - \theta)}$$

$$t = \frac{mcL}{KA}\left|\frac{\ln(\theta_0 - \theta)}{(-1)}\right|_{\theta_1}^{\theta_2}$$

$$t = \frac{mcL}{KA}\ln\left(\frac{\theta_0 - \theta_1}{\theta_0 - \theta_2}\right) \qquad \textit{Ans.}$$

Ex. 6   A rod CD of thermal resistance 5.0 K/W is joined at the middle of an identical rod *AB* as shown in *Fig. 8.16*. The ends *A*, *B* and *D* are maintained at 100°C, 0°C and 25°C respectively. Find the heat current in *CD*.

Sol.   Given, $AC = CB = \dfrac{CD}{2}$

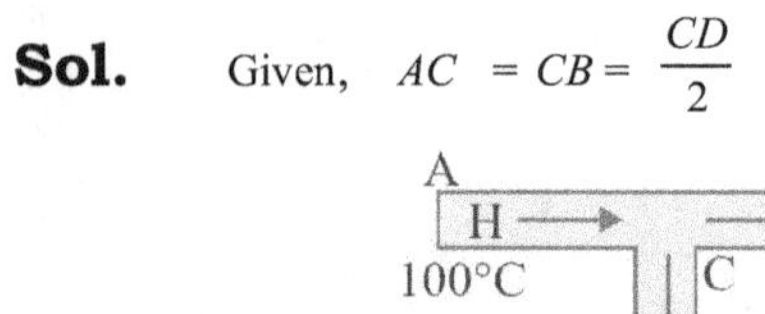

Fig. 8.16

As resistance of the rod is proportional to the length, so

$$R_{AC} = R_{CB} = \frac{R_{CD}}{2} = \frac{5}{2} = 2.5 \text{ K/W}$$

Let H_1 is the heat current in *CD* and H_2 in *CB*, then

$$H_1 = \frac{T_C - T_D}{R_{CD}} = \frac{T_C - 25}{5} \qquad \dots \text{(i)}$$

and

$$H_2 = \frac{T_C - T_B}{R_{CB}} = \frac{T_C - 0}{2.5} \qquad \dots \text{(ii)}$$

If *H* is the heat current through *AC*, then

$$H = \frac{T_A - T_C}{R_{AC}} = \frac{100 - T_C}{2.5}$$

We know that $\qquad H = H_1 + H_2$

$$\therefore \qquad \frac{100 - T_C}{2.5} = \frac{T_C - 25}{5} + \frac{T_C}{2.5}$$

or $\qquad T_C = 45°C$

From (i)

$$H_1 = \frac{45 - 25}{5} = 4.0 \text{ W} \qquad \textit{Ans.}$$

Ex. 7   Consider the situation shown in *Fig. 8.17*. The frame is made of the same material and has a uniform cross-sectional area everywhere. Calculate the amount of heat flowing per second through a cross-section of the bent part if the total heat taken out per second from the end at 100°C is 130 J.

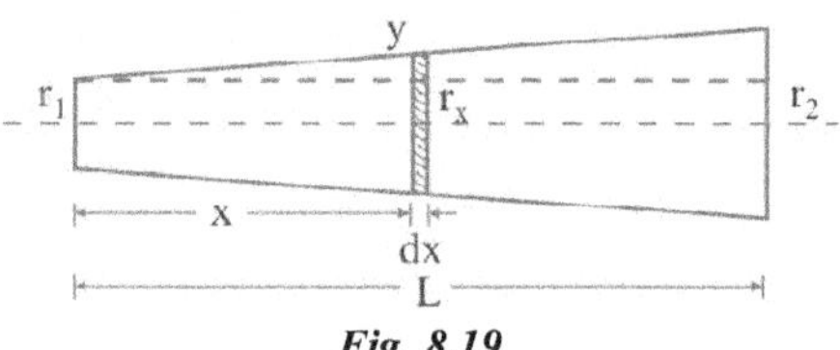

Fig. 8.17

Sol.

Suppose resistance of 10 cm length of frame is R, then

$$R_{AB} = R_{EF} = 2R, \; R_{BE} = 6R$$

Resistance of bent part (length = 60 + 5 + 5 = 70 cm) $R = 7R$

The equivalent network of resistors is shown in figure

Let H_1 and H_2 are the heat in straight and bent parts of the frame, then

$$H_1 \times 6R = H_2 \times 7R$$

or $\qquad 6H_1 = 7H_2 \qquad \dots \text{(i)}$

Given $\quad H_1 + H_1 = 130 \qquad \dots \text{(ii)}$

Solving equations (i) and (ii), we get

$$H_1 = 70 \text{ J/s}$$

and $\qquad H_2 = 60 \text{ J/s} \qquad \textit{Ans.}$

Ex. 8   Find the resistance of the rod as shown in the *Fig. 8.19*. Thermal conductivity of material of the rod is *K*.

Fig. 8.19

Sol.

Choose an element of thickness dx at a distance of x from the left end of the rod. The radius of the element

$$r_x = r_1 + y = r_1 + \left(\frac{r_2 - r_1}{L}\right)x$$

The resistance of the element

$$dR = \frac{\text{length}}{KA_x} = \frac{dx}{K\pi r_x^2}$$

The resistance of whole rod

$$R = \int_0^L \frac{dx}{K\pi r_x^2} = \frac{1}{\pi K}\int_0^L \frac{dx}{\left[r_1 + \left(\frac{r_2 - r_1}{L}\right)x\right]^2}$$

$$= \frac{1}{\pi K}\int_0^L \left[r_1 + \left(\frac{r_2 - r_1}{L}\right)x\right]^{-2} dx$$

$$= \frac{1}{\pi K}\left|\frac{\left[r_1 + \left(\frac{r_2 - r_1}{L}\right)^{-1} x\right]}{(-1)\left(\frac{r_2 - r_1}{L}\right)}\right|_0^L$$

$$= \frac{L}{-\pi K(r_2 - r_1)}\left[\frac{1}{r_1 + \left(\frac{r_2 - r_1}{L}\right)x}\right]_0^L$$

$$= \frac{L}{-\pi K(r_2 - r_1)}\left[\frac{1}{r_2} - \frac{1}{r_1}\right]$$

$$= \frac{L}{\pi K r_1 r_2} \qquad \textit{Ans.}$$

Ex. 9 Two bodies of masses m_1 and m_2 with heat capacities C_1 and C_2 are interconnected by a rod of length L, cross-sectional area A, thermal conductivity K and negligible heat capacity. The whole system is thermally insulated. At time $t = 0$, the temperature of the first body is T_1 and the temperature of the second body is T_2 ($T_1 > T_2$). Find the temperature difference between the two bodies at time t.

Sol.

Let T_1 and T_2 be the instantaneous temperatures of the bodies at time t. If dT_1 is the decrease in temperature of first body and dT_2 is the increase in temperature of the second body, then

$$m_1 C_1\left(-\frac{dT_1}{dt}\right) = KA\left(\frac{T_1 - T_2}{L}\right) \qquad \text{...(i)}$$

$m_1, C_1,$	K	$m_2, C_2,$
T_1	L, A	T_2

Fig. 8.20

$$\text{and} \quad m_2 C_2\left(\frac{dT_2}{dt}\right) = KA\left(\frac{T_1 - T_2}{L}\right) \qquad \text{... (ii)}$$

Equations (i) and (ii) can be written as

$$\frac{dT_1}{dt} = -\frac{KA}{m_1 C_1 L}(T_1 - T_2) \qquad \text{...(iii)}$$

$$\text{and} \quad \frac{dT_2}{dt} = -\frac{KA}{m_2 C_2 L}(T_1 - T_2) \qquad \text{... (iv)}$$

On adding equations (iii) and (iv), we have

$$\frac{d}{dt}(T_1 - T_2) = -\frac{KA}{L}\left(\frac{1}{m_1 C_1} + \frac{1}{m_2 C_2}\right)(T_1 - T_2)$$

$$\text{or} \quad \frac{d(T_1 - T_2)}{T_1 - T_2} = -\frac{KA}{L}\left(\frac{1}{m_1 C_1} + \frac{1}{m_2 C_2}\right)(dt) \qquad \text{... (v)}$$

Integrating equation (v),

$$\int_{(T_1 - T_2)\text{initial}}^{(T_1 - T_2)\text{final}} \frac{d(T_1 - T_2)}{T_1 - T_2} = -\frac{KA}{L}\left(\frac{1}{m_1 C_1} + \frac{1}{m_2 C_2}\right)\int_0^t dt$$

$(T_1 - T_2)$ denotes temperature difference

$$\ln\frac{(T_1 - T_2)\text{final}}{(T_1 - T_2)\text{initial}} = -\frac{KA}{L}\left(\frac{1}{m_1 C_1} + \frac{1}{m_2 C_2}\right)t$$

$$\text{or} \quad (T_1 - T_2)_{\text{final}} = (T_1 - T_2)_{\text{initial}}\, e^{-\frac{KA}{L}\left(\frac{1}{m_1 C_1} + \frac{1}{m_2 C_2}\right)t} \qquad \textbf{Ans.}$$

Ex. 10 n moles of a monoatomic gas at an initial temperature T_0 is enclosed in a cylindrical vessel filled with a light piston. The surrounding air has a temperature T_s ($> T_0$) and the atmospheric pressure is P_a. Heat may be conducted between the surrounding and the gas through the bottom of the cylinder. The bottom has a surface area A, thickness x and thermal conductivity K. Assuming all changes to be slow, find the distance moved by the piston in time t.

Sol.

Light piston will maintain the pressure of the gas equal to the atmospheric pressure (P_a).

Let at any instant, the temperature of the gas is θ. In next small time dt, its temperature increases by $d\theta$.

Heat gained by gas = Heat conducted into the cylinder

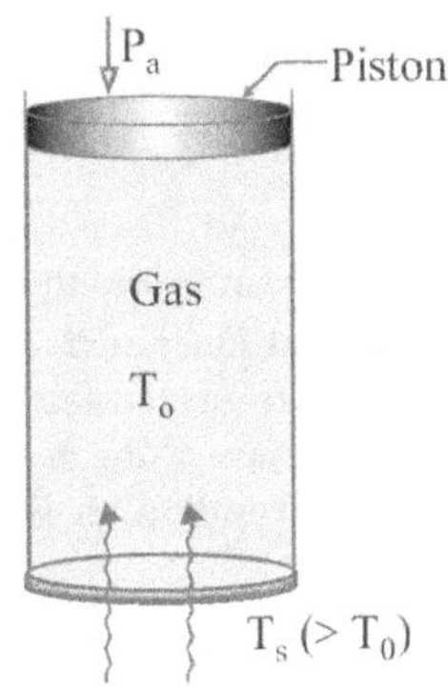

Fig. 8.21

$$\text{or} \quad nC_p(d\theta) = KA\left(\frac{T_s - \theta}{x}\right)dt$$

For monoatomic gas,

$$C_p = \frac{5R}{2}$$

$$\therefore \quad n \times \frac{5R}{2}(d\theta) = KA\left(\frac{T_s - \theta}{x}\right)dt$$

$$\text{or} \quad \frac{d\theta}{(T_s - \theta)} = \frac{2KA}{5nRx}(dt) \qquad \text{... (i)}$$

Let after time t, the temperature of the gas is T, then

$$\int_{T_0}^{T} \frac{d\theta}{(T_s - \theta)} = \frac{2KA}{5nRx}\int_0^t (dt)$$

$$\text{or} \quad -\big|\ln(T_s - \theta)\big|_{T_0}^{T} = \frac{2KA}{5nRx}t$$

$$\text{or} \quad \ln\left(\frac{T_s - T}{T_s - T_0}\right) = -\frac{2KAt}{5nRx}$$

$$\text{or} \quad (T_s - T) = (T_s - T_0)e^{-\left(\frac{2KAt}{5nRx}\right)}$$

If we write $T_s - T = \Delta T$, then

$$\Delta T = (T_s - T_0)e^{-\left(\frac{2KAt}{5nRx}\right)} \qquad \text{...(ii)}$$

By equation of state, we have

$$P\Delta V = nR\Delta T$$

$$\text{or} \quad \Delta V = \frac{nR}{P}\Delta T \qquad \text{... (iii)}$$

From equations (ii) and (iii), we get

$$\Delta V = \frac{nR}{P}\left[(T_s - T_0)e^{-\left(\frac{2KAt}{5nRx}\right)}\right]$$

Let y is the displacement of the piston in time t, then

$$Ay = \Delta V$$

$$\therefore \qquad y = \frac{\Delta V}{A} = \frac{nR}{PA}\left[(T_s - T_0)e^{-\left(\frac{2KAt}{5nRx}\right)}\right] \qquad \textbf{\textit{Ans.}}$$

Ex. 11 A monoatomic ideal gas is contained in a rigid container of volume V with walls of total inner surface area A, thickness x and thermal conductivity K. The gas is at an initial temperature T_0 and pressure P_0. Find the pressure of the gas as a function of time if the temperature of the surrounding air is T_s. All temperatures are in absolute scale.

Sol.

The volume of the gas is constant, so $C_v = \dfrac{3R}{2}$. If the temperature of the gas at time t is θ and next time dt, let temperature of the gas increases by $d\theta$ then

Heat gained by gas = Heat conducted into the container

or $\qquad nC_V(d\theta) = \dfrac{KA(T_s - \theta)}{x}\,dt$

or $\qquad n \times \dfrac{3}{2}R(d\theta) = KA\dfrac{(T_s - \theta)}{x}\,dt$

or $\qquad \dfrac{d\theta}{(T_s - \theta)} = \left(\dfrac{2KA}{3xR}\right)dt$

Integrating above equation, we have

$$\int_{T_0}^{T}\frac{d\theta}{(T_s - \theta)} = \left(\frac{2KA}{3xR}\right)\int_0^t dt$$

or $\qquad -\left|\ln(T_s - \theta)\right|_{T_0}^{T} = \left(\dfrac{2KA}{3xR}\right)t$

or $\qquad \ln\left(\dfrac{T_s - T}{T_s - T_0}\right) = -\left(\dfrac{2KA}{3xR}\right)t$

or $\qquad T_s - T = (T_s - T_0)e^{-\frac{2KA}{3xR}t}$

or $\qquad T = T_s - (T_s - T_0)e^{-\frac{2KA}{3xR}t}$

As the volume remains constant, so

$$\frac{P}{T} = \frac{P_0}{T_0}$$

or $\qquad P = \dfrac{P_0}{T_0}T$

$$= \frac{P_0}{T_0}\left[T_s - (T_s - T_0)e^{-\frac{2KA}{3xR}t}\right] \qquad \textbf{\textit{Ans.}}$$

Ex. 12 A closed cubical box is made of perfectly insulating material and the only way for heat to enter or leave the box is through two solid cylindrical metal plugs, each of cross-sectional area 12 cm² and length 8 cm fixed in the opposite walls of the box. The outer surface of one plug is kept at a temperature of 100°C while the outer surface of the other plug is maintained at a temperature of 4°C. The thermal conductivity of the material of the plug is 2.0 W/m-°C. A source of energy generating 13W is enclosed inside the box. Find the equilibrium temperature of the inner surface of the box assuming that it is the same at all points on the inner surface.

Sol.

Let the temperature of the interior of the box is θ. If H_1 and H_2 are the rate of flow of heats from left and right plugs respectively, then at equilibrium

$$H_1 + P = H_2 \qquad \qquad \ldots \text{(i)}$$

Here P is the power of the source inside the box.

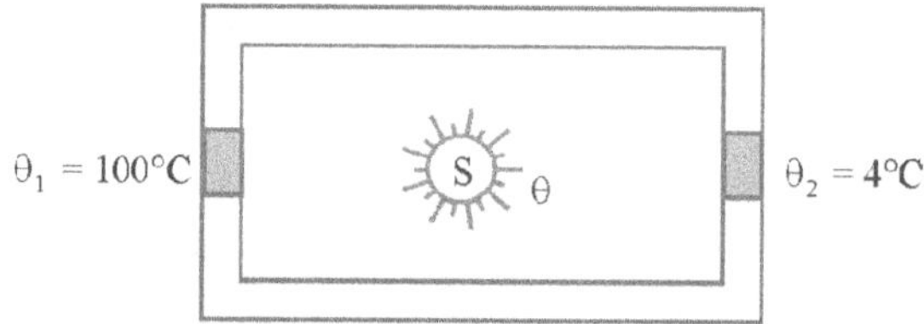

Fig. 8.22

We know that,

$$H_1 = \frac{KA(\theta_1 - \theta)}{x} \quad \text{and} \quad H_2 = \frac{KA(\theta - \theta_2)}{x}$$

Substituting these values in equation (i), we have

$$KA\frac{(\theta_1 - \theta)}{x} + P = \frac{KA(\theta - \theta_2)}{x}$$

Here $\theta_1 = 100°C$, $\theta_2 = 4°C$ and $P = 13W$,

$$K = 2.0 \text{ W/m-C}, A = 12 \times 10^{-4}\,\text{m}^2, x = 0.08\text{ m}$$

$$\therefore \quad 2 \times \frac{(12 \times 10^{-4}) \times (100 - \theta)}{0.08} + 13 = \frac{2 \times (12 \times 10^{-4}) \times (\theta - 4)}{0.08}$$

$$3 \times 10^{-2}(100 - \theta) = 3 \times 10^{-2}(\theta - 4) - 13$$

After solving, we get

$$\theta = 268.67°C \qquad \textbf{\textit{Ans.}}$$

8.11 APPLICATION OF CONDUCTIVITY IN DAILY LIFE

1. **A new quilt is warmer than an old quilt :** New quilts and bed clothing filled with cotton become bad conductor of heat due to air traps in pores. This prevent the conduction of heat from the surroundings and therefore we feel warmer.

2. **Ice is packed in saw dust :** Saw dust and air trapped inside it becomes poor conductors of heat. This prevents the conduction of heat from surroundings to the ice and therefore ice will not melt.

3. **In winter, a metallic handle appears colder than the wooden door :** In winter, the temperature of human body remains higher than the surrounding objects. When we touch the metallic handle, heat flows from our body to the handle and feels cold. But in case of wooden door, on being bad conductor, heat does not flow, so it does not feel as cold as the metallic handle.

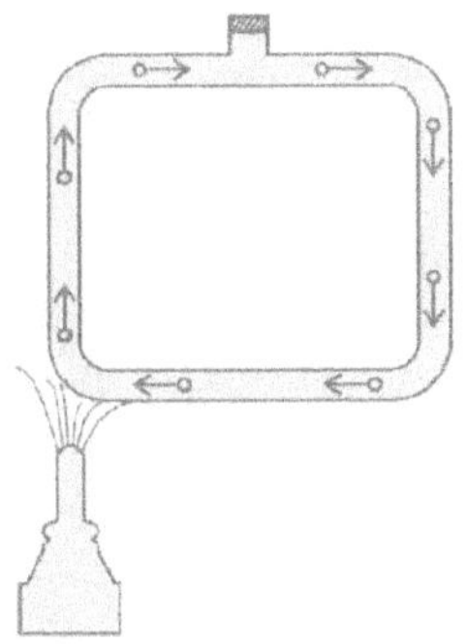

Fig. 8.23

8.12 CONVECTION

It is the process by which heat flows from the region of higher temperature to the region of lower temperature by the actual movement of the particles of the medium. There is no simple equation for convective heat transfer as there is for conduction. Convective heat transfer depends on many factors, such as the shape and orientation of the surface, the mechanical and thermal properties of the fluid. For practical calculations, we can define heat current due to convection as ;

$$H = hA\Delta T$$

where h is called convection coefficient. A is the surface area and ΔT is the temperature difference between the surface and the main body of the fluid.

Experiment1 : Take a glass tube, filled with water and put some charcoal powder in the tube, and starts heating it from one of its sides (see *Fig. 8.23*). The heated water molecules rise up (due to low density) and cold water molecules take their places, coming from the side tube and therefore a convection current is set-up in the whole tube. The direction of movement of water molecules is indicated by the movement of the charcoal particles.

Experiment 2 : Take a flask containing water and put some crystals of potassium permagnet. When flask starts heating, coloured streaks of water rise up due to lower density. The denser cold water takes its place by moving downwards. Thus convection current is setup in the water.

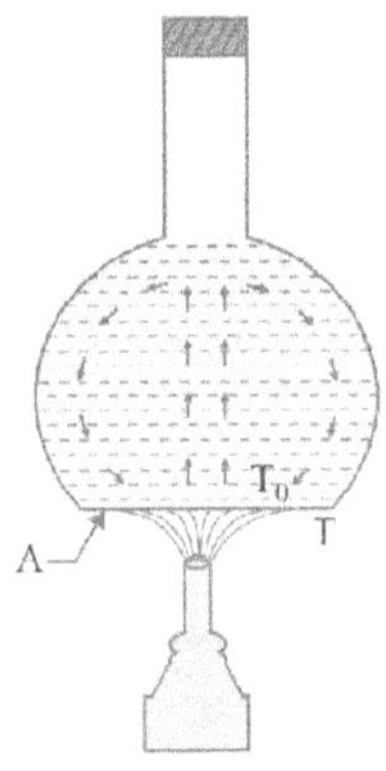

Fig. 8.24

Natural convection : If the material of the medium moves due to difference in density caused by difference in temperature, the process of heat transfer is called natural or free convection. Natural convection currents always move upward due to difference in density and gravity. Different types of winds in the atmosphere are originated due to natural convection.

Forced convection : If the heated material is forced to move by a machine like a blower or a pump, the process of heat transfer is called forced convection. Heat convector, hair drier, air-conditioning are the examples of forced convection.

8.13 PHENOMENON BASED ON CONVECTION

(i) **Monsoon :** In summer, the surface of the earth of the Indian subcontinent becomes hotter than the Indian ocean. This sets up convection current with hot air from the land rising and moving towards the Indian Ocean, while the moisture laden air from the ocean moves towards the land. When obstructed by mountains, the moist air rushes upwards to great height and gets cooled. In this process moisture condenses and causes rains in all over India.

(ii) **Trade winds :** The surface of the earth gets heated more at the equator than at the poles. Warm air at the equator moves up and cold air from the poles moves towards the equator. In the northern hemisphere, it is coming from the north and due to the rotation of the earth from west to east, the wind appears to come from north-east. In the southern hemisphere, the wind appears to be from south-west. These winds are called trade winds because they were used by traders for sailing their vessels in ancient days.

(iii) Land and sea breezes : Sun shines almost uniformly on the land mass near coastal regions, giving equal amount of heat energy. However the temperature of land rises more rapidly as compared to sea, because specific heat capacity of land is much smaller than that of water. Thus the air above the land becomes hot and light and hence rises up. This results decrease in pressure over land mass. So the colder air starts blowing from sea towards land and thereby setting up sea breeze.

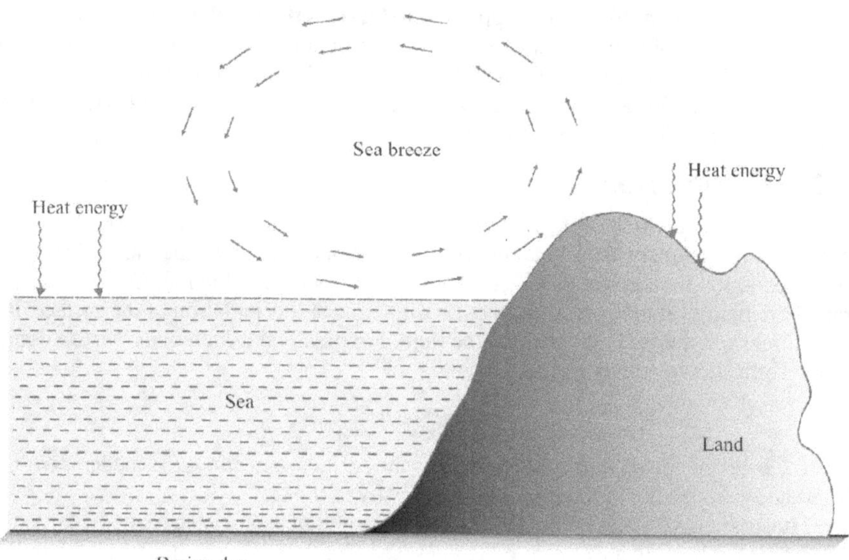

Fig. 8.25

During night the land as well as sea water radiate out heat energy. However the temperature of land decreases more paridly as compared to sea water due to higher specific heat of water. Thus at night the temperature of sea water becomes more than land. The air above sea water become warm and light and rises up. The cold air from land takes its place. This set-up land breeze.

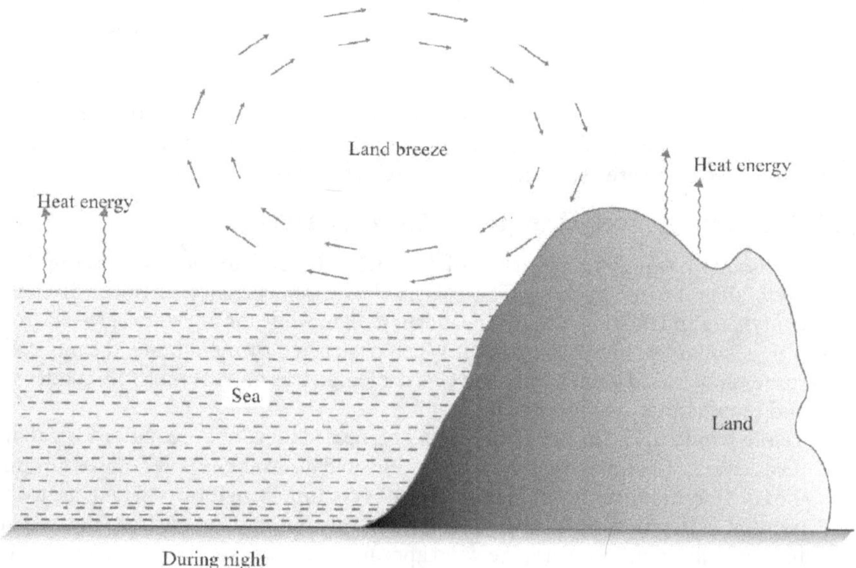

Fig. 8.26

8.14 RADIATION

Radiation is the process by which heat is transmitted from one place to another without heating and transferring the intervening medium.

Properties of thermal radiation

(i)   These are electromagnetic waves having wavelength range from $1\,\mu m$ to $100\,\mu m$. There are also called infrared waves.

(ii)   Thermal radiations travel in straight line with the speed of light.

(iii)   They obey the laws of reflection and refraction like light does.

(iv)   They show the phenomenon of interference, diffraction and polarisation.

Note: Word 'radiation' uses for process and energy both.

Reflectance, absorptance and transmittance

When thermal radiations falls on a body, they are partly reflected, absorbed and rest get transmitted. Let Q amount of thermal energy is incident on a body. Suppose the part R is reflected, A is absorbed and T is transmitted, then

$$R + A + T \;=\; Q \qquad \dots (1)$$

Dividing both sides of equation (1), by Q we have

$$\frac{R}{Q} + \frac{A}{Q} + \frac{T}{Q} \;=\; 1 \qquad \dots (2)$$

where $\dfrac{R}{Q} = r$, is called reflectance

$\dfrac{A}{Q} = a$, is called absorptance and

$\dfrac{T}{Q} = t$, is called transmittance.

Thus equation (2) takes the form $r + a + t \;=\; 1$

For any specific wavelength λ, we can write,

$$r_\lambda + a_\lambda + t_\lambda \;=\; 1.$$

Special cases :

(i)   If a body does not transmit the radiations, $t = 0$, then $r + a = 1$. It shows that if r is more, a is less and vice versa. That is good reflectors will be bad absorbers and viceversa.

(ii)   If a body neither reflects nor transmits any radiation, $r = 0$ and $t = 0$, then $a = 1$, such a body is called a black body.

8.15 SPECTRAL ABSORPTIVE POWER

The absorptive power of any body for a given wavelength λ is defined as the ratio of amount of heat energy absorbed by certain surface area of the body in a given time to the total heat energy incident on that area and in same time within a unit wavelength range around the wavelength λ. It can be denoted by a_λ.

If dQ is the quantity of heat radiations incident on the surface in one second and Q_1 is the quantity of heat absorbed by the surface in a wavelength range λ to $\lambda + d\lambda$, then

$$a_\lambda = \frac{Q_1}{(dQ)} \text{ or } Q_1 = a_\lambda (dQ)$$

8.16 SPECTRAL EMISSIVE POWER

The emissive power of a body at a given temperature and for a given wavelength λ is defined as the amount of radiant energy emitted by unit surface area of the body per unit time within a unit wavelength range around the wavelength λ. If e_λ is the emissive power of the body, then the radiant energy emitted by it in one second = $e_\lambda (d\lambda)$.

The SI unit of emissive power is W/m^2-Å.

8.17 EMISSIVITY

It is defined as the ratio of the heat energy radiated per unit surface area per second by the given body to the amount of the heat energy radiated per unit area per second by a black body of the same temperature. If e and E are the emissive powers of any body and black body respectively, then emissivity

$$\varepsilon = \frac{e}{E}$$

It is a dimensionless quantity. Its value ranges from 0 to 1. For a black body, it is 1.

8.18 BLACK BODY

A perfectly black body is one which absorbs all the heat radiation incident on it. When such a body is placed inside an isothermal enclosure, it will emit all the radiations of the enclosure after it is in equilibrium with the enclosure.

Fery's black body

It is not possible to construct a perfectly black body, but a body showing close approximation to a perfectly black body can be constructed. Fery constructed such a black body. It has a hollow copper sphere and coated with lamp black on its inner surface. A fine hole is made and a pointed projection is made just in front of the hole. When the radiations enter the hole, they suffer multiple reflections and are completely absorbed. This body behaves as a black body.

When this body is heated, the heat radiations come out of the hole. It should be remembered that only the hole, not the walls of the body, acts as the black body emitter.

8.19 KIRCHHOFF'S LAW

It states that at any temperature, the ratio of the emissive power to the absorptive power of any body is a constant, and equal to the emissive power of the perfectly black body at the same temperature.

Consider any body (not black body) which is suspended in a hollow enclosure maintained at a constant temperature.

The amount of energy absorbed per unit area per unit time $= a_\lambda\,(dQ)$

The amount of energy emitted per unit area per second $= e_\lambda\,(d\lambda)$

As the body is in thermal equilibrium, so $e_\lambda\,(d\lambda) = a_\lambda\,(dQ)$ ...(1)

Suppose a black body at the same temperature is suspended in the enclosure. For this body, $a_\lambda = 1$ and $e_\lambda = E_\lambda$, so equation (1) becomes

$$E_\lambda\,(d\lambda) = (dQ) \qquad \text{...(2)}$$

Dividing equation (1) by (2), we get

$$\frac{e_\lambda}{E_\lambda} = a_\lambda \qquad \text{...(3)}$$

or
$$\frac{e_\lambda}{a_\lambda} = E_\lambda \ (\text{constant})$$

The above equation can be stated as ; good emitter is a good absorber.

As
$$\frac{e_\lambda}{E_\lambda} = \varepsilon,$$

∴   from equation (3), we have

$$a_\lambda = \varepsilon$$

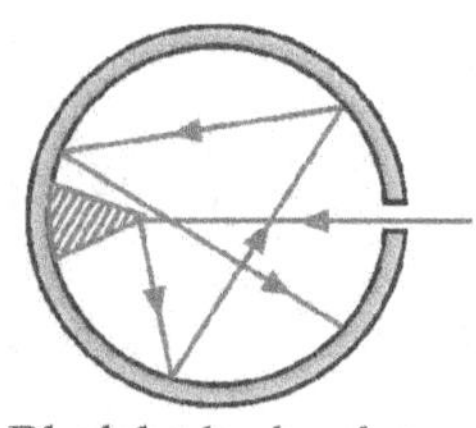

Black body absorber

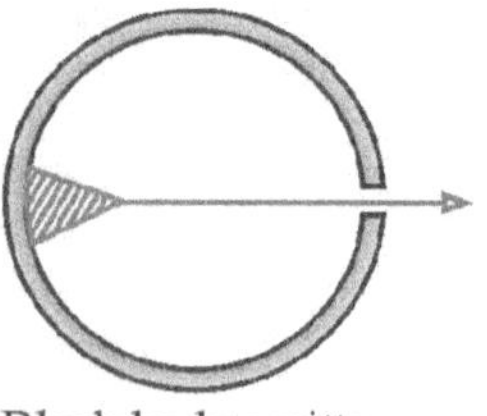

Black body emitter

Fig. 8.27

Thermos flask

A thermos flask is constructed by a double walled glass bottle. The space in between the two walls is evacuated and sealed. By doing this, heat can not go out by conduction and convection. The inner surface of the outer wall and outer surface of inner wall are highly polished, to prevent heat loss by radiation. When a hot liquid is kept in the bottle, it remains hot for a long time. Similarly ice kept inside the flask will not melt for a long time.

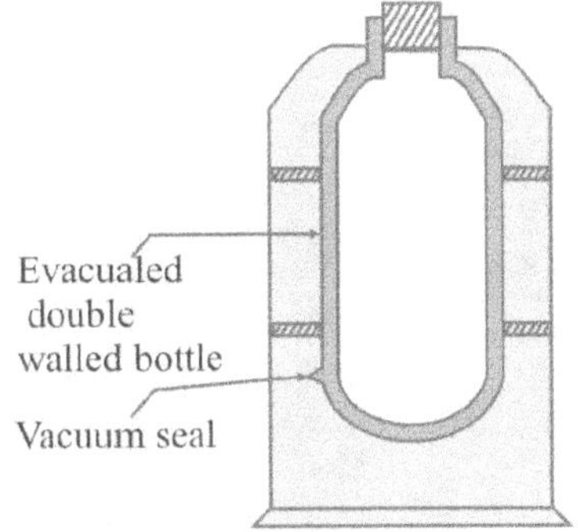

Fig. 8.28

8.20 PREVOST THEORY OF HEAT EXCHANGE (1792)

According to this theory, all bodies radiate thermal radiation at all temperatures. Besides, body also absorbs radiations from its surroundings. This is known as theory of heat exchange. According to this theory:

(i) All bodies at temperature above 0 K emit radiation to the surroundings and gain from the surroundings at all the time.

(ii) The amount of heat radiated per second depends on the nature of the surface, its area and its temperature, and it does affect by the presence of surrounding bodies.

(iii) The rise or fall in temperature of a body is the net result of exchange of heat radiations between body and the surroundings.

8.21 STEFAN -BOLTZMANN LAW

According to this law, the rate of emission of heat energy by unit area of a perfectly black body is proportional to the fourth power of its absolute temperature of its surface. Thus

$$E \propto T^4$$

or

$$E = \sigma T^4 \ \text{W/m}^2$$

Here σ is a universal constant called Stefan's constant. Its values is 5.67×10^8 W/m^2-K^4. If H is the rate of energy radiated by a blackbody of surface area A, then

$$H = EA = \sigma A T^4$$

If T_0 is the temperature of the surrounding and ε is the emissivity of the body, then the net rate of loss of energy per unit area will be ;

$$E_{net} = \varepsilon\sigma(T^4 - T_0^{\ 4}) \ \text{W/m}^2$$

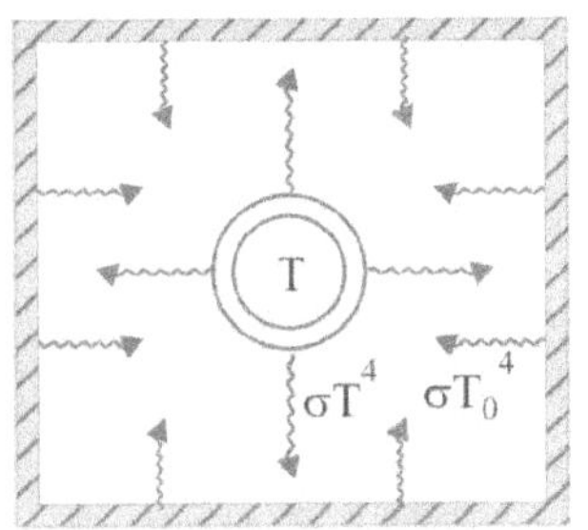

Fig. 8.29

8.22 NEWTON'S LAW OF COOLING

It states that the rate of cooling of the body is directly proportional to the temperature difference between body and the surrounding, provided it to be small.

If T and T_0 are the temperatures of the body and the surrounding respectively and A is the surface area of the body, then by Stefan-Boltzmann law, the rate of loss of heat due to radiation

$$H_1 = \varepsilon\sigma A(T^4 - T_0^{\ 4})$$

If ΔT is the temperature difference between body and surroundings, then we can write

$$\Delta T = T - T_0 \ \text{ or } \ T = T_0 + \Delta T$$

$$\therefore \quad H_1 = \varepsilon\sigma A\left[(T_0 + \Delta T)^4 - T_0^{\ 4}\right]$$

$$= \varepsilon\sigma A\left[T_0^{\ 4}\left(1 + \frac{\Delta T}{T_0}\right)^4 - T_0^{\ 4}\right]$$

If ΔT is small, then

$$\left(1 + \frac{\Delta T}{T_0}\right)^4 \simeq 1 + 4\frac{\Delta T}{T_0}$$

Thus, we have

$$H_1 = \varepsilon\sigma A\left[T_0^4\left(1+\frac{4\Delta T}{T_0}\right) - T_0^4 \right]$$

$$= \varepsilon\sigma A\left[T_0^4 + 4T_0^3\Delta T - T_0^4 \right]$$

or
$$H_1 = 4\varepsilon\sigma AT_0^3(\Delta T)$$

or
$$H_1 = k_1 A(T - T_0) \qquad \ldots(1)$$

where k_1 is a constant. The body may loose heat due to convection also. The rate of loss of heat by convection can be written as

$$H_2 = k_2 A(T - T_0) \qquad \ldots(2)$$

The net rate of loss of heat energy

$$H = H_1 + H_2 = (k_1 + k_2)A(T - T_0) \qquad \ldots(3)$$

If c is the specific heat capacity of the body and m its mass, then

$$H = mc\left(-\frac{dT}{dt}\right)$$

or
$$-\frac{dT}{dt} = \frac{H}{mc} = \frac{(k_1 + k_2)A(T - T_0)}{mc} \qquad \ldots(4)$$

or
$$\frac{dT}{dt} = -k(T - T_0) \qquad \ldots(5)$$

The constant k depends on the surface involved and the surrounding conditions.

Note:

1. From equation (3), it is clear that the rate of loss of heat $H \propto A$. Thus if two bodies of equal surface areas, one solid and other hollow are kept at same temperature difference, then their ratio of loss of heat will be equal.

2. For spherical body, $A = 4\pi r^2$. $\therefore H \propto r^2$

3. From equation (4), $-\dfrac{dT}{dt} \propto \dfrac{A}{mc}(T - T_0)$. Thus two bodies of same material and equal surface areas, one solid other hollow $(m_s > m_H)$, then rate of cooling of solid body will be less.

4. For spherical body, $\dfrac{A}{mc} = \left[\dfrac{4\pi r^2}{\frac{4}{3}\pi r^3 \rho c}\right] \propto \left(\dfrac{1}{r}\right).$

   $\therefore$ Rate of cooling of body is inversely proportional to its radius, provided other things remain constant.

5. If temperature of the body falls from T_1 and T_2 in time t, then we can write

   $$T = \frac{T_1 + T_2}{2},$$

   and
   $$\frac{T_1 - T_2}{t} = k\left[\frac{T_1 + T_2}{2} - T_0\right]$$

6. We have,
$$-\frac{dT}{dt} = k(T - T_0)$$

or
$$\int_{T_i}^{T_f} \frac{dT}{T - T_0} = -\int_0^t k\,dt$$

$$\left|\ln(T - T_0)\right|_{T_i}^{T_f} = -kt$$

or
$$\ln\left(\frac{T_f - T_0}{T_i - T_0}\right) = -kt$$

or
$$(T_f - T_0) = (T_i - T_0)e^{-kt}$$

or
$$T_f = T_0 + (T_i - T_0)e^{-kt}$$

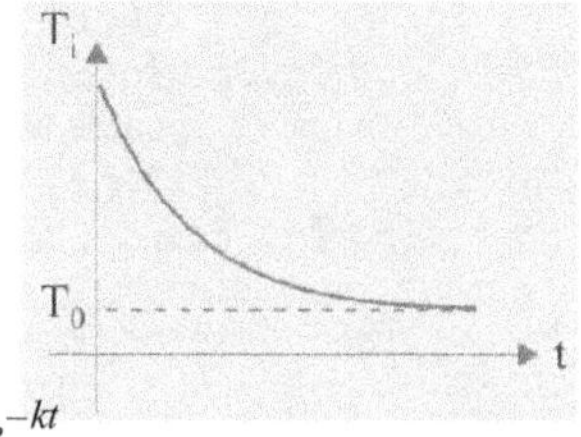

Fig. 8.30

Ex. 13 A spherical body with radius 12 cm radiates 450 W power at 500 K. If the radius were halved and the temperature doubled, what would be the power radiated?

Sol.

By Stefan's law, power radiated
$$E = \varepsilon\sigma AT^4 = \varepsilon\sigma(4\pi r^2)T^4$$

When radius is halved and temperature is doubled, power radiates
$$E = E' = \varepsilon\sigma\left[4\pi\left(\frac{r}{2}\right)^2\right](2T)^4 = 4E$$

$$= 4 \times 450 = 1800 \text{ W}$$

Ex. 14 A thin brass rectangular sheet of sides 15.0 and 12.0 cm is heated in a furnace to 600°C, and taken out. How much electric power is needed to maintain the sheet at this temperature, given that its emissivity is 0.250 ? Neglect heat loss due to convection (Stefan - Boltzmann constant, $\sigma = 5.67 \times 10^{-8}$ W/m^2 - k^4).

Sol.

Area of the both sides of the plate
$$A = 2 \times (15.0) \times (12.0) \times 10^{-4}\,\text{m}^2$$
$$= 3.60 \times 10^{-2}\,\text{m}^2$$

The energy radiated by the plate
$$= \varepsilon\sigma AT^4$$
$$= 0.250 \times 5.67 \times 10^{-8} \times 3.60 \times 10^{-2} \times$$
$$(600 + 273)^4$$
$$= 5.10 \times 10^{-12} \times 873^4 = 296.4 \ W \qquad \textbf{\textit{Ans.}}$$

Ex. 15 A body cools in 7 minute from 60°C to 40°C. What will be its temperature after the next 7 minute? The temperature of the surroundings is 10°C. Assume that Newton's law of cooling holds good throughout the process.

Sol.

Newton's law of cooling can be written as :
$$\frac{T_1 - T_2}{t} = k\left[\frac{T_1 + T_2}{2} - T_0\right]$$

In first case ; $T_1 = 60$°C, $T_2 = 40$°C, $T_0 = 10$°C and $t = 7$ minute

$$\therefore \qquad \frac{60 - 40}{7} = k\left[\frac{60 + 40}{2} - 10\right]$$

or
$$k = \frac{1}{14}$$

In second case; $T_1 = 40$°C and $T_2 = ?$, $T = 7$ minute

$$\therefore \qquad \frac{40 - T_2}{7} = \frac{1}{14}\left[\frac{40 + T_2}{2} - 10\right]$$

or
$$80 - 2T_2 = 20 + \frac{T_2}{2} - 10$$

or
$$T_2 = 28\text{°C} \qquad \textbf{\textit{Ans.}}$$

Ex. 16 A hot body placed in air is cooled down according to Newton's law of cooling, the rate of decrease of temperature being k times the temperature difference from the surrounding. Starting from $t = 0$, find the time in which the body will lose half the maximum heat it can lose.

Sol.

We have,
$$-\frac{dT}{dt} = k(T - T_0)$$

where T_0 is the temperature of the surrounding. If T_1 is the initial temperature and T is the temperature at any time t, then

$$\int_{T_1}^{T} \frac{dT}{(T - T_0)} = -k\int_0^t dt$$

or
$$\left|\ln(T - T_0)\right|_{T_1}^{T} = -kt$$

or
$$\ln\left[\frac{T - T_0}{T_1 - T_0}\right] = -kt$$

or
$$T = T_0 + (T_1 - T_0)e^{-kt} \qquad \ldots\text{(i)}$$

The body continues to lose heat till its temperature becomes equal to that of the surrounding. The loss of heat
$$Q = mc(T_1 - T_0)$$

If the body loss half of the maximum lose that it can, then decrease in temperature

$$\frac{Q}{2} = mc\left(\frac{T_1 - T_0}{2}\right)$$

If body loses this heat in time t, then its temperature at time t' will be

$$T_1 - \left(\frac{T_1 - T_0}{2}\right) = \frac{T_1 + T_0}{2}$$

Putting these values in equation (i), we have

$$\frac{T_1 + T_0}{2} = T_0 + (T_1 - T_0)e^{-kt'}$$

or

$$\frac{T_1 - T_0}{2} = (T_1 - T_0)e^{-kt'}$$

or

$$e^{-kt'} = \frac{1}{2}$$

or

$$t' = \frac{\ln 2}{k} \qquad\qquad \textbf{\textit{Ans.}}$$

Ex. 17 *Fig. 8.31 shows water in a container having 2.0 mm thick walls made of a material of thermal conductivity 0.50 W/m-°C. The container is kept in a melting ice bath at 0°C. The total surface area in contact with water is 0.05 m². A wheel is clamped inside the water and is coupled to a block of mass M as shown in the figure. As the block goes down, the wheel rotates. It is found that after some time a steady state is reached in which the block goes down with a constant speed of 10 cm/s and the temperature of the water remains constant at 1.0°C. Find the mass M of the block. Assume that the heat flows out of the water only through the walls in contact. Take g = 10 m/s².*

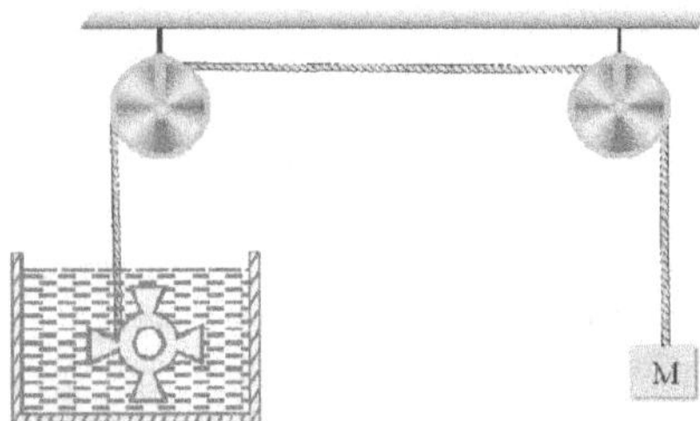

Fig. 8.31

Sol.

At steady state, Rate of doing work by gravity on block
$$M = \text{Rate of energy produced}$$

or

$$\frac{d}{dt}[Mgh] = \frac{d}{dt}\left[Q + \frac{1}{2}Mv^2\right]$$

or

$$Mg\left(\frac{dh}{dt}\right) = \frac{dQ}{dt} + \frac{M}{2} \times 2v\frac{dv}{dt} \qquad \dots \text{(i)}$$

As block goes down with constant velocity, so $\dfrac{dh}{dt} = v$ and $\dfrac{dv}{dt} = 0$

$\therefore$

$$Mgv = \frac{dQ}{dt} \qquad\qquad \dots\text{(ii)}$$

Here

$$\frac{dQ}{dt} = KA\frac{\Delta T}{L}$$

$\therefore$

$$Mgv = KA\frac{\Delta T}{L}$$

or

$$M \times 10 \times (0.1) = 0.50 \times 0.50\frac{(1.0 - 0)}{2 \times 10^{-3}}$$

or

$$M = 12.5\,\text{kg} \qquad\qquad \textbf{\textit{Ans.}}$$

Ex. 18 A copper sphere is suspended in an evacuated chamber maintained at 300 K. The sphere is maintained at a constant temperature of 500 K by heating it electrically. A total of 210 W of electric power is needed to do it. When the surface of the copper sphere is completely blackened, 700 W is needed to maintain the same temperature of the sphere. Calculate the emissivity of copper.

Sol.

Let ε is the emissivity of the sphere then by Stefan's law

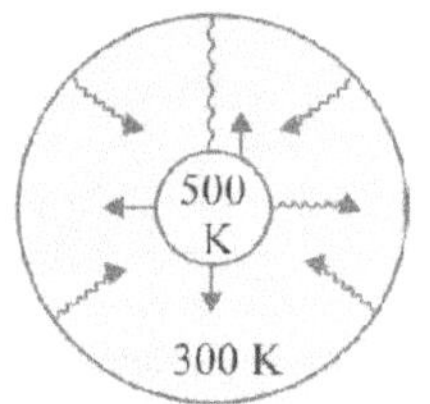

Fig. 8.32

$$E = \varepsilon\sigma A(T^4 - T_0^{\,4})$$

or

$$210 = \varepsilon\sigma A(500^4 - 300^4) \qquad \dots \text{(i)}$$

When sphere is blackened, it behaves like a perfectly blackbody, so we have

$$700 = \sigma A(500^4 - 300^4) \qquad \dots \text{(ii)}$$

Dividing equation (i) and (ii), we get

$$\varepsilon = 0.3 \qquad\qquad \textbf{\textit{Ans.}}$$

Ex. 19 A solid copper sphere (density ρ and specific heat c) of radius r at an initial temperature 200 K is suspended inside a chamber whose walls are almost at 0 K. Calculate the time required for the temperature of sphere to drop to 100 K.

Sol.

Let T is the temperature at any time and $\left(\dfrac{dT}{dt}\right)$ is the rate of fall of temperature. Then the rate of loss of heat

$$= mc\left(-\frac{dT}{dt}\right) \qquad \dots \text{(i)}$$

The rate of heat lost by sphere due to radiation only

$$E = \sigma AT^4 \qquad \dots \text{(ii)}$$

Equating equations (i) and (ii), we have

$$mc\left(-\frac{dT}{dt}\right) = \sigma A(T^4 - 0^4) = \sigma AT^4$$

or

$$\frac{dT}{T^4} = \frac{-\sigma A}{mc}dt$$

Integrating both sides of above equation

$$\int_{200}^{100} T^{-4}dT = -\frac{\sigma A}{mc}\int_0^t dt$$

$$\left.\frac{T^{-3}}{-3}\right|_{200}^{100} = -\frac{\sigma A}{mc}t$$

$\therefore$

$$t = \frac{mc}{3\sigma A}\left[\frac{1}{T^3}\right]_{200}^{100}$$

$$= \frac{\left(\frac{4}{3}\pi r^3 \rho\right)c}{3\sigma \times 4\pi r^2}\left[\frac{1}{100^3} - \frac{1}{200^3}\right]$$

$$= \frac{r\rho c}{\sigma \times 9 \times 10^{+6}}\left[1 - \frac{1}{8}\right]$$

$$= \frac{7}{72}\frac{r\rho c}{\sigma} \times 10^{-6} \; s \qquad\qquad \textbf{\textit{Ans.}}$$

Ex. 20 One end of a rod of length L and cross-sectional area A is kept in a furnace of temperature T_1. The other end of the rod is kept at a temperature T_2. The thermal conductivity of the material of the rod is K and emissivity is ε. It is given that $T_2 = T_s + \Delta T$, where $\Delta T \ll T_s$, T_s being the temperative of surrounding. If $\Delta T \propto (T_1 - T_s)$, find the proportionality constant. Consider that heat is lost only by radiation at the end where the temperature of the rod is T_2.

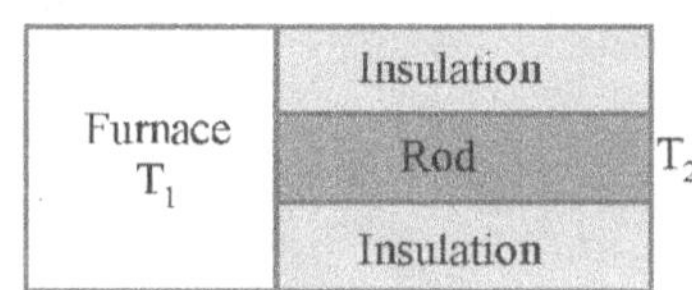

Fig. 8.33

Sol. At steady state rate of heat gained by left end of the rod
$=$ Rate of heat radiates by right end of the rod

or $\qquad KA\dfrac{(T_1 - T_2)}{L} = \varepsilon A\sigma(T_2^{\;4} - T_s^{\;4}) \qquad \ldots \text{(i)}$

Given $\qquad T_2 = T_s + \Delta T$

$\therefore \qquad T_2^{\;4} = (T_s + \Delta T)^4 = T_s^{\;4}\left(1 + \dfrac{\Delta T}{T_s}\right)^4$

As $\Delta T \ll T_s$, so by Binomial theorem, we get

$$T_2^{\;4} = T_s^{\;4}\left(1 + 4\frac{\Delta T}{T_s}\right)$$

or $\qquad T_2^{\;4} - T_s^{\;4} = 4T_s^{\;3}\Delta T$

Also $\qquad T_2 = T_s + \Delta T$

Substituting these values in equation (i), we have

$$KA\frac{[T_1 - (T_s + \Delta T)]}{L} = \varepsilon A\sigma(4T_s^{\;3}\Delta T)$$

or $\qquad K\dfrac{(T_1 - T_s)}{L} - \dfrac{K}{L}\Delta T = 4\varepsilon\sigma T_s^{\;3}\Delta T$

or $\qquad K\dfrac{(T_1 - T_s)}{L} = \left(4\varepsilon\sigma T_s^{\;3} + \dfrac{K}{L}\right)\Delta T$

or $\qquad \Delta T = \dfrac{K(T_1 - T_s)}{(4\varepsilon\sigma L T_s^{\;3} + K)} \qquad \ldots \text{(ii)}$

It is given that $\qquad \Delta T = C(T_1 - T_s)$

$\therefore \qquad$ Constant of proportionality

$$C = \left[\frac{K}{4\varepsilon\sigma L T_s^{\;3} + K}\right] \qquad\qquad \textbf{\textit{Ans.}}$$

8.23 WIEN'S DISPLACEMENT LAW

The intensity of energy radiated by a black body is not uniformly distributed over all the wavelengths but it is maximum for a particular wavelength λ_m. The value of λ_m decreases with the increase of temperature.

According to Wien's law the product of the wavelength corresponding to maximum intensity and absolute temperature is a constant i.e.,

$$\lambda_m T = b \text{ (constant)}$$

where b is Wien's constant. Its value is 2.9×10^{-3} m-K.

8.24 SOLAR CONSTANT

It is the amount of radiant energy that a unit area of a perfectly black body placed at a mean distance of the earth from the sun would receive per second in the absence of the atmosphere with its surface held perpendicular to the sun rays.

Temperature of the sun

Let R_s be the radius and T be the temperature of sun, then the solar energy radiated per second $\qquad E = \sigma A T^4 = 4\pi R_s^{\;2}\sigma T^4$

If r is the mean distance of the earth from the sun then surface area over which solar energy will spread $\qquad\qquad = 4\pi r^2$

Let S is the solar constant, then by the definition

$$S = \frac{E}{4\pi r^2} = \frac{4\pi R_s^{\;2}\sigma T^4}{4\pi r^2}$$

or $\qquad S = \sigma T^4\left(\dfrac{R_s}{r}\right)^2$

or $\qquad T = \left[\dfrac{r^2 S}{R_s^{\;2}\sigma}\right]^{1/4}$

By this formula the surface temperature of sun is found to be 5742 K.

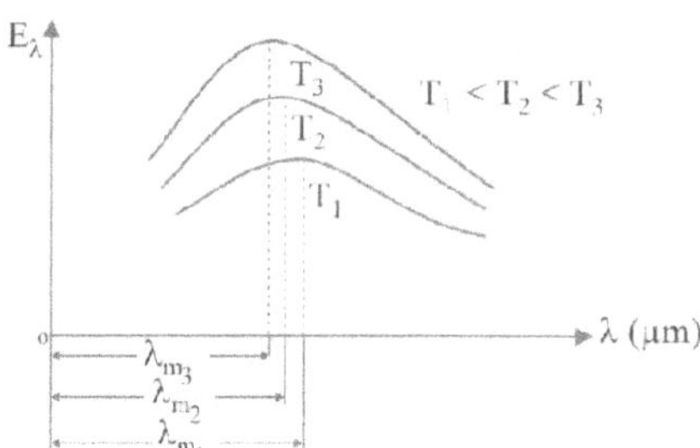

Fig. 8.34

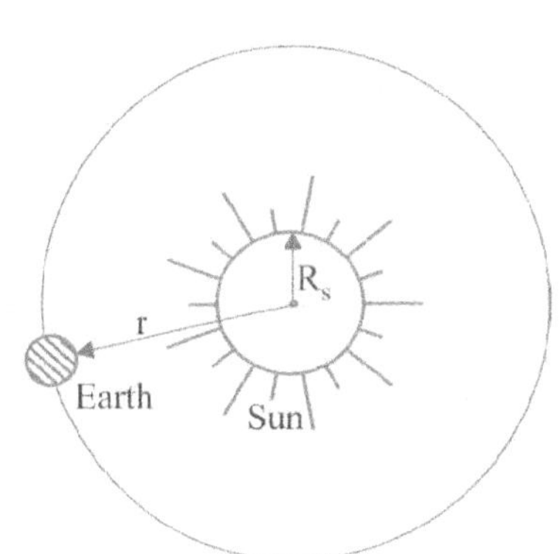

Fig. 8.35

Ex. 21 The spectral energy distribution of the sun has a maximum at 4753 $\mathring{A}$. If the temperature of the sun is 6050 K, what is the temperature of a star for which this maximum is at 9506 $\mathring{A}$?

Sol. Given $\qquad \lambda_m = 4753\ \mathring{A}$, $T = 6050\ K$

$$\lambda'_m = 9506\ \mathring{A}$$

If T' is the temperature of star, then

$$\lambda_m T = \lambda'_m T'$$

or $\qquad T' = \dfrac{\lambda_m T}{\lambda'_m} = \dfrac{4753 \times 6050}{9506} = 3025\ K$ ***Ans.***

Ex. 22 An indirectly heated filament is radiating maximum energy of wavelength 2.16×10^{-5} cm. Find the net amount of heat energy lost per second per unit area, the temperature of surrounding air is 13°C. Given $b = 0.288$ cm - K, $\sigma = 5.77 \times 10^{-5}$ erg/s - cm^2 - K^4.

Sol.

If T is the surface temperature of the filament, then

$$\lambda_m T = b$$

or $\qquad T = \dfrac{b}{\lambda_m} = \dfrac{0.288}{2.16 \times 10^{-5}} = 13333.3\ K$

The temperature of surrounding air $T_0 = 13 + 273 = 286 K$

The net amount of energy radiated per unit area per second

$$E = \sigma(T^4 - T_0^4)$$

$$= 5.77 \times 10^{-5} \left[(13333.3)^4 - (286)^4 \right]$$

$$= 1.824 \times 10^{12}\ \text{erg/s-cm}^2 \text{d} \qquad\qquad ***Ans.***$$

Ex. 23 Two bodies A and B have thermal emissivity of 0.01 and 0.81, respectively. The outer surface areas of the two bodies are the same. The two bodies emit total radiant power at the same rate. The wavelength λ_B corresponding to maximum spectral radiancy in the radiation from B is shifted from the wavelength corresponding to maximum spectral radiancy in the radiation from A by 1.00 μm. The temperature of A is 5802 K. Find temperature of B and wavelength corresponding to maximum spectral radiancy.

Sol.

If T_A and T_B are the temperatures of the bodies A and B respectively, then

$$\varepsilon_A \sigma T_A^{\ 4} = \varepsilon_B \sigma T_B^{\ 4}$$

$$\therefore \quad T_B = \left(\dfrac{\varepsilon_A}{\varepsilon_B}\right)^{1/4} T_A = \left(\dfrac{0.01}{0.81}\right)^{1/4} \times 5802$$

$$= 1934\ \text{K}$$

By Wien's displacement law, we have

$$\lambda_A T_A = \lambda_B T_B$$

or $\qquad \lambda_A \times 5802 = \lambda_B \times 1934$

or $\qquad \lambda_A = \dfrac{\lambda_B}{3} \qquad\qquad\qquad \ldots \text{(i)}$

It is also given

$$\lambda_B - \lambda_A = 10^{-6} \qquad\qquad \ldots \text{(ii)}$$

Solving equations (i) and (ii) , we get

$$\lambda_B = 1.5 \times 10^{-6} m = 1.5 \mu m \qquad\qquad ***Ans.***$$

Note :

Solar spectrum : When light from the sun is seen through a spectrometer, there observed several dark lines over continuous spectrum. These dark lines are called Franhoffer lines. By comparing the wavelengths of these dark lines with those emitted by elements on the earth, we have identified various elements like H, He, Na, N_2 etc. in the atmosphere of the sun.

Review of formulae & Important Points

1. **Rate of heat flow in conduction**

$$H = KA\dfrac{(T_1 - T_2)}{L} = -KA\dfrac{\Delta T}{L}$$

2. **Thermal resistance** $R_H = \dfrac{L}{KA}$

3. **Equivalent thermal conductivity :** When two rods of thermal conductivities K_1 and K_2 are placed in

(i)   Series : $\qquad K = \left(\dfrac{2K_1 K_2}{K_1 + K_2}\right)$

(ii)   Parallel : $\qquad K = \left(\dfrac{K_1 A_1 + K_2 A_2}{A_1 + A_2}\right)$

4. **In radial flow of heat** $\quad K = \dfrac{H(r_2 - r_1)}{4\pi r_1 r_2 (T_1 - T_2)}$

5. **Cylindrical flow of heat** $K = \dfrac{H \ln\left(\frac{r_2}{r_1}\right)}{2\pi \ell (T_2 - T_1)}$

6. **Formation of ice on pond**

$$t = \dfrac{\rho L}{2KT}\left(y_2^2 - y_1^2\right)$$

7. **Radiation** is the universal and fastest mode of heat transfer.

8. **Kirchoff's law :** $\dfrac{e_\lambda}{a_\lambda} = $ constant

9. **Stefan's-Boltzmann law :** Net loss of heat

$$E_{net} = \varepsilon\sigma(T^4 - T_0^4)\ \text{W/m}^2$$

10. **Newtons's law of cooling**

$$\dfrac{dT}{dt} = -k(T - T_0)$$

here $(T - T_0)$ is small.

11. **Wien's displacement law**

$$\lambda_m T = \text{constant}$$

12. **Solar constant,** $S = \sigma T^4 \left(\dfrac{R_s}{r}\right)^2$

MCQ Type 1

LEVEL - 1

Only one option correct

1. The temperature of the two outer surfaces of a composite slab consisting of two materials having coefficient of thermal conductivities K and $2K$, thickness x and $4x$ respectively are T_2 and T_1 ($T_2 > T_1$). The rate of heat transfer through the slab, in a steady state is $f\left[\dfrac{A(T_2 - T_1)K}{x}\right]$, the value of f is

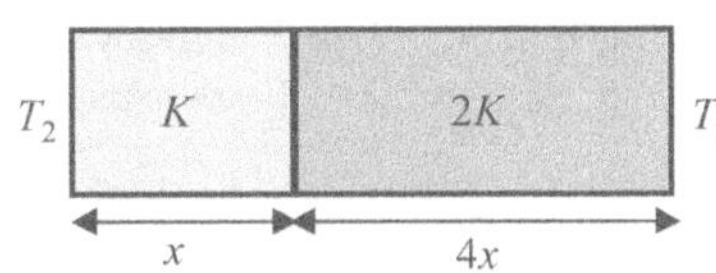

  (a) 1   (b) $\dfrac{1}{2}$

  (c) $\dfrac{2}{3}$ (d) $\dfrac{1}{3}$

2. A black body at a high temperature T K radiates energy at the rate of E W/m^2. When the temperature falls to $\dfrac{T}{2}$ K, the radiated energy in W/m^2 will be

  (a) $\dfrac{E}{4}$ (b) $\dfrac{E}{2}$

  (c) $2E$ (d) $\dfrac{E}{16}$

3. The following solid objects made of the same material are maintained at a temperature of 300 K in an environment whose temperature is 400 K : a cube of edge r, a sphere of radius, r and a hemisphere of radius r. The object in which the heat exchange is the greatest ?

  (a) Cube   (b) Sphere

  (c) Hemisphere   (d) Equal in all

4. Two identical rods of metal are welded end to end as shown in figure (i), 20 calories of heat flows through it in 4 minutes. If the rods are welded as shown in figure (ii), the same amount of heat will flow through the rods in

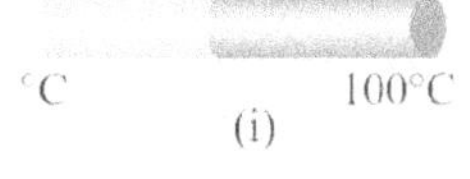

  (a) 1 minute   (b) 2 minute

  (c) 4 minute   (d) 16 minute

5. For cooking the food, which of the following type of utensil is most suitable?

  (a) High specific heat and low conductivity

  (b) High specific heat and high conductivity

  (c) Low specific heat and low conductivity

  (d) Low specific heat and high conductivity

6. A slab consists of two parallel layers of copper and brass of the same thickness and having thermal conductivities in the ratio 1 : 4. If the free face of brass is at 100°C and that of copper at 0°C, the temperature of interface is

  (a) 80°C   (b) 20°C

  (c) 60°C   (d) 40°C

7. Two metal cubes A and B of same size are arranged as shown in the figure. The extreme ends of the combination are maintained at the indicated temperatures. The arrangement is thermally insulated. The coefficients of thermal conductivity of A and B are 300 W/m°C and 200 W/m°C, respectively. After steady state is reached, the temperature of the interface will be

  (a) 45°C

  (b) 90°C

  (c) 30°C

  (d) 60°C

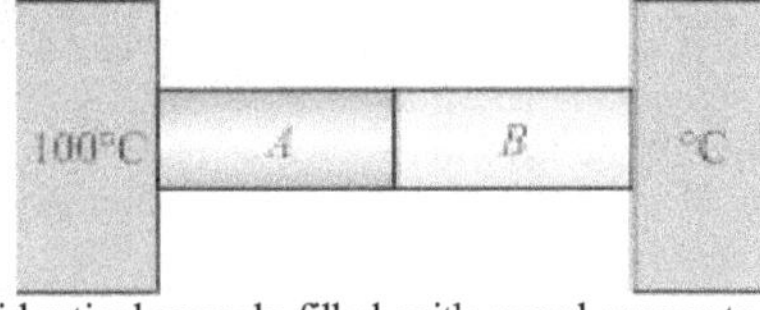

8. There are two identical vessels filled with equal amounts of ice. The vessels are of different metals. If the ice melts in the two vessels in 20 and 35 minutes respectively, the ratio of the coefficients of thermal conductivity of the two metals is

  (a) 4 : 7   (b) 7 : 4

  (c) 16 : 49   (d) 49 : 16

9. In which of the following process, convection does not take place primarily?

  (a) Sea and land breeze

  (b) Boiling of water

  (c) Warming of glass of bulb due to filament

  (d) Heating air around a finance

10. There is a rough black spot on a polished metallic plate. It is heated upto 1400 K approximately and then at once taken in a dark room. Which of the following statements is true?

  (a) In comparison with the plate, the spot will shine more

  (b) In comparison with the plate, the spot will appear more black

  (c) The spot and the plate will be equally bright

  (d) The plate and the black spot can not be seen in the dark room

11. An ideal black body at room temperature is thrown into a furnace. It is observed that

  (a) Initially it is the darkest body and at later times the brightest

  (b) It is the darkest body at all times

  (c) It cannot be distinguished at all times

  (d) Initially it is the darkest body and at later times it cannot be distinguished

Answer Key	1	(d)	3	(b)	5	(d)	7	(d)	9	(c)	11	(a)
Sol. from page 561	2	(d)	4	(a)	6	(a)	8	(b)	10	(a)		

12. Colour of shining bright star is an indication of its
    (a) Distance from the earth   (b) Size
    (c) Temperature   (d) Mass

13. A metal ball of surface area 200 cm^2 and temperature 527°C is surrounded by a vessel at 27°C. If the emissivity of the metal is 0.4, then the rate of loss of heat from the ball is
    ($\sigma = 5.67 \times 10^{-8}$ J/m^2 – s – K^4)
    (a) 108 joule approx.   (b) 168 joule approx.
    (c) 182 joule approx.   (d) 192 joule approx.

14. Assuming the sun to be a spherical body of radius R at a temperature of T K, evaluate the total radiant power, incident on Earth, at a distance r from the Sun
    (a) $\pi r_0^2 R^2 \sigma T^4 / r^2$
    (b) $r_0^2 R^2 \sigma T^4 / 4\pi r^2$
    (c) $R^2 \sigma T^4 / r^2$
    (d) $4\pi r_0^2 R^2 \sigma T^4 / r^2$
    where r_0 is the radius of the earth and σ is stefan's constant.

15. Suppose the sun expands so that its radius becomes 100 times its present radius and its surface temperature becomes half of its present value. The total energy emitted by it then will increase by a factor of
    (a) 10^4 (b) 625
    (c) 256   (d) 16

16. Two rods (one semi-circular and other straight) of same material and of same cross-sectional area are joined as shown in the figure. The points A and B are maintained at different temperature. The ratio of the heat transferred through a cross-section of a semi-circular rod to the heat transferred through a cross section of the straight rod in a given time is
    (a) $2 : \pi$
    (b) $1 : 2$
    (c) $\pi : 2$
    (d) $3 : 2$

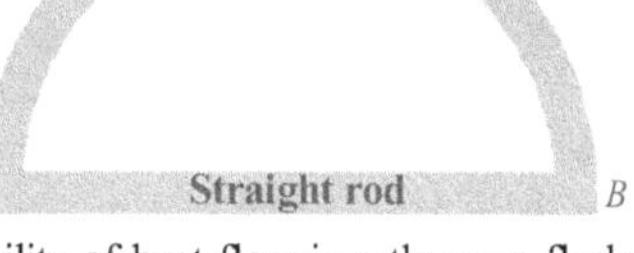

17. The only possibility of heat flow in a thermos flask is through its cork which is 75 cm^2 in area and 5 cm thick. Its thermal conductivity is 0.0075 cal/cmsec°C. The outside temperature is 40°C and latent heat of ice is 80 cal g^{-1}. Time taken by 500 g of ice at 0°C in the flask to melt into water at 0°C is
    (a) 2.47 hr
    (b) 4.27 hr
    (c) 7.42 hr
    (d) 4.72 hr

18. One end of a copper rod of length 1.0 m and area of cross-section 10^{-3} m^2 is immersed in boiling water and the other end in ice. If the coefficient of thermal conductivity of copper is 92 cal/m–s–°C and the latent heat of ice is 8×10^4 cal/kg, then the amount of ice which will melt in one minute is
    (a) 9.2×10^{-3} kg   (b) 8×10^{-3} kg
    (c) 6.9×10^{-3} kg   (d) 5.4×10^{-3} kg

19. Five rods of same dimensions are arranged as shown in the figure. They have thermal conductivities K_1, K_2, K_3, K_4 and K_5. When points A and B are maintained at different temperatures, no heat flows through the central rod if

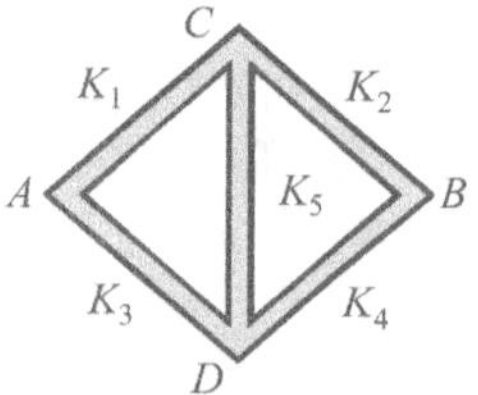

    (a) $K_1 = K_2$ and $K_2 = K_3$
    (b) $K_1 K_4 = K_2 K_3$
    (c) $K_1 K_2 = K_3 K_4$
    (d) $\dfrac{K_1}{K_4} = \dfrac{K_2}{K_3}$

20. Radius of a conductor increases uniformly from left end to right end as shown in fig.

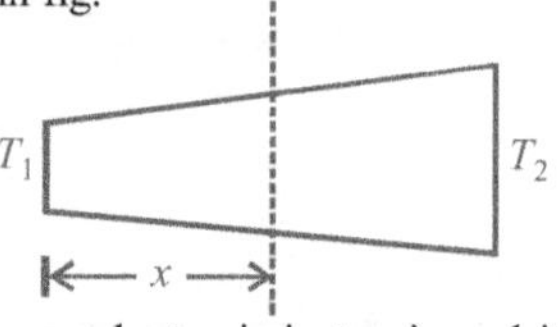

    Material of the conductor is isotropic and its curved surface is thermally insulated from surrounding. Its ends are maintained at temperatures T_1 and T_2 ($T_1 > T_2$) : If, in steady state, heat flow rate is equal to H, then which of the following graphs is correct

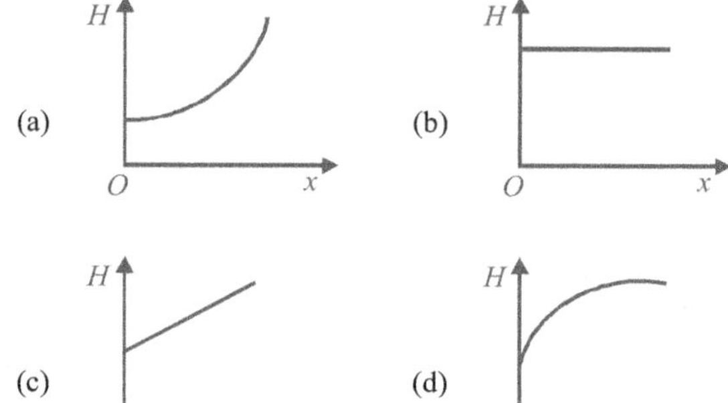

21. A long metallic bar is carrying heat from one of its ends to the other end under steady-state. The variation of temperature θ along the length x of the bar from its hot end is best described by which of the following figures?

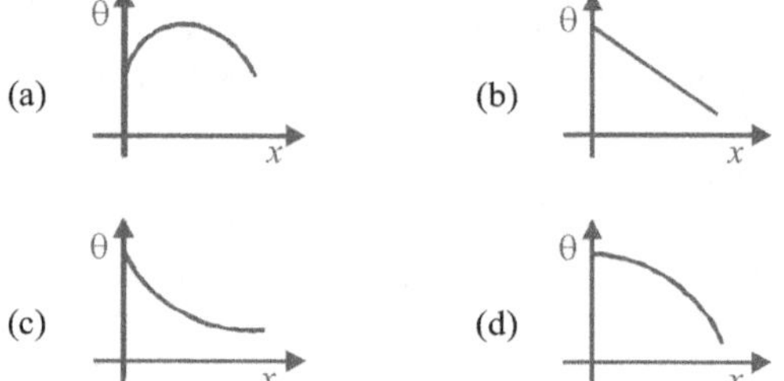

22. Three metal rods made of copper, aluminium and brass, each 1 m long and 4 cm in diameter, are placed end to end with aluminium between the other two. The free ends of copper and brass are maintained at 100°C and 0°C respectively. Assume that thermal conductivity of copper is twice that of aluminium and four times that of brass. The equilibrium temperature of copper-aluminium and aluminium-brass junction are
    (a) 68° C and 75° C   (b) 75° C and 68° C
    (c) 57° C and 86° C   (d) 86° C and 57° C

Answer Key	12	(c)	14	(d)	16	(a)	18	(c)	20	(b)	22	(d)
Sol. from page 561	13	(c)	15	(b)	17	(a)	19	(b)	21	(b)		

23. A 100 W lamp is immersed in an insulated container holding 500 g of alcohol at 20°C. The time it takes to warm the alcohol to 50°C is (specific heat of alcohol 0.572 cal/g°C)

(a) 150 s   (b) 360 s

(c) 100 s   (d) 200 s

24. A boiler is made of a copper plate 2.4 mm thick with an inside coating of a 0.2 mm thick layer of tin. The surface area exposed to gases at 700°C is 400 cm². The maximum amount of steam that could be generated per hour at atmospheric pressure is (K_{cu} = 0.9 and K_{tin} = 0.15 cal/s-cm-°C and L_{steam} = 540 cal/g)

(a) 500 kg   (b) 1000 kg

(c) 4000 kg   (d) 5000 kg

Answer Key

Sol. from page 561

23	(b)	24	(c)

LEVEL -2

Only one option correct

1. A wall has two layers A and B, each made of a different material. Both the layers have the same thickness. The thermal conductivity of the material of A is twice that of B. Under thermal equilibrium, the temperature difference across the wall is 36°C. The temperature difference across the layer A is

(a) 6°C   (b) 12°C

(c) 18°C   (d) 24°C

2. A cylinder of radius R made of a material of thermal conductivity K_1 is surrounded by a cylindrical shell of inner radius R and outer radius $2R$ made of material of thermal conductivity K_2. The two ends of the combined systems are maintained at two different temperatures. There is no loss of heat across the cylindrical surface and the system is in steady state. The effective thermal conductivity of the system is

(a) $K_1 + K_2$ (b) $\dfrac{K_1 + 3K_2}{4}$

(c) $\dfrac{K_1 K_2}{K_1 + K_2}$ (d) $\dfrac{3K_1 + K_2}{4}$

3. The graph shown in figure represents the variation of temperature (T) of two bodies x and y having same surface area with time (t) due to emission of radiation. Find the correct relation between the emissive power and absorptive power of two bodies

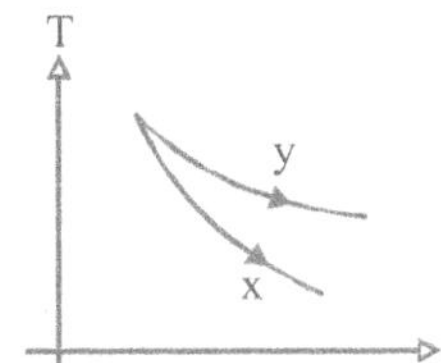

(a) $e_x > e_y, a_x < a_y$ (b) $e_x < e_y, a_x > a_y$

(c) $e_x > e_y$ and $a_x > a_y$ (d) $e_x < e_y$ and $a_x < a_y$

4. A sphere of density ρ, specific heat capacity c and radius r is hung by a thermally insulating thread in an enclosure which is kept at a lower temperature than the sphere. The temperature of the sphere starts to drop at a rate which depends upon the temperature difference between the sphere and the enclosure and the nature of the surface of sphere and is proportional to

(a) $\dfrac{c}{r^3 \rho}$ (b) $\dfrac{1}{r^3 \rho c}$

(c) $3r^3 \rho c$ (d) $\dfrac{1}{r \rho c}$

5. A black body is at a temperature of 2880 K. The energy of radiation emitted by this body with wavelengths between 499 nm and 500 nm is U_1, between 999 nm and 1000 nm is U_2 and between 1499 nm and 1500 nm is U_3. The Wien constant $b = 2.88 \times 10^6$ nm K. Then

(a) $U_1 = 0$ (b) $U_3 = 0$

(c) $U_1 > U_2$ (d) $U_2 > U_1$

6. A spherical black body with a radius of 12 cm radiates 450 W power at 500 K. If the radius were halved and the temperature doubled, the power radiated in watt would be

(a) 225   (b) 450

(c) 900   (d) 1800

7. Two metallic spheres S_1 and S_2 are made of the same material and have got identical surface finish. The mass of S_1 is thrice that of S_2. Both the spheres are heated to the same high temperature and placed in the same room having lower temperature, but are thermally insulated from each other. The ratio of initial rate of cooling of S_1 to that of S_2 is

(a) $\dfrac{1}{3}$ (b) $\dfrac{1}{\sqrt{3}}$

(c) $\dfrac{\sqrt{3}}{1}$ (d) $\left(\dfrac{1}{3}\right)^{1/3}$

8. Three rods of identical cross-sectional area and made from the same metal form the sides of an isosceles triangle ABC, right angled at B. The points A and B are maintained at temperatures T and $\sqrt{2}\,T$ respectively, in the steady state, the temperature of points C is T_c. Assuming that only heat conduction takes place T_c / T is

(a) $\dfrac{1}{2\left(\sqrt{2}-1\right)}$ (b) $\dfrac{3}{\sqrt{2}+1}$

(c) $\dfrac{1}{\sqrt{3}(\sqrt{2}-1)}$ (d) $\dfrac{1}{\sqrt{2}+1}$

Answer Key

Sol. from page 562

1	(b)	3	(c)	5	(d)	7	(d)
2	(b)	4	(d)	6	(d)	8	(b)

9. Two identical conducting rods are first connected independently to two vessels containing metal at $100°C$ and other containing ice at $0°C$. In the second case the rods are joined end to end and connected to the same vessel. Let q_1 and q_2 g/s be the rate of melting of ice in the two cases respectively, the ratio $\dfrac{q_1}{q_2}$ is

(a) $\dfrac{1}{2}$ (b) $\dfrac{2}{1}$

(c) $\dfrac{4}{1}$ (d) $\dfrac{1}{4}$

10. Three discs A, B and C having radii 2 m, 4 m and 6 m respectively are coated with carbon black on their outer surfaces . The wavelength corresponding to maximum intensity are 300 nm, 400 nm and 500 nm respectively. The power radiated by them are Q_A, Q_B and Q_C respectively

(a) Q_A is maximum   (b) Q_B is maximum

(c) Q_C is maximum   (d) $Q_A = Q_B = Q_C$

11. A spherical body of area A and emissivity 0.6 is kept inside a black body. What is the rate at which energy is radiated per second at temperature T

(a) $0.6\,\sigma\,AT^4$ (b) $0.4\,\sigma\,AT^4$

(c) $0.8\,\sigma\,AT^4$ (d) $1.0\,\sigma\,AT^4$

12. A room is maintained at $20°C$ by a heater of resistance $20\ \Omega$ connected to 200 V mains. The temperature is uniform throughout the room and the heat is transmitted through a glass window of area 1 m^2 and thickness 0.2 cm (K for glass is 0.2 cal/m°C. s). The temperature outside is

(a) $20°C$ (b) $10°C$

(c) $12.2°C$ (d) $15.2°C$

13. A 'cold box' in the shape of a cube of edge 50 cm is made of 'thermocool' material 4.0 cm thick. If the outside temperature is $30°C$, the quantity of ice that will melt each hour inside the 'cold box' is (the thermal conductivity of the thermocool material is 0.050 W/m^2.K)

(a) 1.52 kg   (b) 0.605 kg

(c) 2.520 kg   (d) 0.512 kg

14. The body of an unclothed person has a surface area of 1.50 m^2 and an emissivity of 0.80. His skin temperature is $37°C$. He stands in an air–conditioned room where the temperature is maintained at $17°C$. The amount of heat he loses per minute, is

$$(\sigma = 5.67 \times 10^{-8}\ \text{W/m}^2 \cdot \text{K}^4)$$

(a) 8.8 kJ   (b) 4.4 kJ

(c) 2.2 kJ   (d) 3.3 kJ

15. Water contained in a closed thin walled cylindrical copper tank, of radius 30 cm and height 1 m, is maintained at $60°C$ by means of an electric heater immersed in water, the outside temperature being $20°C$. The tank's outer curved surface is covered with 1 cm thick felt ($K_{felt} = 9 \times 10^{-5}$ cal/s.cm.°C). Neglect all other losses. The wattage of the heater is

(a) 100   (b) 1000

(c) 220   (d) 284

16. An insulated tub is divided into two sections by a watertight partition of dimension 20cm × 40cm made of copper 3 mm thick.On one side is water which is boiling and on the other side is a mixture of 2 kg of crushed ice being constantly stirred in 5 kg of water. All the ice will melt in ($K_{Cu} = 0.92$ cal s^{-1} cm^{-1}°C^{-1}) :

(a) 1.32 s   (b) 1.6 s

(c) 0.33 s   (d) 0.65 s

17. Figure shows a composite slab of three different materials, a, b and c with equal thickness and with thermal conductivities $k_a > k_b > k_c$. The transfer of energy through them as heat is non-zero and steady. The temperature difference is the greatest across

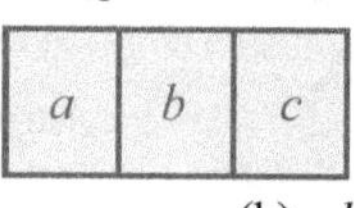

(a) a (b) b

(c) c (d) a and c

18. The intensity of radiation emitted by the sun has its maximum value at a wavelength of 510 nm and that emitted by the north star has the maximum value at 350 nm. If these stars behave like black bodies, then the ratio of the surface temperature of the sun and north star is

(a) 1.46   (b) 0.69

(c) 1.21   (d) 0.83

19. Three rods made of the same material and having the same cross section have been joined as shown in the figure. Each rod is of the same length. The left and right ends are kept at $0°C$ and $90°C$ respectively. The temperature of the junction of the three rods will be

(a) $45°C$

(b) $60°C$

(c) $30°C$

(d) $20°C$

20. Five identical rods are joint as shown in the figure. Point A and C are maintained at temperature $120°C$ and $20°C$ respectively. The temperature of junction B is

(a) $70°C$

(b) $80°C$

(c) $30°C$

(d) $20°C$

21. Three rods of same dimensions are arranged as shown in figure. They have thermal conductivities K_1, K_2 and K_3. The points P and Q are maintained at different temperatures for the heat to flow at the same rate along PRQ and PQ then which of the following options is correct?

(a) $K_3 = \dfrac{1}{2}\left(K_1 + K_2\right)$

(b) $K_3 = K_1 + K_2$

(c) $K_3 = \dfrac{K_1 K_2}{K_1 + K_2}$

(d) $K_3 = 2(K_1 + K_2)$

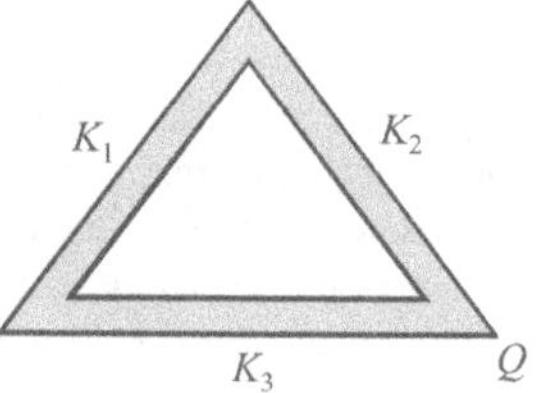

9	(c)	11	(a)	13	(b)	15	(d)	17	(c)	19	(b)	21	(c)
10	(b)	12	(d)	14	(a)	16	(d)	18	(b)	20	(a)		

22. A metal rod AB of length $10x$ has its one end A in ice at $0°C$ and the other end B in water at $100°C$. If a point P on the rod is maintained at $400°C$, then it is found that equal amounts of water and ice evaporate and melt per unit time. The latent heat of evaporation of water is 540 cal/g and latent heat of melting of ice is 80 cal/g. If the point P is at a distance of λx from the ice end A, find the value of λ. [Neglect any heat loss to the surrounding].

(a) 9   (b) 2

(c) 6   (d) 1

23. The figure shows a system of two concentric spheres of radii r_1 and r_2 and kept at temperatures T_1 and T_2, respectively. The radial rate of flow of heat in a substance between the two concentric spheres is proportional to

(a) $\dfrac{r_1 r_2}{(r_2 - r_1)}$

(b) $(r_2 - r_1)$

(c) $(r_2 - r_1)(r_1 r_2)$

(d) $\ln\left(\dfrac{r_2}{r_1}\right)$

24. Which of the following graphs correctly represents the relation between $(\ln E)$ and $(\ln T)$ where E is the amount of radiation emitted per unit time from unit area of a body and T is the absolute temperature

25. A system S receives heat continuously from an electrical heater of power 10W. The temperature of S becomes constant at $50°C$ when the surrounding temperature is $20°C$. After the heater is switched off, S cools from $35°C$ to $34.8°C$ in 1 minute. The heat capacity of S is

(a) 100 J/°C   (b) 300 J/°C

(c) 750 J/°C   (d) 1400 J/°C

26. The sun rays are focussed by a concave mirror of diameter 12 cm fixed with its axis towards the sun onto a copper calorimeter, where they are absorbed. If the thermal capacity of the calorimeter and its contents is 59 cal/°C and the temperature rises by 8°C in 2 minutes, the heat received in 1 minute by a square meter of the earth surface when the rays are incident normaly is

(a) 20860 cal   (b) 25540 cal

(c) 10430 cal   (d) 51180 cal

Answer Key Sol. from page 562	22	(a)	23	(a)	24	(d)	25	(d)	26	(a)

HT   MCQ Type 2   *Exercise 8.2*

Mulitiple options correct

1. Two bodies A and B have thermal emissivities of 0.01 and 0.81 respectively. The outer surface areas of the two bodies are the same. The two bodies emit total radiant power at the same rate. The wavelength λ_B corresponding to maximum spectral radiancy in the radiation from B is shifted from the wavelength corresponding to maximum spectral radiancy in the radiation from A by 1.00 μm. If the temperature of A is 5802 K.

(a) The temperature of B is 1934 K

(b) $\lambda_B = 1.5\ \mu m$

(c) The temperature of B is 11604 K

(d) The temperature of B is 2901 K

2. In a dark room with ambient temperature T_0 a black body is kept at a temperature T. Keeping the temperature of the black body constant (at T) sunrays are allowed to fall on the black body through a hole in the roof of the dark room. Assuming that there is no change in the ambient temperature of the room, which of the following statement is/are correct?

(a) The quantity of radiation absorbed by the black body in unit time will increase.

(b) Since emissivity = absorptivity, hence the quantity of radiation emitted by black body in unit time will increase

(c) Black body radiates more energy in unit time in the visible spectrum

(d) The reflected energy in unit time by the black body remains same

3. For transmission of heat from one place to the other, medium is required in

(a) conduction   (b) convection

(c) radiation   (d) all

Answer Key Sol. from page 564	1	(a, b)	2	(a, b, c, d)	3	(a, b)

4. Three rods of material X and three rods of material Y are connected as shown in the figure. All the rods are of identical length and cross-sectional area. The end A is maintained at 60°C and the junction E at 10°C. The thermal conductivity of X is 0.92 cal/sec-cm-°C and that of Y is 0.46 cal/sec-cm-°C. Choose the correct option(s).

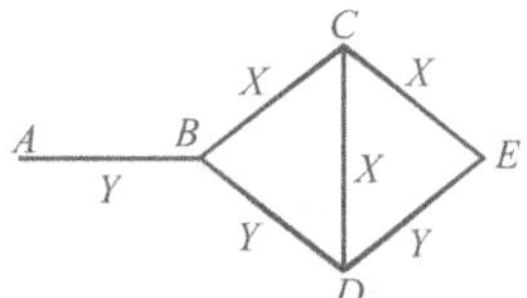

   (a) The temperature of the junction B is 40°C
   (b) The temperature of the junction C is 20°C
   (c) The temperature of the junction D is 20°C
   (d) The temperature of the junction B is 30°C

5. Two identical objects A and B are at temperatures T_A and T_B respectively. Both objects are placed in a room with perfectly absorbing walls maintained at a temperature T ($T_A > T > T_B$). The objects A and B attain the temperature T eventually. Select the correct statements from the following
   (a) A only emits radiations, while B only absorbs it until both attain the temperature T
   (b) A loses more heat by radiation than it absorbs, while B absorbs more radiation than it emits, until they attain the temperature T
   (c) Both A and B only absorb radiation, but do not emit it, until they attain the temperature T
   (d) Each object continues to emit and absorb radiation even after attaining the temperature T

6. A black body of temperature T is inside chamber of temperature T_0 initially. Sun rays are allowed to fall from a hole in the top of chamber. If the temperature of black body (T) and chamber (T_0) remains constant, then

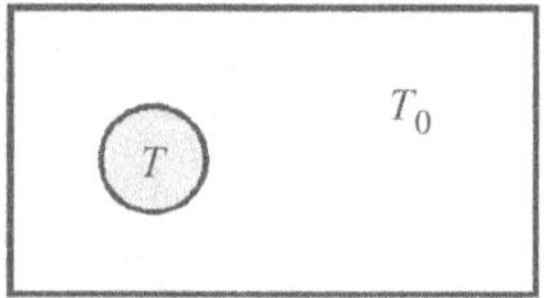

   (a) Black body will absorb more radiation
   (b) Black body will absorb less radiation
   (c) Black body emits more energy
   (d) Black body emits energy equal to energy absorbed by it

7. In Newton's law of cooling, $\dfrac{d\theta}{dt} = -k(\theta - \theta_0)$, the constant k is proportional to
   (a) A, surface area of the body
   (b) S, specific heat of the body
   (c) $1/m$, m being mass of the body
   (d) e, emmisivity of the body

8. A body takes 5 minutes for cooling from 50°C to 40°C. Its temperature comes down to 33.33°C in next 5 minutes. Now, choose the correct statement(s) from the following ?
   (a) The temperature of surrounding is 20°C
   (b) The temperature of surrounding is 25°C
   (c) The temperature of the body in further 5 minutes becomes 18.88°C
   (d) The temperature of the body in further 5 minutes becomes 28.88°C

Answer Key
Sol. from page 564

4	(b, c, d)	5	(b, d)	6	(a, c, d)	7	(a, c)	8	(a, d)

Statement Questions   *Exercise 8.3*

Read the two statements carefully to mark the correct option out of the options given below:
(a) If both the statements are true and the *statement - 2* is the correct explanation of *statement - 1*.
(b) If both the statements are true but *statement - 2* is not the correct explanation of the *statement - 1*.
(c) If *statement - 1* true but *statement - 2* is false.
(d) If *statement - 1* is false but *statement - 2* is true.

1.   *Statement 1*
A body at 25 ° C radiates in a room, where the room temperature is 30° C.
Statement 2
Each body radiates energy at all temperature.

2.   *Statement 1*
If the temperature of a star is doubled then the rate of loss of heat from it becomes 16 times.
Statement 2
Specific heat varies with temperatures

3.   *Statement 1*
Temperature near the sea coast are moderate.
Statement 2
Water has high thermal conductivity.

4.   *Statement 1*
A body that is a good radiator is also a good absorber of radition at a given wavelength.
Statement 2
According to Kirchoff's law the absorptivity of a body is equal to its emissivity at a given wavelength.

5. *Statement 1*

Bodies radiate heat at all temperature.

Statement 2

Rate of radiation of heat is proportional to the fourth power of absolute temperature.

6. *Statement 1*

Woollen cloths keep the body warm in winter.

Statement 2

Air is bad conductor of heat.

7. *Statement 1*

It is hotter over the top of a fire than at the same distance on the sides.

Statement 2

Air surrounding the fire conducts more heat upwards.

8. *Statement 1*

For higher temperature, the peak emission wavelength of a black body shifts to lower wavelengths.

Statement 2

Peak emission wavelength of a blackbody is proportional to the fourth power of absolute temperature.

9. *Statement 1*

The radiation from the sun's surface varies as the fourth power of its absolute temperature.

Statement 2

The sun is not a black body.

10. *Statement 1*

A hollow metallic closed container maintained at a uniform temperature can act as a source of black body radiation.

Statement 2

All metals acts as a black body.

11. *Statement 1*

Blue star is at high temperature than red star.

Statement 2

Wein's displacement law states that $T \propto \dfrac{1}{\lambda_m}$.

Answer Key
Sol. from page 564

1	(a)	2	(b)	3	(b)	4	(a)	5	(b)	6	(a)
7	(c)	8	(c)	9	(c)	10	(c)	11	(a)		

 **HT** Passage & Matrix Exercise 8.4

PASSAGES

Passage for (Q. 1 - 3) :

Hot oil is circulated through an insulated container with a wooden lid at the top whose conductivity $K = 0.149$ J/(m-°C-sec), thickness $t = 5\ mm$, emissivity $= 0.6$. Temperature of the top of the lid is maintained at $T_\ell = 127°C$, if the ambient temperature $T_a = 27°C$.

$$\left(\text{Given } \sigma = \frac{17}{3} \times 10^{-8}\right)$$

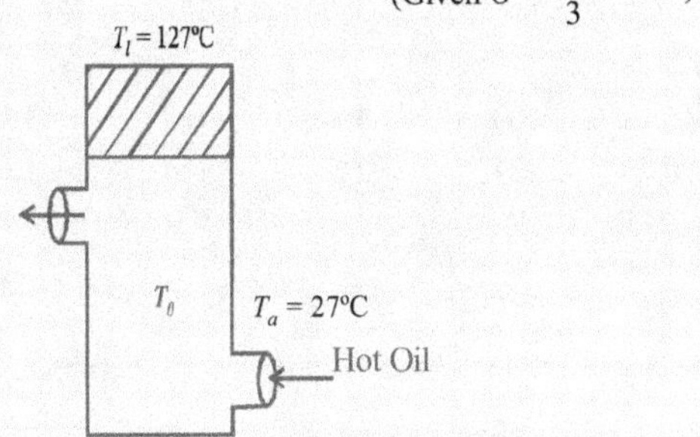

1. The rate of heat loss per unit area due to radiation from the lid is
(a) 415 W / m^2
(b) 555 W / m^2
(c) 595 W / m^2
(d) 315 W / m^2

2. The temperature of the oil is
(a) 439.15 K
(b) 419.83 K
(c) 523 K
(d) 318.2 K

3. If area of the top of the lid be 0.5 m^2 then the rate of heat flow through radiation is
(a) 297.5 W
(b) 595 W
(c) 892.5 W
(d) 669.4 W

Passage for (Q. 4 - 6) :

A hot body placed in air is cooled down according to Newton's law of cooling, the rate of decrease of temperature being k times the temperature difference from the surrounding. Assume that cooling starts at $t = 0$:

4. If T_0 and T_1 be the temperature of the surrounding and the initial temperature of the body respectively, then the temperature of the body at any time t is given by

(a) $T_0 + (T_1 - T_0)e^{-kt}$
(b) $T_0 e^{-kt}$
(c) $T_1(T_0 - T_1)e^{-kt}$
(d) $T_1 + (T_0 - T_1)e^{-kt}$

Answer Key
Sol. from page 565

1	(c)	2	(b)	3	(a)	4	(a)

5. The time in which the body will lose half the maximum heat it can lose is

(a) $\ln 2$

(b) $\dfrac{\ln 2}{k}$

(c) $k \ln 2$

(d) $k + \ln 2$

6. If $k = \ln 2$, then the time (in proper unit) in which the body will lose half the maximum heat it can lose is

(a) 2

(b) 1

(c) 4

(d) 3

Passage for (Q. 7 - 9) :

n moles of a monoatomic gas at an initial temperature T_0 is enclosed in a cylindrical vessel filled with a light piston. The surrounding air has a temperature T_s ($> T_0$) and the atmospheric pressure is P_a. Heat may be conducted between the surrounding and the gas through the bottom of the cylinder. The bottom has a surface area A, thickness x and thermal conductivity K. Assume all changes to be slow.

7. If T be the temperature of gas after time t, then the difference $(T_s - T = \Delta T)$ is given by

(a) $(T_s - T_0)e^{-\left(\frac{2KAt}{5nRx}\right)}$

(b) $(T_s - T_0)e^{-\left(\frac{2KAx}{5nRt}\right)}$

(c) $(T_s - T_0)e^{-\left(\frac{2KtR}{5nAx}\right)}$

(d) $(T_s - T_0)e^{-\left(\frac{3Ktx}{5nRA}\right)}$

8. The change in volume of the gas in cylinder is

(a) $\dfrac{nR}{P_a}\left[(T_s - T_0)e^{-\left(\frac{2KAx}{5nRt}\right)}\right]$

(b) $\dfrac{nR}{P_a}\left[(T_s - T_0)e^{-\left(\frac{2KAt}{5nRx}\right)}\right]$

(c) $\dfrac{nR}{P_a}\left[(T_s - T_0)e^{-\left(\frac{2KA}{5nRtx}\right)}\right]$

(d) $\dfrac{nR}{P_a}\left[(T_s - T_0)e^{-\left(\frac{5KAt}{2nRx}\right)}\right]$

9. The distance moved by the piston in time t is given by

(a) $\dfrac{nR}{P_a A}\left[(T_s - T_0)e^{-\left(\frac{2KAx}{5nRT}\right)}\right]$

(b) $\dfrac{nR}{P_a A}\left[(T_s - T_0)e^{-\left(\frac{2KAt}{5nRx}\right)}\right]$

(c) $\dfrac{nR}{P_a A}\left[(T_s - T_0)e^{-\left(\frac{2KA}{5nRtx}\right)}\right]$

(d) $\dfrac{nR}{P_a A}\left[(T_s - T_0)e^{-\left(\frac{5KAt}{2nRx}\right)}\right]$

Passage for (Q. 10 - 12) :

A metal block of heat capacity 80 J/°C placed in a room at 20°C is heated electrically. The heater is switched off when the temperature reaches 30°C. The temperature of the block rises at the rate of 2°C/s just after the heater is switched on and falls at the rate of 0.2–°C/s just after the heater is switched off. Assume Newton's law of cooling to hold.

10. The power of the heater is

(a) 100 W

(b) 160 W

(c) 190 W

(d) 220 W

11. The power radiated by the block just after the heater is switched off is

(a) 4 W

(b) 8W

(c) 12 W

(d) 16 W

12. The power radiated by the block when the temperature of the block is 25°C is

(a) 4 W

(b) 8 W

(c) 12 W

(d) 16 W

Passage for (Q. 13 - 14) :

The rate at which the radiant energy reaches the surface of earth from the sun is 1.4 kW/m^2. The distance of earth from the sun is 1.5×10^{11} m and the radius of sun is 7×10^8 m. Calculate

13. Rate of radiant energy emitted from sun's surface per unit area per second,

(a) 3.32×10^7 W/m^2

(b) 6.43×10^7 W/m^2

(c) 5.83×10^7 W/m^2

(d) none of these

14. Assuming sun as a black body, what is surface temperature of the sun ?

(a) 4000 K

(b) 5200 K

(c) 5803 K

(d) 6430 K

Answer Key	5	(b)	7	(a)	9	(b)	11	(d)	13	(b)
Sol. from page 565	6	(b)	8	(b)	10	(b)	12	(b)	14	(c)

MATRIX MATCHING

15. A copper rod (initially at room temperature 20°C) of non-uniform cross section is placed between a steam chamber at 100°C and ice-water chamber at 0°C.

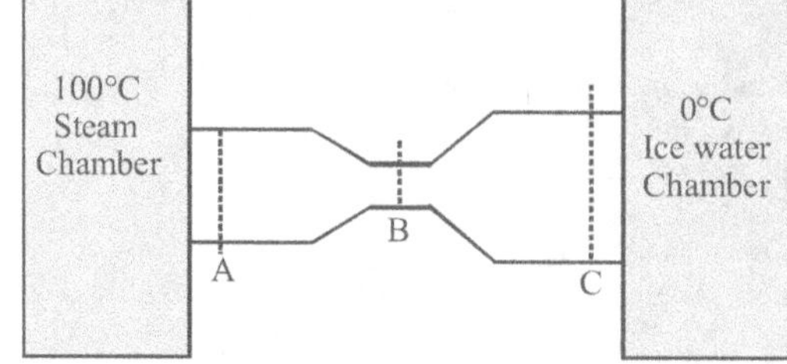

Column I		Column II
A.	Initially, rate of heat flow $\left(\dfrac{dQ}{dt}\right)$ will be	(p) maximum at section A
B.	At steady state, rate of heat flow $\left(\dfrac{dQ}{dt}\right)$ will be	(q) maximum at section B
C.	At steady state, temperature gradient $\left|\left(\dfrac{dT}{dx}\right)\right|$ will be	(r) maximum at section C
D.	At steady state, rate of change of temperature $\left(\dfrac{dT}{dt}\right)$ at a certain point will be	(s) minimum at section B (t) same for all section

16. A ball has surface temperature T initially at time $t = 0$, that is less than surrounding constant temperature T_0. On the vertical axis of the graph shown has either thermal energy radiated/absorbed per unit time or total energy radiated/absorbed till time t by the ball. Correctly match the curves marked in the graph

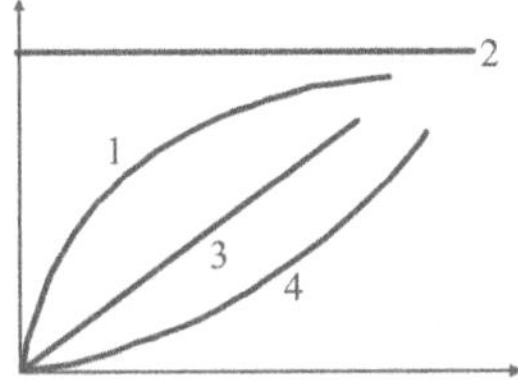

Column I		Column II	
A.	Thermal energy emitted per unit time	(p)	1
B.	Thermal energy absorbed per unit time	(q)	2
C.	Total energy emitted till time t	(r)	3
D.	Total energy absorbed till time t	(s)	4

17. Match columns I and II (regarding Newton's law of cooling)

Column I

A. Curve between $\log(\theta - \theta_0)$ and time, plotted on X- and Y - axes respectively

B. Curve between temperature of body (θ) and time, plotted on X - and Y - axes respectively

C. Curve between the rate of cooling (R) and body temperature (θ), plotted on X-and Y-axes respectively

D. Curve between the rate of cooling (R) and temperature difference between body (θ) and surrounding (θ_0), plotted on X - and Y-axes respectively

Column II

(p) 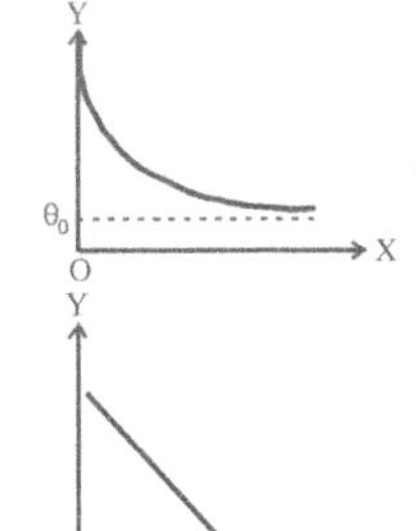

(q)

(r)

(s) 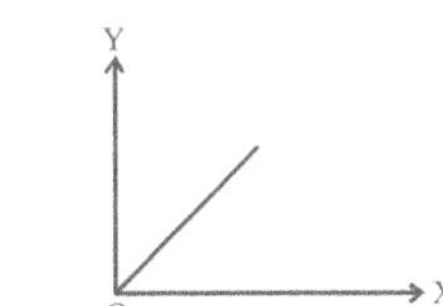

Solution from page 566

1. A pitcher with 1 mm thick porous walls contains 10 kg of water. Water comes to its outer surface and evaporates at the rate of 0.1 g/s. The surface area of the pitcher (one side) = 200 cm². The room temperature = 42°C, latent heat of vaporization = 2.27×10^6 J/kg and the thermal conductivity of the porous walls = 0.80 J/m–s–°C. Calculate the temperature of water in the pitcher when it attains a constant value.   **Ans : 28°C.**

2. A metal rod of cross–sectional area 1.0 cm² is being heated at one end. At one time, the temperature gradient is 5.0 °C/cm at cross–section A and is 2.5°C/cm at cross–section B. Calculate the rate at which the temperature is increasing in the part AB of the rod. The heat capacity of the part AB = 0.40 J/°C, thermal conductivity of the material of the rod = 200 W/m–°C. Neglect any loss of heat to the atmosphere.   **Ans : 12.5°C/s.**

3. Steam at 120°C is continuously passed through a 50 cm long rubber tube of inner and outer radii 1.0 cm and 1.2 cm. The room temperature is 30°C. Calculate the rate of heat flow through the walls of the tube. Thermal conductivity of rubber = 0.15 J/m–s–°C.   **Ans :233 J/s.**

4. A cylindrical rod of length 50 cm and cross–sectional area 1 cm² is fitted between a large ice chamber at 0°C and an evacuated chamber maintained at 27°C as shown in figure. Only small portions of the rod are inside the chambers and the rest is thermally insulated from the surrounding. The cross–section going into the evacuated chamber is blackened so that it completely absorbs any radiation falling on it. The temperature of the blackened end is 17°C when steady state is reached. Stefan's constant $\sigma = 6 \times 10^{-8}$ W/m²–K^4. Find the thermal conductivity of the material of the rod.

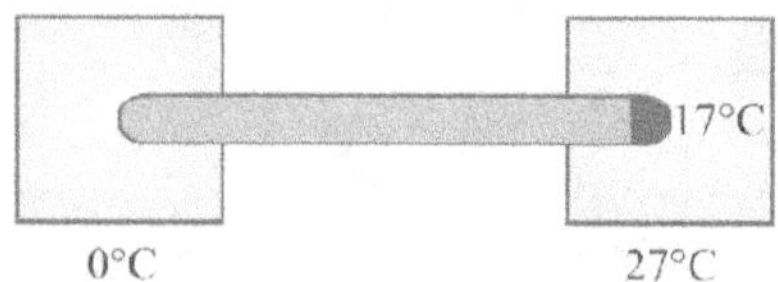

Ans : 1.8 W/m–°C.

5. Three rods of material x and three of material y are connected as shown in figure. All the rods are identical in length and cross–sectional area. If the end A is maintained at 60°C and the junction E at 10°C, calculate the temperature of the junction B. The thermal conductivity of x is 800 W/m–°C and that of y is 400 W/m–°C.

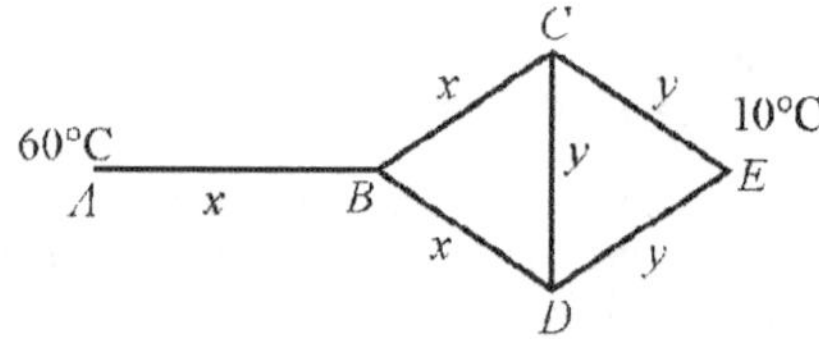

Ans : 40°C.

6. An iron ball having a surface area of 200 cm² and at a temperature of 527°C is placed in an enclosure at 27°C. If the surface emissivity of iron be 0.4, at what rate is heat being lost by radiation by the ball ?

Ans. 44 cal/s.

7. An electric heater is used in a room of total wall area 137 m² to maintain a temperature of + 20°C inside it when the outside temperature is –10°C. The walls have three layers of different materials. The innermost layer is of wood of thickness 2.5 cm, the middle layer is of cement of thickness 1.0 cm and the outermost layer is of brick of thickness 25.0 cm. Find the power of the electric heater. Assume that there is no heat loss through the floor and ceiling. The thermal conductivities of wood, cement and brick are 0.125, 1.5 and 1.0 W/m–°C respectively.

Ans. 9 kW.

Solution from page 567

1. An aluminium container of mass 100 g contains 200 g of ice at $-20°C$. Heat is added to the system at a rate of 100 cal/s. What is the temperature of the system after 4 minutes ? Draw a rough sketch showing the variation in the temperature of the system as a function of time. Specific heat capacity of ice = 0.5 cal/g–°C, specific heat capacity of aluminium = 0.2 cal/g–°C, specific heat capacity of water = 1 cal/g–°C and latent heat of fusion of ice = 80 cal/g.

Ans : 25.5 °C

2. Two vessels A and B of different materials but having identical shape, size and wall–thickness are filled with ice and kept at the same place. Ice melts at the rate of 100 g/min and 150 g/min in A and B respectively. Assuming that heat enters the vessels through the walls only, calculate the ratio of thermal conductivities of their materials. **Ans.** 2 : 3.

3. An electric bulb with tungsten filament having an area of 0.25 cm² is raised to a temperature of 3000 K, when a current passes through it. Calculate the electrical energy being consumed in watt, if the emissivity of the filament is 0.35. Stefan's constant, $\sigma = 5.67 \times 10^{-5}$/erg/cm²–$K^4$. If due to fall in main voltage the filament temperature falls to 2500 K, what will be wattage of the bulb ?

Ans. 40.19 W, 19.38 W.

4. A layer of ice 2 cm thick is formed on a pond. The temperature of air is $-20°C$. Calculate how long it will take for the thickness of ice to increase by 1 mm. [Density of ice = 1 g/cm³, latent heat of ice = 80 cal/g, conductivity of ice = 0.008 cal /cm–s–°C]

Ans : 102.5 s

5. One end of a copper rod of a uniform cross–section and of length 1.5 m is kept in contact with ice and the other end with water at 100°C. At what point along its length should a temperature of 200°C be maintained so that in steady state, the mass of ice melted be equal to that of the steam produced in the same interval of time ? Assume that the whole system is insulated from the surroundings. Latent heat of fusion of ice = 80 cal/g, latent heat of vaporization of water = 540 cal/g.

Ans : 1.396 m.

6. Water is 50°C, is filled in a closed cylindrical vessel of height 10 cm and cross–sectional area 10 cm². The walls of the vessels are adiabatic but the flat parts are made of 1 mm thick aluminium ($K = 200$ J/m–s–°C). Assume that the outside temperature is 20°C. The density of water is 1000 kg/m³ and the specific heat capacity of water = 4200 J/kg–°C. Estimate the time taken for the temperature to fall by 1.0 °C. Make any simplifying assumptions you need but specify them.

Ans : 0.035 s.

7. Three rods of lengths 20 cm each and area of cross–section 1 cm² are joined to form a triangle ABC. The conductivities of the rods are $K_{AB} = 50$ J/m–s–°C, $K_{BC} = 200$ J/m–s–°C and $K_{AC} = 400$ J/m–s–°C. The junctions A, B and C are maintained at 40°C, 80°C and 80°C respectively. Find the rate of heat flowing through the rods AB, AC and BC.

Ans : 1W, 8W, zero.

8. Four identical rods AB, CD, CF and DE are joined as shown in figure. The length, cross–section area and thermal conductivity of each rod are l, A and K respectively. The ends A, E and F are maintained at temperatures T_1, T_2 and T_3 respectively. Assuming no loss of heat to the atmosphere, find the temperature at B.

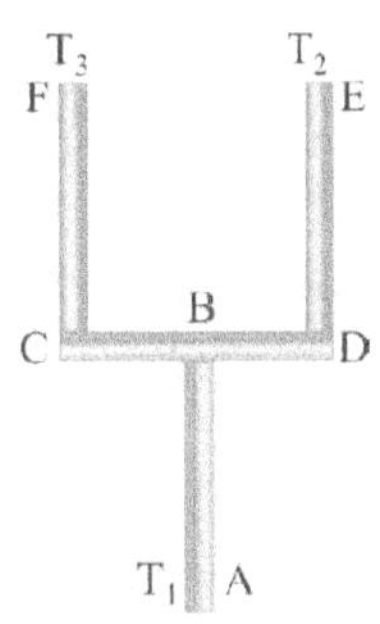

Ans : $\dfrac{3T_1 + 2(T_2 + T_3)}{7}$.

9. A hot body placed in a surrounding of temperature θ_0 obeys Newton's law of cooling $d\theta/dt = -k(\theta - \theta_0)$. Its temperature at $t = 0$ is θ_1. The specific heat capacity of the body is s and its mass is m. Find

(a) the maximum heat that the body can lose and

(b) the time starting from $t = 0$ in which it will lose 90% of this maximum heat.

Ans : (a) $ms\,(\theta_1 - \theta_0)$ (b) $\ln 10 / k$.

10. Consider a cubical vessel of edge a having a small hole in one of its walls. The total thermal resistance of the walls is r. At time $t = 0$, it contains air at atmospheric pressure p_a and temperature T_0. The temperature of the surrounding air is $T_a (> T_0$). Find the amount of the gas (in moles) in the vessel at time t. Take C_v of air to be $5R/2$.

Ans : $n = \dfrac{p_a a^3}{RT_a}\left[1 + \left(\dfrac{T_a}{T_0} - 1\right)e^{-\frac{2T_a}{7rp_a a^3}t}\right]$

11. A cylindrical block of length 0.4 m and area of cross–section 0.04 m² is placed coaxially on a thin metal disc of mass 0.4 kg and of the same cross–section. The upper face of the block is maintained at a constant temperature of 400 K and the initial temperature of the disc is 300 K. If the thermal conductivity of the material of the cylinder is 10W/m–K and the specific heat of the material of the disc is 600 J/kg–K, how long will it take for the temperature of the disc to increase to 350 K ? Assume for purpose of calculation, the thermal conductivity of the disc to be very high and the system to be thermally insulated except for the upper face of the cylinder.

Ans. 2 min. 46 s.

12. A body initially at 80°C cools to 64°C in 5 minutes and to 52°C in 10 minutes. What will be the temperature after 15 minutes and what is the temperature of surroundings ?

Ans. 43°C, 16°C.

13. A solid body X of heat capacity C is kept in an atmosphere whose temperature is $T_A = 300\ K$. At time $t = 0$, the temperature of X is $T_0 = 400\ K$. It cools according to Newton's law of cooling. At time t, the temperature is found to be 350 K. At this time (t_1), the body X is connected to a large box Y at atmospheric temperature T_A, through a conducting rod of length L, cross–sectional area A and thermal conductivity K. The heat capacity of Y is so large that any variation in its temperature may be neglected. The cross-sectional area A of the connecting rod is small compared to the surface area of X. Find the temperature of X at time $t = 3\ t_1$.

$$\textbf{Ans. } T = 300 + 50\exp\left[-2t_1\left\{\frac{KA}{CL} + \frac{\ln 2}{t_1}\right\}\right].$$

14. A rod of length l with thermally insulated lateral surface is made of a material whose thermal conductivity varies as $K = \alpha/T$, where α is a constant. The ends of the rod are kept at temperatures T_1 and T_2. Find the temperature function $T(x)$, where x is the distance from the end whose temperature is T_1 and also find the heat flowing per second per unit cross-sectional area.

$$\textbf{Ans. } T_x = T_1\left(\frac{T_2}{T_1}\right)^{x/\ell}, \quad H = \frac{-\alpha}{\ell}\log_e\frac{T_2}{T_1}$$

15. Find the temperature distribution in a substance placed between two parallel plates kept at temperature T_1 and T_2. The plate separation is equal to l, the coefficient of thermal conductivity of the substance varies as $K \propto \sqrt{T}$.

$$\textbf{Ans. } T = T_1\left[\left\{1 + \frac{x}{\ell}\left(\frac{T_2}{T_1}\right)^{3/2} - 1\right\}\right]^{2/3}$$

Hints & Solutions

1. (d)
$$R = R_1 + R_2$$

or
$$\frac{(x+4x)}{K'A} = \frac{x}{KA} + \frac{4x}{2KA}$$

$$\therefore \quad K' = \frac{5K}{3}$$

The rate of heat flow,

$$H = K'A\left(\frac{T_2 - T_1}{5x}\right)$$

$$= \frac{5K}{3}A\left(\frac{T_2 - T_1}{5x}\right)$$

$$= \frac{K}{3}A\left(\frac{T_2 - T_1}{x}\right).$$

Thus $f = \dfrac{1}{3}$.

2. (d)
$$E = \sigma T^4$$

$$\therefore \quad E' = \sigma\left(\frac{T}{2}\right)^4 = \frac{E}{16}$$

3. (b) The surface area of cube, $A_1 = \pi r^2$; sphere $= 4\pi r^2$

hemisphere $= 2\pi r^2 + \pi r^2 = 3\pi r^2$.

As $E \propto$ surface area, and so heat transfer is greatest for sphere.

4. (a) If R is the resistance of each rod, then

$$R_1 = R + R = 2R \text{ and } R_2 = \frac{R}{2}$$

Like $Q = \dfrac{V^2}{R}t$; $\dfrac{4}{2R} = \dfrac{t}{R/2} \Rightarrow t = 1$ minute

5. (d) For quick and large amount of heat needed low specific heat and high conductivity.

6. (a) If T be the temperature of interface, then

$$KA\left(\frac{T-0}{x}\right) = 4KA\left(\frac{100-T}{x}\right)$$

$$\therefore \quad T = 80° \text{ C}.$$

7. (d) If T be the temperature of interface, then

$$300\,A\left(\frac{100-T}{x}\right) = 200A\left(\frac{T-0}{x}\right)$$

$$\therefore \quad T = 60°$$

8. (b)
$$Q = H_1 t_1 = H_2 t_2$$
or
$$K_1 t_1 = K_2 t_2$$

$$\therefore \quad \frac{K_1}{K_2} = \frac{t_2}{t_1} = \frac{35}{20} = \frac{7}{4}$$

9. (c) Warming of the bulb is due to radiation process.

10. (a) Black spot on heating absorbs radiations from surroundings and so emits them in the dark room while the polished shining part reflects radiation and absorbs nothing and so does not radiate.

11. (a) Initially black body absorbs all the incident energy and so it is the darkest one. Black body radiates maximum energy if conditions are same.

12. (c) Bright body emits colour of short wavelength.

13. (c)
$$E = \varepsilon A\, \sigma\,(T^4 - T_0^4)$$
$$= 0.4 \times 200 \times 10^{-4} \times 5.67 \times 10^{-8} \times [800^4 - 300^4]$$
$$= 182\text{J}.$$

14. (d) The total power radiated by sun

$$= \sigma T^4 \times 4\pi R^2$$

The power incident on earth of surface area $4\pi r_0^2$.

$$= \frac{\sigma T^4 \times 4\pi R^2}{4\pi r^2} \times 4\pi r_0^2$$

$$= \frac{4\pi r_0^2 R^2 \sigma T^4}{r^2}$$

15. (b)
$$E = \left(4\pi R^2\right)\sigma T^4$$

and
$$E' = \left[4\pi(100R)^2\right]\sigma\left[\frac{T}{2}\right]^4$$

$$= 625\,E.$$

16. (a)
$$Q = Ht = CKt = \frac{C't}{R}$$

$$\therefore \quad \frac{Q_1}{Q_2} = \frac{R_2}{R_1} = \frac{2r}{\pi r} = \frac{2}{\pi}$$

17. (a)
$$mL = KA\frac{\Delta T}{\Delta x}$$

or
$$500 \times 80 = 0.0075 \times 75\left(\frac{40}{5}\right)t$$

$$\therefore \quad t = 8888 \text{ s}$$
$$= 2.47 \text{ hr}.$$

18. (c)
$$mL = KA\left(\frac{\Delta T}{\Delta x}\right)t$$

or
$$m \times 8 \times 10^4 = 92 \times 10^{-3} \times \left(\frac{100}{1}\right) \times 60$$

$$\therefore \quad m = 6.9 \times 10^{-3}\text{kg}.$$

19. (b) For no heat flows across CD,

$$\frac{R_1}{R_2} = \frac{R_3}{R_4}$$

or
$$\frac{1/K_1}{1/K_2} = \frac{1/K_3}{1/K_4} \Rightarrow \frac{K_2}{K_1} = \frac{K_4}{K_3}$$

$$\therefore \quad K_2 K_3 = K_1 K_4$$

20. (b) The rate of heat flow does not depend on area of cross-section of specimen.

21. (b)
$$KA\frac{(\theta_1 - \theta)}{x} = KA\frac{(\theta - \theta_2)}{(l - x)}$$

θ_1 θ θ_2

$\longleftarrow x \longrightarrow \longleftarrow \lambda - x \longrightarrow$

$$\therefore \quad \theta = \theta_1 - \left(\frac{\theta_2 - \theta_1}{l}\right)x$$

$\Rightarrow$ It represents straight line with negative slope.

22. (d)

$100°C$ T_1 T_2 $0°C$

Cu   Al   Brass

$$K_{cu}A\frac{100 - T_1}{l} = K_{brass}A\frac{T_2 - 0}{l}$$

$$= K_{Al}A\frac{T_1 - T_2}{l}$$

After substituting the values and simplify,
we get $T_1 = 86°C$ and $T_2 = 57°C$

23. (b)
$$Q = 500 \times 0.572 \times (50 - 20)$$
$$= 8580 \text{ cal.}$$
As $Pt = Q$
$$\therefore \quad t = \frac{Q}{P}$$
$$= 360 \text{ s}$$

24. (c)
$$K_{tin}A\left(\frac{700 - T}{0.2}\right) = K_{cu}A\left(\frac{T - 100}{2.4}\right)$$

$700°C$ T $100°C$

0.2 2.4
mm   mm

$$\therefore \quad T = 500°C$$

$$Q = 0.15 \times (400) \times \left(\frac{700 - 500}{0.2 \times 10^{-1}}\right) \times 3600$$

$$= 2.16 \times 10^9 \text{ cal}$$

$$\therefore \quad m = \frac{Q}{L} = \frac{2.16 \times 10^9}{540} = 4 \times 10^6 \text{ g}$$

$$= 4000 \text{ kg.}$$

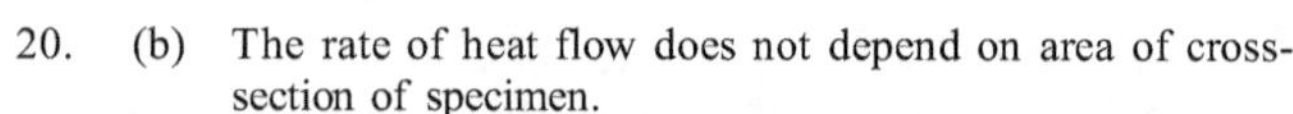
Solutions **EXERCISE 8.1 LEVEL -2**

1. (b)
$$(2K)A\frac{T_1 - T}{x} = KA\frac{T - T_2}{x}$$

T_1 T T_2 | $2K$ | K |

$\longleftarrow x \longrightarrow \longleftarrow x \longrightarrow$

or $2(T_1 - T) = (T - T_2)$
or $3(T_1 - T) = (T - T_2) + T_1 - T$
$$= (T_1 - T_2)$$

$$\therefore \quad T_1 - T = \frac{T_1 - T_2}{3} = \frac{36}{3} = 12$$

2. (b)
$$\frac{1}{R} = \frac{1}{R_1} + \frac{1}{R_2}$$

or $KA = K_1A_1 + K_2A_2$

or $K\left(4\pi R^2\right) = K_1 \times \pi R^2 + K_2 \times \left(4\pi R^2 - \pi R^2\right)$

$$\therefore \quad K = \left(\frac{K_1 + 3K_2}{4}\right)$$

3. (c) The temperature of x is decreasing faster than y, so its emissive power is greater than y.
As $e_x > e_y$, so $a_x > a_y$.

4. (d)
$$\left[\frac{-dT}{dr}\right] = \frac{A}{mc}\left[T - T_0\right]$$

$$= \frac{4\pi r^2}{\rho \times \frac{4}{3}\pi r^3 c}\left[T - T_0\right]$$

$$\therefore \quad \left[\frac{-dT}{dr}\right] \propto \frac{1}{\rho rc}$$

5. (d) The mean wavelength
$$\lambda = \frac{500 + 1500}{2} = 1000 \text{nm}$$

So the intensity of radiation is greatest for 1000 nm.
Thus $U_2 > U_1$ and U_3.

6. (d)
$$E = \sigma T^4 A$$
$$\therefore \quad E_1 = \sigma T^4 \times 4\pi r^2$$

and
$$E_2 = \sigma(2T)^4 \times 4\pi\left(\frac{r}{2}\right)^2$$
$$= 4E_1 = 4 \times 450 = 1800 \text{ W.}$$

7. (d)
$$\rho \times \frac{4}{3}\pi r_1^3 = 3\rho \times \frac{4}{3}\pi r_2^3$$

$$\Rightarrow \quad \frac{r_1}{r_2} = \sqrt[3]{3}$$

$$\therefore \quad \frac{(-dT/dt)_1}{(-dT/dt)_2} = \frac{r_2}{r_1} = \frac{1}{\sqrt[3]{3}}$$

8. (b) For steady state
$$H_1 = H_2$$

$$KA\frac{\sqrt{2}T - T_c}{l} = KA\frac{T_c - T}{\sqrt{2}\,l}$$

$$\therefore \quad \frac{T_c}{T} = \frac{3}{\sqrt{2} + 1}$$

9. (c) In first case $R_1 = R/2$ and in second case $R_2 = 2R$.

Thus, $\dfrac{q_1}{q_2} = \dfrac{R_2}{R_1} = \dfrac{2R}{R/2} = 4$

10. (b)
$$Q_A = \sigma T^4 A = \sigma\left[\frac{b}{\lambda_A}\right]^4 \times A$$

$$= \sigma\left[\frac{b}{300}\right]^4 A = \frac{K}{81}$$

$$Q_B = \sigma\left[\frac{b}{400}\right]^4 \times 4A = \frac{K}{64}$$

$$Q_C = \sigma\left[\frac{b}{500}\right]^4 \times 9A = \frac{9K}{625}$$

$$\Rightarrow \quad Q_B > Q_C > Q_A$$

11. (a) $\quad E = e A \sigma T^4 = 0.6 A \sigma T^4$

12. (d) If T be the outside temperature, then

$$\frac{V^2}{R} = KA\left[\frac{T'-T}{\Delta x}\right]$$

or $\quad \dfrac{200^2}{20} = 0.2 \times 4.2 \times 1\left[\dfrac{20-T}{0.2 \times 10^{-2}}\right]$

$\therefore \quad T = 15.2°\text{C}.$

13. (b) $\quad mL = kA\dfrac{\Delta T}{\Delta x}t$

or $\quad m \times (80 \times 4200) = 0.050 \times \left(6 \times 0.5^2\right)\left(\dfrac{30-0}{0.04}\right) \times 3600$

$\therefore \quad m = 0.605 \text{ kg}.$

14. (a) $\quad E = e A \sigma\left(T^4 - T_0^{\,4}\right)$

$$= 0.80 \times 1.50 \times 5.67 \times 10^{-8}\left(310^4 - 290^4\right) \times 60$$

$$= 8.8 \text{ kJ}$$

15. (d) $\quad P = KA\dfrac{\Delta T}{\Delta x} = K\left[2\pi Rh\right]\left[\dfrac{\Delta T}{\Delta x}\right]$

$$= 9 \times 10^{-5} \times 420\left[2\pi \times 0.30 \times 1\right]\left[\dfrac{60-20}{0.01}\right]$$

$$= 284 \text{ W}.$$

16. (d) $\quad mL = KA\left(\dfrac{\Delta T}{\Delta x}\right)t$

<table>
<tr><td>100°C</td><td></td><td>0°C</td></tr>
</table>

3 mm

or $\quad 2 \times 80 \times 4200$

$$= \left(0.92 \times 420\right) \times \left(0.20 \times 0.40\right) \times \left[\dfrac{100-0}{3 \times 10^{-3}}\right] \times t$$

$\therefore \quad t = 0.65 \text{ s}$

17. (c) $\quad Q = K_a A\dfrac{\Delta T_a}{\Delta x} = K_b A\dfrac{\Delta T_b}{\Delta x} = K_c A\dfrac{\Delta T_c}{\Delta x}$

As K_c is least, so $\Delta T_c \rightarrow$ greatest

18. (b) $\quad \lambda_{sun} T_{sun} = \lambda_{star} T_{star}$

$\therefore \quad \dfrac{T_{sun}}{T_{star}} = \dfrac{\lambda_{star}}{\lambda_{sun}} = \dfrac{350}{510} = \dfrac{35}{51}$

$$= 0.69.$$

19. (b)

$$H = H_1 + H_2$$

$$KA\left(\frac{T-0}{\ell}\right) = KA\left(\frac{90-T}{\ell}\right) \times 2$$

$\therefore \quad T = 60°\text{C}.$

20. (a) The equivalent combination is as follows :

$$H_{AB} = H_{BC}$$

or $\quad \dfrac{120-T}{R} = \dfrac{T-20}{R}$

$\therefore \quad T = 70°\text{C}.$

21. (c) $\quad H_{PRQ} = H_{PQ}$

or $\quad K_{PRQ} = K_{PQ}$

or $\quad \dfrac{K_1 K_2}{K_1 + K_2} = K_3$

22. (a)

$$\left[m_{water}\right]_{evaporate} = \left[m_{ice}\right]_{melt} = m$$

$$m \times 540 = KA\dfrac{\left[400-100\right]}{(10-\lambda)x} \times 1 \quad \dots\dots\dots(i)$$

and $\quad m \times 80 = KA\dfrac{\left[400-0\right]}{\lambda x} \times 1 \quad \dots\dots\dots(ii)$

From above equations, we get

$$\lambda = 9$$

23. (a) The radial flow of heat is given by

$$H = K\left[4\pi r_1 r_2\right]\dfrac{T_1 - T_2}{\left[r_2 - r_1\right]}$$

24. (d) $\quad E = A\left(\sigma T^4\right)$

$\therefore \quad \ell n E = \ell n\left(A\sigma\right) + 4\ell n T$

It represents straight line.

25. (d) If P is the power radiates at 35°C, then

$$10 = \sigma A\left(323^4 - 293^4\right) \quad \dots\dots\dots(i)$$

and $\quad P = \sigma A\left(308^4 - 293^4\right) \quad \dots\dots\dots(ii)$

From above equations, we get

$$P = 4.65 \text{ W}$$

Now $\quad P\,t = mc\Delta T$

or $\quad 4.65 \times 60 = mc \times 0.2$

$\therefore \quad mc = 1400 \text{ J/°C}.$

26. (a) $\quad \sigma T^4 \times \left(\dfrac{\pi d^2}{4}\right) \times 2 \times 60 = 59 \times 8 \quad \dots\dots\dots(i)$

and $\quad Q = \sigma T^4 \times 1 \times 60 \quad \dots\dots\dots(ii)$

After solving above equations, we get

$$Q = 20860 \text{ cal}.$$

Solutions EXERCISE 8.2

1. (a,b)
$$\varepsilon_A \sigma T_A^4 = \varepsilon_B \sigma T_B^4$$

$$\therefore \quad \frac{T_A}{T_B} = \left[\frac{\varepsilon_B}{\varepsilon_A}\right]^{\frac{1}{4}} = \left[\frac{0.81}{0.01}\right]^{\frac{1}{4}} = 3$$

$$\therefore \quad T_B = \frac{T_A}{3} = \frac{5802}{3}$$

$$= 1934 \text{ K}$$

From Wein's displacement law,

$$\lambda_A T_A = \lambda_B T_B$$

or $$\frac{\lambda_A}{\lambda_B} = \frac{T_B}{T_A} = \frac{1934}{5802} = \frac{1}{3} \qquad \ldots\ldots\ldots(i)$$

Also $$\lambda_B - \lambda_A = 1.00 \qquad \ldots\ldots\ldots(ii)$$

After solving above equations, we get

$$\lambda_B = 1.5 \ \mu m.$$

(2). (a,b,c,d) With the incident radiation, the temperature of black body try to increase, so body emits more energy per unit time. To keep the temperature constant it must absorbs incident radiations with increased rate. The reflection depends on the nature of surface not on the temperature.

(3) (a,b) Conduction and convection need medium for transmission of heat.

(4) (b,c,d) $$K_x = 2K_y, \text{ so } R_x = \frac{R_y}{2} = \frac{R}{2}$$

The equivalent circuit is shown in figure.

$$\frac{60 - T_B}{R} = \frac{T_B - 10}{2R/3}$$

$$\therefore \quad T_B = 30°C.$$

Also $$T_C = T_D,$$

and $$\frac{30 - T_C}{R/2} = \frac{T_C - 10}{R/2}$$

$$\therefore \quad T_C = 20°C$$

(5) (b,d) Every object emit and absorb the radiations simultaneously, if energy emitted is more than energy absorbed, temperature falls and vice versa.

(6) (a, c, d) Since sun rays fall on the black body, it will absorb more radiation and since, its temperature is constant it will emit more radiation. The temperature will remain same only when energy emitted is equal to energy absorbed.

(7) (a,c) On comparing the given equation with the equation

$$\left(\frac{-dT}{dt}\right) = \frac{A}{mc}(T - T_0), \text{ we find that}$$

$$K = \frac{A}{mc}$$

$$\therefore \ K \propto A \text{ and } K \propto \frac{1}{m}$$

(8) (a,d)
$$\frac{50 - 40}{5} = k\left[\frac{50 + 40}{2} - T_0\right] \qquad \ldots\ldots\ldots(i)$$

and $$\frac{40 - 33.33}{5} = k\left[\frac{40 + 33.33}{2} - T_0\right] \qquad \ldots\ldots\ldots(ii)$$

on solving above equations, we get

$$T_0 = 20°C$$

Also $$\frac{33.33 - T}{5} = k\left[\frac{33.33 + T}{2} - 20\right] \qquad \ldots\ldots\ldots(iii)$$

$$\therefore \quad T = 28.88°C.$$

Solutions EXERCISE-8.3

(1). (a) According to Stefan's law, the energy radiated per second through unit area

$$E = \varepsilon \sigma T^4$$

(2) (b) $$E = \sigma T^4, \ \therefore \ E' = \sigma(2T)^4 = 16 \ E.$$

(3) (b) Both are experimentally proved.

(4) (a) According to Kirchoff's law

$$\frac{e_\lambda}{a_\lambda} = \text{constant.}$$

(5) (b) $E \propto T^4$, as T is always greater than 0 K, so E always be greater than zero.

(6) (a) Air enclosed inside clothes prevent the heat due to poor conductivity.

(7) (c) Hot air rises up due to smaller density.

(8) (c) $$\lambda \propto \frac{1}{T}$$

(9) (c) Sun is a black body, and so $E \propto T^4$

(10) (c)

(11) (a) The wavelength of blue colour is shorter than red colour, and so temperature of blue star will be higher.

Passage (Q. 1 - 3) :

1. (c) The rate of heat loss per unit area per second due to radiation is given by Stefan's-Boltzmann law

$$E = e\,s\left(T^4 - T_0^4\right)$$

$$= 0.6 \times \frac{17}{3} \times 10^{-8}[(400)^4 - (300)^4] = 595 \text{ watt/m}^2$$

2. (b) Let T_{oil} be the temperature of the oil. Then rate of heat flow through conduction = Rate of heat flow through radiation

$$\frac{KA(T_{oil} - T)}{\ell} = 595 \times A \text{ where A is the area of the top of lid}$$

$$\Rightarrow T_{oil} = \frac{595 \times \ell}{K} + T = \frac{595 \times 5 \times 10^{-3}}{0.149} + 400 = 419.83 \text{ K}$$

3. (a) Rate of heat flow through radiation
$$= (595 \text{ W/m}^2) \times (0.5 \text{ m}^2) = 297.5 \text{ W}.$$

Passage (Q. 4 - 6) :

4. (a)   5. (b)   6. (b)

We have, $-\dfrac{dT}{dt} = k(T - T_0)$

where T_0 is the temperature of the surrounding. If T_1 is the initial temperature and T is the temperature at any time t, then

$$\int_{T_1}^{T} \frac{dT}{(T - T_0)} = -k\int_0^t dt$$

or $$\left|\ln(T - T_0)\right|_{T_1}^{T} = -kt$$

or $$\ln\left[\frac{T - T_0}{T_1 - T_0}\right] = -kt$$

or $$T = T_0 + (T_1 - T_0)e^{-kt} \qquad \dots \text{(i)}$$

The body continues to lose heat till its temperature becomes equal to that of the surrounding. The loss of heat

$$Q = mc(T_1 - T_0)$$

If the body loses half of the maximum loss that it can, then decrease in temperature

$$\frac{Q}{2} = mc\left(\frac{T_1 - T_0}{2}\right)$$

If body loses this heat in time t, then its temperature at time t' will be

$$T_1 - \left(\frac{T_1 - T_0}{2}\right) = \frac{T_1 + T_0}{2}$$

Putting these values in equation (i), we have

$$\frac{T_1 + T_0}{2} = T_0 + (T_1 - T_0)e^{-kt'}$$

or $$\frac{T_1 - T_0}{2} = (T_1 - T_0)e^{-kt'}$$

or $$e^{-kt'} = \frac{1}{2}$$

or $$t' = \frac{\ln 2}{k}$$

If $k = \ln 2$, $t' = 1$ unit

Passage (Q. 7 - 9) :

7. (a)   8. (b)   9. (b)

Light piston will maintain the pressure of the gas equal to the atmospheric pressure (P_a).

Let at any instant, the temperature of the gas be q. In next small time dt, its temperature increases by dq.

Heat gained by gas = Heat conducted into the cylinder

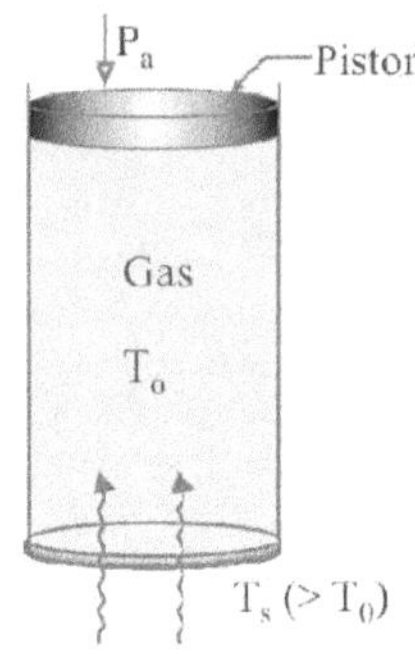

or $nC_p(d\theta) = KA\left(\dfrac{T_s - \theta}{x}\right)dt$

For monoatomic gas, $C_p = \dfrac{5R}{2}$

$$n \times \frac{5R}{2}(d\theta) = KA\left(\frac{T_s - \theta}{x}\right)dt$$

or $$\frac{d\theta}{(T_s - \theta)} = \frac{2KA}{5nRx}(dt) \qquad \dots \text{(i)}$$

Let after time t, the temperature of the gas be T, then

$$\int_{T_0}^{T} \frac{d\theta}{(T_s - \theta)} = \frac{2KA}{5nRx}\int_0^t (dt)$$

or $\qquad -\left|\ln(T_s - \theta)\right|_{T_0}^{T} = \dfrac{2KA}{5nRx}t$

or $\qquad \ln\left(\dfrac{T_s - T}{T_s - T_0}\right) = -\dfrac{2KAt}{5nRx}$

or $\qquad (T_s - T) = (T_s - T_0)e^{-\left(\frac{2KAt}{5nRx}\right)}$

If we write $T_s - T = \Delta T$, then

$$\Delta T = (T_s - T_0)e^{-\left(\frac{2KAt}{5nRx}\right)} \qquad \ldots\text{(ii)}$$

By equation of state, we have

$$P\Delta V = nR\Delta T$$

or $\qquad \Delta V = \dfrac{nR}{P_a}\Delta T \quad (\because P_a = P) \qquad \ldots\text{(iii)}$

From equations (ii) and (iii), we get

$$\Delta V = \dfrac{nR}{P_a}\left[(T_s - T_0)e^{-\left(\frac{2KAt}{5nRx}\right)}\right]$$

Let y is the displacement of the piston in time t, then

$$Ay = \Delta V$$

$$y = \dfrac{\Delta V}{A} = \dfrac{nR}{P_a A}\left[(T_s - T_0)e^{-\left(\frac{2KAt}{5nRx}\right)}\right]$$

Passage for (Q. 10 - 12) :

10. (b)   **11. (d)**   **12. (b)**

(a) Power of the heater $P = (mc)\dfrac{\Delta T}{t}$

$\qquad\qquad = 80 \times 2$

$\qquad\qquad = 160 \text{ W}$

(b) The power radiated by the block,

$$P = (mc)\dfrac{\Delta T}{t}$$

$\qquad\qquad = 80 \times 0.2 = 16 \text{ W}$

(c) Power rediated is proportional to the temperature difference between block and the room.

and so in second case power radiated = 8 W.

(d) The heat energy absorbed by the block

$$Q = (mc)\Delta T$$

$\qquad\qquad = 80 \times 10 = 800 \text{ J}$

Passage for (Q. 13 - 14) :

13. (b)   **14. (c)**

We know that, solar constant $S = \sigma T^4\left[\dfrac{R_s}{r}\right]^2$

or $\qquad 1.4 \times 10^3 = 5.67 \times 10^{-8} \times T^4\left[\dfrac{7\times 10^8}{1.5\times 10^{11}}\right]^2$

$\therefore \qquad\qquad T \simeq 5800 \, K.$ **Ans.**

The energy radiated from the sun per unit area per second

$$E = \sigma T^4$$

$\qquad\qquad = 5.67 \times 10^{-8}[5800]^4$

$\qquad\qquad = 6.43 \times 10^7 \text{ W/m}^2$ **Ans.**

15. (A) $\to$ p, r; (B) $\to$ t; (C) $\to$ q, r; (D) $\to$ t

(A) Initially more heat will enter through section A but the metal will absorb some heat and less heat will leave from C.

(B) At steady state heat accumulation $\Rightarrow \dfrac{dQ}{dt}$ is same for all sections.

(C) At steady state $\dfrac{dQ}{dt} = kA\left|\dfrac{dT}{dx}\right|$ or $\left|\dfrac{dT}{dx}\right| = \dfrac{1}{KA}\left(\dfrac{dQ}{dt}\right)$

$\left|\dfrac{dT}{dx}\right|$ is inversely proportional to area of cross-section. Hence is maximum at B and minimum at C.

(D) At steady state heat accumulation = 0

So $\dfrac{dT}{dx} = 0$ for any section.

16. (A) $\to$ p; (B) $\to$ q; (C) $\to$ s; (D) $\to$ r

17. (A) $\to$ q; (B) $\to$ p; (C) $\to$ s; (D) $\to$ r

Solutions **EXERCISE-8.5**

1. The heat lost in evaporation per second

$\qquad\qquad = (0.1 \times 10^{-3})\times 2.27 \times 10^6$

$\qquad\qquad = 227 \text{ J/s}$

If T is the temperature of the pitcher, then for steady state

$$H = kA\dfrac{\Delta T}{\Delta x}$$

$$227 = 0.80 \times (200 \times 10^{-4})\times \dfrac{\Delta T}{10^{-3}}$$

$\therefore \qquad \Delta T \simeq 14^\circ C$

or $\qquad T_0 - T_i = 14$

$\therefore \qquad\qquad T_i = T_0 - 14$

$\qquad\qquad = 42 - 14$

$\qquad\qquad = 28^\circ C$ **Ans.**

2. We can write

$$C\Delta\theta = KA\frac{\Delta T}{\Delta x}t$$

or

$$C\frac{\Delta\theta}{t} = KA\frac{\Delta T}{\Delta x}$$

$$\therefore \quad \frac{\Delta\theta}{t} = \frac{KA}{C}\frac{\Delta T}{\Delta x}$$

$$= \frac{200\times1\times10^{-4}}{0.40}\times\frac{(5-2.5)}{100}$$

$$= 12.50\ ^\circ\text{C/s} \qquad \textbf{Ans.}$$

3. The rate of flow of heat is given by

$$H = K\frac{2\pi\ell(T_1-T_2)}{\ln\left(\dfrac{r_2}{r_1}\right)}$$

$$= \frac{0.15\times(2\pi\times0.50)[120-30]}{\ln\left(\dfrac{1.2}{1}\right)}$$

$$\simeq 233\ \text{J/s.}\ \textbf{Ans.}$$

4. At steady state

Heat conduct through the rod = heat absorbed at the end

or

$$KA\frac{\Delta T}{\Delta x} = \sigma A(T^4-T_0^4)$$

or

$$K(10^{-4})\left[\frac{17-0}{0.50}\right] = 6\times10^{-8}(10^{-4})\,(300^4-290^4)$$

$$\therefore \quad K = 1.8\ \text{W/m-}^\circ\text{C.} \qquad \textbf{Ans.}$$

5. Suppose the resistance of each of rod of material is r, then resistance of each of material y will be $2r$. The temperature of junction C and D will be equal and so there in no heat flow in between. The equivalent system of rods is shown in figure.

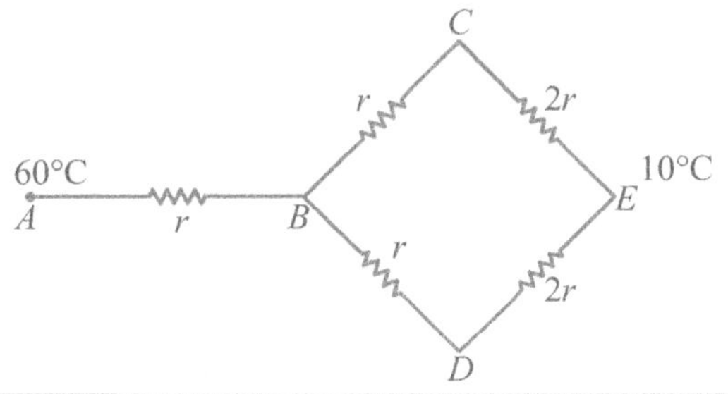

If T_B is the temperature of B, then

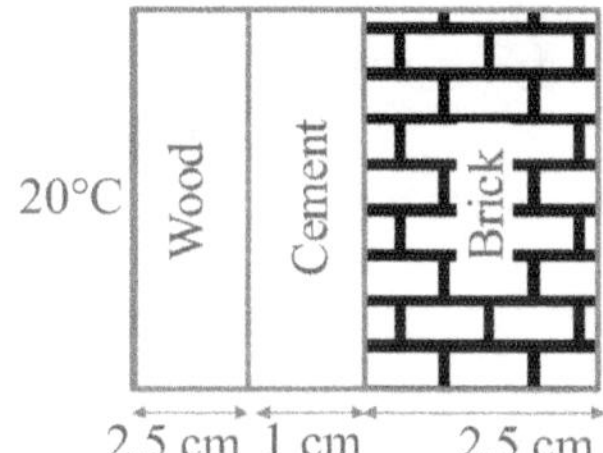

$$\frac{60-T_B}{r} = \frac{T_B-10}{1.5r}$$

$$\therefore \quad T_B = 40^\circ\text{C} \qquad \textbf{Ans.}$$

6. The rate at which heat radiated

$$= \in\sigma A[T^4-T_0^4]$$

$$= 0.4\times5.67\times10^{-8}\times200\times10^{-4}[800^4-300^4]$$

$$= 182.12\ \text{J}$$

$$\simeq 44\ \text{cal/s.}$$

7. The resistance offered by the wall

$$R = R_1+R_2+R_3$$

or

$$\frac{L}{KA} = \frac{L_1}{K_1A}+\frac{L_2}{K_2A}+\frac{L_3}{K_3A}$$

20°C — Wood | Cement | Brick

2.5 cm 1 cm 2.5 cm

or

$$\frac{L_1+L_2+L_2}{K} = \frac{L_1}{K_1}+\frac{L_2}{K_2}+\frac{L_3}{K_3}$$

or

$$\frac{2.5+1+25}{K} = \frac{2.5}{0.125}+\frac{1}{1.5}+\frac{25}{1}$$

$$\therefore \quad K = 0.624\ \text{W/m-}^\circ\text{C}$$

The power of the heater $H = KA\dfrac{\Delta T}{\Delta x}$

$$= 0.624\times137\left(\frac{30}{28.5\times10^{-2}}\right)$$

$$= 9\ \text{kW} \qquad \textbf{Ans.}$$

1. The amount of heat added in 4 min

$$Q = 100\times(4\times60)$$

$$= 2.4\times10^4\ \text{cal.}$$

Suppose temperature of the system becomes T. The heat taken by ice

$$Q_1 = 200\times0.5\times(20)+200\times80+200\times1\times(T-0)$$

Heat taken by aluminimum container

$$Q_2 = 100\times0.2\times(T+20).$$

We can write

$$Q = Q_1+Q_2$$

or

$$2.4\times10^4 = [200\times0.5\times20+200\times80]+[100\times0.2\times(T+20)]$$

$$\therefore \quad T = 25.5^\circ\text{C} \qquad \textbf{Ans.}$$

2. In one minute heat enters into the vessels

$$Q_1 = m_1 L$$

$$= k_1 A \frac{\Delta T}{\Delta x}$$

and

$$Q_2 = m_2 L$$

$$= k_2 A \frac{\Delta T}{\Delta x}$$

$$\therefore \qquad \frac{k_1}{k_2} = \frac{m_1}{m_2}$$

$$= \frac{100}{150}$$

$$= \frac{2}{3} \qquad \textbf{\textit{Ans.}}$$

3. The electrical energy consumed per second

$$E_1 = \varepsilon A \sigma T^4$$

$$= 0.35 \times (0.25) \times 5.67 \times 10^{-5} \times (3000)^4$$

$$= 40.19 \text{ W}. \qquad \textbf{\textit{Ans.}}$$

In the second case

$$E_2 = 0.35 \times 0.25 \times 5.67\,0 \times 10^{-5} \times (2500)^4$$

$$= 19.38 \text{ W} \qquad \textbf{\textit{Ans.}}$$

4. If t be the time taken to form the ice, then

$$t = \frac{\rho L}{2kT}(y_2^2 - y_1^2)$$

After substituting the given values, we get

$$t = 102.5 \text{ s} \qquad \textbf{\textit{Ans.}}$$

5. If m is the mass of ice or steam produced then

$$m \times 80 = KA \frac{(200 - 0)}{x} \qquad \text{...(i)}$$

and

$$m \times 540 = KA \frac{(200 - 100)}{1.5 - x} \qquad \text{...(ii)}$$

$$\begin{array}{ccc} 0°C & 200°C & 100°C \\ \longleftarrow x \longrightarrow & \longleftarrow 1.5 - x \longrightarrow \end{array}$$

From equations (i) and (ii), we get

$$x \simeq 1.4 \text{ m} \qquad \textbf{\textit{Ans.}}$$

6. The mass of the water in the vessel

$$m = \rho V$$

$$= 1000 \times (10 \times 10 \times 10^{-6})$$

$$= 0.1 \text{ kg}.$$

The amount of heat lost in falling the temperature

$$Q = mC\Delta T$$

$$= 0.1 \times 4200 \times 1$$

$$= 420 \text{ J}.$$

If t is the time to fall this temperature, then

$$Q = kA\left(\frac{\Delta T}{\Delta x}\right)t$$

or

$$420 = 200 \times (2 \times 10 \times 10^{-4})\left[\frac{50 - 20}{10^{-3}}\right]t$$

$$\therefore \qquad t = 0.035 \text{ s} \qquad \textbf{\textit{Ans.}}$$

7.

$$H_{AB} = K_{AB} A \frac{\Delta T}{\Delta x}$$

$$= 50 \times (1 \times 10^{-4}) \times \frac{(80 - 40)}{0.20}$$

$$= 1 \text{ W}$$

Similarly,

$$H_{AC} = 8 \text{ W},$$

$$H_{BC} = 0. \qquad \textbf{\textit{Ans.}}$$

8. Suppose resistance of each of AB, CD, CF is r. The resistance of part BDE or BCF is $\dfrac{3r}{2}$. The equivalent system is shown in figure.

By consenation of heat energy, we can write

$$H = H_1 + H_2$$

$$\frac{T_1 - T_B}{r} = \frac{T_B - T_3}{3r/2} + \frac{T_B - T_2}{3r/2}$$

$$\therefore \qquad T_B = \frac{3T_1 + 2(T_2 + T_3)}{7} \qquad \textbf{\textit{Ans.}}$$

9. (a) The maximum heat lost by the body

$$Q = ms\,\Delta T$$

$$= ms\,(\theta_1 - \theta_0)$$

(b) If ΔT be the fall in temperature in lossing 90% of the maximum heat, then

$$0.90\,ms\,(\theta_1 - \theta_0) = ms\,\Delta T$$

$$\therefore \qquad \Delta T = 0.90\,(\theta_1 - \theta_0).$$

Thus final temperature $= \theta_1 - 0.90\,(\theta_1 - \theta_0)$

$$= (0.1\,\theta_1 + 0.9\,\theta_0)$$

Now by Newton's law of cooling

$$\frac{d\theta}{dt} = -k\,(\theta - \theta_0)$$

or $\displaystyle \int_{\theta_1}^{(0.1\theta_1+0.9\theta_0)} \frac{d\theta}{(\theta-\theta_0)} = -k\int_0^t dt$

or $\displaystyle \left| \ln(\theta-\theta_0)\right|_{\theta_1}^{(0.1\theta_1+0.9\theta_0)} = -kt$

$\therefore \qquad t = \dfrac{\ln 10}{k}$ **Ans.**

10. As the gas can leak out from the hole, so the pressure in the vessel becomes equal to atomspheric pressure P_a. Let n be the number of moles in the vessel at time t. Let an amount ΔQ of heat is given to the gas in time dt, its temperature increases by dT, then

$$\Delta Q = nC_p dT$$

If the temperature of the gas is T at time t, then

$$\frac{\Delta Q}{dt} = \frac{T_a-T}{r}$$

or $\displaystyle \frac{nC_p dt}{dt} = \frac{T_a-T}{r}$ ... (i)

By Gas law, $\qquad PV = nRT,$

We have $\qquad P_a(a^3) = nRT$

$\therefore \qquad T = P_a a^3/nR$ .... (ii)

or $\qquad ndT + Tdn = 0$

or $\qquad ndT = -Tdn$ .... (iii)

The initial amount of gas $n_0 = \dfrac{P_a a^3}{RT_0}$.

From above equations, we have

$$\int_{n_0}^{n} \frac{dn}{(nRT_a - P_a a^3)} = -\int_0^t \frac{dt}{C_p r P_a a^3}$$

$\therefore \qquad n = \dfrac{P_a a^3}{RT_a}\left[1+\left(\dfrac{T_a}{T_0}-1\right)e^{-\frac{2T_a t}{kP_a a^3}}\right]$

Ans.

11. Suppose T is the temperature of the lower face of the cylinder, and in time dt the temperature of disc increases by dT, then

$$mc\frac{dT}{dt} = KA\left[\frac{400-T}{\ell}\right]$$

or $\qquad t = \dfrac{mcl}{kA}\displaystyle\int_{300}^{350} \frac{dT}{(400-T)}$

After simplifying and substituting the given values, we get

$\qquad t = 2\text{ min }46\text{ s}$ **Ans.**

12. If T_0 be the temperature of the surroundings, then

$$-\frac{dT}{dt} = k(T-T_0)$$

or $\qquad \dfrac{80-64}{5} = k\left(\dfrac{80+64}{2}-T_0\right)$ ...(i)

and $\qquad \dfrac{80-52}{10} = k\left(\dfrac{80+52}{2}-T_0\right)$ ...(ii)

After simplifying above equations, we get $T_0 = 16°C$

If T' be the temperature after 15 minutes, then

$$\frac{80-T'}{15} = k\left(\frac{80+T'}{2}-16\right) \quad ...(iii)$$

From equations (i) and (iii), we get

$\qquad T' = 43°C.$ **Ans.**

13. If T is the temperature of the body at a time t, then by Newton's law of cooling

$$\frac{dT}{dt} = -k(T-T_A)$$

or $\qquad C\dfrac{dT}{dt} = -kC(T-T_A)$

Substituting $\qquad kC = -b,$

We have $\qquad C\dfrac{dT}{dt} = -b(T-T_A)$

or $\displaystyle \int_{400}^{350} \frac{dT}{(T-T_A)} = -\frac{b}{C}\int_0^{t_1} dt$

or $\qquad \left|\ln(T-T_A)\right|_{400}^{350} = -\dfrac{b}{C}t_1$

$\therefore \qquad b = \dfrac{C\ln 2}{t_1}$

Now when the body X is connected to body Y, the body X loses heat by radiation and by conduction. Thus

$$CdT = -\frac{KA}{L}(T-T_A)dt + \frac{b\ln 2}{t_1}(T-T_A)dt$$

After integrating and substituting the known values, we get

$$T = 300+50\exp\left[-2t_1\left\{\frac{KA}{CL}+\frac{\ln 2}{t_1}\right\}\right]$$

Ans.

14. If A is the cross-sectional area of the rod, then

$$H = KA\left(\frac{-dT}{dx}\right)$$

$$= -\frac{\alpha}{T}A\left(\frac{dT}{dx}\right)$$

or $\displaystyle \int_0^x dx = -\frac{\alpha A}{H}\int_{T_1}^{T} \frac{dT}{T}$ ...(i)

or $\qquad x = -\dfrac{\alpha A}{H}\ln\dfrac{T}{T_1}$

For $x = \ell$,

$$T = T_2$$

$\therefore \qquad \ell = -\dfrac{\alpha A}{H}\cdot\ln\dfrac{T_2}{T_1}$

From equation (i) and (ii), we have

$$T = T_1\left(\frac{T_1}{T_1}\right)^{x/\ell} \qquad \textbf{Ans.}$$

Also heat flow per second, per unit area

$$H = \frac{\alpha}{\ell}\ln\frac{T_1}{T_2} \qquad \textbf{Ans.}$$

15. We have

$$H = -KA\frac{dT}{dx}$$

$$= -C\sqrt{T}\,A\frac{dT}{dx}$$

or

$$\int_0^x dx = -\frac{CA}{H}\int_{T_1}^{T} T^{1/2}dT$$

or

$$x = \frac{2}{3}\frac{CA}{H}\left[T_1^{3/2} - T_2^{3/2}\right] \quad …(i)$$

For $x = \ell$,

$$T = T_2$$

$$\therefore \qquad \ell = \frac{2}{3}\frac{CA}{H}\left[T_1^{3/2} - T_2^{3/2}\right] \quad …(ii)$$

From equations (i) and (ii), we have

$$\frac{x}{\ell} = \frac{T_1^{3/2} - T^{3/2}}{T_1^{3/2} - T_2^{3/2}}$$

or

$$T = T_1\left[1 + \frac{x}{\ell}\left(\frac{T_2}{T_1}\right)^{3/2} - 1\right]^{2/3} \qquad \textbf{Ans.}$$